ART HISTORY

VOLUME TWO | FOURTH EDITION

ART HISTORY

MARILYN STOKSTAD

Judith Harris Murphy Distinguished Professor of Art History Emerita
The University of Kansas

MICHAEL W. COTHREN

Scheuer Family Professor of Humanities
Department of Art, Swarthmore College

CONTRIBUTORS

Frederick M. Asher, David A. Binkley, Claudia L. Brittenham,

Claudia Brown, Patricia J. Darish, Patricia J. Graham,

Carol S. Ivory, D. Fairchild Ruggles, and Joy Sperling

Prentice Hall

Boston Columbus Indianapolis New York San Francisco Upper Saddle River
Amsterdam Cape Town Dubai London Madrid Milan Munich Paris Montréal Toronto
Delhi Mexico City São Paulo Sydney Hong Kong Seoul Singapore Taipei Tokyo

Editorial Director: Craig Campanella
Editor-in-Chief: Sarah Touborg
Senior Sponsoring Editor: Helen Ronan
Editorial Project Manager: David Nitti
Editorial Assistant: Carla Worner
Editor-in-Chief, Development: Rochelle Diogenes
Development Editors: Margaret Manos and Cynthia Ward
Media Director: Brian Hyland
Media Editor: Dave Alick
Media Project Manager: Rich Barnes
Director of Marketing: Brandy Dawson
Senior Marketing Manager: Kate Mitchell
Marketing Assistant: Craig Deming
Senior Managing Editor: Ann Marie McCarthy
Assistant Managing Editor: Melissa Feimer
Production Project Managers: Barbara Cappuccio and Marlene Gassler
Senior Operations and Manufacturing Manager: Nick Sklitsis
Senior Operations Specialist: Brian Mackey
Manager of Design Development: John Christiana
Art Director and Interior Design: Kathy Mrozek
Cover Design: Kathy Mrozek
Site Supervisor, Pearson Imaging Center: Joe Conti
Pearson Imaging Center: Corin Skidds, Robert Uibelhoer, and Ron Walko
Cover Printer: Lehigh-Phoenix Color
Printer/Binder: Courier/Kendallville

This book was designed by Laurence King Publishing Ltd, London
www.laurenceking.com

Commissioning Editor: Kara Hattersley-Smith
Senior Editors: Melissa Danny/Sophie Page
Production Manager: Simon Walsh
Production File Preparation: Jo Fernandes
Page Design: Nick Newton/Randell Harris
Photo Researcher: Emma Brown
Copy Editors: Tessa Clark/Jenny Knight/Robert Shore/
Johanna Stephenson
Proofreader: Jennifer Speake
Indexer: Sue Farr

Cover photo: Peter Paul Rubens, *Self-Portrait with Isabella Brandt.* 1609–1610. Oil on canvas, 5′9″ × 4′5″ (1.78 × 1.36 m). Alte Pinakothek, Munich. Blauel/Gnamm/Artothek.

Credits and acknowledgments borrowed from other sources and reproduced, with permission, in this textbook appear on the appropriate page within text or on the credit pages in the back of this book.

Library of Congress Cataloging-in-Publication Data
Stokstad, Marilyn
    Art History / Marilyn Stokstad, Michael W. Cothren; contributors, Frederick M. Asher … [eg al.]. —4th ed.
    p. cm.
    Includes bibliographical references and index.
    ISBN-13: 978-0-205-74422-0 (hardcover : alk. paper)
    ISBN-10: 0205-74422-2 (hardcover : alk. paper)
    1. Art—History. I. Cothren, Michael Watt. II. Asher, Frederick M. III Title.
N5300.S923 2011
709—dc22   2010001489

10 9 8 7 6 5 4 3 2

Prentice Hall
is an imprint of

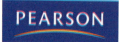
www.pearsonhighered.com

ISBN 10: 0-205-74421-4
ISBN 13: 978-0-205-74421-3

BRIEF CONTENTS

CONTENTS

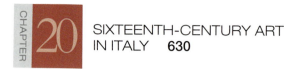

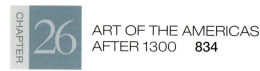

BOXES

CHAPTER 32 THE INTERNATIONAL SCENE SINCE 1950   **1082**

BOXES

This new edition of *Art History* is the result of a happy and productive collaboration between two scholar-teachers who share a common vision. In certain ways, we also share a common history. Neither of us expected to become professors of art history. Marilyn Stokstad took her first art history course as a requirement of her studio arts program. Michael Cothren discovered the discipline almost by chance during a semester abroad in Provence when a painting instructor sent him on a field trip to learn from the formal intricacies of Romanesque sculpture. Perhaps as a result of the unexpected delight we found in these revelatory formative experiences, we share a conviction that first courses in the history of art should be filled with as much enjoyment as erudition, that they should foster an enthusiastic, as well as an educated, public for the visual arts. With this end firmly in mind we will continue to create books intended to help students enjoy learning the essentials of a vast and complex field of study. For millennia human beings have embodied their most cherished ideas and values in visual and tangible form. We have learned that by engaging with these works from the past, we can all enrich our lives in the present, especially because we are living in a present when images have become an increasingly important aspect of how we communicate with each other.

Like its predecessors, this new edition seeks to balance formal and iconographic analysis with contextual art history in order to craft interpretations that will engage with a diverse student population. Throughout the text, the visual arts are treated as part of a larger world, in which geography, politics, religion, economics, philosophy, social life, and the other fine arts were related components of a vibrant cultural landscape. Art and architecture have played a central role in human history, and they continue to do so today. Our book will fulfill its purpose if it introduces a broad spectrum of students to some of the richest human achievements created through the centuries and across the globe, and if it inspires those students both to respect and to cherish their historical legacy in the visual arts. Perhaps it will convince some to dedicate themselves to assuring that our own age leaves a comparable artistic legacy, thereby continuing the ever evolving history of art.

So ... Why Use This New Edition?

We believe that even an established introductory art history text should continually respond to the changing needs of its audience—both students and educators. In this way it is more likely to make a greater difference in the role that art can and will assume in its readers' lives, both at the time of use and long into the future—indeed, long after the need for the next revision arises.

Our goal was to make this revised text an improvement over its earlier incarnations in sensitivity, readability, and accessibility without losing anything in comprehensiveness, in scholarly precision, or in its ability to engage the reader. Incorporating feedback from our many users and reviewers, we believe we have succeeded.

SOME HIGHLIGHTS OF THE NEW EDITION INCLUDE THE FOLLOWING:

- Every chapter now opens with a **Learn About It** feature (key learning objectives) and ends with a corresponding set of **Think About It** questions that probe back to the objectives and help students think through and apply what they have learned.
- The chapters are keyed to **MyArtsLab** resources that enrich and reinforce student learning (see p. xviii).
- **Newly colorized line art and 3D renderings** throughout the book provide the opportunity for students to better visualize architectural principles and key art processes.
- New **Recovering the Past boxes** document the discovery, restoration, or conservation of works of art. Some examples include discussions of the Rosetta stone, the Riace bronzes, and the Sutton Hoo find.
- There is **increased contextual emphasis** now visible with the linking of three key box categories by means of a "target" icon:
  - The new **Closer Look** feature, at the center of the target, pulls in for more specificity within the work of art itself, helping the student understand issues of usage, iconography, and style.
  - The **Object Speaks** box focuses on an in-depth contextual treatment of a work of art.
  - The **Art and Its Contexts** feature at the outer ring of the target represents discussions of ideas about art that are placed within the broad context of the chapter, or the history of art in general.
- **Global coverage has been deepened** with the addition of new works of art and revised discussions that incorporate new scholarship.
- A **new series of maps** has been created to enhance the clarity and accuracy of the relationship between the art discussed and its geographical location and political affiliation.
- Throughout, **images have been updated** whenever new and improved images were available. **New works have been added** to the discussion in many chapters to enhance and enrich what is said in the text.
- The **language used to characterize works of art**—especially those that attempt to capture the lifelike appearance of the natural world—has been **refined and clarified** to bring greater precision and nuance.
- In response to readers' requests, **discussion of many major monuments** has been expanded. For example, the Palette of

Narmer, Sainte Chapelle, Bosch's *Garden of Earthly Delights*, and the Contarelli Chapel.

- **Several chapters have been reorganized** for greater clarity and coherence. Prehistoric Art is now global in scope, the early nineteenth century has been incorporated into the chapter containing the eighteenth century to avoid breaking up the discussion of Neoclassicism and Romanticism, and the last two chapters now break at 1950.
- In keeping with this book's tradition of inclusivity, **an even broader spectrum of media is addressed** here, with expanded attention, for example, to Gothic stained glass, Renaissance tapestries, and Navajo textiles.

NEW SCHOLARSHIP

Over the many years we have taught undergraduate beginners, we have always enjoyed sharing—both with our students and our fellow educators—the new discoveries and fresh interpretive perspectives that are constantly enriching the history of art. We relished the opportunity here to incorporate some of the latest thinking and most recent discoveries—whether this involved revising the dating and interpretation of well-known Prehistoric monuments like Stonehenge (fig. 1–21), presenting fascinating new recreations of familiar masterworks such as the "colorized" Aegina archer from Ancient Greece (p.113), or including a new theory on the meaning of Jan van Eyck's masterful Double Portrait (fig. 18-1). Indeed, changes have been made on many levels—from the introduction to the bibliography, and from captions to chapter introductions. Every change aims to make the text more useful to the instructors and more vibrant for the students in today's art history classrooms.

Chapter by Chapter Revisions

Some of the key highlights of this new edition include the following:

Introduction

Completely rewritten, the introduction orients students to the process and nature of art historical investigation that underlies and, in essence, produced the historical narrative of the text itself.

Chapter 1: Prehistoric Art

Extensive revisions reflect the most current scholarship and broaden scope to global coverage. Key sections of the chapter rewritten to accommodate up-to-date interpretations, with new objects included. Thorough reworking of Stonehenge incorporates new thinking about the monument and landscape. Çatalhöyük and 'Ain Ghazal moved to this chapter.

Chapter 2: Art of the Ancient Near East

New chapter opener with *Stele of Naram-Sin* sets the stage for the chapter material. An historical photograph with a view of the guardian figures from the Citadel of Saragon II places the monument in context. New "Object Speaks" box on the "Great Lyre" includes a discussion of its archaeological discovery. Treatment of key monuments expanded.

Chapter 3: Art of Ancient Egypt

Historical and contextual material reduced to allow for richer discussions of the works of art. Sphinx moved from the Introduction to this chapter. Discussion of the Egyptian canon/grid system refined and updated. New images include stele of the sculptor Userwer and statue of Queen Karomama in the Louvre.

Chapter 4: Art of the Ancient Aegean

Completely revised discussion of Cycladic figures in light of recent research, including two new figures. Reworked Knossos complex text acknowledges its probable role as a ceremonial center. Treatment of *Harvester Rhyton* expanded. New box on Schliemann and the "Mask of Agamemnon" outlines reasons for suspicions about both. Discussion of Mycenaean tombs reorganized to include metalwork found in the shaft graves, with tholos tombs explanation now following.

Chapter 5: Art of Ancient Greece

Historical preludes reduced to focus on cultural and historical factors related to the history of art. Reorganized for greater clarity and coherence, including box placement. Expanded discussion of Aegina architecture and sculpture, and box on color in Greek sculpture focuses on Aegina, thus making it a model analysis for the basic points in architecture and architectural sculpture. Moved ceramic painting technique box to Archaic section in relation to the vessels where most relevant and added detailed views of use of each technique.

Chapter 6: Etruscan and Roman Art

Expanded treatment of the Etruscans with addition of a wall painting, a sarcophagus lid, and the *Ficoroni Cista*. Added clarity to discussions of representational modes—classicizing and veristic. Added box on portraiture using the Polybius text and the *Barberini Togatus*. Expanded treatment of tetrarchic sculpture, concentrating on introduction of a new ideal along with verism and classicism. Reorganized discussion of Constantinian art.

Chapter 7: Jewish, Early Christian, and Byzantine Art

New chapter opener introduces the eclecticism of Byzantine art and foregrounds the continuity of the classical heritage in the Byzantine world. Expanded treatment of Jewish art. Extensively revised Ravenna monuments, especially San Vitale. Reorganized Middle Byzantine discussion for clearer sense of chronology as well as geography. Much expanded section on the Chora church as a late Byzantine monument.

Chapter 8: Islamic Art

Revised to bring greater emphasis on art and society with simpler historical periodization. New chapter opener features *Maqamat* image of a preacher in a mosque, with many new images of art and architecture throughout. Expanded material on Mughal South Asia. Added new box on the topic of ornament with exemplary illustrations. New "Object Speaks" with in-depth explanation of the Mosque at Cordoba.

Chapter 9: Art of South and Southeast Asia before 1200

New coverage of sites, including Bamiyan whose Buddha images were destroyed in 2001. Period divisions updated for greater clarity and comprehension.

Chapter 10: Chinese and Korean Art before 1279

New illustrations of bronze-casting technique for improved understanding of process. New images include Neolithic cong, bronze *guang*, Tang equestrian pair, and detail of *Admonitions of the Imperial Instructress to Court Ladies*. "A Closer Look" examines in detail a section of stone relief in Wu family shrine.

Chapter 11: Japanese Art before 1333

New illustrations and discussion of art and architecture at the Great Buddha Hall (*Daibutsuden*) at Todaiji in "Recovering the Past" box. New discussion of Japan in the eighth century as the eastern terminus of the Silk Route. Increased emphasis on Japan's native religion of Shinto with addition of a Shinto painting. Expanded discussion of Chinese emigrant monks and their influence in section on Zen art.

Chapter 12: Art of the Americas before 1300

Substantially revised and updated sections on Mesoamerican and ancient Andean art. New images include Maya stela, Moche portrait vessel, Olmec sculptural offering, and cylinder vase with image of the Maya ballgame. Expanded discussion of Maya hieroglyphic writing.

Chapter 13: Early African Art

Revised and expanded discussion of Ife portraiture to emphasize idea that among earliest known examples of African sculpture, naturalistic representations of human body were not uncommon. Added treatment of the Ethiopian ancient sites of Lalibela, Gondar and Aksum. Fifteenth-century ivory hunting horn speaks to European contact and trade to west and central Africa that included the export of objects made in Africa for European aristocracy.

Chapter 14: Early Medieval Art in Europe

Added new "Recovering the Past" box on the Sutton Hoo find. New "Object Speaks" box on the Lindisfarne Gospels allows comparison between the Matthew portrait and the Ezra from the Codex Amiatinus. Moved reduced discussion of Vikings before the Carolingians to permit continuity between Carolingians and Ottonians. Carolingian discussion enhanced with addition of bronze equestrian emperor, Corvey façade, new drawing of Aachen chapel, and expanded Saint Gall plan.

Chapter 15: Romanesque Art

Abbreviated and condensed historical discussions not directly related to the situation in the art. Added Canigou to flesh out and clarify the opening discussion of "First Romanesque." Discussion of painting and mosaics at San Clemente in Rome and Saint-Savin-sur-Gartempe moved from a media-based section to the discussion of the buildings themselves. Expanded discussion of Moissac to give sense of one ensemble in some detail.

Chapter 16: Gothic Art of the Twelfth and Thirteenth Centuries

Significant revisions in French Gothic discussion with removal of Amiens and expansion of Saint-Denis, Chartres, and Reims. Stained-glass technique box moved to coincide with the discussion of Saint-Denis and a full panel of glass from that church illustrated. Consolidated and expanded treatment of Assisi.

Chapter 17: Fourteenth-Century Art in Europe

Discussion of Giotto and Duccio reworked to include new focus work in each program, the *Kiss of Judas* for Giotto and the *Raising of Lazarus* for Duccio. Added Simone Martini with discussion of his *Annunciation*. Introduced Hedwig Codex for more variety in German section.

Chapter 18: Fifteenth-Century Art in Northern Europe

More developed discussion of *Hours of Mary of Burgundy* to elaborate on its evidence of new devotional practices. Expanded treatment of *Unicorn* tapestry to include technique and effect, as well as iconography. New box on the processs of oil painting. Transformed discussion of Mérode Altarpiece based on new views about authorship. Revised discussion of Jan van Eyck's *Man in a Red Turban* as self-portrait. Reworked discussion of Fouquet's Melun Diptych.

Chapter 19: Renaissance Art in Fifteenth-Century Italy

New "Art and its Contexts" boxes on the Florentine Baptistery competition reliefs and *cassoni*. Expanded treatment of Orsanmichele including new image of building. Developed discussion of Donatello's David. Revised box on Renaissance perspective and moved to correspond with Masaccio. Expanded discussion of the Sistine mural project.

Chapter 20: Sixteenth-Century Art in Italy

Added Leonardo's *The Virgin of the Rocks*, Raphael portraits of Agnelo Doni and Maddalena Strozzi, and Michelangelo's Laurentian Library. Enhanced discussion of Palazzo del Tè with attention to social and political context. Reoriented treatment of Titian's "Venus" of Urbino in light of Rona Goffen's work. Discussion of Mannerism and Council of Trent reversed to conform with chronology and history.

Chapter 21: Sixteenth-Century Art in Northern Europe and the Iberian Peninsula

Expanded discussion of *Garden of Earthly Delights* includes new interpretive ideas and incorporates exterior wing panels. New addition and discussion of Quentin Massys's *Money Changer and his Wife*. "Object Speaks" box explores two Bruegel paintings as part of a series of the months. Added "Closer Look" box for Holbein's *The French Ambassadors*.

Chapter 22: Seventeenth-Century Art in Europe

New images include Artemisia Gentileschi's *Susannah and the Elders*, a Murillo *Immaculate Conception*, Rubens's *Self-Portrait with Isabella Brandt*, Ruisdael's *View of Haarlem from the Dunes at Overveen* and Le Nain's *A Peasant Family in an Interior*. Added technique box on etchings and drypoint.

Chapter 23: Art of South and Southeast Asia after 1200

Expanded Southeast Asia coverage to include Islamic art. Incorporated discussion of European engagement with Mughal art. Added discussion of South Asian artists working in the Diaspora and Indian architect Charles Correa.

Chapter 24: Chinese and Korean Art after 1279

New image by Yun Shouping, *Amaranth*. New "Closer Look" feature for detail of section of *Spring Dawn in the Han Palace*.

Chapter 25: Japanese Art after 1333

Greater emphasis on importance of crafts with addition of porcelain plate, *kosode*, and contemporary lacquer box. New "Closer Look" highlights techniques used in creation of a *kosode* robe. Increased discussion of Japan's integration of foreign, particularly Western, influences in its art and culture. New emphasis on architecture and crafts in the postwar period. Tea Ceremony discussion consolidated into one section.

Chapter 26: Art of the Americas after 1300

New chapter opener focuses on Navajo textile woven by Julia Jumbo. Additional contemporary Native American art incorporated into chapter. Revised and updated sections on Aztec and Inca art.

Chapter 27: Art of Pacific Cultures

Revised and updated introduction to Australia. Reworked Melanesia section to broaden range of culture areas: added New Britain Tubuan mask, discussions of role of women and different uses of masks. Revamped Polynesia introduction to be Polynesian-centered, not European-centered. New "Object Speaks" for Maori meetinghouse with additional images to show regional difference and change over time (time depth) in Maori art. Contemporary art in Oceania included.

Chapter 28: Art of Africa in the Modern Era

Incorporated image of 1897 British punitive expedition to Benin with short discussion of development of major collections of African art in Europe and America. Collection development tied to European expansion, political and economic interests. New "Object Speaks" created for Kuba mask with additional photographs to help to integrate the mask within its performance and meaning contexts. Moved discussion of divination among the Chokwe closer to discussion of Yoruba divination.

Chapter 29: Eighteenth- and Early Nineteenth-Century Art in Europe and North America

Reorganized chapter now encompasses the early nineteenth century to avoid breaking up the discussion of Neoclassicism and Romanticism. Revised and expanded discussion of how courtly system of individual patronage transformed, first into a Salon system, and then into an academic system of training, exhibition, and sale of art. New images include Fragonard's *The Swing* and Boucher's *Girl Reclining: Louise O'Murphy*.

Chapter 30: Mid- to late Nineteenth-Century Art in Europe and the United States

Revised and updated to emphasize the varying ways the academy and avant-garde envisaged and expressed modernity. Expanded discussion also includes exploration of differing concepts of modernity in France, England, the United States, and elsewhere. Photography moved to early part of chapter. Works by Manet now discussed together and in relation to Realism.

Chapter 31: Modern Art in Europe and the Americas, 1900–1950

Reworked to extend to 1950 so chapter covers the years of Modernism more fully. Updated to reflect the early centrality of Paris in the first half of twentieth century as a center of innovation in the art-world and its subsequent displacement by New York.

Chapter 32: The International Scene Since 1950

Reorganized and revised according to a thematic structure. Emphasis placed on the 1960s as a turning point in the global understanding of art and the subsequent globalization of art in the fast-paced communications age. Fifty percent new images reflect themes outlined in the text.

PEARSON CHOICES AND RESOURCES

Ordering Options

Art History is offered in a variety of formats to suit any course need, whether your survey is Western, global, comprehensive or concise, online or on the ground. Please contact your local representative for ordering details or visit www.pearsonhighered.com/art. In addition to this combined hardcover edition, *Art History* may be ordered in the following formats:

Volume I, Chapters 1–17 (ISBN: 978-0-205-74420-6)
Volume II, Chapters 17–32 (ISBN: 978-0-205-74421-3)

Art History **Portable Edition** has all of the same content as the comprehensive text in six slim volumes. Available in value-package combinations (Books 1, 2, 4, and 6) to suit **Western-focused survey** courses or available individually for period or region specific courses.
Book 1: Ancient Art, Chapters 1–6
Book 2: Medieval Art, Chapters 7, 8, 14–17
Book 3: A View of the World: Part One, Chapters 8–13
Book 4: Fourteenth to Seventeenth Century Art, Chapters 17–22
Book 5: A View of the World: Part Two, Chapters 23–28
Book 6: Eighteenth to Twenty-first Century Art, Chapters 29–32

Books À La Carte Give your students flexibility and savings with the new Books à la Carte edition of *Art History*. This edition features exactly the same content as the traditional textbook in a convenient three-hole-punched, loose-leaf version—allowing students to take only what they need to class. The Books à la Carte edition costs less than a used text—which helps students save about 35% over the cost of a new book.
Volume I, Books à la Carte Edition, 4/e
(ISBN: 978-0-205-79557-4)
Volume II, Books à la Carte Edition, 4/e
(ISBN: 978-0-205-79558-1)

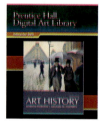

CourseSmart Textbooks Online is an exciting new choice for students looking to save money. As an alternative to purchasing the print textbook, students can subscribe to the same content online and save up to 50% off the suggested list price of the print text. For more information, or to subscribe to the CourseSmart eTextbook, visit www.coursesmart.com.

Combined Volume (ISBN: 978-0-205-80032-2)
Volume I (ISBN: 978-0-205-00189-7)
Volume II (ISBN: 978-0-205-00190-3)

Digital Resources

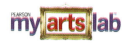

www.myartslab.com This dynamic website provides a wealth of resources geared to meet the diverse teaching and learning needs of today's instructors and students. Keyed specifically to the chapters of *Art History*, Fourth Edition, MyArtsLab's many tools will encourage students to experience and interact with works of art. Here are some of the key features:

- A complete **Pearson e-Text** of the book, enriched with multimedia, including: a unique human scale figure by all works of fine art, an audio version of the text read by the author, primary source documents, video demonstrations, and much more. Students can highlight, make notes and bookmark pages.
- 360 degree **Architectural Panoramas** for most of the major monuments in the book help students understand buildings from the inside and out.
- **Closer Look Tours** These interactive walkthroughs offer an in-depth look at key works of art, enabling the student to zoom in to see detail they could not otherwise see on the printed page or even in person. Enhanced with expert audio, they help students understand the meaning and message behind the work of art.
- A **Gradebook** that reports progress of students and the class as a whole.
- Instructors can also download the Instructor's Manual & Test Item File, PowerPoint questions for Classroom Response Systems, and obtain the PearsonMyTest assessment generation program.
- **MyArtsLab with e-Text** is available for no additional cost when packaged with any version of *Art History*, 4/e; it is also available standalone for less than the cost of a used text, and it is also available without e-Text for an even lower price.

The Prentice Hall Digital Art Library Instructors who adopt *Art History* are eligible to receive this unparalleled resource containing all of the images in *Art History* at the highest resolution (over 300 dpi) and pixellation possible for optimal projection and easy download. This resource features over 1,600 illustrations in jpeg and in PowerPoint, an instant download function for easy import into any presentation software, along with a unique zoom and "Save Detail" feature. (ISBN: 978-0-205-80037-7)

ACKNOWLEDGMENTS AND GRATITUDE

Art History, which was first published in 1995 by Harry N. Abrams, Inc. and Prentice Hall, Inc., continues to rely, each time it is revised, on the work of many colleagues and friends who contributed to the original texts and subsequent editions. Their work is reflected here, and we extend to them our enduring gratitude.

In preparing this fourth edition, we worked closely with two gifted and dedicated editors at Pearson/Prentice Hall, Sarah Touborg and Helen Ronan, whose almost daily support in so many ways was at the center of our work and created the foundation of what we have done. At Pearson, Barbara Cappuccio, Marlene Gassler, Melissa Feimer, Cory Skidds, Brian Mackey, David Nitti, and Carla Worner also supported us in our work. For the design we thank Kathy Mrozek and John Christiana. At Laurence King Publishing, Melissa Danny, Sophie Page, Kara Hattersley-Smith, Julia Ruxton and Simon Walsh oversaw the production of this new edition. We are very grateful for the editing of Cynthia Ward, Margaret Manos, and Robert Shore. For layout design we thank Nick Newton and for photo research we thank Emma Brown. Much appreciation also goes to Brandy Dawson, Director of Marketing, and Kate Stewart Mitchell, Marketing Manager, as well as the entire Social Sciences and Arts team at Pearson.

From Marilyn Stokstad:

The fourth edition of *Art History* represents the cumulative efforts of a distinguished group of scholars and educators. The work done by Stephen Addiss, Chutsing Li, Marylin M. Rhie, and Christopher D. Roy for the original edition has been updated and expanded by David Binkley and Patricia Darish (Africa), Claudia Brown and Robert Mowry (China and Korea), Patricia Graham (Japan), and Rick Asher (South and Southeast Asia). Joy Sperling has reworked the modern material previously contributed by Patrick Frank, David Cateforis and Bradford R. Collins. Dede Ruggles (Islamic), Claudia Brittenham (Americas), and Carol Ivory (Pacific Cultures) also have contributed to the fourth edition.

In addition, I want to thank University of Kansas colleagues Sally Cornelison, Susan Craig, Susan Earle, Charles Eldredge, Kris Ercums, Valija Evalds, Sherry Fowler, Stephen Goddard, Saralyn Reece Hardy, Marsha Haufler, Marni Kessler, Amy McNair, John Pulz, Linda Stone Ferrier, and John Younger for their help and advice. My thanks also to my friends Katherine Giele and Katherine Stannard, David and Nancy Dinneen, William Crowe, David Bergeron, Geraldo de Sousa, and the entire Clement family for their sympathy and encouragement. Of course, my very special thanks go to my sister, Karen Leider, and my niece, Anna Leider.

From Michael Cothren:

Words are barely adequate to express my gratitude to Marilyn Stokstad for welcoming me with such trust, enthusiasm, and warmth into the collaborative adventure of revising this book. Working alongside her—and our extraordinary editors Sarah Touborg and Helen Ronan—has been delightful and rewarding, enriching and challenging. I look forward to continuing the partnership.

My work was greatly facilitated by two extraordinary research assistants, Fletcher Coleman and Andrew Finegold, who found materials and offered opinions just when I needed them. I also have been supported by a host of colleagues at Swarthmore College. Generations of students challenged me to hone my pedagogical skills and steady my focus on what is at stake in telling the history of art. My colleagues in the Art Department—especially Stacy Bomento, June Cianfrana, Randall Exon, Constance Cain Hungerford, Janine Mileaf, Patricia Reilly, and Tomoko Sakomura—have answered all sorts of questions, shared innumerable insights on works in their areas of expertise, and offered unending encouragement and support. I am so lucky to work with them. In Classics, Gil Rose and William Turpin generously shared their expertise in Latin.

Many art historians have provided assistance, often at a moment's notice, and I am especially grateful to Betina Bergman, Claudia Brown, Brigitte Buettner, Madeline Caviness, Cheri Falkenstien-Doyle, Ed Gyllenhaal, Julie Hochstrasser, Penny Jolly, Alison Kettering, Benton Kidd, Ann Kuttner, Cary Liu, Elizabeth Marlowe, Thomas Morton, Mary Shepard, David Simon, Donna Sadler, Jeffrey Chipps Smith, and Mark Tucker.

I was fortunate to have the support of many friends. John Brendler, David Eldridge, Tricia Kramer, Stephen Lehmann, Mary Marissen, Bianca O'Keefe, and Bruce and Carolyn Stephens, patiently listened and truly relished my enjoyment of this work.

My mother and my late father, Mildred and Wat Cothren believed in me and made significant sacrifices to support my education from pre-school to graduate school. My extraordinary daughters Emma and Nora are a constant inspiration. I am so grateful for their delight in my passion for art's history, and for their dedication to keeping me from taking myself too seriously. My deepest gratitude is reserved for Susan Lowry, my wife and soul-mate, who brings joy to every facet of my life. She was not only patient and supportive during the long distraction of my work on this book; she provided help in so very many ways. The greatest accomplishment of my life in art history occurred on the day I met her at Columbia in 1973.

If the arts are ultimately an expression of human faith and integrity as well as human thought and creativity, then writing and producing books that introduce new viewers to the wonders of art's history, and to the courage and visions of the artists and art historians that stand behind it—remains a noble undertaking. We feel honored to be a part of such a worthy project.

Marilyn Stokstad
Lawrence, KS

Michael W. Cothren
Swarthmore, PA

Winter 2010

In Gratitude:

As its predecessors did, this Fourth Edition of *Art History* benefited from the reflections and assessments of a distinguished team of scholars and educators. The authors and Pearson are grateful to the following academic reviewers for their numerous insights and suggestions for improvement:

Craig Adcock, University of Iowa
Kimberly Allen-Kattus, Northern Kentucky University
Susan Jane Baker, University of Houston
Stephen Caffey, Texas A & M University
Charlotte Lowry Collins, Southeastern Louisiana University
Cindy B. Damschroder, University of Cincinnati
Rachael Z. DeLue, Princeton University
Anne Derbes, Hood College
Caroline Downing, State University of New York at Potsdam
Suzanne Eberle, Kendall College of Art & Design of Ferris State University
April Eisman, Iowa State University
Allen Farber, State University of New York at Oneonta
Richard Gay, University of North Carolina - Pembroke
Regina Gee, Montana State University
Mimi Hellman, Skidmore College
Julie Hochstrasser, University of Iowa
Evelyn Kain, Ripon College
Nancy Kelker, Middle Tennessee State University
Patricia Kennedy, Ocean County College
Jennie Klein, Ohio University
Katie Kresser, Seattle Pacific University
Cynthia Kristan-Graham, Auburn University
Barbara Platten Lash, Northern Virginia Community College
Elisa C. Mandell, California State University, Fullerton
Elizabeth C. Mansfield, New York University
Pamela Margerm, Kean University
Elizabeth Marlowe, Colgate University
Marguerite Mayhall, Kean University
Katherine A. McIver, University of Alabama at Birmingham
Janine Mileaf, Swarthmore College
Johanna D. Movassat, San Jose State University
Jacqueline Marie Musacchio, Wellesley College
Lynn Ostling, Santa Rosa Junior College
Ariel Plotek, Clemson University
Patricia V. Podzorski, University of Memphis
Margaret Richardson, George Mason University
James Rubin, Stony Brook University
Donna Sandrock, Santa Ana College
Michael Schwartz, Augusta State University
Joshua A. Shannon, University of Maryland
Karen Shelby, Baruch College
Susan Sidlauskas, Rutgers University
Royce W. Smith, Wichita State University
Jeffrey Chipps Smith, University of Texas - Austin
Stephen Smithers, Indiana State University
Laurie Sylwester, Columbia College (Sonora)
Carolyn Tate, Texas Tech University
Rita Tekippe, University of West Georgia
Amelia Trevelyan, University of North Carolina at Pembroke
Julie Tysver, Greenville Technical College
Jeryn Woodard, University of Houston

This edition has continued to benefit from the assistance and advice of scores of other teachers and scholars who generously answered questions, gave recommendations on organization and priorities, and provided specialized critiques during the course of work on previous editions.

We are grateful for the detailed critiques that the following readers across the country who were of invaluable assistance during work on the third edition:

Charles M. Adelman, University of Northern Iowa; Fred C. Albertson, University of Memphis; Frances Altvater, College of William and Mary; Michael Amy, Rochester Institute of Technology; Jennifer L. Ball, Brooklyn College, CUNY; Samantha Baskind, Cleveland State University; Tracey Boswell, Johnson County Community College; Jane H. Brown, University of Arkansas at Little Rock; Roger J. Crum, University of Dayton; Brian A. Curran, Penn State University; Michael T. Davis,

Mount Holyoke College; Juilee Decker, Georgetown College; Laurinda Dixon, Syracuse University; Laura Dufresne, Winthrop University; Dan Ewing, Barry University; Arne Flaten, Coastal Carolina University; John Garton, Cleveland Institute of Art; Rosi Gilday, University of Wisconsin, Oshkosh; Eunice D. Howe, University of Southern California; Phillip Jacks, George Washington University; William R. Levin, Centre College; Susan Libby, Rollins College; Henry Luttikhuizen, Calvin College; Lynn Mackenzie, College of DuPage; Dennis McNamara, Triton College; Gustav Medicus, Kent State University; Lynn Metcalf, St. Cloud State University; Jo-Ann Morgan, Coastal Carolina University; Beth A. Mulvaney, Meredith College; Dorothy Munger, Delaware Community College; Bonnie Noble, University of North Carolina at Charlotte; Leisha O'Quinn, Oklahoma State University; Willow Partington, Hudson Valley Community College; Martin Patrick, Illinois State University; Albert Reischuck, Kent State University; Jeffrey Ruda, University of California, Davis; Diane Scillia, Kent State University; Stephanie Smith, Youngstown State University; Janet Snyder, West Virginia University; James Terry, Stephens College; Michael Tinkler, Hobart and William Smith Colleges; Reid Wood, Lorain County Community College. Our thanks also to additional expert readers including: Susan Cahan, Yale University; David Craven, University of New Mexico; Marian Feldman, University of California, Berkeley; Dorothy Johnson, University of Iowa; Genevra Kornbluth, University of Maryland; Patricia Mainardi, City University of New York; Clemente Marconi, Columbia University, Tod Marder, Rutgers University; Mary Miller, Yale University; Elizabeth Penton, Durham Technical Community College; Catherine B. Scallen, Case Western University; Kim Shelton, University of California, Berkeley.

Many people reviewed the original edition of *Art History* and have continued to assist with its revision. Every chapter was read by one or more specialists. For work on the original book and assistance with subsequent editions my thanks go to: Barbara Abou-el-Haj, SUNY Binghamton; Roger Aiken, Creighton University; Molly Aitken; Anthony Alofsin, University of Texas, Austin; Christiane Andersson, Bucknell University; Kathryn Arnold; Julie Aronson, Cincinnati Art Museum; Michael Auerbach, Vanderbilt University; Larry Beck; Evelyn Bell, San Jose State University; Janetta Rebold Benton, Pace University; Janet Berlo, University of Rochester; Sarah Blick, Kenyon College; Jonathan Bloom, Boston College; Suzaan Boettger; Judith Bookbinder, Boston College; Marta Braun, Ryerson University; Elizabeth Broun, Smithsonian American Art Museum; Glen R. Brown, Kansas State University; Maria Elena Buszek, Kansas City Art Institute; Robert G. Calkins; Annmarie Weyl Carr; April Claggett, Keene State College; William W. Clark, Queens College, CUNY; John Clarke, University of Texas, Austin; Jaqueline Clipsham; Ralph T. Coe; Robert Cohon, The Nelson-Atkins Museum of Art; Alessandra Comini; James D'Emilio, University of South Florida; Walter Denny, University of Massachusetts, Amherst; Jerrilyn Dodds, City College, CUNY; Lois Drewer, Index of Christian Art; Joseph Dye, Virginia Museum of Art; James Farmer, Virginia Commonwealth University; Grace Flam, Salt Lake City Community College; Mary D. Garrard; Paula Gerson, Florida State University; Walter S. Gibson; Dorothy Glass; Oleg Grabar; Randall Griffey, Amherst College; Cynthia Hahn, Florida State University; Sharon Hill, Virginia Commonwealth University; John Hoopes, University of Kansas; Reinhild Janzen, Washburn University; Wendy Kindred, University of Maine at Fort Kent; Alan T. Kohl, Minneapolis College of Art; Ruth Kolarik, Colorado College; Carol H. Krinsky, New York University; Aileen Laing, Sweet Briar College; Janet LeBlanc, Clemson University; Charles Little, The Metropolitan Museum of Art; Laureen Reu Liu, McHenry County College; Loretta Lorance; Brian Madigan, Wayne State University; Janice Mann, Bucknell University; Judith Mann, St. Louis Art Museum; Richard Mann, San Francisco State University; James Martin,; Elizabeth Parker McLachlan; Tamara Mikailova, St. Petersburg, Russia, and Macalester College; Anta Montet-White; Anne E. Morganstern, Ohio State University; Winslow Myers, Bancroft School; Lawrence Nees, University of Delaware; Amy Ogata, Cleveland Institute of Art; Judith Oliver, Colgate University; Edward Olszewski, Case Western Reserve University; Sara Jane Pearman; John G. Pedley, University of Michigan; Michael Plante, Tulane University; Eloise Quiñones-Keber, Baruch College and the Graduate Center, CUNY; Virginia Raguin, College of the Holy Cross; Nancy H. Ramage, Ithaca College; Ann M. Roberts, Lake Forest College; Lisa Robertson, The Cleveland Museum of Art; Barry Rubin; Charles Sack, Parsons, Kansas; Jan Schall, The Nelson-Atkins Museum of Art; Tom Shaw, Kean College; Pamela Sheingorn, Baruch College, CUNY; Raechell Smith, Kansas City Art Institute; Lauren Soth; Anne R. Stanton, University of Missouri, Columbia; Michael Stoughton; Thomas Sullivan, OSB, Benedictine College (Conception Abbey); Pamela Trimpe, University of Iowa; Richard Turnbull, Fashion Institute of Technology; Elizabeth Valdez del Alamo, Montclair State College; Lisa Vergara; Monica Visoná, University of Kentucky; Roger Ward, Norton Museum of Art; Mark Weil, St. Louis; David Wilkins; Marcilene Wittmer, University of Miami.

The various features of this book reinforce each other, helping the reader to become comfortable with terminology and concepts that are specific to art history.

Starter Kit and Introduction   The Starter Kit is a highly concise primer of basic concepts and tools. The Introduction explores the way they are used to come to an understanding of the history of art.

Captions   There are two kinds of captions in this book: short and long. Short captions identify information specific to the work of art or architecture illustrated:

> artist (when known)
> title or descriptive name of work date
> original location (if moved to a museum or other site)
> material or materials a work is made of
> size (height before width) in feet and inches, with meters and centimeters in parentheses
> present location

The order of these elements varies, depending on the type of work illustrated. Dimensions are not given for architecture, for most wall paintings, or for most architectural sculpture. Some captions have one or more lines of small print below the identification section of the caption that gives museum or collection information. This is rarely required reading; its inclusion is often a requirement for gaining permission to reproduce the work.

Longer, discursive captions contain information that complements the narrative of the main text.

Definitions of Terms   You will encounter the basic terms of art history in three places:

> **In the Text**, where words appearing in boldface type are defined, or glossed, at their first use. Some terms are boldfaced and explained more than once, especially those that experience shows are hard to remember.
>
> **In Boxed Features**, on technique and other subjects, where labeled drawings and diagrams visually reinforce the use of terms.
>
> **In the Glossary**, at the end of the volume (p. 1137), which contains all the words in boldface type in the text and boxes.

Maps   At the beginning of each chapter you will find a map with all the places mentioned in the chapter.

Boxes   Special material that complements, enhances, explains, or extends the narrative text is set off in six types of tinted boxes.

Art and its Contexts and The Object Speaks boxes expand on selected works or issues related to the text. A Closer Look boxes use leader-line captions to focus attention on specific aspects of important works. Elements of Architecture boxes clarify specifically architectural features, often explaining engineering principles or building technology. Technique boxes outline the techniques and processes by which certain types of art are created. Recovering the Past boxes highlight the work of archaeologists who uncover and conservators who assure the preservation and clear presentation of art.

Bibliography   The bibliography at the end of this book beginning on page 1146 contains books in English, organized by general works and by chapter, that are basic to the study of art history today, as well as works cited in the text.

Learn About It   Placed at the beginning of each chapter, this feature captures in bulleted form the key learning objectives, or outcomes, of the chapter. They point to what will have been accomplished upon its completion.

Think About It   These critical thinking questions appear at the end of each chapter and help students assess their mastery of the learning objectives (Learn About It) by asking them to think through and apply what they have learned.

MyArtsLab prompts   These notations are found throughout the chapter and are keyed to MyArtsLab resources that enrich and reinforce student learning.

Dates, Abbreviations, and Other Conventions   This book uses the designations BCE and CE, abbreviations for "Before the Common Era" and "Common Era," instead of BC ("Before Christ") and AD ("Anno Domini," "the year of our Lord"). The first century BCE is the period from 99 BCE to 1 BCE; the first century CE is from the year 1 CE to 99 CE. Similarly, the second century CE is the period from 199 BCE to 100 BCE; the second century CE extends from 100 CE to 199 CE.

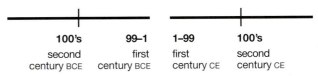

100's	99–1	1–99	100's
second century BCE	first century BCE	first century CE	second century CE

Circa ("about") is used with approximate dates, spelled out in the text and abbreviated to "c." in the captions. This indicates that an exact date is not yet verified.

An illustration is called a "figure," or "fig." Thus, figure 6–7 is the seventh numbered illustration in Chapter 6, and fig. Intro-3 is the third figure in the Introduction. There are two types of figures: photographs of artworks or of models, and line drawings. Drawings are used when a work cannot be photographed or when a diagram or simple drawing is the clearest way to illustrate an object or a place.

When introducing artists, we use the words *active* and *documented* with dates, in addition to "b." (for "born") and "d." (for "died"). "Active" means that an artist worked during the years given. "Documented" means that documents link the person to that date.

Accents are used for words in French, German, Italian, and Spanish only. With few exceptions, names of cultural institutions in Western European countries are given in the form used in that country.

Titles of Works of Art   It was only over the last 500 years that paintings and works of sculpture created in Europe and North America were given formal titles, either by the artist or by critics and art historians. Such formal titles are printed in italics. In other traditions and cultures, a single title is not important or even recognized.

In this book we use formal descriptive titles of artworks where titles are not established. If a work is best known by its non-English title, such as Manet's *Le Déjeuner sur l'Herbe (The Luncheon on the Grass)*, the original language precedes the translation.

Art history focuses on the visual arts—painting, drawing, sculpture, prints, photography, ceramics, metalwork, architecture, and more. This Starter Kit contains basic information and addresses concepts that underlie and support the study of art history. It provides a quick reference guide to the vocabulary used to classify and describe art objects. Understanding these terms is indispensable because you will encounter them again and again in reading, talking, and writing about art.

Let us begin with the basic properties of art. A work of art is a material object having both form and content. It is often described and categorized according to its *style* and *medium*.

FORM

Referring to purely visual aspects of art and architecture, the term *form* encompasses qualities of *line, shape, color, light, texture, space, mass, volume,* and *composition.* These qualities are known as *formal elements.* When art historians use the term *formal,* they mean "relating to form."

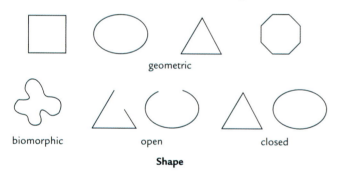

geometric

biomorphic   open   closed

Shape

Line and **shape** are attributes of form. Line is an element—usually drawn or painted—the length of which is so much greater than the width that we perceive it as having only length. Line can be actual, as when the line is visible, or it can be implied, as when the movement of the viewer's eyes over the surface of a work follows a path determined by the artist. Shape, on the other hand, is the two-dimensional, or flat, area defined by the borders of an enclosing *outline* or *contour.* Shape can be *geometric, biomorphic* (suggesting living things; sometimes called *organic), closed,* or *open.* The *outline* or *contour* of a three-dimensional object can also be perceived as line.

Color has several attributes. These include *hue, value,* and *saturation.*

Hue is what we think of when we hear the word *color,* and the terms are interchangeable. We perceive hues as the result of differing wavelengths of electromagnetic energy. The visible spectrum, which can be seen in a rainbow, runs from red through violet. When the ends of the spectrum are connected through the hue red-violet, the result may be diagrammed as a color wheel. The primary hues (numbered 1) are red, yellow, and blue. They are known as primaries because all other colors are made by combining these hues. Orange, green, and violet result from the mixture of two primaries and are known as secondary hues (numbered 2). Intermediate hues, or tertiaries (numbered 3), result from the mixture of a primary and a secondary. Complementary colors are the two colors directly opposite one another on the color

wheel, such as red and green. Red, orange, and yellow are regarded as warm colors and appear to advance toward us. Blue, green, and violet, which seem to recede, are called cool colors. Black and white are not considered colors but neutrals; in terms of light, black is understood as the absence of color and white as the mixture of all colors.

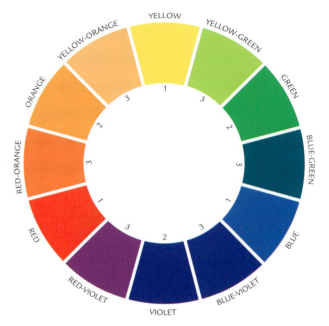

Value is the relative degree of lightness or darkness of a given color and is created by the amount of light reflected from an object's surface. A dark green has a deeper value than a light green, for example. In black-and-white reproductions of colored objects, you see only value, and some artworks—for example, a drawing made with black ink—possess only value, not hue or saturation.

Value scale from white to black.

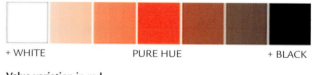

+ WHITE   PURE HUE   + BLACK

Value variation in red.

Saturation, also sometimes referred to as *intensity,* is a color's quality of brightness or dullness. A color described as highly saturated looks vivid and pure; a hue of low saturation may or look a little muddy or greyed.

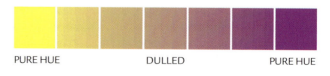

PURE HUE   DULLED   PURE HUE

Intensity scale from bright to dull.

Texture, another attribute of form, is the tactile (or touch-perceived) quality of a surface. It is described by words such as *smooth*, *polished*, *rough*, *prickly*, *grainy*, or *oily*. Texture takes two forms: the texture of the actual surface of the work of art and the implied (illusionistically described) surface of objects represented in the work of art.

Space is what contains forms. It may be actual and three-dimensional, as it is with sculpture and architecture, or it may be fictional, represented illusionistically in two dimensions, as when artists represent recession into the distance on a flat surface—such as a wall or a canvas--by using various systems of perspective.

Mass and volume are properties of three-dimensional things. Mass is solid matter—whether sculpture or architecture—that takes up space. Volume is enclosed or defined space, and may be either solid or hollow. Like space, mass and volume may be illusionistically represented on a two-dimensional surface, such as in a painting or a photograph.

Composition is the organization, or arrangement, of forms in a work of art. Shapes and colors may be repeated or varied, balanced symmetrically or asymmetrically; they may be stable or dynamic. The possibilities are nearly endless and artistic choice depends both on the time and place where the work was created as well as the objectives of individual artists. Pictorial depth (spatial recession) is a specialized aspect of composition in which the three-dimensional world is represented on a flat surface, or *picture plane*. The area "behind" the picture plane is called the *picture space* and conventionally contains three "zones": *foreground*, *middle ground*, and *background*.

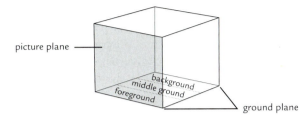

Various techniques for conveying a sense of pictorial depth have been devised by artists in different cultures and at different times. A number of them are diagrammed here. In some European art, the use of various systems of *perspective* has sought to create highly convincing illusions of recession into space. At other times and in other cultures, indications of recession are actually suppressed or avoided to emphasize surface rather than space.

TECHNIQUE | Pictorial devices for depicting recession in space

overlapping

In overlapping, partially covered elements are meant to be seen as located behind those covering them.

diminution

In diminution of scale, successively smaller elements are perceived as being progressively farther away than the largest ones.

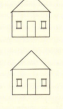

vertical perspective

Vertical perspective stacks elements, with the higher ones intended to be perceived as deeper in space.

atmospheric perspective

Through atmospheric perspective, objects in the far distance (often in bluish-gray hues) have less clarity than nearer objects. The sky becomes paler as it approaches the horizon.

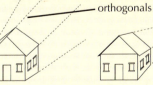

orthogonals

divergent perspective

In divergent or reverse perspective, forms widen slightly and imaginary lines called orthogonals diverge as they recede in space.

intuitive perspective

Intuitive perspective takes the opposite approach from divergent perspective. Forms become narrower and orthogonals converge the farther they are from the viewer, approximating the optical experience of spatial recession.

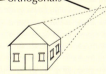

vanishing point · horizon line · vanishing point

one-point · two-point

linear perspective

Linear perspective (also called scientific, mathematical, one-point and Renaissance perspective) is a rationalization or standardization of intuitive perspective that was developed in fifteenth-century Italy. It uses mathematical formulas to construct images in which all elements are shaped by, or arranged along, orthogonals that converge in one or more vanishing points on a horizon line.

CONTENT

Content includes *subject matter*, but not all works of art have subject matter. Many buildings, paintings, sculptures, and other art objects include no recognizable references to things in nature nor to any story or historical situation, focusing instead on lines, colors, masses, volumes, and other formal elements. However, all works of art—even those without recognizable subject matter—have content, or meaning, insofar as they seek to communicate ideas, convey feelings, or affirm the beliefs and values of their makers, their patrons, and usually the people who originally viewed or used them.

Content may derive from the social, political, religious, and economic *contexts* in which a work was created, the *intention* of the artist, and the *reception* of the work by beholders (the audience). Art historians, applying different methods of *interpretation*, often arrive at different conclusions regarding the content of a work of art, and single works of art can contain more than one meaning because they are occasionally directed at more than one audience.

The study of subject matter is called *iconography* (literally, "the writing of images") and includes the identification of *symbols*—images that take on meaning through association, resemblance, or convention.

STYLE

Expressed very broadly, *style* is the combination of form and composition that makes a work distinctive. *Stylistic analysis* is one of art history's most developed practices, because it is how art historians recognize the work of an individual artist or the characteristic manner of groups of artists working in a particular time or place. Some of the most commonly used terms to discuss *artistic styles* include *period style*, *regional style*, *representational style*, *abstract style*, *linear style*, and *painterly style*.

Period style refers to the common traits detectable in works of art and architecture from a particular historical era. It is good practice not to use the words "style" and "period" interchangeably. Style is the sum of many influences and characteristics, including the period of its creation. An example of proper usage is "an American house from the Colonial period built in the Georgian style."

Regional style refers to stylistic traits that persist in a geographic region. An art historian whose specialty is medieval art can recognize Spanish style through many successive medieval periods and can distinguish individual objects created in medieval Spain from other medieval objects that were created in, for example, Italy.

Representational styles are those that describe the appearance of recognizable subject matter in ways that make it seem lifelike.

> **Realism** and **Naturalism** are terms that some people used interchangeably to characterize artists' attempts to represent the observable world in a manner that appears to describe its visual appearance accurately. When capitalized, Realism refers to a specific period style discussed in Chapter 30.

> **Idealization** strives to create images of physical perfection according to the prevailing values or tastes of a culture. The artist may work in a representational style and idealize it to capture an underlying value or expressive effect.

> **Illusionism** refers to a highly detailed style that seeks to create a convincing illusion of physical reality by describing its visual appearance meticulously.

Abstract styles depart from mimicking lifelike appearance to capture the essence of a form. An abstract artist may work from nature or from a memory image of nature's forms and colors, which are simplified, stylized, perfected, distorted, elaborated, or otherwise transformed to achieve a desired expressive effect.

> **Nonrepresentational (or Nonobjective) Art** is a term often used for works of art that do not aim to produce recognizable natural imagery.

> **Expressionism** refers to styles in which the artist exaggerates aspects of form to draw out the beholder's subjective response or to project the artist's own subjective feelings.

Linear describes both styles and techniques. In linear styles artists use line as the primary means of definition. But linear paintings can also incorporate *modeling*—creating an illusion of three-dimensional substance through shading, usually executed so that brushstrokes nearly disappear.

Painterly describes a style of representation in which vigorous, evident brushstrokes dominate, and outlines, shadows, and highlights are brushed in freely.

MEDIUM AND TECHNIQUE

Medium (plural, *media*) refers to the material or materials from which a work of art is made. Today, literally anything can be used to make a work of art, including not only traditional materials like paint, ink, and stone, but also rubbish, food, and the earth itself.

Technique is the process that transforms media into a work of art. Various techniques are explained throughout this book in Technique boxes. Two-dimensional media and techniques include painting, drawing, prints, and photography. Three-dimensional media and techniques are sculpture (for example, using stone, wood, clay or cast metal), architecture, and many small-scale arts (such as jewelry, containers, or vessels) in media such as ceramics, metal, or wood.

Painting includes wall painting and fresco, illumination (the decoration of books with paintings), panel painting (painting on wood panels), painting on canvas, and handscroll and hanging scroll painting. The paint in these examples is pigment mixed with a liquid vehicle, or binder. Some art historians also consider pictorial media such as mosaic and stained glass—where the pigment is arranged in solid form—as a type of painting.

Graphic arts are those that involve the application of lines and strokes to a two-dimensional surface or support, most often paper. Drawing is a graphic art, as are the various forms of printmaking. Drawings may be sketches (quick visual notes, often made in preparation for larger drawings or paintings); studies (more carefully drawn analyses of details or entire compositions); cartoons (full-scale drawings made in preparation for work in another medium, such as fresco, stained glass, or tapestry); or complete artworks in themselves. Drawings can be made with ink, charcoal, crayon, or pencil. Prints, unlike drawings, are made in multiple copies. The various forms of printmaking include woodcut, the intaglio processes (engraving, etching, drypoint), and lithography.

Photography (literally, "light writing") is a medium that involves the rendering of optical images on light-sensitive surfaces. Photographic images are typically recorded by a camera.

Sculpture is three-dimensional art that is *carved*, *modeled*, *cast*, or *assembled*. Carved sculpture is subtractive in the sense that the image is created by taking away material. Wood, stone, and ivory are common materials used to create carved sculptures. Modeled sculpture is considered additive, meaning that the object is built up from a material, such as clay, that is soft enough to be molded and shaped. Metal sculpture is usually cast or is assembled by welding or a similar means of permanent joining.

Sculpture is either free-standing (that is, surrounded by space) or in pictorial relief. Relief sculpture projects from the background surface of the same piece of material. High-relief sculpture projects far from its background; low-relief sculpture is only slightly raised; and sunken relief, found mainly in ancient Egyptian art, is carved into the surface, with the highest part of the relief being the flat surface.

Ephemeral arts include processions, ceremonies, or ritual dances (often with décor, costumes, or masks); performance art; earthworks; cinema and video art; and some forms of digital or computer art. All impose a temporal limitation—the artwork is viewable for a finite period of time and then disappears forever, is in a constant state of change, or must be replayed to be experienced again.

Architecture creates enclosures for human activity or habitation. It is three-dimensional, highly spatial, functional, and closely bound with developments in technology and materials. Since it is difficult to capture in a photograph, several types of schematic drawings are commonly used to enable the visualization of a building:

> **Plans** depict a structure's masses and voids, presenting a view from above of the building's footprint or as if it had been sliced horizontally at about waist height.

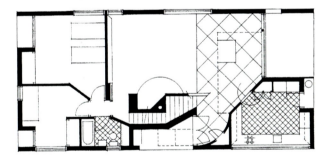

Plan: Philadelphia, Vanna Venturi House

Sections reveal the interior of a building as if it had been cut vertically from top to bottom.

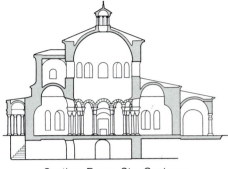

Section: Rome, Sta. Costanza

Isometric Drawings show buildings from oblique angles either seen from above ("bird's-eye view") to reveal their basic three-dimensional forms (often cut away so we can peek inside) or from below ("worm's-eye view") to represent the arrangement of interior spaces and the upward projection of structural elements.

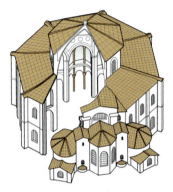

Isometric cutaway from above: Ravenna, San Vitale

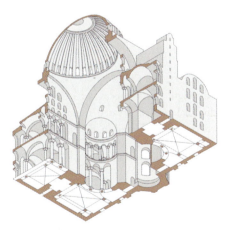

Isometric projection from below: Istanbul, Hagia Sophia

INTRODUCTION

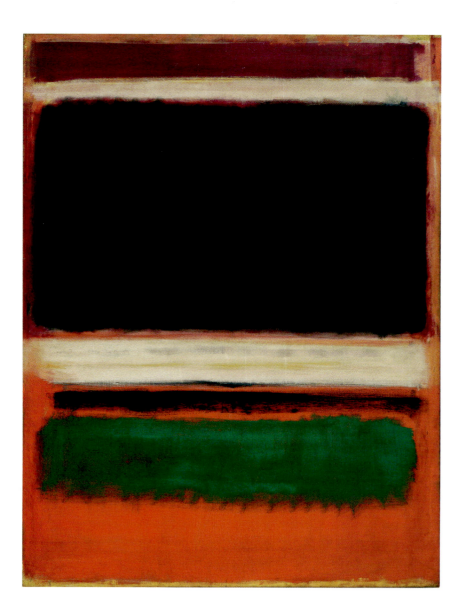

INTRO-1 • Mark Rothko
**NO. 3/NO. 13 (MAGENTA,
BLACK AND GREEN ON
ORANGE)**
1949. Oil on canvas, 7′1⅜″ × 5′5″
(2.165 × 1.648 m). Museum of
Modern Art, New York.

The title of this book seems clear. It defines a field of academic study and scholarly research that has achieved a secure place in college and university curricula across North America. But *Art History* couples two words—even two worlds—that are less well focused when separated. What is art? In what sense does it have a history? Students of art and its history should pause and engage, even if briefly, with these large questions before beginning the journey surveyed in the following chapters.

WHAT IS ART?

Artists, critics, art historians, and the general public all grapple with this thorny question. The *Random House Dictionary* defines "art" as "the quality, production, expression, or realm of what is beautiful, or of more than ordinary significance." Others have characterized "art" as something human-made that combines creative imagination and technical skill and satisfies an innate desire for order and harmony—perhaps a human hunger for the

---

LEARN ABOUT IT

I.1 Consider the criteria used to identify and characterize those cultural artifacts that are labeled as "art."

I.2 Survey the methods used by art historians to analyze works of art and interpret their meaning within their original cultural contexts.

I.3 Explore the methods and objectives of visual analysis.

I.4 Assess the way art historians identify conventional subject matter and symbols in a process called iconography.

I.5 Trace the process of art-historical interpretation in a case study.

HEAR MORE: Listen to an audio file of your chapter **www.myartslab.com**

beautiful. This seems relatively straightforward until we start to look at modern and contemporary art, where there has been a heated and extended debate concerning "What is Art?" The focus is often far from questions of transcendent beauty, ordered design, or technical skill, and centers instead on the meaning of a work for an elite target audience or the attempt to pose challenging questions or unsettle deep-seated cultural ideas.

The works of art discussed in this book represent a privileged subset of artifacts produced by past and present cultures. They were usually meant to be preserved, and they are currently considered worthy of conservation and display. The determination of which artifacts are exceptional—which are works of art— evolves through the actions, opinions, and selections of artists, patrons, governments, collectors, archaeologists, museums, art historians, and others. Labeling objects as art is usually meant to signal that they transcended or now transcend in some profound way their practical function, often embodying cherished cultural ideas or foundational values. Sometimes it can mean they are considered beautiful, well designed, and made with loving care, but this is not always the case, especially in the twentieth and twenty-first centuries when the complex notion of what is art has little to do with the idea of beauty. Some critics and historians argue that works of art are tendentious embodiments of power and privilege, hardly sublime expressions of beauty or truth. After all, art can be unsettling as well as soothing, challenging as well as reassuring, whether made in the present or surviving from the past.

Increasingly we are realizing that our judgments about what constitutes art—as well as what constitutes beauty—are conditioned by our own education and experience. Whether acquired at home, in classrooms, in museums, at the movies, or on the internet, our responses to art are learned behaviors, influenced by class, gender, race, geography, and economic status as well as education. Even art historians find that their definitions of what constitutes art—and what constitutes artistic quality—evolve with additional research and understanding. Exploring works by twentieth-century painter Mark Rothko and nineteenth-century quiltmakers Martha Knowles and Henrietta Thomas demonstrates how definitions of art and artistic value are subject to change over time.

Rothko's painting, **MAGENTA, BLACK AND GREEN ON ORANGE (FIG. INTRO–1)**, is a well-known example of the sort of abstract painting that was considered the epitome of artistic sophistication by the mid-twentieth-century New York art establishment. It was created by an artist who meant it to be a work of art. It was acquired by the Museum of Modern Art in New York, and its position on the walls of that museum is a sure sign that it was accepted as such by a powerful cultural institution. However, beyond the context of the American artists, dealers, critics, and collectors who made up Rothko's art world, such paintings were often received with skepticism. They were seen by many as incomprehensible—lacking both technical skill and recognizable subject matter, two criteria that were part of the general public's definition of art at the time. Abstract paintings

soon inspired a popular retort: "That's not art; my child could do it!" Interestingly enough, Rothko saw in the childlike character of his own paintings one of the qualities that made them works of art. Children, he said, "put forms, figures, and views into pictorial arrangements, employing out of necessity most of the rules of optical perspective and geometry but without the knowledge that they are employing them." He characterized his own art as childlike, as "an attempt to recapture the freshness and naiveté of childish vision." In part because they are carefully crafted by an established artist who provided these kinds of intellectual justifications for their character and appearance, Rothko's abstract paintings are broadly considered works of art and are treasured possessions of major museums across the globe.

Works of art, however, do not always have to be created by individuals who perceive themselves as artists. Nor are all works produced for an art market surrounded by critics and collectors ready to explain, exhibit, and disperse them, ideally to prestigious museums. Such is the case with this quilt **(FIG. INTRO–2)**, made by Martha Knowles and Henrietta Thomas a century before Rothko's painting. Their work is similarly composed of blocks of color, and like Rothko, they produced their visual effect by arranging these flat chromatic shapes carefully and regularly on a rectangular field. But this quilt was not meant to hang on the wall of an art museum. It is the social product of a friendship, intended as an intimate gift, presented to a loved one for use in her home. An inscription on the quilt itself makes this clear—"From M. A. Knowles to her Sweet Sister Emma, 1843." Thousands of such friendship quilts

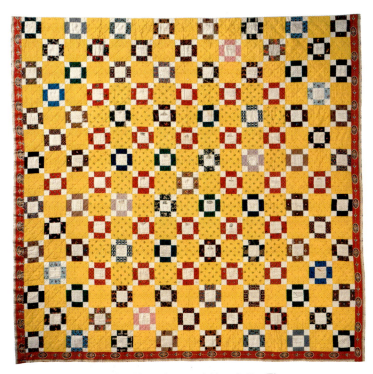

INTRO-2 • Martha Knowles and Henrietta Thomas
MY SWEET SISTER EMMA
1843. Cotton quilt, 8′11″ × 9′1″ (2.72 × 2.77 m). International Quilt Studies Center, University of Nebraska, Lincoln, Nebraska.

Art and Architecture

This book contains much more than paintings and textiles. Within these pages you will also encounter sculpture, vessels, books, jewelry, tombs, chairs, photographs, architecture, and more. But as with Rothko's *Magenta, Black, and Green on Orange* (SEE FIG. INTRO–1) and Knowles and Thomas's *My Sweet Sister Emma* (SEE FIG. INTRO–2), criteria have been used to determine which works are selected for inclusion in a book titled *Art History*. Architecture presents an interesting case.

Buildings meet functional human needs by enclosing human habitation or activity. Many works of architecture, however, are considered "exceptional" because they transcend functional demands by manifesting distinguished architectural design or because they embody in important ways the values and goals of the culture that built them. Such buildings are usually produced by architects influenced, like painters, by great works and traditions from the past. In some cases they harmonize with, or react to, their natural or urban surroundings. For such reasons, they are discussed in books on the history of art.

Typical of such buildings is the church of Nôtre-Dame-du-Haut in Ronchamp, France, designed and constructed between 1950 and 1955 by Swiss architect Charles-Edouard Jeanneret, better known by his pseudonym, Le Corbusier. This building is the product of a significant historical moment, rich in global cultural meaning. A pilgrimage church on this site had been destroyed during World War II, and the creation here of a new church symbolized the end of a devastating war, embodying hopes for a brighter global future. Le Corbusier's design—drawing on sources that ranged from Algerian mosques to imperial Roman villas, from crab shells to airplane wings—is sculptural as well as architectural. It soars at the crest of a hill toward the sky but at the same time seems solidly anchored in the earth. And its coordination with the curves of the natural landscape complement the creation of an outdoor setting for religious ceremonies (to the right in the figure) to supplement the church interior that Le Corbusier characterized as a "container for intense concentration." In fact, this building is so renowned today as a monument of modern architecture, that the bus-loads of pilgrims who arrive at the site are mainly architects and devotees of architectural history.

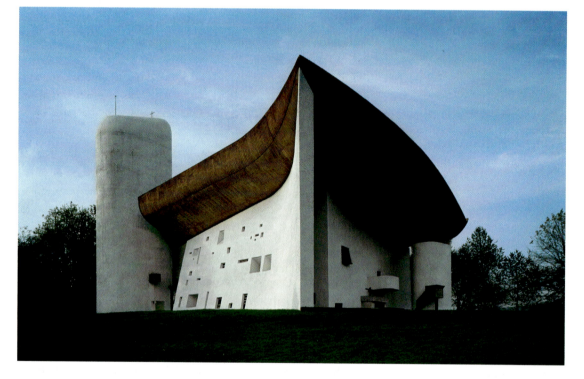

Le Corbusier **NÔTRE-DAME-DU-HAUT**
1950–1955. Ronchamp, France.

were made by women during the middle years of the nineteenth century for use on beds, either to provide warmth or as a covering spread. Whereas quilts were sometimes displayed to a broad and enthusiastic audience of producers and admirers at competitions held at state and county fairs, they were not collected by art museums or revered by artists until relatively recently.

In 1971, at the Whitney Museum in New York—an establishment bastion of the art world in which Rothko moved and worked—art historians Jonathan Holstein and Gail van der Hoof mounted an exhibition entitled "Abstract Design in American Quilts," demonstrating the artistic affiliation we have already noted in comparing the way Knowles and Thomas, like Rothko, create abstract patterns with fields of color. Quilts were later accepted—or should the word be "appropriated?"—as works of art and hung on the walls of a New York art museum because of their visual similarities with the avant-garde, abstract works of art created by establishment, New York artists.

Art historian Patricia Mainardi took the case for quilts one significant step further in a pioneering article of 1973 published in *The Feminist Art Journal*. Entitled, "Quilts: The Great American Art," her argument was rooted not only in the aesthetic affinity of quilts with the esteemed work of contemporary abstract painters, but also in a political conviction that the definition of art had to be broadened. What was at stake here was historical veracity. Mainardi began, "Women have always made art. But for most women, the arts highest valued by male society have been closed to them for just that reason. They have put their creativity instead into the needlework arts, which exist in fantastic variety wherever there are women, and which in fact are a universal female art, transcending race, class, and national borders." She argued for the inclusion of quilts within the history of art to give deserved attention to the work of women artists who had been excluded from discussion because they created textiles and because they worked outside the male-dominated professional structures of the art world—because they were women. Quilts now hang as works of art on the walls of museums and appear with regularity in books that survey the history of art.

As these two examples demonstrate, definitions of art are rooted in cultural systems of value that are subject to change. And as they change, the list of works considered by art historians is periodically revised. Determining what to study is a persistent part of the art historian's task.

WHAT IS ART HISTORY?

There are many ways to study or appreciate works of art. Art history represents one specific approach, with its own goals and its own methods of assessment and interpretation. Simply put, art historians seek to understand the meaning of art from the past within its original cultural contexts, both from the point of view of its producers—artists, architects, and patrons—as well as from the point of view of its consumers—those who formed its original audience. Coming to an understanding of the cultural meaning of a work of art requires detailed and patient investigation on many levels, especially with art that was produced long ago and in societies distinct from our own. This is a scholarly rather than an intuitive exercise. In art history, the work of art is seen as an embodiment of the values, goals, and aspirations of its time and place of origin. It is a part of culture.

Art historians use a variety of theoretical perspectives and a host of interpretive strategies to come to an understanding of works of art within their cultural contexts. But as a place to begin, the work of art historians can be divided into four types of investigation:

1. assessment of physical properties,
2. analysis of visual or formal structure,
3. identification of subject matter or conventional symbolism, and
4. integration within cultural context.

ASSESSING PHYSICAL PROPERTIES

Of the methods used by art historians to study works of art, this is the most objective, but it requires close access to the work itself. Physical properties include shape, size, materials, and technique. For instance, many pictures are rectangular (e.g., SEE FIG. INTRO–1), but some are round (see page xxxi, FIG. C). Paintings as large as Rothko's require us to stand back if we want to take in the whole image, whereas some paintings (see page xxx, FIG. A) are so small that we are drawn up close to examine their detail. Rothko's painting and Knowles and Thomas's quilt are both rectangles of similar size, but they are distinguished by the materials from which they are made—oil paint on canvas versus cotton fabric joined by stitching. In art history books, most physical properties can only be understood from descriptions in captions, but when we are in the presence of the work of art itself, size and shape may be the first thing we notice. To fully understand medium and technique, however, it may be necessary to employ methods of scientific analysis or documentary research to elucidate the practices of artists at the time when and place where the work was created.

ANALYZING FORMAL STRUCTURE

Art historians explore the visual character that artists bring to their works—using the materials and the techniques chosen to create them—in a process called **formal analysis**. On the most basic level, it is divided into two parts:

- assessing the individual visual elements or formal vocabulary that constitute pictorial or sculptural communication, and
- discovering the overall arrangement, organization, or structure of an image, a design system that art historians often refer to as **composition**.

THE ELEMENTS OF VISUAL EXPRESSION. Artists control and vary the visual character of works of art to give their subjects and ideas meaning and expression, vibrancy and persuasion, challenge or delight (see "A Closer Look," pages xxx–xxxi). For example, the motifs, objects, figures, and environments within paintings can be sharply defined by line (SEE FIGS. INTRO–2 and INTRO–3), or they can be suggested by a sketchier definition (SEE FIGS. **INTRO**–1 and INTRO–4). Painters can simulate the appearance of three-dimensional form through **modeling** or shading (SEE FIG. INTRO–3 and page xxxi, FIG. C), that is by describing the way light from a single source will highlight one side of a solid while leaving the other side in shadow. Alternatively, artists can avoid any strong sense of three-dimensionality by emphasizing patterns on a surface rather than forms in space (SEE FIG. INTRO–1 and page xxx, FIG. A). In addition to revealing the solid substance of forms through modeling, dramatic lighting can guide viewers to specific areas of a

A CLOSER LOOK

Visual Elements of Pictorial Expression ▸ Line, Light, Form, and Color.

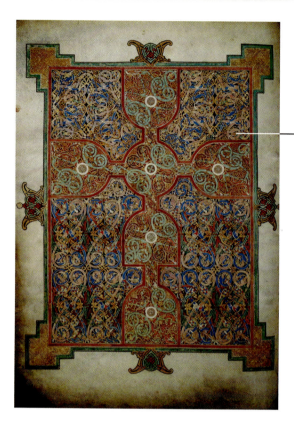

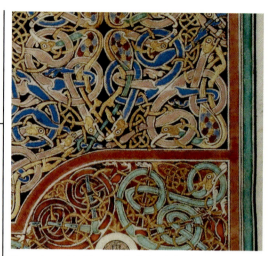

LINE

A. *Carpet Page* **from the Lindisfarne Gospels**
From Lindisfarne, England. c. 715–720. Ink and tempera on vellum, 13⅜ × 9⁷⁄₁₆″ (34 × 24 cm). British Library, London. Cotton MS Nero D.IV fol. 26v

Every element in this complicated painting is sharply outlined by abrupt barriers between light and dark or between one color and another; there are no gradual or shaded transitions. Since the picture was created in part with pen and ink, the linearity is a logical feature of medium and technique. And although line itself is a "flattening" or two-dimensionalizing element in pictures, a complex and consistent system of overlapping gives the linear animal forms a sense of shallow but carefully worked-out three-dimensional relationships to one another.

LIGHT

B. **Georges de la Tour** *The Education of the Virgin*
c. 1650. Oil on canvas, 33 × 39½″ (83.8 × 100.4 cm). The Frick Collection, New York.

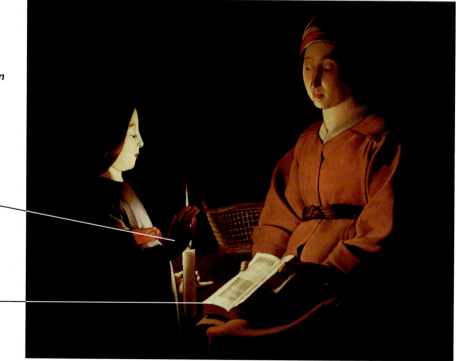

The source of illumination is a candle depicted within the painting. The young girl's upraised right hand shields its flame, allowing the artist to demonstrate his virtuosity in painting the translucency of human flesh.

Since the candle's flame is partially concealed, its luminous intensity is not allowed to distract from those aspects of the painting most brilliantly illuminated by it—the face of the girl and the book she is reading.

FORM

C. Michelangelo *The Holy Family* (*Doni Tondo*)
c. 1503. Oil and tempera on panel, diameter 3'11¼" (1.2 m). Galleria degli Uffizi, Florence.

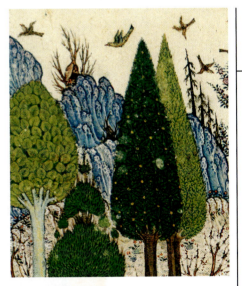

The complex overlapping of their highly three-dimensionalized bodies conveys the somewhat contorted spatial positioning and relationship of these three figures.

Through the use of modeling or shading—a gradual transition from lights to darks—Michelangelo imitates the way solid forms are illuminated from a single light source—the side closest to the light source is bright while the other side is cast in shadow—and gives a sense of three-dimensional form to his figures.

The actual three-dimensional projection of the sculpted heads in medallions around the frame—designed for this painting by Michelangelo himself—heightens the effect of fictive three-dimensionality in the figures painted on its flat surface.

In a technique called **foreshortening**, the carefully calculated angle of the Virgin's elbow makes it seem to project out toward the viewer.

Junayd chose to flood every aspect of his painting with light, as if everything in it were illuminated from all sides at once. As a result, the emphasis here is on jewel-like color. The vibrant tonalities and dazzling detail of the dreamy landscape are not only more important than the simulation of three-dimensional forms distributed within a consistently described space; they actually upstage the human drama taking place against a patterned, tipped-up ground in the lower third of the picture.

COLOR

D. Junayd *Humay and Humayun*, **from a manuscript of the** *Divan* **of Kwaju Kirmani**
Made in Baghdad, Iraq. 1396. Color, ink, and gold on paper, 12⅝ × 9⁷⁄₁₆" (32 × 24 cm). British Library, London. MS Add. 18113, fol. 31r

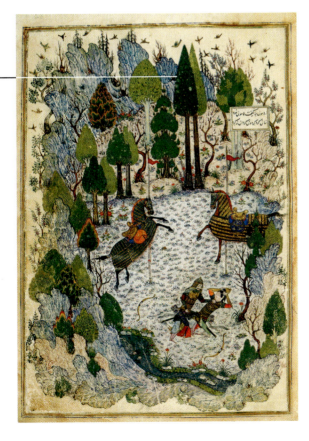

picture (see page xxx, FIG. B), or it can be lavished on every aspect of a picture to reveal all its detail and highlight the vibrancy of its color (see page xxxi, FIG. D). Color itself can be muted or intensified, depending on the mood artists want to create or the tastes and expectations of their audiences.

Thus artists communicate with their viewers by making choices in the way they use and emphasize the elements of visual expression, and art historical analysis seeks to reveal how artists' decisions bring meaning to a work of art. For example in two paintings of women with children (SEE FIGS. INTRO–3 and INTRO–4), Raphael and Renoir work with the same visual elements of line, form, light, and color in the creation of their images, but they employ these shared elements to differing expressive ends. Raphael concentrates on line to clearly differentiate each element of his picture as a separate form. Careful modeling describes these outlined forms as substantial solids surrounded by space. This gives his subjects a sense of clarity, stability, and grandeur. Renoir, on the other hand, foregrounds the flickering of light and the play of color as he downplays the sense of three-dimensionality in individual forms. This gives his image a more ephemeral, casual sense. Art historians pay close attention to such variations in the use of visual elements—the building blocks of artistic expression—and use visual analysis to characterize the expressive effect of a particular work, a particular artist, or a general period defined by place and date.

COMPOSITION. When art historians analyze composition, they focus not on the individual elements of visual expression but on the overall arrangement and organizing design or structure of a work of art. In Raphael's **MADONNA OF THE GOLDFINCH (FIG. INTRO–3)**, for example, the group of figures has been arranged in a triangular shape and placed at the center of the picture. Raphael emphasized this central weighting by opening the clouds to reveal a patch of blue in the middle of the sky, and by flanking the figural group with lace-like trees. Since the Madonna is

at the center and since the two boys are divided between the two sides of the triangular shape, roughly—though not precisely—equidistant from the center of the painting, this is a bilaterally symmetrical composition: on either side of an implied vertical line at the center of the picture, there are equivalent forms on left and right, matched and balanced in a mirrored correspondence. Art historians refer to such an implied line—around which the elements of a picture are organized—as an **axis**. Raphael's painting has not only a vertical, but also a horizontal axis, indicated by a line of demarcation between light and dark—as well as between degrees of color saturation—in the terrain of the landscape. The belt of the Madonna's dress is aligned with this horizontal axis, and this correspondence, taken with the coordination of her head with the blue patch in the sky, relates her to the order of the natural world in which she sits, lending a sense of stability, order, and balance to the picture as a whole.

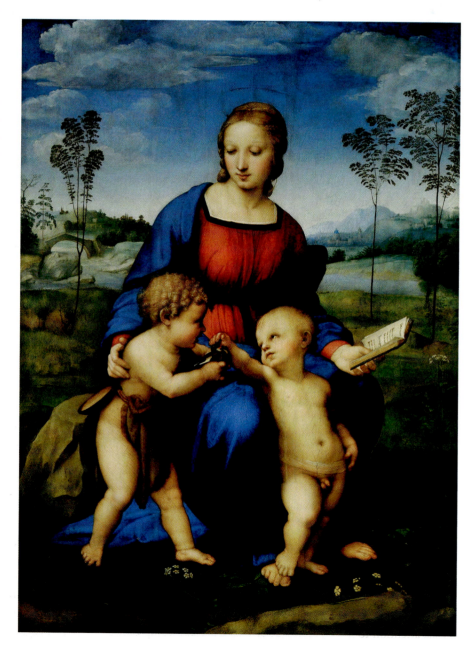

INTRO-3 • Raphael MADONNA OF THE GOLDFINCH (MADONNA DEL CARDELLINO)
1506. Oil on panel, 42 × 29½″ (106.7 × 74.9 cm). Galleria degli Uffizi, Florence.

The vibrant colors of this important work were revealed in the course of a careful, ten-year restoration, completed only in 2008.

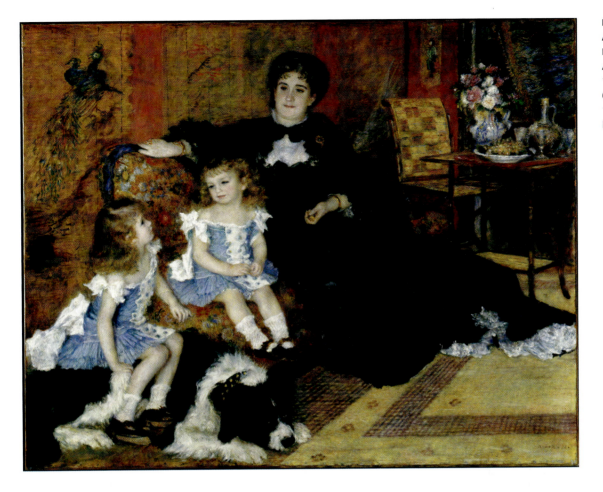

INTRO-4 •
Auguste Renoir
**MME. CHARPENTIER
AND HER CHILDREN**
1878. Oil on canvas,
60½ × 74⅞″ (153.7 ×
190.2 cm). Metropolitan
Museum of Art, New York.

The main axis in Renoir's painting of **MME. CHARPENTIER AND HER CHILDREN (FIG. INTRO–4)** is neither vertical, nor horizontal, but diagonal, running from the upper right to the lower left corner of the painting. All major elements of the composition are aligned along this axis—dog, children, mother, and the table and chair that represent the most complex and detailed aspect of the setting. The upper left and lower right corners of the painting balance each other on either side of the diagonal axis as relatively simple fields of neutral tone, setting off and framing the main subjects between them. The resulting arrangement is not bilaterally symmetrical, but blatantly asymmetrical, with the large figural mass pushed into the left side of the picture. And unlike Raphael's composition, where the spatial relationship of the figures and their environment is mapped by the measured placement of elements that become increasingly smaller in scale and fuzzier in definition as they recede into the background, the relationship of Renoir's figures to their spatial environment is less clearly defined as they recede into the background along the dramatic diagonal axis. Nothing distracts us from the bold informality of this family gathering.

Both Raphael and Renoir arrange their figures carefully and purposefully, but they follow distinctive compositional systems that communicate different notions of the way these figures interact with each other and the world around them. Art historians pay special attention to how pictures are arranged because composition is one of the principal ways artists charge their paintings with expressive meaning.

IDENTIFYING SUBJECT MATTER

Art historians have traditionally sought subject matter and meaning in works of art with a system of analysis that was outlined by Irwin Panofsky (1892–1968), an influential German scholar who was expelled from his academic position by the Nazis in 1933 and spent the rest of his career of research and teaching in the United States. Panofsky proposed that when we seek to understand the subject of a work of art, we derive meaning initially in two ways:

- First we perceive what he called "natural subject matter" by recognizing forms and situations that we know from our own experience.
- Then we use what he called "**iconography**" to identify the conventional meanings associated with forms and figures as bearers of narrative or symbolic content, often specific to a particular time and place.

Some paintings, like Rothko's abstractions, do not contain subjects drawn from the world around us, from stories, or from conventional symbolism, but Panofsky's scheme remains a standard method of investigating meaning in works of art that present narrative subjects, portray specific people or places, or embody cultural values with iconic imagery or allegory.

Iconography

The study and identification of conventional themes, motifs, and symbols to elucidate the subject matter of works of art.

These grapes sit on an imported, Italian silver *tazza*, a luxury object that may commemorate Northern European prosperity and trade. This particular object recurs in several of Peeters's other still lifes.

An image of the artist herself appears on the reflective surface of this pewter tankard, one of the ways that she signed her paintings and promoted her career.

Luscious fruits and flowers celebrate the abundance of nature, but because these fruits of the earth will eventually fade, even rot, they could be moralizing references to the transience of earthly existence.

Detailed renderings of insects showcased Peeters's virtuosity as a painter, but they also may have symbolized the vulnerability of the worldly beauty of flowers and fruit to destruction and decay.

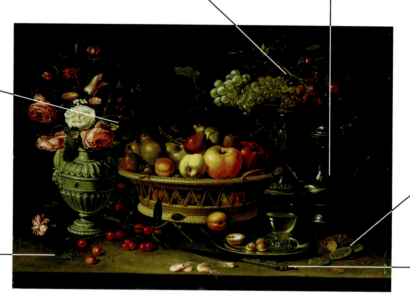

These coins, including one minted in 1608–1609, help focus the dating of this painting. The highlighting of money within a still life could reference the wealth of the owner—or it could subtly allude to the value the artist has crafted here in paint.

This knife—which appears in several of Peeters's still lifes—is of a type that is associated with wedding gifts.

A. Clara Peeters Still Life with Fruit and Flowers
c. 1612. Oil on copper, 25⅕ × 35″ (64 × 89 cm). Ashmolean Museum, Oxford.

Quince is an unusual subject in Chinese painting, but the fruit seems to have carried personal significance for Zhu Da. One of his friends was known as the Daoist of Quince Mountain, a site in Hunan province that was also the subject of a work by one of his favorite authors, Tang poet Li Bai.

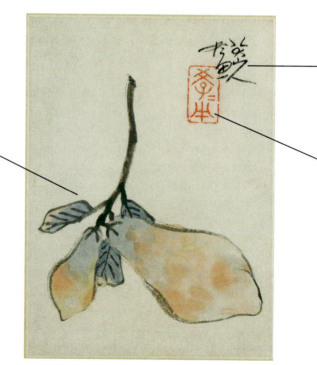

The artist's signature reads "Bada Shanren painted this," using a familiar pseudonym in a formula and calligraphic style that the artist ceased using in 1695.

This red block is a seal with an inscription drawn from a Confucian text: "teaching is half of learning." This was imprinted on the work by the artist as an aspect of his signature, a symbol of his identity within the picture, just as the reflection and inscribed knife identify Clara Peeters as the painter of her still life.

B. Zhu Da (Bada Shanren) Quince (Mugua)
1690. Album leaf mounted as a hanging scroll; ink and colors on paper, 7⅞ × 5¾″ (20 × 14.6 cm). Princeton University Art Museum.

NATURAL SUBJECT MATTER.   We recognize some things in works of visual art simply by virtue of living in a world similar to that represented by the artist. For example, in the two paintings by Raphael and Renoir just examined (SEE FIGS. INTRO–3 and INTRO–4), we immediately recognize the principal human figures in both as a woman and two children, boys in the case of Raphael's painting, girls in Renoir's. We can also make a general identification of the animals: a bird in the hand of Raphael's boys, and a pet dog under one of Renoir's girls. And natural subject matter can extend from an identification of figures to an understanding of the expressive significance of their postures and facial features. We might see in the boy who snuggles between the knees of the woman in Raphael's painting, placing his own foot on top of hers, an anxious child seeking the security of physical contact with a trusted caretaker—perhaps his mother—in response to fear of the bird he reaches out to touch. Many of us have seen insecure children take this very pose in response to potentially unsettling encounters.

The closer the work of art is in both time and place to our own situation temporally and geographically, the easier it sometimes is to identify what is represented. But although Renoir painted his picture over 125 years ago in France, the furniture in the background still looks familiar, as does the book in the hand of Raphael's Madonna, painted five centuries before our time. But the object hanging from the belt of the scantily clad boy at the left in this painting will require identification for most of us. Iconographic investigation is necessary to understand the function of this form.

ICONOGRAPHY.   Some subjects are associated with conventional meanings established at a specific time or place; some of the human figures portrayed in works of art have specific identities; and some of the objects or forms have symbolic or allegorical meanings in addition to their natural subject matter. Discovering these conventional meanings of art's subject matter is called iconography. (See "A Closer Look," opposite.)

For example, the woman accompanied in the outdoors by two boys in Raphael's Madonna of the Goldfinch (SEE FIG. INTRO–3) would have been immediately recognized by members of its intended sixteenth-century Florentine audience as the Virgin Mary. Viewers would have identified the naked boy standing between her knees as her son Jesus, and the boy holding the bird as Jesus' cousin John the Baptist, sheathed in the animal skin garment that he would wear in the wilderness and equipped with a shallow cup attached to his belt, ready to be used in baptisms. Such attributes of clothing and equipment are often critical in making iconographic identifications. The goldfinch in the Baptist's hand was at this time and place a symbol of Christ's death on the cross, an allegorical implication that makes the Christ Child's retreat into secure contact with his mother—already noted on the level of natural subject matter—understandable in relation to a specific story. The comprehension of conventional meanings in this painting would have been almost automatic among those for whom it was painted, but for us,

separated by time and place, some research is necessary to recover associations that are no longer part of our everyday world.

Although it may not initially seem as unfamiliar, the subject matter of Renoir's 1878 portrait of Mme. Charpentier and her Children (SEE FIG. INTRO–4) is in fact even more obscure. Although there are those in twenty-first-century American culture for whom the figures and symbols in Raphael's painting are still recognizable and meaningful, Marguérite-Louise Charpentier died in 1904, and no one living today would be able to identify her based on the likeness Renoir presumably gave to her face in this family portrait commissioned by her husband, wealthy and influential publisher George Charpentier. We need the painting's title to make that identification. And Mme. Charpentier is outfitted here in a gown created by English designer Charles Frederick Worth, the dominant figure in late nineteenth-century Parisian high fashion. Her clothing was a clear attribute of her wealth for those who recognized its source; most of us need to investigate to uncover its meaning. But a greater surprise awaits the student who pursues further research on her children. Although they clearly seem to our eyes to represent two daughters, the child closest to Mme. Charpentier is actually her son Paul, who at age three, following standard Parisian bourgeois practice, has not yet had his first hair cut and still wears clothing comparable to that of his older sister Georgette, perched on the family dog. It is not unusual in art history to encounter situations where our initial conclusions on the level of natural subject matter will need to be revised after some iconographic research.

INTEGRATION WITHIN CULTURAL CONTEXT

Natural subject matter and iconography were only two of three steps proposed by Panofsky for coming to an understanding of the meaning of works of art. The third step he labeled "**iconology**," and its aim is to interpret the work of art as an embodiment of its cultural situation, to place it within broad social, political, religious, and intellectual contexts. Such integration into history requires more than identifying subject matter or conventional symbols; it requires a deep understanding of the beliefs and principles or goals and values that underlie a work of art's cultural situation as well as the position of an artist and patron within it.

In "A Closer Look" (opposite), the subject matter of two **still life** paintings (pictures of inanimate objects and fruits or flowers taken out of their natural contexts) is identified and elucidated, but to truly understand these two works as bearers of cultural meaning, more knowledge of the broader context and specific goals of artists and audiences is required. For example, the fact that Zhu Da (1626–1705) became a painter was rooted more in the political than the artistic history of China at the middle of the seventeenth century. As a member of the imperial family of the Ming dynasty, his life of privilege was disrupted when the Ming were overthrown during the Manchu conquest of China in 1644. Fleeing for his life, he sought refuge in a Buddhist monastery, where he wrote poetry and painted. Almost 40 years later, in the aftermath of a nervous breakdown (that could have been staged to avoid retribution for his family background), Zhu Da abandoned his monastic life and developed a career as a professional painter, adopting a series of descriptive pseudonyms—most notably Bada Shanren ("mountain man of eight greatnesses") by which he is most often known today. His paintings are at times saturated with veiled political commentary; at times they seek to accommodate the expectations of collectors to assure their marketability; and in paintings like the one illustrated here (see page xxxiv, FIG. B), the artist seems to hark back to the contemplative, abstract, and spontaneous paintings associated with great Zen masters such as Muqi (c. 1201–after 1269), whose calligraphic pictures of isolated fruits seem almost like acts of devotion or detached contemplations on natural forms, rather than the works of a professional painter.

Clara Peeters's still life (see page xxxiv, FIG. A), on the other hand, fits into a developing Northern European painting tradition within which she was an established and successful professional, specializing in portrayals of food and flowers, fruit and reflective objects. Still-life paintings in this tradition could be jubilant celebrations of the abundance of the natural world and the wealth of luxury objects available in the prosperous mercantile society of the Netherlands. Or they could be moralizing "*vanitas*" paintings, warning of the ephemeral meaning of those worldly possessions, even of life itself. But this painting has also been interpreted in a more personal way. Because the type of knife that sits in the foreground near the edge of the table was a popular wedding gift, and since it is inscribed with the artist's own name, some have suggested that this still life could have celebrated Peeters's marriage. Or it could simply be a witty way to sign her picture. It certainly could be both personal and participate in the broader cultural meaning of still-life paintings at the same time. Mixtures of private and public meanings have been proposed for Zhu Da's paintings as well. The picture of quince illustrated here (see page xxxiv, FIG. B) has been seen as one in a series of allegorical "self-portraits" that extend across his career as a painter. Art historians frequently reveal multiple meanings when interpreting single works of art. They usually represent complex cultural and personal situations.

A CASE STUDY: ROGIER VAN DER WEYDEN'S PHILADELPHIA CRUCIFIXION

The basic, four-part method of art historical investigation and interpretation just outlined and explored, becomes clearer when its extended use is traced in relation to one specific work of art. A particularly revealing subject for such a case study is a seminal and somewhat perplexing painting now in the Philadelphia Museum of Art—the **CRUCIFIXION WITH THE VIRGIN AND ST. JOHN THE EVANGELIST (FIG. INTRO–5)** by Rogier van der Weyden (c. 1400–1464), a Flemish artist who will be featured in Chapter 18. Each of the four levels of art historical inquiry reveals important information about this painting, information that has been used by

art historians to reconstruct its relationship to its artist, its audience, and its broader cultural setting. The resulting interpretation is rich, but also complex. An investigation this extensive will not be possible for all the works of art in the following chapters, where the text will focus only on one or two facets of more expansive research. Because of the amount and complexity of information involved in a thorough art-historical interpretation, it is sometimes only in a second reading that we can follow the subtleties of its argument, after the first reading has provided a basic familiarity with the work of art, its conventional subjects, and its general context.

PHYSICAL PROPERTIES

Perhaps the most striking aspect of this painting's physical appearance is its division into two separate tall rectangular panels, joined by a frame to form a coherent, almost square composition. These are oak panels, prepared with chalk to form a smooth surface on which to paint with mineral pigments suspended in oil. A technical investigation of the painting in 1981 used infra-red reflectography to reveal a very sketchy underdrawing beneath the surface of the paint, proving to the investigators that this painting is almost entirely the work of Rogier van der Weyden himself. Famous and prosperous artists of this time and place employed many assistants to work in large production workshops, and they would render detailed underdrawings to assure that assistants replicated the style of the master. But in cases where the masters themselves intended to execute the work, only summary compositional outlines were needed. This modern technical investigation of Rogier's painting also used **dendrochronology** (the dating of wood based on the patterns of the growth rings) to date the oak panels and consequently the painting itself, now securely situated near the end of the artist's career, c. 1460.

The most recent restoration of the painting—during the early 1990s by Mark Tucker, Senior Conservator at the Philadelphia Museum of Art—returned it, as close as possible, to current views of its original fifteenth-century appearance (see "Recovering the Past," page xxxviii). This project included extensive technical analysis of almost every aspect of the picture, during which a critical clue emerged, one that may lead to a sharper understanding of its original use. X-rays revealed dowel holes and plugs running in a horizontal line about one-fourth of the way up from the bottom across the entire expanse of the two-panel painting. Tucker's convincing research suggests that the dowels would have attached these two panels to the backs of wooden boxes that contained sculptures in a complex work of art that hung over the altar in a fifteenth-century church.

FORMAL STRUCTURE

The visual organization of this two-part painting emphasizes both connection and separation. It is at the same time one painting and two. Continuing across both panels is the strip of midnight blue sky and the stone wall that constricts space within the picture to a shallow corridor, pushing the figures into the foreground and close

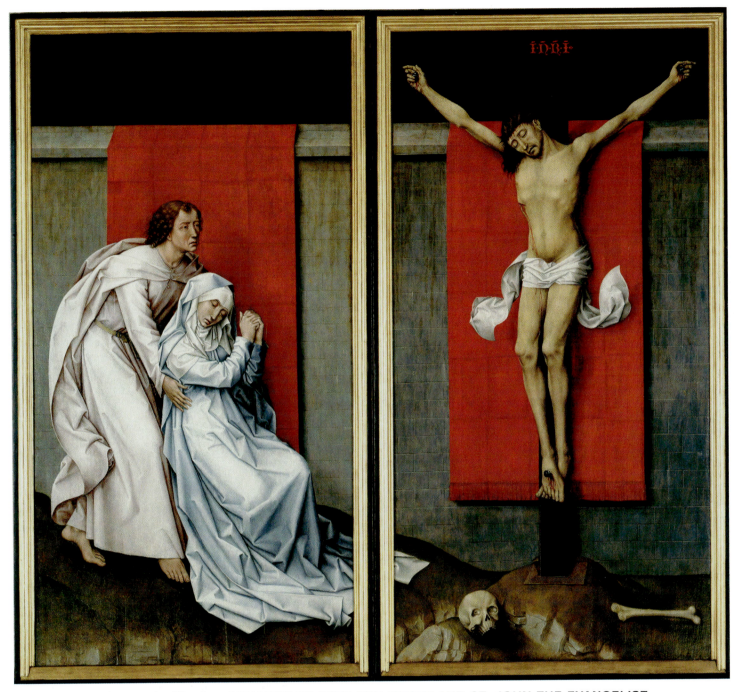

INTRO–5 • Rogier van der Weyden **CRUCIFIXION WITH THE VIRGIN AND ST. JOHN THE EVANGELIST**
c. 1460. Oil on oak panels, 71 × 73″ (1.8 × 1.85 m). John G. Johnson Collection, Philadelphia Museum of Art.

to the viewer. The platform of mossy ground under the two-figure group in the left panel continues its sloping descent into the right panel, as does the hem of the Virgin's ice-blue garment. We look into this scene as if through a window with a mullion down the middle and assume that the world on the left continues behind this central strip of frame into the right side.

On the other hand, strong visual forces isolate the figures within their respective panels, setting up a system of "compare and contrast" that seems to be at the heart of the painting's design. The striking red cloths that hang over the wall are centered directly behind the figures on each side, forming internal frames that

highlight them as separate groups and focus our attention back and forth between them rather than on the pictorial elements that unite their environments. As we begin to compare the two sides, it becomes increasingly clear that the relationship between figures and environment is quite distinct on each side of the divide.

The dead figure of Christ on the cross, elevated to the very top of the picture, is strictly centered within his panel, as well as against the cloth that hangs directly behind him. The grid of masonry blocks and creases in the cloth emphasizes his rectilinear integration into a system of balanced, rigid regularity. His head is aligned with the cap of the wall, his flesh largely contained within

Ever since Rogier van der Weyden's strikingly asymmetrical, two-panel rendering of the *Crucifixion* (SEE FIG. INTRO–5) was purchased by Philadelphia lawyer John G. Johnson in 1906 for his spectacular collection of European paintings, it has been recognized not only as one of the greatest works by this master of fifteenth-century Flemish painting, but as one of the most important European paintings in North America. Soon after the Johnson Collection became part of the Philadelphia Museum of Art in 1933, however, this painting's visual character was significantly transformed. In 1941 the museum employed freelance restorer David Rosen to work on the painting. Deciding that Rogier's work was seriously marred by later overpainting and disfigured by the discoloration of old varnish, he subjected the painting to a thorough cleaning. He also removed the strip of dark blue paint forming the sky above the wall at the top—identifying it as an 18th-century restoration—and replaced it with gold leaf to conform with remnants of gold in this area that he assessed as surviving fragments of the original background. Rosen's restoration of Rogier's painting was uncritically accepted for almost half a century, and the gold background became a major factor in the interpretations of art historians as distinguished as Irwin Panofsky and Meyer Schapiro.

In 1990, in preparation for a new installation of the work, Rogier's painting received a thorough technical analysis by Mark Tucker, the museum's Senior Conservator. There were two startling discoveries:

- The dark blue strip that had run across the top of the picture before Rosen's intervention was actually original to the painting. Remnants of paint left behind in 1941 proved to be the same azurite blue that also appears in the clothing of the Virgin, and in no instance did the traces of gold discovered in 1941 run under aspects of the original paint surface. Rosen had removed Rogier's original midnight blue sky.

- What Rosen had interpreted as disfiguring varnish streaking the wall and darkening the brilliant cloths of honor hanging over it were actually Rogier's careful painting of lichens and water stains on the stone and his overpainting on the fabric that had originally transformed a vermillion undercoat into deep crimson cloth.

In meticulous work during 1992–1993, Tucker cautiously restored the painting based on the evidence he had uncovered. Neither the lost lichens and water stains nor the toning crimson overpainting of the hangings were replaced, but a coat of blue-black paint was laid over Rosen's gold leaf at the top of the panels, taking care to apply the new layer in such a way that should a later generation decide to return to the gold leaf sky, the midnight tonalities could be easily removed. That seems an unlikely prospect. The painting as exhibited today comes as close as possible to the original appearance of Rogier's *Crucifixion*. At least we think so.

the area defined by the cloth. His elbows mark the juncture of the wall with the edge of the hanging, and his feet extend just to the end of the cloth, where his toes substitute for the border of fringe they overlap. The environment is almost as balanced. The strip of dark sky at the top is equivalent in size to the strip of mossy earth at the bottom of the picture, and both are visually bisected by centered horizontals—the cross bar at the top and the alignment of bone and skull at the bottom. A few disruptions to this stable, rectilinear, symmetrical order draw the viewers' attention to the panel at the left: the downward fall of the head of Christ, the visual weight of the skull, the downturn of the fluttering loin cloth, and the tip of the Virgin's gown that transgresses over the barrier to move in from the other side.

John and Mary merge on the left into a single figural mass that could be inscribed into a half-circle. Although set against a rectilinear grid background comparable to that behind Jesus, they contrast with, rather than conform to, the regular sense of order. Their curving outlines offer unsettling unsteadiness, as if they are toppling to the ground, jutting into the other side of the frame. This instability is reinforced by their postures. The projection of Mary's knee in relation to the angle of her torso reveals that she is collapsing into a curve, and the crumpled mass of drapery circling underneath her only underlines her lack of support. John reaches out to catch her, but he has not yet made contact with her body. He strikes a stance of strident instability without even touching the ground, and he looks blankly out into space with an unfocused expression, distracted from, rather than concentrating on, the task at hand. Perhaps he will come to his senses and grab her. But will he be able to catch her in time, and even then support her given his unstable posture? The moment is tense; the outcome is unclear. But we are moving into the realm of natural subject matter. The poignancy of this concentrated portrayal seems to demand it.

ICONOGRAPHY

The subject of this painting is among the most familiar themes in the history of European art. The dead Jesus has been crucified on the cross, and two of his closest associates—his mother and John, one of his disciples—mourn his loss. Although easily recognizable, the austere and asymmetrical presentation is unexpected. More usual is an earlier painting of this subject by the same artist, **CRUCIFIXION TRIPTYCH WITH DONORS AND SAINTS (FIG. INTRO–6)**, where he situates the crucified Christ at the center of a symmetrical arrangement, the undisputed axial focus of the composition. The scene unfolds here within an expansive landscape, populated with a wider cast of participants, each of whom takes a place with symmetrical decorum on either side of the cross. Because most crucifixions follow some variation on this pattern, Rogier's two-panel portrayal (SEE FIG. INTRO-5) in which the cross is asymmetrically displaced to one side, with a spare cast of attendants relegated to a separately framed space, severely restricted by a stark stone wall, requires some explanation. As does the mysterious dark world beyond the wall, and the artificial backdrop of the textile hangings.

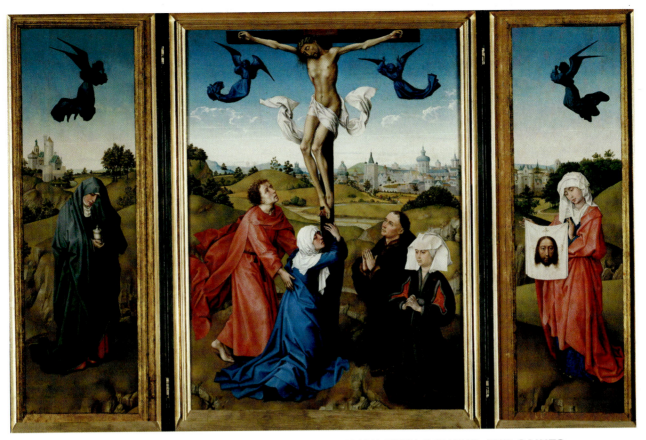

INTRO–6 • Rogier van der Weyden CRUCIFIXION TRIPTYCH WITH DONORS AND SAINTS
c. 1440. Oil on wooden panels, 39¾ × 55″ (101 × 140 cm). Kunsthistorisches Museum, Vienna.

This scene is not only austere and subdued; it is sharply focused, and the focus relates it to the specific moment in the story that Rogier decided to represent. The Christian Bible contains four accounts of Jesus' crucifixion, one in each of the four Gospels. Rogier took two verses in John's account as his painting's text (John 19:26–27), cited here in the Douay-Rheims literal English translation of the Latin Vulgate Bible used by Western European Christians during the fifteenth century:

> When Jesus therefore had seen his mother and the disciple standing whom he loved, he saith to his mother: Woman, behold thy son. After that, he saith to the disciple: Behold thy mother. And from that hour, the disciple took her to his own.

Even the textual source uses conventions that need explanation, specifically the way the disciple John is consistently referred to in this Gospel as "the disciple whom Jesus loved." Rogier's painting, therefore, seems to focus on Jesus' call for a newly expanded relationship between his mother and a beloved follower. More specifically, he has projected us slightly forward in time to the moment when John needs to respond to that call—Jesus has died; John is now in charge.

There are, however, other conventional iconographic associations with the crucifixion that Rogier has folded into this spare portrayal. Fifteenth-century viewers would have understood the skull and femur that lie on the mound at the base of the cross as

the bones of Adam—the first man in the Hebrew Bible account of creation—on whose grave Jesus' crucifixion was believed to have taken place. This juxtaposition embodied the Christian belief that Christ's sacrifice on the cross redeemed believers from the death that Adam's original sin had brought to human existence.

Mary's swoon and presumed loss of consciousness would have evoked another theological idea, the *co-passio*, in which Mary's anguish while witnessing Jesus' suffering and death was seen as a parallel passion of mother with son, both critical for human salvation. Their connection in this painting is underlined visually by the similar bending of their knees, inclination of their heads, and closing of their eyes. They even seem to resemble each other in facial likeness, especially when compared to John.

CULTURAL CONTEXT

In 1981 art historian Penny Howell Jolly published an interpretation of Rogier's Philadelphia *Crucifixion* as a product of a broad personal and cultural context. In addition to building on the work of earlier art historians, she pursued two productive lines of investigation to explain the rationale for this unusually austere presentation:

- the prospect that Rogier was influenced by the work of another artist, and
- the possibility that the painting was produced for an institutional context that called for a special mode of visual presentation and a particular iconographic focus.

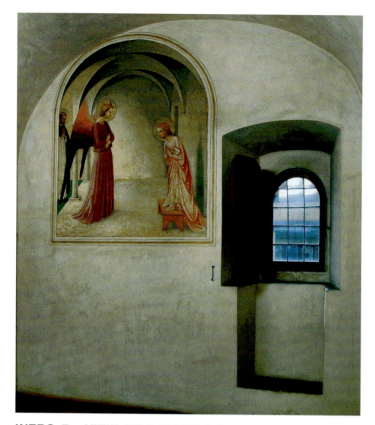

INTRO-7 • VIEW OF A MONK'S CELL IN THE MONASTERY OF SAN MARCO, FLORENCE
Including Fra Angelico's fresco of the *Annunciation*, c. 1438–1445.

FRA ANGELICO AT SAN MARCO. We know very little about the life of Rogier van der Weyden, but we do know that in 1450, when he was already established as one of the principal painters in northern Europe, he made a pilgrimage to Rome. Either on his way to Rome, or during his return journey home, he stopped off in Florence and saw the altarpiece, and presumably also the frescos, that Fra Angelico (c. 1400–1455) and his workshop had painted during the 1440s at the monastery of San Marco. The evidence of Rogier's contact with Fra Angelico's work is found in a work Rogier painted after he returned home, based on a panel of the San Marco altarpiece. For the Philadelphia *Crucifixion*, however, it was Fra Angelico's devotional frescos on the walls of the monks' individual rooms (or cells) that seem to have had the greatest impact **(FIG. INTRO–7)**. Jolly compared the Philadelphia *Crucifixion* with a scene of

the Man of Sorrows at San Marco to demonstrate the connection **(FIG. INTRO–8)**. Fra Angelico presented the sacred figures with a quiet austerity that recalls Rogier's unusual composition. More specific parallels are the use of an expansive stone wall to restrict narrative space to a shallow foreground corridor, the description of the world beyond that wall as a dark sky that contrasts with the brilliantly illuminated foreground, and the use of a draped cloth of honor to draw attention to a narrative vignette from the life of Jesus, to separate it out as an object of devotion.

THE CARTHUSIANS. Having established a possible connection between Rogier's unusual late painting of the crucifixion and frescos by Fra Angelico that he likely saw during his pilgrimage to Rome in 1450, Jolly reconstructed a specific context of patronage and meaning within Rogier's own world in Flanders that could explain why the paintings of Fra Angelico would have had such an impact on him at this particular moment in his career.

During the years around 1450, Rogier developed a personal and profession relationship with the monastic order of the Carthusians, and especially with the Belgian Charterhouse (or Carthusian monastery) of Hérrines, where his only son was invested as a monk in 1450. Rogier gave money to Hérrines, and

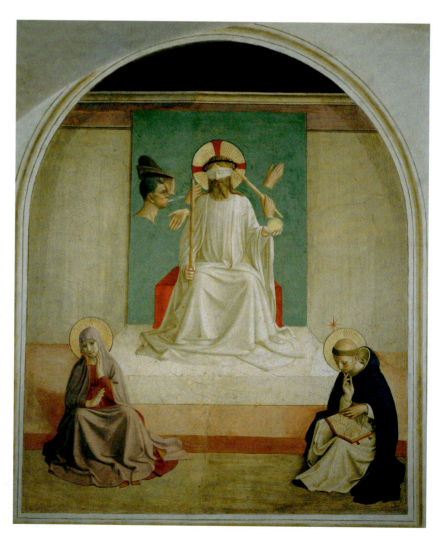

INTRO-8 • Fra Angelico MAN OF SORROWS FRESCO IN CELL 7
c. 1441–1445. Monastery of San Marco, Florence.

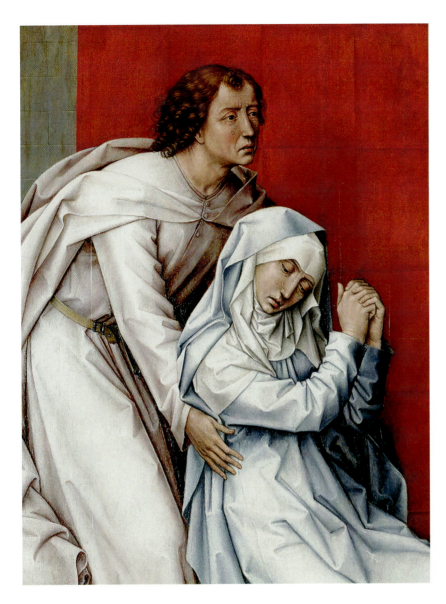

a poignant moment in the life of St. John (FIG INTRO-9) could have been especially meaningful to the artist himself at the time this work was painted?

A CONTINUING PROJECT. The final word has not been spoken in the interpretation of this painting. Mark Tucker's recent work on the physical evidence revealed by x-ray analysis points toward seeing these two panels as part of a large sculptured altarpiece. Even if this did preclude the prospect that it is the panel painting Rogier donated to the chapel of St. Catherine at Hérinnes, it does not negate the relationship Jolly drew with Fra Angelico, nor the Carthusian context she outlined for the work's original situation. It simply reminds us that our historical understanding of works such as this will evolve when new evidence about them emerges.

As the history of art unfolds in the ensuing chapters of this book, it will be important to keep two things in mind as you read the characterizations of individual works of art and the larger story of their integration into the broader cultural contexts of those who made them and those for whom they were initially made. Art-historical interpretations are built on extended research comparable to that we have just summarily surveyed for Rogier van der Weyden's Philadelphia *Crucifixion*. But the work of interpretation is never complete. Art history is a continuing project, a work perpetually in progress.

texts document his donation of a painting to its chapel of Saint Catherine. Jolly suggested that the Philadelphia *Crucifixion* could be that painting. Its subdued colors and narrative austerity are consistent with Carthusian aesthetic attitudes, and the walled setting of the scene recalls the enclosed gardens that were attached to the individual dormitory rooms of Carthusian monks. The reference in this painting to the *co-passio* of the Virgin provides supporting evidence since this theological idea was central to Carthusian thought and devotion. The *co-passio* was even reflected in the monks' own initiation rites, during which they reenacted and sought identification with both Christ's sacrifice on the cross and the Virgin's parallel suffering.

In Jolly's interpretation, the religious framework of a Carthusian setting for the painting emerges as a personal framework for the artist himself, since this *Crucifixion* seems to be associated with important moments in his own life—his religious pilgrimage to Rome in 1450 and the initiation of his only son as a Carthusian monk at about the same time. Is it possible that the sense of loss and separation that Rogier evoked in his portrayal of

THINK ABOUT IT

I.1 How would you define a work of art?

I.2 What are the four separate steps proposed here for characterizing the methods used by art historians to interpret works of art?

I.3 Choose a painting illustrated in this chapter and analyze its composition.

I.4 Characterize the difference between natural subject matter and iconography, focusing your discussion on one work discussed in this chapter.

I.5 What aspect of the case study of Rogier van der Weyden's Philadelphia *Crucifixion* was especially interesting to you? Explain why. How did it broaden your understanding of what you will learn in this course?

PRACTICE MORE: Compose answers to these questions, get flashcards for images and terms, and review chapter material with quizzes
www.myartslab.com

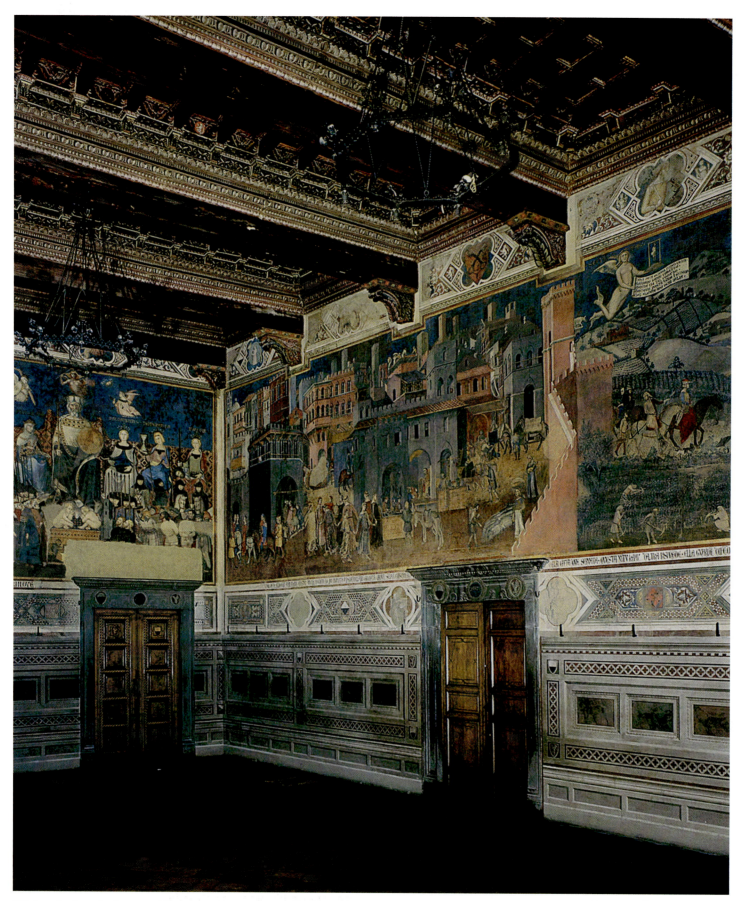

17–1 • Ambrogio Lorenzetti FRESCOS OF THE SALA DEI NOVE (OR SALA DELLA PACE)
Palazzo Pubblico, Siena, Italy. 1338–1339. Length of long wall about 46′ (14 m).

EXPLORE MORE: Gain insight from a primary source related to the frescos in the Palazzo Pubblico
www.myartslab.com

FOURTEENTH-CENTURY ART IN EUROPE

In 1338, the Nine—a council of merchants and bankers that governed Siena as an oligarchy—commissioned frescos from renowned Sienese painter Ambrogio Lorenzetti (c. 1295–c. 1348) for three walls in the chamber within the Palazzo Pubblico where they met to conduct city business. This commission came at the moment of greatest prosperity and security since the establishment of their government in 1287.

Lorenzetti's frescos combine allegory with panoramic landscapes and cityscapes, communicating ideology to visualize the justification for and positive effects of Sienese government. The moral foundation of the rule of the Nine is outlined in a complicated allegory in which seated personifications (far left in FIG. 17–1) of Concord, Justice, Peace, Strength, Prudence, Temperance, and Magnanimity not only diagram good governance but actually reference the Last Judgment in a bold assertion of the relationship between secular rule and divine authority. This tableau contrasts with a similar presentation of bad government, where Tyranny is flanked by the personified forces that keep tyrants in power—Cruelty, Treason, Fraud, Fury, Division, and War. A group of scholars would have devised this complex program of symbols and meanings; it is unlikely that Lorenzetti would have known the philosophical works that underlie them.

Lorenzetti's fame, however, and the wall paintings' secure position among the most remarkable surviving mural programs of the period, rests on the other part of this ensemble—the effects of good and bad government in city and country life (SEE FIG. 17–15).

Unlike the tableau showing the perils of life under tyrannical rule, the panoramic view of life under good government—which in this work of propaganda means life under the rule of the Nine—is well preserved. A vista of fourteenth-century Siena—identifiable by the cathedral dome and tower peeking over the rooftops in the background—details carefree life within shops, schools, taverns, and worksites, as the city streets bustle with human activity. Outside, an expansive landscape highlights agricultural productivity.

Unfortunately, within a decade of the frescos' completion, life in Siena was no longer as stable and carefree. The devastating bubonic plague visited in 1348—Ambrogio Lorenzetti himself was probably one of the victims—and the rule of the Nine collapsed in 1355. But this glorious vision of joyful prosperity preserves the dreams and aspirations of a stable government, using some of the most progressive and creative ideas in fourteenth-century Italian art, ideas whose development we will trace over the next two centuries.

LEARN ABOUT IT

17.1 Assess the close connections between works of art and their patrons in fourteenth-century Europe.

17.2 Compare and contrast the Florentine and Sienese narrative painting traditions as exemplified by Giotto and Duccio.

17.3 Discover the rich references to everyday life and human emotions that begin to permeate figural art in this period.

17.4 Explore the production of small-scale works, often made of precious materials and highlighting extraordinary technical virtuosity, that continues from the earlier Gothic period.

17.5 Evaluate the regional manifestations of the fourteenth-century Gothic architectural style.

HEAR MORE: Listen to an audio file of your chapter www.myartslab.com

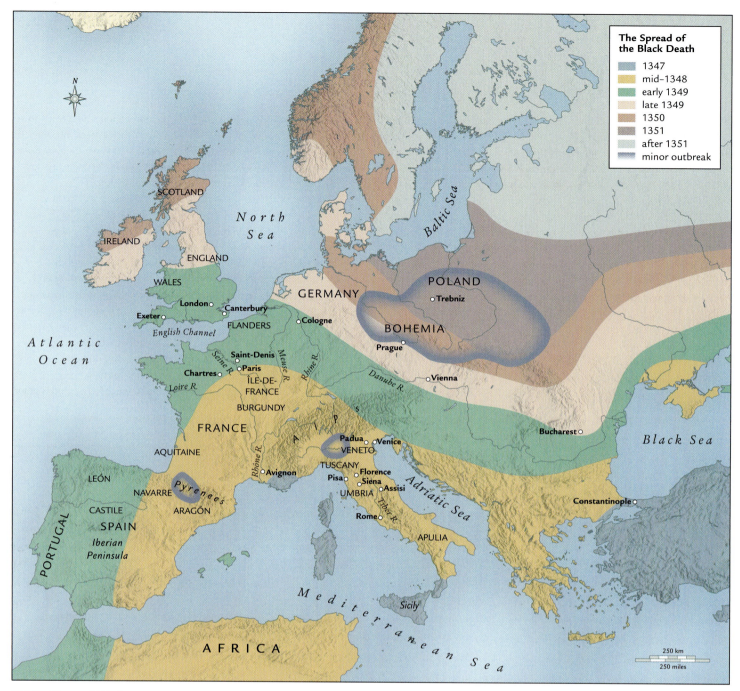

MAP 17–1 • EUROPE IN THE FOURTEENTH CENTURY

From its outbreak in the Mediterranean the Black Death in 1347 swept across the European mainland over the next four years.

FOURTEENTH-CENTURY EUROPE

Literary luminaries Dante, Petrarch, Boccaccio, Chaucer, and Christine de Pizan (see "A New Spirit in Fourteenth-Century Literature," opposite) and the visionary painters Cimabue, Duccio, Jean Pucelle, and Giotto participated in a cultural explosion that swept through fourteenth-century Europe, and especially Italy. The poet Petrarch (1304–1374) was a towering figure in this change, writing his love lyrics in Italian, the language of everyday life, rather than Latin, the language of ceremony and high art. Similarly the deeply moving murals of Florentine painter Giotto di Bondone (c. 1277–1337) were rooted in his observation of the people around him, giving the participants in sacred narratives both great dignity and striking humanity, thus making them familiar, yet new, to the audiences that originally experienced them. Even in Paris—still the artistic center of Europe as far as refined taste and technical

A New Spirit in Fourteenth-Century Literature

For Petrarch and his contemporaries, the essential qualifications for a writer were an appreciation of Greek and Roman authors and an ability to observe the people living around them. Although fluent in Latin, they chose to write in the language of their own time and place—Italian, English, French. Leading the way was Dante Alighieri (1265–1321), who wrote *The Divine Comedy*, his great summation of human virtue and vice, and ultimately human destiny, in Italian, establishing his daily vernacular as worthy to express great literary themes.

Francesco Petrarca, called simply Petrarch (1304–1374), raised the status of secular literature with his sonnets to his unobtainable beloved, Laura, his histories and biographies, and his writings on the joys of country life in the Roman manner. Petrarch's imaginative updating of Classical themes in a work called *The Triumphs*—which examines the themes of Chastity triumphant over Love, Death over Chastity, Fame over Death, Time over Fame, and Eternity over Time—provided later Renaissance poets and painters with a wealth of allegorical subject matter.

More earthy, Giovanni Boccaccio (1313–1375) perfected the art of the short story in *The Decameron*, a collection of amusing and moralizing tales told by a group of young Florentines who moved to the countryside to escape the Black Death. With wit and sympathy, Boccaccio presents the full spectrum of daily life in Italy. Such secular literature, written in Italian as it was then spoken in Tuscany, provided a foundation for fifteenth-century Renaissance writers.

In England, Geoffrey Chaucer (c. 1342–1400) was inspired by Boccaccio to write his own series of stories, *The Canterbury Tales*, told by pilgrims traveling to the shrine of St. Thomas à Becket (1118?–1170) in Canterbury. Observant and witty, Chaucer depicted the pretensions and foibles, as well as the virtues, of humanity.

Christine de Pizan (1364–c. 1431), born in Venice but living and writing at the French court, became an author out of necessity when she was left a widow with three young children and an aged mother to support. Among her many works are a poem in praise of Joan of Arc and a history of famous women—including artists—from antiquity to her own time. In *The Book of the City of Ladies*, she defended women's abilities and argued for women's rights and status.

These writers, as surely as Giotto, Duccio, Peter Parler, and Master Theodoric, led the way into a new era.

---

sophistication were concerned—the painter Jean Pucelle began to show an interest in experimenting with established conventions.

Changes in the way that society was organized were also under way, and an expanding class of wealthy merchants supported the arts as patrons. Artisan guilds—organized by occupation—exerted quality control among members and supervised education through an apprenticeship system. Admission to the guild came after examination and the creation of a "masterpiece"—literally, a piece fine enough to achieve master status. The major guilds included cloth finishers, wool merchants, and silk manufacturers, as well as pharmacists and doctors. Painters belonged to the pharmacy guild, perhaps because they used mortars and pestles to grind their colors. Their patron saint, Luke, who was believed to have painted the first image of the Virgin Mary, was also a physician—or so they thought. Sculptors who worked in wood and stone had their own guild, while those who worked in metals belonged to another. Guilds provided social services for their members, including care of the sick and funerals for the deceased. Each guild had its patron saint, maintained a chapel, and participated in religious and civic festivals.

Despite the cultural flourishing and economic growth of the early decades, by the middle of the fourteenth century much of Europe was in crisis. Prosperity had fostered population growth, which began to exceed food production. A series of bad harvests compounded this problem with famine. To make matters worse, a prolonged conflict known as the Hundred Years' War (1337–1453) erupted between France and England. Then, in mid century, a lethal plague known as the Black Death swept across Europe (**MAP 17–1**), wiping out as much as 40 percent of the population. In spite of these catastrophic events, however, the strong current of cultural change still managed to persist through to the end of the century and beyond.

ITALY

As great wealth promoted patronage of art in fourteenth-century Italy, artists began to emerge as individuals, in the modern sense, both in their own eyes and in the eyes of patrons. Although their methods and working conditions remained largely unchanged from the Middle Ages, artists in Italy contracted freely with wealthy townspeople and nobles as well as with civic and religious bodies. Perhaps it was their economic and social freedom that encouraged ambition and self-confidence, individuality and innovation.

FLORENTINE ARCHITECTURE AND METALWORK

The typical medieval Italian city was a walled citadel on a hilltop. Houses clustered around the church and an open city square. Powerful families added towers to their houses, both for defense

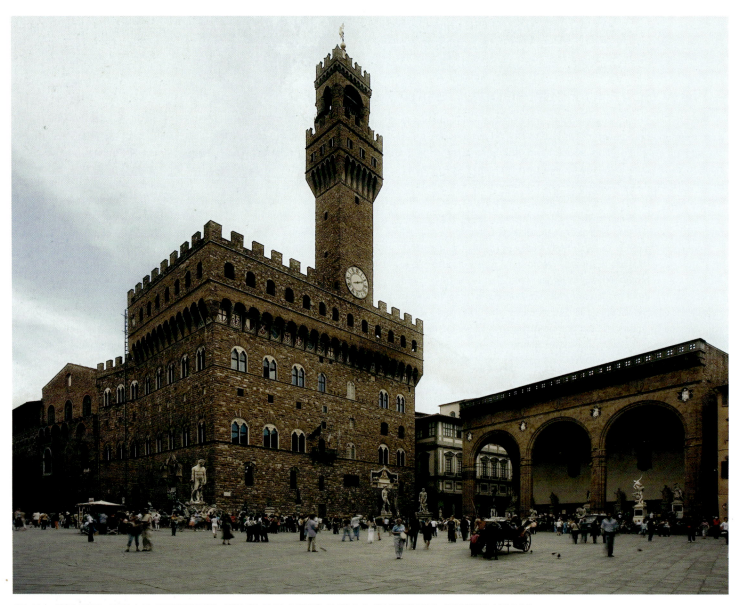

17-2 • PIAZZA DELLA SIGNORIA WITH PALAZZO DELLA SIGNORIA (TOWN HALL) 1299-1310, AND LOGGIA DEI LANZI (LOGGIA OF THE LANCERS), 1376-1382
Florence.

SEE MORE: Click the Google Earth link for the Palazzo della Signoria www.myartslab.com

and as expressions of family pride. In Florence, by contrast, the ancient Roman city—with its axial rectangular plan and open city squares—formed the basis for civic layout. The cathedral stood northeast of the ancient forum and a street following the Roman plan connected it with the Piazza della Signoria, the seat of the government.

THE PALAZZO DELLA SIGNORIA. The Signoria (ruling body, from *signore*, meaning "Lord") that governed Florence met in the **PALAZZO DELLA SIGNORIA**, a massive fortified building with a tall bell tower 300 feet high **(FIG. 17–2)**. The building faces a large square, or piazza, which became the true center of Florence. The town houses around the piazza often had benches along their walls to provide convenient public seating. Between 1376 and 1382,

master builders Benci di Cione and Simone Talenti constructed a huge **loggia** or covered open-air corridor at one side—now known as the Loggi dei Lanzi (Loggia of the Lancers)—to provide a sheltered locale for ceremonies and speeches.

THE BAPTISTERY DOORS. In 1330, Andrea Pisano (c. 1290–1348) was awarded the prestigious commission for a pair of gilded bronze doors for the Florentine Baptistery of San Giovanni, situated directly in front of the cathedral. (Andrea's "last" name means "from Pisa;" he was not related to Nicola and Giovanni Pisano.) The doors were completed within six years and display 20 scenes from the **LIFE OF JOHN THE BAPTIST** (the San Giovanni to whom the baptistery is dedicated) set above eight personifications of the Virtues **(FIG. 17–3)**. The overall effect is two-dimensional and

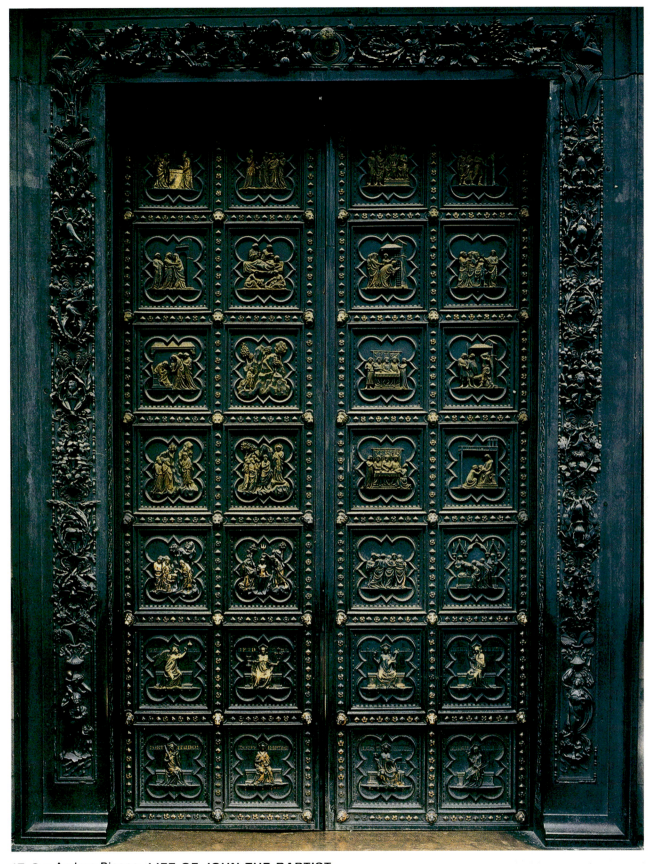

17-3 • Andrea Pisano LIFE OF JOHN THE BAPTIST
South doors, Baptistery of San Giovanni, Florence. 1330–1336. Gilded bronze, each panel 19¼ × 17″ (48 × 43 cm). Frame, Ghiberti workshop, mid-15th century.

The bronze vine scrolls filled with flowers, fruits, and birds on the lintel and jambs framing the door were added in the mid fifteenth century.

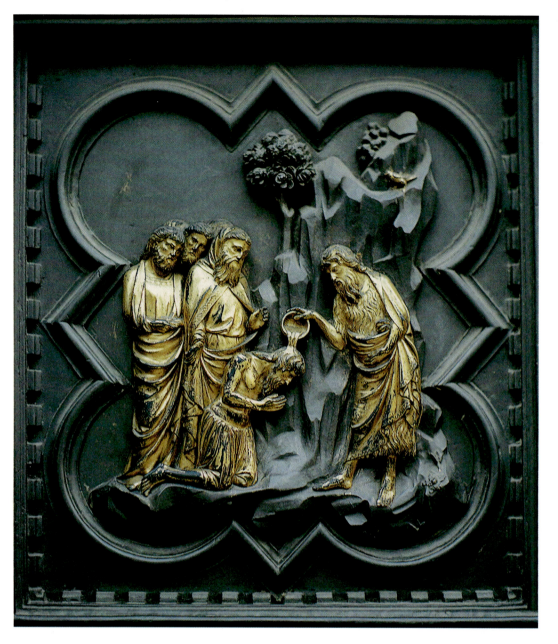

17-4 • Andrea Pisano
THE BAPTISM OF THE MULTITUDE
From the south doors, Baptistery of San Giovanni, Florence. 1330–1336. Gilded bronze, 19¼ × 17″ (48 × 43 cm).

decorative: a grid of 28 rectangles with repeated quatrefoils filled by the graceful, patterned poses of delicate human figures. Within the quatrefoil frames, however, the figural compositions create the illusion of three-dimensional forms moving within the described spaces of natural and architectural worlds.

The scene of John baptizing a multitude (**FIG. 17–4**) takes place on a shelflike stage created by a forward extension of the rocky natural setting, which also expands back behind the figures into a corner of the quatrefoil frame. Composed as a rectangular group, the gilded figures present an independent mass of modeled forms. The illusion of three-dimensionality is enhanced by the way the curving folds of their clothing wrap around their bodies. At the same time, their graceful gestures and the elegant fall of their drapery reflect the soft curves and courtly postures of French Gothic art. Their quiet dignity, however, seems particular to the work of Andrea himself.

FLORENTINE PAINTING

Florence and Siena, rivals in so many ways, each supported a flourishing school of painting in the fourteenth century. Both grew out of thirteenth-century painting traditions and engendered individual artists who became famous in their own time. The Byzantine influence—the *maniera greca* ("Greek style")—continued to provide models of dramatic pathos and narrative iconography, as well as stylized features including the use of gold for drapery folds and striking contrasts of highlights and shadows in the modeling of individual forms. By the end of the fourteenth century, the painter and commentator Cennino Cennini (see "Cennino Cennini on Panel Painting," page 544) would be struck by the accessibility and modernity of Giotto's art, which, though it retained traces of the *maniera greca*, was moving toward the depiction of a lifelike, contemporary world anchored in three-dimensional forms.

CIMABUE. In Florence, this transformation to a more modern style began a little earlier than in Siena. About 1280, a painter named Cenni di Pepi (active c. 1272–1302), better known by his nickname "Cimabue," painted a panel portraying the **VIRGIN AND CHILD ENTHRONED** (FIG. **17–5**), perhaps for the main altar of the church of Santa Trinità in Florence. At over 12 feet tall, this enormous painting set a new precedent for monumental altar-pieces. Cimabue surrounds the Virgin and Child with angels and places a row of Hebrew Bible prophets beneath them. The hieratically scaled figure of Mary holds the infant Jesus in her lap. Looking out at the viewer while gesturing toward her son as the path to salvation, she adopts a formula popular in Byzantine iconography since at least the seventh century (SEE FIG. 7–29).

Mary's huge throne, painted to resemble gilded bronze with inset enamels and gems, provides an architectural framework for the figures. Cimabue creates highlights on the drapery of Mary, Jesus, and the angels with thin lines of gold, as if to capture their divine radiance. The viewer seems suspended in space in front of the image, simultaneously looking down on the projecting elements of the throne and Mary's lap, while looking straight ahead at the prophets at the base of the throne and the angels at each side. These spatial ambiguities, the subtle asymmetries within the

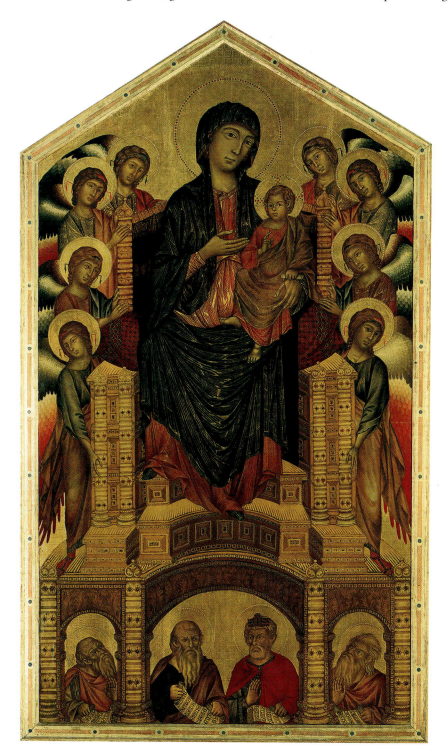

17-5 • Cimabue VIRGIN AND CHILD ENTHRONED
Most likely painted for the high altar of the church of Santa Trinità, Florence. c. 1280. Tempera and gold on wood panel, 12'7" × 7'4" (3.53 × 2.2 m). Galleria degli Uffizi, Florence.

SEE MORE: See a video about the egg tempera process **www.myartslab.com**

centralized composition, the Virgin's engaging gaze, and the individually conceived faces of the old men give the picture a sense of life and the figures a sense of presence. Cimabue's ambitious attention to spatial volumes, his use of delicate modeling in light and shade to simulate three-dimensional form, and his efforts to give naturalistic warmth to human figures had an impact on the future development of Italian painting.

GIOTTO DI BONDONE. According to the sixteenth-century chronicler Giorgio Vasari, Cimabue discovered a talented shepherd boy, Giotto di Bondone, and taught him to paint—and "not only did the young boy equal the style of his master, but he became such an excellent imitator of nature that he completely banished that crude Greek [i.e., Byzantine] style and revived the modern and excellent art of painting, introducing good drawing from live natural models, something which had not been done for more than two hundred years" (Vasari, translated by Bondanella and Bondanella, p. 16). After his training, Giotto may have collaborated on murals at the prestigious church of St. Francis in Assisi. We know he worked for the Franciscans in Florence and absorbed facets of their teaching. St. Francis's message of simple, humble devotion, direct experience of God, and love for all creatures was

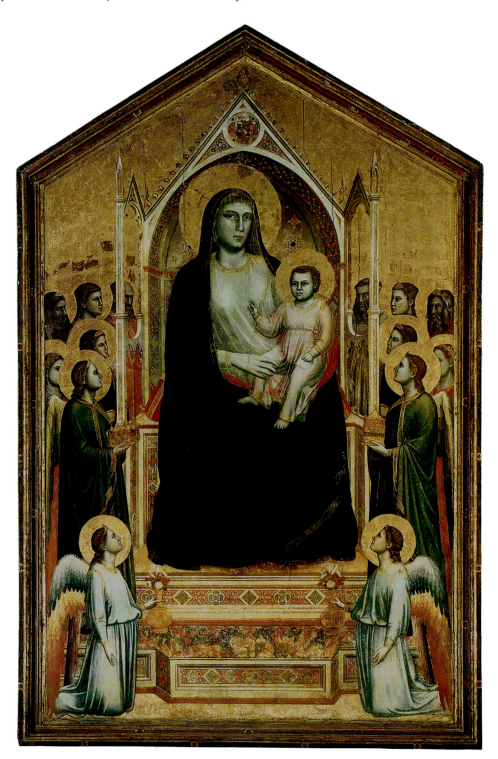

17-6 • Giotto di Bondone VIRGIN AND CHILD ENTHRONED
Most likely painted for the high altar of the church of the Ognissanti (All Saints), Florence. 1305–1310. Tempera and gold on wood panel, 10′8″ × 6′8¼″ (3.53 × 2.05 m). Galleria degli Uffizi, Florence.

EXPLORE MORE: Gain insight from a primary source by Dante Alighieri that references Giotto di Bondone
www.myartslab.com

The two techniques used in mural painting are *buon* ("true") *fresco* ("fresh"), in which paint is applied with water-based paints on wet plaster, and *fresco secco* ("dry"), in which paint is applied to a dry plastered wall. The two methods can be used on the same wall painting.

The advantage of *buon fresco* is its durability. A chemical reaction occurs as the painted plaster dries, which bonds the pigments into the wall surface. In *fresco secco*, by contrast, the color does not become part of the wall and tends to flake off over time. The chief disadvantage of *buon fresco* is that it must be done quickly without mistakes. The painter plasters and paints only as much as can be completed in a day, which explains the Italian term for each of these sections: **giornata**, or a day's work. The size of a *giornata* varies according to the complexity of the painting within it. A face, for instance, might take an entire day, whereas large areas of sky can be painted quite rapidly. In Giotto's Scrovegni Chapel, scholars have identified 852 separate *giornate*, some worked on concurrently within a single day by assistants in Giotto's workshop.

In medieval and Renaissance Italy, a wall to be frescoed was first prepared with a rough, thick undercoat of plaster known as the *arriccio*. When this was dry, assistants copied the master painter's composition onto it with reddish-brown pigment or charcoal. The artist made any necessary adjustments. These underdrawings, known as **sinopia**, have an immediacy and freshness lost in the finished painting. Work proceeded in irregularly shaped *giornate* conforming to the contours of major figures and objects. Assistants covered one section at a time with a fresh, thin coat of very fine plaster—the *intonaco*—

over the *sinopia*, and when this was "set" but not dry, the artist worked with pigments mixed with water, painting from the top down so that drips fell on unfinished portions. Some areas requiring pigments such as ultramarine blue (which was unstable in *buon fresco*), as well as areas requiring gilding, would be added after the wall was dry using the *fresco secco* technique.

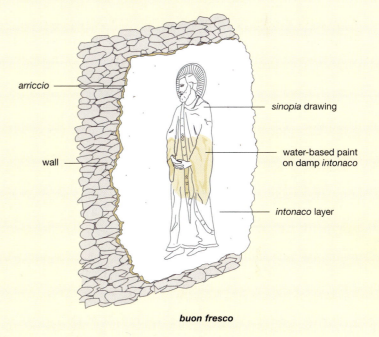

buon fresco

arriccio

sinopia drawing

wall

water-based paint on damp *intonaco*

intonaco layer

---

gaining followers throughout western Europe, and it had a powerful impact on thirteenth- and fourteenth-century Italian literature and art.

Compared to Cimabue's *Virgin and Child Enthroned*, Giotto's panel of the same subject (**FIG. 17–6**), painted about 30 years later for the church of the Ognissanti (All Saints) in Florence, exhibits greater spatial consistency and sculptural solidity while retaining some of Cimabue's conventions. The position of the figures within a symmetrical composition reflects Cimabue's influence. Gone, however, are Mary's modestly inclined head and the delicate gold folds in her drapery. Instead, light and shadow play gently across her stocky form, and her action—holding her child's leg instead of pointing him out to us—seems less contrived. This colossal Mary overwhelms her slender Gothic tabernacle of a throne, where figures peer through openings and haloes overlap faces. In spite of the hieratic scale and the formal, enthroned image and flat, gold background, Giotto has created the sense that these are fully three-dimensional beings, whose plainly draped, bulky bodies inhabit real space. The Virgin's solid torso is revealed by her thin tunic, and Giotto's angels are substantial solids whose foreshortened postures project from the foreground toward us, unlike those of Cimabue, which stay on the surface along lateral strips composed of overlapping screens of color.

Although he was trained in the Florentine tradition, many of Giotto's principal works were produced elsewhere. After a sojourn in Rome during the last years of the thirteenth century, he was called to Padua in northern Italy soon after 1300 to paint frescos (see "Buon Fresco," above) for a new chapel being constructed at the site of an ancient Roman arena—explaining why it is usually referred to as the Arena Chapel. The chapel was commissioned by Enrico Scrovegni, whose family fortune was made through the practice of usury—which at this time meant charging interest when loaning money, a sin so grave that it resulted in exclusion from the Christian sacraments. Enrico's father, Regibaldo, was a particularly egregious case (he appears in Dante's *Inferno* as the prototypical usurer), but evidence suggests that Enrico followed in his father's footsteps, and the building of the Arena Chapel next to his new palatial residence seems to have been conceived at least in part as a penitential act, part of Enrico's campaign not only to atone for his father's sins, but also to seek absolution for his own. He was pardoned by Pope Benedict XI (pontificate 1303–1304).

That Scrovegni called two of the most famous artists of the time—Giotto and Giovanni Pisano (SEE FIG. 16–33)—to decorate his chapel indicates that his goals were to express his power, sophistication, and prestige, as well as to atone for his sins. The building itself has little architectural distinction. It is a simple,

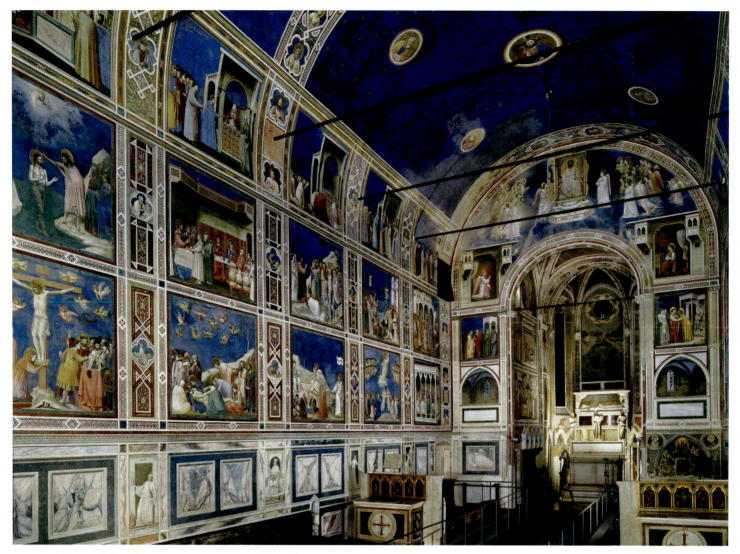

17-7 • Giotto di Bondone **SCROVEGNI (ARENA) CHAPEL**
Padua. 1305–1306. Frescos. View toward east wall.

barrel-vaulted room that provides broad walls, a boxlike space to showcase Giotto's paintings **(FIG. 17–7)**. Giotto covered the entrance wall with the *Last Judgment* (not visible here), and the sanctuary wall with three highlighted scenes from the life of Christ. The Annunciation spreads over the two painted architectural frameworks on either side of the high arched opening into the sanctuary itself. Below this are, to the left, the scene of Judas receiving payment for betraying Jesus, and, to the right, the scene of the Visitation, where the Virgin, pregnant with God incarnate, embraces her cousin Elizabeth, pregnant with John the Baptist. The compositions and color arrangement of these two scenes create a symmetrical pairing that encourages viewers to relate them, comparing the ill-gotten financial gains of Judas (a rather clear reference to Scrovegni usury) to the miraculous pregnancy that brought the promise of salvation.

Giotto subdivided the side walls of the chapel into framed pictures. A dado of faux-marble and allegorical **grisaille** (monochrome paintings in shades of gray) paintings of the Virtues and

Vices support vertical bands painted to resemble marble inlay into which are inserted painted imitations of carved medallions. The central band of medallions spans the vault, crossing a brilliant, lapis-blue, star-spangled sky in which large portrait disks float like glowing moons. Set into this framework are three horizontal bands of rectangular narrative scenes from the life of the Virgin and her parents at the top, and Jesus along the middle and lower registers, constituting together the primary religious program of the chapel.

Both the individual scenes and the overall program display Giotto's genius for distilling complex stories into a series of compelling moments. He concentrates on the human dimensions of the unfolding drama—from touches of anecdotal humor to expressions of profound anguish—rather than on its symbolic or theological weight. His prodigious narrative skills are apparent in a set of scenes from Christ's life on the north wall **(FIG. 17–8)**. At top left Jesus performs his first miracle, changing water into wine at the wedding feast at Cana. The wine steward—looking very much like the jars of new wine himself—sips the results. To the right is the

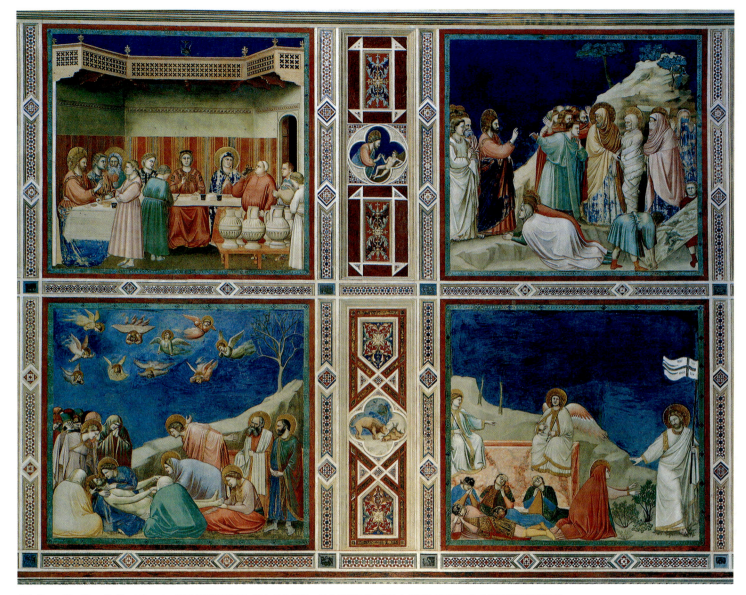

17–8 • Giotto di Bondone **MARRIAGE AT CANA, RAISING OF LAZARUS, LAMENTATION, AND RESURRECTION / NOLI ME TANGERE**
North wall of Scrovegni (Arena) Chapel, Padua. 1305–1306. Fresco, each scene approx. 6'5" × 6' (2 × 1.85 m).

Raising of Lazarus, where boldly modeled and individualized figures twist in space. Through their postures and gestures they react to the human drama by pleading for Jesus' help, or by expressing either astonishment at the miracle or revulsion at the smell of death. Jesus is separated from the crowd. His transforming gesture is highlighted against the dark blue of the background, his profile face locked in communication with the similarly isolated Lazarus, whose eyes—still fixed in death—let us know that the miracle is just about to happen.

On the lower register, where Jesus' grief-stricken followers lament over his dead body, Giotto conveys palpable human suffering, drawing viewers into a circle of personal grief. The stricken Virgin pulls close to her dead son, communing with mute intensity, while John the Evangelist flings his arms back in convulsive despair and others hunch over the corpse. Giotto has

linked this somber scene—much as he linked the scene of Judas' pact and the Visitation across the sanctuary arch—to the mourning of Lazarus on the register above through the seemingly continuous diagonal implied by the sharply angled hillside behind both scenes and by the rhyming repetition of mourners in each scene—facing in opposite directions—who throw back their arms to express their emotional state. Viewers would know that the mourning in both scenes is resolved by resurrection, portrayed in the last picture in this set.

Following traditional medieval practice, the fresco program is full of scenes and symbols like these that are intended to be contemplated as coordinated or contrasting juxtapositions. What is new here is the way Giotto draws us into the experience of these events. This direct emotional appeal not only allows viewers to imagine these scenes in relation to their own life experiences; it

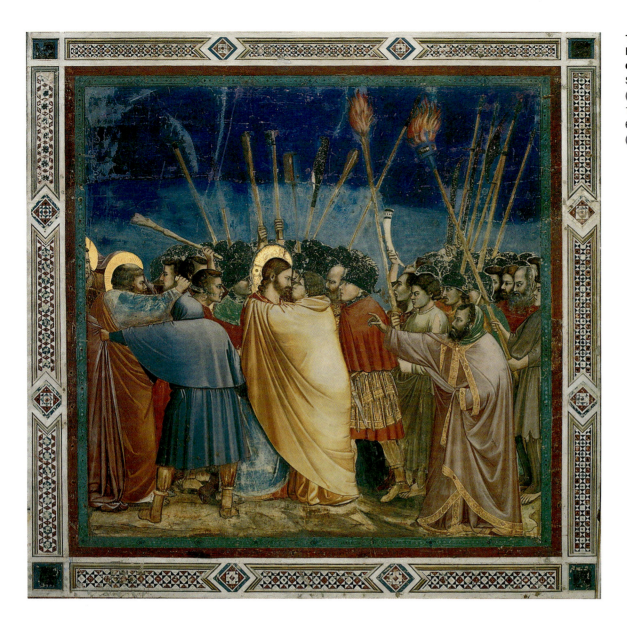

17-9 • Giotto di Bondone **KISS OF JUDAS**
South wall of Scrovegni (Arena) Chapel, Padua. 1305–1306. Fresco, 6′6¾″ × 6′7⅞″ (2 × 1.85 m).

also embodies the new Franciscan emphasis on personal devotion rooted in empathetic responses to sacred stories.

One of the most gripping paintings in the chapel is Giotto's portrayal of the **KISS OF JUDAS**, the moment of betrayal that represents the first step on Jesus' road to the Crucifixion (**FIG. 17–9**). Savior and traitor are slightly off-center in the near foreground. The expansive sweep of Judas' strident yellow cloak— the same outfit he wore at the scene of his payment for the betrayal on the strip of wall to the left of the sanctuary arch—almost completely swallows Christ's body. Surrounding them, faces glare from all directions. A bristling array of weapons radiating from the confrontation draws attention to the encounter between Christ and Judas and documents the militarism of the arresting battalion. Jesus stands solid, a model of calm resolve that recalls his visual characterization in the Resurrection of Lazarus, and forms a striking foil to the noisy and chaotic aggression that engulfs him. Judas, in simian profile, purses his lips for the treacherous kiss that will betray Jesus to his captors, setting up a mythic confrontation of

good and evil. In a subplot to the left, Peter lunges forward to sever the ear of a member of the arresting retinue. They are behind another broad sweep of fabric, this one extended by an ominous figure seen from behind and completely concealed except for the clenched hand that pulls at Peter's mantle. Indeed, a broad expanse of cloth and lateral gestures creates a barrier along the picture plane—as if to protect viewers from the compressed chaos of the scene itself. Rarely has this poignant event been visualized with such riveting power.

SIENESE PAINTING

Like their Florentine rivals, Sienese painters were rooted in thirteenth-century pictorial traditions, especially those of Byzantine art. Sienese painting emphasized the decorative potential of narrative painting, with brilliant, jewel-like colors and elegantly posed figures. For this reason, some art historians consider Sienese art more conservative than Florentine art, but we will see that it has its own charm, and its own narrative strategy.

DUCCIO DI BUONINSEGNA. Siena's foremost painter was Duccio di Buoninsegna (active 1278–1318), whose creative synthesis of Byzantine and French Gothic sources transformed the tradition in which he worked. The format of a large altarpiece he painted for the church of Santa Maria Novella in Florence after 1285 **(FIG. 17–10)** is already familiar from the Florentine altarpieces of Cimabue and Giotto (SEE FIGS. 17-5 and 17-6). A monumental Virgin and Child sit on an elaborate throne, set against a gold ground and seemingly supported by flanking angels. But in striking contrast both with Cimabue's Byzantine drapery stylizations and sense of three-dimensional form and space, and with Giotto's matter-of-fact emphasis on weightiness and references to an earthly setting, Duccio's figural composition foregrounds gracefulness of pose and gesture and a color scheme rich in luminous pastels. Drapery not only models his figures into convincing forms; it also falls into graceful lines and patterns, especially apparent in the sinuous golden edge of the Virgin's deep blue mantle and the ornamental extravagance of the brocade hangings on her throne.

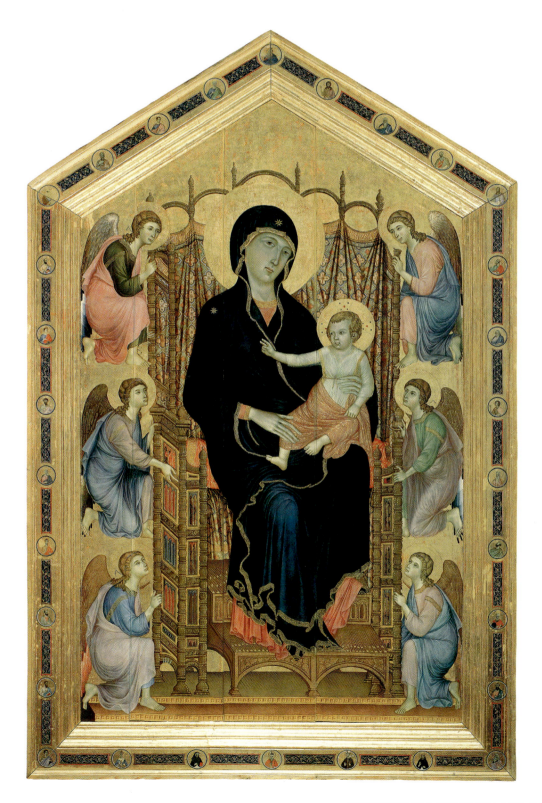

17–10 • Duccio di Buoninsegna
VIRGIN AND CHILD ENTHRONED (RUCELLAI MADONNA)
Commissioned in 1285. Tempera and gold on wood panel, 14'9⅛" × 9'6⅛" (4.5 × 2.9 m). Galleria degli Uffizi, Florence.

This altarpiece, commissioned in 1285 for the church of Santa Maria Novella in Florence by the Society of the Virgin Mary, is now known as the *Rucellai Madonna* because it was installed at one time in the Rucellai family's chapel within the church.

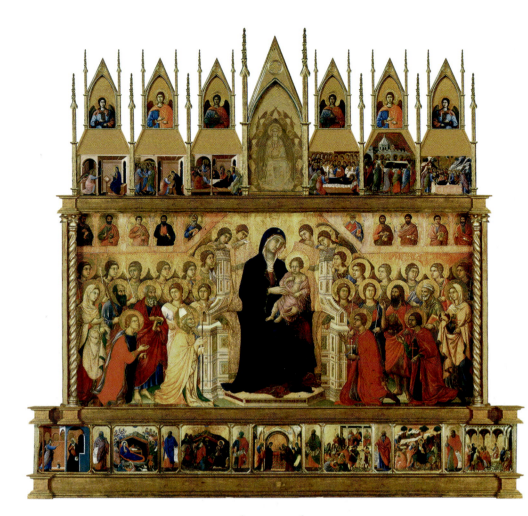

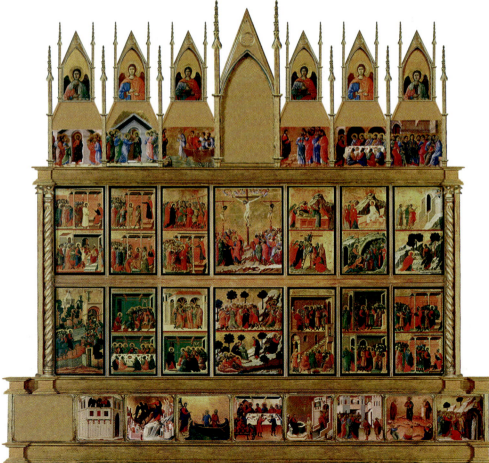

17–11b • Duccio di Buoninsegna
CONJECTURAL RECONSTRUCTION OF THE BACK OF THE MAESTÀ ALTARPIECE

Between 1308 and 1311, Duccio and his workshop painted a huge altarpiece commissioned by Siena Cathedral and known as the *Maestà* ("Majesty") **(FIG. 17–11)**. Creating this altarpiece—assembled from many wood panels bonded together before painting—was an arduous undertaking. The work was not only large—the central panel alone was 7 by 13 feet—but it had to be painted on both sides since it could be seen from all directions when installed on the main altar at the center of the sanctuary.

Because the *Maestà* was dismantled in 1771, its power and beauty can only be imagined from scattered parts, some still in Siena but others elsewhere. **FIG. 17–11a** is a reconstruction of how the front of the original altarpiece might have looked. It is dominated by a large representation of the Virgin and Child in Majesty (thus its title of *Maestà*), flanked by 20 angels and ten saints, including the four patron saints of Siena kneeling in the foreground. Above and below this lateral tableau were small narrative scenes from the last days of the life of the Virgin (above) and the infancy of Christ (spread across the predella). An inscription running around the base of Mary's majestic throne places the artist's signature within an optimistic framework: "Holy Mother of God, be thou the cause of peace for Siena and life to Duccio because he painted thee thus." This was not Duccio's first work for the cathedral. In 1288 he had designed a stunning stained-glass window portraying the Death, Assumption, and Coronation of the Virgin for the huge circular

opening in the east wall of the sanctuary. It would have hovered over the installed *Maestà* when it was placed on the altar in 1311.

On the back of the *Maestà* **(FIG. 17–11b)** were episodes from the life of Christ, focusing on his Passion. Sacred narrative unfolds in elegant episodes enacted by graceful figures who seem to dance their way through these stories while still conveying emotional content. Characteristic of Duccio's narrative style is the scene of the **RAISING OF LAZARUS (FIG. 17–12)**. Lyrical figures enact the event with graceful decorum, but their highly charged glances and expressive gestures—especially the bold reach of Christ—convey a strong sense of dramatic urgency that contrasts with the tense stillness that we saw in Giotto's rendering of this same moment of confrontation (SEE FIG. 17–8). Duccio's shading of drapery, like his modeling of faces, faithfully describes the figures' three-dimensionality, but the crisp outlines of the jewel-colored shapes created by their drapery, as well as the sinuous continuity of folds and gestures, generate rhythmic patterns across the surface. Experimentation with the portrayal of space extends from the receding rocks of the mountainous landscape to carefully studied interiors, here the tomb of Lazarus whose heavy door was removed by the straining hug of a bystander to reveal the shrouded figure of Jesus' resurrected friend, propped up against the door jamb.

The enthusiasm with which citizens greeted a great painting or altarpiece like the *Maestà* demonstrates the power of images as

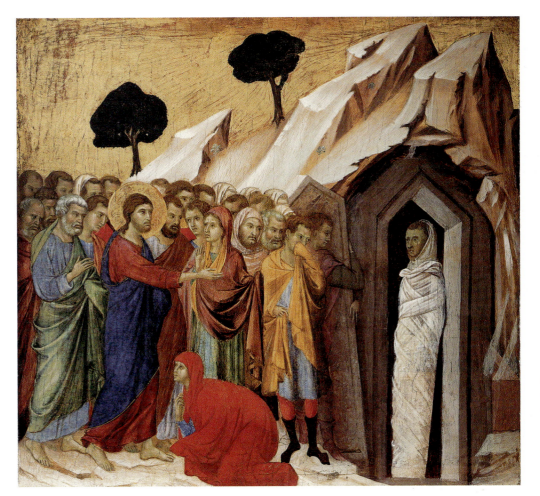

17–12 • Duccio di Buoninsegna RAISING OF LAZARUS
From the back of the *Maestà* altarpiece (lower right corner of FIG. 17–9b), made for Siena Cathedral. 1308–1311. Tempera and gold on wood, 17⅛ × 18¼" (43.5 × 46.4 cm). Kimbell Art Museum, Fort Worth, Texas.

TECHNIQUE | Cennino Cennini on Panel Painting

Il Libro dell' Arte (*The Book of Art*) of Cennino Cennini (c. 1370–1440) is a compendium of Florentine painting techniques from about 1400 that includes step-by-step instructions for making panel paintings, a process also used in Sienese paintings of the same period.

The wood for the panels, he explains, should be fine-grained, free of blemishes, and thoroughly seasoned by slow drying. The first step in preparing such a panel for painting was to cover its surface with clean white linen strips soaked in a **gesso** made from gypsum, a task, he tells us, best done on a dry, windy day. Gesso provided a ground, or surface, on which to paint, and Cennini specified that at least nine layers should be applied. The gessoed surface should then be burnished until it resembles ivory. Only then could the artist sketch the composition of the work with charcoal made from burned willow twigs. At this point, advised Cennini, "When you have finished drawing your figure, especially if it is in a very valuable [altarpiece], so that you are counting on profit and reputation from it, leave it alone for a few days, going back to it now and then to look it over and improve it wherever it still needs something. When it seems to you about right (and bear in mind that you may copy and examine things done by other good masters; that it is no shame to you) when the figure is satisfactory, take the feather and rub it over the drawing very lightly, until the drawing is practically effaced" (Cennini, trans. Thompson, p. 75). At this point, the final design would be inked in with a fine squirrel-hair brush. Gold leaf, he advises, should be affixed on a humid day, the tissue-thin sheets carefully glued down with a mixture of fine powdered clay and egg white on the reddish clay ground called bole. Then the gold is burnished with a gemstone or the tooth of a carnivorous animal. Punched and incised patterning should be added to the gold leaf later.

Fourteenth- and fifteenth-century Italian painters worked principally in tempera paint, powdered pigments mixed with egg yolk, a little water, and an occasional touch of glue. Apprentices were kept busy grinding pigments and mixing paints, setting them out for more senior painters in wooden bowls or shell dishes.

Cennini outlined a detailed and highly formulaic painting process. Faces, for example, were always to be done last, with flesh tones applied over two coats of a light greenish pigment and highlighted with touches of red and white. The finished painting was to be given a layer of varnish to protect it and intensify its colors.

EXPLORE MORE: Gain insight from a primary source by Cennino Cennini www.myartslab.com

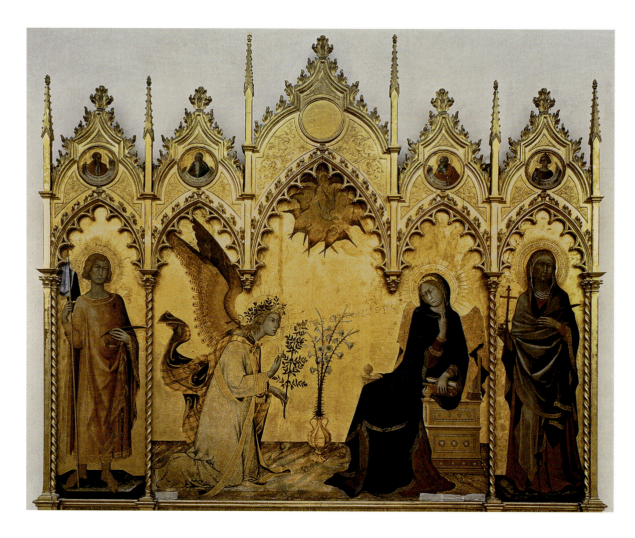

17–13 • Simone Martini and Lippo Memmi ANNUNCIATION Made for Siena Cathedral. 1333. Tempera and gold on wood, 10′ × 8′9″ (3 × 2.67 m). Galleria degli Uffizi, Florence.

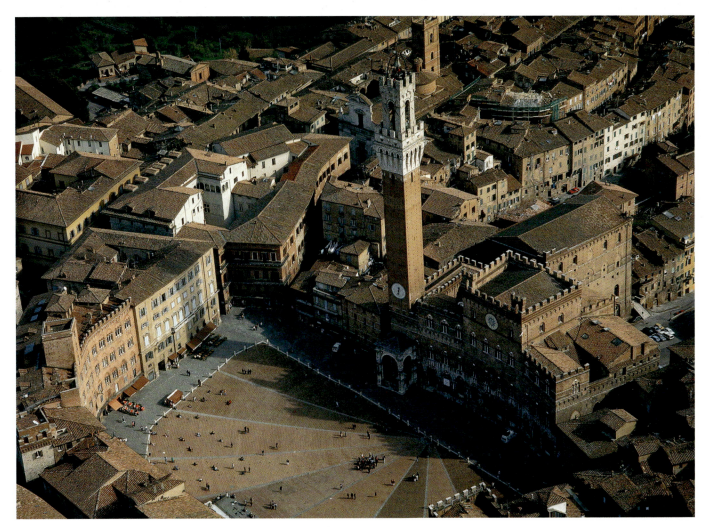

17–14 • AERIAL VIEW OF THE CAMPO IN SIENA WITH THE PALAZZO PUBBLICO (CITY HALL INCLUDING ITS TOWER) FACING ITS STRAIGHT SIDE
Siena. Palazzo Pubblico 1297–c. 1315; tower 1320s–1340s.

well as the association of such magnificent works with the glory of the city itself. According to a contemporary account, on December 20, 1311, the day that Duccio's altarpiece was carried from his workshop to the cathedral, all the shops were shut, and everyone in the city participated in the procession, with "bells ringing joyously, out of reverence for so noble a picture as is this" (Holt, p. 69).

SIMONE MARTINI. The generation of painters who followed Duccio continued to paint in the elegant style he established, combining the evocation of three-dimensional form with a graceful continuity of linear pattern. One of Duccio's most successful and innovative followers was Simone Martini (c. 1284–1344), whose paintings were in high demand throughout Italy, including in Assisi where he covered the walls of the St. Martin Chapel with frescos between 1312 and 1319. His most famous work, however, was commissioned in 1333 for the cathedral of his native Siena, an altarpiece of the **ANNUNCIATION** flanked by two saints **(FIG. 17–13)** that he painted in collaboration with his brother-in-law, Lippo Memmi.

The smartly dressed figure of Gabriel—the extended flourish of his drapery behind him suggesting he has just arrived, and with some speed—raises his hand to address the Virgin. The words of his message are actually incised into the gold-leafed gesso of the background, running from his opened mouth toward the Virgin's ear: *Ave gratia plena dominus tecum* (Luke 1:28: "Hail, full of grace, the Lord is with thee"). Seemingly frightened—at the very least startled—by this forceful and unexpected celestial messenger, Mary recoils into her lavish throne, her thumb inserted into the book she had been reading to safeguard her place, while her other hand pulls at her clothing in an elegant gesture of nobility ultimately deriving from the courtly art of thirteenth-century Paris (see Solomon, second lancet from the right in FIG. 16–13).

AMBROGIO LORENZETTI. The most important civic structure in Siena was the **PALAZZO PUBBLICO (FIG. 17–14)**, the town hall which served as the seat of government, just as the Palazzo della Signoria did in rival Florence. There are similarities between these two buildings. Both are designed as strong, fortified structures sitting on the edge of a public piazza; both have a tall tower, making them visible signs of the city from a considerable distance. The Palazzo Pubblico was constructed from 1297 to 1310, but the tower was not completed until 1348, when the bronze bell, which rang to signal meetings of the ruling council, was installed.

The interior of the Palazzo Pubblico was the site of important commissions by some of Siena's most famous artists. In c. 1315, Simone Martini painted a large mural of the Virgin in Majesty surrounded by saints—clearly based on Duccio's recently installed *Maestà*. Then, in 1338, the Siena city council commissioned Ambrogio Lorenzetti to paint frescos for the council room of the Palazzo known as the Sala della Pace (Chamber of Peace) on the theme of the contrast between good and bad government (SEE FIG. 17–1).

Ambrogio painted the results of both good and bad government on the two long walls. For the expansive scene of the **EFFECTS OF GOOD GOVERNMENT IN THE CITY AND IN THE COUNTRY**, and in tribute to his patrons, Ambrogio created an idealized but recognizable portrait of the city of Siena and its immediate environs (FIG. 17–15). The cathedral dome and the distinctive striped campanile are visible in the upper left-hand corner; the streets are filled with the bustling activity of productive citi-zens who also have time for leisurely diversions. Ambrogio shows the city from shifting viewpoints so we can see as much as possible, and renders its inhabitants larger in scale than the buildings around them so as to highlight their activity. Featured in the foreground is a circle of dancers—probably a professional troupe of male entertainers masquerading as women as part of a spring festival—and above them, at the top of the painting, a band of masons stand on exterior scaffolding constructing the wall of a new building.

The Porta Romana, Siena's gateway leading to Rome, divides the thriving city from its surrounding countryside. In this panoramic landscape painting, Ambrogio describes a natural world marked by agricultural productivity, showing activities of all seasons simultaneously—sowing, hoeing, and harvesting. Hovering above the gate that separates city life and country life is a woman clad in a wisp of transparent drapery, a scroll in one hand and a miniature gallows complete with a hanged man in the other. She represents Security, and her scroll bids those coming to the city to enter without fear because she has taken away the power of the guilty who would harm them.

The world of the Italian city-states—which had seemed so full of promise in Ambrogio Lorenzetti's *Good Government* fresco—was transformed as the middle of the century approached into uncertainty and desolation by a series of natural and societal disasters—in 1333, a flood devastated Florence, followed by banking failures in the 1340s, famine in 1346–1347, and epidemics of the bubonic plague, especially virulent in the summer of 1348, just a few years after Ambrogio's frescos were completed. Some art historians have traced the influence of these calamities on the visual arts at the middle of the fourteenth century (see "The Black Death," page 548). Yet as dark as those days must have seemed to the men and women living through them, the strong currents of cultural and artistic change initiated earlier in the century would persist. In a relatively short span of time, the European Middle Ages gave way in Florence to a new movement that would blossom in the Italian Renaissance.

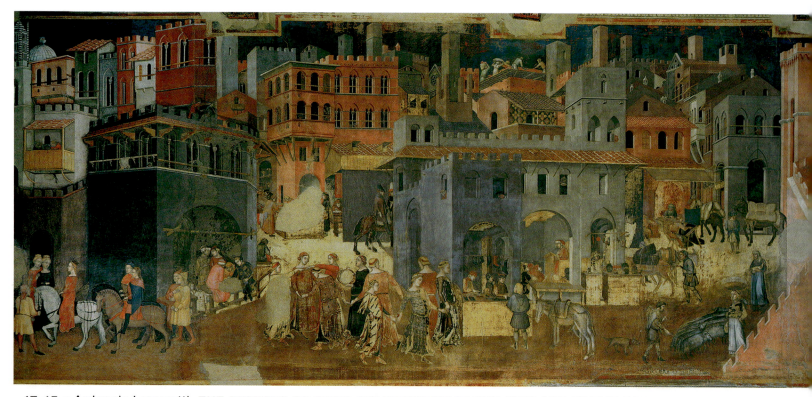

17-15 • Ambrogio Lorenzetti THE EFFECTS OF GOOD GOVERNMENT IN THE CITY AND IN THE COUNTRY
Sala dei Nove (also known as Sala della Pace), Palazzo Pubblico, Siena, Italy. 1338–1339. Fresco, total length about 46′ (14 m).

FRANCE

At the beginning of the fourteenth century, the royal court in Paris was still the arbiter of taste in western Europe, as it had been in the days of King Louis IX (St. Louis). During the Hundred Years' War, however, the French countryside was ravaged by armed struggles and civil strife. The power of the old feudal nobility, weakened significantly by warfare, was challenged by townsmen, who took advantage of new economic opportunities that opened up in the wake of the conflict. As centers of art and architecture, the duchy of Burgundy, England, and, for a brief golden moment, the court of Prague began to rival Paris.

French sculptors found lucrative new outlets for their work—not only in stone, but in wood, ivory, and precious metals, often decorated with enamel and gemstones—in the growing demand among wealthy patrons for religious art intended for homes as well as churches. Manuscript painters likewise created lavishly illustrated books for the personal devotions of the wealthy and powerful. And architectural commissions focused on smaller, exquisitely detailed chapels or small churches, often under private patronage, rather than on the building of cathedrals funded by church institutions.

MANUSCRIPT ILLUMINATION

By the late thirteenth century, private prayer books became popular among wealthy patrons. Because they contained special prayers to be recited at the eight canonical devotional "hours" between morning and night, an individual copy of one of these books came to be called a **Book of Hours**. Such a book included everything the lay person needed for pious practice—psalms, prayers to and offices of the Virgin and other saints (like the owner's patron or the patron of their home church), a calendar of feast days, and sometimes prayers for the dead. During the fourteenth century, a richly decorated Book of Hours was worn or carried like jewelry, counting among a noble person's most important portable possessions.

THE BOOK OF HOURS OF JEANNE D'ÉVREUX.   Perhaps at their marriage in 1324, King Charles IV gave his 14-year-old queen, Jeanne d'Évreux, a tiny Book of Hours—it fits easily when open within one hand—illuminated by Parisian painter Jean Pucelle (see "A Closer Look," page 550). This book was so precious to the queen that she mentioned it and its illuminator specifically in her will, leaving this royal treasure to King Charles V. Pucelle painted the book's pictures in *grisaille*—monochromatic painting in shades of gray with only delicate touches of color. His style clearly derives from the courtly mode established in Paris at the time of St. Louis, with its softly modeled, voluminous draperies gathered loosely and falling in projecting diagonal folds around tall, elegantly posed figures with carefully coiffed curly hair, broad foreheads, and delicate features. But his conception of space, with figures placed within coherent, discrete architectural settings, suggests a firsthand knowledge of contemporary Sienese art.

Jeanne appears in the initial *D* below the Annunciation, kneeling in prayer before a lectern, perhaps using this Book of Hours to guide her meditations, beginning with the words written

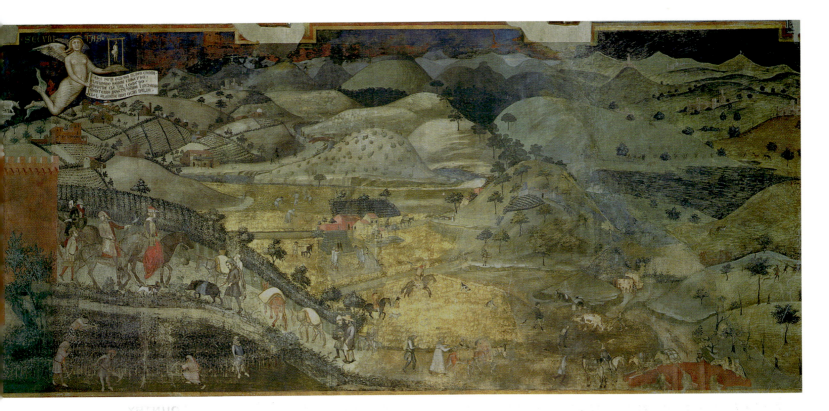

The Black Death

A deadly outbreak of the bubonic plague, known as the Black Death after the dark sores that developed on the bodies of its victims, spread to Europe from Asia, both by land and by sea, in the middle of the fourteenth century. At least half the urban population of Florence and Siena—some estimate 80 percent—died during the summer of 1348, probably including the artists Andrea Pisano and Ambrogio Lorenzetti. Death was so quick and widespread that basic social structures crumbled in the resulting chaos; people did not know where the disease came from, what caused it, or how long the pandemic would last.

Mid-twentieth-century art historian Millard Meiss proposed that the Black Death had a significant impact on the development of Italian art in the middle of the fourteenth century. Pointing to what he saw as a reactionary return to hieratic linearity in religious art, Meiss theorized that artists had retreated from the rounded forms that had characterized the work of Giotto to old-fashioned styles, and that this artistic change reflected a growing reliance on traditional religious values in the wake of a disaster that some interpreted as God's punishment of a world in moral decline.

An altarpiece painted in 1354–1357 by Andrea di Cione, nicknamed Orcagna ("Archangel"), under the patronage of Tommasso Strozzi—the so-called *Strozzi Altarpiece*—is an example of the sort of paintings that led Meiss to his interpretation. The painting's otherworldly vision is dominated by a central figure of Christ, presumably enthroned, but without any hint of an actual seat, evoking the image of the judge at the Last Judgment, outside time and space. The silhouetted outlines of the standing and kneeling saints emphasize surface over depth; the gold expanse of floor beneath them does not offer any reassuring sense of spatial recession to contain them and their activity. Throughout, line and color are more prominent than form.

Recent art historians have stepped back from Meiss's theory of stylistic change in mid-fourteenth-century Italy. Some have pointed out logical relationships between style and subject in the works Meiss cites; others have seen in them a mannered outgrowth of current style rather than a reversion to an earlier style; still others have discounted the underlying notion that stylistic change is connected with social situations. But there is no denying the relationship of works such as the *Strozzi Altarpiece* with death and judgment, sanctity and the promise of salvation. These themes are suggested in the narrative scenes on the **predella** (the lower zone of the altarpiece): Thomas Aquinas's ecstasy during Mass, Christ's miraculous walk on water to rescue Peter, and the salvation of Emperor Henry II because of his donation of a chalice to a religious institution. While these are not uncommon scenes in sacred art, it is difficult not see a relationship between their choice as subject matter here and the specter cast by the Black Death over a world that had just imagined its prosperity in path-breaking works of visual art firmly rooted in references to everyday life.

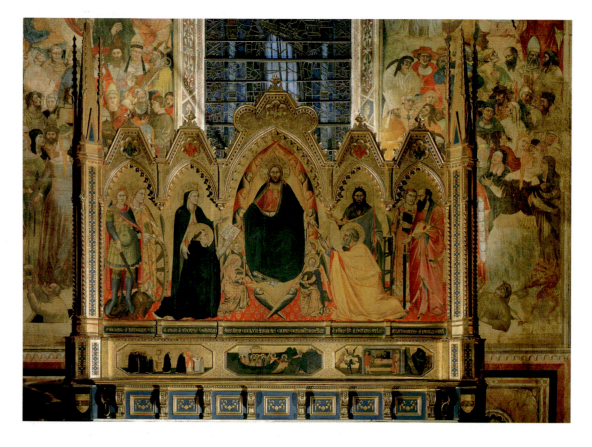

Andrea di Cione (nicknamed Orcagna) **ENTHRONED CHRIST WITH SAINTS, FROM THE STROZZI ALTARPIECE**
Strozzi Chapel, Santa Maria Novella, Florence. 1354–1357. Tempera and gold on wood, 9′ × 9′8″ (2.74 × 2.95 m).

EXPLORE MORE: Gain insight from a primary source related to the Black Death
www.myartslab.com

on this page: *Domine labia mea aperies* (Psalm 51:15: "O Lord, open thou my lips"). The juxtaposition of the praying Jeanne's portrait with a scene from the life of the Virgin Mary suggests that the sacred scene is actually a vision inspired by Jeanne's meditations. The young queen might have identified with and sought to feel within herself Mary's joy at Gabriel's message. Given what we know of Jeanne's own life story and her royal husband's predicament, it might also have directed the queen's prayers toward the fulfillment of his wish for a male heir.

In the Annunciation, Mary is shown receiving the archangel Gabriel in a Gothic building that seems to project outward from the page toward the viewer, while rejoicing angels look on from windows under the eaves. The group of romping children at the bottom of the page at first glance seems to echo the angelic jubilation. Folklorists have suggested, however, that the children are playing "froggy in the middle" or "hot cockles," games in which one child was tagged by the others. To the medieval viewer, if the game symbolized the mocking of Christ or the betrayal of Judas, who "tags" his friend, it would have evoked a darker mood by referring to the picture on the other page of this opening, foreshadowing Jesus' imminent death even as his life is beginning.

METALWORK AND IVORY

Fourteenth-century French sculpture is intimate in character. Religious subjects became more emotionally expressive; objects became smaller and demanded closer scrutiny from the viewer. In the secular realm, tales of love and valor were carved on luxury items to delight the rich (see "An Ivory Chest with Scenes of Romance," pages 552–553). Precious materials—gold, silver, and ivory—were preferred.

THE VIRGIN AND CHILD FROM SAINT-DENIS. A silver-gilt image of a standing **VIRGIN AND CHILD** (FIG. 17–16) is a rare survivor that verifies the acclaim that was accorded Parisian fourteenth-century goldsmiths. An inscription on the base documents the statue's donation to the abbey church of Saint-Denis in 1339 and the donor's name, the same Queen Jeanne d'Évreux whose Book of Hours we have just examined. In a style that recalls the work of artist Jean Pucelle in that Book of Hours, the Virgin holds Jesus in her left arm with her weight on her left leg, standing in a graceful, characteristically Gothic S-curve pose. Mary originally wore a crown, and she still holds a large enameled and jeweled *fleur-de-lis*—the heraldic symbol of royal France—which served as a reliquary container for strands of Mary's hair. The Christ Child, reaching out tenderly to caress his mother's face, is babylike in both form and posture. On the base, minuscule statues of prophets stand on projecting piers to separate 14 enameled scenes from Christ's Infancy and Passion, reminding us of the suffering to come. The apple in the baby's hand carries the theme further with its reference to Christ's role as the new Adam, whose sacrifice on the cross—medieval Christians believed—redeemed humanity from the first couple's fall into sin when Eve bit into the forbidden fruit.

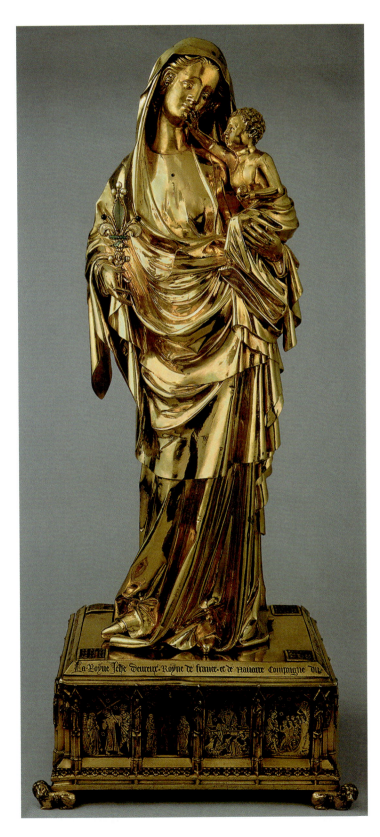

17-16 • VIRGIN AND CHILD
c. 1324–1339. Silver gilt and enamel, height 27⅛" (69 cm).
Musée du Louvre, Paris.

The Hours of Jeanne d'Évreux

by Jean Pucelle, Two-Page Opening with the Kiss of Judas and the Annunciation. Paris. c. 1325–1328. *Grisaille* and color on vellum, each page 3½ × 2¼″ (8.9 × 6.2 cm). Metropolitan Museum of Art, New York. The Cloisters Collection (54.1.2), fols. 15v–16r

In this opening Pucelle juxtaposes complementary scenes drawn from the Infancy and Passion of Christ, placed on opposing pages, in a scheme known as the Joys and Sorrows of the Virgin. The "joy" of the Annunciation on the right is paired with the "sorrow" of the betrayal and arrest of Christ on the left.

Christ sways back gracefully as Judas betrays him with a kiss. The S-curve of his body mirrors the Virgin's pose on the opposite page, as both accept their fate with courtly decorum.

The prominent lamp held aloft by a member of the arresting battalion informs the viewer that this scene takes place at night, in the dark.

The angel who holds up the boxlike enclosure where the Annunciation takes place is an allusion to the legend of the miraculous transportation of this building from Nazareth to Loreto in 1294.

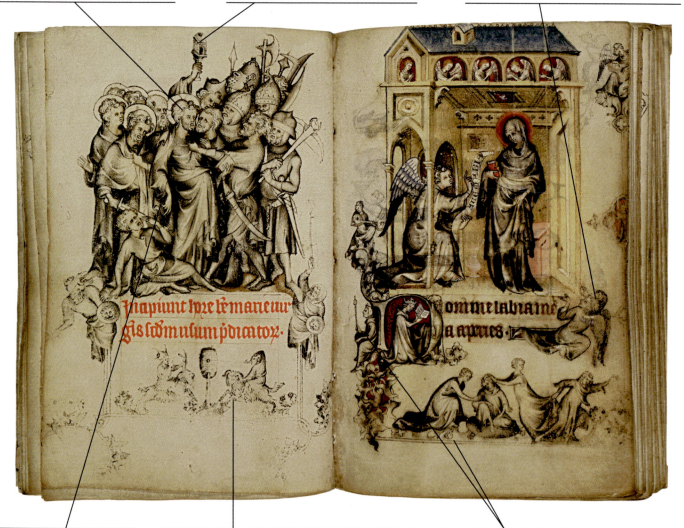

Christ reaches casually down to heal Malchus, the assistant of the high priest whose ear Peter had just cut off in angry retaliation for his participation in the arrest of Jesus.

Scenes of secular amusements from everyday life, visual puns, and off-color jokes appear at the bottom of many pages of this book. Sometimes they relate to the themes of the sacred scenes above them. These comic knights riding goats may be a commentary on the lack of valor shown by the soldiers assaulting Jesus, especially if this wine barrel conjured up for Jeanne an association with the Eucharist.

The candle held by the cleric who guards the "door" to Jeanne's devotional retreat, as well as the rabbit emerging from its burrow in the marginal scene, are sexually charged symbols of fertility that seem directly related to the focused prayers of a child bride required to produce a male heir.

SEE MORE: View the Closer Look feature for The Hours of Jeanne d'Évreux **www.myartslab.com**

ENGLAND

Fourteenth-century England prospered in spite of the ravages of the Black Death and the Hundred Years' War with France. English life at this time is described in the brilliant social commentary of Geoffrey Chaucer in the *Canterbury Tales* (see "A New Spirit in Fourteenth-Century Literature," page 531). The royal family, especially Edward I (r. 1272–1307)—the castle builder—and many of the nobles and bishops were generous patrons of the arts.

EMBROIDERY: OPUS ANGLICANUM

Since the thirteenth century, the English had been renowned for pictorial needlework, using colored silk and gold thread to create images as detailed as contemporary painters produced in manuscripts. Popular throughout Europe, the art came to be called *opus anglicanum* ("English work"). The popes had more than 100 pieces in the Vatican treasury. The names of several prominent embroiderers are known, but in the thirteenth century no one surpassed Mabel of Bury St. Edmunds, who created both religious and secular articles for King Henry III (r. 1216–1272).

THE CHICHESTER-CONSTABLE CHASUBLE. This *opus angicanum* liturgical vestment worn by a priest during Mass **(FIG. 17–17)** was embroidered c. 1330–1350 with images formed by subtle gradations of colored silk. Where gold threads were laid and couched (tacked down with colored silk), the effect resembles the burnished gold-leaf backgrounds of manuscript illuminations. The Annunciation, the Adoration of the Magi, and the Coronation of the Virgin are set in cusped, crocketed **ogee** (S-shape) arches, supported on animal-head corbels and twisting branches sprouting oak leaves with seed-pearl acorns. Because the star and crescent moon in the Coronation of the Virgin scene are heraldic emblems of Edward III (r. 1327–1377), perhaps he or a family member commissioned this luxurious vestment.

During the celebration of the Mass, especially as the priest moved, *opus anglicanum* would have glinted in the candlelight amid treasures on the altar. Court dress was just as rich and colorful, and at court such embroidered garments proclaimed the rank and status of the wearer. So heavy did such gold and bejeweled garments become that their wearers often needed help to move.

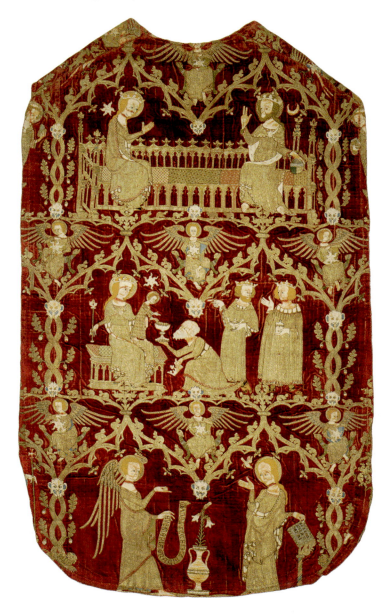

17-17 • LIFE OF THE VIRGIN, BACK OF THE CHICHESTER-CONSTABLE CHASUBLE

From a set of vestments embroidered in *opus anglicanum* from southern England. c. 1330–1350. Red velvet with silk and metallic thread and seed pearls, length 4′3″ (129.5 cm), width 30″ (76 cm). Metropolitan Museum of Art, New York. Fletcher Fund, 1927 (27 162.1)

An Ivory Chest with Scenes of Romance

Fourteenth-century Paris was renowned for more than its goldsmiths (SEE FIG. 17–16). Among the most sumptuous and sought-after Parisian luxury products were small chests assembled from carved ivory plaques that were used by wealthy women to store jewelry or other personal treasures. The entirely secular subject matter of these chests was romantic love. Indeed, they seem to have been courtship gifts from smitten men to desired women, or wedding presents offered by grooms to their brides.

A chest from around 1330–1350, now in the Walters Museum (SEE FIG. A), is one of seven that have survived intact; there are fragments of a dozen more. It is a delightful and typical example. Figural relief covers five exterior sides of the box: around the perimeter and on the hinged top. The assembled panels were joined by metal

hardware—strips, brackets, hinges, handles, and locks—originally wrought in silver. Although some chests tell a single romantic story in sequential episodes, most, like this one, anthologize scenes drawn from a group of stories, combining courtly romance, secular allegory, and ancient fables.

On the lid of the Walters casket (SEE FIG. B), jousting is the theme. Spread over the central two panels, a single scene catches two charging knights in the heat of a tournament, while trumpeting heralds call the attention of spectators, lined up above in a gallery to observe this public display of virility. The panel at right mocks the very ritual showcased in the middle panels by pitting a woman against a knight, battling not with lances but with a long-stemmed rose (symbolizing sexual surrender) and an oak bough (symbolizing fertility). Instead of

observing these silly goings-on, however, the spectators tucked into the upper architecture pursue their own amorous flirtations. Finally, in the scene on the left, knights use crossbows and a catapult to hurl roses at the Castle of Love, while Cupid returns fire with his seductive arrows.

On the front of the chest (SEE FIG. A), generalized romantic allegory gives way to vignettes from a specific story. At left, the long-bearded Aristotle teaches the young Alexander the Great, using exaggerated gestures and an authoritative text to emphasize his point. Today's lesson is a stern warning not to allow the seductive power of women to distract the young prince from his studies. The subsequent scene, however, pokes fun at his eminent teacher, who has become so smitten by the wiles of a young beauty named Phyllis that he lets

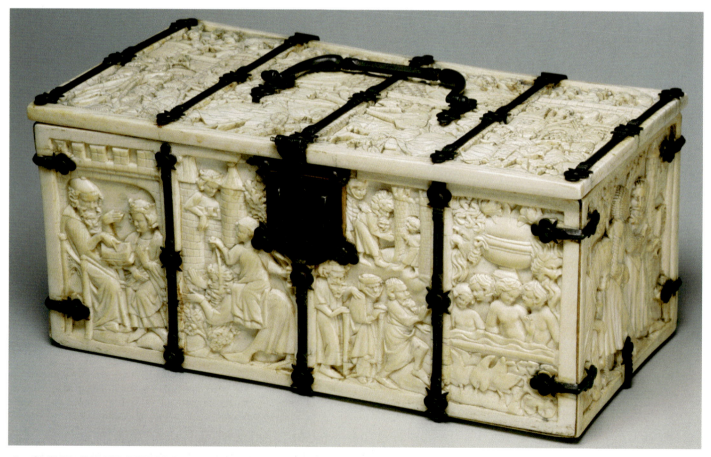

A. SMALL IVORY CHEST WITH SCENES FROM COURTLY ROMANCES
Made in Paris. c. 1330–1350. Elephant ivory with modern iron mounts, height 4½″ (11.5 cm), width 9¹¹⁄₁₆″ (24.6 cm), depth 4⅞″ (12.4 cm). The Walters Art Museum, Baltimore.

her ride him around like a horse, while his student observes this farce, peering out of the castle in the background. The two scenes at right relate to an eastern legend of the fountain of youth, popular in medieval Europe. A line of bearded elders approaches the fountain from the left, steadied by their canes. But after having partaken of its transforming effects, two newly rejuvenated couples, now nude, bathe and flirt within the fountain's basin. The man first in line for treatment, stepping up to climb into the fountain, looks suspiciously like the figure of the aging Aristotle, forming a link between the two stories on the casket front.

Unlike royal marriages of the time, which were essentially business contracts based on political or financial exigencies, the romantic love of the aristocratic wealthy involved passionate devotion. Images of gallant knights and their coy paramours, who could bring intoxicating bliss or cruelly withhold their love on a whim, captured the popular Gothic imagination. They formed the principal subject matter on personal luxury objects, not only chests like this, but mirror backs, combs, writing tablets, even ceremonial saddles. And these stories evoke themes that still captivate us since they reflect notions of desire and betrayal, cruel rejection and blissful folly, at play in our own romantic conquests and relationships to this day. In this way they allow us some access to the lives of the people who commissioned and owned these precious objects, even if we ourselves are unable to afford them.

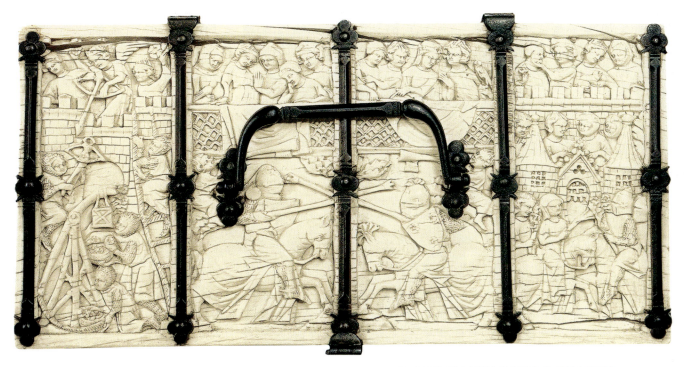

B. ATTACK ON THE CASTLE OF LOVE
Top of the chest.

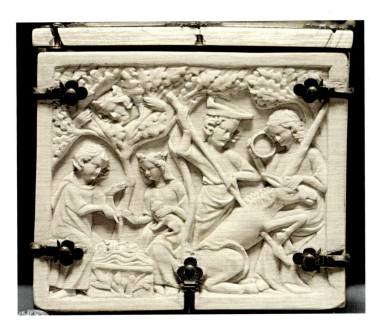

C. TRISTAN AND ISEULT AT THE FOUNTAIN; CAPTURE OF THE UNICORN
Left short side of the chest.

Two other well-known medieval themes are juxtaposed on this plaque from the short side of the ivory chest. At left, Tristan and Iseult have met secretly for an illicit romantic tryst, while Iseult's husband, King Mark, tipped off by an informant, observes them from a tree. But when they see his reflection in a fountain between them, they alter their behavior accordingly, and the king believes them innocent of the adultery he had (rightly) suspected. The medieval bestiary ("book of beasts") claimed that only a virgin could capture the mythical unicorn, which at right lays his head, with its aggressively phallic horn, into the lap of just such a pure maiden so that the hunter can take advantage of her alluring powers over the animal to kill it with his phallic counterpart of its horn, a large spear.

ARCHITECTURE

In the later years of the thirteenth century and early years of the fourteenth, a distinctive and influential Gothic architectural style, popularly known as the "Decorated style," developed in England. This change in taste has been credited to Henry III's ambition to surpass St. Louis, who was his brother-in-law, as a royal patron of the arts.

THE DECORATED STYLE AT EXETER.   One of the most complete Decorated-style buildings is **EXETER CATHEDRAL**. Thomas of Witney began construction in 1313 and remained master mason from 1316 to 1342. He supervised construction of the nave and redesigned upper parts of the choir. He left the towers of the original Norman cathedral but turned the interior into a dazzling stone forest of colonnettes, moldings, and vault ribs (FIG. 17–18). From piers formed by a cluster of colonnettes rise multiple moldings that make the arcade seem to ripple. Bundled colonnettes spring from sculptured foliate **corbels** (brackets that project from a wall) between the arches and rise up the wall to support conical clusters of 13 ribs that meet at the summit of the vault, a modest 69 feet above the floor. The basic structure here is the four-part vault with intersecting cross-ribs, but the designer added additional ribs, called **tiercerons**, to create a richer linear pattern. Elaborately carved **bosses** (decorative knoblike elements)

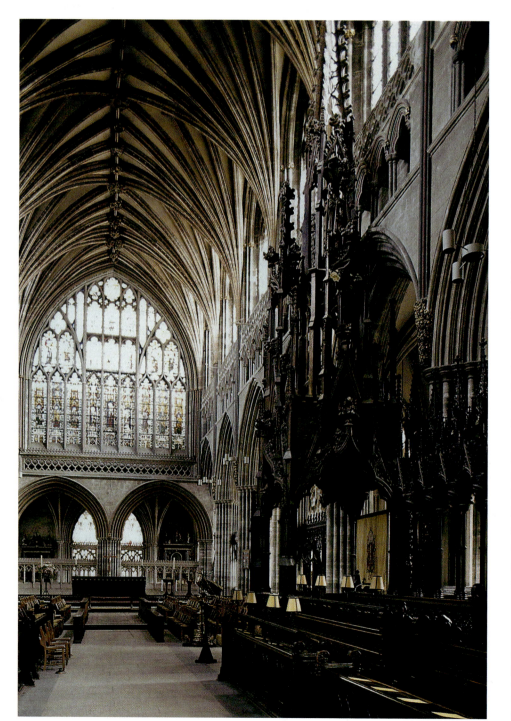

signal the point where ribs meet along the ridge of the vault. Large bar-tracery clerestory windows illuminate the 300-foot-long nave. Unpolished gray marble shafts, yellow sandstone arches, and a white French stone, shipped from Caen, add subtle gradations of color to the upper wall.

Detailed records survive for the building of Exeter Cathedral, documenting work over the period from 1279 to 1514, with only two short breaks. They record where masons and carpenters were housed (in a hostel near the cathedral) and how they were paid (some by the day with extra for drinks, some by the week, some for each finished piece); how materials were acquired and transported (payments for horseshoes and fodder for the horses); and, of course, payments for the building materials (not only stone and wood but rope for measuring and parchment on which to draw forms for the masons). The bishops contributed generously to the building funds. This was not a labor only of love.

Thomas of Witney also designed the intricate, 57-foot-high bishop's throne (at right in FIG. 17–18), constructed by Richard de Galmeton and Walter of Memburg, who led a team of a dozen carpenters. The canopy resembles embroidery translated into wood, with its maze of pinnacles, bursting with leafy crockets and tiny carved animals and

17–18 • EXETER CATHEDRAL
Devon, England. Thomas of Witney, choir, 14th century and bishop's throne, 1313–1317; Robert Lesyngham, east window, 1389–1390.

heads. To finish the throne in splendor, Master Nicolas painted and gilded the wood. When the bishop was seated on his throne wearing embroidered vestments like the Chichester-Constable Chasuble (SEE FIG. 17–17), he must have resembled a golden image in a shrine—more a symbol of the power and authority of the Church than a specific human being.

THE PERPENDICULAR STYLE AT EXETER. During years following the Black Death, work at Exeter Cathedral came to a standstill. The nave had been roofed but not vaulted, and the windows had no glass. When work could be resumed, tastes had changed. The exuberance of the Decorated style gave way to an austere style in which rectilinear patterns and sharp angular shapes replaced intricate curves, and luxuriant foliage gave way to simple stripped-down patterns. This phase is known as the Perpendicular style.

In 1389–1390, well-paid master mason Robert Lesyngham rebuilt the great east window (SEE FIG. 17–18), and he designed the window tracery in the new Perpendicular style. The window fills the east wall of the choir like a glowing altarpiece. A single figure in each light stands under a tall painted canopy that flows into and blends with the stone tracery. The Virgin with the Christ Child stands in the center over the high altar, with four female saints at the left and four male saints on the right, including St. Peter, to whom the church is dedicated. At a distance the colorful figures silhouetted against the silver *grisaille* glass become a band of color, conforming to and thus reinforcing the rectangular pattern of the mullions and transoms. The combination of *grisaille*, silver-oxide stain (staining clear glass with shades of yellow or gold), and colored glass produces a glowing wall, and casts a cool, silvery light over the nearby stonework.

Perpendicular architecture heralds the Renaissance style in its regularity, its balanced horizontal and vertical lines, and its plain wall or window surfaces. When Tudor monarchs introduced Renaissance art into the British Isles, builders were not forced to rethink the form and structure of their buildings; they simply changed the ornament from the pointed cusps and crocketed arches of the Gothic style to the round arches and columns and capitals of Roman Classicism. The Perpendicular style itself became an English architectural vernacular. It remains popular today in the United States for churches and college buildings.

THE HOLY ROMAN EMPIRE

By the fourteenth century, the Holy Roman Empire existed more as an ideal fiction than a fact. The Italian territories had established their independence, and in contrast to England and France, Germany had become further divided into multiple states with powerful regional associations and princes. The Holy Roman emperors, now elected by Germans, concentrated on securing the fortunes of their families. They continued to be patrons of the arts, promoting local styles.

MYSTICISM AND SUFFERING

The by-now-familiar ordeals of the fourteenth century—famines, wars, and plagues—helped inspire a mystical religiosity in Germany that emphasized both ecstatic joy and extreme suffering. Devotional images, known as *Andachtsbilder* in German, inspired worshipers to contemplate Jesus' first and last hours, especially during evening prayers, or vespers, giving rise to the term *Vesperbild* for the image of Mary mourning her son. Through such religious exercises, worshipers hoped to achieve understanding of the divine and union with God.

VESPERBILD. In this well-known example (FIG. 17–19), blood gushes from the hideous **rosettes** that form the wounds of an emaciated and lifeless Jesus who teeters improbably on the lap of his hunched-over mother. The Virgin's face conveys the intensity

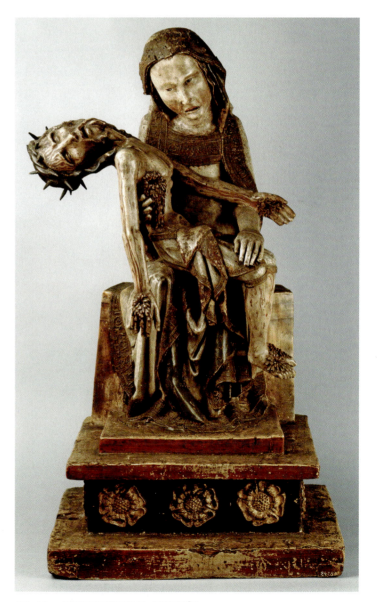

17–19 • VESPERBILD (PIETÀ)
From the Middle Rhine region, Germany. c. 1330. Wood and polychromy, height 34½″ (88.4 cm). Landesmuseum, Bonn.

of her ordeal, mingling horror, shock, pity, and grief. Such images took on greater poignancy since they would have been compared, in the worshiper's mind, to the familiar, almost ubiquitous images of the young Virgin mother holding her innocent and loving baby Jesus.

THE HEDWIG CODEX.   The extreme physicality and emotionalism of the *Vesperbild* finds parallels in the actual lives of some medieval saints in northern Europe. St. Hedwig (1174–1243), married at age 12 to Duke Henry I of Silesia and mother of his seven children, entered the Cistercian convent of Trebniz (in modern Poland) on her husband's death in 1238. She devoted the rest of her life to caring for the poor and seeking to emulate the suffering of Christ by walking barefoot in the snow. As described in her *vita*, she had a

particular affection for a small ivory statue of the Virgin and Child, which she carried with her at all times, and which "she often took up in her hands to envelop it in love, so that out of passion she could see it more often and through the seeing could prove herself more devout, inciting her to even greater love of the glorious Virgin. When she once blessed the sick with this image they were cured immediately" (translation from Schleif, p. 22). Hedwig was buried clutching the statue, and when her tomb was opened after her canonization in 1267, it was said that although most of her body had deteriorated, the fingers that still gripped the beloved object had miraculously not decayed.

A picture of Hedwig serves as the frontispiece **(FIG. 17–20)** of a manuscript of her *vita* (biography) known as the Hedwig Codex, commissioned in 1353 by one her descendants, Ludwig I of

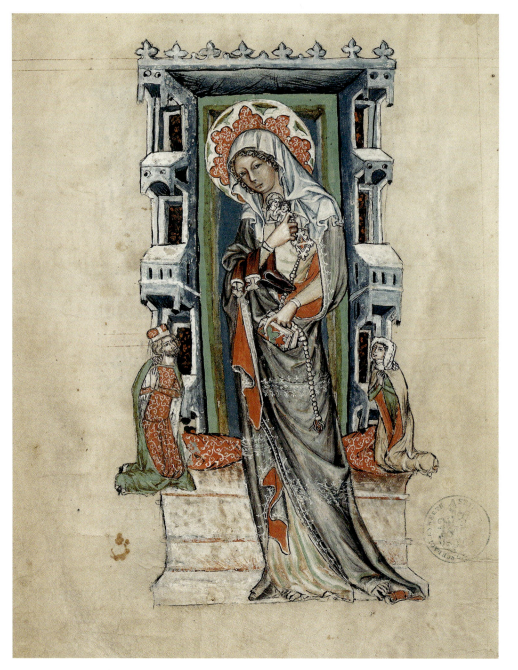

17–20 • ST. HEDWIG OF SILESIA WITH DUKE LUDWIG I OF LIEGNITZ-BRIEG AND DUCHESS AGNES
Dedication page of the Hedwig Codex. 1353. Ink and paint on parchment. 13⁷⁄₁₆ × 9¾" (115 × 94 cm). J. Paul Getty Museum, Los Angeles. MS. Ludwig XI 7, fol. 12v

Liegnitz-Brieg. Duke Ludwig and his wife, Agnes, are shown here kneeling on either side of St. Hedwig, dwarfed by the saint's architectural throne and her own imposing scale. With her prominent, spidery hands, she clutches the famous ivory statue, as well as a rosary and a prayer book, inserting her fingers within it to maintain her place as if our arrival had interrupted her devotions. She has draped her leather boots over her right wrist in a reference to her practice of removing them to walk in the snow. Hedwig's highly volumetric figure stands in a swaying pose of courtly elegance derived from French Gothic, but the fierce intensity of her gaze and posture are far removed from the mannered graciousness of the smiling angel of Reims (see statue at far left in FIG. 16–16), whose similar gesture and extended finger are employed simply to grasp his drapery and assure its elegant display.

THE SUPREMACY OF PRAGUE

Charles IV of Bohemia (r. 1346–1375) was raised in France, and his admiration for the French king Charles IV was such that he changed his own name from Wenceslas to Charles. He was officially crowned king of Bohemia in 1347 and Holy Roman Emperor in 1355. He established his capital in Prague, which, in the view of its contemporaries, replaced Constantinople as the "New Rome." Prague had a great university, a castle, and a cathedral overlooking a town that spread on both sides of a river joined by a stone bridge, a remarkable structure itself.

When Pope Clement VI made Prague an archbishopric in 1344, construction began on a new cathedral in the Gothic style—to be named for St. Vitus. It would also serve as the coronation church and royal pantheon. But the choir was not finished for Charles's first coronation, so he brought Peter Parler from Swabia to complete it.

THE PARLER FAMILY. In 1317, Heinrich Parler, a former master of works on Cologne Cathedral, designed and began building the church of the Holy Cross in Schwäbisch Gmünd, in southwest Germany. In 1351, his son Peter (c. 1330–1399), the most brilliant architect of this talented family, joined the workshop. Peter designed the choir (FIG. 17–21) in the manner of a hall church whose triple-aisled form was enlarged by a ring of deep

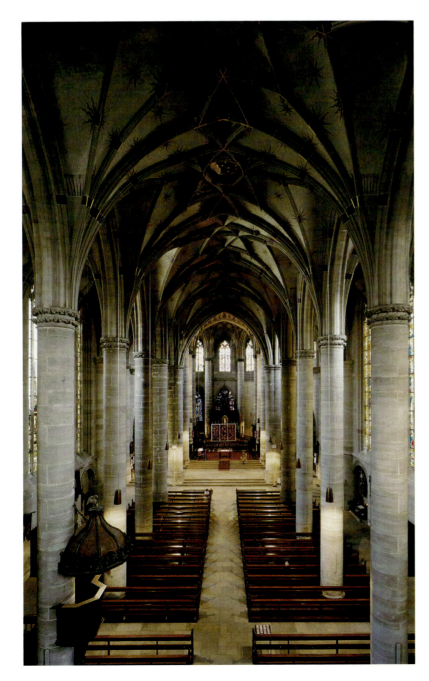

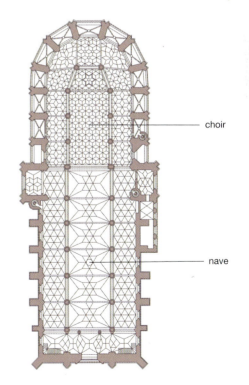

choir

nave

17-21 • Heinrich and Peter Parler PLAN AND INTERIOR OF CHURCH OF THE HOLY CROSS
Schwäbisch Gmünd, Germany. Begun in 1317 by Henrich Parler; choir by Peter Parler begun in 1351; vaulting completed 16th century.

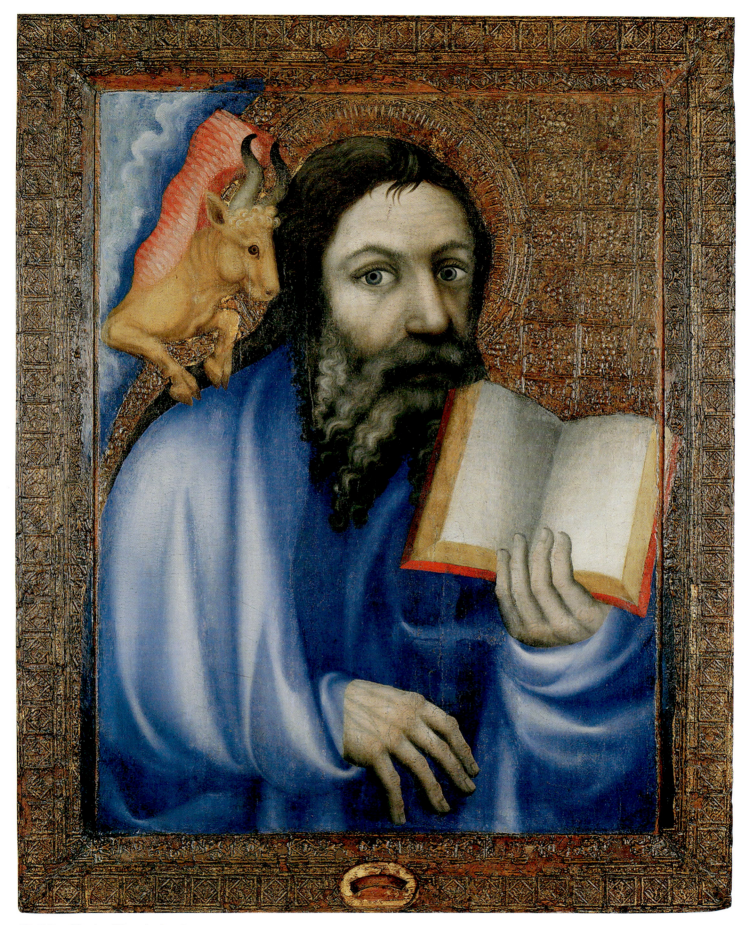

17–22 • Master Theodoric ST. LUKE
Holy Cross Chapel, Karlstejn Castle, near Prague. 1360–1364. Paint and gold on panel. 45¼ × 37″ (115 × 94 cm).

chapels between the buttresses. The contrast between Heinrich's nave and Peter's choir (seen clearly in the plan of FIG. 17–21) illustrates the increasing complexity of rib patterns covering the vaults, which emphasizes the unity of interior space rather than its division into bays.

Called by Charles IV to Prague in 1353, Peter turned the unfinished St. Vitus Cathedral into a "glass house," adding a vast clerestory and glazed triforium supported by double flying buttresses, all covered by net vaults that created a continuous canopy over the space. Because of the success of projects such as this, Peter and his family became the most successful architects in the Holy Roman Empire. Their concept of space, luxurious decoration, and intricate vaulting dominated central European architecture for three generations.

MASTER THEODORIC. At Karlstejn Castle, a day's ride from Prague, Charles IV built another chapel, covering the walls with gold and precious stones as well as with paintings. There were 130 paintings of the saints serving as reliquaries, with relics inserted into their frames. Master Theodoric, the court painter, provided drawings on the wood panels, and he painted about 30 images himself. Figures are crowded into—even extend over—their frames, emphasizing their size and power. Master Theodoric was head of the Brotherhood of St. Luke, and the way that his painting of ST. LUKE (FIG. 17–22), patron saint of painters, looks out at the viewer has suggested to scholars that this may be a self-portrait. His personal style combined a preference for substantial bodies, oversized heads and hands, dour and haunted faces, and soft, deeply modeled drapery, with a touch of grace derived from the French Gothic style. The chapel, consecrated in 1365, so pleased the emperor that in 1367 he gave the artist a farm in appreciation of his work.

Prague and the Holy Roman Empire under Charles IV had become a multicultural empire where people of different religions (Christians and Jews) and ethnic heritages (German and Slav) lived side by side. Charles died in 1378, and without his strong central government, political and religious dissent overtook the empire. Jan Hus, dean of the philosophy faculty at Prague University and a powerful reforming preacher, denounced the immorality he saw in the Church. He was burned at the stake, becoming a martyr and Czech national hero. The Hussite Revolution in the fifteenth century ended Prague's—and Bohemia's—leadership in the arts.

THINK ABOUT IT

17.1 Discuss the circumstances surrounding the construction and decoration of the Scrovegni (Arena) Chapel, with special attention to its relationship to the life and aspirations of its patron.

17.2 Compare and contrast Giotto's and Duccio's renderings of the biblical story of Christ's Raising of Lazarus (FIGS. 17–8, 17–12).

17.3 Discuss Ambrogio Lorenzetti's engagement with secular subject matter in his frescos for Siena's Palazzo Pubblico (FIG. 17–15). How did these paintings relate to their sociopolitical context?

17.4 Choose one small work of art in this chapter that is crafted from precious materials with exceptional technical skill. Explain how it was made and how it was used. How does the work of art relate to its cultural and social context?

17.5 Analyze how the Decorated Gothic style of Exeter Cathedral (FIG. 17–18) preserves certain traditions from the thirteenth-century Gothic that you learned about in Chapter 16, and assess how it departs from the traditional Gothic style.

PRACTICE MORE: Compose answers to these questions, get flashcards for images and terms, and review chapter material with quizzes **www.myartslab.com**

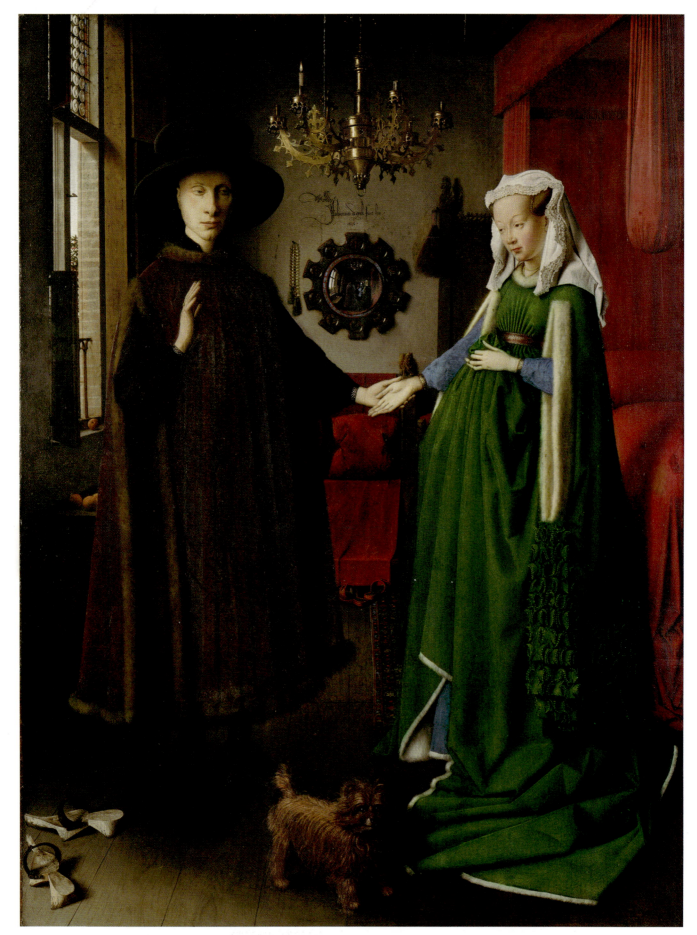

18–1 • Jan van Eyck DOUBLE PORTRAIT OF A GIOVANNI ARNOLFINI AND HIS WIFE
1434. Oil on wood panel, 33 × 22½″ (83.8 × 57.2 cm). The National Gallery, London.

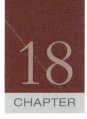

FIFTEENTH-CENTURY ART IN NORTHERN EUROPE

Fifteenth-century Europe saw the emergence of wealthy merchants whose rise to power was fueled by individual accomplishment, rather than hereditary succession within noble families. Certainly Giovanni Arnolfini—the pasty gentleman with the extravagant hat in this double portrait (FIG. 18–1)—earned, rather than inherited, the right to have himself and his wife recorded by renowned artist Jan van Eyck. It was the wealth and connections he made as an Italian cloth merchant providing luxury fabrics to the Burgundian court that put him in the position to commission such a precious picture, in which both patron and painter are identified with conspicuous clarity. Giovanni's face looks more like a personal likeness than anything we have seen since ancient Rome, and not only did Jan van Eyck inscribe his name above the convex mirror ("Jan van Eyck was here, 1434") but his personal painting style carries an equally sure stamp of authorship. The doll-like face of the woman standing next to Giovanni is less individualized. Has she lifted her skirt over her belly so she can follow Giovanni, who has taken her by the hand? Or are most modern observers correct in assuming that she is pregnant? This painting is full of mysteries.

The precise identity of the couple is still open to scholarly debate. And is this a wedding, a betrothal, or perhaps security for a shady financial deal? Recently it has been interpreted as a memorial to a beloved wife lost to death. Only the wealth of the couple is beyond dispute. They are surrounded by luxury objects: lavish bed hangings, sumptuous chandelier, precious oriental carpet, rare oranges, not to mention their extravagant clothing. The man wears a fur-lined, silk velvet *heuque* (sleeveless overgarment). The woman's gown not only employs more costly wool fabric than necessary to cover her slight body; the elaborate cutwork decoration and white fur lining of her sleeves is an ostentatious indicator of cost. In fact, the painting itself—probably hung in the couple's home—was an object of considerable value.

Even within its secular setting, however, the picture resonated with sacred meaning. The Church still provided spiritual grounding for men and women of the Renaissance. The crystal prayer beads hanging next to the convex mirror imply the couple's piety, and the mirror itself—a symbol of the all-seeing eye of God—is framed with a circular cycle of scenes from Christ's Passion. A figure of St. Margaret—protector of women in childbirth—is carved at the top of a post in the high-backed chair beside the bed, and the perky *Affenpinscher* in the foreground may be more than a pet. Dogs served as symbols of fidelity and also have funerary associations, but choosing a rare, ornamental breed for inclusion here may have been yet another opportunity to express wealth.

LEARN ABOUT IT

18.1 Analyze how Flemish painters gave scrupulous attention to describing the textures and luminosity of objects in the natural world and in domestic interiors.

18.2 Trace the development of an extraordinary interest in evoking human likeness in portraits, unlike anything seen since ancient Rome.

18.3 Explore how paintings in northern Europe of the fifteenth century captured in concrete form visions of their meditating donors.

18.4 Uncover the complex symbolic meanings that saturated the settings of Flemish paintings.

18.5 Investigate how prints developed into a major pictorial medium.

HEAR MORE: Listen to an audio file of your chapter **www.myartslab.com**

THE NORTHERN RENAISSANCE

Revitalized civic life and economic growth in the late fourteenth century gave rise to a prosperous middle class that supported scholarship, literature, and the arts. Their patronage resulted in the explosion of learning and creativity we call the Renaissance (French for "rebirth")—a term that was assigned to this period by later historians.

A major manifestation of the Renaissance in northern Europe was a growing and newly intense interest in the natural world manifested in the close observation and detailed recording of nature. Artists depicted birds, plants, and animals with breathtaking descriptive accuracy. They applied the same scrutiny to people and objects, modeling forms with light and shadow to give them the semblance of three-dimensionality. These carefully described subjects were situated into spatial settings, applying an **intuitive perspective** system by diminishing their scale as they receded into the distance. In the portrayal of landscapes—which became a northern specialty—artists used **atmospheric** or **aerial perspective** in which distant elements appear increasingly indistinct and less colorful as they approach the background. The sky, for instance, becomes paler near the horizon and the distant landscape turns bluish-gray.

One aspect of the desire for accurate visual depictions of the natural world was a new interest in individual personalities. Fifteenth-century portraits have an astonishingly lifelike quality, combining careful—sometimes seemingly unflattering—surface description with an uncanny sense of vitality. Indeed, the individual becomes important in every sphere. More names of artists survive from the fifteenth century, for example, than in the entire span from the beginning of the Common Era to the year 1400, and some artists begin regularly to sign their work.

The new power of cities in Flanders and the greater Netherlands (present-day Belgium, Luxembourg, and the Netherlands; SEE MAP 18.1) provided a critical tension and balance with the traditional powers of royalty and the Church. Increasingly, the urban lay public sought to express personal and civic pride by sponsoring secular architecture, sculptured monuments, or paintings directed toward the community. The commonsense values of the merchants formed a solid underpinning for the Northern Renaissance, but their influence remained intertwined with the continuing power of the Church and the royal and noble courts. Giovanni Arnolfini's success at commerce and negotiation provided the funding for his extraordinary double portrait, but he was able to secure the services of Jan van Eyck only with the cooperation of the duke of Burgundy.

ART FOR THE FRENCH DUCAL COURTS

The dukes of Burgundy were the most powerful rulers in northern Europe for most of the fifteenth century. They controlled not only Burgundy itself but also the Flemish and Netherlandish centers of finance and trade, including the thriving cities of Ghent, Bruges, Tournai, and Brussels. The major seaport, Bruges, was the commercial center of northern Europe, rivaling the Italian city-states of Florence, Milan, and Venice as an economic hub. In the late fourteenth century, Burgundian Duke Philip the Bold (r. 1363–1404) had acquired territory in the Netherlands—including the politically desirable region of Flanders—by marrying the daughter of the Flemish count. Though dukes Philip the Bold of Burgundy, Jean of Berry, and Louis of Anjou were brothers of King Charles V of France, their interests rarely coincided. Even the threat of a common enemy, England, during the Hundred Years' War was not a strong unifying factor, since Burgundy and England were often allied because of common financial interests in Flanders.

While the French king held court in Paris, the dukes held even more splendid courts in their own cities. The dukes of Burgundy (including present-day east-central France, Belgium, Luxembourg, and the Netherlands) and Berry (central France), not the king in Paris, were the real arbiters of taste. Especially influential was Jean, duke of Berry, who commissioned many works from Flemish and Netherlandish painters in the fashionable International Gothic style.

This new, composite style emerged in the late fourteenth century from the multicultural papal court in Avignon in southern France, where artists from Italy, France, and Flanders worked side by side. The International Gothic style became the prevailing manner of late fourteenth-century Europe. It is characterized by slender, gracefully posed figures whose delicate features are framed by masses of curling hair and extraordinarily complex headdresses. Noble men and women wear rich brocaded and embroidered fabrics and elaborate jewelry. Landscape and architectural settings are miniaturized; however, details of nature—leaves, flowers, insects, birds—are rendered with nearly microscopic detail. Spatial recession is represented by rising tiled floors in rooms that are open to view like stage sets, by fanciful mountains and meadows with high horizon lines, and by progressive diminution in the size of receding objects and by atmospheric perspective. Artists and patrons preferred light, bright colors and a liberal use of gold in manuscript and panel paintings, tapestries, and polychromed sculpture. The International Gothic was so appealing that it endured well into the fifteenth century.

PAINTING AND SCULPTURE FOR THE CHARTREUSE DE CHAMPMOL

One of Philip the Bold's most lavish projects was the Carthusian monastery, or *chartreuse* ("charterhouse"), at Champmol, near Dijon, his Burgundian capital city. Land was acquired in 1377 and 1383, and construction began in 1385. The monastic church was intended to house the family's tombs, and the monks were expected to pray continuously for the souls of Philip and his family. Carthusian monasteries were particularly expensive to maintain because Carthusian monks did not provide for themselves by farming or other physical work but were dedicated exclusively to prayer and solitary meditation.

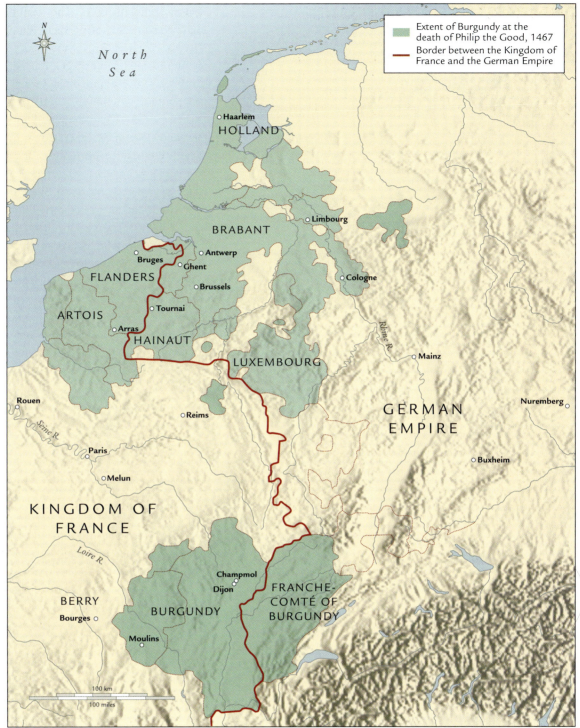

MAP 18-1 •
FIFTEENTH-CENTURY
NORTHERN EUROPE

The dukes of Burgundy—whose territory included much of present-day Belgium and Luxembourg, the Netherlands, and eastern France—became the cultural and political leaders of western Europe. Their major cities of Bruges (Belgium) and Dijon (France) were centers of art and industry as well as politics.

MELCHIOR BROEDERLAM. The duke ordered a magnificent carved and painted altarpiece (see "Altars and Altarpieces," page 564) for the Chartreuse de Champmol. The interior of the altarpiece, carved and gilded by Jacques de Baerze, depicts scenes of the Crucifixion flanked by the Adoration of the Magi and the Entombment. The exteriors of the protective shutters of this triptych were covered not by carvings but by two paintings by Melchior Broederlam (active 1381–1410) showing scenes from the life of the Virgin and the infancy of Christ (FIG. 18–2). Broederlam situates his closely observed, International Style figures within fanciful miniature architectural and landscape settings. His lavish use of brilliantly seductive colors foregrounds one of the features that made International Gothic so popular.

The archangel Gabriel greets Mary while she is at prayer. She sits in a Gothic room with a back door leading into the dark interior of a Romanesque rotunda that symbolizes the Temple of Jerusalem as a repository of the Old Law. According to legend, Mary was an attendant in the Temple prior to her marriage to Joseph. The tiny enclosed garden and conspicuous pot of lilies are symbols of Mary's virginity. In International Gothic fashion, both

Altars and Altarpieces

The altar in a Christian church symbolizes both the table of Jesus' Last Supper and the tombs of Christ and the saints. As a table, the altar is the site where priests celebrate Mass. And as a tomb, it traditionally contained a relic before the Reformation, placed in a reliquary on the altar, beneath the floor on which the altar rests, or even enclosed within the altar itself.

Altarpieces are painted or carved constructions placed at the back of or behind the altar so that altar and altarpiece appear visually to be joined. By the fifteenth century, important altarpieces had evolved into large and elaborate architectural structures filled with images and protected by movable wings that function like shutters. An altarpiece can sit on a base, called a predella. A winged altarpiece can be a **diptych**, in which two panels are hinged together; a **triptych**, in which two wings fold over a center section, forming a diptych when closed; or a **polyptych**, consisting of many panels.

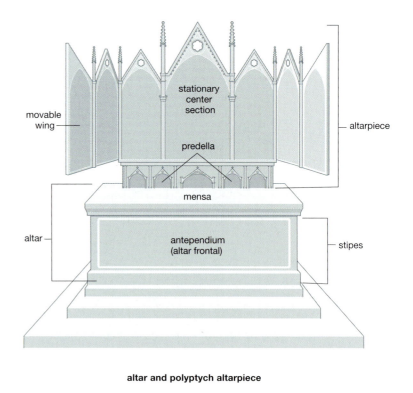

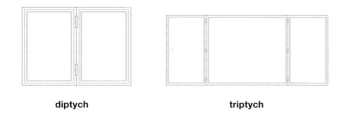

diptych   **triptych**   **altar and polyptych altarpiece**

the interior and exterior of the building are shown, and the floors are tilted up at the back to give clear views of the action. Next, in the Visitation, just outside the temple walls, the now-pregnant Mary greets her older cousin Elizabeth, who will soon give birth to John the Baptist.

On the right shutter is the Presentation in the Temple. Mary and Joseph have brought the newborn Jesus to the Temple for his redemption as a first-born son and for Mary's purification, where Simeon takes the baby in his arms to bless him (Luke 2:25–32). At the far right, the Holy Family flees to Egypt to escape King Herod's order that all Jewish male infants be killed. The family travels along treacherous terrain similar to that in the Visitation scene, where a path leads the viewers' eyes up from the foreground and into the distance along a rising ground plane. Broederlam has created a sense of light and air around his solid figures. Anecdotal details drawn from the real world are scattered throughout the pictures—a hawk flies through the golden sky, the presented baby looks anxiously back at his mother, and Joseph drinks from a flask and carries the family belongings in a satchel over his shoulder on the journey to Egypt. The statue of a pagan god, visible at the upper right, breaks and tumbles from its pedestal as the Christ Child approaches. A new era dawns and the New Law replaces the Old, among both Jews and gentiles.

CLAUS SLUTER. Flemish sculptor Jean de Marville (active 1366–1389) initially directed the decoration of the Chartreuse, and when he died in 1389, he was succeeded by his talented assistant Claus Sluter (c. 1360–1406), from Haarlem, in Holland. Sluter's distinctive work survives in a monumental **WELL OF MOSES** carved for the main cloister (**FIG. 18–3**), begun in 1395 and left unfinished at Sluter's death.

The design of this work is complex. A pier rose from the water to support a large free-standing figure of Christ on the cross, mourned by the Virgin Mary, Mary Magdalen, and John the Evangelist. Forming a pedestal for this Crucifixion group at the viewers' eye level are life-size stone figures from the Hebrew Bible who Christians believe foretold the coming of Christ: Moses, David, and the prophets Jeremiah, Zachariah, Daniel, and Isaiah. This concept may have been inspired by contemporary mystery plays, in which prophets foretell and explain events of Christ's Passion. Sluter's patriarchs and prophets are distinct individuals, physically and psychologically. Moses' sad old eyes blaze out from a memorable face entirely covered with a fine web of wrinkles. Even his horns are wrinkled. (These horns are traditional attributes based on a mistranslation of Exodus 34:29–35 in the Latin Vulgate Bible, where the rays of light radiating from Moses's face become horns.) A mane of curling hair and beard cascades over his heavy

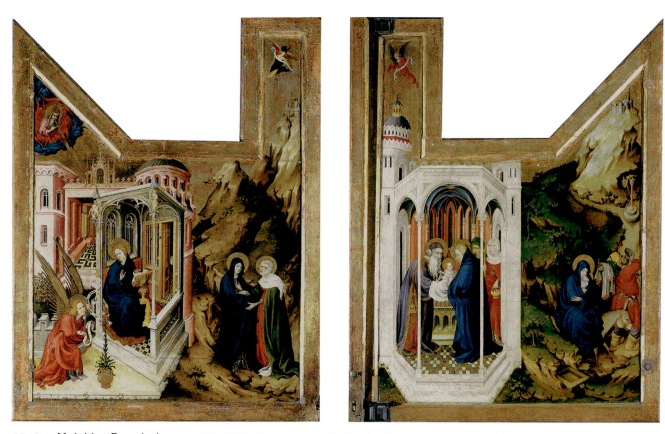

18-2 • Melchior Broederlam ANNUNCIATION, VISITATION, PRESENTATION IN THE TEMPLE, AND FLIGHT INTO EGYPT
Exterior of the wings of the altarpiece of the Chartreuse de Champmol. 1393–1399. Oil on wood panel, 5′5¾″ × 4′1¼″ (1.67 × 1.25 m). Musée des Beaux-Arts, Dijon.

shoulders and chest, and an enormous cloak envelops his body. Beside him stands David, in the voluminous robes of a medieval king, the very personification of nobility.

Sluter looked at human figures in new ways—as a weighty mass defined by voluminous drapery that lies in deep folds and falls in horizontal arcs and cascading lines—both concealing and revealing the body, creating strong highlights and shadows. With these vigorous, imposing, and highly individualized figures of the Well of Moses, Sluter abandoned the idealized faces, elongated figures, and vertical drapery of International Gothic for surface realism and the broad horizontal movement of forms. He retained, however, the detailed naturalism and rich colors (now almost lost but revealed in recent cleaning) and surfaces still preferred by his patrons.

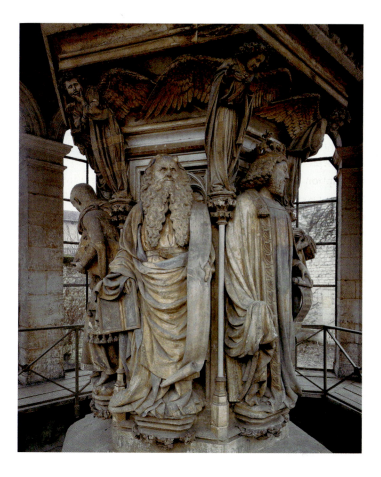

18-3 • Claus Sluter WELL OF MOSES, DETAIL OF MOSES AND DAVID
The Chartreuse de Champmol, Dijon, France. 1395–1406. Limestone with traces of paint, height of figures about 5′8″ (1.69 m).

The sculpture's original details included metal used for buckles and even eyeglasses. It was also painted: Moses wore a gold mantle with a blue lining over a red tunic; David's gold mantle had a painted lining of ermine, and his blue tunic was covered with gold stars and wide bands of ornament.

Women Artists in the Middle Ages and the Renaissance

Since most formal apprenticeships were not open to them, medieval and Renaissance women artists typically learned to paint from their husbands and fathers. Noblewomen, who were often educated in convents, also learned to draw, paint, and embroider. One of the earliest examples of a signed work by a woman is in a tenth-century Spanish manuscript of the Apocalypse illustrated by an artist named Ende (SEE FIG. 14–8), who describes herself as "painter and servant of God." In the twelfth century, a German nun named Guda not only signed her work but also included a self-portrait (SEE FIG. 15–32).

Examples proliferate during the later Middle Ages. In the fourteenth century, Jeanne de Montbaston and her husband, Richart, worked together as book illuminators under the auspices of the University of Paris. After Richart's death, Jeanne maintained the workshop and, following the custom of the time, was sworn in as a *libraire* (publisher) by the university in 1353. Bourgot, the daughter of the miniaturist Jean le Noir, illuminated books for King Charles V of France and Duke Jean of Berry. In the fifteenth century, women could be admitted to guilds in the Flemish towns of Ghent, Bruges, and Antwerp. By the 1480s, one-quarter of the membership in the painters' guild of Bruges was female.

In a French edition of a book by the Italian author Boccaccio entitled *Concerning Famous Women*, there is a picture of Thamyris, an artist of antiquity, at work in her studio. She appears in fifteenth-century dress, painting an image of the Virgin and Child. At the right, an assistant grinds and mixes her colors. In the foreground, her brushes and paints are laid out neatly and conveniently on a table.

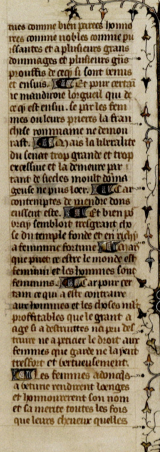

PAGE WITH THAMYRIS
From Giovanni Boccaccio's *De Claris Mulieribus (Concerning Famous Women)*. 1402. Ink and tempera on vellum, 14 × 9½" (35.5 × 24 cm). Bibliothèque Nationale, Paris.

MANUSCRIPT ILLUMINATION

Besides religious texts, wealthy patrons treasured richly illuminated secular writings such as herbals (encyclopedias of plants), health manuals, and works of history and literature. A typical manuscript page might have leafy tendrils framing the text, decorated opening initials, and perhaps a small inset picture (see the illustration in "Women Artists in the Middle Ages and the Renaissance," above). Only the most lavish books would have full-page miniature paintings, set off with frames. These inset pictures are like windows looking into rooms or out onto landscapes with distant horizons.

THE LIMBOURG BROTHERS. Among the finest Netherlandish painters at the beginning of the century were three brothers—Paul, Herman, and Jean Limbourg—their "last" name referring to

their home region. At this time people generally did not have family names in the modern sense, but were known instead by their first names, often followed by a reference to their place of origin, parentage, or occupation.

About 1404 the Limbourg brothers entered the service of avid bibliophile Duke Jean of Berry (1340–1416), for whom they produced their most impressive surviving work, the so-called **TRÈS RICHES HEURES** (Very Sumptuous Book of Hours), between 1413 and 1416 (**FIGS. 18–4, 18–5**). A Book of Hours, in addition to containing prayers and readings used in daily devotion, also included a calendar of holy days. The Limbourgs created full-page illustrations for the calendar in the *Très Riches Heures*, with subjects including both peasant labors and aristocratic pleasures in a framed lower field while elaborate calendar devices, with the chariot of

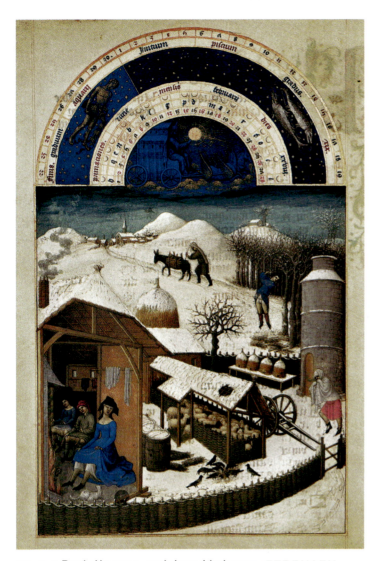

18-4 • Paul, Herman, and Jean Limbourg FEBRUARY, LIFE IN THE COUNTRY. TRÈS RICHES HEURES
1411–1416. Colors and ink on parchment, 11⅜ × 8¼″ (29 × 21 cm). Musée Condé, Chantilly, France.

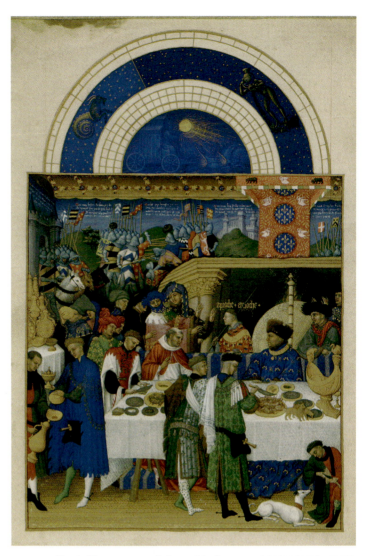

18-5 • Paul, Herman, and Jean Limbourg JANUARY, THE DUKE OF BERRY AT TABLE. TRÈS RICHES HEURES
1411–1416. Colors and ink on parchment, 11⅜ × 8¼″ (29 × 21 cm). Musée Condé, Chantilly, France.

the sun and the zodiac symbols, fill the upper part of the page. Like most European artists of the time, the Limbourgs showed the laboring classes in a light acceptable to aristocrats—that is, happily working for the nobles' benefit or displaying an uncouth lifestyle for aristocratic amusement. At times they also seem to be depicting peasants enjoying the pleasures of their leisure moments.

In the February page (SEE FIG. 18–4), farm folks relax cozily before a blazing fire. Although many country people at this time lived in hovels, this farm looks comfortable and well maintained, with timber-framed buildings, a row of beehives, a sheepfold, and tidy woven wattle fences. In the distance are a village and church. Within this scene, although all are much lower in social standing than the duke himself, there is a hierarchy of class. Largest in scale and most elegantly dressed is the woman closest to us, perhaps the owner of the farm, who carefully lifts her overgarment, balancing it daintily with both hands as she warms herself. She shares her fire with a couple, smaller because farther in the background, who

wear more modest clothing and are considerably less well behaved, especially the uncouth man, who exposes himself as he lifts his clothing to take advantage of the fire's warmth.

One of the most remarkable aspects of this painting is the way it conveys the feeling of cold winter weather: the leaden sky and bare trees, the soft snow and huddled sheep, the steamy breath of the bundled-up worker blowing on his hands, and the comforting smoke curling from the farmhouse chimney. The artists employ several International Gothic conventions: the high placement of the horizon line, the small size of trees and buildings in relation to people, and the cutaway view of the house showing both interior and exterior. The muted palette is sparked with touches of yellowish-orange, blue, and patches of bright red, including the man's turban at the lower left. Scale relationships seem consistent with our experience in the natural world since as the landscape recedes, the size of figures and buildings diminishes progressively in stages from foreground to middle ground to background.

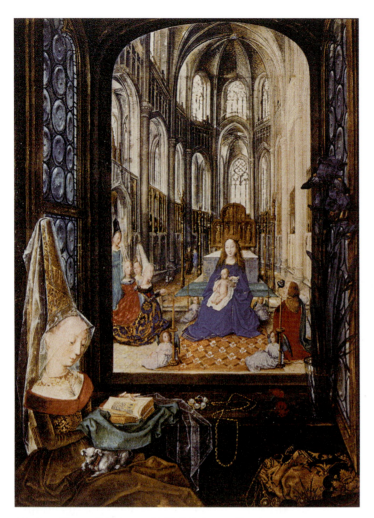

18-6 • Mary of Burgundy Painter MARY AT HER DEVOTIONS, HOURS OF MARY OF BURGUNDY
Before 1482. Colors and ink on parchment, size of image 7½ × 5¼"
(19.1 × 13.3 cm). Österreichische Nationalbibliothek, Vienna.

by 5¼ inches, earthly reality and a religious vision have been rendered equally tangible (**FIG. 18–6**). The painter conjures up a complex pictorial space. We look not only through the "window" of the illustration's frame but through another window in the wall of the room depicted in the foreground of the painting. The artist shows real virtuosity in representing these worlds. Spatial recession leads the viewer into the far reaches of the church interior, past the Virgin and the gilded altarpiece in the sanctuary to two people conversing in the far distance. The filmy veil covering Mary's steeple headdress is exquisitely described, as is the transparency of the glass vase, and the distinctive bull's eye glass (circular panes whose center "lump" was formed by the glassblower's pontil) filling the foreshortened, open window.

Mary of Burgundy appears twice. She is seated in the foreground by a window, reading from, or contemplating a picture within, her Book of Hours, held carefully and protected by a lush green cloth, perhaps from the diminutive dog cuddled into her lap. She appears again in the background, within the representation of the personal vision inspired by her private meditations. For a glorious Gothic church may form the setting for her vision, but it results not from attendance at Mass nor from the direction of a priestly advisor. She experiences it in private, a reward of her personal faith. Christians were encouraged in this period to imagine themselves participating in biblical stories and sacred events so as to feel within bodies and souls the experiences of the protagonists. Secluded into her private space, and surrounded by devotional aids on the window ledge—book, rosary, and symbolic flowers (carnations symbolized the nails of the Crucifixion, the irises Mary's sorrow)—it seems that Mary of Burgundy is doing just that. In her vision, she kneels with attendants and angels in front of a gracefully human Virgin and Child.

TEXTILES

In the fifteenth and sixteenth centuries, the best European tapestries came from Flanders. Major weaving centers at Brussels, Tournai, and Arras produced intricately woven wall hangings for royal and aristocratic patrons across Europe, important church officials including the pope, and even town councils. Among the most common subjects were foliage and flower patterns, scenes from the lives of the saints, and themes from classical mythology and history, such as the Battle of Troy seen hanging on the walls of Duke Jean of Berry's reception room (SEE FIG. 18–5). Tapestries provided both insulation and luxurious decoration for the stone walls of castle halls, churches, and municipal buildings, and because they were much more expensive than wall or panel paintings, they also showed off the owners' wealth. Since they were portable, many were included among aristocratic baggage as courts moved from residence to residence.

The price of a tapestry depended on the artists involved, the work required, and the materials used. Rarely was a fine, commissioned series woven only with wool; instead, tapestry producers enhanced the weaving with silk, and with silver and

In contrast, the illustration for the other winter month—January—depicts an aristocratic household (SEE FIG. 18–5). The duke of Berry sits behind a table laden with food and rich tableware, presiding over his new year's feast and surrounded by servants and allies. His chamberlain invites smartly dressed courtiers to greet the duke (the words written overhead say "approach"), who is himself singled out visually by the red cloth of honor with his heraldic arms—swans and the lilies of France—hanging over him and by a large fire screen that circles his head like a secular halo. Tapestries with battle scenes cover the walls. Such luxury objects attest to the wealth and lavish lifestyle of this great patron of the arts, a striking contrast to the farm life that will be revealed in February when turning the book to its next page.

THE MARY OF BURGUNDY PAINTER. One of the finest painters of Books of Hours later in the century was an artist known as the Mary of Burgundy Painter—so called because he painted a Book of Hours for Mary of Burgundy (1457–1482), only child of Charles the Bold. Within a full-page miniature in a book only 7½

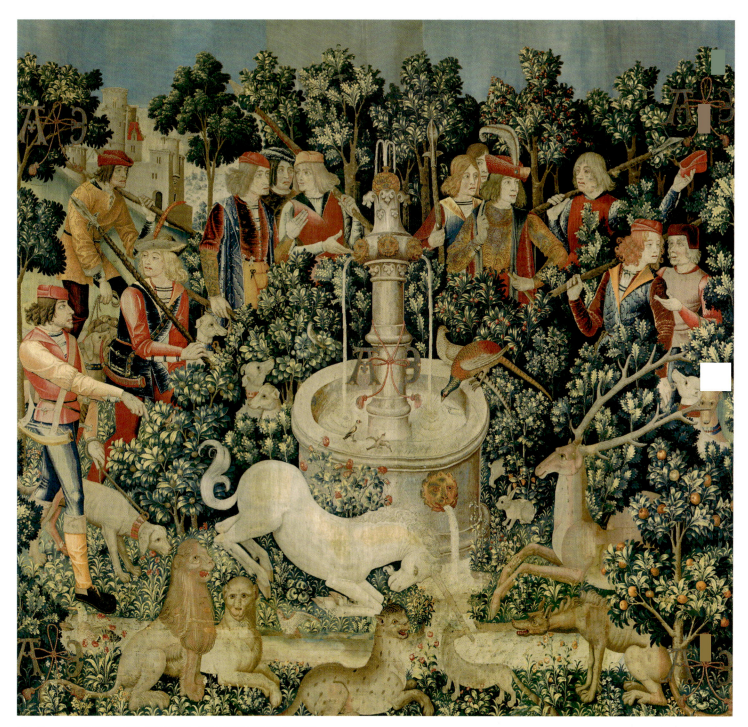

18-7 • UNICORN IS FOUND AT THE FOUNTAIN
From the Hunt of the Unicorn tapestry series. c. 1495–1505. Wool, silk, and silver- and gilt-wrapped thread (13–21 warp threads per inch), 12′1″ × 12′5″ (3.68 × 3.78 m). Metropolitan Museum of Art, New York.
Gift of John D. Rockefeller Jr., The Cloisters Collection, 1937 (37.80.2)

gold threads that must have glittered on the walls of princely residences, especially at night, illuminated by flickering lamps or candles. Because silver and gold threads were made of silk wrapped with real silver and gold, people later burned many tapestries to retrieve the precious materials. As a result, few royal tapestries in France survived the French Revolution. If a greater percentage had survived, these luxurious and monumental textile wall paintings would surely figure more prominently in the history of art.

THE UNICORN TAPESTRY. Tapestries were often produced in series. One of the best known is the Hunt of the Unicorn series from c. 1500. Four of the seven surviving hangings present scenes of people and animals set against a dense field of trees and flowers, with a distant view of a castle, as in the **UNICORN IS FOUND AT THE FOUNTAIN** (FIG. 18–7). The unusually fine condition of the tapestry allows us to appreciate its rich colors and the subtlety in modeling the faces, the tonal variations in the animals' fur, and

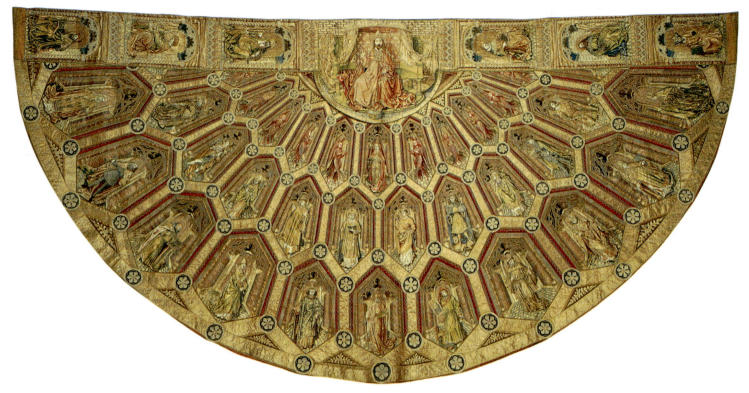

18-8 • COPE OF THE ORDER OF THE GOLDEN FLEECE
Flemish. Mid 15th century. Cloth with gold and colored silk embroidery, 5'4⁹⁄₁₆" × 10'9⁵⁄₁₆" (1.64 × 3.3 m).
Imperial Treasury, Vienna.

even the depiction of reflections in the water. The technical skill of its weavers is astonishing.

In tapestry, designs are woven directly into the fabric. The Unicorn tapestries seem to have been woven on huge, horizontal looms, where weavers interwove fine weft yarn of wool and silk—dyed in a multitude of colors from the creative combination of three vegetal dyes—onto the parallel strands of the coarser wool warp. Weavers worked from behind what would be the front surface of the finished tapestry, following the design on a full-scale cartoon laid on the floor under the loom. They could only see the actual effect of their work by checking the front with mirrors. Making a tapestry panel this large was a collaborative effort that required the organizational skills of a talented production manager and five or six weavers working side by side on a single loom. What is so extraordinary about their work is the skillful way they created curving lines—since the tapestry process is based on a rectilinear network of threads, curves have be simulated—and the lighting effects of shading and reflections, which require using yarn in the same hue with a multitude of values.

The subject of this series concerns the unicorn, a mythical horselike animal with a single long twisted horn, said to be supernaturally swift; it could only be captured by a virgin, to whom it came willingly. Thus, the unicorn became both a symbol of the Incarnation (Christ is the unicorn captured by the Virgin Mary) and also a metaphor for romantic love (see page 553, FIG. C). The capture and killing of the unicorn was also equated with Christ's death on the cross to save humanity.

The natural world represented so splendidly in this tapestry also has potential symbolic meaning. For instance, lions represented valor, faith, courage, and mercy, and even—because they were thought to breathe life into their cubs—the Resurrection of Christ. The stag is another Resurrection symbol (it sheds and grows its antlers) and a protector against poisonous serpents and evil in general. Even today we see rabbits as symbols of fertility, and dogs of fidelity. Many of the easily identifiable flowers and trees also carry both religious and secular meaning. There is a strong theme of marriage: the strawberry is a common symbol of sexual love; the pansy means remembrance; and the periwinkle, a cure for spiteful feelings and jealousy. The trees include oak for fidelity, beech for nobility, holly for protection against evil, hawthorn for the power of love, and pomegranate and orange for fertility.

COPE OF THE ORDER OF THE GOLDEN FLEECE. Surviving vestments of the Order of the Golden Fleece are remarkable examples of Flemish textiles. The Order of the Golden Fleece was an honorary fraternity founded by Duke Philip the Good of Burgundy in 1430 with 23 knights chosen for their moral character and bravery. Religious services were an integral part of the order's meetings, and opulent liturgical and clerical objects were created for the purpose.

The surface of the sumptuous cope (cloak) in **FIG. 18–8** is divided into compartments filled with the standing figures of saints. At the top of the neck edge, as if presiding over the company, is an enthroned figure of Christ, flanked along the front edge by

Whereas Italian artists favored tempera, using it almost exclusively for panel painting until the end of the fifteenth century (see "Cennino Cennini on Panel Painting," page 544), Flemish artists preferred oil paints, in which powdered pigments are suspended in linseed—and occasionally walnut—oil. They exploited the potential of this medium during the fifteenth century with a virtuosity that has never been surpassed.

Tempera had to be applied in a very precise manner because it dried almost as quickly as it was laid down. Shading was restricted to careful overlying strokes in graded tones ranging from white and gray to dark brown and black. Because tempera is opaque—light striking its surface does not penetrate to lower layers of color and reflect back— the resulting surface is **matte**, or dull, taking on a sheen only with burnishing or an overlay of varnish.

On the other hand, oil paint is a viscous medium which takes much longer to dry, and while it is still wet changes can be made easily.

Once applied, the paint has time to smooth out during the drying process, erasing traces of individual brushstrokes on the surface of the finished panel. Perhaps even more importantly, oil paint is translucent when applied in very thin layers, called glazes. Light striking a surface built up of glazes penetrates to the lower layers and is reflected back, creating the appearance of an interior glow. These luminous effects enabled artists to capture jewel-like colors and the varying effects of light on changing textures, enhancing the illusion that viewers are looking at real objects rather than their painted imitation.

So brilliant was Jan van Eyck's use of oil paint that he was credited by Giorgio Vasari with inventing the medium. Actually, it had been in use at least since the twelfth century, when it is described in Theophilus Presbyter's *De diversis artibus* (see "Stained Glass Windows," page 497).

SEE MORE: View videos about the processes of oil painting and grinding oil paint www.myartslab.com

---

scholar-saints in their studies. The embroiderers worked with great precision to match the illusionistic effects of contemporary Flemish painting. The particular stitch used here is known as couching. Gold threads are tacked down using unevenly spaced colored silk threads to create images and an iridescent effect.

PAINTING IN FLANDERS

A strong economy based on the textile industry and international trade provided stability and money for a Flemish efflorescence in the arts. Civic groups, town councils, and wealthy merchants were important patrons in the Netherlands, where the cities were self-governing and largely independent of landed nobility. Guilds oversaw nearly every aspect of their members' lives, and high-ranking guild members served on town councils and helped run city governments. Even experienced artists who moved from one city to another usually had to work as assistants in a local workshop until they met the requirements for guild membership.

Throughout most of the fifteenth century, Flemish art and artists were greatly admired across Europe. Artists from abroad studied Flemish works, and their influence spread even to Italy. Only at the end of the fifteenth century did a pervasive preference for Netherlandish painting give way to a taste for the new styles of art and architecture developing in Italy.

THE FOUNDERS OF THE FLEMISH SCHOOL

Flemish panel painters preferred using an oil medium rather than the tempera paint that was standard in the works of Italian artists. Since it was slow to dry, oil paint provided flexibility, and it had a luminous quality (see "Oil Painting," above). Like manuscript illuminations, Flemish panel paintings provided a window onto a scene rendered with keen attention to describing individual

features—people, objects, or aspects of the natural world—with consummate skill.

THE MASTER OF FLÉMALLE. Some of the earliest and most outstanding exponents of the new Flemish style were painters in the workshop of an artist known as the Master of Flémalle, identified by some art historians as Robert Campin (active 1406–1444). About 1425–1430, these artists painted the triptych now known as the **MÉRODE ALTARPIECE**, after its later owners (FIG. 18–9). Its relatively small size—slightly over 2 feet tall and about 4 feet wide with the wings open—suggests that it was probably made for a small private chapel.

The Annunciation of the central panel is set in a Flemish home and incorporates common household objects, many invested with symbolic religious meaning. The lilies in the **majolica** (glazed earthenware) pitcher on the table, for example, often appear in Annunciations to symbolize Mary's virginity. The hanging water pot in the background niche refers to Mary's purity and her role as the vessel for the Incarnation of God. What seems at first to be a towel hung over the prominent, hinged rack next to the niche may be a tallis (Jewish prayer shawl). Some art historians have referred to these as "hidden" or "disguised" symbols because they are treated as a normal part of the setting, but their routine religious meanings would have been obvious to the intended audience.

Some have interpreted the narrative episode captured in the central panel as the moment immediately following Mary's acceptance of her destiny. A rush of wind riffles the book pages and snuffs the candle (the flame, symbolic of God's divinity, extinguished at the moment he takes human form) as a tiny figure of Christ carrying a cross descends on a ray of light. Having accepted the miracle of the Incarnation (God assuming human

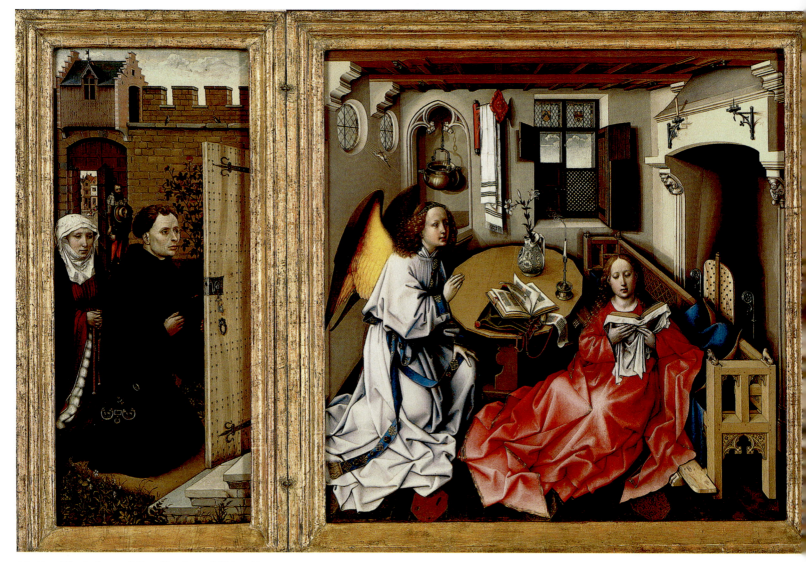

18–9 • Workshop of the Master of Flémalle
MÉRODE ALTARPIECE (TRIPTYCH OF THE ANNUNCIATION) (OPEN)
c. 1425–1430s. Oil on wood panel, center 25¼ × 24⅞″ (64.1 × 63.2 cm); each wing approx. 25⅜ × 10¾″ (64.5 × 27.6 cm). Metropolitan Museum of Art, New York. The Cloisters Collection, 1956 (56.70)

In the late nineteenth century, this triptych was associated with a group of stylistically related works and assigned to an artist called the Master of Flémalle, who was subsequently identified by some art historians as a documented artist named Robert Campin. Recently, however, experts have questioned this association and proposed that the triptych we now see was the work of several artists working within the workshop that created the stylistic cluster. Current opinion holds that the Annunciation was initially created as an independent panel, and a short time later expanded into a triptych with the addition of the side panels under the patronage of the donor in the foreground at left. Finally, some time later in the 1430s, the figure of his wife was added behind him, presumably on the occasion of his marriage.

form), Mary reads her Bible while sitting humbly on the footrest of the long bench. Her position becomes a symbol of her submission to God's will. Other art historians have proposed that the scene represents the moment just prior to the Annunciation. In this view, Mary is not yet aware of Gabriel's presence, and the rushing wind is the result of the angel's rapid entry into the room, where he appears before her, half kneeling and raising his hand in salutation.

In the left wing of the triptych, the donors—presumably a married couple—kneel in an enclosed garden, another symbol of Mary's virginity, before the open door of the house where the Annunciation is taking place, implying that the scene is a vision brought on by their faithful meditations, comparable to the vision we have already seen in the Hours of Mary of Burgundy (SEE FIG. 18–6). Such presentations, very popular with Flemish patrons, allowed those who commissioned a religious work to appear in the same space and time, and often on the same scale, as religious figures. The donors' eyes, which seem oddly unfocused, are directed not outward but inward, intent on the spiritual exercise of imagining their own presence within this sacred narrative.

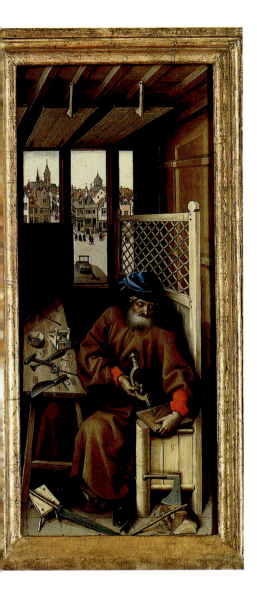

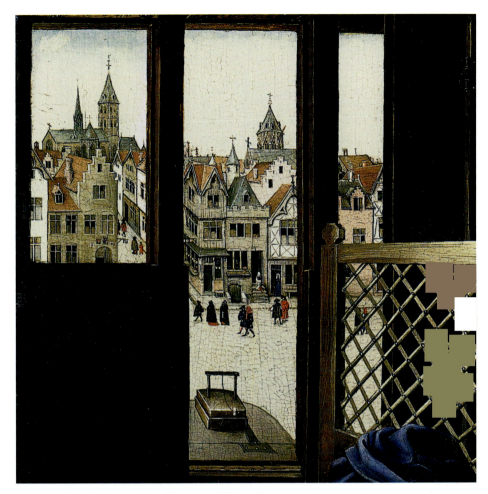

18–10 • Workshop of the Master of Flémalle A FLEMISH CITY
Detail of the right wing of the Mérode Altarpiece in FIG. 18–9.

On the right wing, Joseph is working in his carpentry workshop. A prosperous Flemish city is exquisitely detailed in the view through the shop window, with people going about their daily business **(FIG. 18–10)**. Even here there is religious symbolism. On the windowsill of Joseph's shop is a mousetrap (another sits on the workbench next to him), which fifteenth-century viewers would understand as a reference to Christ as the bait in a trap set by God to catch Satan. Joseph is drilling holes in a small board used as a drainboard for making wine, calling to mind the Eucharist and Christ's Passion.

The complex and consistent treatment of light in the Mérode Altarpiece represents a major preoccupation of Flemish painters. The strongest illumination comes from an unseen source at the upper left in front of the **picture plane** (the picture's front surface) as if sunlight were entering through the opened front of the room. More light comes from the rear windows, and a few painted, linear rays come from the round window at left, a symbolic vehicle for the Christ Child's descent. Jesus seems to slide down the rays of light linking God with Mary, carrying the cross of human salvation

over his shoulder. The light falling on the Virgin's lap emphasizes this connection, and the transmission of the symbolic light through a transparent panel of glass (which remains intact) recalls the virginal nature of Jesus' conception.

JAN VAN EYCK. In 1425 Jan van Eyck (active 1420s–1441) became court painter to Duke Philip the Good of Burgundy (r. 1419–1467), who was the uncle of the king of France and one of the most sophisticated men in Europe. He made Jan one of his confidential employees and even sent him on a diplomatic mission to Portugal, charged with painting a portrait of a prospective bride for Philip. The duke alluded to Jan's remarkable technical skills in a letter of 1434–1435, saying that he could find no other painter equal to his taste or so excellent in art and science. So brilliant was Jan's use of oil glazes that he was mistakenly credited with the invention of oil painting (see "Oil Painting," page 571).

Jan's 1433 portrait of a **MAN IN A RED TURBAN** (FIG. 18–11) projects a particularly strong sense of personality, and the signed and dated frame also bears Jan's personal motto—"As I can, [but

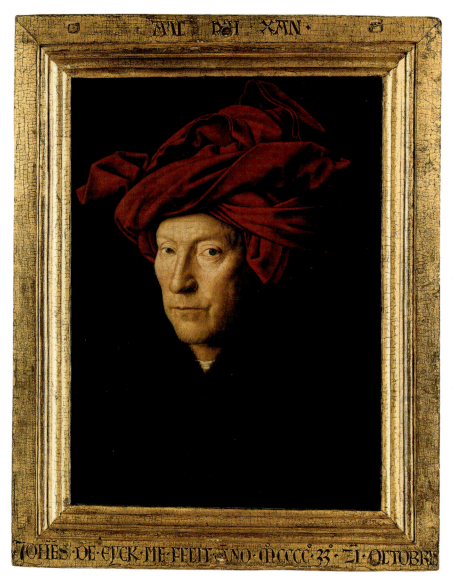

18–11 • Jan van Eyck MAN IN A RED TURBAN
1433. Oil on wood panel, 13⅛ × 10¼″ (33.3 × 25.8 cm). National Gallery, London.

not as I would]"—in Greek letters at the top. Since these letters also form an anagram of his own name, most scholars see this painting as a self-portrait in which physical appearance seems recorded in a magnifying mirror. We see the stubble of a day's growth of beard on his chin and cheeks, and every carefully described wrinkle around the artist's eyes, reddened from the strain of his work, and reflecting light that seems to emanate from our own space. That same light source gives the inscriptions the *trompe l'oeil* sense of having been engraved into the frame, heightening the illusionistic wizardry of Jan's painting. Is Jan looking out directly at us, or are we seeing his reflection in a mirror?

In his lifetime, one of the most famous works of Jan van Eyck was a huge polyptych with a very complicated and learned theological program that he (perhaps in collaboration with his brother Hubert) painted for a chapel in what is now the Cathedral of St. Bavo in Ghent (see "The Ghent Altarpiece," pages 576–577). The three-dimensional mass of the figures, the voluminous draperies

as well as their remarkable surface realism, and the scrupulous attention to the luminous details of textures as variable as jewels and human flesh, are magnificent examples of Jan's artistic wizardry. He has carefully controlled the lighting within this multi-panel ensemble to make it appear that the objects represented are illuminated by sunlight coming through the window of the very chapel where it was meant to be installed. Jan's painting is firmly grounded in the terrestrial world even when he is rendering a visionary subject.

The Ghent altarpiece may have been Jan's most famous painting during his lifetime, but his best-known painting today is a distinctive double portrait of a couple identified as a Giovanni Arnolfini and his wife (SEE FIG. 18–1). Early interpreters saw this fascinating work as a wedding or betrothal. Above the mirror on the back wall (FIG. 18–12), the artist inscribed the words: *Johannes de eyck fuit hic 1434* ("Jan van Eyck was here 1434"). More normal on a signature would have been, "Jan van Eyck made this," so the words "was here" might suggest that Jan served as a witness to a matrimonial episode portrayed in the painting. Jan is not the only witness recorded in the painting. The convex mirror between the figures reflects not only the back of the couple but a front view of two visitors standing in the doorway, entering the room. Perhaps one of them is the artist himself.

New research has complicated the developing interpretation of this painting by revealing that the Giovanni Arnolfini traditionally identified as the man in this painting married his wife Giovanna Cenami only in 1447, long after the date on the wall and Jan van Eyck's own death. One scholar has proposed that the picture is actually a prospective portrait of Giovanni and Giovanna's marriage in the future, painted in 1434 to secure the early transfer of the dowry from her father to her future husband. Others have more recently suggested the man portrayed here is a different Giovanni Arnolfini, accompanied either by his putative second wife or a memorial portrait of his first wife, Costanza Trenta, who died the year before this picture was painted, perhaps in childbirth. The true meaning of this fascinating masterpiece may remain a mystery, but it is doubtful that scholars will stop trying to solve it.

ROGIER VAN DER WEYDEN. Little as we know about Jan van Eyck, we know even less about the life of Rogier van der Weyden (c. 1400–1464). Not a single existing work of art bears his name. He may have studied under the Master of Flémalle, but the relationship is not altogether clear. First establishing himself in

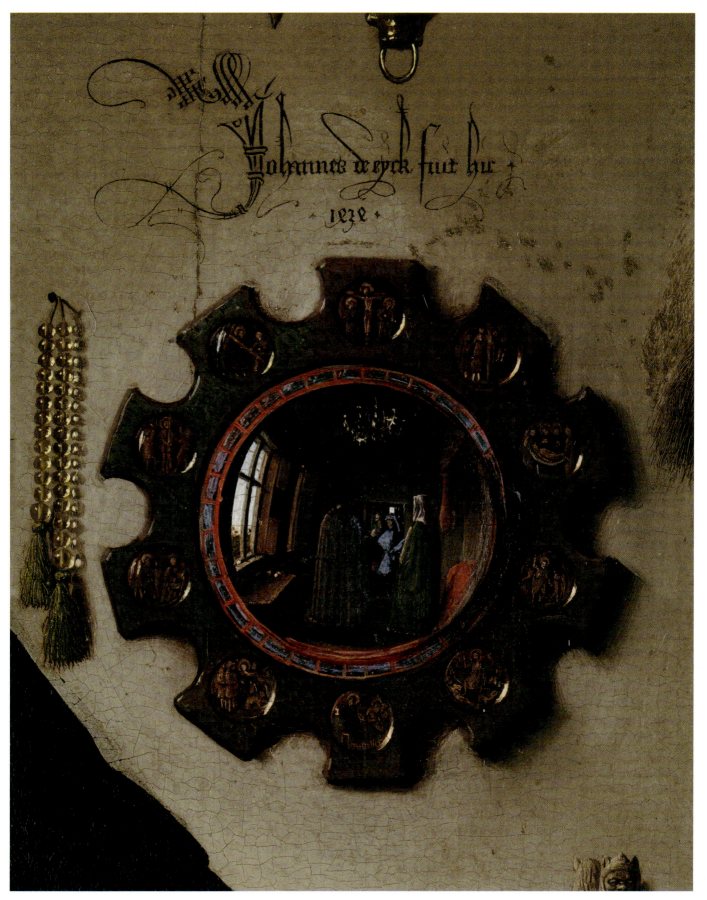

18–12 • Jan van Eyck **DETAIL OF MIRROR AND SIGNATURE IN A DOUBLE PORTRAIT OF A GIOVANNI ARNOLFINI AND HIS WIFE (FIG. 18–1)**

1434. Oil on wood panel. The National Gallery, London.

The Ghent Altarpiece

An inscription on the frame of the Ghent Altarpiece seems to identify both Jan and Hubert van Eyck as its artists: "The painter Hubert van Eyck, greater than whom no one was found, began [this work]; and Jan, his brother, second in art, having carried through the task at the expense of Jodocus Vyd, invites you by this verse, on the sixth of May [1432], to look at what has been done."

Many art historians believe Hubert began this altarpiece, and after his death in 1426, Jan completed it, when free of ducal responsibilities in 1430–1432. Others believe the entire painting was produced by Jan and his workshop, Hubert perhaps being responsible for the frame. At least commission and situation are clear. Jodocus Vijd, who appears with his wife Isabella Borluut on the outside of the polyptych's shutters—both visible only when the altarpiece is closed—commanded the work. Part of a wealthy family of financiers, Jodocus was a city official in Ghent—holding an office comparable to mayor in 1433–1434—and the altarpiece was part of a renovation he funded in the family chapel at the parish church of St. John (now the Cathedral of St. Bavo). He also endowed daily Masses in the chapel for the couple's salvation, and that of their ancestors.

When the altarpiece was closed, the exterior of the shutters displayed the striking likenesses of the donor couple kneeling to face painted statues of SS. John the Baptist (patron of Ghent) and John the Evangelist (patron of this church) that recall those on Sluter's Well of Moses (SEE FIG. 18–3). Above this row is an expansive rendering of the Annunciation—whose somber color scheme coordinates with the *grisaille* statues painted below—situated in an upstairs room that looks out over a panoramic cityscape. As in Simone Martini's Annunciation altarpiece (SEE FIG. 17–13), the words that issue from Gabriel's mouth ("Hail, full of grace, the Lord is with thee") appear on the painting's surface, and here there is Mary's response as well ("Behold the handmaid of the Lord"), only it is painted upside down since it is

directed to God, who hovers above her head as the dove of the Holy Spirit. Prophets and sibyls perch in the irregular compartments at the top, unfurling scrolls recording their predictions of Christ's coming.

When the shutters were opened on Sundays and feast days, the mood changed. The effect is no longer muted, but rich in both color and implied sound. Dominating the altarpiece by size, central location, and brilliant color is the enthroned figure of God, wearing the triple papal crown, with an earthly crown at his feet, and flanked by the Virgin Mary and John the Baptist, each holding an open book. To either side are first angel musicians and then Adam and Eve,

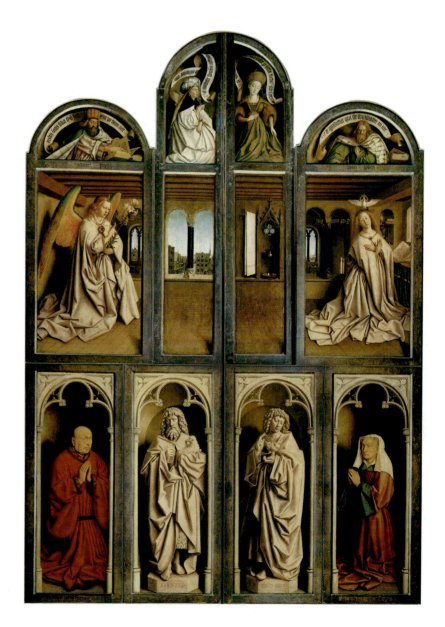

A. Jan and Hubert (?) van Eyck **GHENT ALTARPIECE (CLOSED), ANNUNCIATION WITH DONORS**
Completed 1432. Oil on panel, height 11′5¾″ (3.5 m). Cathedral of St. Bavo, Ghent.

represented as lifelike nudes. Adam seems to have been painted from a model, from whom Jan reproduced even the "farmer's tan" of his hands and face. Eve displays clear features of the female anatomy; the pigmented line running downward from her navel appears frequently during pregnancy. Each of the three themes of the upper register—God with Mary and John, musical angels, and Adam and Eve—is set in a distinct space: the holy trio in a golden shrine, angels against a blue sky, Adam and Eve in shallow stone niches.

The five lower panels present a unified field. A vast landscape with meadows, woods, and distant cities is set against a continuous horizon. A diverse array of saints—apostles, martyrs, confessors, virgins, hermits, pilgrims, warriors, judges—assemble to adore the Lamb of God as described in the book of Revelation. The Lamb stands on an altar, blood flowing into a chalice, ultimately leading to the fountain of life.

The Ghent altarpiece became a famous work of art almost as soon as it was completed. To celebrate Duke Philip the Good's visit to the city in 1458, citizens of Ghent welcomed him with *tableaux vivants* (living pictures) of its scenes. German artist Albrecht Dürer traveled to Ghent to see the altarpiece in 1521. During the French occupation of Flanders in 1794 it was transferred to Paris (returned in 1815), and during World War II it was confiscated by the Nazis. It is now displayed within a secure glass case in the baptismal chapel of the church for which it was made.

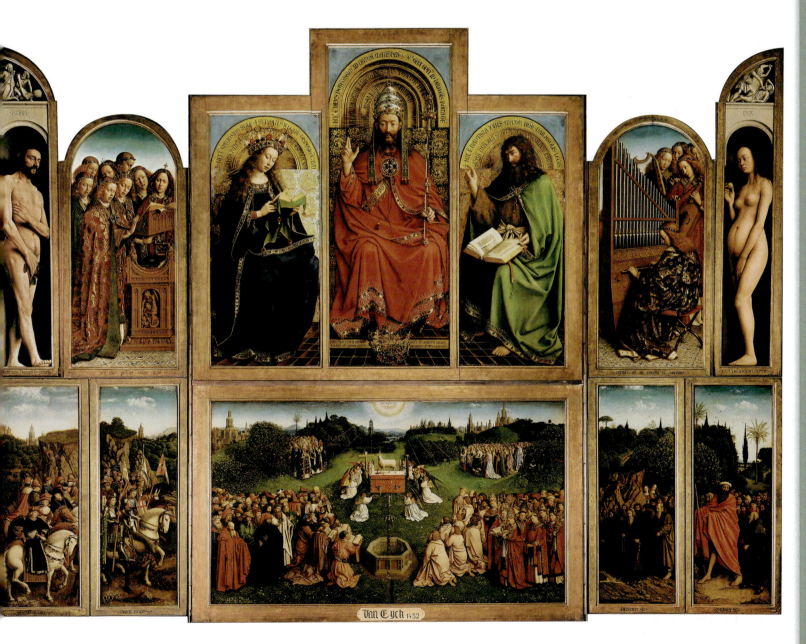

B. Jan and Hubert (?) van Eyck **GHENT ALTARPIECE (OPEN), ADORATION OF THE MYSTIC LAMB**
Completed 1432. Oil on panel, 11′5¾″ × 15′1½″ (3.5 × 4.6 m). Cathedral of St. Bavo, Ghent.

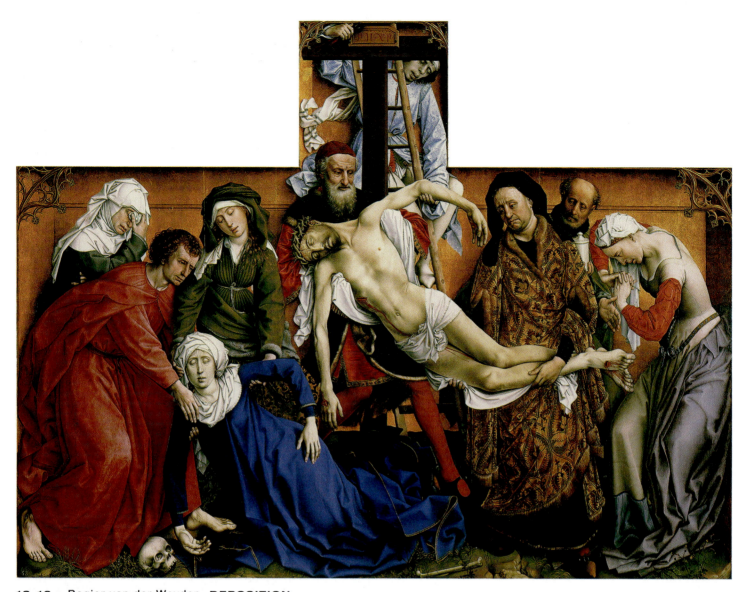

18–13 • Rogier van der Weyden DEPOSITION
From an altarpiece commissioned by the crossbowmen's guild, Louvain, Belgium. Before 1443, possibly
c. 1435–1438. Oil on wood panel, 7′2⅝″ × 8′7⅛″ (2.2 × 2.62 m). Museo del Prado, Madrid.

EXPLORE MORE: Gain insight from a primary source regarding Rogier van der Weyden
www.myartslab.com

1432 as an independent master in Tournai, at the peak of his career, Rogier maintained a large workshop in Brussels, where he was the official city painter, attracting apprentices and shop assistants from as far away as Italy. To establish the stylistic characteristics of Rogier's art, scholars have turned to a painting of the **DEPOSITION** (**FIG. 18–13**), an altarpiece commissioned by the Louvain crossbowmen's guild (crossbows can be seen in the tracery painted in the upper corners) sometime before 1443, the date of the earliest known copy of it by another artist.

The Deposition was a popular theme in the fifteenth century because of its potential for dramatic, personally engaging portrayal. Rogier sets the act of removing Jesus' body from the cross on the shallow stage of a gilt wooden box, just like the case of a carved and painted altarpiece. The ten solid, three-dimensional figures, however, are not simulations of polychromed wood carving, but near life-size renderings of actual human figures who seem to press forward into the viewer's space, allowing them no escape from the forceful expressions of heartrending grief. Jesus' friends seem palpably real, with their portraitlike faces and scrupulously described contemporary dress, as they tenderly and sorrowfully remove his body from the cross for burial. Jesus' corpse dominates the center of the composition, drooping in a languid curve, framed by jarringly thin, angular arms. His pose is echoed by the rhyming form of the swooning Virgin. It is as if mother and son share in the redemptive passion of his death on the cross, encouraging viewers to identify with them both, or join their assembled companions in mourning their fate. Although united by their sorrow, the mourning figures react in personal ways, from the intensity of Mary Magdalen at far right, wringing her hands in anguish, to John the Evangelist's blank stare at left, lost in grief as he reaches to support the collapsing Virgin. The anguish of the woman behind him, mopping her tear-soaked eyes with the edge of her veil, is almost unbearably poignant.

Rogier's choice of color and pattern balances and enhances his composition. The complexity of the gold brocade worn by Joseph of Arimathea, who offered his new tomb for the burial, and the contorted pose and vivid dress of Mary Magdalen increase the visual impact of the right side of the panel to counter the pictorial weight of the larger number of figures at the left. The palette contrasts subtle, slightly muted colors with brilliant expanses of blue and red, while white accents focus the viewers' attention on the main subjects. The whites of the winding cloth and the tunic of the youth on the ladder set off Jesus' pale body, as the white turban and shawl emphasize the ashen face of Mary.

Another work by Rogier, painted at about the same time as the Deposition, is both quieter and more personal. It represents the evangelist St. Luke executing a preparatory drawing in silverpoint for a painting of the Virgin and Child who seem to have materialized to pose for him (FIG. 18–14). The painting is based on a legend with origins in sixth-century Byzantium of a miraculous appearance of the Virgin and Child to Luke so he could record their appearance and pass on his authentic witness to his Christian followers. Rogier's version takes place in a carefully defined interior

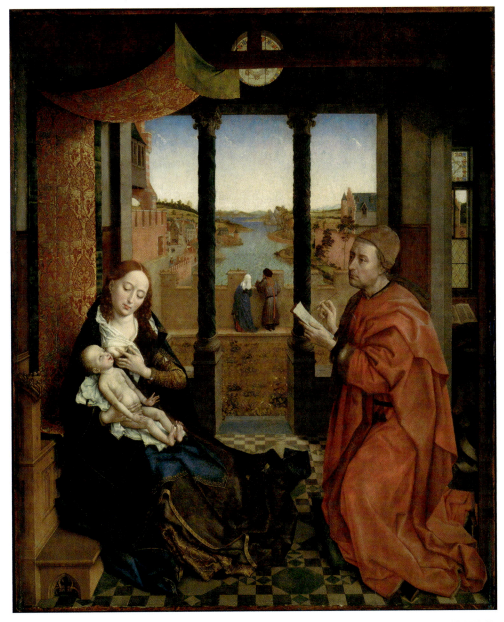

18–14 • Rogier van der Weyden **ST. LUKE DRAWING THE VIRGIN AND CHILD**
c. 1435–1440. Oil and tempera on wood panel, 54¼ × 43⅝″ (137.7 × 110.8 cm). Museum of Fine Arts, Boston.

space that opens onto a garden, and from there into a distant vista of urban life before dissolving into the countryside through which a winding river guides our exploration all the way to the horizon. The Virgin is preoccupied with a routine maternal activity. Her baby has pulled away from her breast, producing a smile and flexing his hand—familiar gestures of actual babies during nursing. The good mother and happy baby are observed by Luke, who perches on his knees and captures the scene in a silverpoint sketch, a common preliminary step used by fifteenth-century Flemish painters in the planning of their paintings, especially portraits. And the portraitlike quality of Luke's face here has led scholars to propose that this image of a saint is a self-portrait of its artist.

Art historians have traditionally interpreted this painting in two ways. Some see it—especially if it is a self-portrait—as a document of Rogier's sense of his own profession. They see him distancing himself and his fifteenth-century Flemish colleagues from identification with the laboring artisans of the Middle Ages, and staking a claim for his special role as an inspired creator who recorded sacred visions in valuable, individualistic works of art. The notion of Rogier's own identification with Luke in this painting is supported by the fact that later artists emulated his composition in creating their own self-portraits as the century progressed. But other art historians, proposing that this painting was created for the chapel of the guildhall of the painters in Brussels (the evidence is suggestive but unclear), have interpreted it as a claim for the importance of the painters' profession because it is rooted in saintly legend. Perhaps this extraordinary picture was both self-fashioning and professional propaganda. But it was also a devotional image.

Luke's tenuous, half-kneeling perch, and his dreamy, introspective gaze certainly remind us that one of the tasks of painters in this period was to create inspiring pictures of religious visions that are also materialized by meticulous references to the real world. This most certainly is that.

PAINTING AT MID CENTURY: THE SECOND GENERATION

The extraordinary accomplishments of the Master of Flémalle, Jan van Eyck, and Rogier van der Weyden attracted many followers in Flanders. The work of this second generation of Flemish painters may have been simpler, more direct, often easier to understand than that of their predecessors, but they produced extraordinary works of great emotional power. They were in large part responsible for the rapid spread of the Flemish style throughout Europe.

PETRUS CHRISTUS.   Among the most interesting of these painters was Petrus Christus (active 1444–c. 1475/1476), who became a citizen of Bruges in 1444 and signed and dated six paintings in a career that extended over three decades.

In 1449, Christus painted a portrait of a goldsmith, serving two well-dressed customers in his shop (see "A Closer Look," opposite). A halo around the head of the seated figure—not originally a part of the painting—was removed by restorers in 1993. This coincided with a reevaluation of the subject matter of the work, now seen as a vocational portrait of an actual goldsmith, rather than an image of St. Eloi, patron saint of goldsmiths, set in the present. Both finished products and raw materials of the jeweler's trade sit on the shelves behind the goldsmith: containers, rings, brooches, a belt buckle, a string of beads, pearls, gemstones, coral, and crystal cylinders. A betrothal belt curls across the counter. Such a combination of objects suggests that the painting expresses the hope for health and well-being for the couple who may be in the process of procuring rings for their upcoming marriage.

As in Jan van Eyck's double portrait, a convex mirror extends the viewer's field of vision, in this instance to the street outside, where two men appear. One is stylishly dressed in red and black, and the other holds a falcon, another indication of high status. Whether or not the reflected image has symbolic meaning, the mirror would have had practical value in a goldsmith's shop, allowing him to observe the approach of potential customers to the counter outside his shop window.

DIRCK BOUTS.   Dirck Bouts (active c. 1444–1475) is best known among Flemish painters as a storyteller, and he exercised those skills in a series of large altarpieces, with narrative scenes drawn from the life of Christ and the lives of the saints. But he also created more intimate pictures, such as this tender rendering of the **VIRGIN AND CHILD**, just 8½ inches tall **(FIG. 18–15)**. Even it evokes a story. Mary holds her baby securely, using both of her plain, strong hands to surround completely the lower part of his body. The baby reaches across his mother's chest and around her neck, pulling himself closer to press his face next to hers, cheek to cheek,

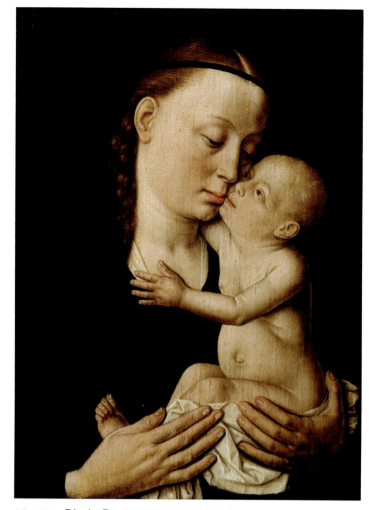

18–15 • Dieric Bouts VIRGIN AND CHILD
c. 1455–1460. Oil on wood panel, 8½ × 6½" (21.6 × 16.5 cm). Metropolitan Museum of Art, New York.

nose to nose, mouth to mouth, eyes locked together, forming a symmetrical system that links them in pattern and almost melds them into a single mirrored form. It is as if a fifteenth-century St. Luke had captured a private moment between the Virgin and Child—a dimpled mother and baby looking very much like the actual people in the artist's world—during their miraculous appearance to sit as his model (compare FIG. 18–14). The concept is actually not so far fetched. Bouts's painting is modeled after a fourteenth-century Italian image in the cathedral of Cambrai that in the fifteenth century was believed to have been painted by St. Luke himself.

HUGO VAN DER GOES.   Hugo van der Goes (c. 1440–1482), dean of the painters' guild in Ghent (1468–1475), united the intellectual prowess of Jan van Eyck with the emotional sensitivity of Rogier van der Weyden to create an entirely new personal style. Hugo's major work was an exceptionally large altarpiece, more than 8 feet tall, of the Nativity **(FIG. 18–16)**, commissioned by Tommaso Portinari, head of the Medici bank in Bruges. Painted probably

A Goldsmith in his Shop ▶
by Petrus Christus. 1449. Oil on oak panel, 38⅝ × 33½″ (98 × 85 cm).
Metropolitan Museum of Art, New York, Robert Lehman Collection, 1975. 1975.1.110

The coat of arms of the dukes of Guelders hangs from a chain around this man's neck, leading some to speculate that the woman, who is the more active of the pair, is Mary of Guelders, niece of Duke Philip the Good, who married King James II of the Scots the same year this picture was painted.

Goldsmiths were expected to perform all their transactions, including the weighing of gold, in public view to safeguard against dishonesty. Here the scales tip toward the couple, perhaps an allusion to the scales of the Last Judgment, which always tip to the side of the righteous.

Three types of coins rest on the shop counter: "florins" from Mainz, "angels" from English King Henry VI's French territories, and "riders" minted under Philip the Good. Such diversity of currency could show the goldsmith's cosmopolitanism, or they could indicate his participation in money changing, since members of that profession belonged to the same guild as goldsmiths.

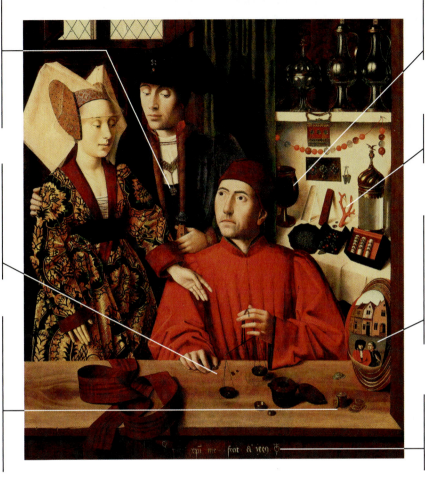

This coconut cup was supposed to neutralize poison. The slabs of porphyry and rock crystal were "touchstones," used to test gold and precious stones.

The red coral and serpents' tongues (actually fossilized sharks' teeth) were intended to ward off the evil eye.

Two men, one with a falcon on his arm, are reflected in the obliquely placed mirror as they stand in front of the shop. The edges of the reflection catch the red sleeve of the goldsmith and the door frame, uniting the interior and exterior spaces and drawing the viewer into the painting.

The artist signed and dated his work in a bold inscription that appears just under the tabletop at the bottom of the painting: "Master Petrus Christus made me in the year 1449."

SEE MORE: View the Closer Look feature for *A Goldsmith in his Shop* **www.myartslab.com**

between 1474 and 1476, the triptych was sent to Florence and installed in 1483 in the Portinari family chapel, where it had a noticeable impact on Florentine painters.

Tommaso, his wife Maria Baroncelli, and their three oldest children are portrayed kneeling in prayer on the side panels of the wing interiors. On the left wing, looming larger than life behind Tommaso and his son Antonio, are the saints for whom they are named, St. Thomas and St. Antony. Since the younger son, Pigello, born in 1474, was apparently added after the original composition was set, his name saint is lacking. On the right wing, Maria and her daughter Margherita are presented by SS. Mary Magdalen and Margaret.

The theme of the altarpiece is the Nativity as told by Luke (2:10–19). The central panel represents the Adoration of the newborn Christ Child by Mary and Joseph, a host of angels, and the shepherds who have rushed in from the fields. In the middle ground of the wings are additional scenes. Winding their way through the winter landscape are two groups headed for Bethlehem. On the left wing, Mary and Joseph travel there to take part in a census. Near term in her pregnancy, Mary has dismounted from her donkey and staggers, supported by Joseph. On the right wing, a servant of the three Magi, who are coming to honor the awaited Savior, asks directions from a peasant.

Hugo paints meadows and woods meticulously, and he used atmospheric perspective to approximate distance in the landscape. He shifts figure size for emphasis: The huge figures of Joseph, Mary, and the shepherds are the same size as the patron saints on the wings, in contrast to the much smaller Portinari family and still

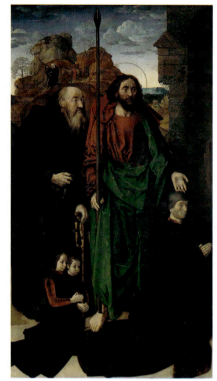

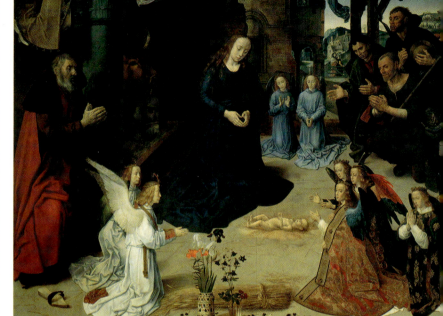

18-16 • Hugo van der Goes PORTINARI ALTARPIECE (OPEN)

c. 1474–1476. Tempera and oil on wood panel; center 8′3½″ × 10′ (2.53 × 3.01 m), wings each 8′3½″ × 4′7½″ (2.53 × 1.41 m). Galleria degli Uffizi, Florence.

smaller angels. Hugo also uses light, as well as the gestures and gazes of the figures, to focus our eyes on the center panel where the mystery of the Incarnation takes place. Instead of lying swaddled in a manger or in his mother's arms, Jesus rests naked and vulnerable on the barren ground. Rays of light emanate from his body. This image was based on the visionary writing of the medieval Swedish mystic St. Bridget (who composed her work c. 1360–1370), which describes Mary kneeling to adore the Christ Child immediately after giving birth.

As in the work of Jan van Eyck, aspects of the setting of this painting are infused with symbolic meaning. In the foreground, the wheatsheaf refers both to the location of the event at Bethlehem, which in Hebrew means "house of bread," and to the Eucharistic Host, which represents the body of Christ. The majolica albarello is decorated with vines and grapes, alluding to the Eucharistic wine, which represents the blood of Christ. It holds a red lily for Christ's blood and three irises—white for purity and purple for Christ's royal ancestry. The seven blue columbines in the glass vessel remind the viewer of the Virgin's future sorrows, and scattered on the ground are violets, symbolizing humility. But Hugo's artistic vision transcends such formal religious symbolism. For example, the shepherds, who stand in unaffected awe before the miraculous event, are among the most sympathetically rendered images of common people to be found in the art of any period, and the portraits of the Portinari children are unusually sensitive renderings of the delicate features of youthful faces.

HANS MEMLING. The artist who seems to summarize and epitomize painting in Flanders during the second half of the fifteenth century is German-born Hans Memling (c. 1435–1494). Memling combines the intellectual depth and virtuoso rendering of his predecessors with a delicacy of feeling and exquisite grace, a "prettiness" that made his work exceptionally popular. Memling may have worked in Rogier van der Weyden's Brussels workshop in the 1460s, but soon after Rogier's death in 1464, Memling moved to Bruges, where he developed an international clientele that supported a thriving workshop. He also worked for local patrons.

In 1487, the 24-year-old Maarten van Nieuwenhove (1463–1500), member of a powerful political family in Bruges (he would himself become mayor of Bruges in 1497), commissioned from Memling a diptych that combined a meticulously detailed portrait with a visionary apparition of the Virgin and Child, presented as a powerful fiction of their physical encounter in Maarten's own home (**FIG. 18–17**). This type of devotional diptych was a specialty of Rogier van der Weyden, but Memling transforms the type into something more intimate by placing it in a domestic setting. An expensively outfitted figure of Maarten appears in the right wing of the diptych, seen from an oblique angle, hands folded in prayer. He seems caught in a moment of introspection inspired by personal devotions—his Book of Hours lies still open on the table in front of him. The window just over his shoulder holds a stained-glass rendering of his name saint, Martin, in the top pane, while a recognizable landmark in Bruges can be seen through the pane below. The Virgin and Child on the adjacent panel are presented frontally, and the strong sense of specific likeness characterizing Maarten's portrait has given way to an idealized delicacy and grace in the visage of the Virgin that complements the extravagance of her clothing. Although she does not seem to be

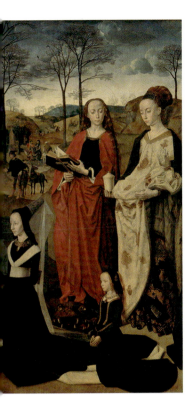

focusing on him, a completely nude Jesus stretches out on the silk pillow in front of her; she stabilizes him with one hand and offers him an apple with the other. This seems a clear reference to their roles as the new Adam and Eve, ready to redeem the sin brought into the world by the first couple. The stained glass behind them is filled with heraldry, devices, and a motto associated with Maarten's family.

Memling's construction of a coherent interior space for these figures is both impressive and meaningful. We are looking through two windows into a rectangular room containing this devotional group. The pillow under the Christ Child casts a shadow, painted on the lower frame of the left panel, to intensify the illusion, and the Virgin's scarlet mantle extends under the division between the two wings of the diptych to reappear on Maarten's side of the painting underneath his Book of Hours. This mantle not only connects the two sides of the painting spatially but also relates Maarten's devotional exercise and the apparition of the Virgin and Child. This relationship is also documented with a device already familiar to us in paintings by Jan van Eyck (SEE FIG. 18–12) and Petrus Christus (see "A Closer Look," page 581). On the shadowy back wall, over the Virgin's right shoulder and set against the closed shutters of a window, is a convex mirror that reflects the backs of both Maarten and Mary, bearing visual witness to their presence together within his domestic space and undoing the division between them that is endemic to the diptych format. Maarten's introspective gaze signals that for him the encounter is internal and spiritual, but Memling transforms Maarten's private devotion into a public statement that promotes an image of his piety and freezes him in perpetual prayer. We bear witness to his vision as an actual event.

EUROPE BEYOND FLANDERS

Flemish art—its complex symbolism, its coherent configurations of atmospheric space, its luminous colors and sensuous surface textures—delighted wealthy patrons and well-educated courtiers both inside and outside Flanders. At first, Flemish artists worked in foreign courts or their works were commissioned and exported abroad. Flemish manuscripts, tapestries, altarpieces, and portraits

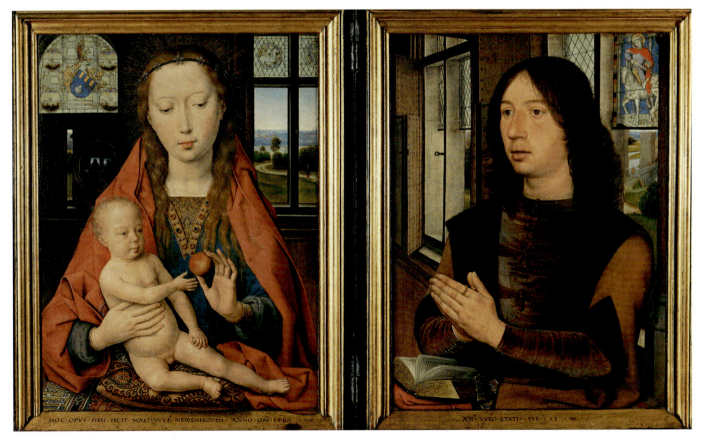

18-17 • Hans Memling DIPTYCH OF MAARTEN VAN NIEUWENHOVE
1487. Oil on wood panel, each panel (including frames) 20½ × 16¼″ (52 × 41.5 cm). Hans Memling Museum, Musea Brugge, Sint-Jans Hospital, Bruges.

appeared in palaces and chapels throughout Europe. Soon regional artists traveled to Flanders to learn oil-painting techniques and practice emulating the Flemish style. By the end of the fifteenth century, distinctive regional variations of Flemish art could be found throughout Europe, from the Atlantic Ocean to the Danube.

FRANCE

The centuries-long struggle for power and territory between France and England continued well into the fifteenth century. When King Charles VI of France died in 1422, England claimed the throne for the king's 9-month-old grandson, Henry VI of England. The plight of Charles VII, the late French king's son, inspired Joan of Arc to lead a crusade to return him to the throne. Thanks to Joan's efforts, Charles was crowned at Reims in 1429. Although Joan was burned at the stake in 1431, the revitalized French forces drove the English from French lands. In 1461, Louis XI succeeded his father, Charles VII, as king of France. Under his rule the French royal court again became a major source of patronage for the arts.

JEAN FOUQUET. The leading court artist of fifteenth-century France, Jean Fouquet (c. 1425–1481), was born in Tours and may have trained in Paris as an illuminator and in Bourges in the workshop of Jacob de Littemont, Flemish court painter to Charles VII. He was part of a French delegation to Rome in 1446–1448, but by mid century he had established a workshop in Tours and was a renowned painter. Fouquet drew from contemporary Italian

Classicism, especially in rendering architecture, and he was also strongly influenced by Flemish illusionism. He painted pictures of Charles VII, the royal family, and courtiers, and he illustrated manuscripts and designed tombs.

Among the court officials who commissioned paintings from Fouquet was Étienne Chevalier, treasurer of France under Charles VII. Fouquet painted a diptych for him that was installed over the tomb of Chevallier's wife Catherine Budé (d. 1452) in the church of Notre-Dame in Melun (FIG. 18–18). Chevalier appears in the left panel, kneeling in prayer with clasped hands and an introspective, meditative gaze within an Italianate palace, accompanied by his name saint Stephen (Étienne in French). Fouquet describes the courtier's ruddy features with a mirrorlike precision that is reminiscent of Flemish art. He is expensively dressed in a heavy red wool garment lined with fur, and his "bowl cut" represents the latest Parisian fashion in hair styling. St. Stephen's features convey a comparable sense of likeness and sophistication. A deacon in the Early Christian church in Jerusalem, Stephen was the first Christian martyr, stoned to death for defending his beliefs. Here he wears the fifteenth-century liturgical, or ritual, vestments of a deacon and carries a large stone on a closed Gospel book as evidence of his martyrdom. A trickle of blood can be seen on his tonsured head (male members of religious orders shaved the tops of their heads as a sign of humility). Placing his arm around Étienne Chevalier's back, the saint seems to be introducing the treasurer to the Virgin and Child in the adjacent panel.

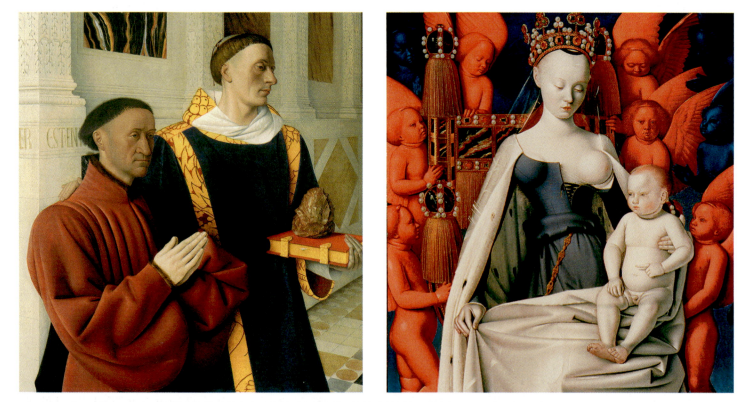

18–18 • Jean Fouquet **ÉTIENNE CHEVALIER AND ST. STEPHEN, VIRGIN AND CHILD**
The Melun Diptych. c. 1452–1455. Oil on oak panel. Left wing: 36½ × 33½″ (92.7 × 85.5 cm), Staatliche Museen zu Berlin, Preussischer Kulturbesitz, Gemäldegalerie; right wing: 37¼ × 33½″ (94.5 × 85.5 cm). Koninklijk Museum voor Schone Kunsten, Antwerp, Belgium.

The Virgin and Child, however, exist in another world. A supernatural vision unfolds here as the queen of heaven is enthroned surrounded by red and blue seraphim and cherubim, who form a tapestrylike background. Even the Virgin seems a celestial being, conceived by Fouquet as a hybrid of careful description and powerful abstraction. Her fashionable, tightly waisted bodice has been unlaced so she can present her spherical breast to a substantial, seated baby, who points across the juncture between the two wings of the diptych to acknowledge Chevalier. According to tradition, Fouquet gave this image of the Virgin the features of the king's much loved and respected mistress, Agnès Sorel, who died in 1450. The original frame that united these two panels—now divided between two museums—into a diptych is lost, but among the fragments that remain is a stunning medallion self-portrait that served as the artist's signature.

JEAN HEY, THE MASTER OF MOULINS. Perhaps the greatest French follower of Jean Fouquet is an artist who for many years was known as the Master of Moulins after a large triptych he painted at the end of the fifteenth century under the patronage of Duke Jean II of Bourbon, for the Burgundian Cathedral of Moulins. This triptych combines the exuberance of Flemish attention to brilliant color and the differentiation of surface texture with a characteristically French air of reserved detachment. Recently the work of this artist has been associated with the name Jean Hey, a painter of Flemish origin, who seems to have been trained in the workshop of Hugo van der Goes, but who pursued his career at the French court.

This charming portrait (FIG. 18–19)—which may have been one half of a devotional diptych comparable to that painted by Memling for Maarten van Nieuwenhove (SEE FIG. 18–17)—portrays Margaret of Austria (1480–1530), daughter of Emperor Maximilian I, who had been betrothed to the future French king Charles VIII (r. 1483–1498) at age 2 or 3 and was being brought up at the French court. She would return home to her father in 1493 after Charles decided to pursue another, more politically expedient marriage (after two political marriages of her own, the widowed Margaret would eventually become governor of the Habsburg Netherlands), but Hey captures her at a tender moment a few years before those troubled times. She kneels in front of a strip of wall between two windows that open onto a lush country landscape, fingering the pearl beads of her rosary. Details of her lavish velvet and ermine outfit not only proclaim her wealth but provide the clues to her identity—the *Cs* and *Ms* embroidered on her collar signal her betrothal to Charles and the ostentatious *fleur-de-lis* pendant set with large rubies and pearls proclaims her affiliation with the French court. But it is the delicacy and sweet vulnerability of this 10-year-old girl that are most arresting. They recall Hugo van der Goes's sensitivity to the childlike qualities of the young members of donor families (SEE FIG. 18–16) and provide one strong piece of evidence for ascribing Hey's training to the workshop of this Flemish master.

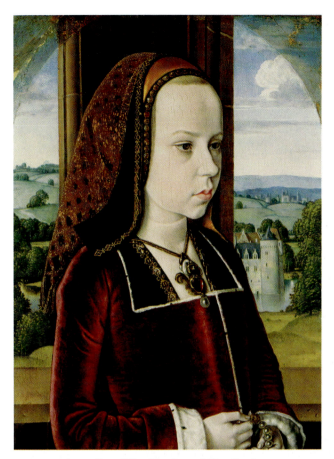

18–19 • Jean Hey (The Master of Moulins)
PORTRAIT OF MARGARET OF AUSTRIA
c. 1490. Oil on wood panel, 12⅞ × 9⅛″ (32.7 × 23 cm). Metropolitan Museum of Art, New York, Robert Lehman Collection.

FLAMBOYANT ARCHITECTURE. The great age of cathedral building that had begun in the mid twelfth century was essentially over by the end of the fourteenth century, but growing urban populations needed houses, city halls, guildhalls, and more parish churches. It was in buildings such as these that late Gothic architecture took form in a style we call "Flamboyant" because of its repeated, twisted, flamelike tracery patterns. Late Gothic masons covered their buildings with increasingly elaborate, complex, and at times playful architectural decoration. Like painters, sculptors also turned to describing the specific nature of the world around them, and they covered capitals and moldings with ivy, hawthorn leaves, and other vegetation, not just the conventional acanthus motifs rooted in the Classical world.

The church of Saint-Maclou in Rouen, which was begun after a fund-raising campaign in 1432 and dedicated in 1521, is an outstanding and well-preserved example of Flamboyant Gothic (FIG. 18–20) probably designed by the Paris architect Pierre Robin. A projecting porch bends to enfold the façade of the church in a screen of tracery. Sunlight on the flame-shape openings casts ever-changing shadows across the intentionally complex surface. **Crockets**—small, knobby leaflike ornaments that line the steep gables and slender buttresses—break every defining line. In

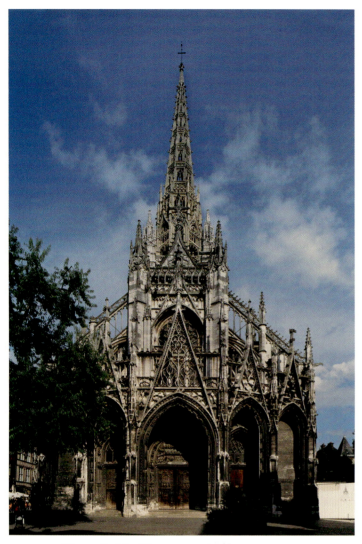

18-20 • Pierre Robin (?) **CHURCH OF SAINT-MACLOU, ROUEN**
Normandy, France. West façade, 1432–1521; façade c. 1500–1514.

SEE MORE: Click the Google Earth link for Saint-Maclou
www.myartslab.com

GERMANY AND SWITZERLAND

Present-day Germany and Switzerland were situated within the Holy Roman Empire, a loose confederation of primarily German-speaking states. Artisan guilds grew powerful and trade flourished under the auspices of the Hanseatic League, an association of cities and trading outposts, stimulating a strengthening of the merchant class. The Fugger family, for example, began their spectacular rise

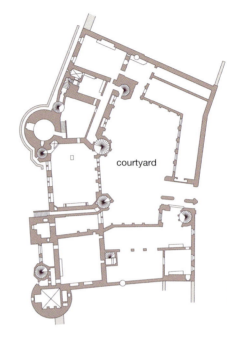

18-21 • **PLAN OF JACQUES COEUR HOUSE**
Bourges, France. 1443–1451.

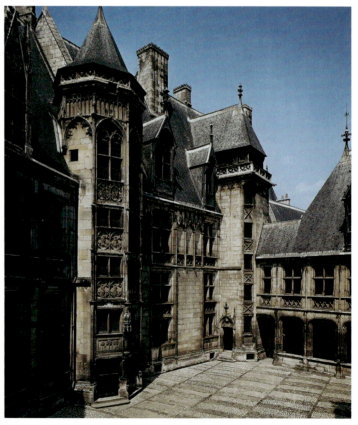

18-22 • **INTERIOR COURTYARD OF JACQUES COEUR HOUSE**
Bourges, France. 1443–1451.

the Flamboyant style, decoration sometimes disguises structural elements with an overlay of tracery and ornament in geometric and natural shapes, all to dizzying effect.

The house of Jacques Coeur, a fabulously wealthy merchant in Bourges, reflects the popularity of the Flamboyant style for secular architecture (**FIGS. 18–21, 18–22**). Built at great expense between 1443 and 1451, it survives almost intact, although it has been stripped of its rich furnishings. The rambling, palatial house is built around an irregular open courtyard, with spiral stairs in octagonal towers giving access to the upper-floor rooms. Tympana over doors indicate the function of the rooms within; for example, over the door to the kitchen a cook stirs the contents of a large bowl. Among the carved decorations are puns on the patron's surname, Coeur (meaning "heart" in French). The house was also Jacques Coeur's place of business, so it had large storerooms for goods and a strongroom for treasure.

W
sculptu
panel p
opened
by Pac
actual
create
queen
use of
in the
and go
the cha
candles

THE

Printm
century
local m
used by
and en;
590). **W**
on clot
images
copies
of each
often ill

SINGLI

Large q
and en;
century.
to cut fi

THE Bu
souveni
was fou
Germar
manusci
and pro
river. H
guide h
millers
quality
strength
(facial f
inner si
was one
survive.
some ev

MARTIN
goldsmi

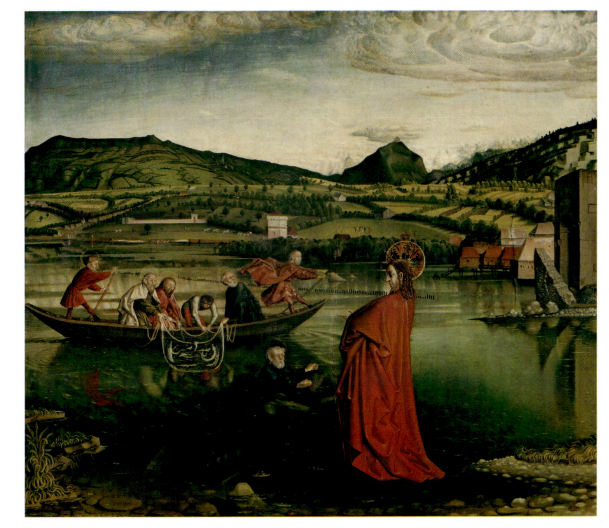

18-23 • Konrad Witz MIRACULOUS DRAFT OF FISHES
From an altarpiece for the Cathedral of St. Peter, Geneva, Switzerland. 1444. Oil on wood panel,
4'3" × 5'1" (1.29 × 1.55 m). Musée d'Art et d'Histoire, Geneva.

from simple textile workers and linen merchants to bankers for the Habsburgs and the popes.

KONRAD WITZ. Germanic fifteenth-century artists worked in two very different styles. Some, clustered around Cologne, continued the International Gothic style with increased prettiness, softness, and sweetness of expression. Other artists began an intense investigation and detailed description of the physical world. The major exponent of the latter style was Konrad Witz (active 1434–1446). A native of Swabia in southern Germany, Witz moved to Basel (in present-day Switzerland), where he found a rich source of patronage in the Church.

Witz's last large commission before his early death in 1446 was an altarpiece dedicated to St. Peter for the Cathedral of Geneva, signed and dated to 1444. In one of its scenes—the **MIRACULOUS DRAFT OF FISHES** (FIG. 18–23)—Jesus appears posthumously to his disciples as they fish on the Sea of Galilee and Peter leaps from the boat to greet him. But Witz sets the scene on the Lake of Geneva, with the distinctive dark mountain (the Mole) rising on the north

shore and the snow-covered Alps shining in the distance. Witz records every nuance of light and water—the rippling surface, the reflections of boats, figures, and buildings, even the lake bottom. Peter's body and legs, visible through the water, are distorted by the refraction. For one of the earliest times in European art, an artist captures both the appearance and the spirit of nature.

MICHAEL PACHER. In Germanic lands, patrons preferred altarpieces that featured polychromed wood carvings rather than the large ensembles of panel paintings that we saw in Flanders (see, for example, "The Ghent Altarpiece," pages 576–577). One of the greatest artists working in this tradition was painter and sculptor Michael Pacher (1435–1498), based in Bruneck, now in the Italian Alps. In 1471, Benedict Eck, abbot of Mondsee, commissioned from Pacher for the pilgrimage church of St. Wolfgang a grand high altarpiece that is still installed in its original church setting (FIG. 18–24). The surviving contract specifies materials and subject matter and even documents the cost—1,200 Hungarian florins—but sets no time limit for its completion. Pacher and his shop worked on it for ten years.

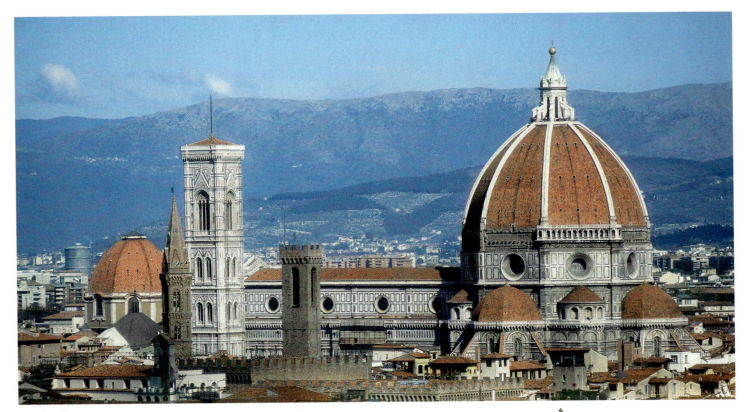

19-2 • Filippo Brunelleschi DOME OF FLORENCE CATHEDRAL (SANTA MARIA DEL FIORE)
1420–1436; lantern completed 1471.

SEE MORE: View a simulation about doming
www.myartslab.com

19-3 • SCHEMATIC DRAWING OF THE CATHEDRAL OF FLORENCE
The separate, central-plan building in front of the façade is the Baptistery. Adjacent to the façade is a tall tower designed by Giotto in 1334.

18-24 •
St. Wolfgan

FILIPPO BRUNELLESCHI. Filippo Brunelleschi (1377–1446), whose father had been involved in the original plans for the cathedral dome in 1367, achieved what many considered impossible: He solved the problem of the dome. Brunelleschi had originally trained as a goldsmith (see "The Competition Reliefs," page 601). To further his education, he traveled to Rome to study ancient Roman sculpture and architecture, and it was on his return to Florence that he tackled the dome. After the completion of a tall octagonal drum in 1412, Brunelleschi designed the dome itself in 1417, and it was built between 1420 and 1436 (FIGS. 19–2, 19–3). A revolutionary feat of engineering, the dome is a double shell of masonry 138 feet across. The octagonal outer shell is supported on eight large and 16 lighter ribs. Instead of using a costly and even dangerous scaffold and centering, Brunelleschi devised a system in which temporary wooden supports were cantilevered out from the drum. He moved these supports up as building progressed. As the dome was built up course by course, each portion of the structure reinforced the next one. Vertical marble ribs interlocked with horizontal sandstone rings, connected and reinforced with iron rods and oak beams. The inner and outer shells were linked internally by a system of arches. When completed, this self-buttressed unit required no external support to keep it standing.

An oculus (round opening) in the center of the dome was surmounted by a lantern designed in 1436. After Brunelleschi's death, this crowning structure, made up of Roman architectural forms, was completed by another Florentine architect, Michelozzo di Bartolomeo (1396–1472). The final touch—a gilt bronzed ball—was added in 1468–1471.

Other commissions came quickly after the cathedral dome project established Brunelleschi's fame. From about 1418 until his death in 1446, Brunelleschi was involved in a series of influential projects. In 1419, he designed a foundling hospital for the city (see "The Foundling Hospital," pages 598–599). Between 1419 and 1423, he built the elegant Capponi Chapel in the church of Santa Felicità (SEE FIG. 20–25). For the Medicis' parish church of San Lorenzo, he designed and built a centrally planned sacristy (a room where ritual attire and vessels are kept), from 1421 to 1428, and also conceived plans for a new church.

Brunelleschi's **SAN LORENZO** has a basilican plan with a long nave flanked by side aisles that open into shallow lateral chapels (FIG. 19–4). A short transept and square crossing lead to a square sanctuary flanked by additional chapels opening off the transept. Projecting from the left transept, as one faces the altar, are Brunelleschi's sacristy and the older Medici tomb. Brunelleschi based his mathematically regular plan on a square **module**—a basic unit of measure that could be multiplied or divided and

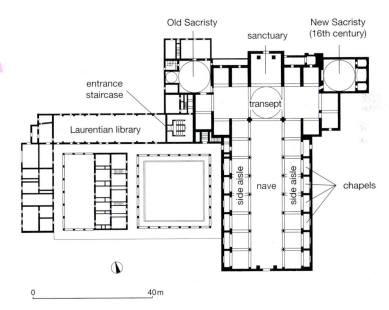

19-4 • Filippo Brunelleschi; continued by Michelozzo di Bartolomeo **INTERIOR AND PLAN OF CHURCH OF SAN LORENZO, FLORENCE** c. 1421–1428; nave (designed 1434?) 1442–1470.

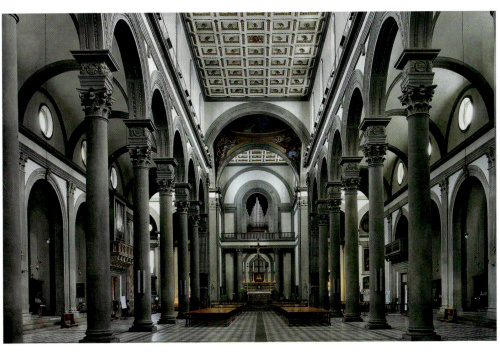

The Foundling Hospital

In 1419, the guild of silk manufacturers and goldsmiths (Arte della Seta) in Florence undertook a significant public service: It established a large public orphanage and commissioned the brilliant young architect Filippo Brunelleschi to build it next to the church of the Santissima Annunziata (Most Holy Annunciation), which housed a miracle-working painting of the Annunciation, making it a popular pilgrimage site. Completed in 1444, the Foundling Hospital—*Ospedale degli Innocenti*—was unprecedented in terms of scale and design (FIG. A).

Brunelleschi created a building that paid homage to traditional forms while introducing features that we associate with the Italian Renaissance style. Traditionally, a charitable foundation's building had a portico open to the street to provide shelter, and Brunelleschi built an arcade of unprecedented lightness and elegance, using smooth round columns and richly carved capitals—his own interpretation of the Classical Corinthian order. Although we might initially assume that the sources for this arcade lay in the Roman architecture of Classical antiquity, columns were not actually used in antiquity to support free-standing arcades, only to support straight architraves. In fact, it was local Romanesque architecture that was the source for Brunelleschi's graceful design. It is the details of capitals and moldings that bring an air of the antique to this influential building.

The underlying mathematical basis for Brunelleschi's design—traced to the same Pythagorean proportional systems that were believed to create musical harmony—creates a distinct sense of harmony in this graceful arcade. Each bay encloses a cube of space defined by the 10-*braccia* (20-foot) height of the columns and the diameter of the arches. Hemispherical pendentive domes, half again as high as the columns, cover the cubes. The bays at the end of the arcade are slightly larger than the rest, creating a subtle frame for the composition. Brunelleschi defined the perfect squares and semicircles of his building with dark gray stone (*pietra serena*) against plain white walls. His training as a goldsmith and sculptor (see "The

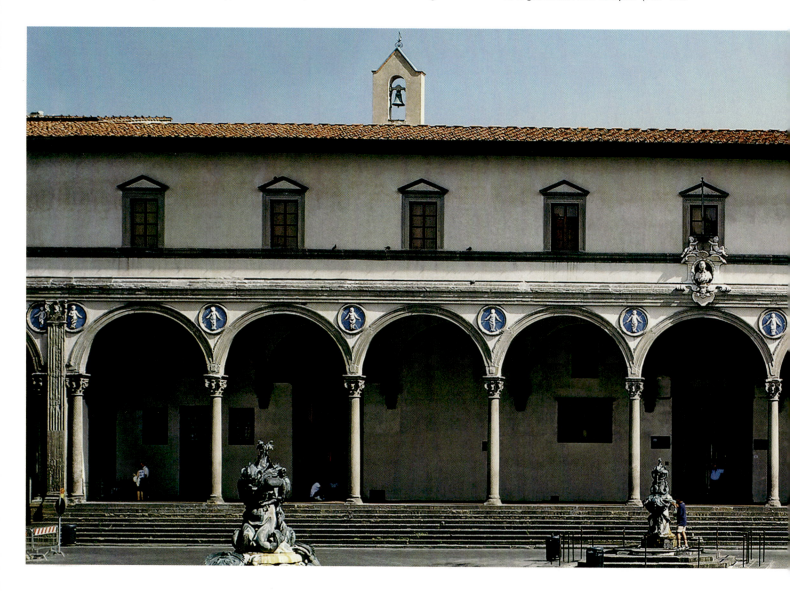

Competition Reliefs," page 601) served him well as he led his artisans to carve crisp, elegantly detailed capitals and moldings for the covered gallery.

A later addition to the building seems eminently suitable: About 1487, Andrea della Robbia, who had inherited the family firm and its secret glazing formulas from his uncle Luca, created for the interstices between the arches glazed terra-cotta medallions (FIG. B) that signified the building's function. Molds were used in the ceramic workshop to facilitate the production of the series of identical babies in swaddling clothes that float at the center of each medallion. The molded terra-cotta forms were covered with a tin glaze to make the sculptures both weatherproof and decorative, and the baby-blue ceramic backgrounds—a signature color for the della Robbia family workshop—makes them seem to float as celestial apparitions. This is not altogether inappropriate: They are meant to evoke the "innocent" baby boys martyred by King Herod in his attempt to rid his realm of the potential rival the Magi had journeyed to venerate (Matthew 2:16).

Andrea della Robbia's adorable ceramic babies—which remain among the most beloved images of the city of Florence—seem to lay claim to the human side of Renaissance humanism, reminding viewers that the city's wealthiest guild cared for the most helpless members of society. Perhaps the Foundling Hospital spoke to fifteenth-century Florentines of an increased sense of social responsibility. Or perhaps, by so publicly demonstrating social concerns, the wealthy guild that sponsored it solicited the approval and support of the lower classes in the cut-throat power politics of the day.

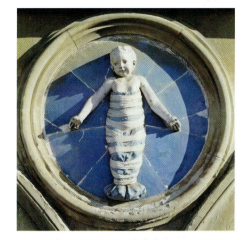

B. Andrea della Robbia INFANT IN SWADDLING CLOTHES (ONE OF THE HOLY INNOCENTS MASSACRED BY HEROD)
Ospedale degli Innocenti (Foundling Hospital), Florence. 1487. Glazed terra cotta.

A. Filippo Brunelleschi OSPEDALE DEGLI INNOCENTI (FOUNDLING HOSPITAL), FLORENCE
Designed 1419; built 1421–1444.

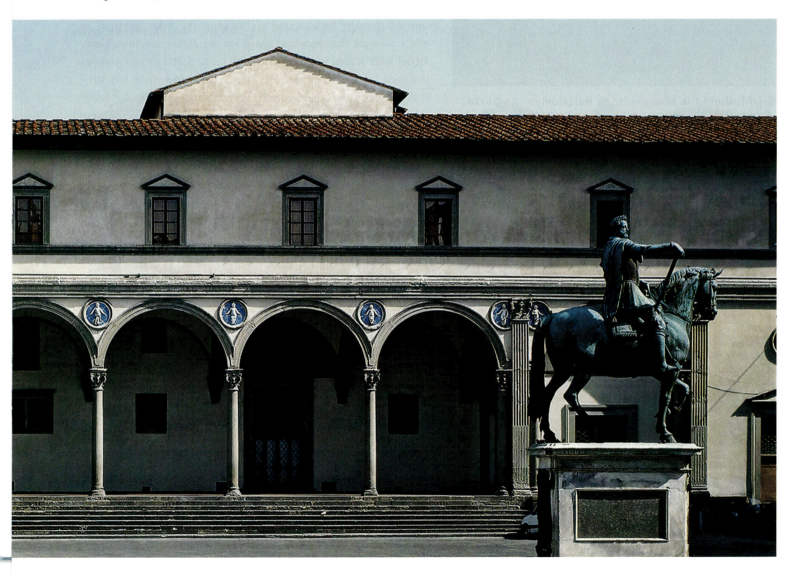

in the second story match the exterior windows on this same level. Disks bearing the Medici arms surmount each arch in a frieze decorated with swags in **sgraffito** work (decoration produced by scratching through a darker layer of plaster or glaze). Such classicizing elements, inspired by the study of Roman ruins, gave the great house an aura of dignity and stability that enhanced the status of its owners. The Medici Palace inaugurated a new fashion for monumentality and regularity in residential Florentine architecture. Wealthy Florentine families soon emulated it in their own houses.

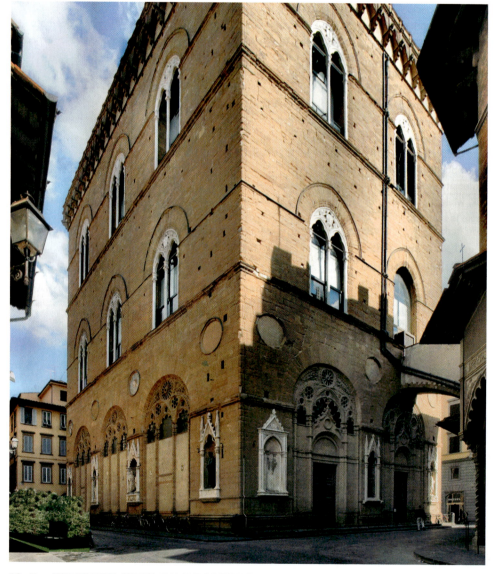

19-7 • EXTERIOR VIEW OF ORSANMICHELE SHOWING SCULPTURE IN NICHES
Florence, begun in 1337.

At street level, Orsanmichele was constructed originally as an open loggia (similar to the Loggia dei Lanzi in FIG. 17–2); in 1380 the spaces under the arches were filled in. In this view of the southeast corner, appearing on the receding wall to the left is first (in the foreground on the corner pier) Donatello's *St. George*, then, Nanni di Banco's *Four Crowned Martyrs*. However, the sculptures seen in this photograph are modern replicas; the originals have been removed to museums for safekeeping.

SEE MORE: Click the Google Earth link for Orsanmichele
www.myartslab.com

SCULPTURE

The new architectural language inspired by ancient Classical forms was accompanied by a similar impetus in sculpture. By 1400, Florence had enjoyed internal stability and economic prosperity for over two decades. However, until 1428, the city and its independence were challenged by two great antirepublican powers: the duchy of Milan and the kingdom of Naples. In an atmosphere of wealth and civic patriotism, Florentines turned to commissions that would express their self-esteem and magnify the importance of their city. A new attitude toward realism, space, and the Classical past set the stage for more than a century of creativity. Sculptors led the way.

ORSANMICHELE. In 1339, 14 of Florence's most powerful guilds had been assigned to fill the ground-floor niches that decorated the exterior of **ORSANMICHELE**—a newly completed loggia that served as a grain market—with sculpted images of their patron saints (FIG. 19–7). By 1400, only three had fulfilled this responsibility. In the new climate of republicanism and civic pride, the government pressured the guilds to furnish their niches with statuary. In the wake of this directive, Florence witnessed a dazzling display of sculpture produced by the most impressive local practitioners, including Nanni di Banco, Lorenzo Ghiberti, and Donatello, each of whom took responsibility for filling three niches.

In about 1409, Nanni di Banco (c. 1385–1421), son of a sculptor in the Florence Cathedral workshop, was commissioned by the stonecarvers and woodworkers' guild (to which he himself belonged) to produce **THE FOUR CROWNED MARTYRS** (FIG. 19–8). According to tradition, these third-century Christian martyrs were sculptors, executed for refusing to make an image of a pagan Roman god for Emperor Diocletian. Although the architectural setting is Gothic in style, Nanni's figures—with their solid bodies, heavy, form-revealing togas, noble hair and beards, and portraitlike features—reveal his interest in ancient Roman sculpture, particularly portraiture. They stand as a testimony to this sculptor's role in the Florentine revival of interest in antiquity.

The saints convey a new spatial relationship to the building and to the viewer. They stand in a semicircle, with feet and drapery protruding beyond the floor of the niche and into the viewer's space. The saints appear to be four individuals interacting within their own world, but a world that opens to engage with pedestrians (SEE FIG. 19–7). The relief panel below the niche shows the four sculptors at work, embodied with a similar solid vigor. Nanni deeply undercut both figures and objects to cast shadows that enhance the illusion of three-dimensionality.

Donatello (Donato di Niccolò di Betto Bardi, c. 1386/1387–1466) also received three commissions for the niches at Orsanmichele during the first quarter of the century. A member of

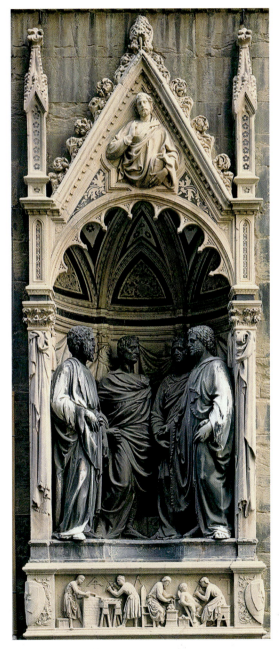

19-8 • Nanni di Banco THE FOUR CROWNED MARTYRS
c. 1409–1417. Marble, height of figures 6' (1.83 m). Orsanmichele, Florence (photographed before removal of figures to a museum).

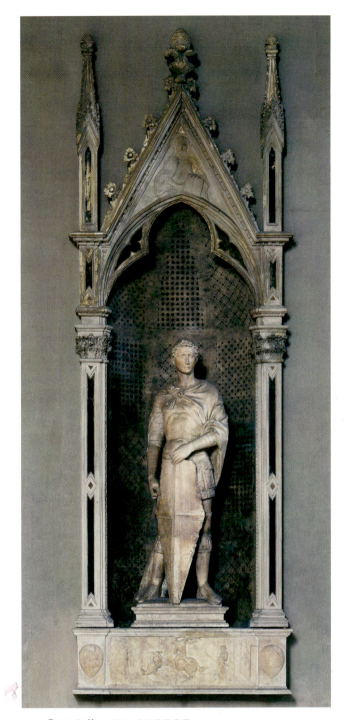

19-9 • Donatello ST. GEORGE
1417–1420. Marble, height 6'5" (1.95 m). Bargello, Florence. Formerly Orsanmichele, Florence.

the guild of stonecarvers and woodworkers, he worked in both media, as well as in bronze. During a long and productive career, he developed into one of the most influential and distinguished figures in the history of Italian sculpture, approaching each commission as if it were the opportunity for a new experiment. One of Florence's lesser guilds—the armorers and sword-makers—called on Donatello to carve a majestic and self-assured St. George for their niche (FIG. 19–9). As originally conceived, the saint would have been a standing advertisement for their trade, carrying a metal

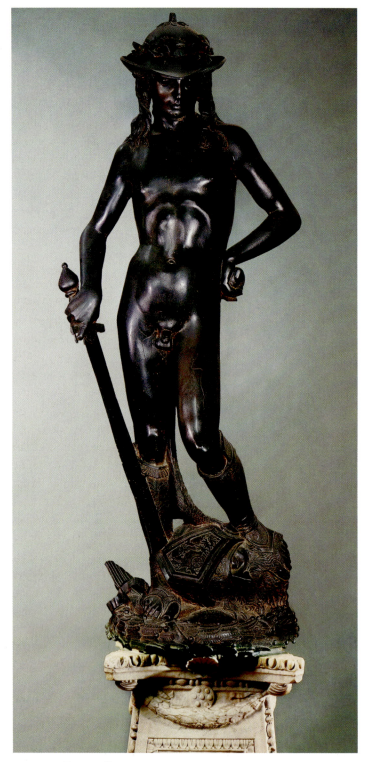

19-10 • Donatello DAVID
c. 1446–1460(?). Bronze, height 5'2¼" (1.58 m). Museo Nazionale del Bargello, Florence.

This sculpture is first recorded as being in the courtyard of the Medici Palace in 1469, where it stood on a base inscribed with these lines:

The victor is whoever defends the fatherland.
All-powerful God crushes the angry enemy.
Behold, a boy overcomes the great tyrant.
Conquer, O citizens!

SEE MORE: View a video about the process of lost-wax casting **www.myartslab.com**

sword in his right hand and probably wearing a metal helmet and sporting a scabbard, all now lost. The figure has remarkable presence, even without his accessories. St. George stands in solid contrapposto, legs braced to support his armor-heavy torso, the embodiment of alertness and determination. He seems to be staring out into our world, perhaps surveying his most famous adversary—a dragon that was holding a princess captive—lurking unsettlingly in the space behind us. With his wrinkled brow and fierce expression, he is tense, alert, focused, if perhaps also somewhat worried. Donatello's complex psychological characterization of this warrior-saint particularly impressed Donatello's contemporaries, not least among them his potential patrons.

For the base of the niche, Donatello carved a remarkable shallow relief showing St. George slaying the dragon and saving the princess, the next scene in his story. The contours of the foreground figures are slightly undercut to emphasize their mass, while the landscape and architecture are in progressively lower relief until they are barely incised rather than carved, an ingenious emulation of the painters' technique of atmospheric perspective. This is also a pioneering example of linear perspective (see "Renaissance Perspective," page 608), in which the orthogonals converge on the figure of the saint himself, using this burgeoning representational system not only to simulate spatial recession but also to provide narrative focus.

DONATELLO. Donatello's long career as a sculptor in a broad variety of media established him as one of the most successful and admired sculptors of the Italian Renaissance. He excelled in part because of his attentive exploration of human emotions and expression, as well as his ability to solve the technical problems posed by various media—from lost-wax casting in bronze and carved marble to polychromed wood. In a bronze **DAVID**, he produced the first life-size male nude since antiquity (**FIG. 19–10**), and in his portrait of the soldier Erasmo da Narni, one of the first life-size bronze equestrian portraits of the Renaissance (SEE FIG. 19–11).

Since nothing is known about the circumstances of its creation, the *David* has been the subject of continuing inquiry and speculation. Although the statue clearly draws on the Classical tradition of heroic nudity, the meaning of this sensuous, adolescent boy in a jaunty laurel-trimmed shepherd's hat and boots has long piqued interest. Some art historians have stressed an overt homoeroticism, especially in the openly effeminate conception of David and the way a wing from the helmet on Goliath's severed head caresses the young hero's inner thigh. Others have seen in David's angular pose and boyish torso a sense that he is poised between childish interests and adult responsibility, an image of improbable heroism. David was a potent political image in Florence, a symbol of the citizens' resolve to oppose tyrants regardless of their superior power, since virtue brings divine support and preternatural strength. Indeed, an inscription engraved into the base where the sculpture once stood suggests that it could have celebrated the

Florentine triumph over the Milanese in 1425, a victory that brought resolution to a quarter-century struggle with despots and helped give Florence a vision of itself as a strong, virtuous republic.

In 1443, Donatello was probably called to Padua to execute an **EQUESTRIAN STATUE (FIG. 19–11)** to commemorate the Paduan general of the Venetian army, Erasmo da Narni, nicknamed "Gattamelata" (meaning "Honeyed Cat"—a reference to his mother, Melania Gattelli). If any image could be said to characterize the self-made men of the Italian Renaissance, surely it would be those of the *condottieri*—the brilliant generals such as Gattamelata and Niccolò da Tolentino (SEE FIG. 19–1) who organized the armies and fought for any city-state willing to pay for their services. As guardians for hire, they were tough, opportunistic mercenaries. But they also subscribed to an ideal of military and civic virtue. Horsemanship was more than a necessary skill for the *condottieri*.

The horse, a beast of enormous brute strength, symbolized animal passions, and skilled horsemanship demonstrated physical and intellectual control—self-control, as well as control of the animal—the triumph of the intellect, of "mind over matter."

Donatello's sources for this statue were surviving Roman bronze equestrian portraits, notably the famous image of Marcus Aurelius (SEE FIG. 6–52), which the sculptor certainly knew from his stay in Rome. Viewed from a distance, Donatello's man–animal juggernaut, installed on a high marble base in front of the church of Sant'Antonio in Padua, seems capable of thrusting forward at the first threat. Seen up close, however, the man's sunken cheeks, sagging jaw, ropy neck, and stern but sad expression suggest a warrior grown old and tired from the constant need for military vigilance and rapid response.

THE GATES OF PARADISE. The bronze doors that Lorenzo Ghiberti (1381?–1455) produced for the Florentine Baptistery after winning his famous competition with Brunelleschi in 1401 (see "The Competition Reliefs," page 601) were such a success that in 1425 he was awarded the commission for yet another set of bronze doors for the east side of the Baptistery, and his first set was moved to the north side. The new door panels, funded by the wool manufacturers' guild, were a significant conceptual leap from the older schemes of 28 small scenes employed for Ghiberti's earlier doors and those of Andrea Pisano in the fourteenth century (SEE FIG. 17–3). Ghiberti departed entirely from the old arrangement, producing a set of ten scenes from the Hebrew Bible—from the Creation to the reign of Solomon—composed in rectangular fields, like a set of framed paintings. Michelangelo reportedly said that the results, installed in 1452, were worthy of the **"GATES OF PARADISE"**—the name by which they are now commonly known **(FIG. 19–12)**.

Ghiberti organized the space in the ten square reliefs either by a system of linear perspective with obvious orthogonal lines (see "Renaissance Perspective," page 608)

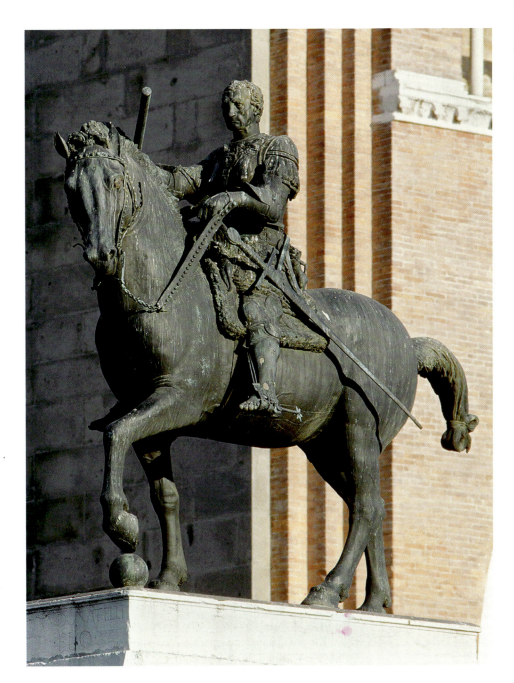

19-11 • Donatello EQUESTRIAN STATUE OF ERASMO DA NARNI (GATTAMELATA)
Piazza del Santo, Padua. 1443–1453. Bronze, height approx. 12′2″ (3.71 m).

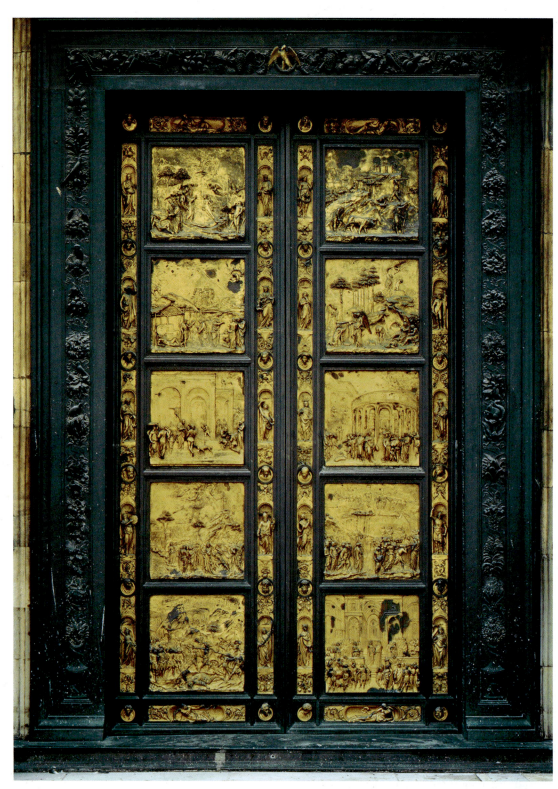

19–12 • Lorenzo Ghiberti "GATES OF PARADISE" (EAST DOORS), BAPTISTERY OF SAN GIOVANNI, FLORENCE
1425–1452. Gilt bronze, height 15′ (4.57 m). Museo dell'Opera del Duomo, Florence.

The door panels, commissioned by the wool manufacturers' guild, depict ten scenes from the Hebrew Bible beginning with the Creation in the upper left panel. The murder of Abel by his brother, Cain, follows in the upper right panel, succeeded in the same left–right paired order by the Flood and the drunkenness of Noah, Abraham sacrificing Isaac, the story of Jacob and Esau, Joseph sold into slavery by his brothers, Moses receiving the Tablets of the Law, Joshua and the fall of Jericho, David and Goliath, and finally Solomon and the queen of Sheba. Ghiberti placed his own portrait as a signature in the frame at the lower right corner of the Jacob and Esau panel. He wrote in his *Commentaries* (c. 1450–1455): "I strove to imitate nature as clearly as I could, and with all the perspective I could produce, to have excellent compositions with many figures."

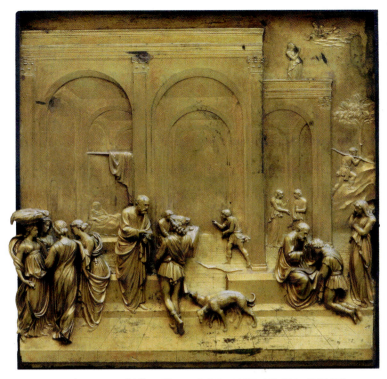

19-13 • Lorenzo Ghiberti **JACOB AND ESAU, PANEL OF THE "GATES OF PARADISE" (EAST DOORS)** Formerly on the Baptistery of San Giovanni, Florence. c. 1435. Gilded bronze, 31¼" (79 cm) square. Museo dell'Opera del Duomo, Florence.

or more intuitively by a series of arches or rocks or trees charting the path into the distance. Foreground figures are grouped in the lower third of each panel, while the other figures decrease gradually in size to map their positioning in deep space. The use of a system of perspective, with clearly differentiated background and foreground, also helped Ghiberti combine a series of related events, separated by narrative time, within a single pictorial frame.

The story of Jacob and Esau (Genesis 25 and 27) fills the center panel of the left door. Ghiberti creates a coherent and measurable space peopled by graceful, idealized figures (FIG. 19–13). He pays careful attention to one-point perspective in laying out the architectural setting. Squares in the pavement establish the receding lines of the orthogonals that converge to a central vanishing point under the loggia, while towering arches overlap and gradually diminish in size from foreground to background to define the receding space above the figures. The story unfolds in a series of individual episodes and begins in the background. On the rooftop (upper right) Rebecca stands, listening as God warns of her unborn sons' future conflict; under the left-hand arch she gives birth to the twins. The adult Esau sells his rights as oldest son to his brother Jacob, and when he goes hunting (center right), Rebecca and Jacob plot against him. Finally, in the right foreground, Jacob receives Isaac's blessing, while in the center, Esau faces his father. Ghiberti's portrayal of the scene relates more closely to developments in painting than to contemporary sculpture. Ghiberti not only signed his work, but also included his self-portrait in the medallion beside the lower right-hand corner of this panel.

POLLAIUOLO. Sculptors in the fifteenth century not only worked on a monumental scale in the public sphere; they also created small works, each designed to inspire the mind and delight the eye of its private owner. The ambitious and multi-talented Antonio del Pollaiuolo—goldsmith, embroiderer, printmaker, sculptor, and painter—who came to work for the Medici family in Florence about 1460, mostly created small bronze sculptures. His **HERCULES AND ANTAEUS** of about 1475 is one of the largest (FIG. 19–14). This study of complex interlocking figures has an explosive energy that can best be appreciated by viewing it from every angle.

Statuettes of religious subjects were still popular, but humanist patrons began to collect bronzes of Classical subjects. Many sculptors, especially those trained as goldsmiths, started to cast small copies after well-known ancient works. Some artists also executed

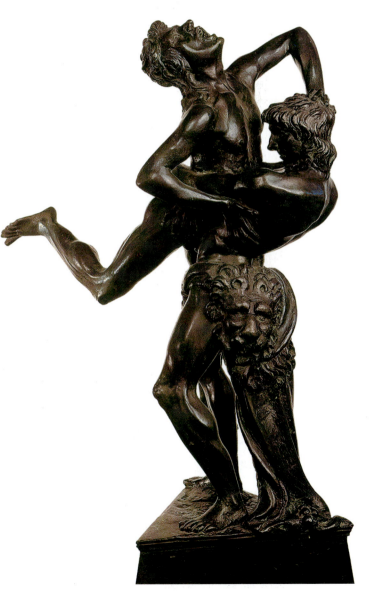

19-14 • Antonio del Pollaiuolo **HERCULES AND ANTAEUS** c. 1475. Bronze, height with base 18" (45.7 cm). Museo Nazionale del Bargello, Florence.

Fifteenth-century Italian artists developed a system known as linear, or mathematical perspective that enabled them to represent three dimensions on a two-dimensional surface, simulating the recession of space in the visible world pictorially in a way they found convincing. The sculptor and architect Filippo Brunelleschi first demonstrated the system about 1420, and the theorist and architect Leon Battista Alberti codified it in 1436 in his treatise *Della Pittura* (*On Painting*).

For Alberti, in one-point linear perspective a picture's surface was conceived as a flat plane that intersected the viewer's field of vision at right angles. This highly artificial concept presumed a viewer standing dead center at a prescribed distance from a work of art. From this single fixed vantage point, everything would appear to recede into the distance at the same rate, following imaginary lines called

orthogonals that met at a single **vanishing point** on the horizon. By using orthogonals in concert with controlled diminution of scale as forms move back toward the vanishing point, artists could replicate the optical illusion that things appear to grow smaller, rise higher, and come closer together as they get farther away from us. Linear perspective makes pictorial spaces seem almost like extensions of the viewer's real space, creating a compelling, even exaggerated sense of depth.

Linear perspective is not the only way to simulate spatial recession in two-dimensional painting. In atmospheric perspective, variations in color and clarity convey the feeling of distance when objects and landscape are portrayed less clearly, and colors become grayer, in the background, imitating the natural effects of a loss of clarity and color when viewing things in the distance through an atmospheric haze.

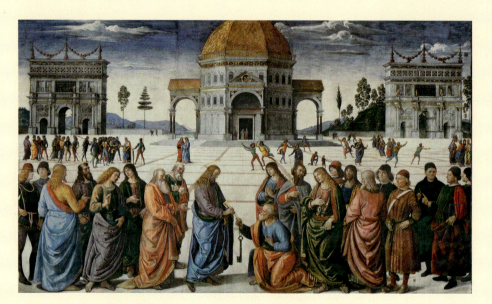

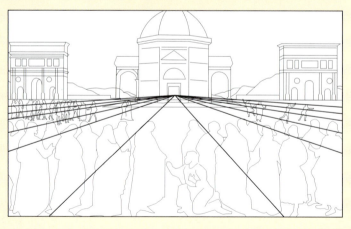

Perugino THE DELIVERY OF THE KEYS TO ST. PETER, WITH A SCHEMATIC DRAWING SHOWING THE ORTHOGONALS AND VANISHING POINT
Fresco on the right wall of the Sistine Chapel, Vatican, Rome. 1481. 11'5½" × 18'8½" (3.48 × 5.70 m).

The Delivery of the Keys to St. Peter is a remarkable study in linear perspective. The clear demarcation of the paving stones of the piazza provides a network of orthogonal and horizontal lines for the measured placement of the figures. People and buildings become increasingly, and logically, smaller as the space recedes. Horizontally, the composition is divided between the foreground frieze of figures and the widely spaced background buildings, vertically by the open space at the center between Christ and Peter and by the symmetrical architectural forms on either side of this central axis. Perugino's painting is, among other things, a representation of Alberti's ideal city, described in *De re aedificatoria* as having a "temple" (that is, a church) at the very center of a great open space raised on a dais and separate from any other buildings that might obstruct its view.

original designs *all'antica* ("in the antique style") to appeal to a cultivated humanist taste. Hercules was always a popular figure; as a patron of Florence, he was on the city seal. Among the many courageous acts by which Hercules gained immortality was the slaying of the evil Antaeus in a wrestling match by lifting him off the earth, the source of the giant's great physical power.

An engraving by Pollaiuolo, **THE BATTLE OF THE NUDES (FIG. 19–15)**, reflects two interests of Renaissance scholars—the study of Classical sculpture and anatomical research. Pollaiuolo may have intended this, his only known—but highly influential—print, as a study in composition involving the human figure in action. The naked men, fighting each other ferociously against a tapestrylike

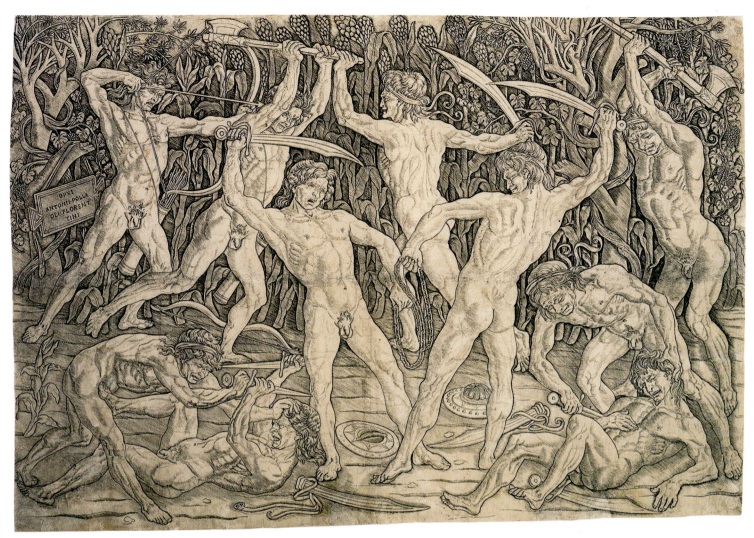

19–15 • Antonio del Pollaiuolo THE BATTLE OF THE NUDES
c. 1465–1470. Engraving, 15⅛ × 23¼″ (38.3 × 59 cm). Cincinnati Art Museum, Ohio. Bequest of Herbert Greer French. 1943.118

background of foliage, seem to have been drawn from a single model in a variety of poses, many of which were taken from Classical sources. Like the artist's *Hercules and Antaeus*, much of the engraving's fascination lies in how it depicts muscles of the male body reacting under tension.

PAINTING

Italian patrons commissioned murals and large altarpieces for their local churches and smaller panel paintings for their houses and private chapels. Artists experienced in fresco were in great demand and traveled widely to execute wall and ceiling decorations. At first the Italians showed little interest in oil painting, for the most part using tempera even for their largest works. But, in the last decades of the century, oil painting became popular in Venice.

MASACCIO.   Even though his brief career lasted less than a decade, Tommaso di Ser Giovanni di Mone Cassai (1401–1428/ 1429?), nicknamed "Masaccio" (meaning "Big Tom"), established a new direction in Florentine painting, much as Giotto had a

century earlier. He did this by integrating monumental and consistently scaled figures into rational architectural and natural settings using linear perspective. The chronology of Massaccio's works is uncertain, but his fresco of the **TRINITY** in the church of Santa Maria Novella in Florence must have been painted around 1426, the date on the Lenzi family tombstone that once stood in front of it **(FIGS. 19–16, 19–17)**.

Masaccio's fresco was meant to give the illusion of a stone funerary monument and altar table set below a deep **aedicula** (framed niche) in the wall. The effect of looking up into a barrel-vaulted niche was made plausible through precisely rendered linear perspective. The eye level of an adult viewer standing within the church determined the horizon line on which the vanishing point was centered, just below the kneeling figures above the altar. And the painting demonstrates not only Masaccio's intimate knowledge of Brunelleschi's perspective experiments (see "Renaissance Perspective," opposite), but also his architectural style (SEE FIG. 19–4). The painted architecture is an unusual combination of Classical orders. On the wall surface, Corinthian pilasters support a plain architrave below a cornice, while inside the niche Renaissance variations on Ionic columns support arches on all four sides. The "source" of the consistent illumination of the architecture lies in front of the picture, casting reflections on the coffers, or sunken panels, of the ceiling.

The figures are organized in a measured progression through space. At the near end of the recessed, barrel-vaulted space is the Trinity—Jesus on the cross, the dove of the Holy Spirit poised in downward flight above his tilted halo, and God the Father, who stands behind to support the cross from his elevated perch on a high platform, apparently supported on the rear columns. As in many scenes of the Crucifixion, Jesus is flanked by the Virgin Mary and John the Evangelist, who contemplate the scene on either side of the cross. Mary gazes calmly out at us, her raised hand drawing our attention to the Trinity. Members of the Lenzi family kneel in front of the pilasters—thus closer to us than the Crucifixion; the red robes of the male donor signify that he was a member of the governing council of Florence. Below these donors, in an open sarcophagus, is a skeleton, a grim reminder of the Christian belief that since death awaits us all, our only hope is redemption and the promise of life in the hereafter, rooted in Christ's sacrifice on the cross. The inscription above the skeleton reads: "I was once that which you are, and what I am you also will be."

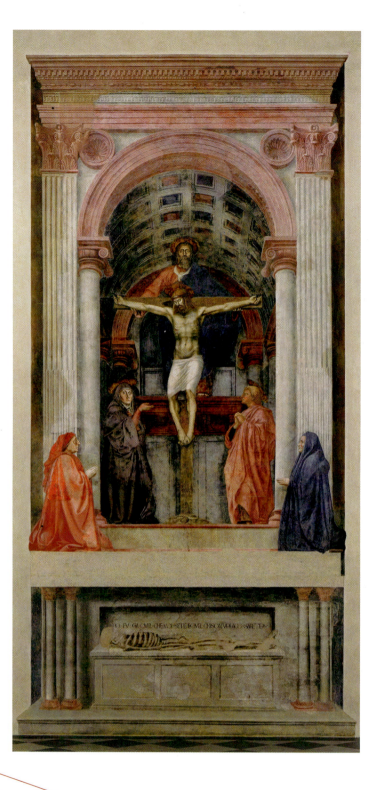

19–16 • Masaccio TRINITY WITH THE VIRGIN, ST. JOHN THE EVANGELIST, AND DONORS
Church of Santa Maria Novella, Florence. c. 1425–1427/1428. Fresco, 21′ × 10′5″ (6.4 × 3.2 m).

19–17 • SECTION DIAGRAM OF THE ILLUSIONISTIC SPATIAL WORLD PORTRAYED IN MASACCIO'S TRINITY
After Gene Brucker, *Florence: The Golden Age*, Berkeley, 1998.

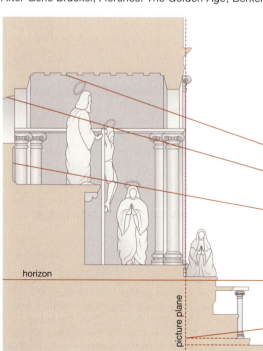

horizon

picture plane

viewing point

THE BRANCACCI CHAPEL. Masaccio's brief career culminated in the frescos he painted on the walls of the Brancacci Chapel in the church of Santa Maria del Carmine in Florence. Reproduced here are two of the best-known scenes: **THE EXPULSION OF ADAM AND EVE FROM PARADISE** (FIG. 19–18) and **THE TRIBUTE MONEY** (FIG. 19–19). In *The Expulsion*, he presented Adam and Eve as monumental nude figures, combining his studies of the human figure with an intimate knowledge of ancient Roman sculpture. In contrast to Flemish painters, who sought to record every visible detail of a figure's surface (compare Adam and Eve from the Ghent Altarpiece, page 577, FIG. B), Masaccio focused on the mass of bodies formed by the underlying bone and muscle structure, and a single light source emphasizes their tangibility with modeled forms and cast shadows. Departing from earlier interpretations of the event that emphasized wrongdoing and the fall from grace, Masaccio concerns himself with the psychological impact of shame on these first humans, who have been cast out of paradise mourning and protesting, thrown naked into the world.

In *The Tribute Money* (SEE FIG. 19–19), Masaccio portrays an incident from the life of Jesus that highlights St. Peter (Matthew 17: 24–27), to whom this chapel was dedicated. In the central scene a tax collector (dressed in a short red tunic and seen from behind) asks Peter (in the left foreground with the short gray beard) if Jesus pays the Jewish temple tax (the "tribute money" of the title). Set against the stable backdrop of a semicircular block of apostolic observers, a masterful series of dynamic diagonals in the postures and gestures of the three main figures interlocks them in a compositional system that imbues their interaction with a sense of tension calling out for resolution. Jesus instructs Peter to "go to the sea, drop in a hook, and take the first fish that comes up," which Peter does at the far left. In the fish's mouth is a coin worth twice the tax demanded, which Peter gives to the tax collector at the far right. The tribute story was especially significant for Florentines because in 1427, to raise money for defense against military aggression, the city enacted a graduated tax, based on the value of people's personal property.

The Tribute Money is particularly remarkable for its early use of both linear and atmospheric perspective to integrate figures, architecture, and landscape into a consistent whole. The group of disciples around Jesus and his disciples forms a clear central focus, from which the landscape seems to recede naturally into the far distance. To foster this illusion, Masaccio used linear perspective in the depiction of the house, and then reinforced it by diminishing the sizes of the barren trees and reducing the size of the crouching Peter at far left. At the central vanishing point established by the orthogonals of the house is the head of Jesus. A second vanishing point determines the position of the steps and stone rail at the right.

The cleaning of the painting in the 1980s revealed that it was painted in 32 *giornate* (a *giornata* is a section of fresh plaster that could be prepared and painted in a single day; see "Buon Fresco," page 537). The cleaning also uncovered Masaccio's subtle use of

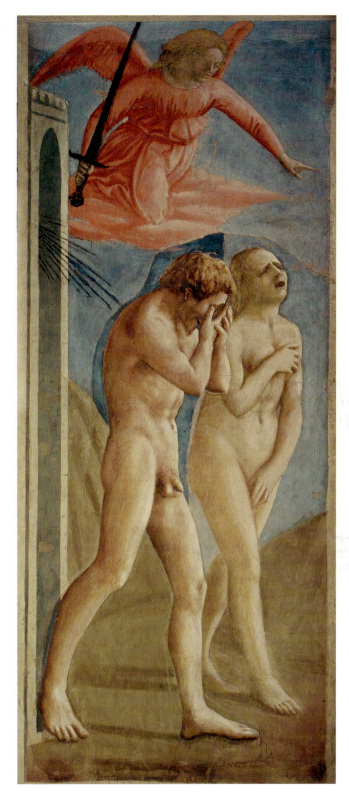

19–18 • Masaccio THE EXPULSION OF ADAM AND EVE FROM PARADISE
Brancacci Chapel, church of Santa Maria del Carmine, Florence. c. 1427. Fresco, 7′ × 2′11″ (214 × 90 cm).

Cleaning and restoration of the Brancacci Chapel paintings revealed the remarkable speed and skill with which Masaccio worked. He painted Adam and Eve in four *giornate* (each *giornata* of fresh plaster representing a day's work). Working from the top down and left to right, he painted the angel on the first day; on the second day, the portal; Adam on the third day; and Eve on the fourth.

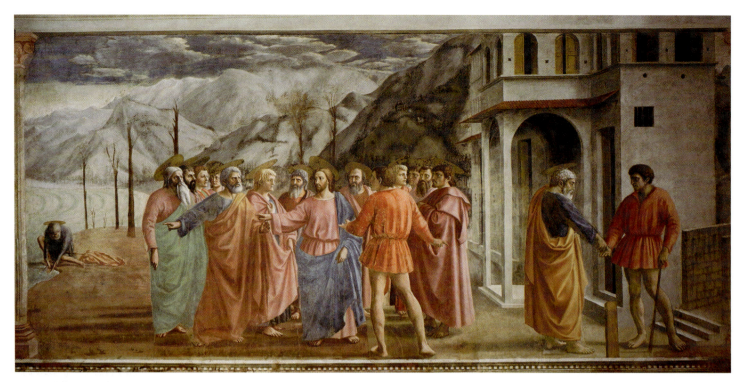

19-19 • Masaccio THE TRIBUTE MONEY
Brancacci Chapel, church of Santa Maria del Carmine, Florence. c. 1427. Fresco, 8'1" × 19'7" (2.46 × 6 m).

color to create atmospheric perspective in the distant landscape, where mountains fade from grayish-green to grayish-white and the houses and trees on their slopes are loosely sketched to simulate the lack of clear definition when viewing things in the distance through a haze. Green leaves were painted on the branches *al secco* (meaning "on the dry plastered wall").

As in *The Expulsion*, Masaccio modeled the foreground figures here with bold highlights and long shadows on the ground toward the left, giving a strong sense of volumetric solidity and implying a light source at the far right, as if the scene were lit by the actual window in the rear wall of the Brancacci Chapel. Not only does the lighting give the forms sculptural definition, but the colors vary in tone according to the strength of the illumination. Masaccio used a wide range of hues—pale pink, mauve, gold, blue-green, seafoam-green, apple-green, peach—and a sophisticated shading technique using contrasting colors, as in Andrew's green robe which is shaded with red instead of darker green. The figures of Jesus and the apostles originally had gold-leaf haloes, several of which have flaked off. Rather than silhouette the heads against consistently flat gold circles in the medieval manner, however, Masaccio conceived of haloes as gold disks hovering in space above each head that moved with the heads as they moved, and he foreshortened them depending on the angle from which each head is seen.

Some stylistic innovations take time to be fully accepted, and Masaccio's innovative depictions of volumetric solidity, consistent lighting, and spatial integration were best appreciated by a later generation of painters. Many important sixteenth-century Italian artists, including Michelangelo, studied and sketched Masaccio's Brancacci Chapel frescos, as they did Giotto's work in the Scrovegni Chapel. In the meantime, painting in Florence after Masaccio's death developed along somewhat different lines.

PAINTING IN FLORENCE AFTER MASACCIO

The tradition of covering walls with paintings in fresco continued uninterrupted through the fifteenth century. Between 1438 and 1445, the decoration of the Dominican monastery of San Marco in Florence, where Fra Angelico lived, was one of the most extensive projects.

FRA ANGELICO. Guido di Piero da Mugello (c. 1395/1400–1455), earned his nickname "Fra Angelico" ("Angelic Brother") through his piety as well as his painting: in 1984, he was beatified, the first step toward sainthood. Fra Angelico is first documented painting in Florence in 1417–1418, and he remained an active painter after taking vows as a Dominican monk in nearby Fiesole between 1418 and 1421.

Between 1438 and 1445, in the monastery of San Marco, Fra Angelico and his assistants—probably working under the patronage of Cosimo de' Medici—created paintings to inspire meditation in each monk's cell (44 in all; SEE FIGS INTRO-7, INTRO-8), in the chapter house (meeting room), and even in the corridors (hallways). At the top of the stairs in the north corridor, where the monks would pass frequently on their way to their individual cells, Fra Angelico painted a serene picture of the **ANNUNCIATION (FIG. 19–20)**. To describe the quiet, measured space where the demure

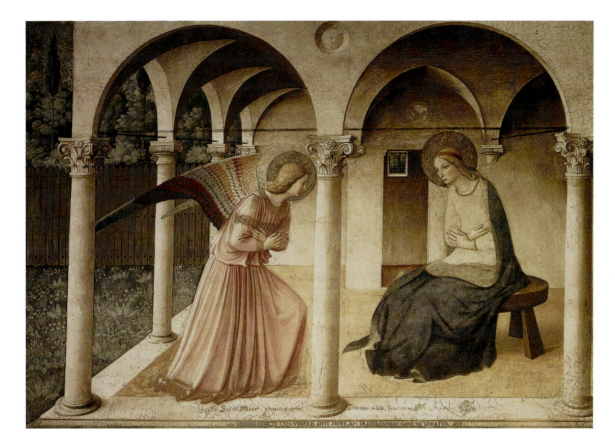

archangel greets the unassuming, youthful Mary, Fra Angelico used linear perspective with unusual skill, extending the monks' stairway and corridor outward into an imagined portico and garden beside the Virgin's home. The slender, graceful figures, wearing quietly flowing draperies, assume modest poses. Natural light falling from the left models their forms gently, casting an almost supernatural radiance over their faces and hands. The scene is a sacred vision rendered in a contemporary setting, welcoming the monks to the most intimate areas of the monastery and preparing them for their private meditations.

UCCELLO. At mid century, when Fra Angelico was still painting his radiant visions of Mary and Jesus in the monastery of San Marco, a new generation of artists began to emerge. Thoroughly conversant with the theories of Brunelleschi and Alberti, they had mastered the techniques (and tricks) of depicting figures in a constructed architectural space. Some artists became specialists, among them Paolo Uccello, who devoted his life to the study of linear perspective (FIG. 19–21; SEE ALSO FIG. 19–1). Vasari

devoted a chapter in his biographies of Italian artists to Uccello, whom he described as a man so obsessed with the science of perspective that he neglected his painting, his family, and even his pet birds (his *uccelli*). According to Vasari, Uccello's wife complained that he sat up drawing all night and when she called to him to come to bed he would say, "Oh, what a sweet thing this perspective is!" (Vasari, trans. Bondanella and Bondanella, p. 83).

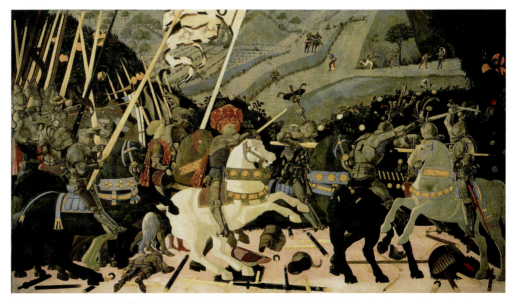

19–21 • Paolo Uccello **THE BATTLE OF SAN ROMANO**
1438–1440. Tempera on wood panel, approx. 6′ × 10′7″ (1.83 × 3.23 m). National Gallery, London.

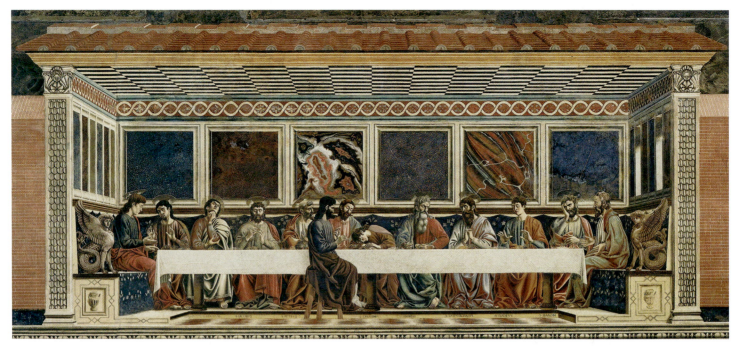

19-22 • Andrea del Castagno THE LAST SUPPER
Refectory, convent of Sant'Apollonia, Florence. 1447. Fresco, width approx. 16 × 32′ (4.6 × 9.8 m).

CASTAGNO. Notable Florentine painter Andrea del Castagno (c. 1417/19–1457) painted a fresco of **THE LAST SUPPER** for a convent of Benedictine nuns in 1447 **(FIG. 19–22)**. The Last Supper was often painted in monastic refectories (dining halls) to remind the monks or nuns of Christ's Last Supper with his first followers and encourage them to see their daily gatherings for meals almost as a sacramental act rooted in this biblical tradition. Here Castagno has not portrayed the scene in the biblical setting of an "upper room." Rather, the humble house of the original account has become a great palace with sumptuous marble revetment. The most brilliantly colored and wildly patterned marble panel frames the heads of Christ and Judas to focus viewers on the most important part of the picture. Judas sits on the viewer's side of the table, separated from the other apostles, and St. John sleeps, head collapsed onto the tabletop. The strong perspective lines of floor tiles, ceiling rafters, and paneled walls draw viewers into the scene, especially the nuns

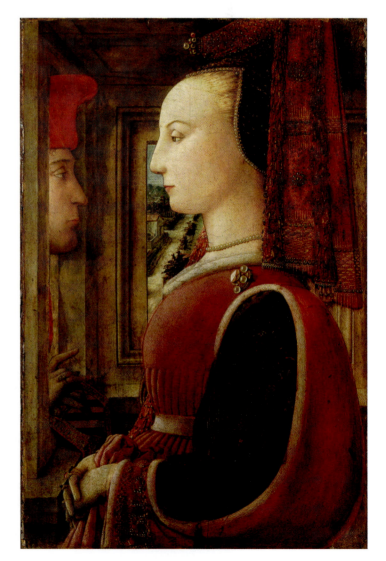

19-23 • Fra Filippo Lippi PORTRAIT OF A WOMAN AND MAN (ANGIOLA DI BERNARDO SAPITI AND LORENZO DI RANIERI SCOLARI?)
c. 1435–1445. Tempera on wood panel, 25¼ × 16½″ (64.1 × 41.9 cm). Metropolitan Museum of Art, New York

Some art historians have seen in the sumptuousness of this woman's costume an indication that she is a newlywed, especially since the pearls sewn with gold threads into the embroidery on her sleeve spell out the word *lealtà*, meaning "loyalty." But since technical evidence shows that the face of the man was added after the portrait of the woman, and since he is unable to meet her gaze, others speculate that this was transformed into a memorial portrait after her death.

who would have seen the painting as an extension of their own dining hall. At first, the lines of the orthogonals seem perfectly logical, but close examination reveals that only the lines of the ceiling converge to a single point, below the hands of St. John. Two windows light the painting's room from the direction of the actual refectory windows, further unifying the two spaces. Castagno worked quickly, completing this huge mural in at most 32 days.

FRA FILIPPO LIPPI. Not all Florentine paintings of the mid fifteenth century were sacred scenes on the walls of religious buildings. It is during this period that portraiture comes into its own as a major artistic form in Italy, and among the most extraordinary—if enigmatic—examples is this **PORTRAIT OF A WOMAN AND MAN** (FIG. 19–23), an early work of Fra Filippo Lippi (c. 1406–1469). This painting is also the earliest surviving double portrait of the Italian Renaissance. Lippi grew up as an orphan in the Carmelite church where Masaccio had painted frescos in the Brancacci Chapel, and art historians have stressed the impact this work had on Lippi's development as an artist. But although he may have absorbed Massacio's predilection for softly rounded forms situated in carefully mapped spaces, in Lippi's hands these artistic tools became the basis for pictures that often ask more questions than they answer, by stressing outline at the same time as form, and by creating complex and often confusing spatial systems.

The emphasis in this double portrait is squarely on the woman. She is spotlighted in the foreground, sharply profiled against a window that serves as an unsettling internal frame, not big enough to contain her. This window opens onto a vista, clearly a fragment of a larger world, but one that highlights an orthogonal to emphasize a spatial recession only partially revealed. The woman blocks most of this vista with her shining visage and sumptuous costume—notably its embroidered velvet, fur lining, and luminous pearls. There is no engagement with the viewer and little sense of likeness. And it is not at all clear where or to what she directs her attention, especially since the gaze of the man in the background does not meet hers. He is even more of a mystery. We see only a masklike sliver of his profile, although the substantiality of his face is reinforced by the strong shadow it casts against the window casement through which he looks. Unlike the woman, who clasps her inert hands in front of her as if to highlight her rings, this man fidgets with his fingers, perhaps to draw our attention to the heraldic device below him that may identify him as a member of the Scolari family. This could be a double portrait of Lorenzo di Ranieri Scolari and Angiola di Bernardo Sapiti, who married in 1436. But what does the painting say about them? Does it commemorate their marriage, celebrate the birth of their child, or memorialize one of their deaths? All have been proposed by art historians as an explanation for this innovative double portrait, but it remains a puzzle to be pondered. Could that pondering be the point of the picture?

ITALIAN ART IN THE SECOND HALF OF THE FIFTEENTH CENTURY

In the second half of the fifteenth century, the ideas and ideals of artists like Brunelleschi, Donatello, and Masaccio began to spread from Florence to the rest of Italy, as artists who had trained or worked in Florence traveled to other cities to work, carrying the style with them. Northern Italy embraced the new Classical ideas swiftly, especially in the ducal courts at Urbino and Mantua. Venice and Rome also emerged as innovative art centers in the last quarter of the century.

URBINO

Under Federico da Montefeltro, Urbino developed into a thriving artistic center. A new palace was under construction, and prominent architects and artists were brought into the court to make the new princely residence a showcase of ducal splendor.

THE PALACE AT URBINO. Construction of the palace had been under way for about 20 years in 1468 when Federico hired Luciano Laurana (c. 1420/1425–1479) to direct the work. Among Laurana's major contributions to the palace were closing the courtyard with a fourth wing and redesigning the courtyard façades (FIG. 19–24). The result is a superbly rational solution to the problems

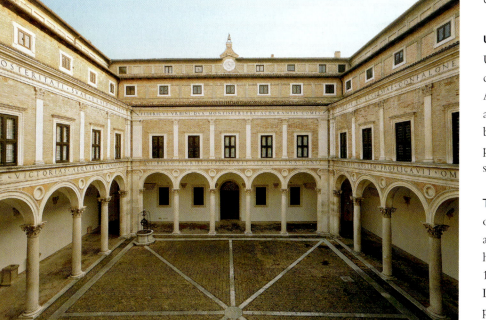

19-24 • Luciano Laurana **COURTYARD, DUCAL PALACE, URBINO**
Courtyard c. 1467–1472; palace begun c. 1450.

The altarpiece Ghirlandaio painted for the Sassetti Chapel portrays the **NATIVITY AND ADORATION OF THE SHEPHERDS (FIG. 19–33)**. It is still in its original frame, still in the place for which it was painted (SEE FIG. 19–32). The influence of Hugo's Portinari Altarpiece (SEE FIG. 18–16), which had been placed on the high altar of the church of Sant'Egidio two years earlier, in 1483, is strong. Ghirlandaio's Christ Child also lies on the ground, adored by the Virgin while rugged shepherds kneel at the right. Ghirlandaio even copies some of Hugo's flowers—although here the iris, a symbol of the Passion, springs not from a vase, but from the earth in the lower right corner. But Ghirlandaio highlights references to Classical Rome. First to catch the eye are the two

Classical pilasters with Corinthian capitals, one of which has the date 1485 on it. The manger is an ancient sarcophagus with an inscription that promises resurrection (as in the fresco directly above the altarpiece where St. Francis is reviving a child); and in the distance a Classical arch inscribed with a reference to the Roman general Pompey the Great frames the road along which the Magi travel. Weighty, restrained actors replace the psychologically intense figures of Hugo's painting. Ghirlandaio joins a clear foreground, middle ground, and background in part by the road and in part by aerial perspective, which creates a seamless transition of color, from the sharp details and primary hues of the Adoration to the soft gray mountains in the distance.

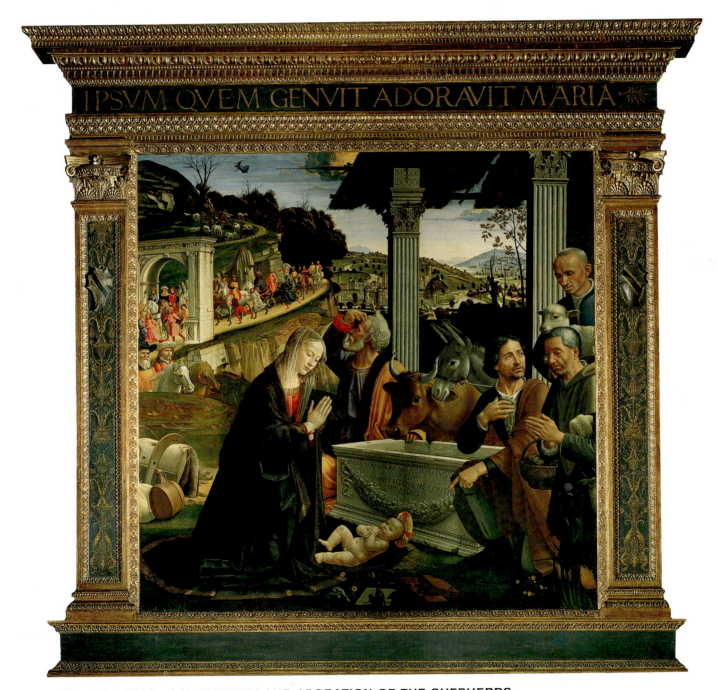

19-33 • Domenico Ghirlandaio NATIVITY AND ADORATION OF THE SHEPHERDS
Altarpiece in the Sassetti Chapel, Santa Trinità, Florence, 1485. Panel, 65¾" square (1.67 m square).

BOTTICELLI. Like most artists in the second half of the fifteenth century, Sandro Botticelli (1445–1510) learned to draw and paint sculptural figures that were modeled by light from a consistent source and placed in a setting rendered illusionistic by linear perspective. An outstanding portraitist, he, like Ghirlandaio, often included recognizable contemporary figures among the saints and angels in religious paintings. He worked in Florence, often for the Medici, then was called to Rome in 1481 by Pope Sixtus IV to help decorate the new Sistine Chapel along with Ghirlandaio, Perugino, and other artists.

Botticelli returned to Florence that same year and entered a new phase of his career. Like other artists working for patrons steeped in Classical scholarship and humanistic thought, he was exposed to philosophical speculations on beauty—as well as to the examples of ancient art in his employers' collections. For the Medici, Botticelli produced secular paintings of mythological subjects inspired by ancient works and by contemporary Neoplatonic thought. Art historian Michael Baxandall has shown that these works were also patterned on the slow movements of fifteenth-century Florentine dance, in which figures acted out their relationships to one another in public performances that would have influenced the thinking and viewing habits of both painters and their audience.

The overall appearance of Botticelli's *Primavera*, or *Spring* (see "A Closer Look," page 626), recalls Flemish tapestries (SEE FIG. 18–7), which were very popular in Italy at the time. And its subject—like the subjects of many tapestries—is a highly complex allegory (a symbolic illustration of a concept or principle), interweaving Neoplatonic ideas with esoteric references to Classical sources. In simple terms, Neoplatonic philosophers and poets conceived Venus, the goddess of love, as having two natures.

The first ruled over earthly, human love and the second over universal, divine love. In this way the philosophers could argue that Venus was a Classical equivalent of the Virgin Mary. *Primavera* was painted at the time of the wedding of Lorenzo di Pierfrancesco de' Medici and Semiramide d'Appiano in 1482. The theme suggests love and fertility in marriage, and the painting can be read as a lyrical wish for a similar fecundity in the union of Lorenzo and Semiramide—a sort of highly refined fertility dance.

Several years later, some of the same mythological figures reappeared in Botticelli's **BIRTH OF VENUS** (FIG. 19–34), in which the central image represents the Neoplatonic idea of divine love in the form of a nude Venus based on an antique statue type known as the "modest Venus" that ultimately derives from Praxiteles' *Aphrodite of Knidos* (SEE FIG. 5–45). Botticelli's Classical goddess of love and beauty, born of sea foam, averts her eyes from our gaze as she floats ashore on a scallop shell, gracefully arranging her hands and hair to hide—but actually drawing attention to—her sexuality. Indeed, she is an arrestingly alluring figure, with voluminous hair highlighted with gold. Blown by the wind—Zephyr (with his love, the nymph Chloris)—Venus arrives at her earthly home. She is welcomed by a devotee who offers Venus a garment embroidered with flowers. The circumstances of this commission are uncertain. It is painted on canvas, which suggests that it may have been a banner or a painted tapestrylike wall hanging.

Botticelli's later career was affected by a profound spiritual crisis. While the artist was creating his mythologies for the Medici, a Dominican monk, Fra Girolamo Savonarola (active in Florence 1490–1498), had begun to preach impassioned sermons denouncing the worldliness of Florence. Many Florentines reacted with orgies of self-recrimination, and processions of weeping penitents wound through the streets. Botticelli, too, fell into a state of religious fervor.

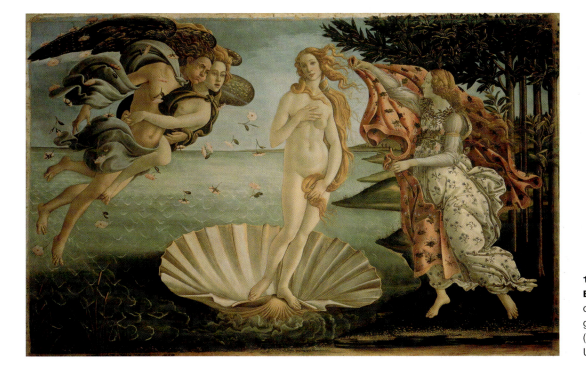

19–34 • Sandro Botticelli
BIRTH OF VENUS
c. 1484–1486. Tempera and gold on canvas, 5′8⅞″ × 9′1⅞″ (1.8 × 2.8 m). Galleria degli Uffizi, Florence.

Primavera ▸ by Sandro Botticelli, c. 1482. Tempera on wood panel. 6′8″ × 10′4″ (2.03 × 3.15 m). Galleria degli Uffizi, Florence.

Mercury, the sign for the month of May, disperses the winter clouds with his caduceus. This staff wound with serpents became a symbol for the medical profession. The name Medici means "doctors."

Venus, clothed in contemporary costume and crowned with a marriage wreath, appears in her role as the goddess of wedded love. The presence of both Venus and Mercury may be an astrological reference; prominent Neoplatonist Marsilio Ficino told Lorenzo de Pierfrancesco de' Medici that these planets were aligned in his horoscope.

The setting of the painting is a grove of orange trees. These hold a double meaning—both suggestive of Venus's Garden of the Hesperides, with its golden fruit, and perhaps an allusion to the Medici, whose coat of arms featured golden orbs.

This three-figure grouping tells a story. Zephyrus, the west wind, is accosting the virgin nymph Chloris, identifiable from the roses pouring out of her mouth. Once Zephyrus makes her his bride, Chloris is transformed into the goddess Flora, the elaborately dressed personification of spring at the front of the group.

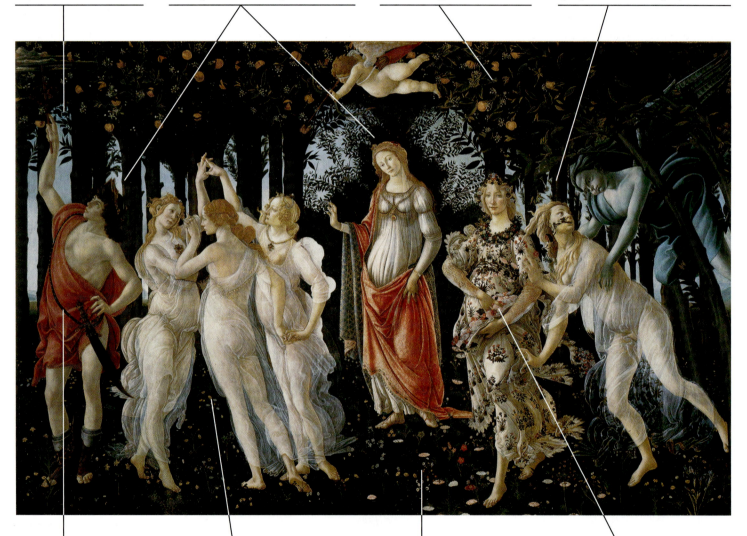

These gold flames are also an attribute of St. Lawrence, the namesake of Lorenzo di Pierfrancesco de' Medici, for whom this painting was made. The laurel tree (laurus in Latin) behind Zephyrus also alludes to Lorenzo's name.

The Three Graces symbolize ideal female virtues—Chastity, Beauty, Love. Venus' son Cupid—the embodiment of romantic desire—playfully aims his arrow at them.

So accurate is their representation, 138 of the 190 flowering plants depicted in the painting have been identified. Almost all grow in the neighborhood of Florence between the months of March and April, and most carry symbolic associations with love and marriage.

Flora scatters flowers held in a fold of her dress at the level of her womb, equating the fecundity brought about by changing seasons with female procreative fertility.

SEE MORE: View the Closer Look feature for *Primavera* **www.myartslab.com**

In a dramatic gesture of repentance, he burned many of his earlier paintings and began to produce highly emotional pictures pervaded by an intense religiosity.

VENICE

In the last quarter of the fifteenth century, Venice emerged as a major Renaissance art center. Ruled as an oligarchy (government by a select few) with an elected duke (*doge* in the Venetian dialect), the city government was founded at the end of the Roman Empire and survived until the Napoleonic era. In building their city, the Venetians had turned marshes into a commercial seaport, and they saw the sea as a resource, not a threat. They depended on naval power and on the natural defense of their lagoons rather than city walls. Venice turned toward the east, especially after the crusaders' conquest of 1204, designing the church of St. Mark as a great Byzantine building sheathed in mosaics (SEE FIG. 7–36). Venice excelled in the arts of textiles, gold and enamel, glass and mosaic, and fine printing as well as bookbinding.

VENETIAN PALACES.   Venice was a city of waterways with few large public spaces. Even palaces had only small interior courtyards and tiny gardens, and were separated by narrow alleys. Their façades overlooked the canals, whose waters gave protection and permitted the owners to project on these major thoroughfares the large portals, windows, and loggias that proclaimed their importance through the lavishness of their residences—a sharp contrast to the fortresslike character of most Florentine town houses (SEE FIG. 19–5). But, as with the Florentine great houses, Venician owners combined in these structures a place of business with a dwelling.

The Ca d'Oro (House of Gold), home of the wealthy nobleman Marino Contarini, has a splendid front with three super-imposed loggias facing the Grand Canal (FIG. 19–35). The house was constructed between 1421 and 1437, and its asymmetrical elevation is based on a traditional Byzantine plan. A wide central hall ran from front to back all the way through the building to a small inner courtyard with a well and garden. An outside stair led to the main floor on the second level. The entrance on the canal permitted goods to be delivered directly into the warehouse that constituted the ground floor. The principal floor, on the second level, had a salon and reception room opening on the richly decorated loggia. It was filled with light from large windows, and more light reflected off the polished terrazzo floor. Private family rooms filled the upper stories. Contarini's instructions to his contractors and workers specified that the façade was to be painted with white enamel and ultramarine blue and that the red stones in the patterned wall should be oiled to make them even brighter. Details of carving, such as coats of arms and balls on the crest at the roofline, were to be gilded. Beautiful as the palace is today, in the fifteenth and sixteenth centuries it must have been truly spectacular.

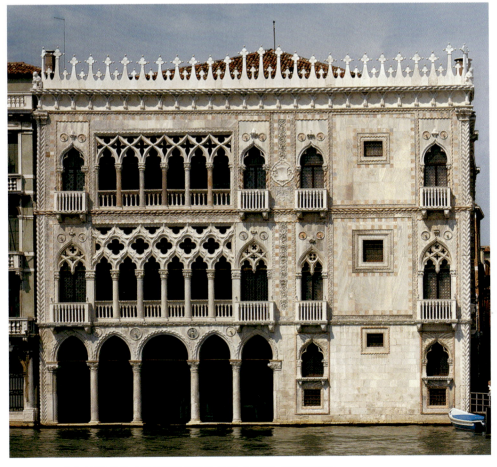

19-35 • CA D'ORO (CONTARINI PALACE), VENICE
1421–1437.

SEE MORE: Click the Google Earth link for the Ca d'Oro www.myartslab.com

THE BELLINI BROTHERS.   The domes of the church of St. Mark dominated the city center, and the rich colors of its glowing mosaics captured painters' imaginations. Perhaps it was their love of color that encouraged the Venetian painters to embrace the oil medium for both panel and canvas painting.

The most important Venetian artists of this period were two brothers: Gentile (c. 1429–1507) and Giovanni (c. 1430–1516) Bellini, whose father, Jacopo (c. 1400–1470), had also been a central figure in Venetian art. Andrea Mantegna was also part of this circle, for he had married Jacopo's daughter in 1453.

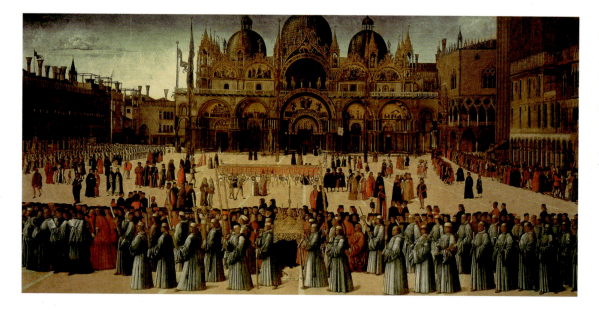

19–36 • Gentile Bellini
PROCESSION OF THE RELIC OF THE TRUE CROSS BEFORE THE CHURCH OF ST. MARK
1496. Oil on canvas, 12′ × 24′5″ (3.67 × 7.45 m). Galleria dell'Accademia, Venice.

Gentile Bellini celebrated the daily life of the city in large, lively narratives, such as the **PROCESSION OF THE RELIC OF THE TRUE CROSS BEFORE THE CHURCH OF ST. MARK** (FIG. 19–36). Every year on the feast of St. Mark (April 25), the Confraternity of St. John the Evangelist carried the miracle-working relic of the true cross in a procession through the square in front of the church. Bellini's painting of 1496 depicts an event that had occurred in 1444: the miraculous recovery of a sick child whose father (the man in red kneeling to the right of the relic) prayed for help as the relic passed by. Gentile has rendered the cityscape with great attention to detail. The mosaic-encrusted Byzantine Cathedral of St. Mark (SEE FIG. 7–36) forms a backdrop for the procession, and the doge's palace and base of the bell tower can be seen at the right. The gold reliquary is carried under a canopy, surrounded by marchers with giant candles, led by a choir and followed at the far right by the doge and other officials. Gentile's procession serves as a reminder that fifteenth-century piazzas and buildings were sites of ritual ceremony, and it was in moments such as this that they were brought to life.

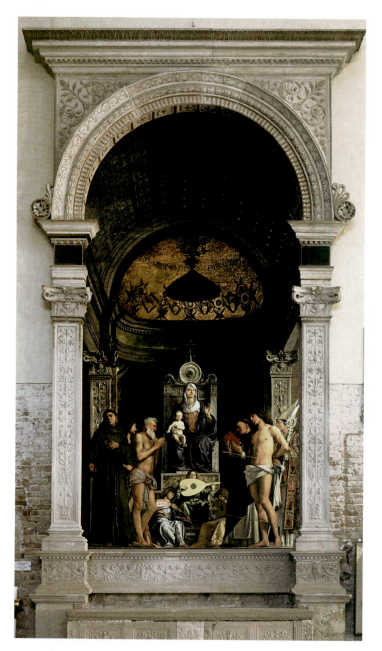

19–37 • Giovanni Bellini VIRGIN AND CHILD ENTHRONED WITH SS. FRANCIS, JOHN THE BAPTIST, JOB, DOMINIC, SEBASTIAN, AND LOUIS OF TOULOUSE
(Computer reconstruction). Originally commissioned for the chapel of the Hospital of San Giobbe, Venice. c. 1478. Oil on wood panel, 15′4″ × 8′4″ (4.67 × 2.54 m). Galleria dell'Accademia, Venice. The original frame is in the chapel of the Hospital of San Giobbe, Venice.

Art historians have given the special name *sacra conversazione* ("holy conversation") to this type of composition that shows saints, angels, and sometimes even the painting's donors in the same pictorial space with the enthroned Virgin and Child. Despite the name, no "conversation" or spoken interaction takes place in a literal sense. Instead, the individuals portrayed are joined in a mystical and eternal communion that occurs outside human time and space.

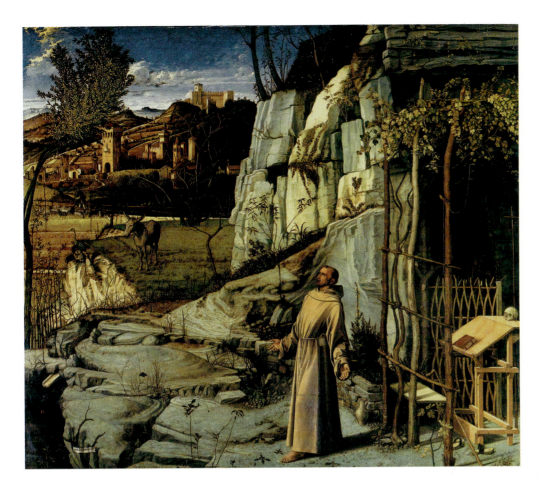

19–38 • Giovanni Bellini
ST. FRANCIS IN ECSTASY
c. 1470s. Oil and tempera on wood
panel, 49 × 55⅞" (125 × 142 cm).
The Frick Collection, New York.

sylvan delight. Like most of the fifteenth-century religious art we have seen, however, Bellini presents viewers with a natural world saturated in symbolism. Here a relationship between St. Francis and Moses is outlined. The tree symbolizes the burning bush; the stream, the miraculous spring brought forth by Moses. The crane and donkey represent the monastic virtue of patience. The detailed description, luminous palette, and symbolic surroundings suggest Flemish art, but the golden light suffusing the painting is unmistakably Venetian.

Gentile's brother Giovanni amazed and attracted patrons with his artistic virtuosity for almost 60 years. The **VIRGIN AND CHILD ENTHRONED WITH SS. FRANCIS, JOHN THE BAPTIST, JOB, DOMINIC, SEBASTIAN, AND LOUIS OF TOULOUSE** (FIG. 19–37), painted about 1478 for the chapel of the Hospital of San Giobbe (St. Job), exhibits a dramatic perspectival view up into a tunnel vault that leads to an apse. Giovanni may have known his brother-in-law Mantegna's early experiments in radical foreshortening and in the use of a low vanishing point. Here Giovanni positions the vanishing point for the rapidly converging lines of the architecture at bottom center, on the feet of the lute-playing angel. His figures stand in a Classical architectural interior with a coffered barrel vault reminiscent of Masaccio's *Trinity* (SEE FIG. 19–16). The gold mosaic, with its identifying inscription and stylized seraphim (angels of the highest rank), recalls Byzantine art and the long tradition of Byzantine-inspired painting and mosaics produced in Venice.

Giovanni Bellini's early painting of **ST. FRANCIS IN ECSTASY** (FIG. 19–38), painted in the 1470s, recalls Flemish painting in the fine detail with which he rendered the natural world. The saint stands bathed in early morning sunlight, his outspread hands showing his stigmata. Francis had moved to a cave in the barren wilderness in his search for communion with God, but in the world Giovanni creates for him, the fields blossom and flocks of animals graze. The grape arbor over his desk adds to the atmosphere of

THINK ABOUT IT

19.1 Discuss Masaccio's use of linear perspective in either *The Tribute Money* or *Trinity with the Virgin, St. John the Evangelist, and Donors*. How does he use this technique? Illustrate your points with a comparative reference to a work discussed earlier in this chapter or in a previous chapter.

19.2 Explain how one Florentine sculptor discussed in this chapter helped establish the increasing naturalism and growing emulation of Classical models that would be central to the early Italian Renaissance.

19.3 Choose a wealthy merchant or *condottiere* and discuss how his patronage fostered the emergence of the Renaissance in fifteenth-century Italy. Make reference to specific works in forming your answer.

19.4 Discuss the 1401 competition to choose an artist to create the bronze doors of the Florence Baptistery. How did the competition affect the careers of the two finalists, Ghiberti and Brunelleschi?

19.5 Discuss the role of the Classical past in Brunelleschi's architecture, focusing on one of the buildings he designed in Florence.

PRACTICE MORE: Compose answers to these questions, get flashcards for images and terms, and review chapter material with quizzes **www.myartslab.com**

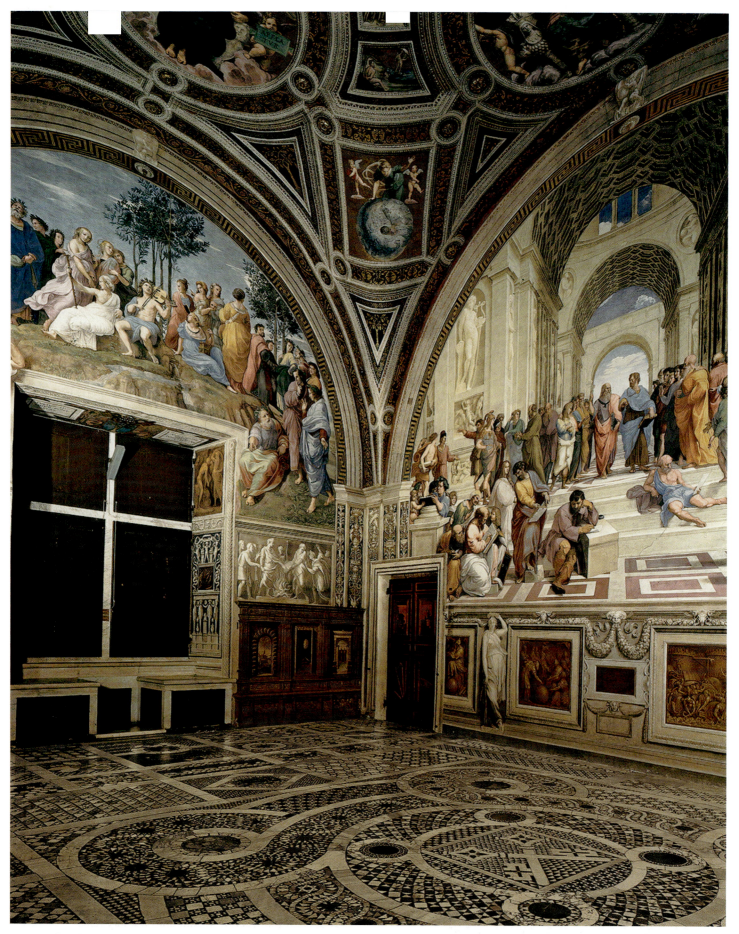

20-1 • Raphael STANZA DELLA SEGNATURA Vatican, Rome. Fresco in the left lunette, *Parnassus*; in the right lunette, *The School of Athens*. 1510–1511.

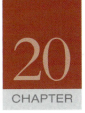

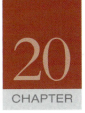

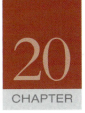

SIXTEENTH-CENTURY ART IN ITALY

Two young artists—Raphael and Michelangelo—although rivals in almost every sense, were linked in service to Pope Julius II (pontificate 1503–1513) in the early years of the sixteenth century. Raphael was painting the pope's private library (1509–1511) while, nearby, Michelangelo painted the ceiling of his Sistine Chapel (1508–1512). The pope demanded an art that reflected his imperial vision of a new, worldwide Church based on humanistic ideas, which he would lead as a new St. Peter, founding a second great age of papal dominion. In fulfilling this proud demand, Raphael and Michelangelo united Renaissance principles of harmony and balance with a new monumentality based on Classical ideals, and they knit these elements into a dynamic and synthetic whole, rich in color and controlled by cohesive design. Working alongside the architect Donato Bramante and the multifaceted genius Leonardo da Vinci, they created a style we call the High Renaissance.

Julius II intended the **STANZA DELLA SEGNATURA**, or Room of the Signature, to be his personal study (**FIG. 20–1**). Raphael sought to create an ideal setting for papal activities, with murals proclaiming that all human knowledge exists under the power of divine wisdom. He organized the mural program itself like a library, separated into divisions of theology, philosophy, the arts, and justice. He created pictorial allegories to illustrate each theme. On one wall, churchmen discussing the sacraments represent theology, while across the room ancient philosophers led by Plato and Aristotle debate in the School of Athens. Plato holds his book *Timaeus*, in which creation is seen in terms of geometry, and in which humanity encompasses and explains the universe. Aristotle holds his *Nicomachean Ethics*, a decidedly human-centered book concerned with relations among people. Ancient representatives of the academic curriculum—Grammar, Rhetoric, Dialectic, Arithmetic, Music, Geometry, and Astronomy—surround them. On a window wall, Justice, holding a sword and scales, assigns each his due. Across the room, Poetry and the Arts are represented by Apollo and the Muses, and the poet Sappho reclines against the fictive frame of an actual window. Raphael included his own portrait among the onlookers on the extreme lower right in the *School of Athens* fresco and signed the painting with his initials—a signal that both artists and patrons were becoming increasingly aware of their individual significance.

Raphael achieved a lofty style in keeping with papal ambition—using ideals of Classical grandeur, professing faith in human rationality and perfectibility, and celebrating the power of the pope as God's earthly administrator. But when Raphael died at age 37 on April 6, 1520, the grand moment was already passing: Luther and the Protestant Reformation were challenging papal authority, and the world would never be the same again.

LEARN ABOUT IT

20.1 Trace the shift in the artistic center of Italy from Florence to Rome, and recognize the efforts of Pope Julius II to create a new "golden age."

20.2 Understand the Vatican as a site for the creative energies of the most important artists of the Italian Renaissance.

20.3 Explore the intentional subversion of Classical style and decorum in the work of Mannerist artists.

20.4 Compare and contrast the emphasis on drawing and clearly structured compositions in the work of Roman and Florentine painters with the expressive potential of color that characterizes the work of their Venetian counterparts.

20.5 Examine the architectural creativity lavished on the design of both grand churches and pleasurable retreats for the wealthy in sixteenth-century Italy.

HEAR MORE: Listen to an audio file of your chapter **www.myartslab.com**

EUROPE IN THE SIXTEENTH CENTURY

The sixteenth century was an age of social, intellectual, and religious ferment that transformed European culture. It was marked by continual warfare triggered by the expansionist ambitions of warring rulers. The humanism of the fourteenth and fifteenth centuries, with its medieval roots and its often uncritical acceptance of the authority of Classical texts, slowly developed into a critical exploration of new ideas, the natural world, and distant lands. Cartographers began to acknowledge the Earth's curvature and the degrees of distance, giving Europeans a more accurate understanding of their place within the world. The printing press sparked an explosion in book production, spreading new ideas through the translation and publication of ancient and contemporary texts, broadening the horizons of educated Europeans and encouraging the development of literacy. Since travel was growing more common, artists and their work became mobile, and the world of art was transformed into a more international community.

At the start of the sixteenth century, England, France, and Portugal were nation-states under strong monarchs. German-speaking central Europe was divided into dozens of principalities, counties, free cities, and small territories. But even states as powerful as Saxony and Bavaria acknowledged the supremacy of the Habsburg Holy Roman Empire—in theory the greatest power in Europe. Charles V, elected emperor in 1519, also inherited Spain, the Netherlands, and vast territories in the Americas. Italy, which was divided into numerous small states, was a diplomatic and military battlefield where, for much of the century, the Italian city-states, Habsburg Spain, France, and the papacy fought each other in shifting alliances. Popes behaved like secular princes, using diplomacy and military force to regain control over central Italy and in some cases to establish family members as hereditary rulers.

The popes' incessant demands for money, to finance the rebuilding of St. Peter's as well as their self-aggrandizing art projects and luxurious lifestyles, aggravated the religious dissent that had long been developing, especially north of the Alps. Early in the century, religious reformers within the established Church challenged beliefs and practices, especially Julius II's sale of indulgences promising forgiveness of sins and assurance of salvation in exchange for a financial contribution to the Church. Because they protested, these northern European reformers came to be called Protestants; their demand for reform gave rise to a movement called the Reformation.

The political maneuvering of Pope Clement VII (pontificate 1523–1534) led to a direct clash with Holy Roman Emperor Charles V. In May 1527, Charles's German mercenary troops attacked Rome, beginning a six-month orgy of killing, looting, and burning. The Sack of Rome, as it is called, shook the sense of stability and humanistic confidence that until then had characterized the Renaissance, and it sent many artists fleeing from the ruined city. Nevertheless, Charles saw himself as the leader of the Catholic forces—and he was the sole Catholic ally Clement had at the time. In 1530, Clement VII crowned Charles emperor in Bologna.

Sixteenth-century patrons valued artists highly and rewarded them well, not only with generous commissions but sometimes even with high social status. Charles V, for example, knighted the painter Titian. Some painters and sculptors became entrepreneurs and celebrities, selling prints of their works on the side and creating international reputations for themselves. Many artists recorded their activities—professional and private—in diaries, notebooks, and letters that have come down to us. In addition, contemporary writers began to report on the lives of artists, documenting their physical appearance and assessing their individual reputations. In 1550, Giorgio Vasari wrote the first survey of Italian art history—*Lives of the Best Architects, Painters, and Sculptors*—organized as a series of critical biographies but at its core a work of critical judgment. Vasari also commented on the role of patrons, and argued that art had become more realistic and more beautiful over time, reaching its apex of perfection in his own age. From his characterization developed our notion of this period as the High Renaissance—that is, as a high point in art since the early experiments of Cimabue and Giotto, marked by a balanced synthesis of Classical ideals and a lifelike rendering of the natural world.

During this period, the fifteenth-century humanists' notion of painting, sculpture, and architecture not as manual arts but as liberal (intellectual) arts, requiring education in the Classics and mathematics as well as in the techniques of the craft, became a topic of intense interest. And from these discussions arose the Renaissance formulation—still with us today—of artists as divinely inspired creative geniuses, a step above most of us in their gifts of hand and mind. This idea weaves its way through Vasari's work like an organizing principle. And this newly elevated status to which artists aspired favored men. Although few artists of either sex had access to the humanist education required by the sophisticated, often esoteric, subject matter used in paintings (usually devised by someone other than the artist), women were denied even the studio practice necessary to draw lifelike nude figures in foreshortened poses. Furthermore, it was almost impossible for an artist to achieve international status without traveling extensively and frequently relocating to follow commissions—something most women could not do. Still, some European women managed to follow their gifts and establish careers as artists during this period despite the obstacles that blocked their entrance into the profession.

ITALY IN THE EARLY SIXTEENTH CENTURY: THE HIGH RENAISSANCE

Italian art from the 1490s to about the time of the Sack of Rome in 1527 has been called the "High Renaissance." As we have already seen with the "High Classical" period in ancient Athens, the term "High Renaissance" encapsulates an art-historical

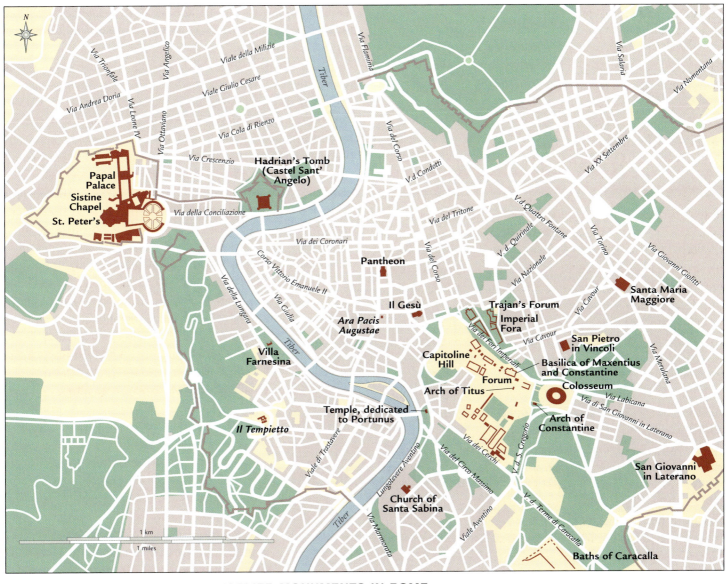

MAP 20-1 • RENAISSANCE AND EARLIER MONUMENTS IN ROME

In addition to situating the principal works of the Roman Renaissance that emerged from Julius II's campaign to revitalize the papal city, this map also locates the surviving works of Roman antiquity that would have been available to the Renaissance artists and architects who masterminded the Classical revival.

judgment, claiming that what happened in Rome at this time represents a pinnacle of achievement within a longer artistic movement, and that it set standards for the future (MAP 20–1). High Renaissance art is characterized by a sense of gravity and decorum, a complex but ordered relationship of individual parts to the whole, and an emulation of the principles artists saw in ancient Classical art. Art historian Sydney Freedberg has stressed the way High Renaissance art fuses the real and the ideal, characterizing Leonardo's *Mona Lisa*, for example, as "a rare perfection between art and reality; an image in which a breathing instant and a composure for all time are held in suspension" (Freedberg, p. 28).

Two important practical developments at the turn of the sixteenth century affected the arts in Italy. Technically, the use of tempera gave way to the more flexible oil painting medium; and economically, commissions from private sources increased so that

artists no longer depended so exclusively on the patronage of the Church, the court, or civic associations.

THREE GREAT ARTISTS OF THE EARLY SIXTEENTH CENTURY

Florence's renowned artistic tradition attracted a stream of young artists to that city, traveling there to study Masaccio's solid, monumental figures, with their eloquent facial features, poses, and gestures, in the Brancacci Chapel paintings. The young Michelangelo's sketches of the chapel frescos document the importance of Masaccio to his developing style. In fact, Michelangelo, Leonardo, and Raphael—the three leading artists of the High Renaissance—all began their careers in Florence, although they soon moved to other centers of patronage and their influence spread well beyond that city, even beyond Italy.

LEONARDO DA VINCI. Leonardo da Vinci (1452–1519) was 12 or 13 when his family moved to Florence from the Tuscan village of Vinci. After an apprenticeship in the shop of the Florentine painter and sculptor Verrocchio, and a few years on his own, Leonardo traveled to Milan in 1481 or 1482 to work for the ruling Sforza family.

Leonardo spent much of his time in Milan on military and civil engineering projects, including both urban-renewal and fortification plans for the city, but he also created a few key monuments of Renaissance painting. In April 1483, Leonardo contracted with the Confraternity of the Immaculate Conception to paint an altarpiece for their chapel in the church of San Francesco Grande in Milan, a painting now known as *The Virgin of the Rocks* (FIG. 20–2). The contract stipulates a painting of the Virgin and Child with angels, but Leonardo added a figure of the young John the Baptist, who balances the composition at the left, pulled into dialogue with his younger cousin Jesus by the long, protective arm of the Virgin. She draws attention to her child by extending her other hand over his head, while the enigmatic figure of the angel—who looks out without actually making eye contact with the viewer—points to the center of interaction. The stable, balanced, pyramidal figural group—a compositional formula that will become a standard feature of High Renaissance Classicism—is set against an exquisitely detailed landscape that dissolves mysteriously into the misty distance.

To assure their dominance in the picture, Leonardo picks out the four figures with spotlights, creating a strong **chiaroscuro** (from the Italian words *chiaro*, meaning "light," and *oscuro*, meaning "dark") that enhances their modeling as three-dimensional forms. This painting is an excellent early example of a specific variant of this technique, called **sfumato** ("smoky"), in which there are subtle, almost imperceptible, transitions between light and dark in shading, as if the picture were seen through smoke or fog. *Sfumato* becomes a hallmark of Leonardo's style, and the effect is artificially enhanced in this painting by the yellowing of its thick varnish, which masks the original vibrancy of its color.

At Duke Ludovico Sforza's request, Leonardo painted THE LAST SUPPER (FIGS. 20–3, 20–4) in the refectory, or dining hall, of the monastery of Santa Maria delle Grazie in Milan between 1495 and 1498. In fictive space defined by a coffered ceiling and four pairs of tapestries that seem to extend the refectory itself into another room, Jesus and his disciples are seated at a long table placed parallel to the picture plane and to the monastic diners who would have been seated in the hall below. In a sense, Jesus' meal with his disciples prefigures the daily gathering of this local monastic community at mealtimes. The stagelike space recedes from the table to three windows on the back wall, where the vanishing point of the one-point linear perspective lies behind Jesus' head. A stable, pyramidal Jesus at the center is

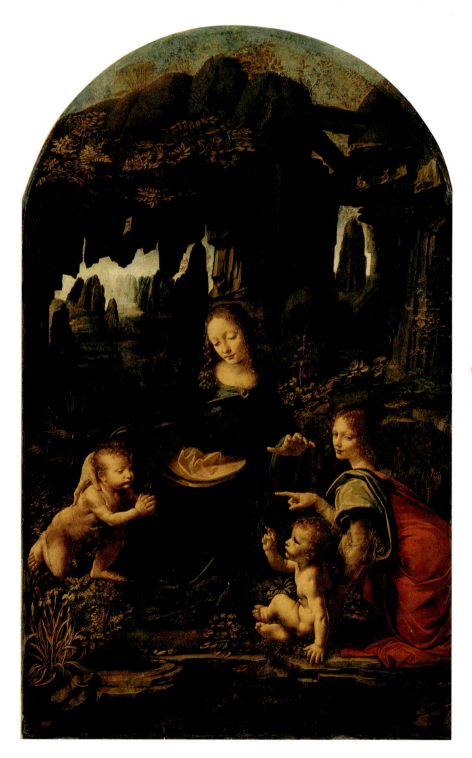

20-2 • Leonardo da Vinci THE VIRGIN OF THE ROCKS
c. 1485. Oil on wood panel (now transferred to canvas), 6′6″ × 4′ (1.9 × 1.2 m). Musée du Louvre, Paris.

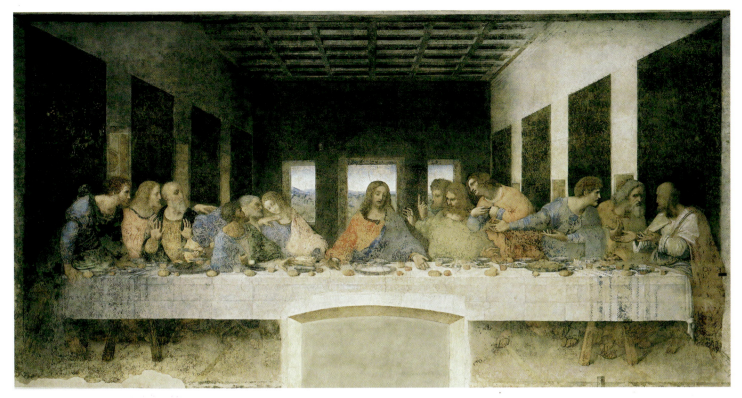

20-3 • Leonardo da Vinci THE LAST SUPPER
Refectory of the monastery of Santa Maria delle Grazie, Milan, Italy. 1495–1498. Tempera and oil on plaster, 15′2″ × 28′10″ (4.6 × 8.8 m).

SEE MORE: View a video about Leonardo da Vinci's *The Last Supper* www.myartslab.com

20-4 • REFECTORY OF THE MONASTERY OF SANTA MARIA DELLE GRAZIE, SHOWING LEONARDO'S LAST SUPPER
Milan, Italy.

Instead of painting in fresco, Leonardo devised an experimental technique for this mural. Hoping to achieve the freedom and flexibility of painting on wood panel, he worked directly on dry *intonaco*— a thin layer of smooth plaster—with an oil-and-tempera paint for which the formula is unknown. The result was disastrous. Within a short time, the painting began to deteriorate, and by the middle of the sixteenth century its figures could be seen only with difficulty. In the seventeenth century, the monks saw no harm in cutting a doorway through the lower center of the composition. The work has barely survived the intervening period, despite many attempts to halt its deterioration and restore its original appearance. The painting narrowly escaped complete destruction in World War II, when the refectory was bombed to rubble. The coats of arms at the top are those of patron Ludovico Sforza, the duke of Milan (r. 1494–1499), and his wife, Beatrice.

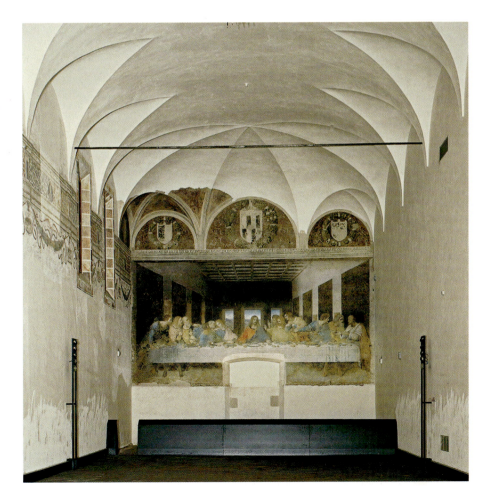

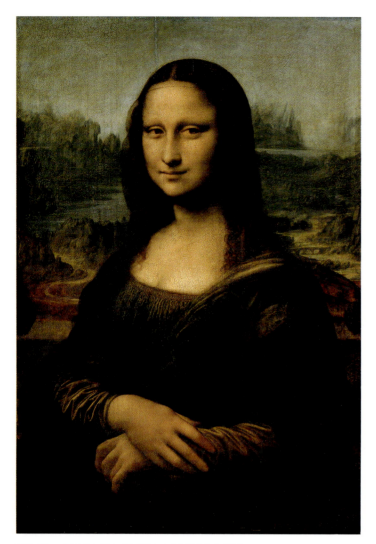

20–5 • Leonardo da Vinci MONA LISA
c. 1503–1506. Oil on wood panel, 30¼ × 21″ (77 × 53 cm).
Musée du Louvre, Paris. (INV. 779)

EXPLORE MORE: Gain insight from a primary source by
Leonardo **www.myartslab.com**

flanked by his 12 disciples, grouped in four interlocking sets of three.

On one level, Leonardo has painted a scene from a story—one that captures the individual reactions of the apostles to Jesus' announcement that one of them will betray him. Leonardo was an acute observer of human behavior, and his art captures human emotions with compelling immediacy. On another level, *The Last Supper* is a symbolic evocation of Jesus' coming sacrifice for the salvation of humankind, the foundation of the institution of the Mass. Breaking with traditional representations of the subject (SEE FIG. 19–22), Leonardo placed the traitor Judas—clutching his money bags in the shadows—within the first triad to the left of Jesus, along with the young John the Evangelist and the elderly Peter, rather than isolating him on the opposite side of the table. Judas, Peter, and John were each to play an essential role in Jesus' mission: Judas set in motion the events leading to Jesus' sacrifice; Peter led the Church after Jesus' death; and John, the visionary, foretold the Second Coming and the Last Judgment in the book of Revelation.

The painting's careful geometry, the convergence of its perspective lines, the stability of its pyramidal forms, and Jesus' calm demeanor at the mathematical center of all the commotion together reinforce the sense of gravity, balance, and order. The clarity and stability of this painting epitomize High Renaissance style.

Leonardo returned to Florence in 1500, after the French, who had invaded Italy in 1494, claimed Milan by defeating Leonardo's Milanese patron, Ludovico Sforza. Perhaps the most famous of his Florentine works is the portrait he painted between about 1503 and 1506 known as the **MONA LISA (FIG. 20–5)**. The subject may have been 24-year-old Lisa Gherardini del Giocondo, the wife of a prominent Florentine merchant. Leonardo never delivered the painting and kept it with him for the rest of his life. In a departure from tradition, the young woman is portrayed without jewelry, not even a ring. The solid pyramidal form of her halflength figure—another departure from traditional portraiture, which was limited to the upper torso—is silhouetted against distant hazy mountains, giving the painting a sense of mystery reminiscent of *The Virgin of the Rocks* (SEE FIG. 20–2). Mona Lisa's facial expression has been called "enigmatic" because her gentle smile is not accompanied by the warmth one would expect to see in her eyes, which have boldly—perhaps flirtatiously—shifted to the side to look straight out at the viewer. It is this expressive complexity, and the sense of psychological presence it gives the human face—especially in the context of the masklike detachment that was more characteristic of Renaissance portraiture (compare FIG. 19–27, or even FIG. 20–8)—that makes the innovative *Mona Lisa* so arresting and haunting, even today.

A fiercely debated topic in Renaissance Italy was the question of the relative merits of painting and sculpture. Leonardo insisted on the supremacy of painting as the best and most complete means of creating an illusion of the natural world, while Michelangelo argued for sculpture. Yet in creating a painted illusion, Leonardo considered color to be secondary to the depiction of sculptural volume, which he achieved through his virtuosity in *sfumato*. He also unified his compositions by covering them with a thin, lightly tinted varnish, which enhanced the overall smoky haze. Because early evening light tends to produce a similar effect naturally, Leonardo considered dusk the finest time of day and recommended that painters set up their studios in a courtyard with black walls and a linen sheet stretched overhead to reproduce twilight.

Leonardo's fame as an artist is based on only a few works, for his many interests took him away from painting. Unlike his humanist contemporaries, he was not particularly interested in Classical literature or archaeology. Instead, his passions were mathematics, engineering, and the natural world. He compiled volumes of detailed drawings and notes on anatomy, botany, geology, meteorology, architectural design, and mechanics. In his drawings of human figures, he sought not only the precise details of anatomy but also the geometric basis of perfect proportions (see "The Vitruvian Man," opposite). Leonardo's searching mind is

The Vitruvian Man

Artists throughout history have turned to geometric shapes and mathematical proportions to seek the ideal representation of the human form. Leonardo, and before him the first-century BCE Roman architect and engineer Vitruvius, equated the ideal man with both circle and square. Ancient Egyptian artists laid out square grids as aids to design (see "Egyptian Pictorial Relief," page 65). Medieval artists adapted a variety of figures, from triangles to pentagrams (see "Villard de Honnecourt," page 510).

Vitruvius, in his ten-volume *De architectura* (*On Architecture*), wrote: "For if a man be placed flat on his back, with his hands and feet extended, and a pair of compasses centered at his navel, the fingers and toes of his two hands and feet will touch the circumference of a circle described therefrom. And just as the human body yields a circular outline, so too a square figure may be found from it. For if we measure the distance from the soles of the feet to the top of the head, and then apply that measure to the outstretched arms, the breadth will be found to be the same as the height" (Book III, Chapter 1, Section 3). Vitruvius determined that the ideal body should be eight heads high. Leonardo added his own observations in the reversed writing he always used in his notebooks when he created his well-known diagram for the ideal male figure, called the Vitruvian Man.

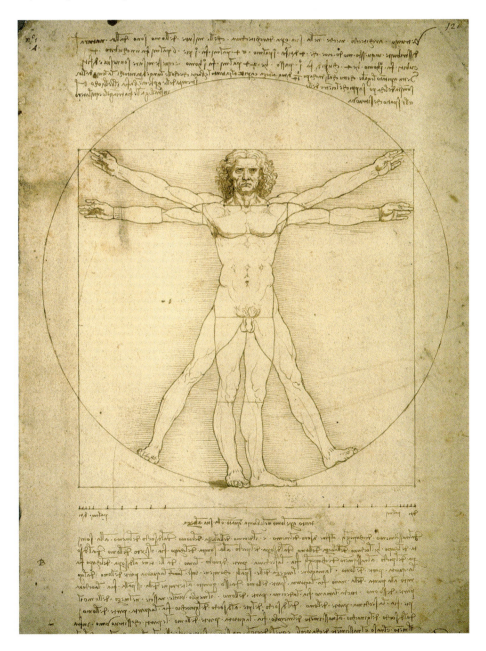

Leonardo da Vinci
VITRUVIAN MAN
c. 1490. Ink, 13½ × 9⅝"
(34.3 × 24.5 cm).
Galleria dell'Accademia, Venice.

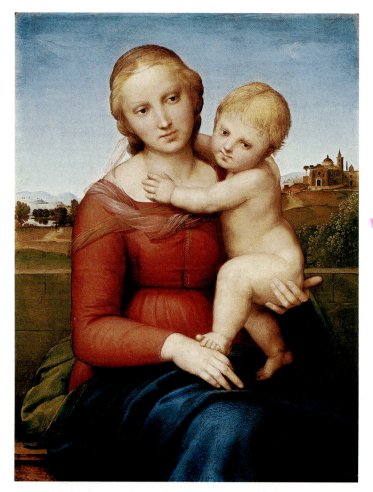

20-6 • Raphael THE SMALL COWPER MADONNA
c. 1505. Oil on wood panel, 23⅜ × 17⅜" (59.5 × 44.1 cm).
National Gallery of Art, Washington, D.C.
Widener Collection (1942.9.57)

In the distance on a hilltop, Raphael has painted a scene he knew
well from his childhood, the domed church of San Bernardino, two
miles outside Urbino. The church contains the tombs of dukes of
Urbino, Federico and Guidobaldo da Montefeltro, and their wives
(SEE FIG. 19–27). Donato Bramante, whose architecture was key in
establishing the High Renaissance style, may have designed the
church.

evident in his drawings, not only of natural objects and human
beings, but also of machines, so clearly and completely worked
out that modern engineers have used them to construct working
models. He designed flying machines, a kind of automobile, a
parachute, and all sorts of military equipment, including a mobile
fortress. His imagination outran his means to bring his creations
into being. For one thing, he lacked a source of power other than
men and horses. For another, he may have lacked focus and
follow-through. His contemporaries complained that he never
finished anything and that his inventions distracted him from his
painting.

Leonardo returned to Milan in 1508 and lived there until
1513. He also lived for a time in the Vatican at the invitation of
Pope Leo X, but there is no evidence that he produced any works
of art during his stay. In 1516, he accepted the French king Francis

I's invitation to relocate to France as an advisor on architecture,
taking the *Mona Lisa* with him. He remained at Francis's court
until his death in 1519.

RAPHAEL. About 1505—while Leonardo was working on the
Mona Lisa—Raphael (Raffaello Santi or Sanzio, 1483–1520)
arrived in Florence from his native Urbino after studying in
Perugia with the city's leading artist, Perugino (SEE FIG. 19–31).
Raphael quickly became successful in Florence, especially with
small, polished paintings of the Virgin and Child, such as THE
SMALL COWPER MADONNA (named for a modern owner) of about
1505 (FIG. 20–6). Already a superb painter technically, the youthful
Raphael shows his indebtedness to his teacher in the delicate tilt of
the figures' heads, the brilliant tonalities, and the pervasive sense of
serenity. But Leonardo's impact is also evident here in the simple
grandeur of these monumental shapes, the pyramidal composition
activated by the spiraling movement of the child, and the draperies
that cling to the Virgin's substantial form. In other Madonnas from
this period, Raphael included the young John the Baptist (SEE FIG.
INTRO–3), experimenting with the multiple figure interactions
pioneered by Leonardo in *The Virgin of the Rocks* (SEE FIG. 20–2).

At the same time as he was producing engaging images
of elegant Madonnas, Raphael was also painting portraits of
prosperous Florentine patrons. To commemorate the marriage in
1504 of 30-year-old cloth merchant Agnelo Doni to Maddalena
Strozzi, the 15-year-old daughter of a powerful banking family,
Doni commissioned from Raphael pendent portraits of the newly-
weds (FIGS. 20–7, 20–8). They are flawlessly executed by the
mature painter at the peak of his illusionistic virtuosity. Like Piero
della Francesca in his portraits of Battista Sforza and Federico da
Montefeltro (SEE FIG. 19–27), Raphael silhouettes Maddalena and
Agnelo against a meticulously described panoramic landscape. But
unlike their predecessors, they turn to address the viewer. Agnelo is
commanding but casual, leaning his arm on a balustrade to add
three-dimensionality to his posture. Maddalena's pose imitates
Leonardo's innovative presentation of his subject in the *Mona Lisa*
(SEE FIG. 20–5), which Raphael had obviously seen in progress,
but with Maddalena there is no sense of mystery, indeed little
psychological presence, and Raphael follows tradition in
emphasizing the sumptuousness of her clothing and making
ostentatious display of her jewelry. Only the wisps of hair
that escape from her sculpted coiffure offer a hint of human
vulnerability in her haughty demeanor.

Raphael left Florence about 1508 for Rome, where Pope
Julius II put him to work almost immediately decorating rooms
(*stanze*, singular *stanza*) in the papal apartments. In the Stanza della
Segnatura (SEE FIG. 20–1)—the papal library—Raphael painted the
four branches of knowledge as conceived in the sixteenth century:
Religion (the *Disputà*, depicting discussions concerning the true
presence of Christ in the Eucharistic Host), Philosophy (the
School of Athens), Poetry (Parnassus, home of the Muses), and Law
(the Cardinal Virtues under Justice).

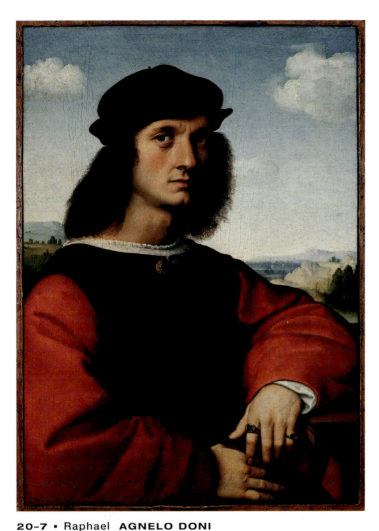

20–7 • Raphael AGNELO DONI
c. 1506. Oil on wood panel, 24½ × 17¼" (63 × 45 cm). Palazzo Pitti, Florence.

These portraits were not the only paintings commissioned by Agnelo Doni to commemorate his upwardly mobile marriage alliance with Maddalena Strozzi. He ordered a *tondo* portraying the holy family from rival artist Michelangelo (see Introduction, "A Closer Look"). Tradition holds that Doni tried to haggle with Michelangelo over the cost of the painting, but ultimately had to pay the price demanded by the artist.

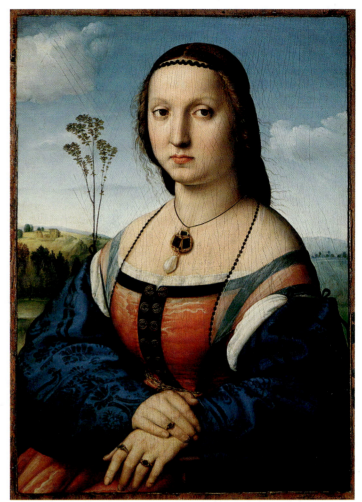

20–8 • Raphael MADDALENA STROZZI
c. 1506. Oil on wood panel, 24½ × 17¼" (63 × 45 cm). Palazzo Pitti, Florence.

Raphael's most influential achievement in the papal rooms was *The School of Athens*, painted about 1510–1511 (see "A Closer Look," page 640). Here, the painter seems to summarize the ideals of the Renaissance papacy in a grand conception of harmoniously arranged forms in a rational space, as well as in the calm dignity of the figures that occupy it. If the learned Julius II did not actually devise the subjects, he certainly must have approved them. Greek philosophers Plato and Aristotle take center stage—placed to the right and left of the vanishing point—silhouetted against the sky and framed under three successive barrel vaults. Surrounding Plato and Aristotle are mathematicians, naturalists, astronomers, geographers, and other philosophers, debating and demonstrating their theories with and to onlookers and each other. The scene takes place in an immense barrel-vaulted interior, flooded with a clear, even light from a single source, and seemingly inspired by the

new design for St. Peter's, under construction at the time. The grandeur of the building is matched by the monumental dignity of the philosophers themselves, each of whom has a distinct physical and intellectual presence. The sweeping arcs of the composition are activated by the variety and energy of their poses and gestures, creating a dynamic unity that is a prime characteristic of High Renaissance art.

In 1515, Raphael was commissioned by Pope Leo X (pontificate 1513–1521) to provide designs on themes from the Acts of the Apostles to be woven into tapestries for the strip of blank wall below the fifteenth-century wall paintings of the Sistine Chapel (SEE FIG. 19–30). For the production of the tapestries, woven in Brussels, Raphael and his large workshop of assistants made full-scale charcoal drawings, then painted over them with color for the weavers to match (see "Raphael's Cartoons for Tapestries in the Sistine Ceiling," pages 646–647). Pictorial weaving was the most prestigious and expensive kind of wall decoration. With murals by the leading painters of the fifteenth century above and Michelangelo's work circling over all, Raphael must have felt both honored and challenged. The pope had given him the place of honor among the artists in the papal chapel.

The School of Athens ▸ by Raphael, fresco in the Stanza della Segnatura, Vatican, Rome. c. 1510–1511. 19 × 27′ (5.79 × 8.24 m).

Looking down from niches in the walls are sculptures of Apollo, the god of sunlight, rationality, poetry, music, and the fine arts; and of Minerva, the goddess of wisdom and the mechanical arts.

Plato points upward to the realm of ideas and pure forms that were at the center of his philosophy. His pupil Aristotle gestures toward his surroundings, signifying the empirical world that for him served as the basis for understanding.

The figure bent over a slate with a compass is Euclid, the father of geometry. Vasari claimed that Raphael gave this mathematician the portrait likeness of Bramante, the architect whose redesigned St. Peter's was under construction not far from this room.

Raphael placed his own portrait in a group that includes the geographer Ptolemy, who holds a terrestrial globe, and the astronomer Zoroaster, who holds a celestial globe.

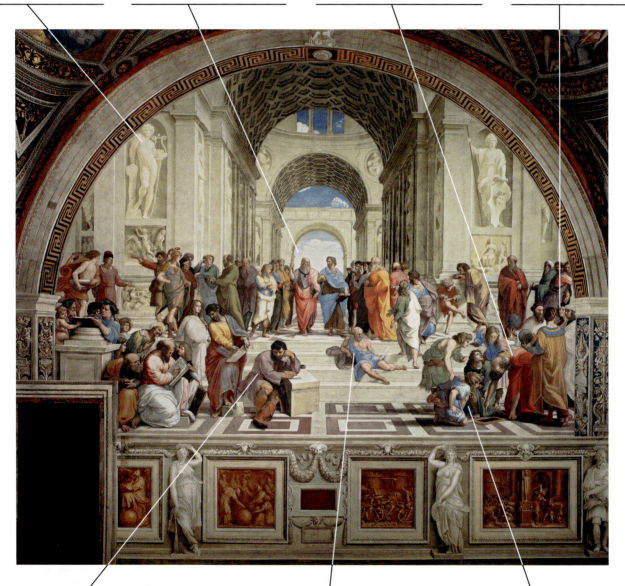

The brooding figure of Heraclitus, a late addition to the composition, is a portrait of Michelangelo, who was working next door on the ceiling of the Sistine Chapel, and whose monumental figural style is here appropriated (or is it mimicked?) by Raphael. The stonecutter's boots on his feet refer to Michelangelo's self-identification—or Raphael's insistence that he be seen—as a sculptor rather than a painter.

This figure is usually identified as Diogenes the Cynic following Vasari's account of the painting. It is more likely that he is Socrates, however. The cup next to him could refer to his deadly draught of hemlock, and his recumbent position recalls his teaching from his prison bed.

The group of figures gathered around Euclid illustrate the various stages of understanding: literal learning, dawning comprehension, anticipation of the outcome, and assisting the teacher. Raphael received acclaim for his ability to communicate so clearly through the poses and expressions of his figures.

SEE MORE: View the Closer Look feature for *The School of Athens* www.myartslab.com

MICHELANGELO'S EARLY WORK. Michelangelo Buonarroti (1475–1564) was born in the Tuscan town of Caprese into an impoverished Florentine family that laid a claim to nobility—a claim the artist carefully advanced throughout his life. He grew up in Florence, where at age 13 he was apprenticed to Ghirlandaio (SEE FIG. 19–32), in whose workshop he learned the technique of fresco painting and studied drawings of Classical monuments. Soon the talented youth joined the household of Lorenzo the Magnificent, head of the ruling Medici family, where he came into contact with Neoplatonic philosophy and studied sculpture with Bertoldo di Giovanni, a pupil of Donatello. After Lorenzo died in 1492, Michelangelo traveled to Venice and Bologna, then returned to Florence.

Michelangelo's major early work at the turn of the century was a marble sculpture of the **PIETÀ**, commissioned by a French cardinal and installed as a tomb monument in Old St. Peter's **(FIG. 20–9).** The theme of the *pietà* (in which the Virgin supports and mourns the dead Jesus in her lap), long popular in northern Europe (SEE FIG. 17–19), was an unusual theme in Italy at the time. Michelangelo traveled to the marble quarries at Carrara in central Italy to select the block from which to make this large work, a practice he was to continue for nearly all of his sculpture. The choice of stone was important to him because he envisioned his sculpture as already existing within the marble, needing only his tools to set it free. Michelangelo was a poet as well as an artist, and later wrote in his Sonnet 15: "The greatest artist has no conception which a single block of marble does not potentially contain within its mass, but only a hand obedient to the mind can penetrate to this image."

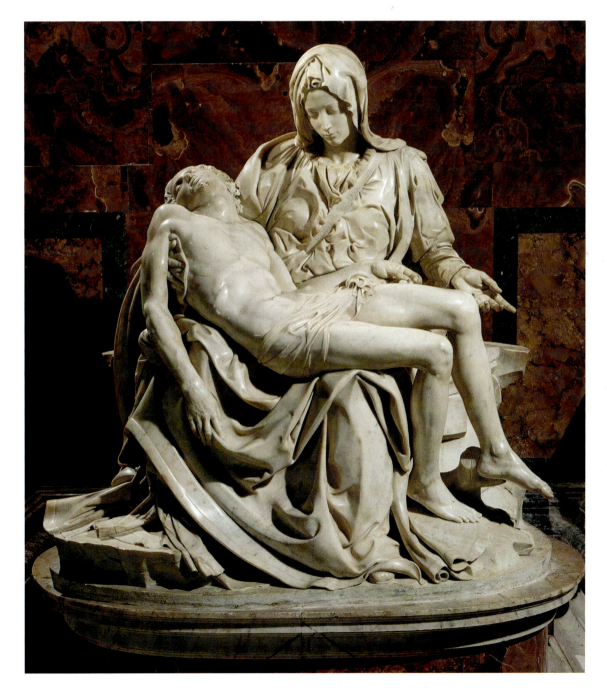

20-9 • Michelangelo PIETÀ
c. 1500. Marble, height 5′8½″ (1.74 m). St. Peter's, Vatican, Rome.

EXPLORE MORE: Gain insight from a primary source by Michelangelo on his *Pietà*
www.myartslab.com

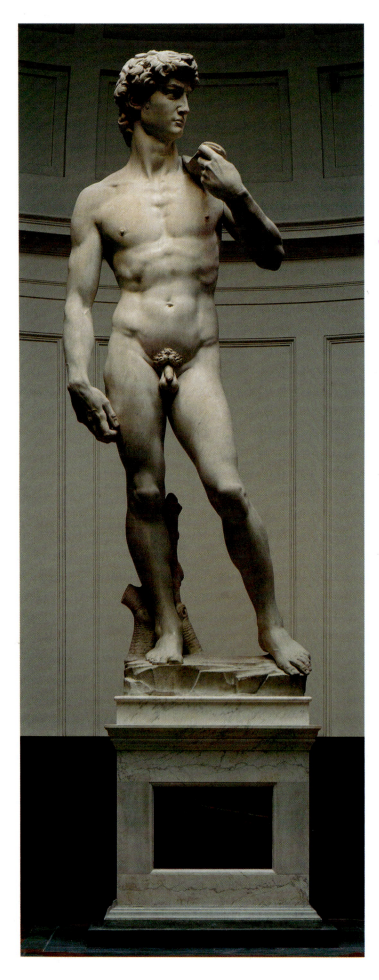

Michelangelo's Virgin is a young woman of heroic stature holding the unnaturally smaller, lifeless body of her grown son. Inconsistencies of scale and age are forgotten, however, when contemplating the sweetness of expression, technical virtuosity of the carving, and smooth modeling of the luscious forms. Michelangelo's compelling vision of beauty was meant to be seen up close so that the viewer can look directly into Jesus' face. The 25-year-old artist is said to have slipped into the church at night to sign the statue on a strap across the Virgin's breast after it was finished, answering directly questions that had come up about the identity of its creator.

In 1501, Michelangelo accepted a Florentine commission for a statue of the biblical hero **DAVID** (FIG. 20–10), to be placed high atop a buttress of the cathedral. But when it was finished in 1504, the *David* was so admired that the city council instead placed it in the principal city square, next to the Palazzo della Signoria (SEE FIG. 17–2), the seat of Florence's government. There it stood as a reminder of Florence's republican status, which was briefly reinstated after the expulsion of the powerful Medici oligarchy in 1494. Although in its muscular nudity Michelangelo's *David* embodies the antique ideal of the athletic male nude, the emotional power of its expression and its concentrated gaze are entirely new. Unlike Donatello's bronze *David* (SEE FIG. 19–10), this is not a triumphant hero with the trophy head of the giant Goliath already under his feet. Slingshot over his shoulder and a rock in his right hand, Michelangelo's *David* knits his brow and stares into space, seemingly preparing himself psychologically for the danger ahead, a mere youth confronting a gigantic experienced warrior. No match for his opponent in experience, weaponry, or physical strength, Michelangelo's powerful *David* stands for the supremacy of right over might—a perfect emblem for the Florentines, who had recently fought the forces of Milan, Siena, and Pisa, and still faced political and military pressure.

THE SISTINE CHAPEL. Despite Michelangelo's contractual commitment to Florence Cathedral for additional statues, in 1505, Pope Julius II, who saw Michelangelo as an ideal collaborator in

20-10 • Michelangelo DAVID
1501–1504. Marble, height 17' (5.18 m) without pedestal. Galleria dell'Accademia, Florence.

Michelangelo's most famous sculpture was cut from an 18-foot-tall marble block. The sculptor began with a small model in wax, then sketched the contours of the figure as they would appear from the front on one face of the marble. Then, according to his friend and biographer Vasari, he chiseled in from the drawn-on surface, as if making a figure in very high relief. The completed statue took four days to move on tree-trunk rollers down the narrow streets of Florence from the premises of the cathedral shop where he worked to its location outside the Palazzo della Signoria (SEE FIG. 17–2). In 1504, the Florentines gilded the tree stump and added a gilded wreath to the head and a belt of 28 gilt-bronze leaves, since removed. In 1873, the statue was replaced by a copy, and the original was moved into the museum of the Florence Academy.

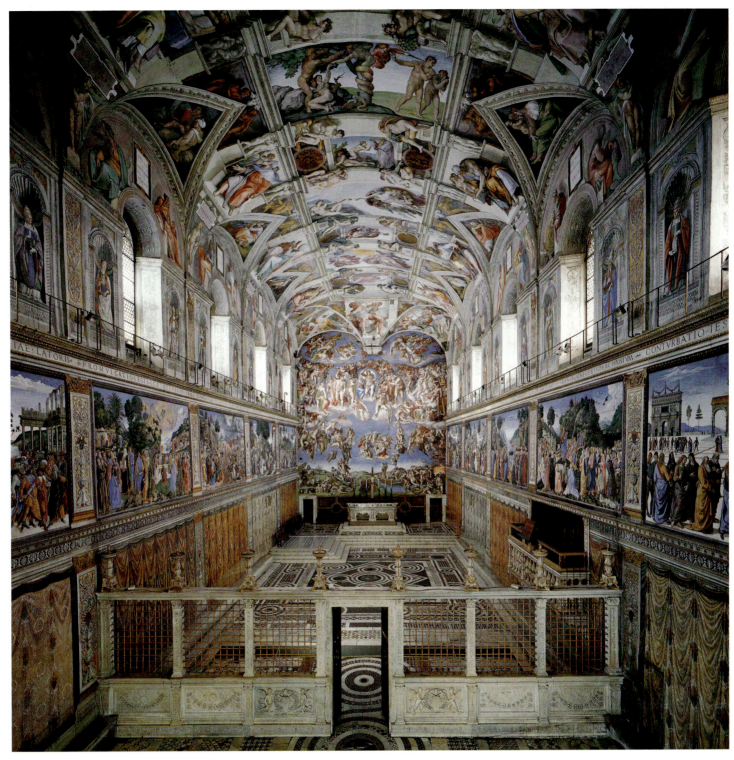

20–11 • INTERIOR, SISTINE CHAPEL

Vatican, Rome. Built 1475–1481; ceiling painted 1508–1512; end wall, 1536–1541. The ceiling measures 45 × 128′ (13.75 × 39 m).

the artistic aggrandizement of the papacy, arranged for him to come to Rome to work on the spectacular tomb Julius planned for himself. Michelangelo began the tomb project, but two years later the pope ordered him to begin painting the ceiling of the SISTINE CHAPEL instead (FIG. 20–11).

Michelangelo considered himself a sculptor, but the strong-minded pope wanted paintings; work began in 1508. Michelangelo

complained bitterly in a sonnet to a friend: "This miserable job has given me a goiter….The force of it has jammed my belly up beneath my chin. Beard to the sky….Brush splatterings make a pavement of my face…. I'm not a painter." Despite his physical misery as he stood on a scaffold, painting the ceiling just above him, the results were extraordinary, and Michelangelo established a new and remarkably powerful style in Renaissance painting.

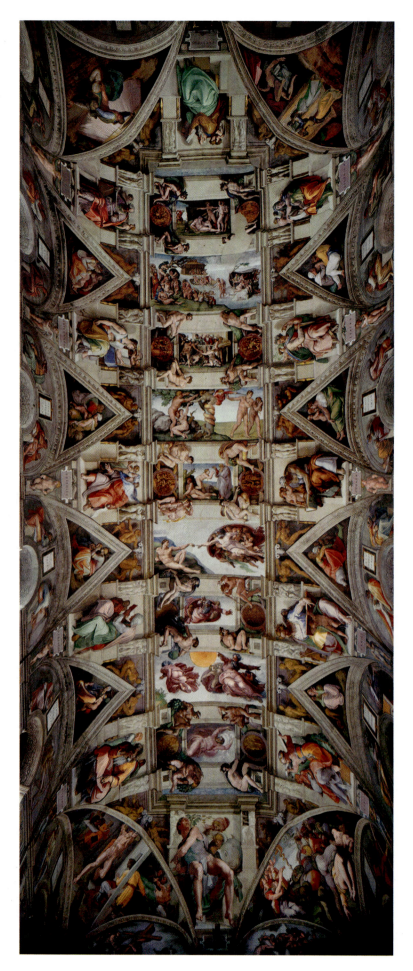

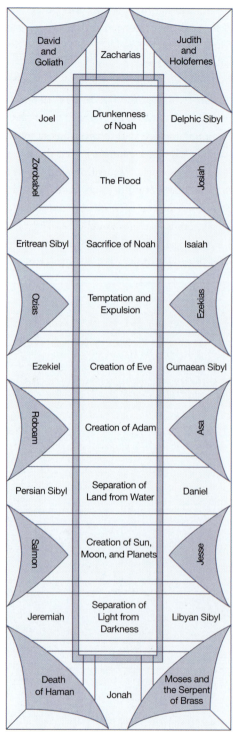

David and Goliath	Zacharias	Judith and Holofernes
Joel	Drunkenness of Noah	Delphic Sibyl
Zorobabel	The Flood	Josiah
Eritrean Sibyl	Sacrifice of Noah	Isaiah
Ozias	Temptation and Expulsion	Ezekias
Ezekiel	Creation of Eve	Cumaean Sibyl
Roboam	Creation of Adam	Asa
Persian Sibyl	Separation of Land from Water	Daniel
Salmon	Creation of Sun, Moon, and Planets	Jesse
Jeremiah	Separation of Light from Darkness	Libyan Sibyl
Death of Haman	Jonah	Moses and the Serpent of Brass

ALTAR

20–12 • Michelangelo SISTINE CHAPEL CEILING WITH DIAGRAM IDENTIFYING SCENES
1508–1512. Fresco.

Julius's initial order for the ceiling was simple: *trompe-l'oeil* coffers to replace the original star-spangled blue decoration. Later he wanted the 12 apostles seated on thrones on the triangular spandrels between the lunettes framing the windows. According to Michelangelo, when he objected to the limitations of Julius's plan, the pope told him to paint whatever he liked. This Michelangelo presumably did, although he was certainly guided by a theological advisor and his plan no doubt required the pope's approval. Then, as master painter, Michelangelo assembled a team of expert assistants to work with him.

In Michelangelo's design, an illusionistic marble architecture establishes a framework for the figures and narrative scenes on the vault of the chapel (**FIG. 20–12**). Running completely around the ceiling is a painted cornice with projections supported by pilasters decorated with "sculptured" *putti*. Between the pilasters are figures of prophets and sibyls (female seers from the Classical world) who were believed to have foretold Jesus' birth. Seated on the fictive cornice are heroic figures of nude young men (called **ignudi**, singular, *ignudo*), holding sashes attached to large gold medallions. Rising behind the *ignudi*, shallow bands of fictive stone span the center of the ceiling and divide it into nine compartments containing successive scenes from Genesis—the Creation, the Fall, and the Flood—beginning over the altar and ending near the chapel entrance. God's earliest acts of creation are therefore closest to the altar, the Creation of Eve at the center of the ceiling, followed by the imperfect actions of humanity: Temptation, Fall, Expulsion from Paradise, and God's eventual destruction of all people except Noah and his family by the Flood. The eight triangular spandrels over the windows contain paintings of the ancestors of Jesus.

Perhaps the most familiar scene on the ceiling is the **CREATION OF ADAM** (**FIG. 20–13**), where Michelangelo captures the moment when God charges the languorous Adam with the spark of life. As if to echo the biblical text, Adam's heroic body, outstretched arm, and profile almost mirror those of God, in whose image he has been created. Emerging under God's other arm, and looking across him in the direction of her future mate, is the robust and energetic figure of Eve before her creation. Directly below Adam, an *ignudo* grasps a bundle of oak leaves and giant acorns, which refer to Pope Julius's family name (della Rovere, or "of the oak") and possibly also to a passage in the prophecy of Isaiah (61:3): "They will be called oaks of justice, planted by the Lord to show his glory."

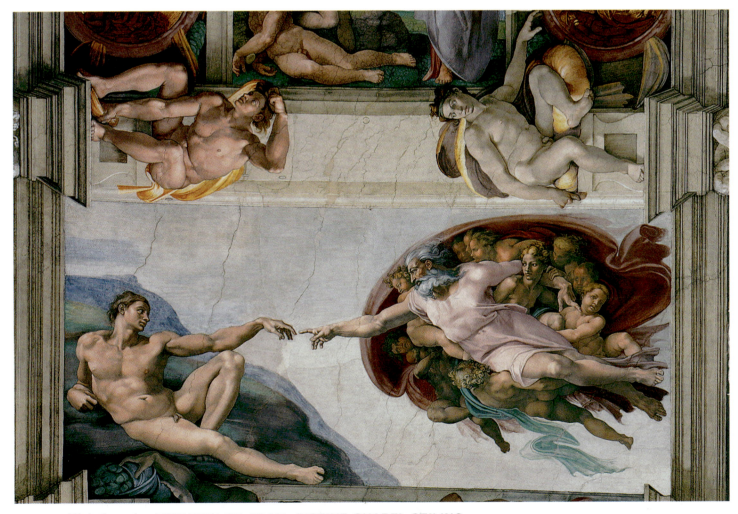

20–13 • Michelangelo CREATION OF ADAM, SISTINE CHAPEL CEILING
1511–1512. Fresco. 9′2″ × 18′8″ (2.8 × 5.7 m).

Raphael's Cartoons for Tapestries in the Sistine Chapel

The Sistine Chapel was a major focus of papal patronage during the Renaissance. The building was constructed in 1475–1481 by Sixtus IV, who also began its painted embellishment by calling a constellation of illustrious artists to Rome in the early 1480s to create a band of framed frescos recounting the life of Moses on one wall and the life of Christ on the other (SEE FIG. 19–30). Between 1508 and 1512, Michelangelo painted the chapel's ceiling at the behest of Julius II. And soon after he became pope in 1513, Leo X commissioned Raphael to produce ten cartoons (full-size preparatory designs for a work of art executed in another medium) for a lavish set of tapestries portraying scenes from the lives of SS. Peter and Paul that would complete the decorative program on the chapel's lower level. At the time, these would have been considered its most prestigious and expensive works of art. The tapestry program cost Leo X more than five times what Julius II had paid Michelangelo to paint the ceiling. For designing the program and producing the cartoons, however, Raphael only received a sixteenth of the total cost of the tapestries; the expense here involved production more than design.

The cartoons were created in Raphael's workshop between 1515 and 1516. Raphael was clearly the intellect behind the compositions, and he participated in the actual preparation and execution. This was a prestigious commission that would reflect directly on the reputation of the master. But he could not have accomplished this imposing task in a little over a year without the collaboration of numerous assistants working in his thriving workshop. The completed cartoons—first drawn with charcoal on paper (160–170 separate sheets were glued together to form the expanse of a single tapestry) and then overpainted with color—were sent to Brussels, where they were woven into tapestries in the workshop of Pieter van Aelst. The first was complete in 1517, seven were hanging in the chapel for Christmas 1519, and the entire cycle was installed by Leo X's death in 1521.

The process of creation, from design through production, can be charted by examining the tapestry portraying *Christ's Charge to Peter* (John 21:15–17; Matthew 16:17–19) at three stages in its development. We have Raphael's preliminary drawing (FIG. A), where models—it is tempting to see these as Raphael's assistants, stripped to their drawers to help the master work out his composition—are posed to enact the moment when Jesus addresses his apostles. This is a preliminary idea for the pose of Christ. In the final cartoon (FIG. B), Raphael changes Christ's gesture so that he addresses the kneeling Peter specifically rather than the whole apostolic group; for the patron, this would be an important detail since papal power rested in the belief that Christ had transferred authority to Peter, who was considered the first pope, with subsequent popes inheriting this authority in unbroken succession. Comparison of drawing and cartoon also reveals an important aspect of the design process.

The cartoon reverses the figural arrangement of the drawing because in the production process the tapestry would be woven from the back, and if the weavers followed the reversed version of the composition on the cartoon, the resulting tapestry (FIG. C) would show the scene in its intended orientation. Comparison of cartoon and tapestry also indicates that the weavers were not required to follow their models slavishly. They have embellished the costume of Christ, perhaps in an attempt to assure that the viewers' attention will be immediately directed to this most important figure in the scene.

After they had been used to create the tapestries hung in the Sistine Chapel, Raphael's cartoons remained in Brussels, where several additional sets of tapestries were made from them—one for Henry VIII of England, another for Francis I of France—before seven surviving cartoons were acquired in 1623 by the future Charles I of England. They remain in the British Royal Collection. The tapestries themselves, although still in the Vatican, are displayed in the museum rather than on the walls of the chapel for which they were originally conceived, as one of the most prestigious artistic projects from the peak of the Roman High Renaissance.

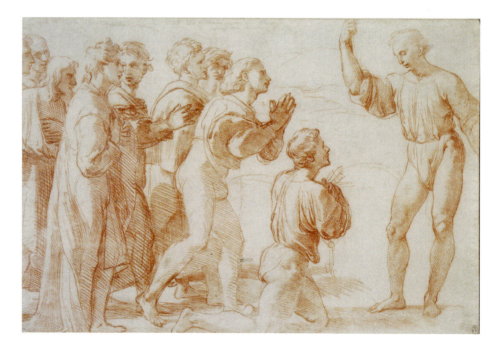

A. Raphael **STUDY FOR CHRIST'S CHARGE TO PETER** c. 1515. Red chalk. Royal Library, Windsor Castle.

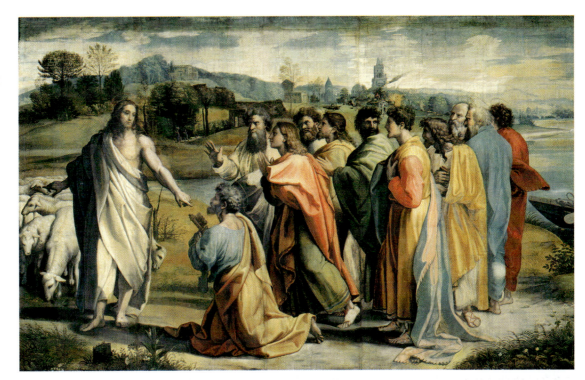

B. Raphael
CARTOON FOR TAPESTRY PORTRAYING CHRIST'S CHARGE TO PETER
c. 1515–1516. Distemper on paper (now transferred to canvas), 11'1″ × 17'4″ (3.4 × 5.3 m). Lent by Her Majesty the Queen to the Victoria & Albert Museum, London

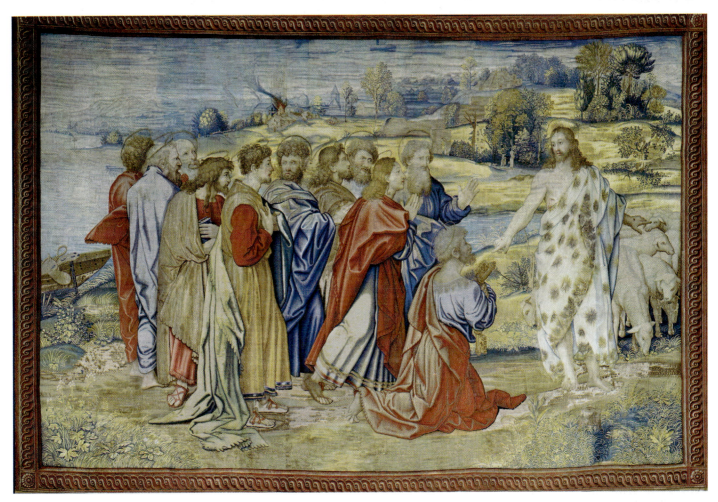

C. Shop of Pieter van Aelst, Brussels, after cartoons by Raphael and assistants **CHRIST'S CHARGE TO PETER**
Woven 1517, installed 1519 in the Sistine Chapel. Wool and silk with silver-gilt wrapped threads. Musei Vaticani, Pinacoteca, Rome.

MICHELANGELO AT SAN LORENZO. After the Medici regained power in Florence in 1512, and Leo X succeeded Julius in 1513, Michelangelo became chief architect for Medici family projects at the church of San Lorenzo in Florence—including a new chapel for the tombs of Lorenzo the Magnificent, his brother Giuliano, and two younger dukes, also named Lorenzo and Giuliano, ordered in 1519 for the so-called New Sacristy (SEE FIG. 19–4). The older men's tombs were never built to Michelangelo's designs, but the unfinished tombs for the younger relatives were placed on opposite side walls (FIG. 20–14).

Each of the two monuments consists of an idealized portrait of the deceased, who turns to face the family's unfinished ancestral tomb. The men are dressed in a sixteenth-century interpretation of Classical armor and seated in wall niches above pseudo-Classical sarcophagi. Balanced precariously atop the sarcophagi are male and female figures representing the times of day. Their positions would not seem so unsettling had reclining figures of river gods been installed below them, as originally planned, but even so there is a conspicuous tension here between the substantiality of the figures and the limitations imposed on them by their architectural surrounds. In the tomb illustrated here, Michelangelo represents Giuliano as the Active Life, and his sarcophagus figures are allegories of Night and Day. Night at left is accompanied by her symbols: a star and crescent moon on her tiara; poppies, which induce sleep; and an owl under the arch of her leg. The huge mask at her back may allude to Death, since Sleep and Death were said to be the children of Night. Some have seen in this mask that glares out at viewers in the chapel a self-portrait of the artist, serving both as signature and as a way of proclaiming his right to be here because of his long relationship with the family. On the other tomb, Lorenzo, representing the Contemplative Life, is supported by Dawn and Evening.

Concurrent with work on the Medici tombs was the construction of a new library at San Lorenzo. The idea for the library belongs to Cardinal Giulio de' Medici and dates to 1519, but it was only after he was elected Pope Clement VII in 1523 that the money became available to realize it. Michelangelo was commissioned to design and also supervise construction of the new **VESTIBULE** (FIG. 20–15) and reading room and to spare no expense in making them both grand and ambitious. The pope paid keen attention to the library's progress—not, he said, to verify the quality of the design, but because the project had a special interest for him.

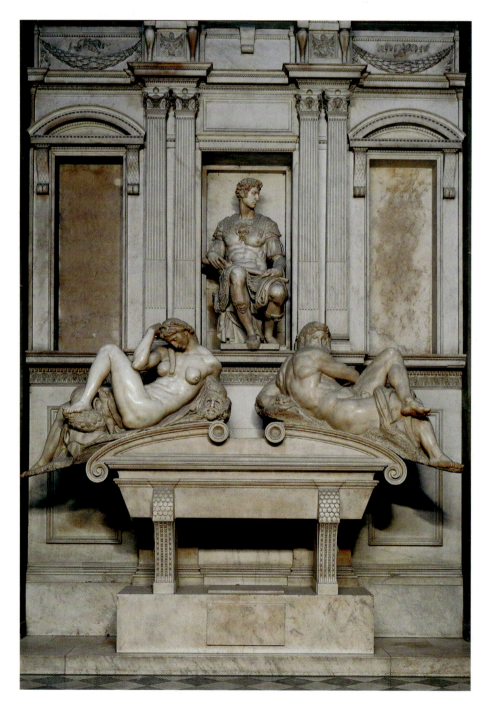

20–14 • Michelangelo TOMB OF GIULIANO DE' MEDICI WITH ALLEGORICAL FIGURES OF NIGHT AND DAY
New Sacristy (Medici Chapel), church of San Lorenzo, Florence. 1519–1534. Marble, height of seated figure approx. 5'10" (1.8 m).

Michelangelo coordinated his work within a decorative tradition established at San Lorenzo when Brunelleschi designed the church itself a century earlier (SEE FIG. 19–4), using stylized architectural elements carved in dark gray *pietra serena*, set against and within a contrasting white wall. However, Michelangelo plays with the Classical architectural etiquette that Brunelleschi had used to create such clarity, harmony, and balance in the nave. In Michelangelo's vestibule, chunky columns are recessed into rectangular wall niches that can barely contain them. They are crowded and overlapped by the aggressive lateral extension of the pediment over the door. The door itself is broken into parts, sides jutting forward as fluted pilasters that are then partially obscured by the frame around the opening. The three flights of stairs leading up to the reading room almost fill the vestibule, and the central stairs cascade forward forcefully toward visitors, hardly encouraging them to go against the flow and step up. Through their playfulness, these creative combinations of architectural forms draw attention to themselves and their design rather than the function of the building or the comfortable accommodation of its users.

Fearing for his life when ongoing political struggles flared up in Florence, Michelango returned to Rome in 1534 and settled permanently. He had left both the Medici chapel and the library unfinished. In 1557, he sent a plaster model of the library staircase to Florence to assure that its completion conformed to his design. In 1545, his students had assembled the tomb sculptures, including unfinished figures of the times of day, into the composition we see today.

The figures of the dukes are finely finished, but the times of day are notable for their contrasting areas of rough unfinished and polished marble. These are the only unfinished sculptures Michelangelo apparently permitted to be put in place, and we do not know what his reasons were. Michelangelo specialists, characterizing these works with the word *nonfinito* ("unfinished"), propose that Michelangelo had begun to view his artistic creations as symbols of human imperfection. Indeed, Michelangelo's poetry often expressed his belief that humans could achieve perfection only in death.

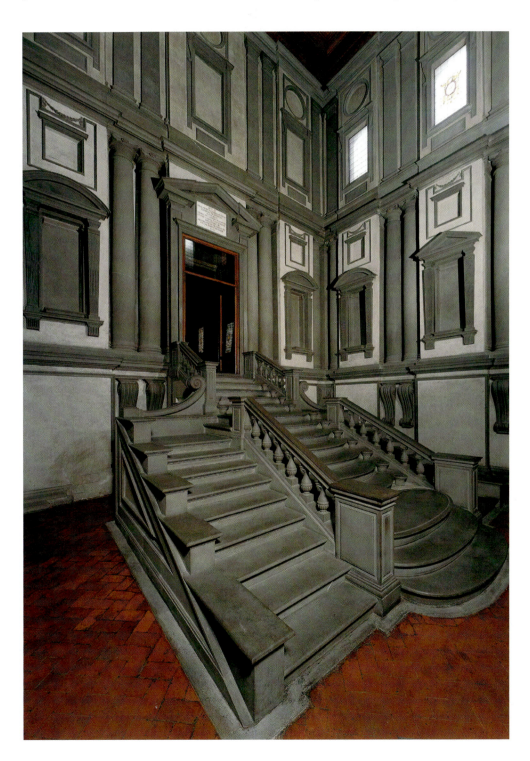

20–15 • Michelangelo
VESTIBULE OF THE LAURENTIAN LIBRARY
Church of San Lorenzo, Florence. Begun 1524; stairway designed 1550s.

ARCHITECTURE IN ROME AND THE VATICAN

The election of Julius II as pope in 1503 crystallized a resurgence of papal power, but France, Spain, and the Holy Roman Empire all had designs on Italy. During his ten-year papacy, Julius fought wars and formed alliances to consolidate his power. He also enlisted Bramante, Raphael, and Michelangelo as architects to carry out his vision of a revitalized Rome as the center of a new Christian architecture, inspired by the achievements of their fifteenth-century predecessors as well as the monuments of antiquity. Although most commissions were for churches, opportunities also arose to build urban palaces and country villas.

BRAMANTE.   Donato Bramante (1444–1514) was born near Urbino and trained as a painter, but turned to architectural design early in his career. About 1481, he became attached to the Sforza

court in Milan, where he would have known Leonardo da Vinci. In 1499, Bramante settled in Rome, but work came slowly. The architect was nearing 60 when Julius II asked him to redesign St. Peter's (see "St. Peter's Basilica,"opposite) and the Spanish rulers Queen Isabella and King Ferdinand commissioned a small shrine over the spot in Rome where the apostle Peter was believed to have been crucified **(FIG. 20–16)**. In this tiny building, known as *Il Tempietto* ("Little Temple"), Bramante combined his interpretation of the principles of Vitruvius and Alberti from the stepped base, to the Doric columns and frieze (Vitruvius had advised that the Doric order be used for temples to gods of particularly forceful character), to the elegant balustrade. The centralized plan and the tall drum (circular wall) supporting a hemispheric dome recall Early Christian shrines built over martyrs' relics, as well as ancient Roman circular temples. Especially notable is the sculptural effect of the building's exterior, with its deep wall niches and sharp contrasts of light and shadow. Bramante's design called for a circular cloister around the church, but the cloister was never built.

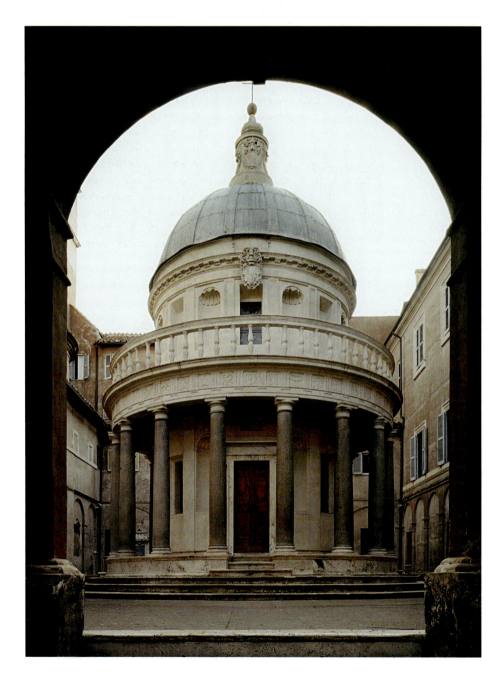

ARCHITECTURE, PAINTING, AND SCULPTURE IN NORTHERN ITALY

While Rome was Italy's preeminent arts center at the beginning of the sixteenth century, wealthy and powerful families elsewhere also patronized the arts and letters just as the Montefeltro and Gonzaga had in Urbino and Mantua during the fifteenth century. The architects and painters working for these sixteenth-century patrons created fanciful structures and developed a new colorful, illusionistic painting style. The result was witty, elegant, and finely executed art designed to appeal to the jaded taste of the intellectual elite in cities such as Mantua, Parma, and Venice.

GIULIO ROMANO.   In Mantua, Federigo II Gonzaga (r. 1519–1540) continued the family tradition of patronage when, in 1524, he lured a Roman follower of Raphael, Giulio Romano (c. 1499–1546), to Mantua to build him a pleasure palace. Indeed, the Palazzo del

20–16 • Donato Bramante
IL TEMPIETTO, CHURCH OF SAN PIETRO IN MONTORIO
Rome. 1502–1510; dome and lantern were restored in the 17th century.

St. Peter's Basilica

The history of St. Peter's in Rome is an interesting case of the effects of individual and institutional demands on a religious building of major sacred significance. The original church, now referred to as Old St. Peter's, was built in the fourth century by Constantine, the first Christian Roman emperor, to mark the grave of the apostle Peter, the first bishop of Rome and therefore considered the first pope. Because the site was so holy, Constantine's architect had to build a structure large enough to hold the crowds of pilgrims who came to visit St. Peter's tomb. To provide a platform for the church, a huge terrace was cut into the side of the Vatican Hill, across the Tiber River from the city. Here Constantine's architect erected a basilica with a new feature, a transept, to allow large numbers of visitors to approach the shrine at the front of the apse. The rest of the church was, in effect, a covered cemetery, carpeted with the tombs of believers who wanted to be buried near the apostle's grave. When it was built, Constantine's basilica, as befitted an imperial commission, was one of the largest buildings in the Roman world (interior length 368 feet, width 190 feet). For more than a thousand years it was the most important pilgrimage site in Europe.

In 1506, Pope Julius II made the astonishing decision to demolish the Constantinian basilica, which had fallen into disrepair, and to replace it with a new building. That anyone, even a pope, should have had the nerve to pull down such a venerated building is an indication of the extraordinary self-assurance of the Renaissance—and of Julius himself. To design and build the new church, the pope appointed Donato Bramante, who envisioned the new St. Peter's as a central-plan building, in this case a Greek cross (with four arms of equal length) crowned by an enormous dome. This design was intended to emulate the Early Christian tradition of constructing domed and round buildings over the tombs of martyrs (SEE FIG. 7–20), itself derived from the Roman practice of building centrally planned tombs (see "Central-Plan Churches," page 228). In Renaissance thinking, the central plan and dome symbolized the perfection of God.

The deaths of pope and architect in 1513–1514 put a temporary halt to the project. Successive plans by Raphael, Antonio da Sangallo, and others changed the Greek cross into a Latin cross (with three shorter arms and one long one) to provide the church with an extended nave. However, when Michelangelo was appointed architect in 1546, he returned to the Greek-cross plan and simplified Bramante's design to create a single, unified space covered with a hemispherical dome. The dome was finally completed some years after Michelangelo's death by Giacomo della Porta, who retained Michelangelo's basic design but gave the dome a taller profile (SEE FIG. 20–35).

During the Counter-Reformation, the Catholic Church emphasized congregational worship; as a result, more space was needed to house the congregation and allow for processions. To expand the church—and to make it more closely resemble Old St. Peter's—Pope Paul V in 1606 commissioned the architect Carlo Maderno to change Michelangelo's Greek-cross plan back once again into a Latin-cross plan. Maderno extended the nave to its final length of slightly more than 636 feet and added a new façade, thus completing St. Peter's as we see it is today. Later in the seventeenth century, the sculptor and architect Gianlorenzo Bernini changed the approach to the basilica by surrounding it with a great colonnade, like a huge set of arms extended to embrace the faithful as they approach the principal church of Western Christendom.

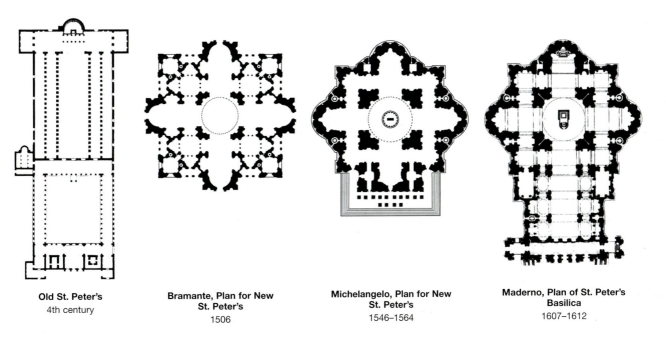

Old St. Peter's
4th century

Bramante, Plan for New St. Peter's
1506

Michelangelo, Plan for New St. Peter's
1546–1564

Maderno, Plan of St. Peter's Basilica
1607–1612

SEE MORE: View a simulation about plans for St. Peter's Basilica www.myartslab.com

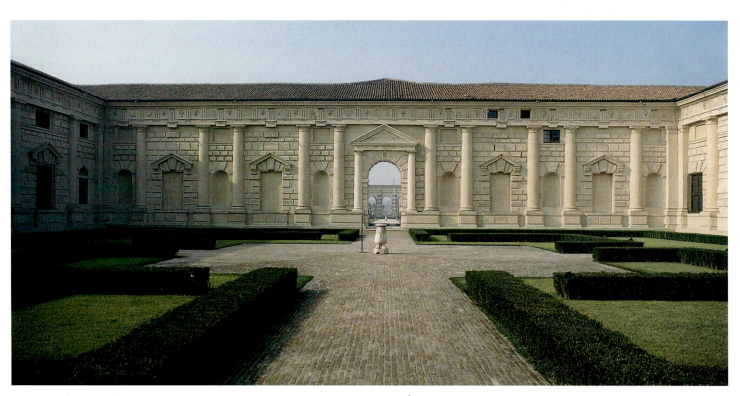

20–17 • Giulio Romano **COURTYARD FAÇADE, PALAZZO DEL TÈ, MANTUA**
1527–1534.

SEE MORE: Click the Google Earth link for the Palazzo del Tè **www.myartslab.com**

Tè **(FIG. 20–17)** devoted more space to gardens, pools, and stables than to rooms for residential living. Since Federigo and his erudite friends would have known Classical orders and proportions, they could appreciate the playfulness with which they are used here. The building is full of visual jokes, such as lintels masquerading as arches and triglyphs that slip sloppily out of place. Like the similar, if more sober, subversions of Classical architectural decorum in Michelangelo's contemporary Laurentian Library (SEE FIG. 20–15), its sophisticated humor and exquisite craft have been seen as a precursor to Mannerism or as a manifestation of Mannerism itself.

Giulio Romano continued his witty play in the decoration of the two principal rooms. One, dedicated to the loves of the gods, depicted the marriage of Cupid and Psyche. The other room is a remarkable feat of *trompe-l'oeil* painting in which the entire building seems to be collapsing about the viewer as the gods defeat the giants **(FIG. 20–18)**. Here, Giulio Romano accepted the challenge Andrea Mantegna had laid down in the Camera Picta of the Gonzaga Palace (SEE FIG. 19–29), painted for Federigo's grandfather: to dissolve architectural barriers and fantasize a world of playful delight beyond the walls and ceilings. But the Palazzo del Tè was not just fun and games. The unifying

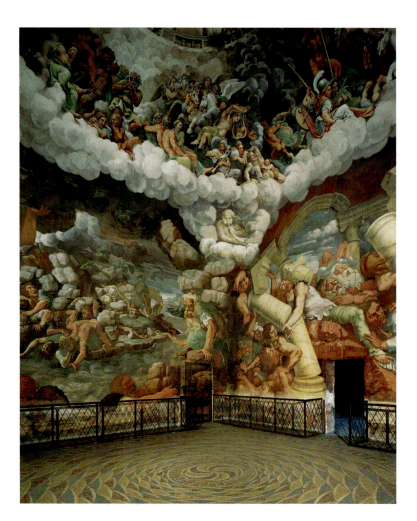

20–18 • Giulio Romano **FALL OF THE GIANTS**
Sala dei Giganti, Palazzo del Tè. 1530–1532. Fresco.

themes were love and politics, the former focused on the separate apartments built to house Federigo's mistress, Isabella Boschetti. The palace was constructed in part as a place where they could meet beyond the watchful gaze of her husband. But the decoration also seems to reflect Federigo's dicey alliance with Charles V, who stayed in the palace in 1530 and again in 1532, when the scaffolding was removed from the Sala dei Giganti so the emperor could see the paintings in progress. He must have been impressed with his host's lavish new residence, and doubtless he saw a connection between these reeling paintings and his own military successes.

CORREGGIO. At about the same time that Giulio Romano was building and decorating the Palazzo del Tè, in nearby Parma an equally skillful master, Correggio (Antonio Allegri da Correggio, c. 1489–1534), was creating similarly theatrical effects with dramatic foreshortening in Parma Cathedral. Correggio's great work, the **ASSUMPTION OF THE VIRGIN (FIG. 20–19)**, a fresco painted between about 1526 and 1530 in the cathedral's dome, distantly recalls the illusionism of Mantegna's ceiling in the Gonzaga Palace, but Correggio has also assimilated Leonardo da Vinci's use of *sfumato* and Raphael's idealism into his personal style. Correggio's

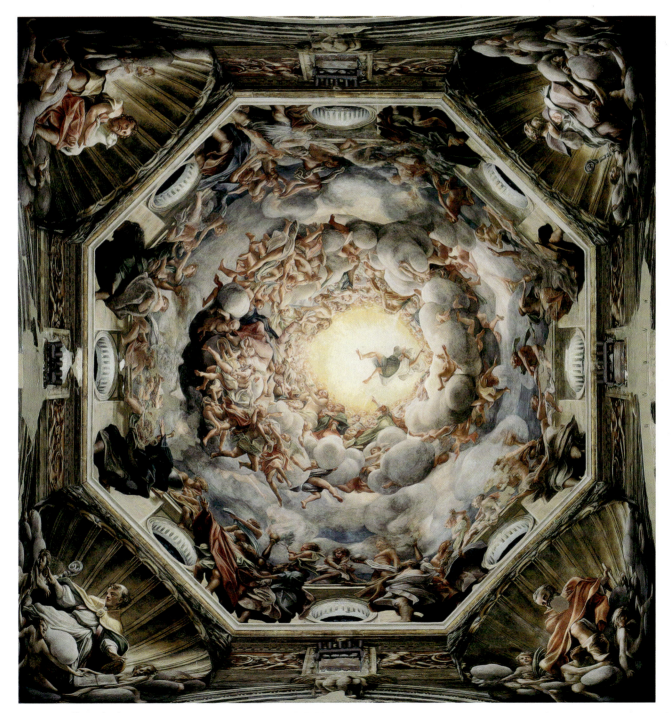

20–19 • Correggio ASSUMPTION OF THE VIRGIN
Main dome, interior, Parma Cathedral, Italy. c. 1526–1530. Fresco, diameter of base of dome approx. 36′ (11 m).

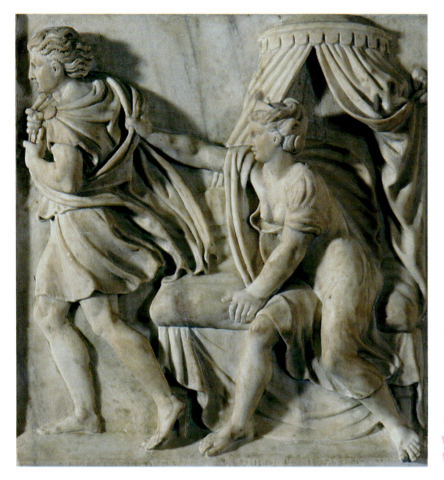

VENICE AND THE VENETO

In the sixteenth century the Venetians did not see themselves as rivals of Florence and Rome, but rather as their superiors. Their city was the greatest commercial sea power in the Mediterranean; they had challenged Byzantium and now they confronted the Muslim Turks. Favored by their unique geographical situation—protected by water and controlling sea routes in the Adriatic Sea and the eastern Mediterranean—the Venetians became wealthy and secure patrons of the arts. Their Byzantine heritage, preserved by their conservative tendencies, encouraged an art of rich patterned surfaces emphasizing light and color.

The idealized style and oil-painting technique initiated by the Bellini family in the late fifteenth century (see Chapter 19) were developed further by sixteenth-century Venetian painters. Venetians were the first in Italy to use oils for painting on both wood panel and canvas. Possibly because they were a seafaring people accustomed to working with large sheets of canvas, and possibly because humidity made their walls crack and mildew, the Venetians were also the first to cover walls with large canvas paintings instead of frescos. Because oils dried slowly, errors could be corrected and changes made easily during the work. The flexibility of the canvas support, coupled with the radiance and depth of oil-suspended pigments, eventually made oil on canvas the preferred medium, especially since it was particularly well suited to the rich color and lighting effects favored by Giorgione and Titian, two of the city's major painters of the sixteenth century.

Assumption is a dazzling illusion—the architecture of the dome seems to dissolve and the forms seem to explode through the building, drawing viewers into the swirling vortex of saints and angels who rush upward amid billowing clouds to accompany the Virgin as she soars into heaven. Correggio's sensual rendering of the figures' flesh and clinging draperies contrasts with the spirituality of the theme (the miraculous transporting of the Virgin to heaven at the moment of her death). The viewer's strongest impression is of a powerful, upward-spiraling motion of alternating cool clouds and warm, alluring figures.

PROPERZIA DE' ROSSI. Very few women had the opportunity or inclination to become sculptors. Properzia de' Rossi (c. 1490–1529/30), who lived in Bologna, was an exception. She mastered many arts, including engraving, and was famous for her miniature sculptures, including an entire *Last Supper* carved on a peach pit! She carved several pieces in marble—two sibyls, two angels, and this relief of **JOSEPH AND POTIPHAR'S WIFE**—for the Cathedral of San Petronio in Bologna (FIG. 20–20). Vasari wrote that a rival male sculptor prevented her from being paid fairly and from securing additional commissions. This particular relief, according to Vasari, was inspired by her own love for a young man, which she got over by carving this panel. Joseph escapes, running, as the partially clad seductress snatches at his cloak. Properzia is the only woman Vasari included in the 1550 edition of *Lives of the Artists*.

GIORGIONE. The career of Giorgione (Giorgio da Castelfranco, c. 1475–1510) was brief—he died from the plague—and most scholars accept only four or five paintings as entirely by his hand. But his importance to Venetian painting is critical. He introduced new, enigmatic pastoral themes, known as *poesie* (or "painted poems"), that were inspired by the contemporary literary revival of ancient pastoral verse. He is significant for his sensuous nude figures, and, above all, for his appreciation of nature in his landscape painting. His early life and training are undocumented, but his work suggests that he studied with Giovanni Bellini. Perhaps Leonardo da Vinci's subtle lighting system and mysterious, intensely observed landscapes also inspired him.

Giorgione's most famous work, called today **THE TEMPEST** (FIG. 20–21), was painted shortly before his death, potentially in response to personal, private impulses—as with many modern artists—rather than to fulfill an external commission. Simply trying to understand what is happening in the picture piques our interest. At the right, a woman is seated on the ground, nude except for the end of a long white cloth thrown over her shoulders. Her nudity seems maternal rather than erotic as she nurses the baby at her side. Across the dark, rock-edged spring stands a man wearing the uniform of a German mercenary soldier. His head is turned in the direction of the woman, but he only appears to have paused for a moment before continuing to turn toward the viewer. X-rays of the painting show that Giorgione altered his composition while he was still at work on it—the soldier replaces a second woman. Inexplicably, a spring gushes forth between the figures to feed a lake surrounded by substantial houses, and in the far distance a bolt of lightning splits the darkening sky. Indeed, the artist's attention seems more focused on the landscape and the unruly elements of nature than on the figures.

TITIAN. In 1507, Giorgione took on a new assistant, Tiziano Vecellio, better known today as Titian (c. 1488–1576). For the next

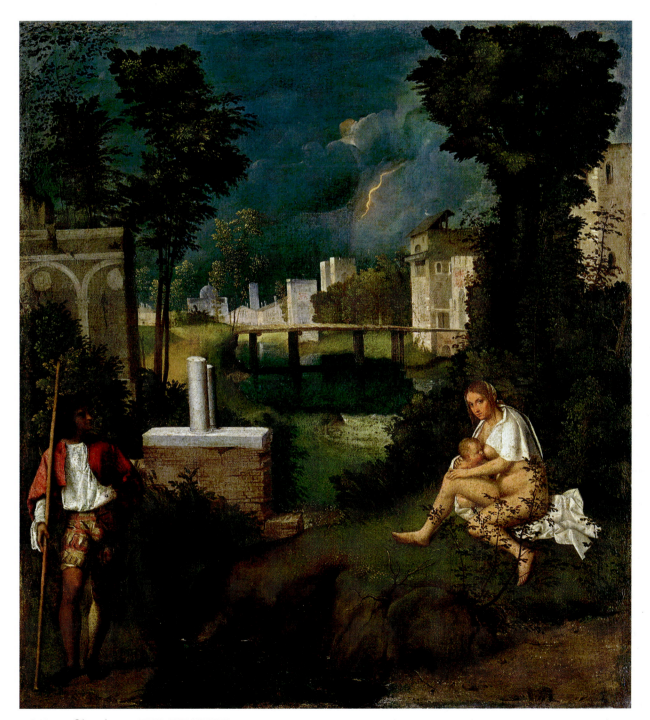

20-21 • Giorgione THE TEMPEST
c. 1506. Oil on canvas, 32 × 28¾″ (82 × 73 cm). Galleria dell'Accademia, Venice.

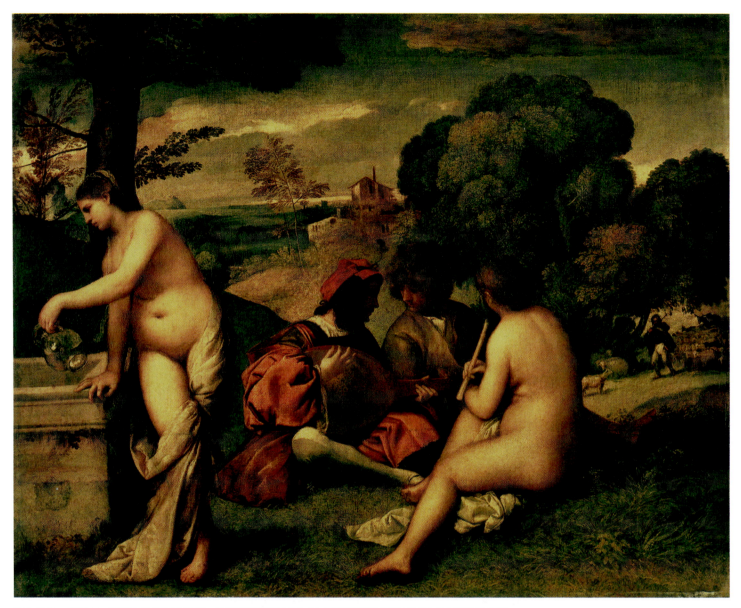

20–22 • Titian **THE PASTORAL CONCERT OR ALLEGORY ON THE INVENTION OF PASTORAL POETRY**
c. 1510. Oil on canvas, 41¼ × 54¾″ (105 × 136.5 cm). Musée du Louvre, Paris.

three years, before Giorgione's untimely death, the two artists' careers were closely bound together. The painting known as **THE PASTORAL CONCERT (FIG. 20–22)** has been attributed to both of them, although today scholarly opinion favors Titian. As in Giorgione's *The Tempest*, the idyllic, fertile landscape, here bathed in golden, hazy late-afternoon sunlight, seems to be one of the main subjects of the painting. In this mythic world, two men—an aristocratic musician in rich red silks and a barefoot, singing peasant in homespun cloth—turn toward each other, seemingly unaware of the two naked women in front of them. One woman plays a pipe and the other pours water into a well; their swaths of white drapery sliding to the ground enhance rather than hide their nudity. Are they the musicians' muses? Behind the figures the sunlight illuminates another shepherd and his animals near lush woodland. The painting evokes a golden age of love and innocence recalled in

ancient Roman pastoral poetry. In fact, the painting is now interpreted as an allegory on the invention of poetry. Titian displays here his renowned talent for painting sensuous female nudes whose bodies seem to glow with an incandescent light, inspired by flesh and blood beauty as much as any source from poetry or art.

Titian's early life is obscure. He supposedly began an apprenticeship as a mosaicist, then studied painting under Gentile and Giovanni Bellini. He was about 20 when he began work with Giorgione, and whatever Titian's early work had been, he had completely absorbed Giorgione's style by the time Giorgione died two years later. Titian completed paintings that they had worked on together, and when Giovanni Bellini died in 1516, Titian became the official painter to the republic of Venice.

In 1519, Jacopo Pesaro, commander of the papal fleet that had defeated the Turks in 1502, commissioned Titian to commemorate the victory in a votive altarpiece for a side-aisle chapel in the Franciscan church of Santa Maria Gloriosa dei Frari in Venice. Titian worked on the painting for seven years and changed the concept three times before he finally came up with a revolutionary composition—one that complemented the viewer's approach from the left. He created an asymmetrical setting of huge columns on high bases soaring right out of the frame (FIG. 20–23). Into this architectural setting, he placed the Virgin and Child on a high throne at one side and arranged saints and the Pesaro family below on a diagonal axis, crossing at the central figure of St. Peter (a reminder of Jacopo's role as head of the papal forces in 1502). The red of Francesco Pesaro's brocade garment and of the banner diagonally across sets up a contrast of primary colors against St. Peter's blue tunic and yellow mantle and the red and blue draperies of the Virgin. St. Maurice (behind the kneeling Jacopo at the left) holds the banner with the papal arms, and a cowering

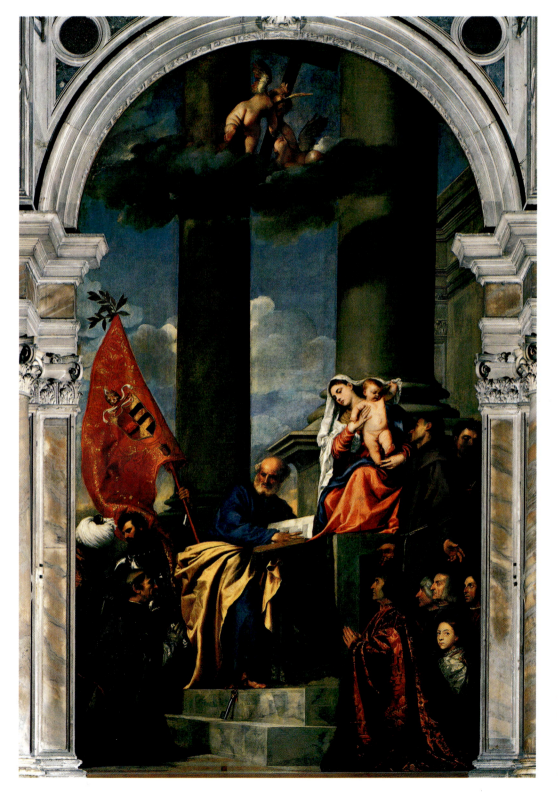

20-23 • Titian
PESARO MADONNA
1519–1526. Oil on canvas,
16′ × 8′10″ (4.9 × 2.7 m).
Side-aisle altarpiece, Santa Maria
Gloriosa dei Frari, Venice.

Women Patrons of the Arts

In the sixteenth century, many wealthy women, from both the aristocracy and the merchant class, were enthusiastic patrons of the arts. The Habsburg princesses Margaret of Austria and Mary of Hungary presided over brilliant humanist courts. The marchesa of Mantua, Isabella d'Este (1474–1539), became a patron of painters, musicians, composers, writers, and literary scholars. Married to Francesco II Gonzaga at age 15, she had great beauty, great wealth, and a brilliant mind that made her a successful diplomat and administrator. A true Renaissance woman, her motto was the epitome of rational thinking—"Neither through Hope nor Fear." An avid collector of manuscripts and books, she sponsored the publication of an edition of Virgil while still in her twenties. She also collected ancient art and objects, as well as works by contemporary Italian artists such as Mantegna, Leonardo, Perugino, Correggio, and Titian. Her study in her Mantuan palace was a veritable museum. The walls above the storage and display cabinets were painted in fresco by Mantegna, and the carved wood ceiling was covered with mottoes and visual references to Isabella's impressive literary interests.

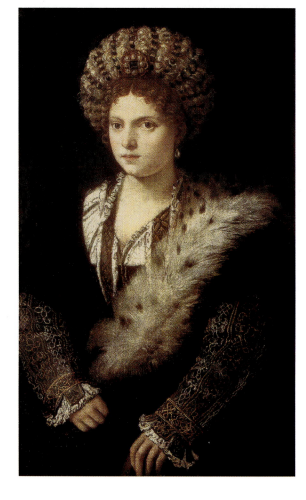

Titian **ISABELLA D'ESTE**
1534–1536. Oil on canvas, 40⅛ × 25⁹⁄₁₆″ (102 × 64.1 cm).
Kunsthistorisches Museum, Vienna.

Turkish captive reminds the viewer of the Christian victory. The arresting image of the youth who turns to meet our gaze at lower right guarantees our engagement, and light floods in from above, illuminating not only this and other faces, but also the great columns, where *putti* in the clouds carry a cross. Titian was famous for his mastery of light and color even in his own day, but this altarpiece demonstrates that he also could draw and model as solidly as any Florentine. The perfectly balanced composition, built on diagonals instead of a vertical and horizontal grid, looks forward to the art of the seventeenth century.

In 1529, Titian, who was well known outside Venice, began a long professional relationship with Emperor Charles V, who vowed to let no one else paint his portrait and ennobled Titian in 1533. The next year Titian was commissioned to paint a portrait of Isabella d'Este (see "Women Patrons of the Arts," above). Isabella was past 60 when Titian portrayed her in 1534–1536, but she asked to appear as she had in her twenties. Titian was able to satisfy her wish by referring to an early portrait by another

artist, but he also conveyed the mature Isabella's strength, self-confidence, and energy.

No photograph can convey the vibrancy of Titian's paint surfaces, which he built up in layers of pure colors, chiefly red, white, yellow, and black. A recent scientific study of Titian's paintings revealed that he ground his pigments much finer than had earlier wood-panel painters. The complicated process by which he produced many of his works began with a charcoal drawing on the prime coat of lead white that was used to seal the pores and smooth the surface of the rather coarse Venetian canvas. The artist then built up the forms with fine glazes of different colors, sometimes in as many as 10 to 15 layers. Titian and others had the advantage of working in Venice, the first place to have professional retail "color sellers." These merchants produced a wide range of specially prepared pigments, even mixing their oil paints with ground glass to increase their glowing transparency. Not until the second half of the sixteenth century did color sellers open their shops in other cities.

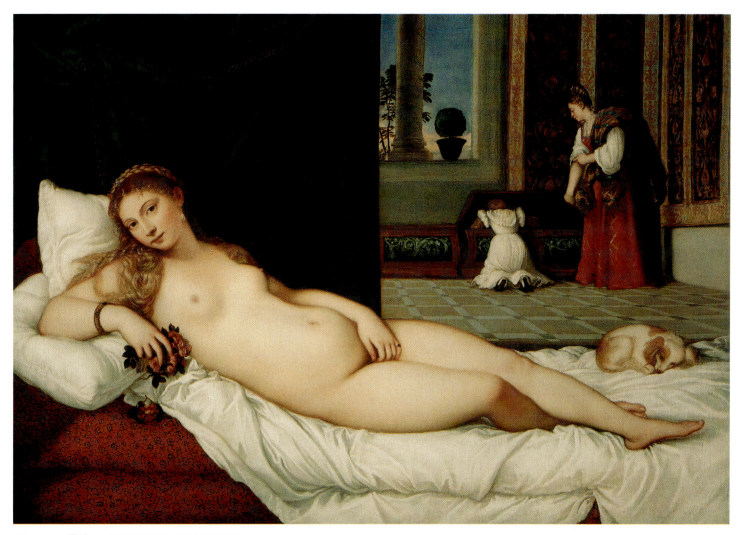

20-24 • Titian "VENUS" OF URBINO
c. 1538. Oil on canvas, 3'11" × 5'5" (1.19 × 1.65 m). Galleria degli Uffizi, Florence.

Paintings of nude reclining women became especially popular in sophisticated court circles, where male patrons could enjoy and appreciate the "Venuses" under the cloak of respectable Classical mythology. Seemingly typical of such paintings is the **"VENUS"** Titian delivered to Guidobaldo della Rovere, duke of Urbino, in spring 1538 (**FIG. 20–24**). Here, we seem to see a beautiful Venetian courtesan, with deliberately provocative gestures, stretching languidly on her couch in a spacious palace, her glowing flesh and golden hair set off by white sheets and pillows. But for its original audience, art historian Rona Goffen has argued, the painting was more about marriage than mythology or seductiveness. The multiple matrimonial references in this work include the pair of *cassoni* (see "The Morelli–Nerli Wedding Chests," page 616) where servants are removing or storing the woman's clothing in the background, the bridal symbolism of the myrtle and roses she holds in her hand, and even the spaniel snoozing at her feet—a traditional symbol of fidelity and domesticity, especially when sleeping so peacefully. Titian's picture might be associated with Duke Guidobaldo's marriage in 1534 to the 10-year-old Giulia Verano. Four years later, when this painting arrived, she would have been considered an adult rather

than a child bride. It seems to represent not a Roman goddess nor a Venetian courtesan, but a physically and emotionally mature bride welcoming her husband into their lavish bedroom.

In his late work from a very lengthy career, Titian sought the essence of form and idea, not the surface perfection of his youthful paintings, in part because he was beset by failing eyesight and a trembling hand. Like Michelangelo, Titian outlived the Classical phase of the Renaissance and his late style profoundly influenced Italian art of the later years of the sixteenth century.

MANNERISM

A new style developed in Florence and Rome in the 1520s that art historians have associated with the death of Raphael and labeled "Mannerism," a word deriving from the Italian *maniera* (meaning "style"). Mannerism was an anti-Classical movement in which artificiality, grace, and elegance took priority over the ordered balance and lifelike references that were hallmarks of High Renaissance art. Patrons favored esoteric subjects, displays of extraordinary technical virtuosity, and the pursuit of beauty for its own sake. Painters and sculptors quoted from ancient and modern works of art in the same self-conscious manner that contemporary poets and authors were quoting from ancient and modern literary classics. Architects working in the Mannerist style designed buildings that defied uniformity and balance and used Classical orders in unconventional ways.

PAINTING

Painters working in the Mannerist style fearlessly manipulated and distorted accepted formal conventions, creating contrived compositions and irrational spatial environments. Figures take on elongated proportions, complicated artificial poses, enigmatic gestures, and dreamy expressions. The pictures are full of quoted references to the works of illustrious predecessors.

PONTORMO. The frescos and altarpieces painted between 1525 and 1528 by Jacopo da Pontormo (1494–1557) for the 100-year-old **CAPPONI CHAPEL** in the church of Santa Felicità in Florence (**FIG. 20–25**) bear the hallmarks of early Mannerist painting. Open on two sides, Brunelleschi's chapel forms an interior loggia in which frescos on the right-hand wall depict the Annunciation and **tondi** (circular paintings) under the cupola represent the four evangelists. In the *Annunciation* the Virgin accepts the angel's message but also seems moved by the adjacent vision of her future sorrow, as she sees her son's body lowered from the cross in the **ENTOMBMENT**, portrayed in the altarpiece on the adjoining wall (**FIG. 20–26**).

Pontormo's ambiguous composition in the *Entombment* enhances the visionary quality of the altarpiece. Shadowy ground

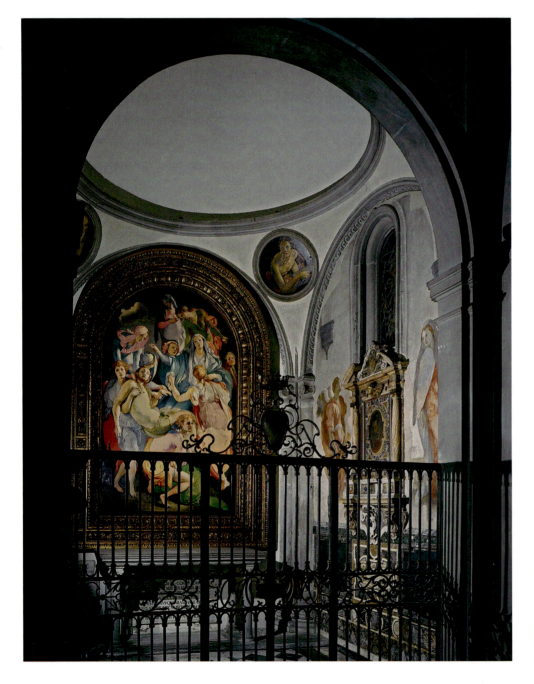

20-25 • CAPPONI CHAPEL, CHURCH OF SANTA FELICITÀ, FLORENCE
Chapel by Filippo Brunelleschi for the Barbadori family, 1419–1423; acquired by the Capponi family, who ordered paintings by Pontormo, 1525–1528.

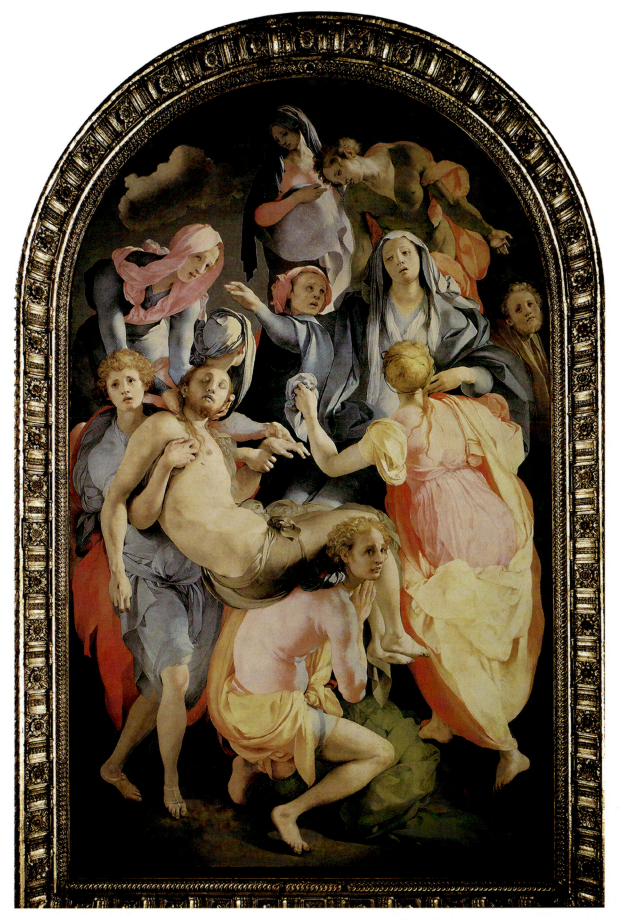

20-26 • Pontormo ENTOMBMENT
Altarpiece in Capponi Chapel, church of Santa Felicità, Florence. 1525–1528. Oil and tempera on wood
panel, 10′3″ × 6′4″ (3.1 × 1.9 m).

and cloudy sky give no sense of a specific location, and little sense of grounding for the figures. Some press forward into the viewer's space, while others seem to levitate or stand precariously on tiptoe. Pontormo chose a moment just after Jesus' removal from the cross, when the youths who have lowered him pause to regain their hold on the corpse, which recalls Michelangelo's Vatican *Pietà* (SEE FIG. 20–9). Odd poses and drastic shifts in scale charge the scene emotionally, but perhaps most striking is the use of weird colors in odd juxtapositions—baby blue and pink with accents of olive-green, yellow, and scarlet. The overall tone of the picture is set by the unstable youth crouching in the foreground, whose skintight bright pink shirt is shaded in iridescent, pale gray-green, and whose anxious expression is projected out of the painting, directly at the viewer.

PARMIGIANINO. When Parmigianino (Francesco Mazzola, 1503–1540) left his native Parma in 1524 for Rome, the strongest influence on his work was Correggio. In Rome, however, Parmigianino met

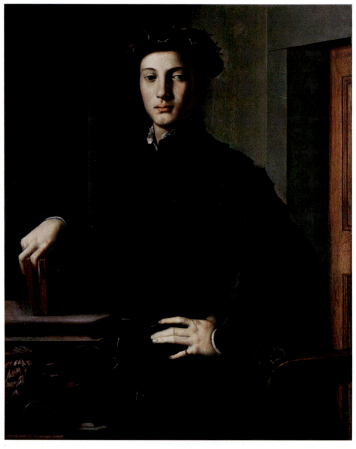

20-28 • Bronzino **PORTRAIT OF A YOUNG MAN**
c. 1540–1545. Oil on wood panel, 37½ × 29½″ (95.5 × 74.9 cm). Metropolitan Museum of Art, New York. The H. O. Havemayer Collection 29.100.16

Giulio Romano; he also studied the work of Raphael and Michelangelo. What he assimilated developed into a distinctive Mannerist style, calm but strangely unsettling. After the Sack of Rome in 1527, he moved to Bologna and then back to Parma.

Left unfinished at the time of his early death is a disconcerting painting known as the **MADONNA WITH THE LONG NECK** (FIG. 20–27). The unnaturally proportioned figure of Mary, whose massive legs and lower torso contrast with her narrow shoulders and long neck and fingers, is presumably seated on a throne, but there is no seat in sight. The languid expanse of the sleeping child recalls the pose of the ashen Christ in a *pietà*. The plunge into a deep background to the right reveals a startlingly small St. Jerome, who unrolls a scroll in front of huge white columns that support absolutely nothing, whereas at the left a crowded mass of blushing boys blocks any view into the background. Like Pontormo, Parmigianino presents a well-known image in a challenging manner calculated to unsettle viewers.

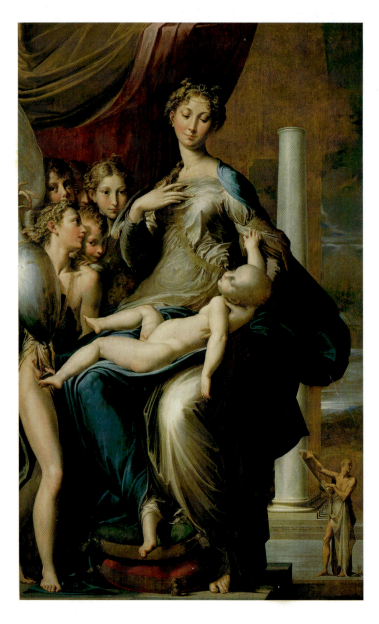

20-27 • Parmigianino **MADONNA WITH THE LONG NECK**
1534–1540. Oil on wood panel, 7′1″ × 4′4″ (2.16 × 1.32 m). Galleria degli Uffizi, Florence.

BRONZINO. About 1522, Agnolo di Cosimo (1503–1572), whose nickname of "Bronzino" means "copper-colored" (just as we might call someone "Red"), became Pontormo's assistant, probably helping with the tondi in the corners of the Capponi Chapel (SEE FIG. 20–25). In 1530, he established his own workshop, though he continued to work with Pontormo on occasional large projects. In 1540, Bronzino became court painter to the Medici. Although he was a versatile artist who produced altarpieces, fresco decorations, and tapestry designs over his long career, he is best known today for his elegant portraits. Bronzino's virtuosity in rendering costumes and settings creates a rather cold and formal effect, but the self-contained demeanor of his subjects admirably conveys their haughtiness. **PORTRAIT OF A YOUNG MAN (FIG. 20–28)** demonstrates Bronzino's characteristic portrayal of his subjects as intelligent, aloof, elegant, and self-assured. The youth's spidery fingers toy with a book, suggesting his scholarly interests, but his wall-eyed stare creates a slightly unsettling, artificial effect, associating his face with the carved masks on the furniture. His costume seems more present than his personality.

Bronzino's **ALLEGORY WITH VENUS AND CUPID** is one of the strangest paintings of the sixteenth century (FIG. 20–29). It contains all the formal, iconographical, and psychological characteristics of Mannerist art and could almost stand alone as a summary of the movement. Seven figures, two masks, and a dove interweave in an intricate, claustrophobic formal composition pressed breathlessly into the foreground plane. Taken as individual images, they display the exaggerated poses, graceful forms, polished surfaces, and delicate colors that characterize Mannerist art. But a closer look into this composition uncovers disturbing erotic attachments and bizarre irregularities. The painting's complex allegory and relentless ambiguity probably delighted mid-sixteenth-century courtiers who enjoyed equally sophisticated wordplay and esoteric Classical references, but for us it defies easy explanation. Nothing is quite what it seems.

Venus and her son Cupid engage in an unsettlingly lascivious dalliance, encouraged by a *putto* sauntering in from the right—representing Folly, Jest, or Playfulness—who is about to throw pink roses at them while stepping on a thorny branch that draws blood from his foot. Cupid gently kisses his mother and pinches her erect nipple while Venus snatches an arrow from his quiver, leading some scholars to suggest that the painting's title should be *Venus Disarming Cupid*. Venus holds the golden apple of discord given to her by Paris; her dove conforms to the shape of Cupid's foot without actually touching it, while a pair of masks lying at her feet reiterates the theme of duplicity. An old man, Time or Chronos, assisted by an outraged Truth or Night, pulls back a curtain to expose the couple. Lurking just behind Venus a monstrous serpent—which has the upper body and head of a beautiful young girl and the legs and claws of a lion—crosses her hands to hold a honeycomb and the stinger at the end of her tail. This strange hybrid has been identified both as Fraud and Pleasure.

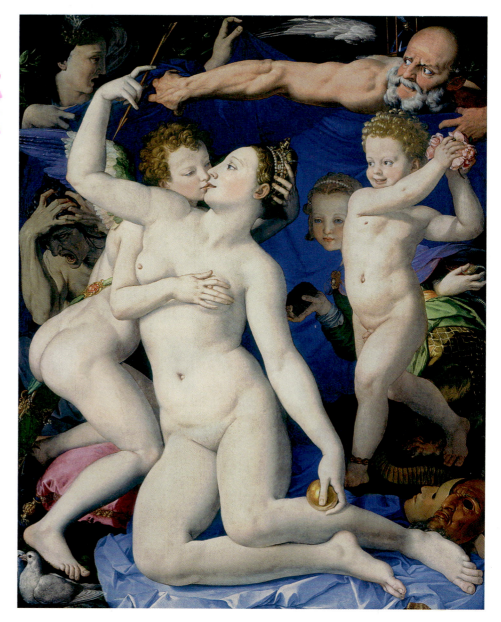

20-29 • Bronzino ALLEGORY WITH VENUS AND CUPID
Mid 1540s. Oil on panel, 57½ × 46″ (1.46 × 1.16 m). National Gallery, London.
Reproduced by courtesy of the Trustees of the National Gallery, London

In the shadows to the left, a pale and screaming man tearing at his hair has recently been identified as a victim of syphilis, which raged as an epidemic during this period. This interpretation suggests that the painting could be a warning of the dangers of this disease, believed in the sixteenth century to be spread principally by coitus, kissing, and breast feeding, all of which are alluded to in the intertwined Cupid and Venus. But the complexity of the painting makes room for multiple meanings, and deciphering them would be typical of the sorts of games enjoyed by sixteenth-century intellectuals. Perhaps the allegory tells of the impossibility of constant love and the folly of lovers, which becomes apparent across time. Or perhaps it is an allegorical warning of the dangers of illicit sexual liaisons, including the pain, hair loss, and disfiguration of venereal disease. Maybe it is both, and even more. Duke Cosimo ordered the painting himself, and presented it as a diplomatic gift to King Francis I of France, who would doubtless have relished its overt eroticism and flawless execution.

SOFONISBA ANGUISSOLA.   Northern Italy, more than any other part of the peninsula, produced a number of gifted women artists. In the latter half of the sixteenth century, Bologna, for example, boasted some two dozen women painters and sculptors, as well as a number of learned women who lectured at the university. Sofonisba Anguissola (c. 1532–1625), born into a noble family in Cremona (between Bologna and Milan), was unusual in that she was not the daughter of an artist. Her father gave all his children a humanistic education and encouraged them to pursue careers in literature, music, and especially painting. He consulted Michelangelo about Sofonisba's artistic talents in 1557, asking for a drawing that she might copy and return to be critiqued. Michelangelo evidently obliged because Sofonisba Anguissola's father wrote an enthusiastic letter of thanks.

Anguissola was a gifted portrait painter who also created miniatures, an important aspect of portraiture in the sixteenth century, when people had few means of recording the features of a lover, friend, or family member. Anguissola painted a miniature **SELF-PORTRAIT** holding a medallion, the border of which spells out her name and home town, Cremona **(FIG. 20–30)**. The interlaced letters at the center of the medallion pose a riddle; they seem to form a monogram with the first letters of her sisters' names: Minerva, Europa, Elena. Such names are further evidence of the Anguissola family's enthusiasm for the Classics.

In 1560, Anguissola accepted the invitation of the queen of Spain to become a lady-in-waiting and court painter, a post she held for 20 years. Unfortunately, most of her Spanish works were lost in a seventeenth-century palace fire, but a 1582 Spanish inventory described her as "an excellent painter of portraits above all the painters of this time"—extraordinary praise in a court that patronized Titian. After her years at court, she returned to Sicily (a Spanish territory), where she died at age 92. Anthony Van Dyck met her in Palermo in 1624, where he sketched her and claimed that she was then 96 years old. He wrote that she

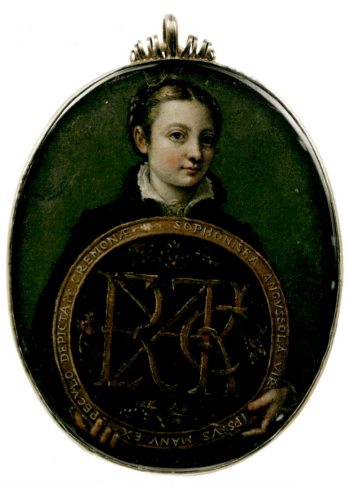

20–30 • Sofonisba Anguissola SELF-PORTRAIT
c. 1552. Oil on parchment on cardboard, 2½ × 3¼″ (6.4 × 8.3 cm). Museum of Fine Arts, Boston. Emma F. Munroe Fund 60.155

advised him on positioning the light for her portrait, asking that it not be placed too high because the strong shadows would bring out her wrinkles.

LAVINIA   FONTANA.   Bolognese   artist   Lavinia   Fontana (1552–1614) learned to paint from her father. By the 1570s, her success was so well rewarded that her husband, the painter Gian Paolo Zappi, gave up his own painting career to care for their large family and help his wife with the technical aspects of her work, such as framing. In 1603, Fontana moved to Rome as an official painter to the papal court. She also soon came to the attention of the Habsburgs, who became major patrons.

While still in her twenties, Fontana painted a **NOLI ME TANGERE (FIG. 20–31)**, where Christ reveals himself for the first time to Mary Magdalen following his Resurrection, warning her not to touch him (John 20:17). Christ's broad-brimmed hat and spade refer to the passage in the Gospel of John that tells us that Mary Magdalen at first thought Christ was the gardener. In the middle distance Fontana portrays a second version of the Resurrection, where women followers of Christ discover an angel in his empty tomb. This secondary scene's dizzying diagonal plunge into depth is a typical feature of late Mannerist painting in Italy.

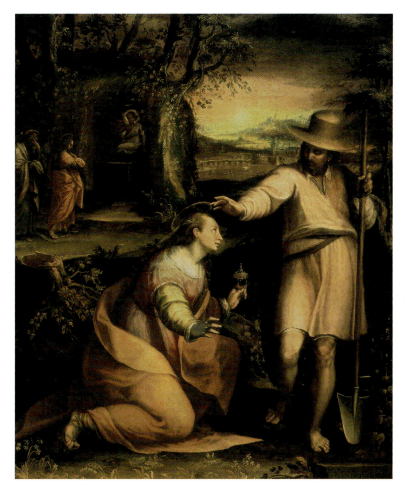

20-31 • Lavinia Fontana NOLI ME TANGERE
1581. Oil on canvas, 47⅜ × 36⅝″ (120.3 × 93 cm).
Galleria degli Uffizi, Florence.

SCULPTURE

Mannerist sculpture—often small in size and made from precious metals—stylizes body forms and foregrounds displays of technical skill in ways that are reminiscent of Mannerist painting.

CELLINI. The Florentine goldsmith and sculptor Benvenuto Cellini (1500–1571), who wrote a dramatic—and scandalous—autobiography and a practical handbook for artists, worked in the French court at Fontainebleau. There he made the famous **SALTCELLAR OF KING FRANCIS I (FIG. 20–32)**, a table accessory transformed into an elegant sculptural ornament by fanciful imagery and superb execution. In gold and enamel, the Roman sea god Neptune, representing the source of salt, sits next to a tiny boat-shape container that carries the seasoning, while a personification of Earth guards the plant-derived pepper, contained in the triumphal arch to her right. Representations of the seasons and the times of day on the base refer to both daily meal schedules and festive seasonal celebrations. The two main figures lean away from each other at impossible angles yet are connected and visually balanced by glance, gestures, and coordinated poses—they mirror each other with one bent and one straight leg. Their supple, elongated bodies and small heads reflect the Mannerist conventions of artists like Parmigianino. Cellini wrote, "I represented the Sea and the Land, both seated, with their legs intertwined just as some branches of the sea run into the land and the land juts into the sea…" (Cellini, *Autobiography*, trans G. Bull, p. 291).

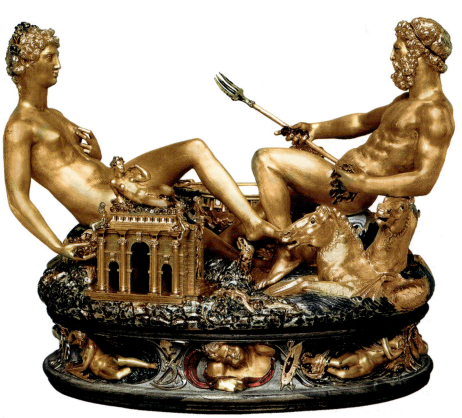

20-32 • Benvenuto Cellini SALTCELLAR OF KING FRANCIS I OF FRANCE
1540–1543. Gold and enamel, 10½ × 13⅛″
(26.67 × 33.34 cm). Kunsthistorisches Museum, Vienna.

EXPLORE MORE: Gain insight from a primary source about Benvenuto Cellini
www.myartslab.com

GIAMBOLOGNA. In the second half of the sixteenth century, probably the most influential sculptor in Italy was Jean de Boulogne, better known by his Italian name, Giovanni da Bologna or Giambologna (1529–1608). Born in Flanders, he had settled by 1557 in Florence, where both the Medici family and the sizable Netherlandish community were his patrons. He not only influenced a later generation of Italian sculptors, he also spread the Mannerist style to the north through artists who came to study his work. Although inspired by Michelangelo, Giovanni favored graceful forms and poses, as in his gilded-bronze **ASTRONOMY, OR VENUS URANIA** (FIG. 20–33) of about 1573. The figure's identity is suggested by the astronomical device on the base of the plinth. Although she is based on a Classical prototype, Giambologna has twisted Venus' upper torso and arms to one side

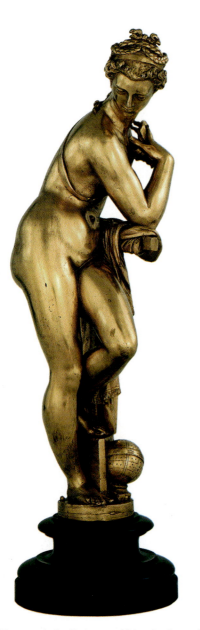

20-33 • Giovanni da Bologna (Giambologna) ASTRONOMY, OR VENUS URANIA
c. 1573. Bronze gilt, height 15¼″ (38.8 cm). Kunsthistorisches Museum, Vienna.

and bent her neck back in the opposite direction so that her chin is over her right shoulder, straining the torsion of the human body to its limits. Consequently, viewers are encouraged to walk around this figure to explore it fully; it cannot be understood from any single viewpoint. The elaborate coiffure and the detailed engraving of drapery texture contrast strikingly with the smooth, gleaming flesh of Venus' body. Following standard practice for cast-metal sculpture, Giambologna replicated this statuette several times for different patrons.

ART AND THE COUNTER-REFORMATION

Pope Clement VII, whose miscalculations had spurred Emperor Charles V to attack and destroy Rome in 1527, also misjudged the threat to the Church and to papal authority posed by the Protestant Reformation. His failure to address the issues raised by the reformers enabled the movement to spread. His successor, Paul III (pontificate 1534–1549), the rich and worldly Roman noble Alessandro Farnese, was the first pope to pursue church reform in response to the rise of Protestantism. In 1536, he appointed a commission to investigate charges of church corruption and convened the Council of Trent (1545–1563) to define Catholic dogma, initiate disciplinary reforms, and regulate the training of clerics.

Pope Paul III also addressed Protestantism through repression and censorship. In 1542, he instituted the Inquisition, a papal office that sought out heretics for interrogation, trial, and sentencing. The enforcement of religious unity extended to the arts. Traditional images of Christ and the saints were sanctioned, but art was scrutinized for traces of heresy and profanity. Guidelines issued by the Council of Trent limited what could be represented in Christian art and led to the destruction of some works. At the same time, art became a powerful weapon of propaganda, especially in the hands of members of the Society of Jesus, a new religious order founded by the Spanish nobleman Ignatius of Loyola (1491–1556) and confirmed by Paul III in 1540. Dedicated to piety, education, and missionary work, the Jesuits, as they are known, spread worldwide and became important leaders of the Counter-Reformation movement and the revival of the Catholic Church.

ART AND ARCHITECTURE IN ROME AND THE VATICAN

To restore the heart of the city of Rome, Paul III began rebuilding the Capitoline Hill as well as continuing work on St. Peter's. His commissions include some of the finest art and architecture of the late Italian Renaissance. His first major commission brought Michelangelo, after a quarter of a century, back to the Sistine Chapel.

MICHELANGELO'S LATE WORK. In his early sixties, Michelangelo complained bitterly of feeling old, but he nonetheless undertook the important and demanding task of painting the **LAST JUDGMENT** on the 48-foot-high end wall above the Sistine Chapel altar between 1536 and 1541 (FIG. 20–34).

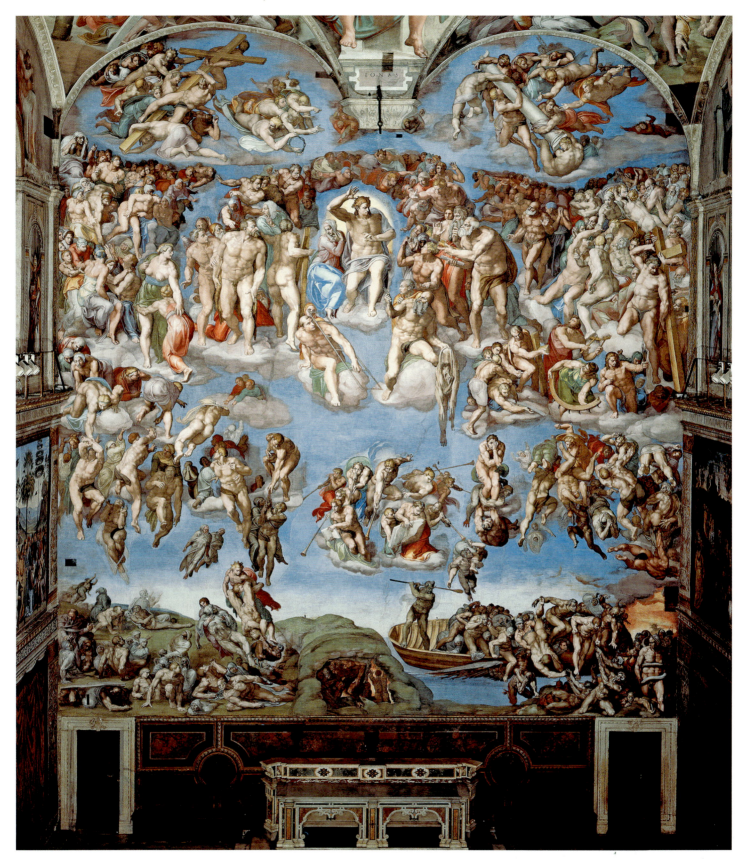

20–34 • Michelangelo LAST JUDGMENT, SISTINE CHAPEL
1536–1541. Fresco, 48 × 44′ (14.6 × 13.4 m).

Dark, rectangular patches left by recent restorers (visible, for example, in the upper left and right corners) contrast with the vibrant colors of the chapel's frescos. These dark areas show just how dirty the walls had become over the centuries before their recent cleaning.

EXPLORE MORE: Gain insight from a primary source of Michelangelo's poetry **www.myartslab.com**

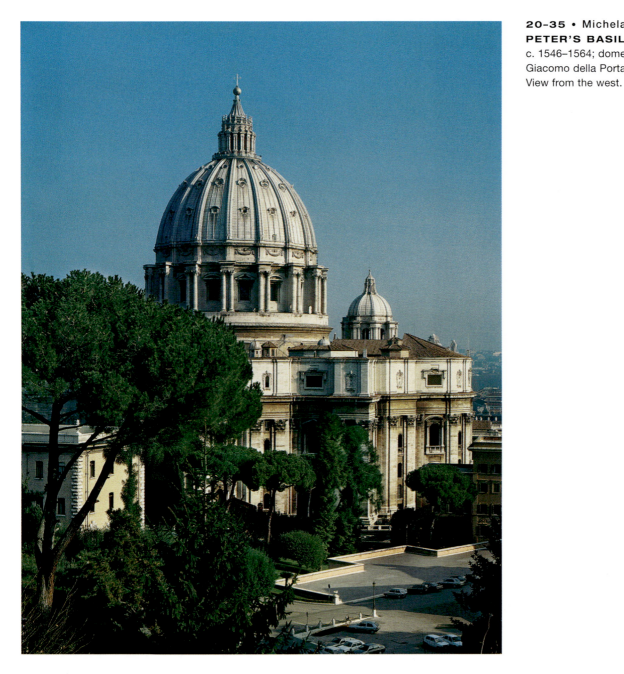

20-35 • Michelangelo **ST. PETER'S BASILICA, VATICAN**
c. 1546–1564; dome completed 1590 by Giacomo della Porta; lantern 1590–1593. View from the west.

Abandoning the clearly organized medieval conception of the Last Judgment, in which the saved are neatly separated from the damned, Michelangelo painted a writhing swarm of resurrected humanity. At left (on Christ's right side), the dead are dragged from their graves and pushed up into a vortex of figures around Christ, who wields his arm like a sword of justice. The shrinking Virgin under Christ's raised right arm represents a change from Gothic tradition, where she had sat enthroned beside, and equal in size to, her son. To the right of Christ's feet is St. Bartholomew, who in legend was martyred by being skinned alive. He holds his flayed skin, and Michelangelo seems to have painted his own distorted features on the skin's face. Despite the efforts of several saints to save them at the last minute, the damned are plunged toward hell on the right, leaving the elect and still-unjudged in a dazed, almost uncomprehending state. On the lowest level of the mural, right above the altar, is the gaping, fiery entrance to hell, toward which Charon, the ferryman of the dead to the underworld, propels his craft. The painting was long interpreted as a grim and constant reminder to celebrants of the Mass—the pope and his cardinals—that ultimately they too would face stern judgment at the end of time. Conservative clergy criticized the painting for its frank nudity, and after Michelangelo's death they ordered bits of drapery to be added by artist Daniele da Volterra to conceal the offending areas, earning Daniele the unfortunate nickname *Il Braghettone* ("breeches painter").

Another of Paul III's ambitions was to complete the new St. Peter's, a project that had been under way for 40 years (see "St. Peter's Basilica," page 651). Michelangelo was well aware of the work done by his predecessors—from Bramante to Raphael to Antonio da Sangallo the Younger. The 71-year-old sculptor, confident of his

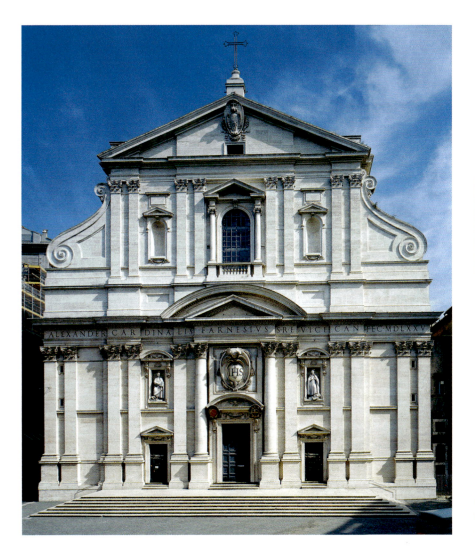

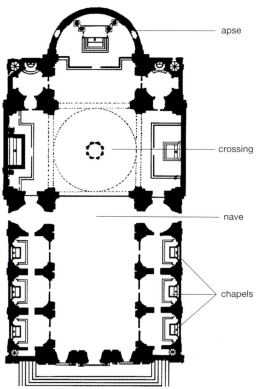

20-36 • Giacomo della Porta and Vignola
FAÇADE AND PLAN OF THE CHURCH OF IL GESÙ, ROME
c. 1573–1584.

architectural expertise, demanded the right to deal directly with the pope, rather than through a committee of construction deputies. Michelangelo further shocked the deputies—but not the pope—by tearing down or canceling parts of Sangallo's design and returning to Bramante's central plan, long associated with shrines of Christian martyrs. Although seventeenth-century additions and renovations dramatically changed the original plan of the church and the appearance of its interior, Michelangelo's **ST. PETER'S** (**FIG. 20–35**) still can be seen in the contrasting forms of the flat and angled exterior walls and the three surviving hemicycles (semicircular structures). Colossal pilasters, blind windows (frames without openings), and niches surround the sanctuary of the church. The current dome, erected by Giacomo della Porta in 1588–1590, retains Michelangelo's basic design: segmented with regularly spaced ribs, seated on a high drum with pedimented windows between paired columns, and surmounted by a tall lantern reminiscent of Bramante's *Il Tempietto* (SEE FIG. 20–16).

Michelangelo—often described by his contemporaries as difficult and even arrogant—alternated between periods of depression and frenzied activity. Yet he was devoted to his friends and helpful to young artists. He believed that his art was divinely inspired; later in life, he became deeply absorbed in religion and

dedicated himself to religious works—many left unfinished—that subverted Renaissance ideals of human perfectibility and denied his own youthful idealism. In the process he pioneered new stylistic directions that would inspire succeeding generations of artists.

VIGNOLA.   A young artist who worked to meet the need for new Roman churches was Giacomo Barozzi (1507–1573), known as Vignola after his native town. He worked in Rome during the late 1530s, surveying ancient Roman monuments and providing illustrations for an edition of Vitruvius. From 1541 to 1543, he was in France with Francesco Primaticcio at the château of Fontainebleau. After returning to Rome, he secured the patronage of the Farnese family and profited from the Counter-Reformation program of church building.

Catholicism's new emphasis on individual, emotional participation brought a focus on sermons and music, requiring churches with wide naves and unobstructed views of the altar, instead of the complex interiors of medieval and earlier Renaissance churches. Ignatius of Loyola was determined to build **IL GESÙ**, the Jesuit headquarters church in Rome, according to these precepts, although he did not live to see it finished (**FIG. 20–36**). The

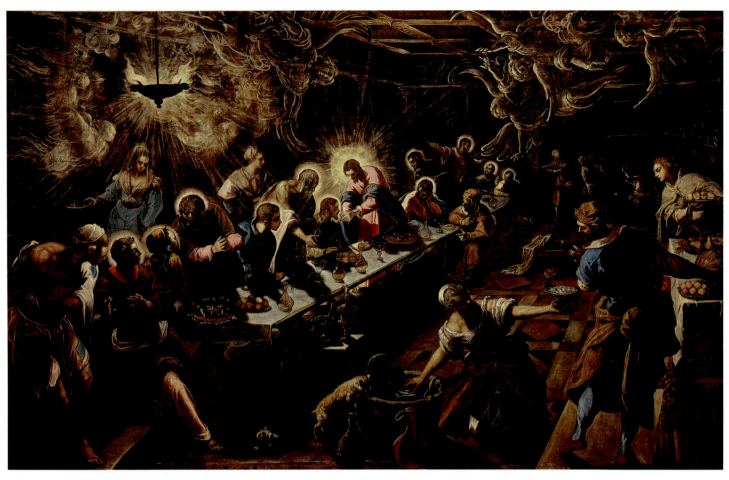

20-37 • Tintoretto THE LAST SUPPER
1592–1594. Oil on canvas, 12′ × 18′8″ (3.7 × 5.7 m). Church of San Giorgio Maggiore, Venice.

Tintoretto, who had a large workshop, often developed a composition by creating a small-scale model like a miniature stage set, which he populated with wax figures. He then adjusted the positions of the figures and the lighting until he was satisfied with the entire scene. Using a grid of horizontal and vertical threads placed in front of this model, he could easily sketch the composition onto squared paper for his assistants to copy onto a large canvas. His assistants also primed the canvas, blocking in the areas of dark and light, before the artist himself, free to concentrate on the most difficult passages, finished the painting. This efficient working method allowed Tintoretto to produce a large number of paintings in all sizes.

also joined the shop. So skillfully did Marietta capture her father's style and technique that today art historians cannot identify her work in the shop.

ARCHITECTURE: PALLADIO

Just as Veronese and Tintoretto expanded upon the rich Venetian tradition of oil painting initiated by Giorgione and Titian, Andrea Palladio dominated architecture during the second half of the century by expanding upon the principles of Alberti and ancient Roman architecture. His buildings—whether villas, palaces, or churches—were characterized by harmonious symmetry and controlled ornamentation. Born Andrea di Pietro della Gondola (1508–1580), probably in Padua, Palladio began his career as a stonecutter. After moving to Vicenza, he was hired by the nobleman, humanist scholar, and amateur architect Giangiorgio Trissino, who gave him the nickname "Palladio" for the Greek goddess of wisdom, Pallas Athena, and the fourth-century Roman

writer Palladius. Palladio learned Latin at Trissino's small academy and accompanied his benefactor on three trips to Rome, where he made drawings of Roman monuments.

Over the years, Palladio became involved in several publishing ventures, including a guide to Roman antiquities and an illustrated edition of Vitruvius. He also published his own books on architecture—including ideal plans for country estates, using proportions derived from ancient Roman buildings—that for centuries would be valuable resources for architectural design. Despite their theoretical bent, his writings were often more practical than earlier treatises. Perhaps his early experience as a stonemason provided him with the knowledge and self-confidence to approach technical problems and discuss them as clearly as he did theories of ideal proportion and uses of the Classical orders. By the eighteenth century, Palladio's *Four Books of Architecture* had been included in the libraries of most educated people. Thomas Jefferson had one of the first copies in America.

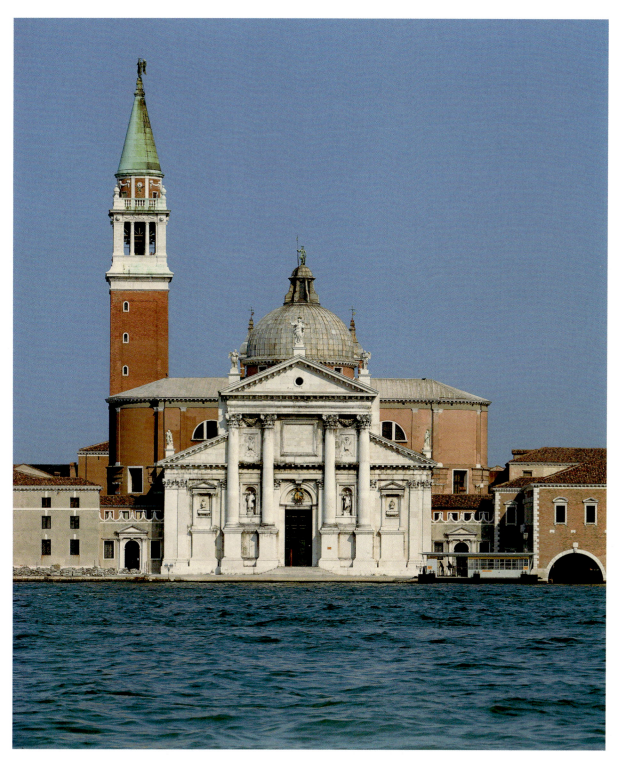

20-38 • Palladio CHURCH OF SAN GIORGIO MAGGIORE, VENICE
Plan 1565; construction 1565–1580; façade 1597–1610; campanile 1791.
Finished by Vincenzo Scamozzi following Palladio's design.

SEE MORE: Click the Google Earth link for San Giorgio Maggiore **www.myartslab.com**

SAN GIORGIO MAGGIORE. By 1559, when he settled in Venice, Palladio was one of the foremost architects in Italy. In 1565, he undertook a major architectural commission: the monastery **CHURCH OF SAN GIORGIO MAGGIORE (FIG. 20–38)**. His variation on the traditional Renaissance façade for a basilica— a wide lower level fronting the nave and side aisles, surmounted by a narrower front for the nave clerestory—creates the illusion of two temple fronts of different heights and widths, one set inside the other. At the center, colossal columns on high pedestals support an entablature and pediment; these columns correspond to

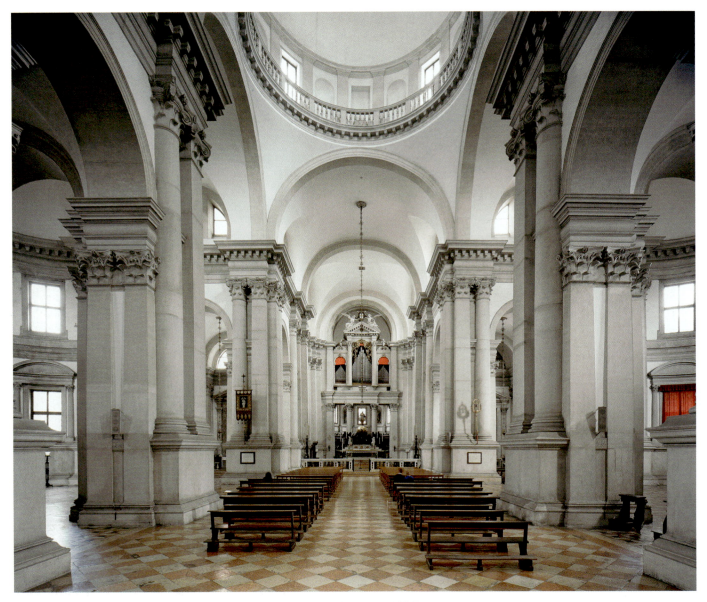

20-39 • NAVE, CHURCH OF SAN GIORGIO MAGGIORE, VENICE
Begun 1566. Tintoretto's *Last Supper* (not visible) hangs to the left of the altar.

the width of the nave within. Behind the taller temple front, a second front consists of pilasters supporting another entablature and pediment; this wider front spans the entire width of the church, including the triple aisle. Although the façade was not built until after the architect's death, his original design was followed.

The interior of **SAN GIORGIO** (FIG. **20–39**) is a fine example of Palladio's harmoniously balanced geometry, expressed here in strong verticals and powerfully opened arches. The tall engaged columns and shorter pilasters of the nave arcade piers echo the two levels of orders on the façade, thus unifying the building's exterior and interior.

THE VILLA ROTONDA. Palladio's versatility was already apparent in numerous villas built early in his career. In the 1560s, he started his most famous and influential villa just outside Vicenza. Although

villas were traditionally working farms, Palladio designed this one as a retreat, literally a party house. To maximize vistas of the countryside, he placed a porch elevated at the top of a wide staircase on each face of the building. The main living quarters are on this second level, and the lower level is reserved for the kitchen, storage, and other utility rooms. Upon its completion in 1569, the building was dubbed the **VILLA ROTONDA** (FIG. **20–40**) because it had been inspired by another round building, the Roman Pantheon. The plan (FIG. **20–41**) shows the geometric clarity of Palladio's conception: a circle inscribed in a small square inside a larger square, with symmetrical rectangular compartments and identical rectangular projections from each of its faces. The use of a central dome on a domestic building was a daring innovation that effectively secularized the dome and initiated what was to become a long tradition of domed country houses, particularly in England and the United States.

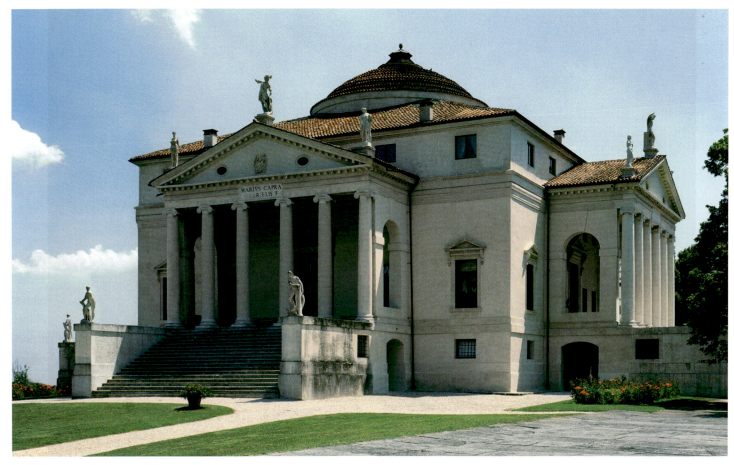

20-40 • Palladio EXTERIOR VIEW OF VILLA ROTONDA, VICENZA
Italy. Begun 1560s.

After its purchase in 1591 by the Capra family, the Villa Rotonda became known as the Villa Capra.

SEE MORE: Click the Google Earth link for the Villa Rotonda, Vicenza www.myartslab.com

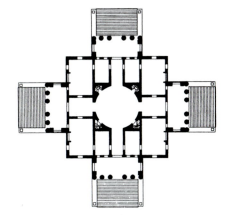

20-41 • Palladio PLAN OF VILLA ROTONDA, VICENZA
Italy. Begun 1560s.

EXPLORE MORE: Gain insight from a primary source by Andrea Palladio www.myartslab.com

THINK ABOUT IT

20.1 Discuss Julius II's efforts to aggrandize the city of Rome and create a new golden age of papal art. Focus your answer on at least two specific works he commissioned.

20.2 Write about either Michelangelo's or Raphael's extensive work in the Sistine Chapel. How did papal commissions push these two established artists in new creative directions?

20.3 Select either Pontormo's *Entombment* (FIG. 20–26) or Parmigianino's *Madonna with the Long Neck* (FIG. 20–27), and explain why the painting characterizes Mannerist style. How does your chosen work depart from the Classical norms of the High Renaissance?

20.4 Elaborate on the idea that whereas Rome and Florence were oriented toward drawing, Venice was oriented toward color. Compare and contrast a specific work from each tradition in forming your answer.

20.5 Analyze either the Palazzo del Tè (FIG. 20–17) or the Villa Rotonda (FIG. 20–40). Explain how the design of the building differs from the design of grand churches during this same period, even though architects clearly used Classical motifs in both sacred and secular contexts.

PRACTICE MORE: Compose answers to these questions, get flashcards for images and terms, and review chapter material with quizzes www.myartslab.com

In Nuremberg, a city known for its master metalworkers, Hans Krug (d. 1519) and his sons Hans the Younger and Ludwig were among the finest. They created marvelous display pieces for the wealthy, such as this silver-gilt apple cup. Made about 1510, a gleaming apple, in which the stem forms the handle of the lid, balances on a leafy branch that forms its base.

The Krug family was responsible for the highly refined casting and finishing of the final product, but several artists worked together to produce such pieces—one drawing designs, another making the models, and others creating the final piece in metal. A drawing by Dürer may have been the basis for the apple cup. Though we know of no piece of goldwork by the artist himself, Dürer was a major catalyst in the growth of Nuremberg as a key center of German goldsmithing. He accomplished this by producing designs for metalwork throughout his career. Designers played an essential role in the metalwork process. With design in hand, the modelmaker created a wooden form for the goldsmith to follow. The result of this artistic collaboration was a technical *tour de force*, an intellectual conceit, and an exquisite object.

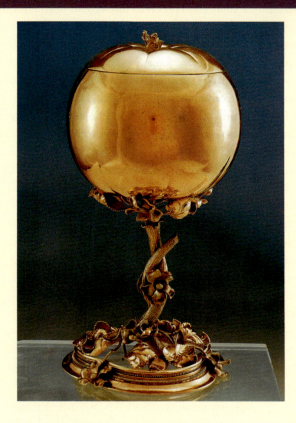

Workshop of Hans Krug (?) APPLE CUP
c. 1510–1515. Gilt silver, height 8½″ (21.5 cm). Germanisches Nationalmuseum, Nuremberg.

Erhart Harschner, a specialist in architectural shrines, had begun work on the elaborate Gothic frame in 1499, and was paid 50 florins for his work. Riemenschneider was commissioned to provide the figures and scenes to be placed within this frame. He was paid 60 florins for the sculpture, giving us a sense of the relative value patrons placed on their contributions.

The main panel of the altarpiece portrays the moment at the Last Supper when Christ revealed that one of his followers would betray him. Unlike Leonardo da Vinci, who chose the same moment (SEE FIG. 20–3), Riemenschneider puts Judas at center stage and Jesus off-center at the left. The disciples sit around the table. As the event is described in the Gospel of John (13:21–30), Jesus extends a morsel of food to Judas, signifying that he will be the traitor who sets in motion the events leading to the Crucifixion. One apostle points down, a strange gesture until we realize that he is pointing to the crucifix in the predella, to the relic of Christ's blood, and to the altar table, the symbolic representation of the table of the Last Supper and the tomb of Christ.

Rather than creating individual portraits of the apostles, Riemenschneider repeated a limited number of facial types. His figures have large heads, prominent features, sharp cheekbones, sagging jowls, baggy eyes, and elaborate hair with thick wavy locks and deeply drilled curls. The muscles, tendons, and raised veins of hands and feet are also especially lifelike. His assistants and apprentices copied these faces and figures, either from drawings or from three-dimensional models made by the master. In the altarpiece, deeply hollowed folds create active patterns in the voluminous draperies whose strong highlights and dark shadows harmonize the figural composition with the intricate carving of the framework. The Last Supper is set in a "real" room containing actual benches for the figures. Windows in the back wall are glazed with bull's-eye glass so that natural light shines in from two directions to illuminate the scene, producing changing effects depending on the time of day and the weather. Although earlier sculpture had been painted and gilded, Riemenschneider introduced the use of a natural wood finish toned with varnish. This meant that details of both figures and environment had to be carved into the wood itself, not quickly added later with paint. Since this required more skillful carvers and more time for them to carve, this new look was a matter of aesthetics, not cost-saving.

In addition to producing an enormous number of religious images for churches, Riemenschneider was politically active in the city's government, and he even served as mayor in 1520. His career ended during the Peasants' War (1524–1526), an early manifestation of the Protestant movement. His support for the peasants led to a fine and imprisonment in 1525, and although he survived, Riemenschneider produced no more sculpture and died in 1531.

NIKOLAUS HAGENAUER. Prayer was the principal source of solace and relief to the ill before the advent of modern medicine. About 1505, the Strasbourg sculptor Nikolaus Hagenauer (active

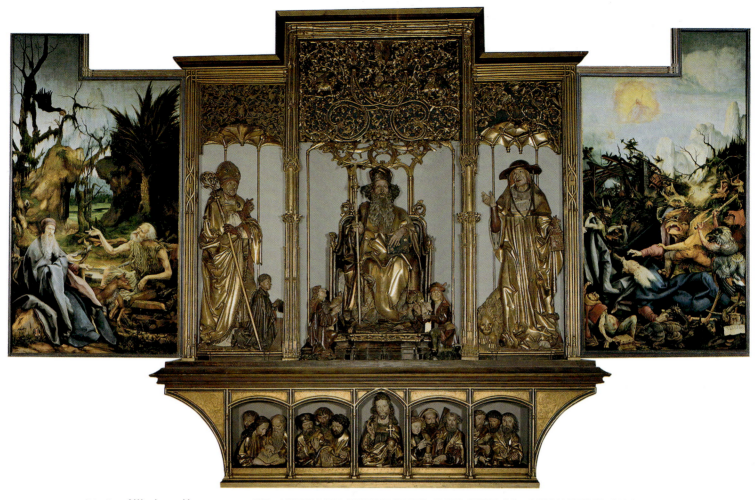

21-3 • Nikolaus Hagenauer ST. ANTHONY ENTHRONED BETWEEN SS. AUGUSTINE AND JEROME, SHRINE OF THE ISENHEIM ALTARPIECE (OPEN, SHOWING GRÜNEWALD WINGS)
From the Community of St. Anthony, Isenheim, Alsace, France. c. 1500. Painted and gilt limewood, center panel 9′9½″ × 10′9″ (2.98 × 3.28 m), predella 2′5½″ × 11′2″ (0.75 × 3.4 m), wings 8′2½″ × 3′½″ (2.49 × 0.93 m). Predella: *Christ and the Apostles*. Wings: *SS. Anthony and Paul the Hermit* (left); *The Temptation of St. Anthony* (right). 1510–1515. Musée d'Unterlinden, Colmar, France.

1493–1530s) carved an altarpiece for the abbey of St. Anthony in Isenheim near Colmar **(FIG. 21–3)** where a hospital specialized in the care of patients with skin diseases, including the plague, leprosy, and St. Anthony's Fire (caused by eating rye and other grains infected with the ergot fungus). The shrine includes images of SS. Anthony, Jerome, and Augustine. Three tiny men—their size befitting their subordinate status—kneel at the feet of the saints: the donor, Jean d'Orliac, and two men offering a rooster and a piglet.

In the predella below, Jesus and the apostles bless the altar, Host, and assembled patients in the hospital. This limewood sculpture was painted in lifelike colors, and the shrine itself was gilded to enhance its resemblance to a precious reliquary. A decade later, Matthias Grünewald painted wooden shutters to cover the shrine (SEE FIGS. 21–4, 21–5).

PAINTING

The work of two very different German artists has come down to us from the first decades of the sixteenth century. Matthias

Grünewald continued currents of medieval mysticism and emotional spirituality to create extraordinarily moving paintings. Albrecht Dürer, on the other hand, used intense observation of the world to render lifelike representations of nature, mathematical perspective to create convincing illusions of space, and a reasoned canon of proportions to standardize depictions of the human figure.

MATTHIAS GRÜNEWALD. As a court artist to the archbishop of Mainz, Matthias Grünewald (Matthias Gothart Neithart, c. 1470/ 1475–1528) was a man of many talents, who worked as an architect and hydraulic engineer as well as a painter. He is best known today for painting the shutters or wings attached to Nikolaus Hagenauer's carved Isenheim Altarpiece (SEE FIG. 21–3). The completed altarpiece is impressive in size and complexity. Grünewald painted one set of fixed wings and two sets of movable ones, plus one set of sliding panels to cover the predella. The altarpiece could be exhibited in different configurations depending upon the church calendar. The wings and carved wooden shrine

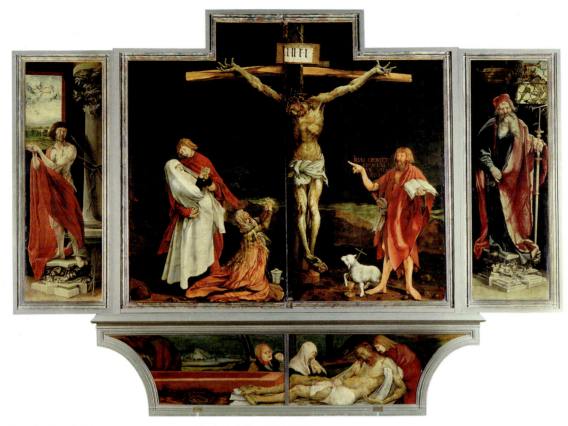

21-4 • Matthias Grünewald ISENHEIM ALTARPIECE (CLOSED)
From the Community of St. Anthony, Isenheim, Alsace, France. Center panels: *Crucifixion*; predella: *Lamentation*; side panels: *SS. Sebastian* (left) and Anthony Abbot (right). c. 1510–1515. Date 1515 on ointment jar. Oil on wood panel, center panels 9′9½″ × 10′9″ (2.97 × 3.28 m) overall; each wing 8′2½″ × 3′1½″ (2.49 × 0.93 m); predella 2′5½″ × 11′2″ (0.75 × 3.4 m). Musée d'Unterlinden, Colmar, France.

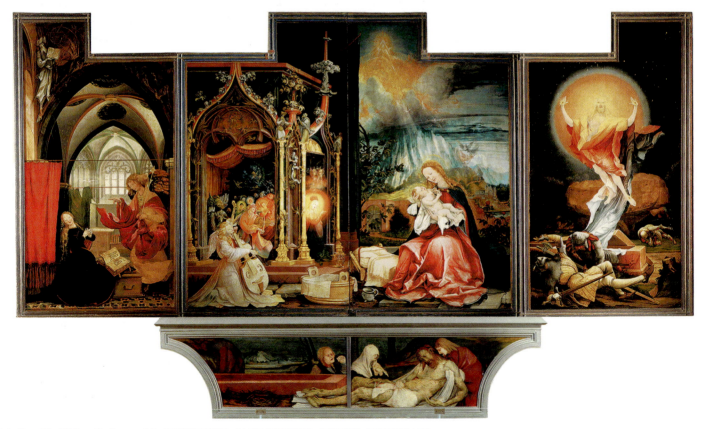

21-5 • Matthias Grünewald ISENHEIM ALTARPIECE (FIRST OPENING)
Left to right: *Annunciation*, *Virgin and Child with Angels*, *Resurrection*. c. 1510–1515. Oil on wood panel, center panel 9′9½″ × 10′9″ (2.97 × 3.28 m), each wing 8′2½″ × 3′1½″ (2.49 × 0.92 m). Musée d'Unterlinden, Colmar, France.

complemented one another, the inner sculpture seeming to bring the surrounding paintings to life, and the painted wings protecting the precious carvings.

On weekdays, when the altarpiece was closed, viewers saw a grisly image of the Crucifixion in a darkened landscape, a *Lamentation* below it on the predella, and life-size figures of SS. Sebastian and Anthony Abbot—both associated with the plague— standing on *trompe l'oeil* pedestals on the fixed wings (FIG. 21–4). The intensity of feeling here has suggested that Grünewald may have been inspired by the visions of St. Bridget of Sweden, a fourteenth-century mystic whose works—including morbidly detailed descriptions of the Crucifixion—were published in Germany beginning in 1492. Grünewald has scrupulously described the horrific character of the tortured body of Jesus, covered with gashes from his beating and pierced by the thorns used to form a crown for his head. His ashen body, clotted blood, open mouth, and blue lips signal his death. In fact, he appears already to be decaying, an effect enhanced by the palette of putrescent green, yellow, and purplish-red—all described by St. Bridget. She wrote, "The color of death spread through his flesh…." An immaculately garbed Virgin Mary has collapsed in the arms of a ghostlike John the Evangelist, and Mary Magdalen has fallen in anguish to her knees; her clasped hands with outstretched fingers seem to echo Jesus' fingers, cramped in rigor mortis. At the right, John the Baptist points to Jesus and repeats his prophecy, "He shall increase." The Baptist and the lamb, holding a cross and bleeding from its breast into a golden chalice, allude to baptism, the Eucharist, and to Christ as the sacrificial Lamb of God. In the predella below, Jesus' bereaved mother and friends prepare his racked body for burial—an activity that must have been a common sight in the abbey's hospital.

In contrast to these grim scenes, the first opening displays events of great joy—the Annunciation, the Nativity, and the Resurrection—appropriate for Sundays and feast days (FIG. 21–5). Praying in front of these pictures, the patients must have hoped for miraculous recovery and taken comfort in these visions of divine rapture and orgiastic color. Unlike the awful darkness of the Crucifixion, the inner scenes are brilliantly illuminated, in part by phosphorescent auras and haloes, and stars glitter in the night sky of the Resurrection. The technical virtuosity of Grünewald's painting alone is enough to inspire euphoria.

The *Annunciation* on the left wing may be related to a special liturgy called the Golden Mass, which celebrated the divine motherhood of the Virgin. The Mass included a staged reenactment of the angel's visit to Mary, as well as readings from the story of the Annunciation (Luke 1:26–38) and the Hebrew Bible prophecy of the Savior's birth (Isaiah 7:14–15), which is inscribed in Latin on the pages of the Virgin's open book.

The central panels show the heavenly and earthly realms joined in one space. In a variation on the northern European visionary tradition, the new mother adores her miraculous Christ Child while envisioning her own future as queen of heaven amid angels and cherubims. Grünewald portrayed three distinct types of angels in the foreground—young, mature, and a feathered hybrid with a birdlike crest on its human head. The range of ethnic types in the heavenly realm may have emphasized the global dominion of the Church, whose missionary efforts were expanding as a result of European exploration. St. Bridget describes the jubilation of the angels as "the glowing flame of love."

The second opening of the altarpiece (SEE FIG. 21–3) reveals Hagenauer's sculpture and was reserved for the special festivals of St. Anthony. The wings in this second opening show to the left the meeting of St. Anthony with the hermit St. Paul, and to the right St. Anthony attacked by horrible demons, perhaps inspired by the horrors of the diseased patients, but also modeled in part on Schongauer's well-known print of the same subject (SEE FIG. 18–26). The meeting of the two hermits in the desert glorifies the monastic life, and in the wilderness Grünewald depicts medicinal plants used in the hospital's therapy. Grünewald painted the face of St. Paul with his own self-portrait, while St. Anthony is a portrait of the donor and administrator of the hospital, the Italian Guido Guersi, whose coat of arms Grünewald painted on the rock next to him.

Like Riemenschneider, Grünewald's involvement with the Peasants' War may have damaged his artistic career. He left Mainz and spent his last years in Halle, whose ruler was the chief protector of Martin Luther and a long-time patron of Grünewald's contemporary Albrecht Dürer.

ALBRECHT DÜRER.   Studious, analytical, observant, and meticulous —and as self-confident as Michelangelo—Albrecht Dürer (1471–1528) was the foremost artist of the German Renaissance. He made his home in Nuremberg, where he became a prominent citizen. Nuremberg was a center of culture as well as of business, with an active group of humanists and internationally renowned artists. It was also a leading publishing center. Dürer's father was a goldsmith and must have expected his son to follow in his trade (see "German Metalwork: A Collaborative Venture," page 680). Dürer did complete an apprenticeship in gold-working, as well as in stained-glass design, painting, and the making of woodcuts—which he learned from Michael Wolgemut, illustrator of the *Nuremberg Chronicle* (SEE FIG. 18–27). But ultimately it was as a painter and graphic artist that he built his artistic fame.

In 1490, Dürer began traveling to extend his education. He went to Basel, Switzerland, hoping to meet Martin Schongauer, but arrived after the master's death. By 1494, Dürer had moved from Basel to Strasbourg. His first trip to Italy (1494–1495) introduced him to Italian Renaissance ideas and attitudes and, as we considered at the beginning of this chapter, to the concept of the artist as an independent creative genius. In his self-portrait of 1500 (SEE FIG. 21–1), Dürer represents himself as an idealized, Christ-like figure in a severely frontal pose, staring directly at the viewer.

On his return to Nuremberg, Dürer began to publish his own prints to bolster his income, and ultimately it was prints, not

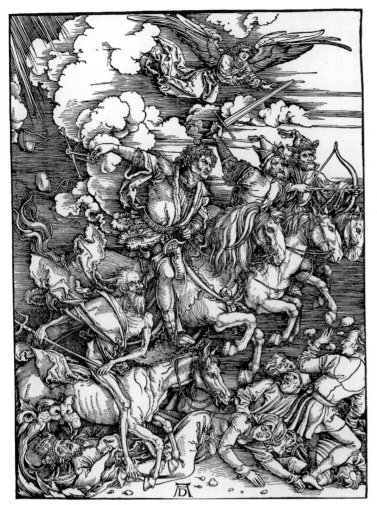

21–6 • Albrecht Dürer THE FOUR HORSEMEN OF THE APOCALYPSE
From *The Apocalypse*. 1497–1498. Woodcut, 15½ × 11⅛"
(39.4 × 28.3 cm). Metropolitan Museum of Art, New York.
Gift of Junius S. Morgan, 1919 (19.73.209)

as a goldsmith is evident in his meticulous attention to detail, and in his decorative cloud and drapery patterns. Following the tradition established by his late fifteenth-century predecessors, he fills the foreground with large, active figures.

Perhaps as early as the summer of 1494, Dürer began to experiment with engravings, cutting the metal plates himself with an artistry rivaling Schongauer's. His growing interest in Italian art and his theoretical investigations are reflected in his 1504 engraving **ADAM AND EVE (FIG. 21–7)**, which represents his first documented use of ideal human proportions based on Roman copies of ancient Greek sculpture. He may have seen figures of Apollo and Venus in Italy, and he would have known ancient sculpture from contemporary prints and drawings. But around these idealized human figures he represents plants and animals with typically northern attention to descriptive detail.

Dürer filled the landscape with symbolic content reflecting the medieval theory that after Adam and Eve disobeyed God, they and their descendants became vulnerable to imbalances in the body fluids that controlled human temperament. An excess of black bile from the liver would produce melancholy, despair, and greed. Yellow bile caused anger, pride, and impatience; phlegm in the lungs resulted in lethargy and disinterest; and an excess of

paintings, that made his fortune. His first major publication, *The Apocalypse*, appeared simultaneously in German and Latin editions in 1497–1498. It consisted of a woodcut title page and 14 full-page illustrations with the text printed on the back of each. Perhaps best known is **THE FOUR HORSEMEN OF THE APOCALYPSE (FIG. 21–6)**, based on figures described in Revelation 6:1–8: a crowned rider, armed with a bow, on a white horse (Conquest); a rider with a sword, on a red horse (War); a rider with a set of scales, on a black horse (Plague and Famine); and a rider on a sickly pale horse (Death). Earlier artists had simply lined up the horsemen in the landscape, but Dürer created a compact, overlapping group of wild riders charging across the world and trampling its cowering inhabitants, men and women, clerical and lay.

Dürer probably did not cut his own woodblocks but employed a skilled carver who followed his drawings faithfully. Dürer's dynamic figures show affinities with Schongauer's *Temptation of St. Anthony* (SEE FIG. 18–26). He adapted Schongauer's metal-engraving technique to the woodcut medium, using a complex pattern of lines to model the forms. Dürer's early training

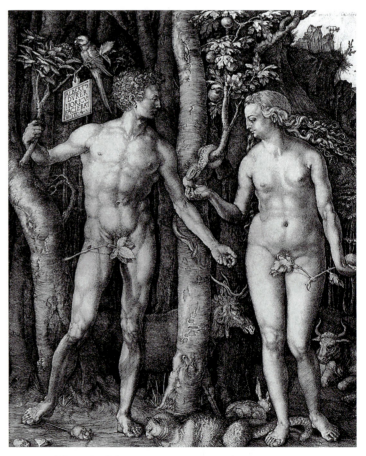

21–7 • Albrecht Dürer ADAM AND EVE
1504. Engraving, 9⅞ × 7⅝" (25.1 × 19.4 cm).
Philadelphia Museum of Art.
Purchased: Lisa Nora Elkins Fund

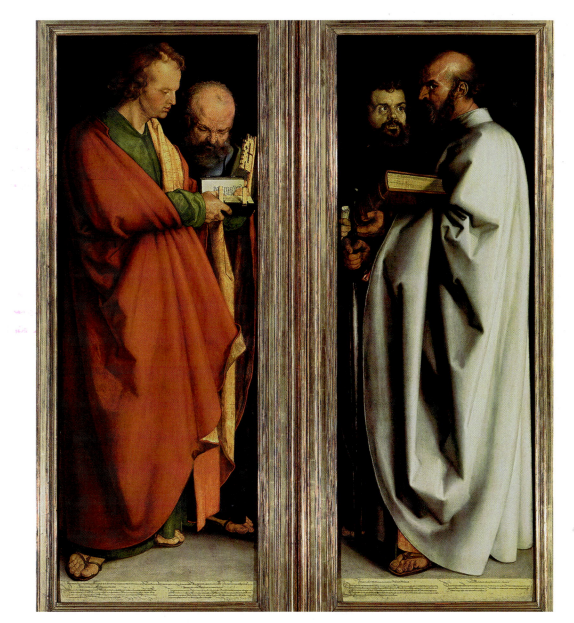

21-8 • Albrecht Dürer
FOUR APOSTLES
1526. Oil on wood panel,
each panel 7′1½″ × 2′6″
(2.15 × 0.76 m).
Alte Pinakothek, Munich.

blood made a person unusually optimistic but also compulsively interested in the pleasures of the flesh. These four human temperaments, or personalities, are symbolized here by the melancholy elk, the choleric cat, the phlegmatic ox, and the sanguine (or sensual) rabbit. The mouse is a symbol of Satan (see the mousetrap in FIG. 18–10), whose earthly power, already manifest in the Garden of Eden, was capable of bringing human beings to a life of woe through their own bad choices. Adam seems to be releasing the mouse into the world of his paradise as he contemplates eating the forbidden fruit that Eve receives from the snake. Dürer placed his signature prominently on a placard hung on a tree branch in Adam's grasp and on which perches a parrot—possibly symbolizing false wisdom, since it can only repeat mindlessly what it hears.

Dürer's familiarity with Italian art was greatly enhanced by a second, leisurely trip over the Alps in 1505–1506. Thereafter, he seems to have resolved to reform the art of his own country by publishing theoretical writings and manuals that discussed Renaissance problems of perspective, ideal human proportions, and the techniques of painting.

Dürer admired Martin Luther, but they never met. In 1526, the artist openly professed his Lutheranism in a pair of inscribed panels, the **FOUR APOSTLES** (FIG. 21–8). On the left panel, the elderly Peter, who normally has a central position as the first pope, has been displaced with his keys to the background by Luther's favorite evangelist, John, who holds an open Gospel that reads "In the beginning was the Word," reinforcing the Protestant emphasis on the Bible. On the right panel, Mark stands behind Paul, whose epistles were particularly admired by the Protestants. A long inscription on the frame warns the viewer not to be led astray by "false prophets" but to heed the words of the New Testament as recorded by these "four excellent men." Below each figure are excerpts from their letters and from the Gospel of Mark—drawn from Luther's German translation of the New Testament—warning

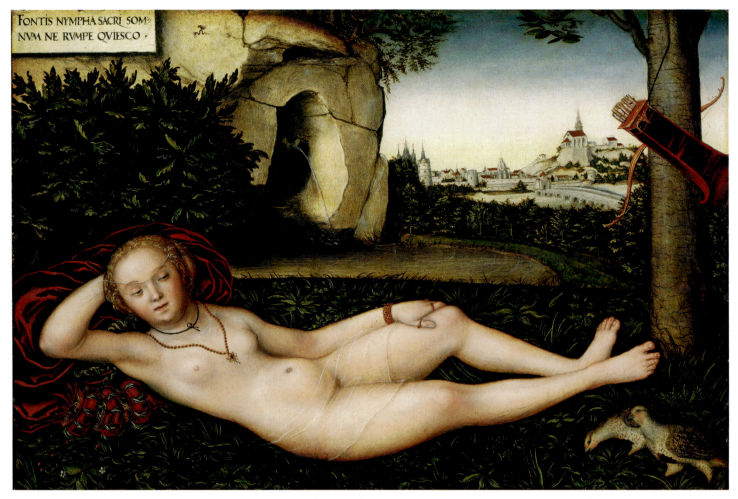

FONTIS NYMPHA SACRI SOM-
NVM NE RVMPE QVIESCO ·

21–9 • Lucas Cranach the Elder NYMPH OF THE SPRING
c. 1537. Oil on panel, 19 × 28½″ (48.5 × 72.9 cm). National Gallery of Art, Washington, D.C.

against those who do not understand the true Word of God. These paintings were surely meant to chart the possibility of a Protestant visual art.

Dürer presented the panels to the city of Nuremberg, which had already adopted Lutheranism as its official religion. Dürer wrote, "For a Christian would no more be led to superstition by a picture or effigy than an honest man to commit murder because he carries a weapon by his side. He must indeed be an unthinking man who would worship picture, wood, or stone. A picture therefore brings more good than harm, when it is honourably, artistically, and well made" (Snyder, p. 333).

LUCAS CRANACH THE ELDER.   Martin Luther's favorite painter, Lucas Cranach the Elder (1472–1553), moved his workshop to Wittenberg in 1504, after a number of years in Vienna. In addition to the humanist milieu of its university and library, Wittenberg offered the patronage of the Saxon court. Appointed court painter to Elector Frederick the Wise, Cranach created woodcuts, altarpieces, and many portraits.

Just how far German artists' style and conception of the figure could differ from Italian Renaissance idealism is easily seen in

Cranach's **NYMPH OF THE SPRING** (FIG. **21–9**), especially when compared with Titian's *"Venus" of Urbino* (SEE FIG. 20–24). The sleeping nymph was a Renaissance theme, not an ancient one. Cranach was inspired by a fifteenth-century inscription on a fountain beside the Danube, cited in the upper left corner of the painting: "I am the nymph of the sacred font. Do not interrupt my sleep for I am at peace." Cranach records the Danube landscape with characteristic northern attention to detail and turns his nymph into a rather provocative young woman, who glances slyly out at the viewer through half-closed eyes. She has cast aside a fashionable red velvet gown, but still wears her jewelry, which together with her transparent veil enhances rather than conceals her nudity—especially those coral beads that fall between her breasts, outlining their contours. Unlike other artists working for Protestant patrons, many of whom looked on earthly beauty as a sinful vanity, Cranach seems delighted by earthly things—the lush foliage that provides the nymph's couch, the pair of partridges (symbols of Venus and married love), and Cupid's bow and quiver of arrows hanging on the tree. Could this nymph be a living beauty from the Wittenburg court? She is certainly not an embodiment of an idealized, Classical Venus.

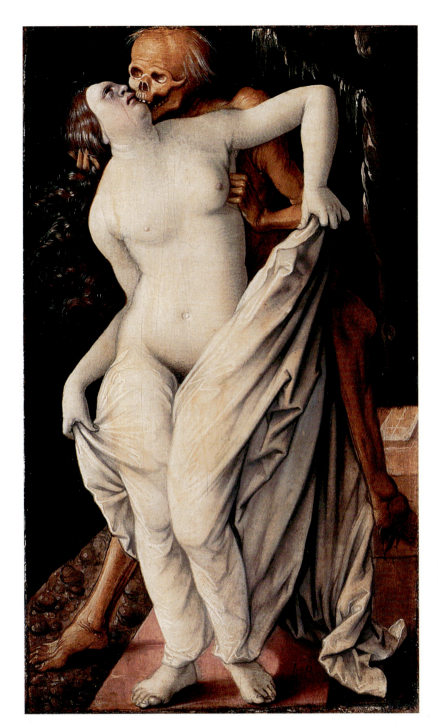

21-10 • Hans Baldung Grien DEATH AND THE MATRON

c. 1520–1525. Oil on wood panel, 12⅜ × 7⅜″ (31.3 × 18.7 cm). Öffentliche Kunstsammlung, Basel.

Although more erotically charged and certainly more dramatic than Dürer's Eve in FIG. 21–7, Baldung's woman is based in certain ways on this famous image, which was engraved while he was assisting in Dürer's workshop. In many respects, the similarities in pose (especially the feet) and form (wide hips with narrowing waist and torso) only point up the differences in expressive content.

HANS BALDUNG GRIEN. Cranach's slightly younger contemporary Hans Baldung (1484/1485–1545)—his nickname tag "Grien" ("green," apparently a favorite color) dates from his apprenticeship days and was used to distinguish him from the numerous other apprentices named Hans—is known for very different visualizations of women. Born into an affluent and well-educated family, Baldung was working in Strasbourg by 1500, before moving to Nuremberg in 1503 and eventually joining Dürer's workshop in 1505–1507. Over the course of his long career, he also worked in Halle and Freiburg, but his principal artistic home was Strasbourg, where he lived out a prosperous professional life as a painter, printmaker, and stained-glass designer.

During the first half of his career, Baldung created a series of paintings on the theme of **DEATH AND THE MATRON** that juxtapose sensuality with mortality, voluptuousness with decay, attraction with repulsion. The example in **FIG. 21–10**—painted in about 1520–1525 for a private collector in Basel—uses brilliant illumination and expansive posture to draw our attention first to the voluptuous nude, fleshier and considerably more sensual than Cranach's nymph (SEE FIG. 21–9) or Dürer's Eve (SEE FIG. 21–7). But this focus is soon overtaken by a sense of surprise that mirrors her own, as she turns her head to discover that the figure stroking her hair and clutching at her breast is not her lover but Death himself. The putrid decay of his yellowing flesh contrasts sharply

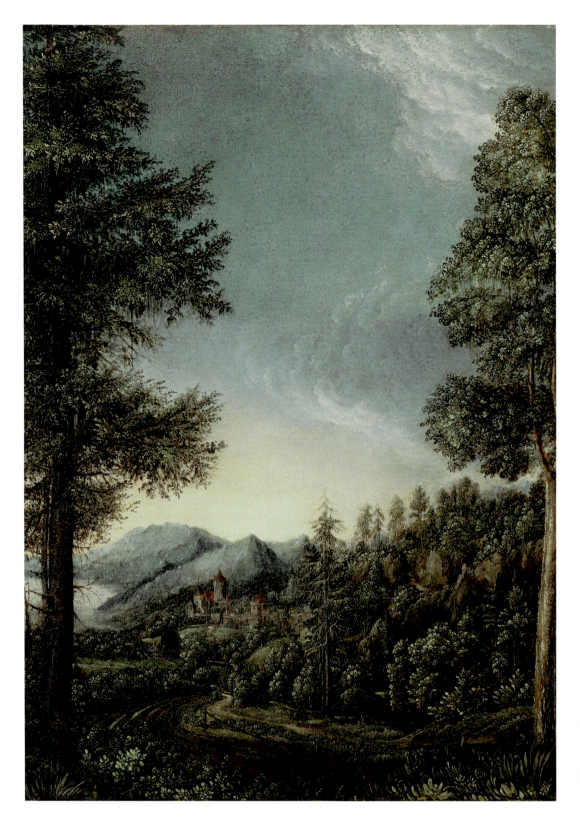

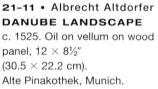

21–11 • Albrecht Altdorfer
DANUBE LANDSCAPE
c. 1525. Oil on vellum on wood panel, 12 × 8½″
(30.5 × 22.2 cm).
Alte Pinakothek, Munich.

with her soft contours, and his bony molting head is the antithesis of her full pink cheeks, flowing tresses, and soft traces of body hair. That the encounter takes place in a cemetery, on top of a tombstone, serves to underline the warning against the transitory pleasures of the flesh, but Baldung also seems to depend on the viewers' own erotic engagement to make the message not only moral but personal.

ALBRECHT ALTDORFER. Landscape, with or without figures, became a popular theme in the sixteenth century. In the fifteenth century, northern artists had examined and recorded nature with the care and enthusiasm of biologists, but painted landscapes were reserved for the backgrounds of figural compositions, usually sacred subjects. In the 1520s, however, religious art found little favor among Protestants. Landscape painting, on the other hand, had no overt religious content, although it could be seen as a reflection or even glorification of God's works on Earth. The most accomplished German landscape painter of the period was Albrecht Altdorfer (c. 1480–1538).

Altdorfer probably received his early training in Bavaria from his father, but he became a citizen of Regensburg in 1505 and remained there painting the Danube River Valley for the rest of his life. **DANUBE LANDSCAPE** of about 1525 (**FIG. 21–11**) is an early example of pure landscape painting, without a narrative subject, human figures, or overt religious significance. A small work on vellum laid down on a wood panel, it shows a landscape that seems to be a minutely detailed reproduction of the natural terrain, but the forest seems far more poetic and mysterious than Dürer's or Cranach's carefully observed views of nature. The low mountains, gigantic lacy pines, neatly contoured shrubberies, and fairyland castle with red-roofed towers at the end of a winding path announce a new sensibility. The eerily glowing yellow–white horizon below moving gray and blue clouds in a sky that takes up more than half the composition prefigures the Romanticism of German landscape painting in later centuries.

FRANCE

Renaissance France followed a different path from that taken in Germany. In 1519, Pope Leo X came to an agreement with French King Francis I (r. 1515–1547) that spared the country the turmoil suffered in Germany. Furthermore, whereas Martin Luther had devoted followers in France, French reformer John Calvin (1509–1564) fled to Switzerland in 1534, where he led a theocratic state in Geneva.

During the second half of the century, however, warring political factions favoring either Catholics or Huguenots (Protestants) competed to exert power over the French crown, with devastating consequences. In 1560, the devoutly Catholic Catherine de' Medici, widow of Henry II (r. 1547–1559), became regent for her young son, Charles IX, and tried, but failed, to balance the warring factions. Her machinations ended in religious polarization and a bloody conflict that began in 1562. When her third son, Henry III (r. 1574–1589), was murdered by a fanatical Dominican friar, a Protestant cousin, Henry, king of Navarre, the first Bourbon king, inherited the throne. Henry converted to Catholicism and ruled as Henry IV. Backed by a country sick of bloodshed, he quickly settled the religious question by proclaiming tolerance of Protestants in the Edict of Nantes in 1598.

A FRENCH RENAISSANCE UNDER FRANCIS I

Immediately after his ascent to the throne, Francis I sought to "modernize" the French court by acquiring the versatile talents of Leonardo da Vinci, who moved to France in 1516. Officially, Leonardo was there to advise the king on royal architectural projects and, the king said, for the pleasure of his conversation. Francis supported an Italian-inspired Renaissance in French art and architecture throughout his long reign.

JEAN CLOUET. Not all the artists working at the court of Francis I, however, were Italian. Flemish artist Jean Clouet (c. 1485–c. 1540) found great favor at the royal court, especially as a portrait painter. About the same time that he became principal court painter in 1527, he produced an official portrait of the king (**FIG. 21–12**). Clouet created a flattering image of Francis by modulating the king's distinctive features with soft shading and highlighting the nervous activity of his fingers. At the same time he conceived an image of pure power. Elaborate, puffy sleeves broaden the king's

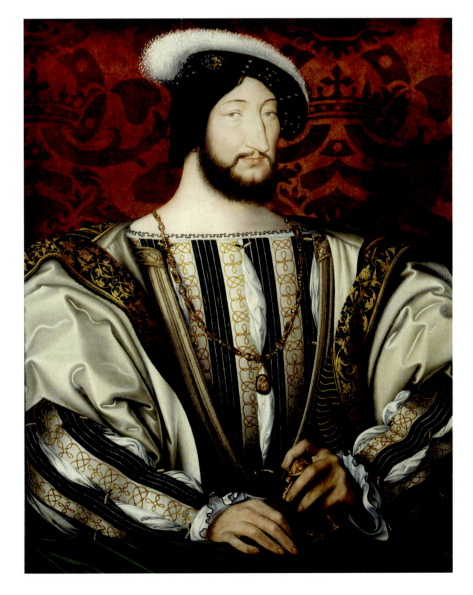

21–12 • Jean Clouet FRANCIS I
1525–1530. Oil and tempera on wood panel, 37¾ × 29⅛" (95.9 × 74 cm). Musée du Louvre, Paris.

The Castle of the Ladies

Women played an important role in the patronage of the arts during the Renaissance. Nowhere is their influence stronger than in the châteaux of the Loire River Valley. At Chenonceau, built beside and literally over the River Cher, a tributary of the Loire, women built, saved, and restored the château. Catherine Briconnet and her husband, Thomas Bohier, originally acquired the property, including a fortified mill, on which they built their country residence. Catherine supervised the construction, which included such modern conveniences as a straight staircase (an Italian and Spanish feature) instead of traditional medieval spiral stairs, and a kitchen inside the château instead of in a distant outbuilding. After Thomas died in 1524 and Catherine in 1526, their son gave Chenonceau to King Francis I.

King Henry II, Francis's son, gave Chenonceau to his mistress Diane de Poitiers in 1547. She managed the estate astutely, increased its revenue, developed the vineyards, added intricately planted gardens in the Italian style, and built a bridge across the Cher. When Henry died in a tournament, his queen, Catherine de' Medici (1519–1589), appropriated the château for herself.

Catherine, like so many in her family a great patron of the arts, added the two-story gallery to the bridge at Chenonceau, as well as outbuildings and additional formal gardens. Her parties were famous:

mock naval battles on the river, fireworks, banquets, dances, and on one occasion two choruses of young women dressed as mermaids in the moat and nymphs in the shrubbery—who were then chased about by young men costumed as satyrs!

When Catherine's third son became king as Henry III in 1574, she gave the château to his wife, Louise of Lorraine, who lived in mourning at Chenonceau after Henry III was assassinated in 1589. She wore only white and covered the walls, windows, and furniture in her room with black velvet and damask. She gave Chenonceau to her niece when she died.

In the eighteenth and nineteenth centuries, the ladies continued to determine the fate of Chenonceau. During the French Revolution (1789–1793), the owner, Madame Dupin, was so beloved by the villagers that they protected her and saved her home. Then, in 1864, Madame Pelouze bought Chenonceau and restored it by removing Catherine de' Medici's Italian "improvements."

Chenonceau continued to play a role in the twentieth century. During World War I, it was used as a hospital. During the German occupation in World War II (1940–1942), when the River Cher formed the border with Vichy "Free" France, the gallery bridge at Chenonceau became an escape route.

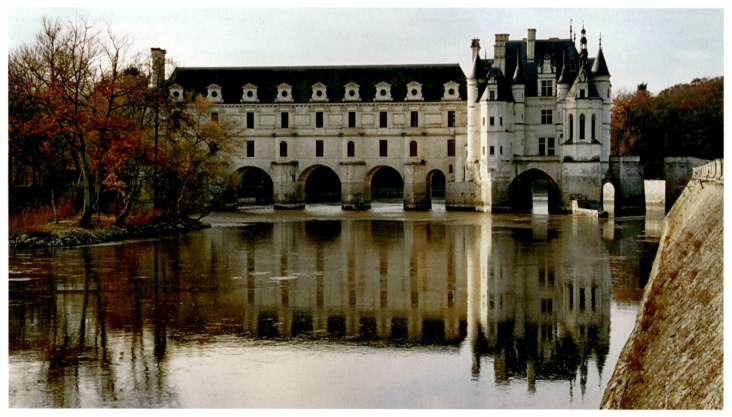

CHÂTEAU OF CHENONCEAU
Touraine, France. Original building (at right) 1513–1521; gallery on bridge at left by Philibert de l'Orme, finished c. 1581.

shoulders to fill the entire width of the panel, much as Renaissance parade armor turned scrawny men into giants. The detailed rendering of the delicately worked costume of silk, satin, velvet, jewels, and gold embroidery could be painted separately from the portrait itself. Royal clothing was often loaned to the artist or modeled by a servant to spare the "sitter" the boredom of posing. In creating such official portraits, the artist sketched the subject, then painted a prototype that, upon approval, became the model for numerous replicas made for diplomatic and family purposes.

THE CHÂTEAU OF CHENONCEAU. With the enthusiasm of Francis for things Italian and the widening distribution of Italian books on architecture, the Italian Renaissance style soon infiltrated French architecture. Builders of elegant rural palaces, called **châteaux**, were quick to introduce Italianate decoration to otherwise Gothic buildings, but French architects soon adapted Classical principles of building design as well.

One of the most beautiful châteaux was not built as a royal residence, although it soon became one. In 1512, Thomas Bohier, a royal tax collector, bought the castle of Chenonceau on the River Cher, a tributary of the Loire (see "The Castle of the Ladies," opposite). He demolished the old castle, leaving only a tower. Using the piers of a water mill on the river bank as part of the foundations, he and his wife erected a new Renaissance home. The plan reflects the Classical principles of geometric regularity and symmetry—a rectangular building with rooms arranged on each side of a wide central hall. Only the library and chapel, which are corbelled out over the water, break the line of the walls. In the upper story, the builders used traditional features of medieval castles—

battlements, corner turrets, steep roofs, and dormer windows. The owners died soon after the château was finished in 1521, and their son gave it to Francis I, who turned it into a hunting lodge.

Later, Roman-trained French Renaissance architect Philibert de l'Orme (d. 1570) designed a gallery on a bridge across the river for Catherine de' Medici, completed about 1581 and incorporating contemporary Italianate window treatments, wall molding, and cornices that harmonized almost perfectly with the forms of the original turreted building.

FONTAINEBLEAU. Having chosen as his primary residence the medieval hunting lodge at Fontainebleau, Francis I began transforming it into a grand country palace. In 1530, he imported a Florentine artist, the Mannerist painter Rosso Fiorentino (1495–1540), to direct the project. After Rosso died, he was succeeded by his Italian colleague Francesco Primaticcio (1504–1570), who had earlier worked with Giulio Romano in Mantua (SEE FIG. 20–18), then joined Rosso in 1532, and would spend the rest of his career working on the decoration of Fontainebleau. During that time, he also commissioned and imported a large number of copies and casts of original Roman sculpture, from the newly discovered Laocoön (SEE FIG. 5–55) to the relief decoration on the Column of Trajan (SEE FIG. 6–44). These works provided an invaluable visual resource of figures and techniques for the northern European artists employed on the Fontainebleau project.

Among Primaticcio's first projects at Fontainebleau was the redecoration, in the 1540s, of the rooms of the king's official mistress, Anne, duchess of Étampes (FIG. 21–13). The artist

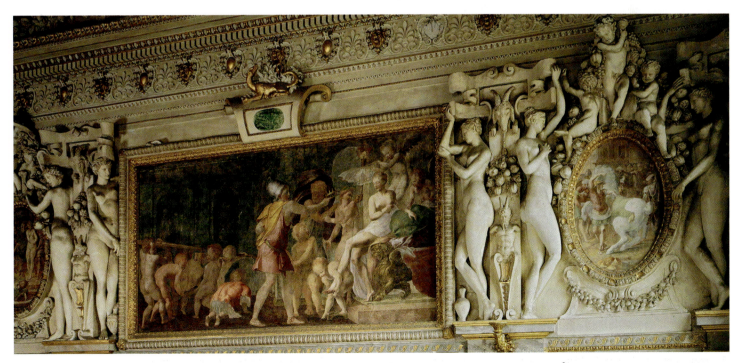

21-13 • Primaticcio STUCCO AND WALL PAINTING, CHAMBER OF THE DUCHESS OF ÉTAMPES, CHÂTEAU OF FONTAINEBLEAU
France. 1540s.

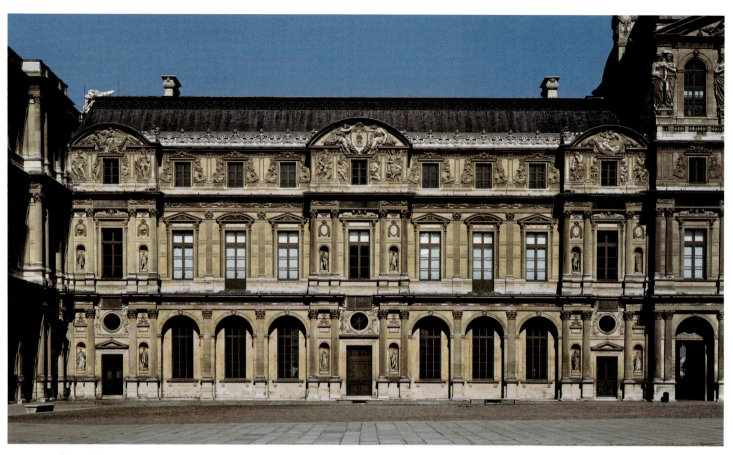

21–14 • Pierre Lescot and Jean Goujon **WEST WING OF THE COUR CARRÉE, PALAIS DU LOUVRE**
Paris. Begun 1546.

combined woodwork, stucco relief, and fresco painting in his complex but whimsical and graceful interior design. The lithe figures of stucco nymphs, with their elongated bodies and small heads, recall Parmigianino's paintings (SEE FIG. 20–27). Their spiraling postures and teasing bits of clinging drapery are playfully erotic. Garlands, mythological figures, and Roman architectural ornament almost overwhelm the walls with visual enrichment, yet the whole remains ordered and lighthearted. The first School of Fontainebleau, as this Italian phase of the palace decoration is called, established an Italianate tradition of Mannerism in painting and interior design that spread to other centers in France and into the Netherlands.

THE LOUVRE. Before the defeat of Francis I at Pavia by Holy Roman Emperor Charles V, and the king's subsequent imprisonment in Spain in 1525, the French court had been a mobile unit, and the locus of French art resided outside Paris in the Loire Valley. After his release in 1526, Francis made Paris his bureaucratic seat, and the Île-de-France—Paris and its region—took the artistic lead. The move to the capital gave birth to a style of French Classicism when Francis I and Henry II decided to modernize the medieval castle of the Louvre. Work began in 1546, with the replacement of the west wing of the square court, or **COUR CARRÉE (FIG. 21–14)**, by architect Pierre Lescot (c. 1510–1578) working with sculptor

Jean Goujon (1510–1568). They designed a building that incorporated Renaissance ideals of balance and regularity with Classical architectural details and rich sculptural decoration. The irregular rooflines seen in a château such as the one at Chenonceau (see "The Castle of the Ladies," page 690, right side of the photograph) gave way to discreetly rounded arches and horizontal balustrades. Classical pilasters and entablatures replaced Gothic buttresses and stringcourses. A round-arched arcade on the ground floor suggests an Italian loggia. On the other hand, the sumptuousness of the decoration recalls the French Flamboyant style (see Chapter 18), only with Classical pilasters and acanthus replacing Gothic colonnettes and cusps.

SPAIN AND PORTUGAL

The sixteenth century saw the high point of Spanish political power. The country had been united in the fifteenth century by the marriage of Isabella of Castile and Ferdinand of Aragon. Only Navarre (in the Pyrenees) and Portugal remained outside the union of the crowns. (See "Sculpture for the Knights of Christ at Tomar," opposite.) When Isabella and Ferdinand's grandson Charles V abdicated in 1556, his son Philip II (r. 1556–1598) became the king of Spain, the Netherlands, and the Americas, as well as ruler of Milan, Burgundy, and Naples, but Spain was

Sculpture for the Knights of Christ at Tomar

One of the most beautiful, if also one of the strangest, sixteenth-century sculptures in Portugal seems to float over the cloisters of the Convent of Christ in Tomar. Unexpectedly, in the heart of the castle-monastery complex, one comes face to face with the Old Man of the Sea. He supports on his powerful shoulders an extraordinary growth—part roots and trunk of a gnarled tree; part tangled mass of seaweed, algae, ropes, and anchor chains. Barnacle- and coral-encrusted piers lead the eye upward, revealing a large lattice-covered window, the great west window of the church of the Knights of Christ.

When, in 1314, Pope Clement V disbanded the Templars (a monastic order of knights founded in Jerusalem after the First Crusade), King Dinis of Portugal offered them a renewed existence as the Knights of Christ. As a result, in 1356, they made the former Templar castle and monastery in Tomar their headquarters. When Prince Henry the Navigator (1394–1460) became the grand master of the order, he invested their funds in the exploration of the African coast and the Atlantic Ocean. The Templar insignia, the squared cross, became the emblem used on the sails of Portuguese ships.

King Manuel I of Portugal (r. 1495–1521) commissioned the present church, with its amazing sculpture by Diogo de Arruda, in 1510. So distinctive is the style developed under King Manuel by artists like the Arruda brothers, Diogo (active 1508–1531) and Francisco (active 1510–1547), that Renaissance art in Portugal is called "Manueline." In the window of Tomar, every surface is carved with architectural and natural detail associated with the sea. Twisted ropes form the corners of the window; the coral pillars support great swathes of seaweed. Chains and cables drop through the watery depths to the place where the head of a man—could this Old Man of the Sea be a self-portrait of Diogo de Arruda?—emerges from the roots of a tree. Above the window, more ropes, cables, and seaweed support the emblems of the patron—armillary spheres at the upper outside corners (topped by pinnacles) and at dead center, the coat of arms of Manuel I with its Portuguese castles framing the five wounds of Christ. Topping the composition is the square cross of the Order of Christ—clearly delineated against the wall of the chapel.

The armillary sphere became a symbol of the era. This complex form of a celestial globe, with the sun at the center surrounded by rings marking the paths of the planets, was a teaching device that acknowledged the new scientific theory that the sun, not the Earth, is the center of the solar system. (Copernicus, teaching in Germany at this time, only published his theories in 1531 and 1543.) King Manuel's use of the armillary sphere as his emblem signals his determination to make Portugal the leader in the exploration of the sea. Indeed, in Manuel's reign the Portuguese reached India and Brazil.

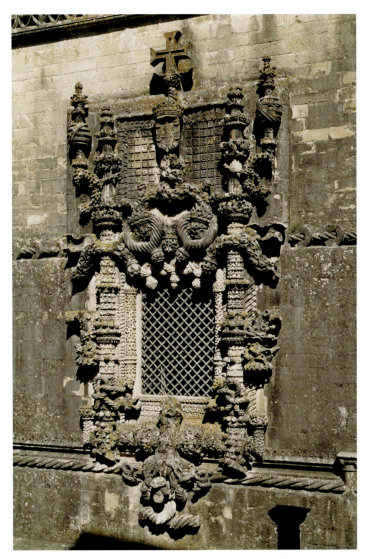

Diogo de Arruda **WEST WINDOW, CHURCH IN THE CONVENT OF CHRIST**
Tomar, Portugal. c. 1510. Commissioned by King Manuel I of Portugal.

Philip's permanent residence. For more than half a century, he supported artists in Spain, Italy, and the Netherlands. His navy, the famous Spanish Armada, halted the advance of Islam in the Mediterranean and secured control of most American territories. Despite enormous effort, however, Philip could not suppress the revolt of the northern provinces of the Netherlands, nor could he prevail in his war against the English, who destroyed his navy in 1588. He was able to gain control of the entire Iberian peninsula, however, by claiming Portugal in 1580, and it remained part of Spain until 1640.

ARCHITECTURE

Philip built **THE ESCORIAL (FIG. 21–15)**, the great monastery-palace complex outside Madrid, partly to comply with his father's direction to construct a "pantheon" in which all Spanish kings might be buried and partly to house his court and government. In 1559, Philip summoned from Italy Juan Bautista de Toledo (d. 1567), who had been Michelangelo's supervisor of work at St. Peter's from 1546 to 1548. Juan Bautista's design for the monastery-palace reflected his indoctrination in Bramante's Classical principles in Rome, but the king himself dictated the severity and size of the structure. The Escorial's grandeur comes from its overwhelming size, fine proportions, and excellent masonry. The complex includes not only the royal residence but also the Royal Monastery of San Lorenzo, a school, a library, and a church, its crypt serving as the royal burial chamber. The plan was said to resemble a gridiron, the instrument of martyrdom of its patron saint, Lawrence, who was roasted alive.

In 1572, Juan Bautista's assistant, Juan de Herrera, was appointed architect, and he immediately changed the design, adding second stories on all wings and breaking the horizontality of the main façade with a central frontispiece that resembled the superimposed temple fronts that were fashionable on Italian churches at this time (SEE FIGS. 20–36, 20–38). Before beginning the church in the center of the complex, Philip solicited the advice of Italian architects—including Vignola and Palladio. The final design combined ideas that Philip approved and Herrera carried out, and it embodies Italian Classicism in its geometric clarity, symmetry, and superimposed temple-front façade. In its austerity, it embodies the deep religiosity of Philip II.

PAINTING

Although Philip II was a great patron of the Venetian painter Titian, and he collected Netherlandish artists such as Bosch, the most famous painter working in Spain during the last quarter of the sixteenth century is Domenikos Theotokopoulos (1541–1614), who arrived in Spain in 1577 after working for ten years in Italy. "El Greco" ("The Greek"), as he is called, was trained as an icon painter in the Byzantine manner in his native Crete, then under Venetian rule. In about 1566, he went to Venice and entered Titian's studio, where he also studied the paintings of Tintoretto and Veronese. From about 1570 to 1577, he worked in Rome, apparently without finding sufficient patronage, although he lived for a time in the Farnese Palace. Probably encouraged by Spanish church officials whom he met in Rome, El Greco settled in Toledo, seat of the Spanish archbishop. He had hoped for a court appointment, but Philip II disliked the painting he had commissioned from El Greco for The Escorial and never again gave him work.

In Toledo, El Greco joined the circle of humanist scholars. He wrote that the artist's goal should be to copy nature, that Raphael relied too heavily on the ancients, and that the Italians' use of mathematics to achieve ideal proportions hindered their painting of nature. At this same time an intense religious revival was under way in Spain, expressed in the impassioned preaching of Ignatius of Loyola, as well as in the poetry of two great Spanish mystics: St. Teresa of Ávila (1515–1582) and her follower St. John of the Cross (1542–1591). El Greco's style—rooted in Byzantine icon painting and strongly reflecting the rich colors and loose brushwork of Venetian painting—was well equipped to express the intense spirituality of these mystics.

In 1586, the Orgaz family commissioned El Greco to paint a large altarpiece honoring an illustrious fourteenth-century ancestor. Count Orgaz had been a great benefactor of the Church, and at his funeral in 1323, SS. Augustine and Stephen were said to have appeared to lower his body into his tomb as his soul was seen ascending to heaven. El Greco's painting the **BURIAL OF COUNT ORGAZ (FIG. 21–16)** captures these miracles. An angel lifts Orgaz's

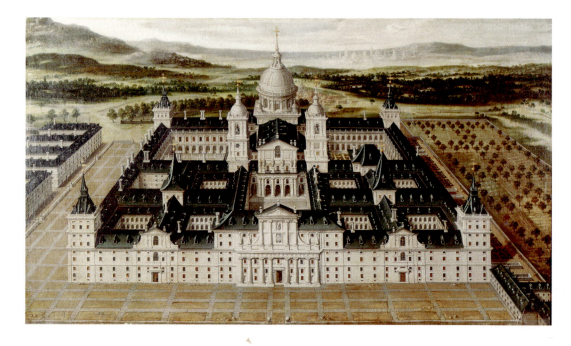

21–15 • Juan Bautista de Toledo and Juan de Herrera THE ESCORIAL
Madrid. 1563–1584. Detail from an anonymous 18th-century painting.

SEE MORE: Click the Google Earth link for The Escorial
www.myartslab.com

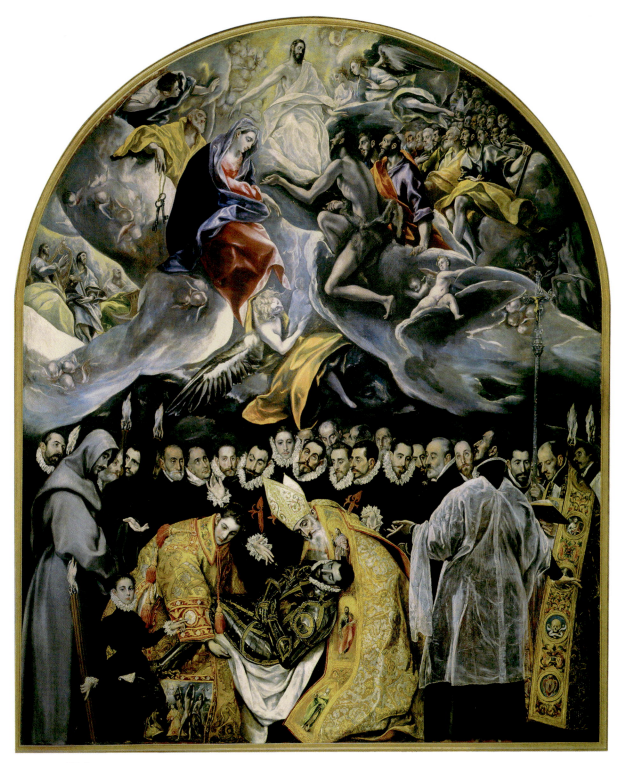

21–16 • El Greco BURIAL OF COUNT ORGAZ
1586. Oil on canvas, 16′ × 11′10″ (4.88 × 3.61 m). Church of Santo Tomé, Toledo, Spain.

ghostly soul along the central axis of the painting toward the enthroned Christ at the apex of the canvas. El Greco filled the space around the burial scene with portraits of the local aristocracy and religious notables. He placed his own 8-year-old son at the lower left next to St. Stephen and signed the painting on the boy's white kerchief. El Greco may also have put his own features on the man just above the saint's head, the only other figure who, like the child, looks straight out at the viewer.

In composing the painting, El Greco used Mannerist devices reminiscent of Pontormo (SEE FIG. 20–26), packing the pictorial field with figures and eliminating specific reference to the spatial setting. Yet he has distinguished between heaven and earth by the light emanating from Christ, whose otherworldly luminescence is quite unlike the natural light below.

THE NETHERLANDS

In the Netherlands, the sixteenth century was an age of bitter religious and political conflict. Despite the opposition of the Spanish Habsburg rulers, the Protestant Reformation took hold in the northern provinces. Seeds of unrest were sown still deeper over the course of the century by continued religious persecution, economic hardship, and inept governors. Widespread iconoclasm characterized 1566–1567, and a long battle for independence began with a revolt in 1568 that lasted until Spain relinquished all claims to the region 80 years later. As early as 1579, when the seven northern Protestant provinces declared themselves the United Provinces, the discord split the Netherlands, eventually dividing it along religious lines into the United Provinces (the present-day Netherlands) and Catholic Flanders (present-day Belgium).

Even with the turmoil, the Netherlanders found the resources to pay for art, and Antwerp and other cities developed into thriving art centers. The Reformation led artists to seek patrons outside the Church. While courtiers and burghers alike continued to commission portraits, the demand arose for small paintings with interesting secular subjects appropriate for homes. For example, some artists became specialists known for their landscapes or satires. In addition to painting, textiles, ceramics, printmaking, and sculpture in wood and metal flourished in the Netherlands. Flemish tapestries were sought after and highly prized across Europe, as they had been in the fifteenth century, and leading Italian artists made cartoons to be woven into tapestries in Flemish workshops (see "Raphael's Cartoons for Tapestries in the Sistine Chapel," pages 646–647). The graphic arts emerged as an important medium, providing many artists with another source of income. Pieter Bruegel the Elder began his career drawing amusing and moralizing images to be printed and published by At the Four Winds, an Antwerp publishing house. Artists such as Hendrick Goltzius, who traveled with sketchbook in hand, turned their experiences to profit when they returned home.

Like Vasari in Italy, Carel van Mander (1548–1606) recorded the lives of his Netherlandish contemporaries in engaging biographies that mix fact and gossip. He, too, intended his 1604 book *Het Schilder-boeck* (*The Painter's Book*) to be a survey of the history of art, and he included material from the ancient Roman writers Pliny and Vitruvius as well as from Vasari's revised and expanded *Lives*, published in 1568.

ART FOR ARISTOCRATIC AND NOBLE PATRONS

Artistic taste among the wealthy bourgeoisie and noble classes in the early sixteenth-century Netherlands was characterized by a striking diversity, encompassing the imaginative and difficult visions of Hieronymus Bosch, as well as the more Italianate compositions of Jan Gossaert. In the later years of his life, Bosch's membership in a local but prestigious confraternity called the Brotherhood of Our Lady seems to have opened doors to noble patrons such as Count Hendrick III of Nassau and Duke Philip the Fair. His younger contemporary Gossaert left the city of Antwerp as a young man to spend the majority of his active years as the court painter for the natural son of Duke Philip the Good. His art also attracted members of the Habsburgs, including Charles V, who were seduced by Gossaert's combination of northern European and Italian styles.

HIERONYMUS BOSCH. Among the most fascinating Netherlandish painters to modern viewers is Hieronymus Bosch (1450–

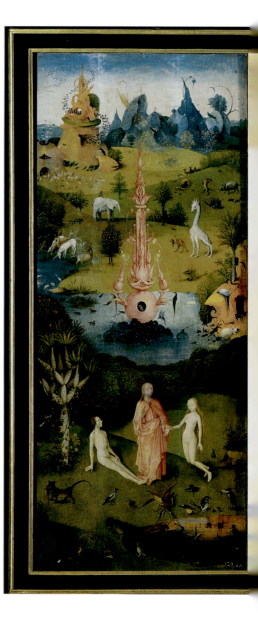

21-17 • Hieronymus Bosch GARDEN OF EARTHLY DELIGHTS (OPEN)
c. 1505–1515. Oil on wood panel, center panel 7′2½″ × 6′4¾″ (2.20 × 1.95 m), each wing 7′2½″ × 3′2″ (2.20 × 0.97 m). Museo del Prado, Madrid.

Despite—or perhaps because of—its bizarre subject matter, this triptych was woven in 1566 into tapestries, and at least one painted copy was made as well. Bosch's original triptych was sold at the onset of the Netherlands Revolt and sent in 1568 to Spain, where it entered the collection of Philip II.

EXPLORE MORE: Gain insight from a primary source on Hieronymus Bosch
www.myartslab.com

1516), who depicted the sort of imaginative fantasies more often associated with medieval than Renaissance art. A superb colorist and virtuoso technician, Bosch spent his career in the town whose name he adopted, 's-Hertogenbosch. Bosch's religious devotion is certain, and his range of subjects shows that he was well educated. Challenging and unsettling paintings such as his GARDEN OF EARTHLY DELIGHTS (FIG. 21–17) have led modern scholars to label Bosch both a mystic and a social critic. The subject of the triptych seems to be founded on Christian belief in the natural state of human sinfulness, but it was not painted for a church.

In the left wing, God introduces doll-like figures of Adam and Eve, under the watchful eye of the owl of perverted wisdom. The owl symbolizes both wisdom and folly. Folly had become an important concept to the northern European humanists, who believed in the power of education. They believed that people would choose to follow the right way once they knew it. Here the owl peers out from an opening in the spherical base of a fantastic pink fountain in a lake from which vicious creatures creep out into the world.

In the central panel, the Earth teems with such monsters, but also with vivacious human revelers and luscious huge fruits, symbolic of fertility and sexual abandon. In hell, at the right, sensual pleasures—eating, drinking, music, and dancing—become instruments of torture in a dark world of fire and ice. The emphasis in the right wing on the torments of hell, with no hint of the rewards of heaven, seems to caution that damnation is the natural outcome of a life lived in ignorance and folly, that humans ensure their damnation through their self-centered pursuit of pleasures of the flesh—the sins of gluttony, lust, greed, and sloth—outlined with such fantastic and graphic abandon in the central panel.

One scholar has proposed that the central panel is a parable on human salvation in which the practice of alchemy—the process that sought to turn common metals into gold—parallels Christ's power to convert human dross into spiritual gold. In this theory, the bizarre fountain at the center of the lake in the middle distance can

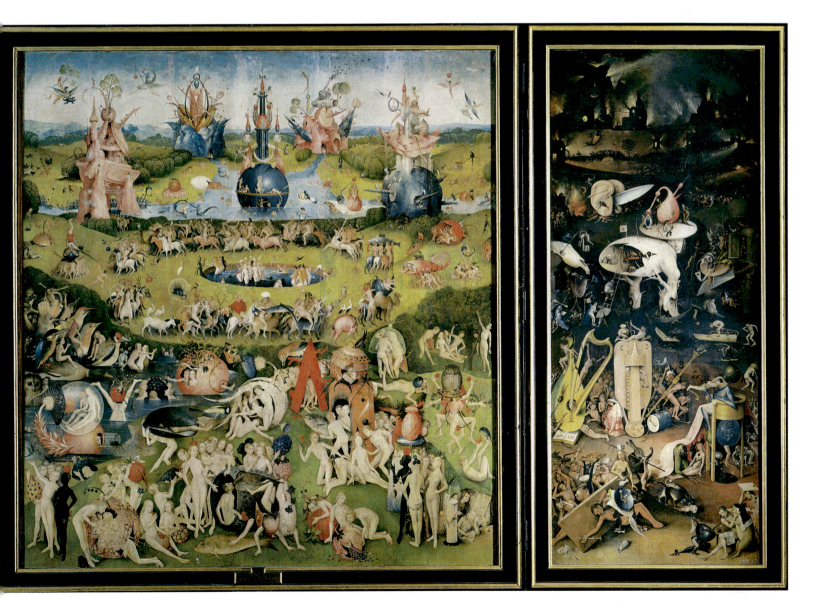

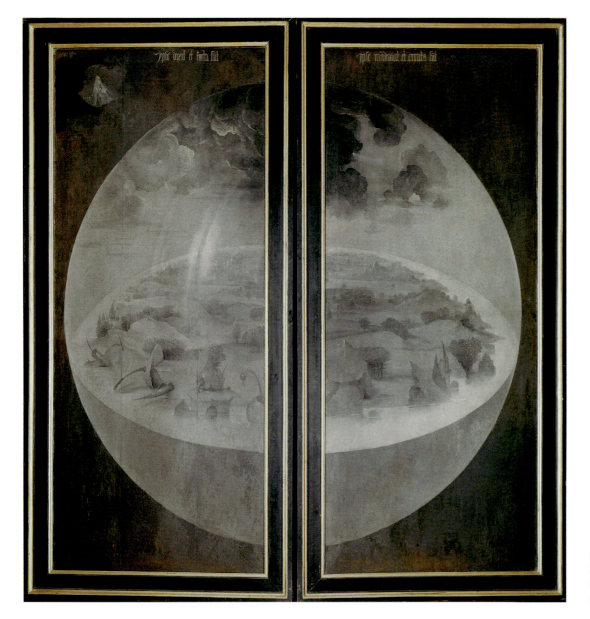

21–18 • Hieronymus Bosch GARDEN OF EARTHLY DELIGHTS (CLOSED)

be seen as an alchemical "marrying chamber," complete with the glass vessels for collecting the vapors of distillation. Others see the theme known as "the power of women." In this interpretation, the central pool is the setting for a display of seductive women and sex-obsessed men. Women frolic alluringly in the pool while men dance and ride in a mad circle trying to attract them. In this strange garden, men are slaves to their own lust. An early seventeenth-century critic focused on the fruit, writing that the triptych was known as *The Strawberry Plant* because it represented the "vanity and glory and the passing taste of strawberries or the strawberry plant and its pleasant odor that is hardly remembered once it has passed." Luscious fruits of obvious sexual symbolism—straw-berries, cherries, grapes, and pomegranates—appear every-where in the garden, serving as food, as shelter, and even as a boat. Is human life as fleeting and insubstantial as the taste of a straw-berry? Yet another modern reading sees the central tableau imagin-ing the course of life in paradise, assuming that Adam and Even had not consigned humanity to sin by eating the forbidden fruit.

Conforming to a long tradition of triptych altarpieces made for churches, Bosch painted a more sober, *grisaille* picture on the reverse of the side wings. When the triptych is closed, a less enigmatic, but equally fascinating, scene is displayed (FIG. 21–18). A transparent, illusionistic rendering of a receding sphere floating within a void encloses the flat circular shelf of Earth on its third day of creation. Fragments of the fantastic fruit that will appear fully formed in the interior pictures float here in the primordial sea, while ominous dark clouds promise the rain that will nurture them into their full seductive ripeness. A tiny crowned figure of God the Creator hovers in a bubble within dark clouds at upper left, displaying a book, perhaps a Bible opened to the words from Psalm 33:9 that are inscribed across the top: "For he spoke, and it came to be; he commanded, and it stood firm."

The *Garden of Earthly Delights* was commissioned by an aristocrat (probably Count Hendrick III of Nassau) for his Brussels town house, and the artist's choice of a triptych format, which suggests an altarpiece, may have been an understated irony. In a private home the painting surely inspired lively discussion, even ribald commentary, much as it does today in the Prado Museum. Perhaps that, rather than a single meaning or interpretation, is the true intention behind this dazzling display of artistic imagination.

JAN GOSSAERT. In contrast to the private visions of Bosch, Jan Gossaert (c. 1478–c. 1533) maintained traditional subject matter and embraced the new Classical art of Italy. Gossaert (who later called himself Mabuse after his native city Maubeuge) entered the service of Philip, the illegitimate son of the duke of Burgundy, accompanying him to Italy in 1508, and remaining in his service after Philip became archbishop of Utrecht in 1517.

Gossaert's "Romanizing" style—inspired by Italian Mannerist paintings and decorative details drawn from ancient Roman art—is evident in his painting of **ST. LUKE DRAWING THE VIRGIN MARY** **(FIG. 21–19)**, a traditional subject we already know from a painting

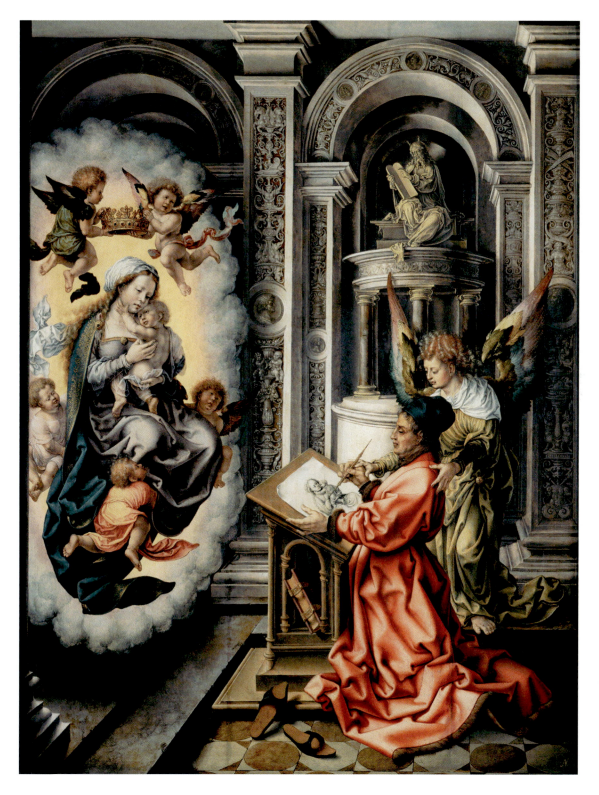

21–19 • Jan Gossaert
ST. LUKE DRAWING THE VIRGIN MARY
1520. Oil on panel, 43⅜ × 32¼″ (110.2 × 81.9 cm). Kunsthistorisches Museum, Vienna.

by Rogier van der Weyden (SEE FIG. 18–14). In Gossaert's version, the artist's studio is an extraordinary structure of Classical piers and arches, carved with a dense ornament of foliage and medallions. Mary and the Christ Child appear in a blaze of golden light and clouds before the saint, who kneels at a desk, his hand guided by an angel as he records the vision in a drawing. Luke's crumpled red robe replicates fifteenth-century drapery conventions in a seeming reference to Rogier's famous picture. Seated above and behind Luke on a round, columnar structure, Moses holds the Tablets of the Law, referencing his own visions of God on Mount Sinai. Just

as Moses had removed his shoes in God's presence, so has Luke in the presence of his vision. Gossaert, like Dürer before him, seems to be staking a claim for the divine inspiration of the artist.

ANTWERP

During the sixteenth century, Antwerp was the commercial and artistic center of the southern Netherlands. Its deep port made it an international center of trade (it was one of the European centers for trade in spices), and it was the financial center of Europe. Painting, printmaking, and book production flourished in this

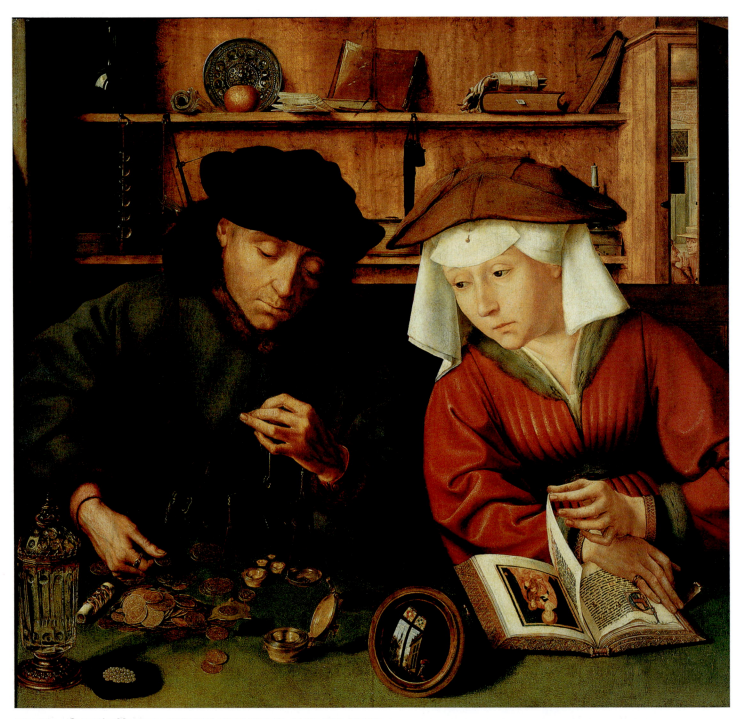

21–20 • Quentin Massys MONEY CHANGER AND HIS WIFE
1514. Oil on panel, 28 × 26¾″ (71.2 × 68 cm). Kunsthistorisches Museum, Vienna.

environment, attracting artists and craftsmen from all over Europe. The demand for luxury goods fostered the birth of the art market, in which art was transformed into a commodity for both local and international consumption. In responding to this market system, many artists became specialists in one area, such as portraiture or landscape, working with art dealers, who emerged as middlemen, further shaping the commodification of art, its production, and its producers.

QUENTIN MASSYS. Early accounts of the prosperous Antwerp artist Quentin Massys (1466–1530) claim that he began working in his native Louvain as a blacksmith (his father's profession) but changed to painting to compete with a rival for the affections of a young woman; Carel van Mander claims he was a self-trained artist. We know he entered the Antwerp painters' guild in 1491, and at his death in 1530 he was among its most prosperous and renowned members, supervising a large workshop to meet the market in this burgeoning art center.

One of his most fascinating paintings— **MONEY CHANGER AND HIS WIFE** (FIG. 21–20)— recalls, like Gossaert's *St. Luke*, a famous fifteenth-century work, in this case the picture of a goldsmith painted for the Antwerp goldsmiths' guild by Petrus Christus (see "A Closer Look," page 581). Here, however, a couple is in charge of business, and they present us with two different profiles of engagement. The soberly dressed proprietor himself focuses intently on weighing coins in a suspended balance. His brightly outfitted wife —dressed in an archaic fifteenth-century costume that harks back to a golden age of Flemish painting—looks to the side, distracted by her husband's activity from the attention she was giving to the meticulously described Book of Hours spread out on the table in front of her. It would be easy to jump to the conclusion that this is a moral fable, warning of the danger of losing "sight" of religious obligations because of a preoccupation with affairs of business. But the painting is not that simple. An inscription that ran around the original frame quoted Leviticus 19:36—"You shall have honest balances and honest weights"—claiming just business practices as a form of righteous living. Is it possible the moral here juxtaposes not worldliness and spirituality, but attentive and distracted devotional practice? The sidetracked wife seems to have been idly flipping through her prayer book before turning to observe what her husband is doing, whereas a man in a red turban reflected in the convex mirror next to her Book of Hours is caught in rapt attention to the book in front of him, and the nature of his reading is suggested by

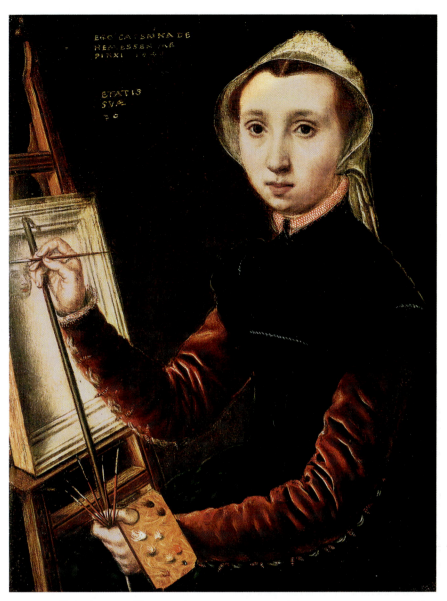

21–21 • Caterina van Hemessen SELF-PORTRAIT
1548. Oil on wood panel, 12¼ × 9¼" (31.1 × 23.5 cm). Öffentliche Kunstsammlung, Basel, Switzerland.

the church steeple through the window behind him. The sermon here concerns the challenge of godly living in a worldly society, but wealth itself is not necessarily the root of the problem.

CATERINA VAN HEMESSEN. Antwerp painter Caterina van Hemessen (1528–1587) developed an illustrious reputation as a portraitist. She had learned to paint from her father, the Flemish Mannerist Jan Sanders van Hemessen, who was dean of the Antwerp painters' guild in 1548, but the quiet realism and skilled rendering of her subjects is distinctively her own. To maintain focus on her foreground subjects, van Hemessen painted them against even, dark-colored backgrounds, on which she identified the sitter by name and age, signing and dating each work. The inscription in her **SELF-PORTRAIT** (FIG. 21–21) reads: "I Caterina van Hemessen painted myself in 1548. Her age 20." In delineating

Bruegel's Cycle of the Months

Cycles, or series, of paintings unified by a developing theme or allegorical subject—for instance, the Times of the Day, the Four Seasons, or the Five Senses—became popular wall decorations in prosperous Flemish homes during the sixteenth century. In 1565, Pieter Bruegel the Elder was commissioned to paint a series of six large paintings, each over 5 feet wide, surveying the months of the year, two months to a picture. They were made to be hung together in a room—probably the dining room since food figures prominently in these pictures—in the suburban villa of wealthy merchant Niclaes Jonghelinck, just outside Antwerp.

Return of the Hunters (FIG. A) represents December and January. The bleak landscape is gripped by winter as hunters return home at dusk with meager results: a single rabbit slung over the largest man's shoulder. But the landscape, rather than the figures, seems to be the principal subject here. A row of trees forms a receding set, consistently diminishing in scale, to draw our attention into the space of the painting along the orthogonal descent on the hillside of houses on the left. Like the calendar illustrations of medieval Books of Hours, the landscape is filled with behavior emblematic of the time of year: the singeing of the pig outside the farmhouse at left, the playful movement of ice skaters across frozen fields. We see it all from an omnipotent elevated viewpoint, like one of the birds that perch in the trees or glide across the snow-covered fantasy of an alpine background.

The mood is very different in the painting representing the hazy late summer days of August and September (FIG. B). Birds still perch and glide, and a silhouetted tree still dominates the foreground—as if Bruegel wanted to set up obvious relationships between the scenes so that viewers would assess them comparatively—but the setting here is more rural than residential. Architecture keeps its distance or is screened by foliage. Agricultural workers trudge through their labor, harvesting grain, and gathering stalks into tidy sheaves, ready for transport. The figural focus, however, is in the foreground, on a

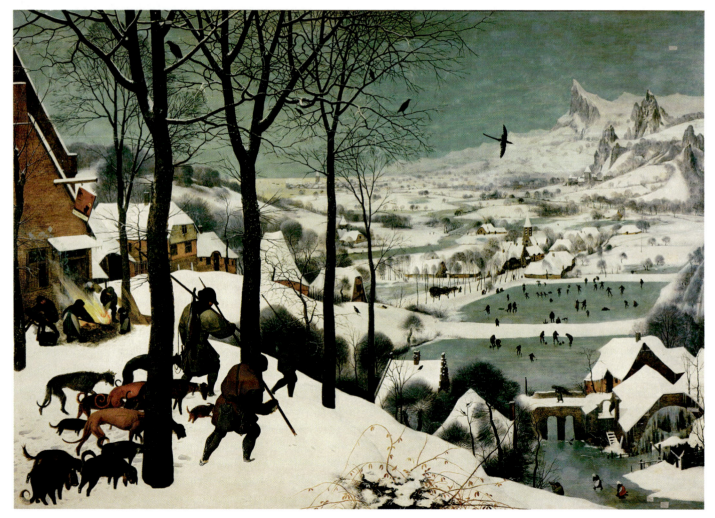

A. Pieter Bruegel the Elder RETURN OF THE HUNTERS
1565. Oil on wood panel, 3'10½" × 5'3¾" (1.18 × 1.61 m). Kunsthistorisches Museum, Vienna.

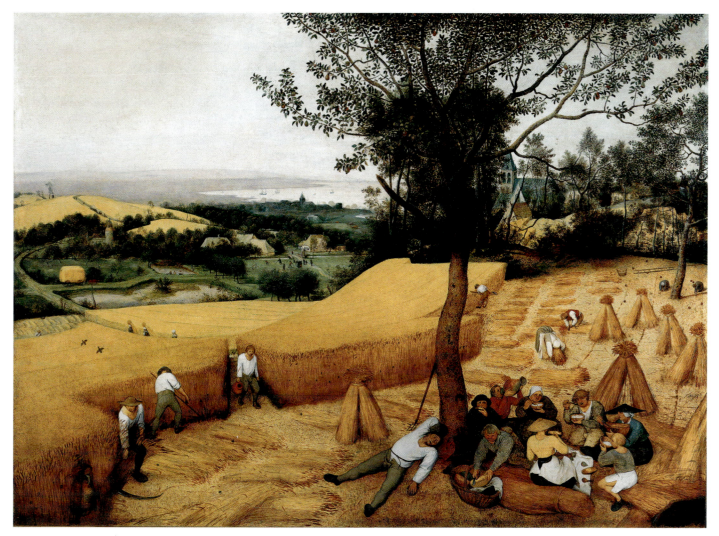

B. Pieter Bruegel the Elder **THE HARVESTERS**
1565. Oil on wood panel, 46⅞ × 63¾″ (1.17 × 1.6 m). Metropolitan Museum of Art, New York.

shift of workers on their lunch break— serving themselves from baskets, gnawing on hard pieces of bread, spooning milk from bowls, or gulping from an uplifted jug. One man takes the opportunity of this break for a quick nap. Some have seen in this lounging figure an emblem of sloth, or a wanton display of uncouth behavior, reminiscent of the embarrassing exposure of the peasant couple invited in to warm themselves before the fire in the farmhouse of the February page of Duke Jean de Berry's *Très Riches Heures* (SEE FIG. 18–4), painted by the Netherlandish Limbourg brothers a century and a half earlier.

Indeed, Bruegel's series of the months invites comparison with this venerable tradition—dating to the early Middle Ages— of showing peasant activity within the calendar cycles of prayer books made for wealthy patrons. Were they amused by peasant behavior? Did they enjoy representations of the productivity of their land and the availability of willing laborers to work it? Or do these vignettes embody their own longings for a simpler life, idealized for them as a harmony between the natural world and the people who live on it, and off it? But the peasants enjoying the good life in this sunny scene of harvesting are only on a lunch break. Another shift is already hard at work in the fields, and the wealth of the patrons who supported the growth of an art market was dependent on the labor of countless folks like them.

EXPLORE MORE: Gain insight from a primary source on Pieter Bruegel **www.myartslab.com**

The French Ambassadors ▶

by Hans Holbein the Younger. 1533. Oil on wood panel.
81⅛ × 82⅝″ (2.07 × 2.1 m). National Gallery, London.

Embossing on the sheath of the dagger tells us that de Dinteville is 28, while an inscription on the edge of the book (Bible?) under de Selve's arm records that he is 24.

This globe has Polisy, the de Dinteville family estate, marked at the center. It was here that this painting was hung when the ambassador returned to France at the end of 1533.

These objects on the top shelf were used to observe natural heavenly phenomena and chart the passage of time. The items displayed on the lower shelf relate more to terrestrial concerns.

Music is a common symbol of harmony in this period, and the broken string on this lute has been understood as an allusion to the discord created by the sweep of Protestant reform across Europe.

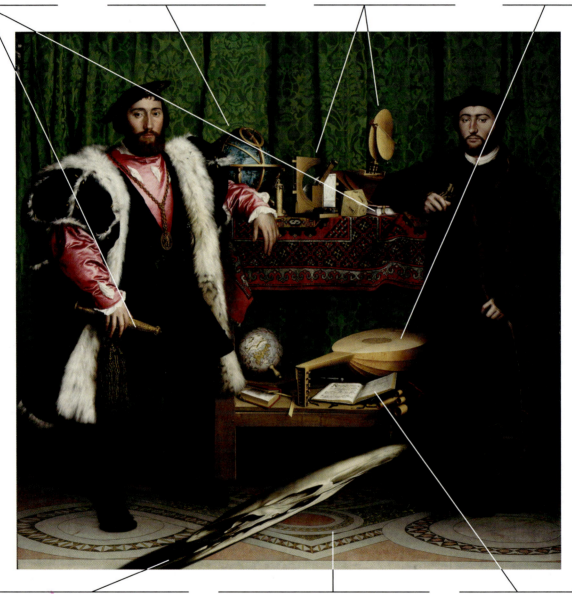

This bizarre, but prominently placed skull—as well as the skull badge that appears on de Dinteville's cap—reminded viewers of their own mortality. The foreground skull is distorted by anamorphosis, in which images are stretched horizontally with the use of a trapezoidal grid so that they must be viewed from the side to appear correctly proportioned.

This pavement—known as "Cosmati work" after the thirteenth-century Italian family that specialized in it—is copied from the floor in Westminster Abbey and may proclaim the ambassadors' involvement in a holy enterprise of reconciliation. The artist signed the painting on the left edge of the floor: "Johannes Holbein pingebat, 1533."

This is a Lutheran hymnal published in 1527, open at one of Luther's best-known compositions: "Come, Holy Ghost, our souls inspire." Neither man was a Protestant, but some of de Selve's contemporaries saw him as sympathetic to the cause of the reformers.

SEE MORE: View the Closer Look feature for *The French Ambassadors* www.myartslab.com

her own features, van Hemessen presented a serious young person who looks up to acknowledge us, interrupting her work on a portrait of a woman client. Between the date of this self-portrait and 1552, she painted ten signed and dated portraits of women, which seems to have been a specialty. She became a favored court artist to Mary of Hungary, sister of Emperor Charles V and regent of the Netherlands, for whom she painted not only portraits but also religious works, and whom she followed back to Spain when Mary ceased to be regent in 1556.

PIETER BRUEGEL THE ELDER. So popular did the works of Hieronymus Bosch remain that, nearly half a century after his death, Pieter Bruegel (c. 1525–1569) began his career by imitating them. Like Bosch, he often painted large narrative works crowded with figures, and he chose moralizing or satirical subject matter. He traveled throughout Italy, but, unlike many Renaissance artists, he did not record the ruins of ancient Rome or the wonders of the Italian cities. Instead, he seems to have been fascinated by the landscape, particularly the formidable jagged rocks and sweeping panoramic views of Alpine valleys, which he recorded in detailed drawings. Back home in his studio, he made an impressive leap of the imagination as he painted the flat and rolling lands of Flanders as broad panoramas, even adding imaginary mountains on the horizon. He also visited country fairs to sketch the farmers and townspeople who became the focus of his paintings, presenting humans not as unique individuals but as well-observed types, whose universality makes them familiar even today.

Bruegel depicted nature in all seasons and in all moods. *Return of the Hunters* (see "Bruegel's Cycle of the Months," pages 702–703, FIG. A) captures the bleak atmosphere of early nightfall during a damp, cold winter, with a freshness that recalls the much earlier paintings of his compatriots the Limbourgs (SEE FIG. 18–4). The hunters are foregrounded before a sharp plunge into space; the juxtaposition of near and far without middle ground is a typically sixteenth-century device. But this is clearly not an accidental image; it is a slice of everyday life faithfully reproduced within a carefully calculated composition. The same can be said of Breugel's portrayal of late summer harvest (SEE "Bruegel's Cycle of the Months," pages 702–703, FIG. B), where the light is warmer, the landscape lush and verdant, the human activity rooted in agricultural labor or a momentary respite from it. As a depiction of Netherlandish life, these peasant scenes focusing on landscape represent a relative calm before the storm. Three years after they were painted, the anguished struggle of the northern provinces for independence from Spain began.

Pieter the Elder died in 1569, leaving two children, Pieter the Younger (1564/1565–1637/1638) and Jan (1568–1625), both of whom became successful painters. And the dynasty continued with Jan's son, Jan the Younger (1601–1678), who changed the family name from Bruegel to Brueghel.

ENGLAND

Tudor England, in spite of the disruption caused by the Reformation, was economically and politically stable enough to provide sustained support for the arts, as Henry VIII strived to compete with the wealthy, sophisticated court of Francis I. Music, literature, and architecture flourished, but painting was principally left to foreigners.

As a young man, Henry VIII (r. 1509–1547) was loyal to the Church, defending it against Luther's attacks. He was rewarded by the pope in 1521 by being granted the title "Defender of the Faith." But when the pope refused to annul his marriage to Catherine of Aragon, Henry broke with Rome. By action of Parliament in 1534 he became the "Supreme Head on Earth of the Church and Clergy of England." He mandated an English translation of the Bible in every church, and in 1536 and 1539, he dissolved the monasteries, confiscating their great wealth and rewarding his followers with monastic lands and buildings. Shrines and altars were stripped of their jewels and precious metals to bolster the royal purse, and in 1548, during the reign of Henry's son, Edward VI, religious images were officially prohibited.

During the brief reign of Mary (r. 1553–1558), England officially returned to Catholicism, but the accession of Elizabeth in 1558 confirmed England as a Protestant country. So effective was Elizabeth, who ruled until 1603, that the last decades of the sixteenth century in England are called the Elizabethan Age.

ARTISTS IN THE TUDOR COURT

A remarkable record of the appearance of Tudor notables survives in portraiture. Since the Tudors had long favored Netherlandish and German artists, it is hardly surprising that it was a German-born painter, Hans Holbein the Younger (c. 1497–1543), who shaped the taste of the English court and upper classes.

HANS HOLBEIN. Holbein first visited London from 1526 to 1528 and was introduced by the Dutch scholar Erasmus to the humanist circle around the English statesman Thomas More. He returned to England in 1532 and was appointed court painter to Henry VIII about four years later. During the 1530s, he created a spectacular series of portraits of nobles and diplomats associated with the Tudor court. The court's climate of international interaction is embodied in a double portrait that Holbein painted in 1533 (see "A Closer Look," opposite)—a German painter's rendering in England of two French diplomats, one of them representing the court of Francis I in the Vatican. The French Ambassadors foregrounds Holbein's virtuosity as a painter and constructs a rich characterization of Jean de Dinteville, French ambassador to England, and his friend Georges de Selve, bishop of Lavaur and ambassador to the Holy See. With a loving detail that recalls the work of Jan van Eyck, the artist describes the surface textures and luminosity of the many objects placed in the painting to reflect the intellectual gifts and symbolize the political accomplishments of these two men. References in these objects to the conflicts

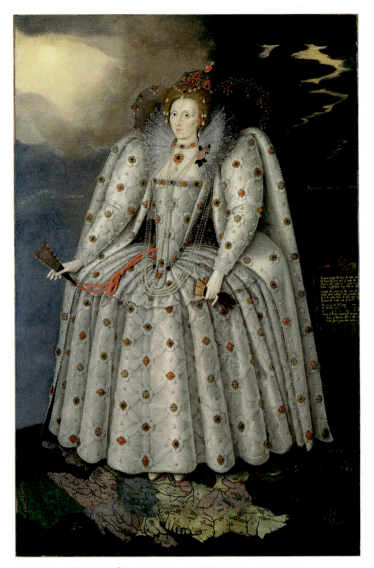

21-22 • Marcus Gheeraerts the Younger QUEEN ELIZABETH I (THE DITCHLEY PORTRAIT)
c. 1592. Oil on canvas, 95 × 60″ (2.4 × 1.5 m). National Portrait Gallery, London.

between European states, and within the Catholic Church itself, imply that these bright and confident young ambassadors will apply their considerable diplomatic skills to finding a resolution.

PORTRAITS OF ELIZABETH. Queen Elizabeth I carefully controlled the way artists represented her in official portraits and was known to have imprisoned artists whose unofficial images did not meet with her approval. A stark and hieratic regal image by Flemish artist Marcus Gheeraerts typifies the look she was after

21-23 • Nicholas Hilliard GEORGE CLIFFORD, THIRD EARL OF CUMBERLAND (1558-1605)
c. 1595. Watercolor on vellum on card, oval 2¾ × 2³⁄₁₆″ (7.1 × 5.8 cm). The Nelson-Atkins Museum of Art, Kansas City, Missouri. Gift of Mr. and Mrs. John W. Starr through the Starr Foundation. F58-60/188

(FIG. 21–22). Called the *Ditchley Portrait* because it seems to have been commissioned for Ditchley, the estate of her courtier Sir Henry Lee, to commemorate the Queen's visit in 1592, the full-length figure of Elizabeth—more costume than body—stands supreme on a map of her realm with her feet in Oxfordshire, near Ditchley. The stark whiteness of her elaborate dress and the pale abstraction of her severe face assert the virginal purity that she cultivated as a part of her image. A storm passes out of the picture on the right while the sun breaks through on the left. It is as if the queen is in control not only of England but of nature itself.

NICHOLAS HILLIARD. In 1570, Nicholas Hilliard (1547–1619) arrived in London from southwest England to pursue a career as a jeweler, goldsmith, and painter of miniatures. Hilliard never received a court appointment, but he created miniature portraits of the queen and court notables, including George Clifford, third earl of Cumberland (FIG. 21–23). Cumberland was a regular participant in the annual tilts and festivals celebrating the anniversary of Elizabeth's ascent to the throne. In Hilliard's miniature, Cumberland, a

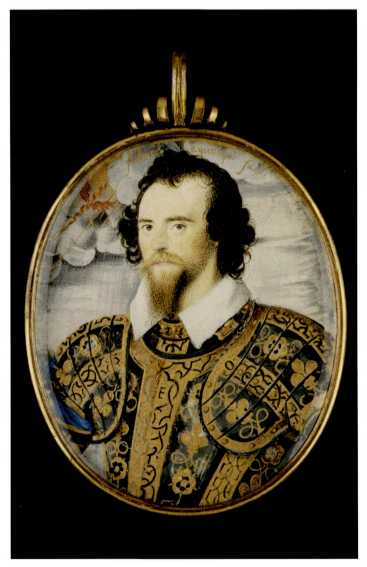

Armor for Royal Games

The medieval tradition of holding tilting, or jousting, competitions at English festivals and public celebrations continued during Renaissance times. Perhaps most famous were the Accession Day Tilts, held annually to celebrate the anniversary of Elizabeth I's coming to the throne. The gentlemen of the court, dressed in armor made especially for the occasion, held mock battles in the queen's honor. They rode their horses from opposite directions, trying to strike each other with long lances during six passes, as judges rated their performances.

The elegant armor worn by George Clifford, third Earl of Cumberland, at the Accession Day Tilts has been preserved in the collection of the Metropolitan Museum of Art in New York. Tudor roses and back-to-back capital *E*s in honor of the queen decorate the armor's surface. As the queen's champion, beginning in 1590, Clifford also wore her jeweled glove attached to his helmet as he met all comers in the tiltyard of Whitehall Palace in London.

Made by Jacob Halder in the royal armories at Greenwich, the 60-pound suit of armor is recorded in the sixteenth-century Almain Armourers' Album along with its "exchange pieces." These allowed the owner to vary his appearance by changing mitts, side pieces, or leg protectors, and also provided backup pieces if one were damaged.

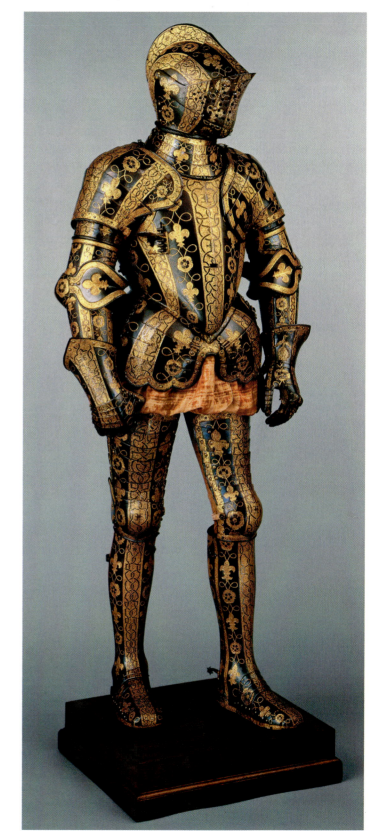

Jacob Halder **ARMOR OF GEORGE CLIFFORD, THIRD EARL OF CUMBERLAND**
Made in the royal workshop at Greenwich, England. c. 1580–1585. Steel and gold, height 5′9½″ (1.77 m). Metropolitan Museum of Art, New York. Munsey Fund, 1932 (32.130.6)

man of about 30, wears a richly engraved and gold-inlaid suit of armor, forged for his first appearance in 1583 (see "Armor for Royal Games," page 707). Hilliard gives him a marked air of courtly jauntiness, with a stylish beard, mustache, and curled hair, but Cumberland is also humanized by his direct gaze and receding hairline. Cumberland's motto—"I bear lightning and water"—is inscribed on a stormy sky, with a lightning bolt in the form of a caduceus, one of his emblems. After all, he was that remarkable Elizabethan type—a naval commander and a gentleman pirate.

ARCHITECTURE

To increase support for the Tudor dynasty, Henry and his successors granted titles to rich landowners. To display their wealth and status, many of these newly created aristocrats embarked on extensive building projects, constructing lavish country residences, which sometimes surpassed the French châteaux in size and grandeur. Rooted in the Perpendicular Gothic style (SEE FIG. 17–18), Elizabethan architecture's severe walls and broad expanses of glass were modernized by replacing medieval ornament with Classical motifs copied from architectural handbooks and pattern books. The first architectural manual in English, published in 1563, was written by John Shute, one of the few builders who had spent time in Italy. Most influential were the treatises on architectural design by the Italian architect Sebastiano Serlio.

HARDWICK HALL. One of the grandest of all the Elizabethan houses was Hardwick Hall, the home of Elizabeth, Countess of Shrewsbury, known as "Bess of Hardwick" (FIG. 21–24). When she was in her seventies, the redoubtable countess—who inherited riches from all four of her deceased husbands—employed Robert Smythson (c. 1535–1614), England's first Renaissance architect, to build Hardwick Hall (1591–1597).

The medieval great hall was transformed into a two-story entrance hall, with rooms arranged symmetrically around it—a nod to Classical balance. A sequence of rooms leads to a grand stair up to the long gallery and high great chamber on the second floor that featured an ornately carved fireplace (FIG. 21–25). It was here the countess received guests, entertained, and sometimes dined. The room seems designed to showcase a precious set of six Brussels tapestries featuring the story of Ulysses and is illuminated by its enormous windows. They serve as yet another reminder of the international character of the lavish decoration of residences created for wealthy patrons across Europe during this Renaissance century.

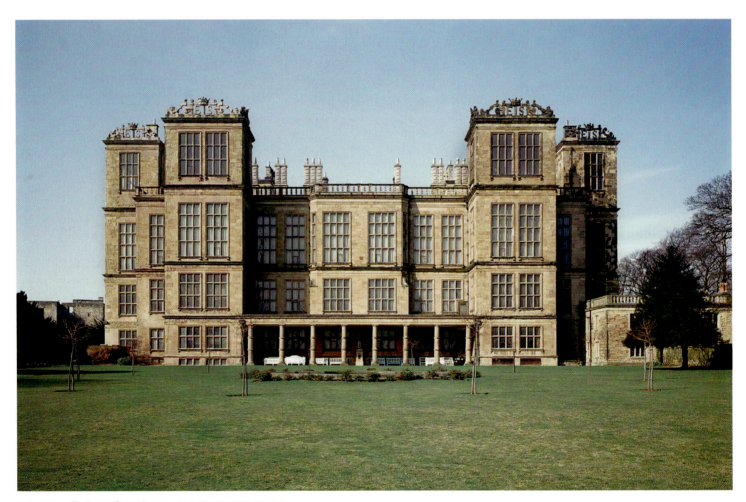

21-24 • Robert Smythson HARDWICK HALL
Derbyshire, England. 1591–1597.

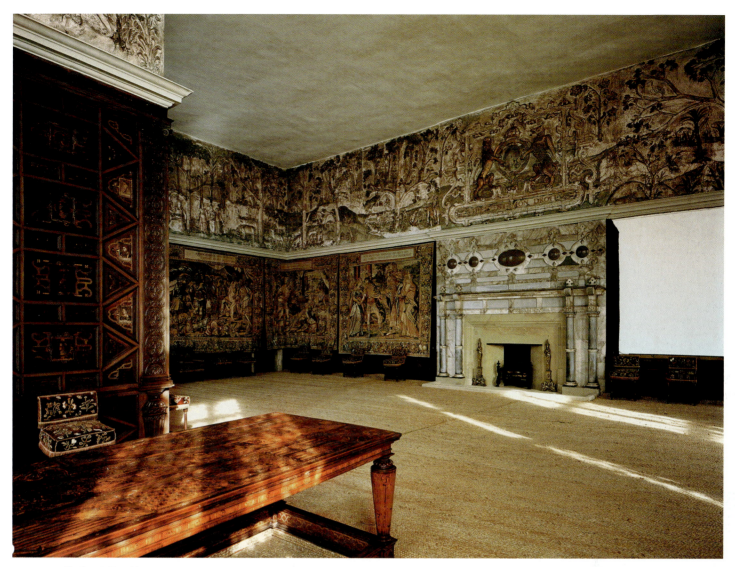

21–25 • Robert Smythson **HIGH GREAT CHAMBER, HARDWICK HALL**
Derbyshire, England. 1591–1597. Brussels tapestries 1550s; painted plaster sculpture by Abraham Smith.

THINK ABOUT IT

21.1 Choose one European court that patronized artists working in a "foreign" tradition from another part of Europe and assess how this internationalism fostered breaking down regional and national boundaries in European art. Be sure to ground your discussion in the work of specific artists.

21.2 Explore the impact of Italian art and ideas on the work and persona of German artist Albrecht Dürer. Choose one of his works from the chapter, and discuss its Italianate features and the ways in which it departs from and draws on earlier northern European traditions.

21.3 Summarize the factors that led to a burgeoning art market in the Netherlands in the sixteenth century. Who are some of the artists who benefited from this more fluid system of patronage? How and why were they successful within it?

21.4 Discuss the impact of the Protestant Reformation on the visual arts in northern Europe, focusing your discussion on types of subject matter that patrons sought.

21.5 Choose a work of art discussed in this chapter that displays extraordinary technical skill in more than one medium. How was its virtuosity achieved, and how is it highlighted as an important factor in the work's significance?

PRACTICE MORE: Compose answers to these questions, get flashcards for images and terms, and review chapter material with quizzes
www.myartslab.com

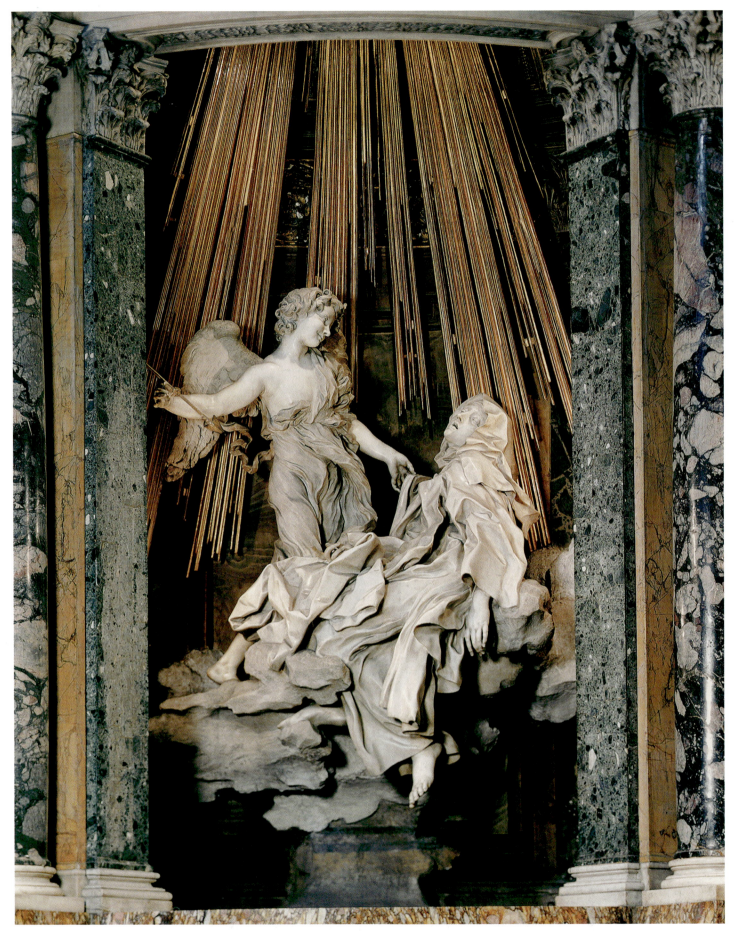

22–1 • Gianlorenzo Bernini **ST. TERESA OF ÁVILA IN ECSTASY**
1645–1652. Marble, height of the group 11′6″ (3.5 m). Cornaro Chapel, church of Santa Maria della Vittoria, Rome.

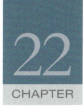

SEVENTEENTH-CENTURY ART IN EUROPE

In the Church of Santa Maria della Vittoria in Rome, the sixteenth-century Spanish mystic St. Teresa of Ávila (1515–1582, canonized 1622) swoons in ecstasy on a bank of billowing marble clouds (FIG. 22–1). A puckish angel tugs open her robe, aiming a gilded arrow at her breast. Gilded bronze rays of supernatural light descend, even as actual light illuminates the figures from a hidden window above. This dramatic scene, created by Gianlorenzo Bernini (1598–1680) between 1645 and 1652, represents a famous vision described with startling physical clarity by Teresa, in which an angel pierced her body repeatedly with an arrow, transporting her to a state of ecstatic oneness with God, charged with erotic associations.

The sculpture is an exquisite example of the emotional, theatrical style perfected by Bernini in response to the religious and political climate in Rome during the period of spiritual renewal known as the Counter-Reformation. Many had seen the Protestant Reformation of the previous century as an outgrowth of Renaissance Humanism with its emphasis on rationality and independent thinking. In response, the Catholic Church took a reactionary, authoritarian position, supported by the new Society of Jesus founded by Ignatius Loyola (d. 1556, canonized 1622). In the "spiritual exercises"

(1522–1523) initiated by St. Ignatius, Christians were enjoined to use all their senses to transport themselves emotionally as they imagined the events on which they were meditating. They were to feel the burning fires of hell or the bliss of heaven, the lashing of the whips and the flesh-piercing crown of thorns. Art became an instrument of propaganda and also a means of leading the spectator to a reinvigorated Christian practice and belief.

Of course, the arts had long been used to convince or inspire, but nowhere more effectively than by the Catholic Church in the seventeenth century. To serve the educational and evangelical mission of the revitalized and conservative Church, paintings and sculpture had to depict events and people accurately and clearly, following guidelines established by religious leaders. Throughout Catholic Europe, painters such as Rubens and Caravaggio created brilliant religious art under official Church sponsorship. And although today some viewers find this sculpture of St. Teresa uncomfortably charged with sexuality, the Church approved of the depictions of such sensational and supernatural mystical visions. They helped worshipers achieve the emotional state of religious ecstasy that was a goal of the Counter-Reformation.

LEARN ABOUT IT

22.1 Assess the impact of the Council of Trent's guidelines for the Counter-Reformation art of the Roman Catholic Church.

22.2 Explore how the work of Bernini and Caravaggio established a new dramatic intensity, technical virtuosity, and unvarnished naturalism that blossomed into the Baroque.

22.3 Trace the broad influence of Caravaggio's style on art across Europe during the seventeenth century.

22.4 Assess the resurgence of Classicism, especially in the work of seventeenth-century French artists and architects.

22.5 Analyze the way that seventeenth-century artists created works that embodied the power and prestige of the monarchy.

22.6 Examine the development of portraiture, still life, landscape, and genre scenes as major subjects for painting, especially within the prosperous art market of the Netherlands.

HEAR MORE: Listen to an audio file of your chapter **www.myartslab.com**

"BAROQUE"

The intellectual and political forces set in motion by the Renaissance and Reformation of the fifteenth and sixteenth centuries intensified during the seventeenth century. Religious wars continued, although gradually the Protestant forces gained control in the north, where Spain recognized the independence of the Dutch Republic in 1648. Catholicism maintained its primacy in southern Europe, the Holy Roman Empire, and France through the efforts of an energized papacy, aided by the new Society of Jesus, also known as the Jesuit Order (MAP 22–1). At the same time, scientific advances compelled people to question their worldview. Of great importance was the growing understanding that the Earth was not the center of the universe but rather was a planet revolving around the sun. As rulers' economic strength began to slip away, artists found patrons in the Church and the secular state, as well as in the newly confident and prosperous urban middle class. What evolved was a style that art historians have called "the Baroque." The label may be related to the Italian word *barocco*, a jeweler's term for an irregularly shaped pearl—something beautiful, fascinating, and strange.

Baroque art deliberately evokes intense emotional responses from viewers. Dramatically lit, theatrical compositions often combine several media within a single work as artists highlight their technical virtuosity. But the seventeenth century also saw its own version of Classicism, a more moving and dramatic variant of Renaissance ideals and principles featuring idealization based on observation of the material world; balanced (though often asymmetrical) compositions; diagonal movement in space; rich, harmonious colors; and the inclusion of visual references to ancient Greece and Rome. Many seventeenth-century artists sought lifelike depiction of their world in portraiture, **genre paintings** (scenes from everyday life), still life (paintings of inanimate objects such as food, fruit, or flowers), and religious scenes enacted by ordinary people in ordinary settings. Intense emotional involvement, lifelike renderings, and Classical references may exist in the same work, and are all part of the stylistic complexion of the seventeenth century.

The role of viewers also changed. Italian Renaissance painters and patrons had been fascinated with the visual possibilities of perspective and treasured idealism of form and subject which kept viewers at a distance, reflecting intellectually on what they were seeing. Seventeenth-century masters, on the other hand, sought to engage viewers as participants in the work of art, and often reached out to incorporate or activate the world beyond the frame into the nature and meaning of the work itself. In Catholic countries, representations of horrifying scenes of martyrdom or the passionate spiritual life of a mystic in religious ecstasy were intended to inspire viewers to a renewed faith by making them feel what was going on, not simply by causing them to think about it. In Protestant countries, images of communal parades and city views sought to inspire pride in civic accomplishments. Viewers participated in works of art like audiences in a theater—vicariously but completely—as the work of art drew them visually and emotionally

into its orbit. The seventeenth-century French critic Roger de Piles (1635–1709) described this exchange when he wrote: "True painting … calls to us; and has so powerful an effect, that we cannot help coming near it, as if it had something to tell us" (Puttfarken, p. 55).

ITALY

Italy in the seventeenth century remained a divided land in spite of a common history, language, and geography, with borders defined by the seas. The Kingdom of Naples and Sicily was Spanish; the Papal States crossed the center; Venice maintained its independence as a republic; and the north remained divided among small principalities. Churchmen and their families remained powerful patrons of the arts, especially as they recognized the visual arts' role in revitalizing the Roman Catholic Church. The Council of Trent (1563) had set guidelines for Church art that went against the arcane, worldly, and often lascivious trends exploited by Mannerism. The clergy's call for clarity, simplicity, chaste subject matter, and the ability to rouse a very Catholic piety in the face of Protestant revolt found a response in the fresh approaches to subject matter and style offered by a new generation of artists.

ARCHITECTURE AND SCULPTURE IN ROME

A major goal of the Counter-Reformation was to embellish churches properly, and Pope Sixtus V (pontificate 1585–1590) had begun the renewal in Rome by cutting long, straight avenues through the city to link the major pilgrimage churches with one another and with the main gates of Rome. Sixtus also ordered open spaces—piazzas—to be cleared in front of major churches, marking each site with an Egyptian obelisk. In a practical vein, he also reopened one of the ancient aqueducts to stabilize the city's water supply. Unchallengeable power and vast financial resources were required to carry out such an extensive plan of urban renewal and to refashion Rome—parts of which had been the victim of rapacity and neglect since the Middle Ages—once more into the center of spiritual and worldly power.

The Counter-Reformation popes had great wealth, although they eventually nearly bankrupted the Church with their building programs. Sixtus began to renovate the Vatican and its library; he completed the dome of St. Peter's and built splendid palaces. The Renaissance ideal of the central-plan church continued to be used for the shrines of saints, but Counter-Reformation thinking called for churches with long, wide naves to accommodate large congregations assembled to hear inspiring sermons as well as to participate in the Mass. In the sixteenth century, the decoration of new churches had been relatively austere, but seventeenth- and eighteenth-century Catholic taste favored opulent and spectacular visual effects to heighten the emotional involvement of worshipers.

ST. PETER'S BASILICA IN THE VATICAN. Half a century after Michelangelo had returned St. Peter's Basilica to Bramante's original

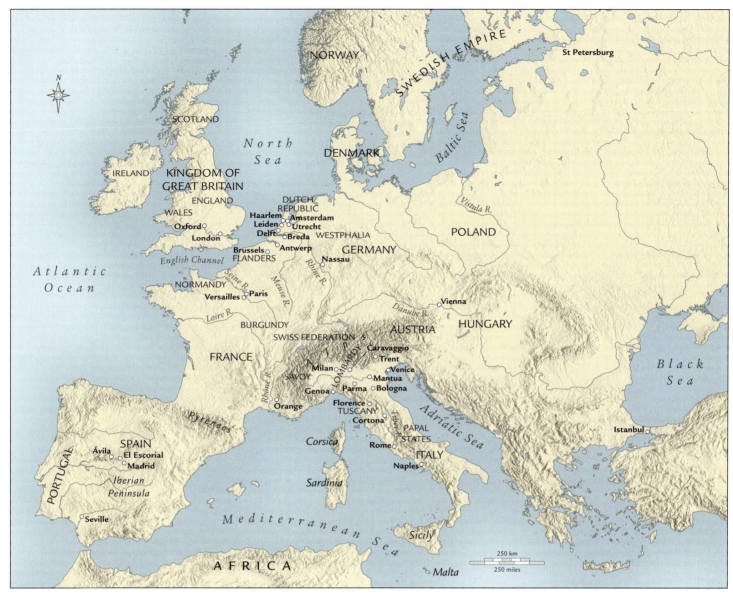

MAP 22-1 • SEVENTEENTH-CENTURY EUROPE

Protestantism still dominated northern Europe, while in the south Roman Catholicism remained strong after the Counter-Reformation. The Habsburg Empire was now divided into two parts, under separate rulers.

vision of a central-plan building, Pope Paul V Borghese (pontificate 1605–21) commissioned Carlo Maderno (1556–1629) to provide the church with a longer nave and a new façade (FIG. 22–2). Construction began in 1607, and everything but the façade bell towers was completed by 1615 (see "St. Peter's Basilica," page 651). In essence, Maderno took the concept of *Il Gesù*'s façade (SEE FIG. 20–36) and enlarged it for the most important church of the Catholic world. Maderno's façade for St. Peter's "steps out" in three progressively projecting planes: from the corners to the doorways flanking the central entrance area, then the entrance area, then the central doorway itself. Similarly, the colossal orders connecting the first and second stories are flat pilasters at the corners but fully round columns where they flank the doorways. These columns support a continuous entablature that also steps out—following the columns—as it moves toward the central door.

When Maderno died in 1629, he was succeeded as Vatican architect by his collaborator of five years, Gianlorenzo Bernini (1598–1680). The latter was taught by his father, and part of his training involved sketching the Vatican collection of ancient sculpture, such as *Laocoön and His Sons* (SEE FIG. 5–55) and the *Farnese Hercules* (SEE FIG. 5–47), as well as the many examples of Renaissance painting in the papal palace. Throughout his life, Bernini admired antique art and, like other artists of this period, considered himself a Classicist. Today, we not only appreciate his strong debt to the Renaissance tradition but also acknowledge the way he broke through that tradition to take us into a new, Baroque style.

When Urban VIII was elected pope in 1623, he unhesitatingly gave the young Bernini the daunting task of designing an enormous bronze baldachin, or canopy, over the high altar of St. Peter's. The church was so large that a dramatic focus on the altar

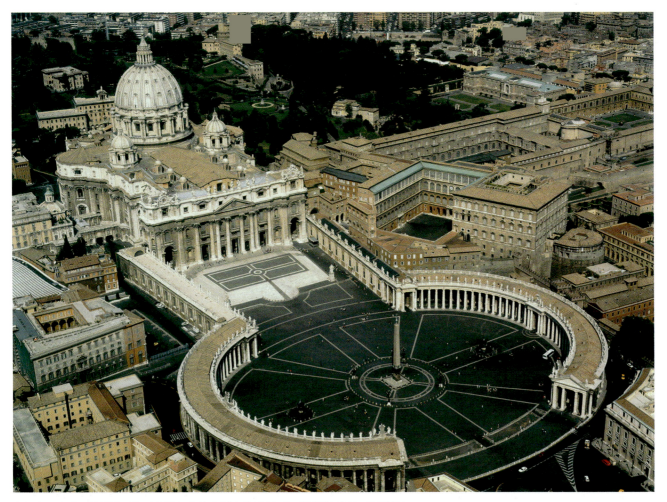

22-2 • ST. PETER'S BASILICA AND PIAZZA, VATICAN, ROME
Carlo Maderno, façade, 1607–1626; Gianlorenzo Bernini, piazza design, c. 1656–1657.

Perhaps only a Baroque artist of Bernini's talents could have unified the many artistic periods and styles that come together in St. Peter's Basilica (starting with Bramante's original design for the building in the sixteenth century). The basilica in no way suggests a piecing together of parts made by different builders at different times but rather presents itself as a triumphal unity of all the parts in one coherent whole.

SEE MORE: Click the Google Earth link for an aerial view of St. Peter's, Vatican City
www.myartslab.com

was essential. The resulting *baldacchino* (**FIG. 22–3**), completed in 1633, stands almost 100 feet high and exemplifies the Baroque objective to create multimedia works, combining architecture and sculpture—and sometimes painting as well—that defy simple categorization. The gigantic corner columns symbolize the union of Christianity and its Jewish tradition—the vine of the Eucharist climbing the twisted columns associated with the Temple of Solomon. They support an entablature with a crowning element topped with an orb (a sphere representing the universe) and a cross (symbolizing the reign of Christ). Figures of angels and *putti* decorate the entablature, which is hung with tasseled panels in imitation of a cloth canopy. This imposing work not only marks the site of the tomb of St. Peter, but also serves as a tribute to Urban VIII and his family, the Barberini, whose emblems— honeybees and suns on the tasseled panels, and laurel leaves on the climbing vines—are prominently displayed.

Between 1627 and 1641, Bernini and several other sculptors, again in multimedia extravaganzas, rebuilt Bramante's crossing piers as giant reliquaries. Statues of SS. Helena, Veronica, Andrew, and Longinus stand in niches below alcoves containing their relics, to the left and right of the *baldacchino*. Visible through the *baldacchino*'s columns in the apse of the church is another reliquary: the gilded-stone, bronze, and stucco shrine made by Bernini between 1657 and 1666 for the ancient wooden throne thought to have belonged to St. Peter as the first bishop of Rome. The Chair of Peter symbolized the direct descent of Christian authority from Peter to the current pope, a belief rejected by Protestants and therefore deliberately emphasized in Counter-Reformation Catholicism. Above the shrine, a brilliant stained-glass window portrays the Holy Spirit as a dove surrounded by an oval of golden rays. Adoring gilded angels and gilt-bronze rays fan out around the window and seem to extend the penetration of the natural light—

made the basilica and its setting an even more awe-inspiring vision. The approach today—along the grand avenue of the Via della Conciliazione running from the Tiber to the Basilica—was conceived by Mussolini in 1936 as part of his masterplan to transform Rome into a grand fascist capital.

BERNINI AS SCULPTOR. Even after Bernini's appointment as Vatican architect in 1629, he was still able to accept outside commissions by virtue of his large workshop. In fact, he first became famous as a sculptor, and he continued to work as one throughout his career, for both the papacy and private clients. A man of many talents, he was also a painter and even a playwright—an interest that dovetailed with his genius for theatrical and dramatic presentation.

Bernini's *David* (FIG. 22–4), made for a nephew of Pope Paul V in 1623, introduced a new type of three-dimensional composition that intrudes forcefully into the viewer's space. The young hero bends at the waist and twists far to one side, ready to launch the lethal rock at Goliath. Unlike Donatello's already victorious sassy

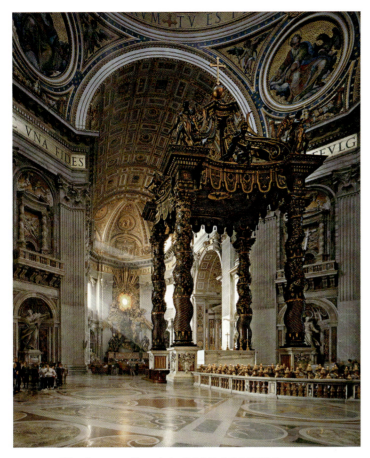

22-3 • Gianlorenzo Bernini BALDACCHINO
1624–1633. Gilt bronze, height approx. 100′ (30.48 m). Chair of Peter shrine, 1657–1666. Gilt bronze, marble, stucco, and glass. Pier decorations, 1627–1641. Gilt bronze and marble. Crossing, St. Peter's Basilica, Vatican, Rome.

and the Holy Spirit—into the apse of the church. The gilding also reflects the light back to the window, creating a dazzling, ethereal effect that the seventeenth century, with its interest in mystics and visions, would equate with the activation of divinity.

At approximately the same time that he was at work on the Chair of Peter, Bernini designed and supervised the building of a colonnade to form a huge double piazza in front of the entrance to St. Peter's (SEE FIG. 22–2). The open space that he had to work with was irregular, and an Egyptian obelisk and a fountain previously installed by Sixtus V had to be incorporated into the overall plan. Bernini's remarkable design frames the oval piazza with two enormous curved porticos, or covered walkways, supported by Doric columns. These curved porticos are connected to two straight porticos, which lead up a slight incline to the two ends of the church façade. Bernini characterized his design as the "motherly arms of the Church" reaching out to the world. He had intended to build a third section of the colonnade closing the side of the piazza facing the church so that only after pilgrims had crossed the Tiber River bridge and made their way through narrow streets, would they encounter the enormous open space before the imposing church. This element of surprise would have

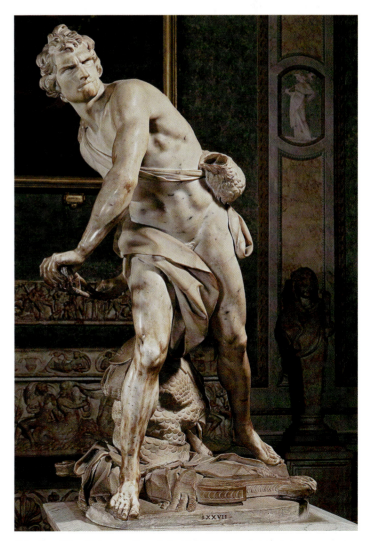

22-4 • Gianlorenzo Bernini DAVID
1623. Marble, height 5′7″ (1.7 m). Galleria Borghese, Rome.

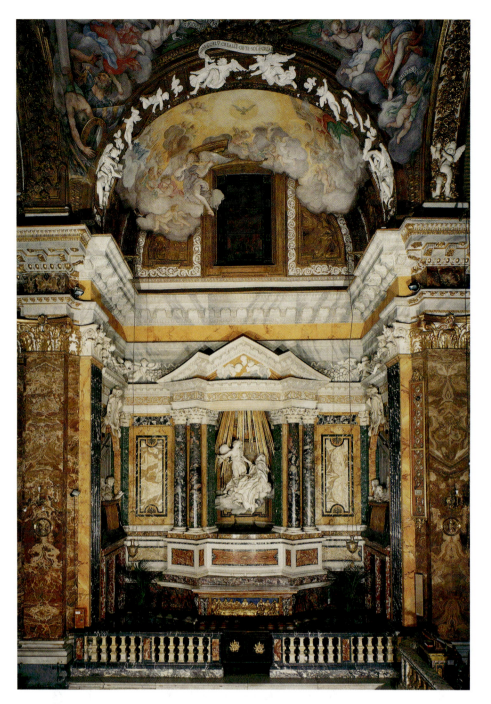

22–5 • Gianlorenzo Bernini
CORNARO CHAPEL, CHURCH OF SANTA MARIA DELLA VITTORIA, ROME
1642–1652.

EXPLORE MORE: Gain insight from a primary source on Gianlorenzo Bernini **www.myartslab.com**

SEE MORE: View a simulation related to the Cornaro Chapel **www.myartslab.com**

was dedicated to the Spanish saint Teresa of Ávila, canonized only 20 years earlier. Bernini designed it as a rich and theatrical setting for the portrayal of a central event in Teresa's life. He covered the walls with multicolored marble panels and crowned them with a projecting cornice supported by marble pilasters.

In the center of the chapel and framed by columns in the huge oval niche above the altar, Bernini's marble group *St. Teresa of Ávila in Ecstasy* (SEE FIG. 22–1) represents a vision described by the Spanish mystic in which an angel pierced her body repeatedly with an arrow, transporting her to a state of indescribable pain, religious ecstasy, and a sense of oneness with God. St. Teresa and the angel, who seem to float upward on clouds of stucco (a moistened mixture of lime and marble dust that can be molded), are cut from a heavy mass of solid marble supported on a seemingly drifting pedestal that was fastened by hidden metal bars to the chapel wall. Bernini's skill at capturing the movements and emotions of these figures is matched by his virtuosity in simulating different textures and colors in the pure white medium of marble; the angel's gauzy, clinging draperies seem silken in contrast with Teresa's heavy woolen monastic robe. Bernini effectively used the configuration of the garment's folds to convey the saint's swooning, sensuous body beneath, even though only Teresa's face, hands, and bare feet are actually visible.

Kneeling against what appear to be balconies on both sides of the chapel are marble portrait sculptures of Federigo, his deceased father (a Venetian doge), and six cardinals of the Cornaro family.

adolescent (SEE FIG. 19–10), or Michelangelo's pensive young man contemplating the task ahead (SEE FIG. 20–10), Bernini's more mature David, with his lean, sinewy body, tightly clenched mouth, and straining muscles, is all tension, action and determination. By creating a twisting figure caught in movement, Bernini incorporates the surrounding space within his composition, implying the presence of an unseen adversary somewhere behind the viewer. Thus, the viewer becomes part of the action, rather than its displaced and dispassionate observer.

From 1642 until 1652, Bernini worked on the decoration of the funerary chapel of Venetian cardinal Federigo Cornaro (**FIG. 22–5**) in the Church of Santa Maria della Vittoria, designed by Carlo Maderno earlier in the century. The Cornaro family chapel

The figures are informally posed and naturalistically portrayed. Two read from their prayer books, others exclaim at the miracle taking place in the light-infused realm above the altar, and one leans out from his seat, apparently to look at someone entering the chapel—perhaps the viewer, whose space these figures share. Bernini's intent was not to produce a spectacle for its own sake, but to capture a critical, dramatic moment at its emotional and sensual height, and by doing so guide viewers to identify totally with the event—and perhaps be transformed in the process.

BORROMINI'S CHURCH OF SAN CARLO. The intersection of two of the wide, straight avenues created by Pope Sixtus V inspired city planners to add a special emphasis, with fountains marking each of the four corners of the crossing. In 1634, Trinitarian monks

decided to build a new church at the site and awarded the commission for **SAN CARLO ALLE QUATTRO FONTANE** (St. Charles at the Four Fountains) to Francesco Borromini (1599–1667). Borromini, a nephew of architect Carlo Maderno, had arrived in Rome in 1619 from northern Italy to enter his uncle's workshop. Later, he worked under Bernini's supervision on the decoration of St. Peter's, and some details of the Baldacchino, as well as its structural engineering, are now attributed to him, but San Carlo was his first independent commission. Unfinished at Borromini's death, the church was nevertheless completed according to his design.

San Carlo stands on a narrow piece of land, with one corner cut off to accommodate one of the four fountains that give the church its name (**FIG. 22–6**). To fit the irregular site, Borromini created an elongated central-plan interior space with undulating walls (**FIG. 22–7**). Robust pairs of columns support a massive entablature, over which an oval dome, supported on pendentives, seems to float (**FIG. 22–8**). The coffers (inset panels in geometric shapes) filling the interior of the oval-shaped dome form an eccentric honeycomb of crosses, elongated hexagons, and octagons. These coffers decrease sharply in size as they approach the apex, or highest point, where the dove of the Holy Spirit hovers in a climax that brings together the geometry used in the chapel: oval, octagon, circle, and—very important—a triangle, symbol of the Trinity as well as of the church's patrons. The dome appears to be shimmering and inflating—almost floating up and away—thanks to light sources placed in the lower coffers and the lantern.

It is difficult today to appreciate how audacious Borromini's design for this small church was. In it he abandoned the modular,

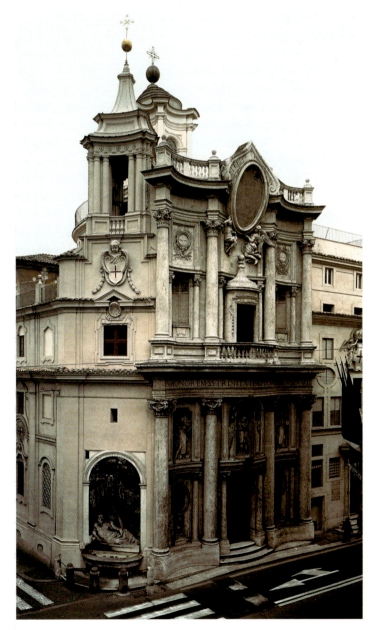

22-6 • Francesco Borromini **FAÇADE, CHURCH OF SAN CARLO ALLE QUATTRO FONTANE, ROME** 1638–1667.

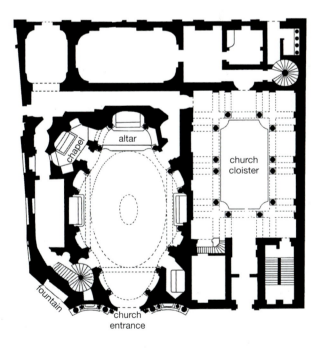

22-7 • Francesco Borromini **PLAN OF THE CHURCH OF SAN CARLO ALLE QUATTRO FONTANE, ROME** 1638–1667.

additive system of planning taken for granted by every architect since Brunelleschi. He worked instead from an overriding geometrical scheme, as a Gothic architect might, subdividing modular units to obtain more complex, rational shapes. For example, the elongated, octagonal plan of San Carlo is composed of two triangles set base to base along the short axis of the plan (SEE FIG. 22–7). This diamond shape is then subdivided into secondary triangular units made by calculating the distances between what will become the concave centers of the four major and five minor niches. Yet Borromini's conception of the whole is not medieval. The chapel is dominated horizontally by a Classical entablature that breaks any surge upward toward the dome. Borromini's treatment of the architectural elements as if they were malleable was also unprecedented. His contemporaries understood immediately what an extraordinary innovation the church represented; the Trinitarian monks who had commissioned it received requests for plans from visitors from all over Europe. Although Borromini's innovative work had little impact on the architecture of Classically minded Rome, it was widely imitated in northern Italy and beyond the Alps.

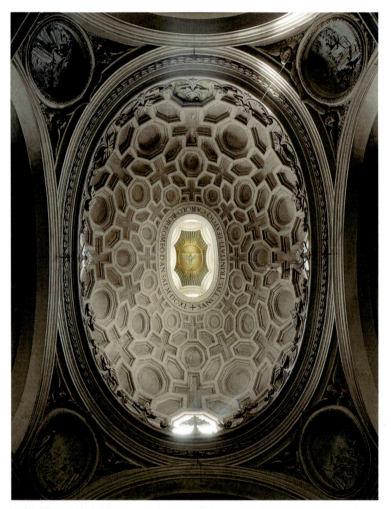

22-8 • Francesco Borromini VIEW INTO THE DOME OF THE CHURCH OF SAN CARLO ALLE QUATTRO FONTANE, ROME
1638–1667.

Borromini's design for San Carlo's façade (SEE FIG. 22–6), executed more than two decades later, was as innovative as his planning of the interior. He turned the building's front into an undulating, sculpture-filled screen punctuated with large columns and deep concave and convex niches that create dramatic effects of light and shadow. Borromini also gave his façade a strong vertical thrust in the center by placing over the tall doorway a statue-filled niche, then a windowed niche covered with a canopy, then a giant, forward-leaning cartouche held up by angels carved in such high relief that they appear to hover in front of the wall. The entire composition is crowned with a balustrade broken by the sharply pointed frame of the cartouche. As with the design of the building itself, Borromini's façade was enthusiastically imitated in northern Italy and especially in northern and eastern Europe.

PAINTING

Painting in seventeenth-century Italy followed one of two principal paths: the ordered Classicism of the Carracci or the dramatic naturalism of Caravaggio. Although the leading exponents of these paths were northern Italians—the Carracci family was from Bologna, and Caravaggio was born in or near Milan— they were all eventually drawn to Rome, the center of power and patronage. The Carracci family, like Caravaggio, were schooled in northern Italian Renaissance traditions, with its emphasis on *chiaroscuro*, as well as in Venetian color and *sfumato*. The Carracci quite consciously rejected the artifice of the Mannerist style and fused their northern roots with the central Italian Renaissance insistence on line (*disegno*), compositional structure, and figural solidity. They looked to Raphael, Michelangelo, and antique Classical sculpture for their ideal figural types and their expressive but decorous compositions. Caravaggio, on the other hand, satisfied the Baroque demand for drama and clarity by developing realism in a powerful new direction. He painted people he saw in the world around him—even the lowlife of Rome—and worked directly from models without elaborate drawings and compositional notes. Unlike the Carracci, he claimed to ignore the influence of the great masters so as to focus steadfastly on a sense of immediacy and invention.

THE CARRACCI. The brothers Agostino (1557–1602) and Annibale Carracci (1560–1609) and their cousin Ludovico (1555–1619) shared a studio in Bologna. As their re-evaluation of the High Renaissance masters attracted interest among their peers, they opened their doors to friends and students and then, in 1582, founded an art academy, where students drew from live models and studied art theory, Renaissance painting, and antique Classical sculpture. The Carracci placed a high value on accurate drawing, complex figure compositions, complicated narratives, and technical expertise in both oil and fresco painting. During its short life, the academy had an impact on

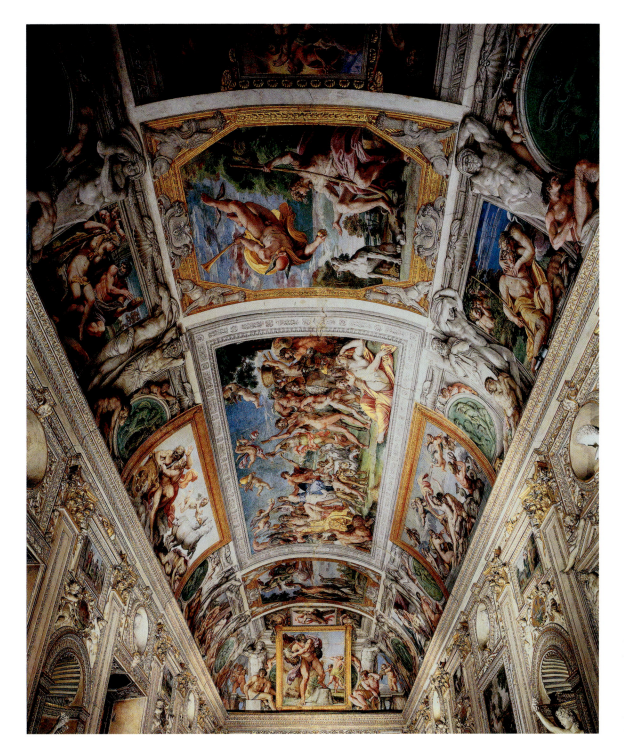

22-9 • Annibale Carracci **CEILING OF GALLERY, PALAZZO FARNESE, ROME** 1597–1601. Fresco, approx. 68 × 21′ (20.7 × 6.4 m).

the development of the arts—and art education—through its insistence on both life drawing (to achieve naturalism) and aesthetic theory (to achieve artistic harmony).

In 1595, Annibale was hired by Cardinal Odoardo Farnese to decorate the principal rooms of his family's immense Roman palace. In the long *galleria* (gallery), to celebrate the wedding of Duke Ranuccio Farnese of Parma to the niece of the pope, the artist was requested to paint scenes of love based on Ovid's *Metamorphoses* (**FIG. 22–9**). Undoubtedly, Annibale and Agostino, who assisted him, felt both inspiration and competition from the important Farnese collection of antique sculpture exhibited throughout the palace.

The primary image, set in the center of the vault, is *The Triumph of Bacchus and Ariadne*, a joyous procession celebrating the wine god Bacchus's love for Ariadne, whom he rescued after her lover, Theseus, abandoned her on the island of Naxos. Annibale combines the great northern Italian tradition of ceiling painting—seen in the work of Mantegna and Correggio (FIGS. 19–29, 20–19)—with his study of central Italian Renaissance painters and the Classical heritage of Rome. Annibale organized his complex theme by using illusionistic devices to create multiple levels of reality. Painted imitations of gold-framed easel paintings called *quadri riportati* ("transported paintings") appear to "rest" on

Caravaggio in the Contarelli Chapel

As soon as he had established himself as an up-and-coming artist during the 1590s, Caravaggio turned to a series of important commissions for religious paintings in the chapels of Roman churches. Unlike in the Renaissance, where frescos were applied directly to the walls, Caravaggio produced large oil paintings on canvas in his studio, only later installing them within the chapels to form coordinated ensembles. Several such installations survive, giving us the precious opportunity to experience the paintings as Caravaggio and his patrons intended. One of these intact programs, in the Contarelli Chapel of San Luigi dei Francesi, was Caravaggio's earliest religious commission in Rome, perhaps obtained through the efforts of Cardinal del Monte, who had supported the artist through the 1590s.

This church served the French community in Rome, and the building itself was constructed between 1518 and 1589, begun under the patronage of Catherine de' Medici, Queen of France. The chapel Caravaggio decorated was founded in 1565 by Mathieu Cointrel—Matteo Contarelli—a French noble at the papal court who would serve as a financial administrator under Gregory XIII (pontificate 1572–1585). Although earlier artists had been called on to provide paintings for the chapel, it was only after Contarelli's death in 1585 that the executors of his will brought the decoration to completion, hiring Giuseppe Cesare in

1591 to paint the ceiling frescos, and Caravaggio in 1599 to provide paintings of scenes from the life of the patron's patron saint: *The Calling of St. Matthew* on the left wall and *The Martyrdom of St. Matthew* on the right (not visible in FIG. A), both installed in July 1600.

The commissioning document was explicit, requiring the artist to show, in *The Calling of St. Matthew* (fig. B), the saint rising from his seat to follow Christ in ministry. But Caravaggio was never very good at following the rules. Among the group of smartly dressed Romans who form Matthew's circle of cohorts seated at the left, no one rises to leave. Art historians have not even been able to agree on which figure is Matthew. Most identify him with a bearded man in the center, interpreting his pointing gesture as a self-referential, questioning response to Jesus' call. But some see Matthew in the figure hunched over the scattered coins at far left, seemingly unmoved by Jesus' presence. In this case, the bearded figure's pointing would question whether this bent-over colleague was the one Jesus

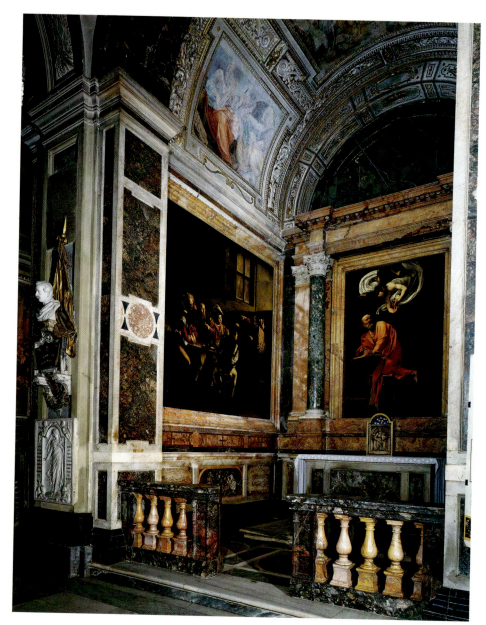

A. CONTARELLI CHAPEL, SAN LUIGI DEI FRANCESI
Rome. Paintings by Caravaggio 1599–1602.

sought. The painting is marked by mystery, not by the clarity sought by Counter-Reformation guidelines.

In February 1602, Caravaggio received a second commission for the Contarelli Chapel, this time for a painting over the altar showing St. Matthew, accompanied by his angelic symbol and writing his Gospel. It was to be completed within three months, but Caravaggio did not receive payment for the picture until September of that year, and the painting he delivered was rejected. The clergy considered Caravaggio's rendering of the saint unacceptably crude and common, his cross-legged pose uncouth and unnecessarily revealing. The fleshiness of the angel, who sidles cozily up to Matthew, was judged inappropriately risqué. In short, the painting was inconsistent with guidelines for saintly decorum set for artists by the Council of Trent. Caravaggio had to paint a second, more decorous altarpiece for the chapel (seen in FIG. A), with a nobler Matthew and a more distant angel. The rejected version was snapped up by Roman collector Vincenzo Giustiniani, who actually paid for the replacement in order to acquire the more sensational original. Unfortunately, this first painting was destroyed in the 1945 bombing of Berlin during World War II.

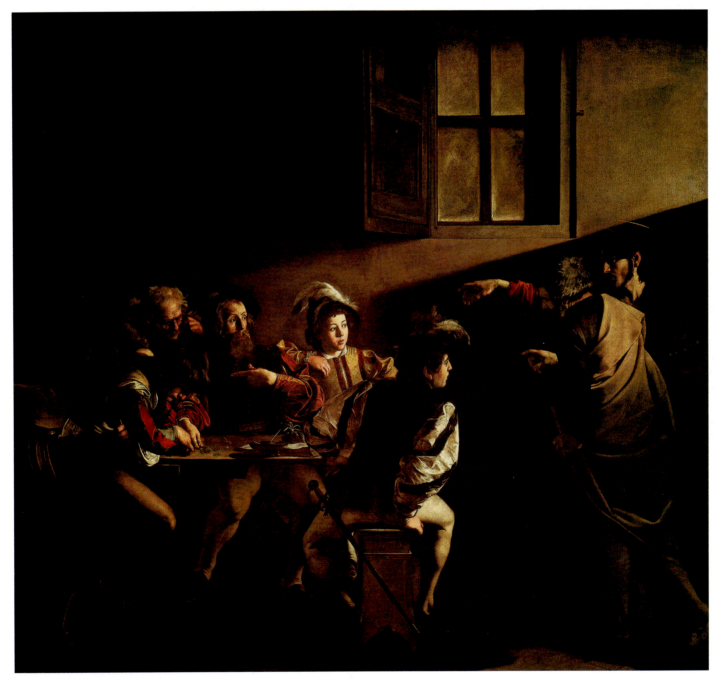

B. Caravaggio THE CALLING OF ST. MATTHEW
Contarelli Chapel, Church of San Luigi dei Francesi, Rome. 1599–1600.
Oil on canvas, 10'7½" × 11'2" (3.24 × 3.4 m).

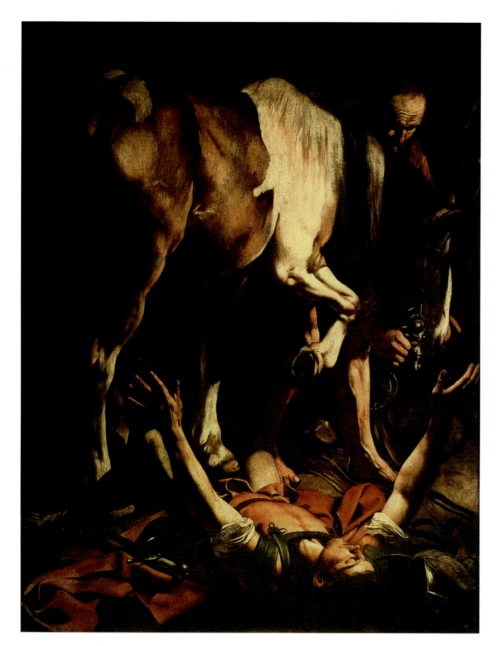

22-12 • Caravaggio THE CONVERSION OF ST. PAUL
Cerasi Chapel, Santa Maria del Popolo, Rome. c. 1601. Oil on canvas, 7′6″ × 5′8″ (2.3 × 1.75 m).

EXPLORE MORE: Gain insight from a primary source on Caravaggio
www.myartslab.com

religious subjects directly and dramatically, combining intensely observed figures, poses, and expressions with strongly contrasting effects of light and color. His knowledge of Lombard painting, where the influence of Leonardo was strong, must have aided him in his development of the technique now known as **tenebrism**, in which forms emerge from a dark background into a strong light that often falls from a single source outside the painting. The effect is that of a theatrical spotlight.

One of Caravaggio's first religious commissions, paintings for the Contarelli Chapel in the French community's church of St. Louis (San Luigi dei Francesi), included *The Calling of St. Matthew*, painted about 1599–1600 (see "Caravaggio in the Contarelli Chapel," pages 722–723). The subject is conversion, a common Counter-Reformation theme. Jesus calls Levi, the tax collector, to join his apostles (Matthew 9:9; Mark 2:14). Levi—who will become St. Matthew—sits at a table, counting or collecting money,

surrounded by elegant young men in plumed hats, velvet doublets, and satin shirts. Nearly hidden behind the back of the beckoning apostle—probably St. Peter—at the right, the gaunt-faced Jesus points dramatically at Levi with a gesture that is repeated in the presumed (other than Jesus, identities are not certain here) tax collector's own surprised response of pointing to himself, as if to say, "Who, me?" An intense raking light enters the painting from upper right, as if it were coming from the chapel's actual window above the altar to spotlight the important features of this darkened scene. Viewers encountering the painting obliquely across the empty space of the chapel interior seem to be witnessing the scene as it is occurring, elevated on a recessed stage opening through the wall before them.

The emotional power of Caravaggio's theatrical approach to sacred narrative is nowhere more evident than in his rendering of **THE CONVERSION OF ST. PAUL** for the Cerasi Chapel of Santa

Maria del Popolo (**FIG. 22–12**). This is one of two paintings commissioned for this chapel in 1600; the other portrayed the Crucifixion of St. Peter. The first pair was rejected when Caravaggio delivered them, and they were acquired by a private collector (see also "Caravaggio in the Contarelli Chapel," pages 722–723). This second version of Paul's conversion is direct and simple. Caravaggio focuses on Paul's internal involvement with a pivotal moment, not its external cause. There is no indication of a heavenly apparition, only Paul's response to it. There is no clear physical setting, only mysterious darkness. And Paul's experience is personal. Whereas he has been flung from his horse and threatens to tumble into the viewers' own space—arms outstretched and legs akimbo, bathed in a strong spotlight—the horse and groom behind him seem oblivious to Paul's experience. The horse actually takes up more space in the painting than the saint, and the unsettling position of its lifted foreleg, precariously poised over the sprawled body of Paul, adds further tension to an already charged presentation.

Despite the great esteem in which Caravaggio was held by some, especially the younger generation of artists, his violent temper repeatedly got him into trouble. During the last decade of his life, he was frequently arrested, initially for minor offenses such as carrying arms illegally or street brawling. But in May of 1606 he killed a man in a duel fought over a disputed tennis match and had to flee Rome as a fugitive under a death sentence. He supported himself on the run by painting in Naples, Malta, and Sicily. The Knights of Malta awarded him the cross of their religious and military order in July 1608, but in October he was imprisoned for insulting one of their number, and again he escaped and fled. Caravaggio died on July 18, 1610, just short of his 39th birthday, of a fever contracted during a journey back to Rome where he expected to be pardoned of his capital offense. Caravaggio's unvarnished realism and tenebrism influenced nearly every important European artist of the seventeenth century.

ARTEMISIA GENTILESCHI. One of Caravaggio's most brilliant Italian followers was Artemisia Gentileschi (1593–c. 1652/1653), whose international reputation helped spread the Caravaggesque style beyond Rome. Artemisia first studied and worked under her father, Orazio, one of the earliest followers of Caravaggio. In 1616, she moved from Rome to Florence, where she worked for the grand duke of Tuscany and was elected, at the age of 23, to the Florentine Academy of Design. But like many great artists, her promise as a painter was already evident in her early work. At the age of 17, while she was still part of her father's studio, she painted a stunning rendering of the popular subject of *Susannah and the Elders* (**FIG. 22–13**), perhaps an intentional "masterpiece," meant to showcase her talent and secure her reputation as one of the preeminent painters of the age.

The subject is biblical, drawn from a part of the Book of Daniel that was excluded from the Protestant Bible, but—perhaps consequently—especially popular as a subject in Roman Catholic art. While bathing alone in her garden, the beautiful young Susannah is observed by two lecherous elders—Peeping Toms—who threaten to claim they saw her engaged in a lovers' tryst unless

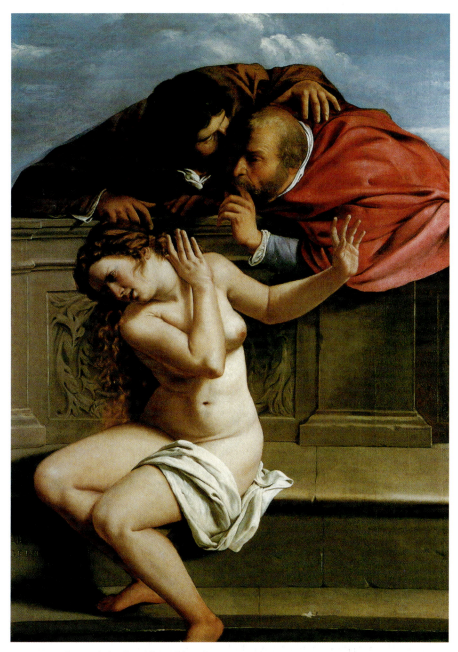

22–13 • Artemisia Gentileschi SUSANNAH AND THE ELDERS
1610. Oil on canvas, 67 × 47⅝″ (1.7 × 1.21 m). Count Schönborn Kunstsammlungen, Pommersfelden.

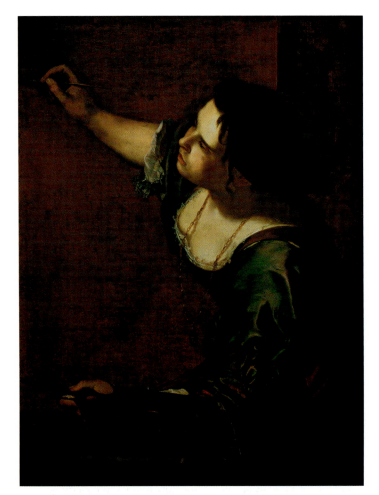

22-14 • Artemisia Gentileschi SELF-PORTRAIT AS THE ALLEGORY OF PAINTING
1630. Oil on canvas, 38 × 29″ (96.5 × 73.7 cm). The Royal Collection, Windsor Castle, England.

EXPLORE MORE: Gain insight from a primary source on Artemisia Gentileschi **www.myartslab.com**

she agrees to have sex with them. Susannah refuses to surrender her chastity, and they make good on their threat. Initially sentenced to death for her supposed sexual transgression, through the intervention of Daniel, she is proven innocent, and the two dishonest voyeurs are executed instead.

Most male artists who painted this scene emphasized Susannah's sexual allure and the elders' lustful stares, but Artemesia shifts the narrative focus to the powerless young woman's vulnerability—and this Susannah actually looks like a woman. Although female artists were excluded from using male models, Artemesia has clearly studied the appearance and anatomy of unclothed women, creating one of the first truly lifelike female nudes in the European tradition. Her interest in unvarnished naturalism is probably derived from Caravaggio. His revolutionary art is also behind the theatricality of the heroine's rhetorical gesture (recalling that of Adam when expelled from paradise in the Sistine Ceiling), the complex interlocking of the figures' postures (note the patterned relationship between the hands), and the crowding of

figures up against the picture plane. But Artemisia has blended her sources and influences into a personal rendering of a traditional subject that moves viewers to empathize with the heroine's condition, and will perhaps inspire them to emulate her righteousness in a world still dominated by overpowering men.

Twenty years after this painting, Artemisia painted a **SELF-PORTRAIT AS THE ALLEGORY OF PAINTING (FIG. 22–14)**. A richly dressed woman, with palette and brushes in hand, is totally immersed in her work. Aspects of the image are derived from Cesare Ripa's sourcebook *Iconologia* (1593), which became an essential tool for creating and deciphering seventeenth- and eighteenth-century art. For instance, *Iconologia* is the source for the woman's gold necklace with its mask pendant: Ripa writes that the mask imitates the human face, as painting imitates nature, and the gold chain symbolizes "the continuity and interlocking nature of painting, each man [*sic*] learning from his master and continuing his master's achievements in the next generation" (Maser, trans. no. 197). By painting her own features on a personification of Painting, Artemisia not only commemorates her profession but also claims her own place within it.

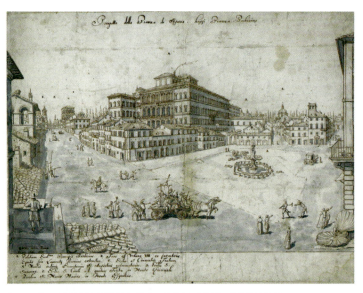

22-15 • BARBERINI PALACE AND SQUARE
1628–1636. Drawing by Lieven Cruyl, 1665. Ink and chalk on paper, 15 × 19¾″ (38.2 × 49.4 cm). Cleveland Museum of Art, Cleveland, Ohio. Dudley P. Allen Fund 1943.265

Maderno, Bernini, and Borromini collaborated on the Barberini Palace between 1628 and 1636, and in the 1670s the structure underwent considerable remodeling. The original plan is unique, having no precedents or imitators in the history of Roman palaces. The structure appears as a single massive pile, but in fact it consists of a central reception block flanked by two residential wings and two magnificent staircases. Designed to house two sides of the family, the rooms are arranged in suites allowing visitors to move through them, achieving increasing intimacy and privacy. Since Cruyl visited the city during Carnival, a float with musicians and actors takes center stage among the strollers. Carnival floats are among the ephemera of art. (Today we might call them "performance art.") Cruyl, who includes his own image at the left, published his drawings as engravings, a set of 15 plates called *Views of Rome*, in 1665.

BAROQUE CEILINGS: CORTONA AND GAULLI. Theatricality, intricacy, and the opening of space reached an apogee in Baroque ceiling decoration—complex constructions combining architecture, painting, and stucco sculpture. These grand illusionistic projects were carried out on the domes and vaults of churches, civic buildings, palaces, and villas, and went far beyond even Michelangelo's Sistine Chapel ceiling (SEE FIG. 20–11) or Correggio's dome (SEE FIG. 20–19). Baroque ceiling painters sought the drama of an immeasurable heaven that extended into vertiginous zones far beyond the limits of High Renaissance taste. To achieve this, they employed the system of *quadratura* (literally, "squaring" or "gridwork"): an architectural setting painted in meticulous perspective and usually requiring that it be viewed from a specific spot to achieve the desired effect of soaring space. The resulting viewpoint is called *di sotto in su* ("from below to above"), which we first saw, in a limited fashion, in Mantegna's ceiling in Mantua (FIG. 19–29). Because it required such careful calculation, figure painters usually had specialists in *quadratura* paint the architectural frame for them.

Pietro Berrettini (1596–1669), called "Pietro da Cortona" after his hometown, carried the development of the Baroque ceiling away from Classicism into a more strongly unified and illusionistic direction. Trained in Florence and inspired by Veronese's ceiling in the Doge's Palace, which he saw on a trip to Venice in 1637, the artist was commissioned in the early 1630s by the Barberini family of Pope Urban VIII to decorate the ceiling of the audience hall of their Roman palace. A drawing by a Flemish artist visiting Rome, Lieven Cruyl (1640–c. 1720), gives us a view of the Barberinis' huge palace, piazza, and the surrounding city. Bernini's Trident Fountain stands in the center of the piazza, and his scallop-shell fountain can be seen at the right (FIG. 22–15).

Pietro da Cortona's great fresco *The Glorification of the Papacy of Urban VIII* became a model for a succession of Baroque illusionistic palace ceilings throughout Europe (FIG. 22–16). He structured his mythological scenes around a vaultlike skeleton of architecture, painted in *quadratura*, that appears to be attached to the actual cornice of the room. But in contrast to Annibale Carracci's neat separations and careful *quadro riportato* framing (SEE FIG. 22–9), Pietro's figures weave in and out of their setting in active and complex profusion; some rest on the actual cornice, while others float weightlessly against the sky. Instead of Annibale's warm, nearly even light, Pietro's dramatic illumination, with its bursts of brilliance alternating with deep shadows, fuses the ceiling into a dense but unified whole.

The subject is an elaborate allegory of the virtues of the pope. Just below the center of the vault, seated at the top of a pyramid of clouds and figures personifying Time and the Fates, Divine Providence (in gold against an open sky) gestures toward three giant bees surrounded by a huge laurel wreath (both Barberini emblems) carried by Faith, Hope, and Charity. Immortality offers a crown of stars, while other figures present the crossed keys and the triple-tiered crown of the papacy. Around these figures are scenes of Roman gods and goddesses, who demonstrate the pope's wisdom and virtue by triumphing over the vices. So complex was the imagery that a guide gave visitors an explanation, and one member of the household published a pamphlet, still in use today, explaining the painting.

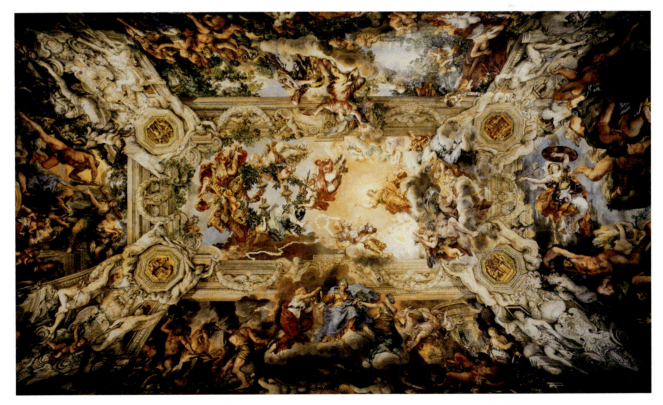

22-16 • Pietro da Cortona THE GLORIFICATION OF THE PAPACY OF URBAN VIII
Ceiling in the Gran Salone, Palazzo Barberini, Rome. 1632–1639. Fresco.

building up his forms with layers of loosely applied paint and finishing off the surfaces with dashing highlights in white, lemon yellow, and pale orange. Rather than using light to model volumes in the time-honored manner, Velázquez tried to depict the optical properties of light reflecting from surfaces. On close inspection his forms dissolve into a maze of individual strokes of paint.

No consensus exists today on the meaning of this monumental painting. It is a royal portrait; it is also a self-portrait of Velázquez standing at his easel. But fundamentally, *Las Meninas* is a personal statement. Throughout his life, Velázquez had sought respect and acclaim for himself and for the art of painting. Here, dressed as a courtier, the Order of Santiago on his chest (added later) and the keys of the palace tucked into in his sash, Velázquez proclaims the dignity and importance of painting itself.

BARTOLOMÉ ESTEBAN MURILLO.   The Madrid of Velázquez was the center of Spanish art. Seville declined after an outbreak of plague in 1649, but it remained a center for trade with the Spanish colonies, where the work of Bartolomé Esteban Murillo (1617–1682) had a profound influence on art and religious iconography. Many patrons wanted images of the Virgin Mary and especially of the Immaculate Conception, the controversial idea that Mary was born free from original sin. Although the Immaculate Conception became Catholic dogma only in 1854, the concept, as well as devotion to Mary, grew during the seventeenth and eighteenth centuries.

Counter-Reformation authorities had provided specific instructions for artists painting the Virgin: Mary was to be dressed in blue and white, her hands folded in prayer, as she is carried upward by angels, sometimes in large flocks. She may be surrounded by an unearthly light ("clothed in the sun") and may stand on a crescent moon in reference to the woman of the Apocalypse (SEE FIG. 14–7). Angels often carry palms and symbols of the Virgin, such as a mirror, a fountain, roses, and lilies, and they may vanquish the serpent, Satan. The Church exported to the New World many paintings faithful to these orthodox guidelines by Murillo, Zurbarán, and others. When the indigenous population began to visualize the Christian story (SEE FIG. 29–45), paintings such as Murillo's **THE IMMACULATE CONCEPTION** provided prompts for their imaginings **(FIG. 22–24)**.

ARCHITECTURE IN SPAIN

Turning away from the severity displayed in the sixteenth-century El Escorial monastery-palace (SEE FIG. 21–15), seventeenth-century Spanish architects again embraced the lavish decoration that had characterized their art since the fourteenth century. Profusions of ornament swept back into fashion, first in huge *retablos* (altarpieces), then in portals (main doors often embellished with sculpture), and finally in entire buildings.

THE CATHEDRAL OF SANTIAGO DE COMPOSTELA.   In the seventeenth century, the role of St. James as patron saint of Spain was challenged by the supporters of St. Teresa of Ávila and then by supporters of St. Michael, St. Joseph, and other popular saints. It became important to the archbishop and other leaders in Santiago de Compostela, where the Cathedral of St. James was located, to establish their primacy. They reinforced their efforts to revitalize the yearly pilgrimage to the city, undertaken by Spaniards since the ninth century, and used architecture as part of their campaign.

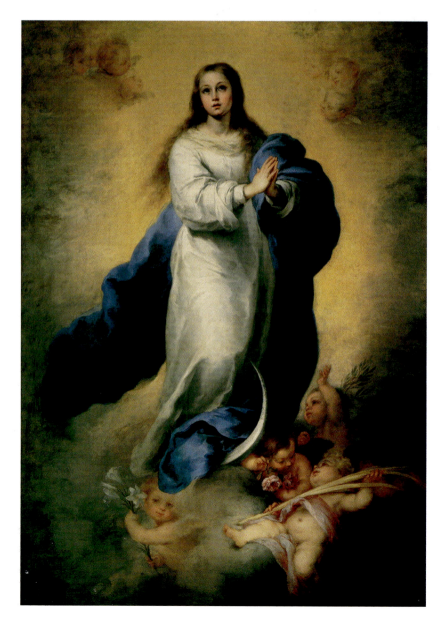

22-24 • Bartolomé Esteban Murillo
THE IMMACULATE CONCEPTION
c. 1660–1665. Oil on canvas, 81⅛ × 56⅝"
(2.06 × 1.44 m). Prado, Madrid.

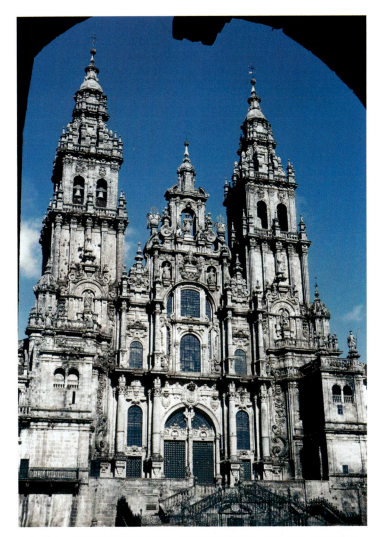

22-25 • WEST FAÇADE, CATHEDRAL OF ST. JAMES, SANTIAGO DE COMPOSTELA, SPAIN
South tower 1667–1680; north tower and central block finished mid-18th century by Fernando de Casas y Nóvoas.

Renewed interest in pilgrimages to the shrines of saints in the seventeenth century brought an influx of pilgrims, and consequently financial security, to the city and the Church. The cathedral chapter ordered a façade of almost unparalleled splendor to be added to the twelfth-century pilgrimage church (**FIG. 22–25**). The twelfth-century portal had already been closed with doors in the sixteenth century. A south tower was built in 1667–1680 and then later copied as the north tower.

The last man to serve as architect and director of works at the cathedral, Fernando de Casas y Nóvoas (active 1711–1749), tied the disparate elements together at the west end—towers, portal, stairs—in a grand design focused on a veritable wall of glass, popularly called "The Mirror." His design culminates in a free-standing gable soaring above the roof, visually linking the towers, and framing a statue of St. James. The extreme simplicity of the cloister walls and the archbishop's palace at each side of the portal heightens the dazzling effect of this enormous expanse of glass windows, glittering, jewel-like, in their intricately carved granite frame.

FLANDERS AND THE NETHERLANDS

Led by the nobleman Prince William of Orange, the Netherlands' Protestant northern provinces (present-day Holland) rebelled against Spain in 1568. The seven provinces joined together as the United Provinces in 1579 and began the long struggle for independence, achieved only in the seventeenth century. The king of Spain considered the Dutch heretical rebels, but finally the Dutch prevailed. In 1648, the United Provinces joined emissaries from Spain, the Vatican, the Holy Roman Empire, and France on equal footing in peace negotiations. The resulting Peace of Westphalia recognized the independence of the northern Netherlands.

FLANDERS

After a period of relative autonomy from 1598 to 1621 under Habsburg regents, Flanders, the southern—and predominantly Catholic—part of the Netherlands, returned to direct Spanish rule. Catholic churches were restored and important commissions went to religious subject matter. As Antwerp, the capital city and major arts center of the southern Netherlands, gradually recovered from the turmoil of the religious wars, artists of great talent flourished there. Painters like Peter Paul Rubens and Anthony van Dyck established international reputations that brought them important commissions from foreign as well as local patrons.

RUBENS. Peter Paul Rubens (1577–1640), whose painting has become synonymous with Flemish Baroque art, was born in Germany, where his father, a Protestant, had fled from his native Antwerp to escape religious persecution. In 1587, after her husband's death, Rubens's mother and her children returned to Antwerp and to Catholicism. Rubens decided in his late teens to become an artist and at age 21 was accepted into the Antwerp painters' guild, a testament to his energy, intelligence, and skill. Shortly thereafter, in 1600, he left for Italy. In Venice, his work came to the attention of the duke of Mantua, who offered him a court post. His activities on behalf of the duke over the next eight years did much to prepare him for the rest of his long and successful career. The duke had him copy famous paintings in collections all over Italy to add to the ducal collection.

Rubens visited every major Italian city, went to Madrid as the duke's emissary, and spent two extended periods in Rome, where he studied the great works of Roman antiquity and the Italian Renaissance. While in Italy, Rubens studied the paintings of two contemporaries, Caravaggio and Annibale Carracci. Hearing of Caravaggio's death in 1610, Rubens encouraged the duke of Mantua to buy the artist's *Death of the Virgin*, which the patron had rejected because of its shocking realism. The duke eventually bought the painting.

In 1608, Rubens returned to Antwerp, where in 1609 he accepted a position as court painter to the Habsburg regents of Flanders, Archduke Albert and Princess Isabella Clara Eugenia, the daughter of Philip II. Ten days after that appointment, he married the 18-year-old Isabella Brandt (1596–1626), an alliance that was

Allegory of Sight ▶

by Jan Brueghel and Peter Paul Rubens, from the Allegories of the Five Senses series. c. 1617–1618. Oil on wood panel, 25⅝ × 43″ (65 × 109 cm). Museo del Prado, Madrid.

Coudenberg, the Brussels residence of the patrons, appears in the background.

The double-headed eagle crowning the brass chandelier is the symbol of the Habsburg Dynasty.

On the top shelf are small-scale reproductions of sculptures by Michelangelo—slaves from the tomb of Julius II and personifications of the times of the day from the Medici tombs—and on the lower shelves are portraits of Roman emperors.

The Tiger Hunt seen on the back wall was a recent painting by Rubens. Along with his *Daniel in the Lions' Den* in the upper left and his and Brueghel's *Madonna and Child in a Garland of Flowers* at right, this seems to have been included to showcase the artists' latest work.

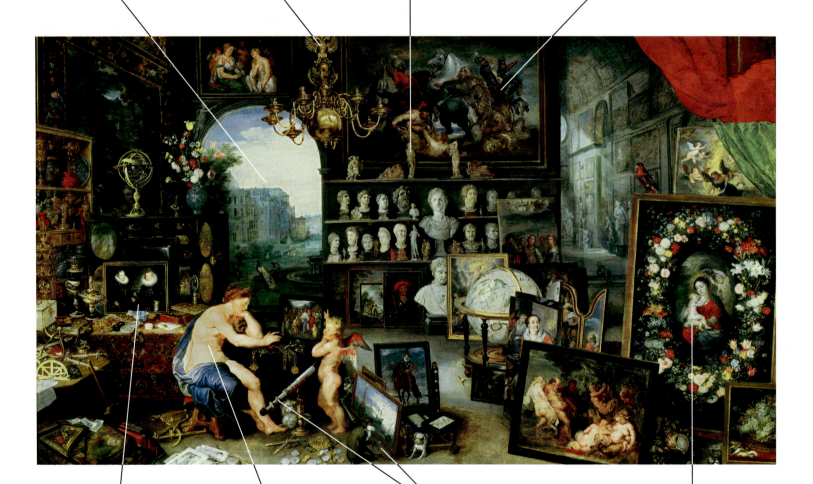

A double portrait of the patrons Albert and Isabella sits on the table, while an equestrian portrait of Albert is seen on the floor at the center of the room. Both copy actual paintings by Rubens.

Personifying sight, Juno Optica— identified by her bird, the peacock, seen in the doorway next to her head— contemplates a painting of *Christ Healing the Blind* that invokes Sight through its opposite, while linking the senses to the doctrine of salvation.

Instruments such as the telescope and magnifying glass, as well as the spectacles worn by the monkey in the immediate foreground, all refer to the sense of sight and its limitations.

This painting—the Madonna and Child is by Rubens and the framing floral wreath by Brueghel—is identical to one now in the Louvre, except it is shown larger here in proportion to the other objects in the room.

SEE MORE: View the Closer Look feature for *Allegory of Sight* **www.myartslab.com**

his association with Rubens as a specialist in painting heads. The need to blend his work seamlessly with that of Rubens enhanced Van Dyck's technical skill. After a trip to the English court of James I (r. 1603–1625) in 1620, Van Dyck traveled to Italy and worked as a portrait painter for seven years before returning to Antwerp. In 1632, he returned to England as the court painter to Charles I (r. 1625–1649), by whom he was knighted and given a studio, a summer home, and a large salary.

Van Dyck's many portraits of the royal family provide a sympathetic record of their features and demeanor. In **CHARLES I AT THE HUNT (FIG. 22–31)**, of 1635, Van Dyck was able, by clever manipulation of the setting, to portray the king truthfully and still present him as an imposing figure. Dressed casually for the hunt and standing on a bluff overlooking a distant view (a device used by Rubens to enhance the stature of Henry IV; SEE FIG. 22–29), Charles, who was in fact very short, appears here taller than his pages and even than his horse, since its head is down and its heavy body is partly off the canvas. The viewer's gaze is diverted from the king's delicate and rather short frame to his pleasant features, framed by his jauntily cocked cavalier's hat and the graceful cascade

of his hair. As if in decorous homage, the tree branches bow gracefully toward him, echoing the circular lines of the hat.

Yet another painter working with Rubens, Jan Brueghel (1568–1625), specialized in settings rather than portraits. Jan was the son of Pieter Bruegel the Elder (see "Breugel's Cycle of the Months," pages 702–703), and it was Jan who added the "h" to the family name. Brueghel's and Rubens's series of allegories of the five senses—five paintings, made for Habsburg regents Princess Isabella Clara Eugenia and Archduke Albert, and illustrating sight, hearing, touch, taste, and smell—in effect invited the viewer to wander in an imaginary space enjoying an amazing collection of works of art and scientific equipment (see "A Closer Look," opposite). Their allegory of sight is a display, a virtual inventory, and a summary of the wealth, scholarship, and **connoisseurship** (the study of style to assess quality and determine authorship) that was made possible through the patronage of the Habsburg rulers of the Spanish Netherlands.

Our term, "still life," for paintings of artfully arranged objects on a table, comes from the Dutch *stilleven*, a word coined about 1650. The Antwerp artist Clara Peeters (1594–c. 1657) specialized

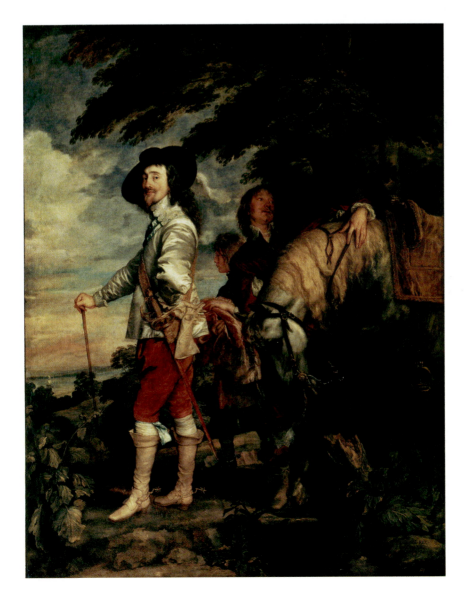

**22–31 • Anthony van Dyck
CHARLES I AT THE HUNT**
1635. Oil on canvas, 8′11″ × 6′11″ (2.75 × 2.14 m). Musée du Louvre, Paris.

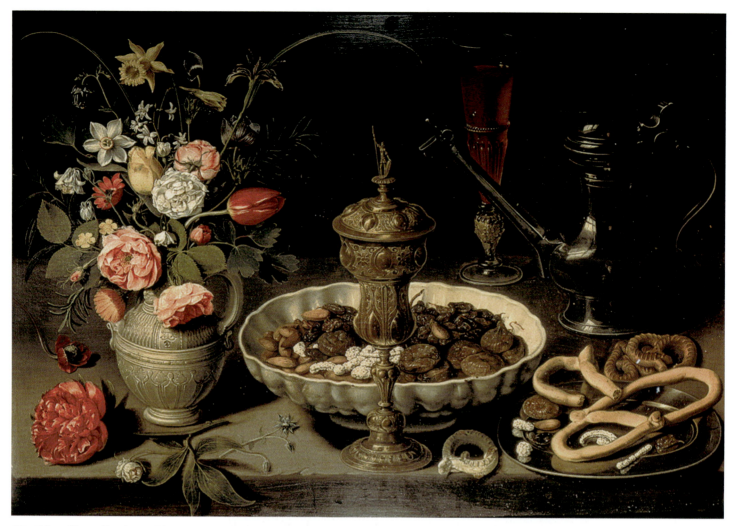

22-32 • Clara Peeters STILL LIFE WITH FLOWERS, GOBLET, DRIED FRUIT, AND PRETZELS
1611. Oil on panel, 20½ × 28¾″ (52 × 73 cm). Museo del Prado, Madrid.

Like many "breakfast pieces," this painting features a pile of pretzels among the elegant tableware. The salty, twisted bread was called *pretzel* (from the Latin *pretiola*, meaning "small reward") because it was invented by German monks to reward children who had learned their prayers. The twisted shapes represented the crossed arms of a child praying.

in still-life tabletop arrangements (see Iconography box in the Introduction, FIG. A). She was a precocious young woman whose career seems to have begun before she was 14. Of some 50 paintings now attributed to her (of which more than 30 are signed), many are of the type called "breakfast pieces," showing a table set for a meal of bread and fruit. Peeters was one of the first artists to combine flowers and food in a single painting, as in her **STILL LIFE WITH FLOWERS, GOBLET, DRIED FRUIT, AND PRETZELS (FIG. 22–32)**, of 1611. Peeters arranged rich tableware and food against neutral, almost black backgrounds, the better to emphasize the fall of light over the contrasting surface textures. In a display of precious objects that must have appealed to her clients, the luxurious goblet and bowl contrast with simple stoneware and pewter, as do the delicate flowers with the homey pretzels. The pretzels, piled on the pewter tray, are a particularly interesting Baroque element, with their complex multiple curves.

THE DUTCH REPUBLIC

The House of Orange was not notable for its patronage of the arts, but patronage improved significantly under Prince Frederick Henry (r. 1625–1647), and Dutch artists found many other eager patrons among the prosperous middle class in Amsterdam, Leiden, Haarlem, Delft, and Utrecht. The Hague was the capital city and the preferred residence of the House of Orange, but Amsterdam was the true center of power, because of its sea trade and the enterprise of its merchants, who made the city an international commercial center. The Dutch delighted in depictions of themselves and their country—the landscape, cities, and domestic life—not to mention beautiful and interesting objects to be seen in still-life paintings and interior scenes. A well-educated people, the Dutch were also fascinated by history, mythology, the Bible, new scientific discoveries, commercial expansion abroad, and colonial exploration.

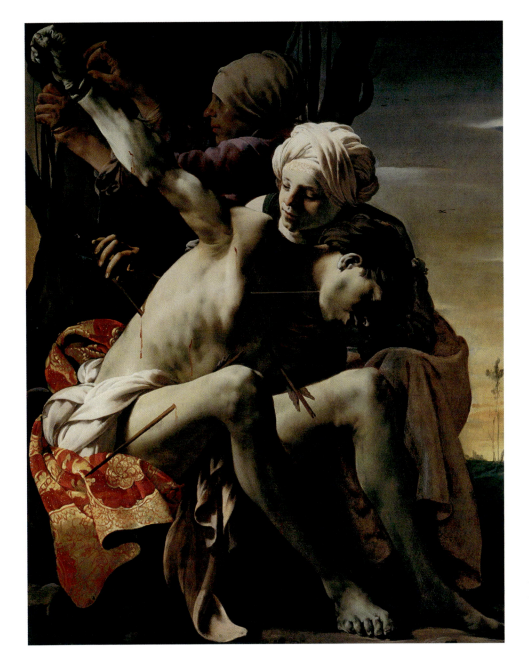

22-33 • Hendrick ter Brugghen
**ST. SEBASTIAN TENDED BY
ST. IRENE**
1625. Oil on canvas, 58¹⁵⁄₁₆ × 47½"
(149.6 × 120 cm). Allen Memorial Art
Museum, Oberlin College, Ohio.

Visitors to the Netherlands in the seventeenth century noted the popularity of art among merchants and working people. Peter Mundy, an English traveler, wrote in 1640 that even butchers, bakers, shoemakers, and blacksmiths had pictures in their houses and shops. This taste for art stimulated a free market for paintings that functioned like other commodity markets. Artists had to compete to capture the interest of the public by painting on speculation. Specialists in particularly popular types of images were most likely to be financially successful, and what most Dutch patrons wanted were paintings of themselves, their country, their homes, their possessions, and the life around them. The demand for art also gave rise to an active market for the graphic arts, both for original compositions and for copies of paintings, since one copperplate could produce hundreds of impressions, and worn-out plates could be reworked and used again.

THE INFLUENCE OF ITALY. Hendrick ter Brugghen (1588–1629) had spent time in Rome, perhaps between 1608 and 1614, where he must have seen Caravaggio's works and became an enthusiastic follower. On his return home, in 1616, he entered the Utrecht painters' guild, bringing Caravaggio's style into the Netherlands. Ter Brugghen's **ST. SEBASTIAN TENDED BY ST. IRENE** introduced the Netherlandish painters to the new art of Baroque Italy (**FIG. 22–33**). The sickly gray-green flesh of the nearly dead St. Sebastian, painted in an almost monochromatic palette, contrasts with the brilliant red and gold brocade of what seems to be his crumpled garment. Actually this is the cope of the bishop of Utrecht, which had survived destruction by Protestants and become a symbol of Catholicism in Utrecht. The saint is cast as a heroic figure, his strong, youthful body still bound to the tree. But St. Irene (the patron saint of nurses) delicately removes one of the

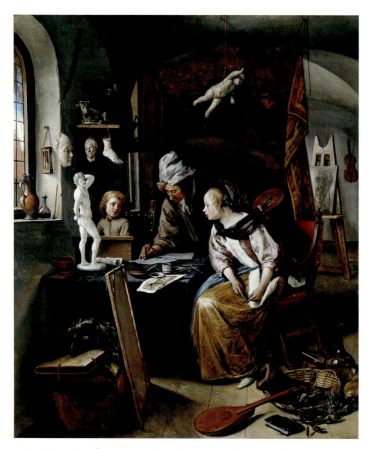

22-44 • Jan Steen THE DRAWING LESSON
1665. Oil on wood panel, 19⅜ × 16¼″ (49.3 × 41 cm).
The J. Paul Getty Museum, Los Angeles.

evoked by touch. Ter Borch was renowned for his exquisite rendition of lace, velvet, and especially satin, and such wealth could be seen as a symbol of excess. One critic has even suggested that the white satin is a metaphor for the women's skin. If there is a moral lesson, it is presented discreetly and ambiguously.

Another important genre painter is Jan Steen (1626–1679), whose larger brushstrokes contrast with the meticulous treatment of Ter Borch. Steen painted over 800 works but never achieved financial success. Most of his scenes used everyday life to portray moral tales, illustrate proverbs and folk sayings, or make puns to amuse the spectator. Steen moved about the country for most of his life, and from 1670 until his death he kept a tavern in Leiden. He probably found inspiration and models all about him. Early in his career Steen was influenced by Frans Hals, but his work could be either very summary or extremely detailed.

Jan Steen's paintings of children are especially remarkable, for he captured not only their childish physiques but also their fleeting moods and expressions with rapid and fluid brushstrokes. His ability to capture such transitory dispositions was well expressed in his painting **THE DRAWING LESSON (FIG. 22–44)**. Here, youthful apprentices—a boy and a well-dressed young woman—observe the master artist correct an example of drawing, a skill widely believed to be the foundation of art. The studio is cluttered with all the supplies the artists need. On the floor at the lower right,

still-life objects such as a lute, wine jug, book, and skull may remind the viewer of the transitory nature of life in spite of the permanence art may seem to offer.

Emanuel de Witte (1617–1692) of Rotterdam specialized in architectural interiors, first in Delft in 1640 and then in Amsterdam after settling there permanently in 1652. Although many of his interiors were composites of features from several locations combined in one idealized architectural view, De Witte also painted faithful "portraits" of actual buildings. One of these is his **PORTUGUESE SYNAGOGUE, AMSTERDAM (FIG. 22–45)** of 1680. The synagogue, which still stands and is one of the most impressive buildings in Amsterdam, is shown here as a rectangular hall divided into one wide central aisle with narrow side aisles, each covered with a wooden barrel vault resting on lintels supported by columns. De Witte's shift of the viewpoint slightly to one side has created an interesting spatial composition, and strong contrasts of light and shade add dramatic movement to the simple interior. The elegant couple and the dogs in the foreground provide a sense of scale for the architecture and add human interest.

Today, this painting is interesting not only as a work of art, but also as a record of seventeenth-century synagogue architecture. It also reflects Dutch religious tolerance in an age when Jews were often persecuted. Expelled from Spain and Portugal from the late

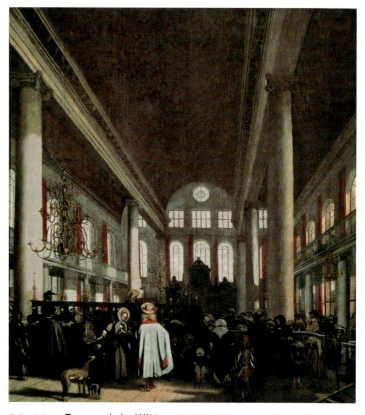

22-45 • Emanuel de Witte PORTUGUESE SYNAGOGUE, AMSTERDAM
1680. Oil on canvas, 43½ × 39″ (110.5 × 99.1 cm). Rijksmuseum, Amsterdam. Architects Daniel Stalpaert and Elias Bouman built the synagogue in 1671–1675.

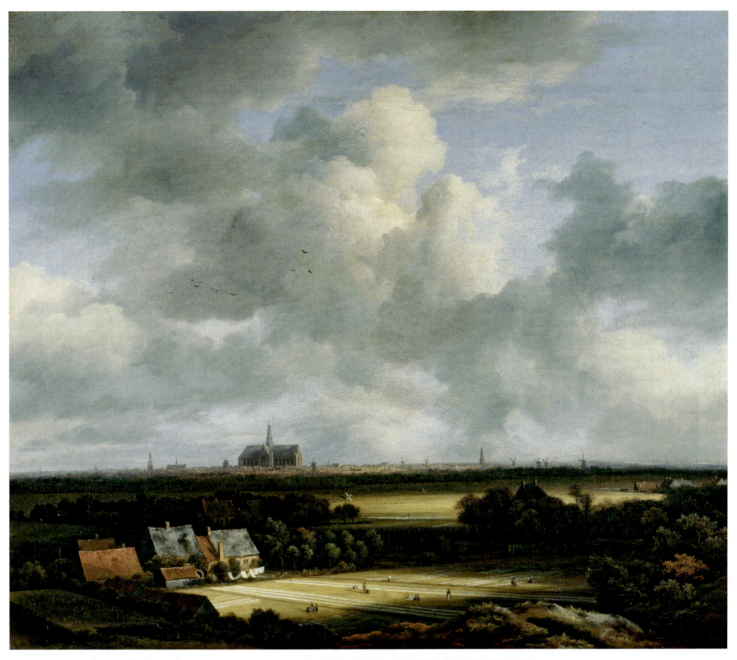

22–46 • Jacob van Ruisdael VIEW OF HAARLEM FROM THE DUNES AT OVERVEEN
c. 1670. Oil on canvas, 22″ × 24¼″ (55.8 × 62.8 cm). Mauritshuis, The Hague.

fifteenth century on, many Jews had settled in Amsterdam, and their community numbered about 2,300 people, most of whom were well-to-do merchants. Fund-raising for a new synagogue began in 1670, and in 1671 Elias Bouman and Daniel Stalpaert began work on the building. With its classical architecture, Brazilian jacaranda-wood furniture, and 26 brass chandeliers, this synagogue was considered one of the most impressive buildings in Amsterdam.

LANDSCAPE. The Dutch loved the landscapes and vast skies of their own country, but landscape painters worked in their studios rather than in nature, and they were never afraid to rearrange, add to, or subtract from a scene in order to give their compositions formal organization or a desired mood. Starting in the 1620s,

landscape painters generally adhered to a convention in which little color was used beyond browns, grays, and beiges. After 1650, they tended to be more individualistic in their styles, but nearly all brought a broader range of colors into play. One continuing motif was the emphasis on cloud-filled expanses of sky dominating a relatively narrow horizontal band of earth below.

The Haarlem landscape specialist Jacob van Ruisdael (1628/29–1682), whose popularity drew many pupils to his workshop, was especially adept at both the invention of dramatic compositions and the projection of moods in his canvases. His **VIEW OF HAARLEM FROM THE DUNES AT OVERVEEN** (FIG. 22–46), painted about 1670, celebrates the flatlands outside Haarlem that had been reclaimed from the sea as part of a massive landfill

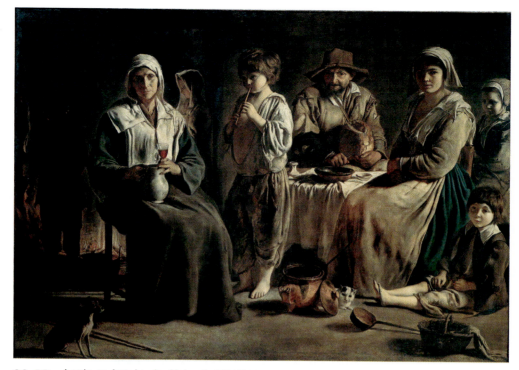

22-53 • Louis or Antoine Le Nain **A PEASANT FAMILY IN AN INTERIOR**
c. 1640. Oil on canvas, 44½ × 62½″ (1.13 × 1.59 m). Musée du Louvre, Paris.

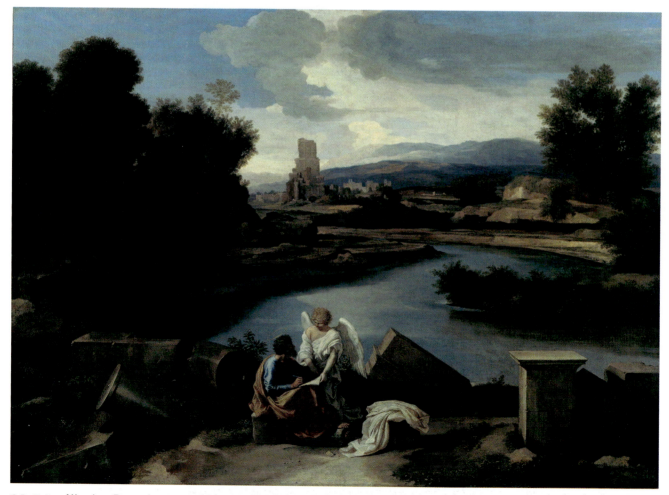

22-54 • Nicolas Poussin **LANDSCAPE WITH ST. MATTHEW AND THE ANGEL**
1639–1640. Oil on canvas, 39 × 53⅛″ (99 × 135 cm). Staatliche Museen, Berlin.

individual styles. They are best known for their painting of genre scenes in which French peasants pause from their honest labor for quiet family diversions. **A PEASANT FAMILY IN AN INTERIOR (FIG. 22–53)** of about 1640, probably by Louis Le Nain, is the largest, and one of the most lyrical, of these noble scenes of peasant life. Three generations of this family are gathered around a table. The adults acknowledge our presence—a spotlighted woman at left even seems to offer us some wine—whereas the children remain lost in their dreams or focused on their play. The casualness of costume and deportment is underlined by the foreground clutter of pets and kitchen equipment. It is only after we survey the frieze of figures illuminated around the table that the painting reveals one of its most extraordinary passages—a boy in the left background, warming himself in front of a fireplace and represented only as a dark silhouette from behind, edged by the soft golden firelight. Why the brothers chose to paint these peasant families, and who bought their paintings, are questions still unresolved.

THE CLASSICAL LANDSCAPE: POUSSIN AND CLAUDE LORRAIN. Painters Nicolas Poussin (1594–1665) and Claude Gellée (called "Claude Lorrain" or simply "Claude," 1600–1682) pursued their careers in Italy although they usually worked for French patrons. They perfected the French ideal of the "Classical" landscape and profoundly influenced painters for the next two centuries. We refer to Poussin and Claude as Classicists because they organized natural elements and figures into gently illuminated, idealized compositions. Both were influenced by Annibale Carracci and to some extent by Venetian painting, yet each evolved an unmistakably personal style that conveyed an entirely different mood from that of their sources and from each other.

Nicolas Poussin was born in Normandy but settled in Paris, where his initial career as a painter was unremarkable. Determined to go to Rome, he arrived there in 1624, and the Barberini became his foremost patrons. Bernini considered Poussin one of the greatest painters in Rome, and others clearly agreed. In 1639, Giovanni Maria Roscioli, secretary to Pope Urban VIII, commissioned from Poussin two large paintings showing the evangelists John and Matthew writing their gospels within expansive landscapes dotted with Classical buildings and antique ruins **(FIGS. 22–54, 22–55)**. The paintings were completed by

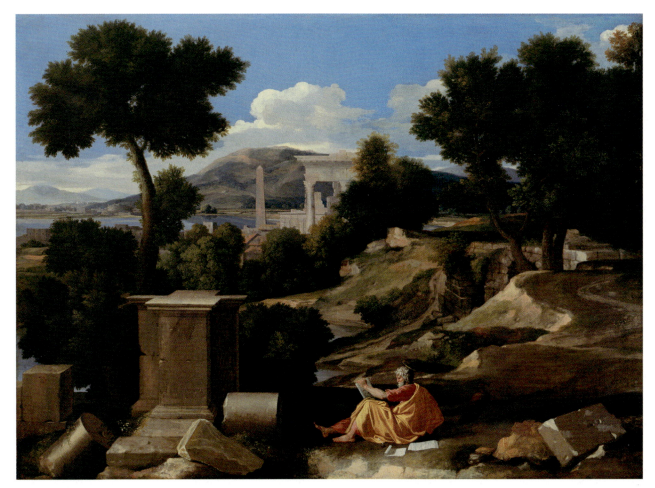

22-55 • Nicolas Poussin LANDSCAPE WITH ST. JOHN ON PATMOS
1640. Oil on canvas, 40 × 53½" (101.8 × 136.3 cm). The Art Institute of Chicago. A. A. Munger Collection, 1930.500

EXPLORE MORE: Gain insight from a primary source by Nicolas Poussin www.myartslab.com

Grading the Old Masters

The members of the French Royal Academy of Painting and Sculpture considered ancient Classical art to be the standard by which contemporary art should be judged. By the 1680s, however, younger artists of the academy began to argue that modern art might equal, or might even surpass, the art of the ancients—a radical thought that sparked controversy.

A debate arose over the relative merits of drawing and color in painting. The conservatives argued that drawing was superior to color because drawing appealed to the mind while color appealed to the senses. They saw Nicolas Poussin as embodying perfectly the Classical principles of subject and design. But the young artists who admired the vivid colors of Titian, Veronese, and Rubens claimed that painting should deceive the eye, and since color achieves this deception more convincingly than drawing, application of color should be valued over drawing. Adherents of the two positions were called *poussinistes* (in honor of Poussin) and *rubénistes* (for Rubens).

The portrait painter and critic Roger de Piles (1635–1709) took up the cause of the *rubénistes* in a series of pamphlets. In *The Principles of Painting*, de Piles evaluated the most important painters on a scale of 0 to 20 in four categories. He gave no score higher than 72 (18 in each category), since no mortal artist could achieve perfection. Caravaggio received a 0 in expression and a 6 in drawing, while Michelangelo and Leonardo both got a 4 in color and Rembrandt a 6 in drawing.

Most of the painters examined here do not do very well. Raphael and Rubens get 65 points (A on our grading scale), Van Dyck comes close with 55 (C+). Poussin and Titian earn 53 and 51 (solid Cs), while Rembrandt slips by with 50 (C–). Leonardo da Vinci gets 49 (D), and Michelangelo and Dürer with 37 and Caravaggio with 28 are resounding failures in de Piles's view. Tastes change. Someday our own ideas may seem just as misguided as those of the academicians.

October 1640, just before Poussin left for two years in Paris to work for Louis XIII. Perhaps they were the first installment of a set of four evangelists within landscapes, but these were the only two painted by the time of the patron's death in 1644.

These two paintings epitomize and are among the earliest examples of the new style of rigorously ordered and highly idealized Classical landscapes with figures. This artistic theme and format, created by Poussin while working in Rome, would have a long history in European painting. Although each painting was individually composed to create an ordered whole on its own, they were designed as a pair. The large clumps of trees at the outside edges form "bookends" that bring lateral closure to the broad panorama that stretches across both canvases. Their unity is signaled by the evangelists' postures, turned inward toward each other, and solidified at the lower inside corners where huge blocks of Classical masonry converge from both pictures as coordinated remains of the same ruined monument. There is a consistent perspective progression in both pictures from the picture plane back into the distance through a clearly defined foreground, middle ground, and background, illuminated by an even light with gentle shadows and highlights. In the middle distance behind St. John are a ruined temple and an obelisk, and the round building in the distant city is Hadrian's Tomb, which Poussin knew from Rome. Precisely placed trees, hills, mountains, water, and even clouds take on a solidity of form that seems almost as structural as this architecture. The subject of Poussin's paintings is not the writing evangelists but the balance and order of nature.

When Claude Lorrain went to Rome in 1613, he first studied with Agostino Tassi, an assistant of Guercino and a specialist in architectural painting. Claude, however, preferred landscape. He sketched outdoors for days at a time, then returned to his studio to compose his paintings. Claude was fascinated with light, and his works are often studies of the effect of the rising or setting sun on colors and the atmosphere. A favorite and much-imitated device was to place one or two large objects in the foreground—a tree, building, a figural group, or hill—past which the viewer's eye enters the scene and proceeds, often by diagonal paths, into the distance.

Claude used this compositional device to great effect in paintings such as **A PASTORAL LANDSCAPE** of the late 1640s **(FIG. 22–56)**. Instead of balancing symmetrically placed elements in a statement of stable order, Claude leads his viewers actively into the painting in a continuing, zigzagging fashion. A conversing couple frames the composition at the right; their gestures and the ambling of the cows they are tending lead our attention toward the left on a slightly rising diagonal, where a bridge and the traveler moving across it establish a middle ground. Across the bridge into the distance is a city, setting up a contrast between the warm, soft contours of the pastoral right foreground and the misty angularity of the fortified walls and blocks composing the distant city. More distant still are the hazy outlines of hills that seem to take this space into infinity. The picture evokes a city dweller's nostalgia and longing for the simpler and more sensuous life of the country, and it is easy to imagine the foreground shepherd extolling to his companion the superior virtues of their own life in contrast to that in the city, toward which he gestures to underline his point.

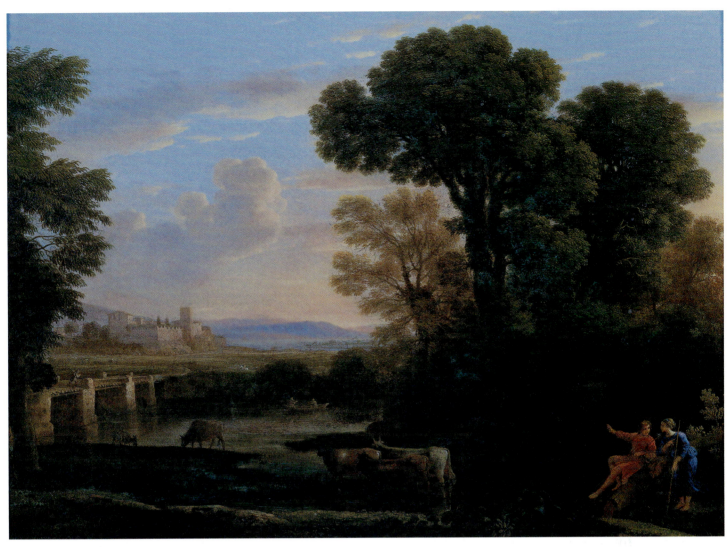

22-56 • Claude Lorrain A PASTORAL LANDSCAPE
c. 1648. Oil on copper, 15½ × 21″ (39.3 × 53.3 cm). Yale University Art Gallery, New Haven, Connecticut.

ENGLAND

England and Scotland were joined in 1603 with the ascent to the English throne of James VI of Scotland, who reigned over Great Britain as James I (r. 1603–1625). James increased royal patronage of British artists, especially in literature and architecture. William Shakespeare wrote *Macbeth*, featuring the king's legendary ancestor Banquo, in tribute to the new royal family, and the play was performed at court in December 1606.

Although James's son Charles I was an important collector and patron of painting, religious and political tensions that erupted into civil war cost Charles his throne and his life in 1649. A succession of republican and monarchical rulers who alternately supported Protestantism or Catholicism followed, until the Catholic king James II was deposed in the Glorious Revolution of 1689 by his Protestant son-in-law and daughter, William and Mary. After Mary's death in 1694, William (the Dutch great-grandson of William of Orange, who had led the Netherlands' independence movement) ruled on his own until his death in 1702. He was succeeded by Mary's sister, Anne (r. 1702–1714).

ARCHITECTURE

In sculpture and painting, the English court patronized foreign artists. The field of architecture, however, was dominated in the seventeenth century by the Englishmen Inigo Jones, Christopher Wren, and Nicholas Hawksmoor. They replaced the country's long-lived Gothic style with Classicism.

INIGO JONES. In the early seventeenth century, Inigo Jones (1573–1652) introduced his version of Renaissance Classicism—based on the style of the architect Andrea Palladio—into England. Jones had studied Palladio's work in Venice, and he filled his copy of Palladio's *Four Books of Architecture*—still preserved—with notes. Appointed surveyor-general in 1615, Jones was commissioned to design the Queen's House in Greenwich and the Banqueting House for the royal palace of Whitehall.

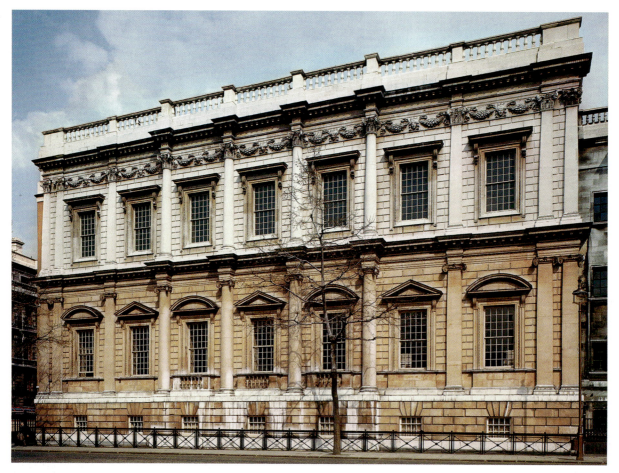

22-57 • Inigo Jones BANQUETING HOUSE, WHITEHALL PALACE
London. 1619–1622.

The **BANQUETING HOUSE** (**FIG. 22–57**), built in 1619–1622 to replace an earlier hall destroyed by fire, was used for court ceremonies and entertainments such as the popular masques—stylized dramas combining theater, music, and dance in spectacles performed by professional actors, courtiers, and even members of the royal family itself. The west front, shown here, consisting of what appears to be two upper stories with superimposed Ionic and Composite orders raised over a plain basement level, exemplifies the understated elegance of Jones's interpretation of Palladian design. Pilasters flank the end bays, and engaged columns subtly emphasize the three bays at the center. These vertical elements are repeated in the balustrade along the roofline. A rhythmic effect results from varying window treatments—triangular and segmental (semicircular) pediments on the first level, cornices with volute (scroll-form) brackets on the second. The sculpted garlands just below the roofline add an unexpected decorative touch, as does the use of different stone colors—pale golden, light brown, and white—for each story (no longer visible after the building was refaced in uniformly white Portland stone).

Although the exterior suggests two stories, the interior of the Banqueting House (**FIG. 22–58**) is actually one large hall divided by a balcony, with antechambers at each end. Ionic pilasters suggest a colonnade but do not impinge on the ideal, double-cube space, which measures 55 feet in width by 110 feet in length by 55 feet in height. In 1630, Charles I commissioned Peter Paul Rubens—who was in England on a peace mission—to decorate the ceiling. Jones had divided the flat ceiling into nine compartments, for which Rubens painted canvases glorifying the reign of James I. Installed in 1635, the paintings show the triumph of the Stuart dynasty with the king carried to heaven on clouds of glory. The large rectangular panel beyond it depicts the birth of the new nation, flanked by allegorical paintings of heroic strength and virtue overcoming vice. In the long paintings on each side, *putti* holding the fruits of the earth symbolize the peace and prosperity of England and Scotland under Stuart rule. So proud was Charles of the result that, rather than allow the smoke of candles and torches to harm the ceiling decoration, he moved evening entertainments to an adjacent pavilion.

CHRISTOPHER WREN. After Jones's death, English architecture was dominated by Christopher Wren (1632–1723). Wren began his professional career in 1659 as a professor of astronomy; for him architecture was a sideline until 1665, when he traveled to France to further his education. While there, he met with French architects and with Bernini, who was in Paris to consult on designs for the Louvre. Wren returned to England with architecture books,

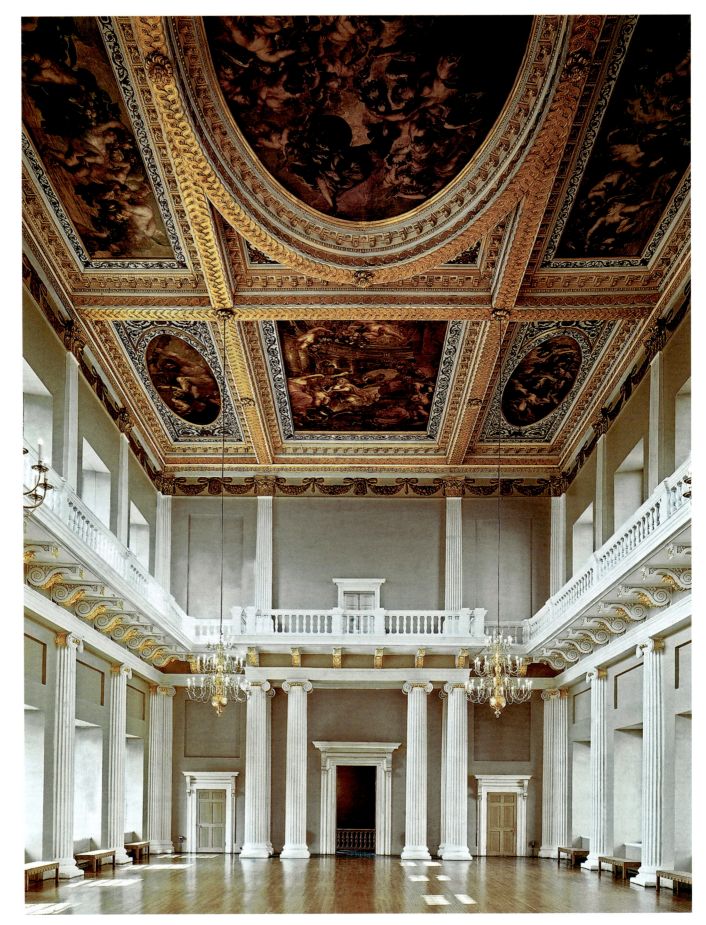

22-58 • INTERIOR, BANQUETING HOUSE, WHITEHALL PALACE
Ceiling paintings of the apotheosis of King James and the glorification of the Stuart monarchy by Peter Paul Rubens. 1630–1635.

ART AND ITS CONTEXTS

Foundations of Indian Culture

The earliest civilization on the Indian subcontinent flourished toward the end of the third millennium BCE along the Indus River in present-day Pakistan. Remains of its expertly engineered brick cities have been uncovered, together with works of art that intriguingly suggest spiritual practices and reveal artistic traits known in later Indian culture.

The decline of the Indus civilization during the mid second millennium BCE coincides with (and may be related to) the arrival from the northwest of a seminomadic people who spoke an Indo-European language and referred to themselves as Aryans. Over the next millennium they were influential in formulating the new civilization that gradually emerged. The most important Aryan contributions to this new civilization included the Sanskrit language and the sacred texts called the Vedas. The evolution of Vedic thought under the influence of indigenous Indian beliefs culminated in the mystical, philosophical texts called the Upanishads, which took shape sometime after 800 BCE.

The Upanishads teach that the material world is illusory; only Brahman, the universal soul, is real and eternal. We—that is, our individual souls—are trapped in this illusion in a relentless cycle of birth, death, and rebirth. The ultimate goal of religious life is to liberate ourselves from this cycle and to unite our individual soul with Brahman.

Buddhism and Jainism are two of the many religions that developed in the climate of Upanishadic thought. Buddhism (see "Buddhism" page 297) is based on the teachings of Shakyamuni Buddha, who lived in central India about 500 BCE; Jainism was shaped about the same time by the followers of the spiritual leader Mahavira. Both religions acknowledged the cyclical nature of existence and taught a means of liberation from it, but they rejected the authority,

rituals, and social strictures of Vedic religion. Whereas the Vedic religion was in the hands of a hereditary priestly class, Buddhist and Jain communities welcomed all members of society, which gave them great appeal. The Vedic tradition eventually evolved into the many sects now collectively known as Hinduism (see "Hinduism" page 298).

Through most of its history India was a mosaic of regional dynastic kingdoms, but from time to time empires emerged that unified large parts of the subcontinent. The first was that of the Maurya dynasty (c. 322–185 BCE), whose great king Ashoka patronized Buddhism. From this time Buddhist doctrines spread widely and its artistic traditions were established.

In the first century CE the Kushans, a central Asian people, created an empire extending from present-day Afghanistan down into central India. Buddhism prospered under Kanishka, the most powerful Kushan king, and spread into central Asia and to east Asia. At this time, under the evolving thought of Mahayana Buddhism, traditions first evolved for depicting the image of the Buddha in art.

Later, under the Gupta dynasty (c. 320–550 CE) in northern India, Buddhist art and culture reached their high point. However, Gupta monarchs also patronized Hindu art, and from this time Hinduism grew to become the dominant Indian religious tradition, with its emphasis on the great gods Vishnu, Shiva, and the Goddess—all with multiple forms.

After the tenth century, numerous regional dynasties prevailed, some quite powerful and long-lasting. Hindu temples, in particular, developed monumental and complex forms that were rich in symbolism and ritual function, with each region of India producing its own variation.

---

paper rather than palm leaf, the material that had previously been used for written documents.

With great economy, the illustration, inserted between blocks of Sanskrit text, depicts the birth of Mahavira. He is shown cradled in his mother's arms as she reclines in her bed under a canopy | connoting royalty, attended by three ladies-in-waiting. Decorative pavilions and a shrine with peacocks on the roof suggest a luxurious palace setting. Everything appears two-dimensional against the brilliant red or blue ground. Vibrant colors and crisp outlines impart an energy to the painting that suggests the arrival of the divine in the mundane world. Transparent garments with variegated designs reveal the swelling curves of the figures, whose alert postures and gestures convey a sense of the importance and excitement of the event. Strangely exaggerated features, such as the protruding eyes, contribute to the air of the extraordinary. With its angles and tense curves, the drawing is closely linked to the aesthetics of Sanskrit calligraphy, and the effect is as if the words themselves had suddenly flared into color and image.

HINDU ART

With the increasing popularity of Hindu sects came the rapid development of Hindu temples. Spurred by the ambitious building programs of wealthy rulers, well-formulated regional styles had evolved by about 900 CE. The most spectacular structures of the era were monumental, with a complexity and grandeur of proportion rarely equaled even in later Indian art.

Emphasis on monumental individual temples gave way to the building of vast temple complexes and more moderately scaled, yet more richly ornamented, individual temples. These developments took place largely in the south of India, although some of the largest temples are in the north, for example, the Sun Temple at Konarak, built in the thirteenth century, and the Govind Deva Temple in Brindavan, built in the sixteenth century under the patronage of the Mughal emperor Akbar. The mightiest of the southern Indian kingdoms was Vijayanagar (c. 1336–1565), whose rulers successfully countered the potential incursions of neighboring dynasties, both Hindu and Muslim, for more than 200 years. Under the patronage of the Vijayanagar kings and their successors, the Nayaks, some of India's most spectacular Hindu architecture was created.

TEMPLE AT MADURAI. The enormous temple complex at Madurai, one of the capitals of the Nayaks, is an example of this fervent expression of Hindu faith. Founded around the thirteenth century, it is dedicated to the goddess Minakshi (the local name for Parvati, the consort of the god Shiva) and to Sundareshvara (the local name for Shiva himself). The temple complex stands in the center of the city and is the focus of Madurai life. At its heart are the two oldest shrines, one to Minakshi and the other to Sundareshvara. Successive additions over the centuries gradually expanded the complex around these small shrines and came to dominate the visual landscape of the city. The most dramatic features of this and similar "temple cities" of the south were the thousand-pillar halls, large ritual-bathing pools, and especially the entrance gateways, **gopuras** in Sanskrit, that tower above the temple site and the surrounding city like modern skyscrapers (**FIG. 23–4**).

Gopuras proliferated as a temple city grew, necessitating new and bigger enclosing walls, and thus new gateways. Successive rulers, often seeking to outdo their predecessors, donated taller and taller *gopuras*. As a result, the tallest structures in temple cities are often at the periphery, rather than at the central temples, which are sometimes totally overwhelmed by the height of the surrounding structures. The temple complex at Madurai has 11 *gopuras*, the largest over 160 feet tall.

Formally, the *gopura* has its roots in the pyramidal tower characteristic of the seventh-century southern temple style. As the *gopura* evolved, it took on the graceful concave silhouette shown here. The exterior is embellished with thousands of sculpted figures, evoking a teeming world of gods and goddesses. Inside, stairs lead to the top for an extraordinary view.

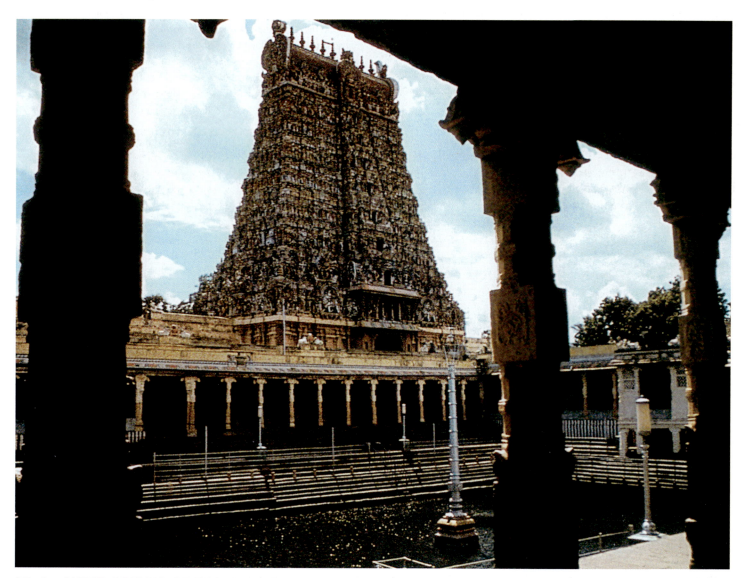

23-4 • OUTER GOPURA OF THE MINAKSHI-SUNDARESHVARA TEMPLE
Madurai, Tamil Nadu, south India. Nayak dynasty, mostly 13th to mid 17th century, with modern renovations.

Tantric Influence in the Art of Nepal and Tibet

The legacy of India's Tantric Buddhist art can be traced in the regions of Nepal and Tibet. Artistic expression of Esoteric Buddhist ideals reached a high point in the seventeenth and eighteenth centuries. Indeed, even today, artists worldwide continue to explore aspects of this tradition.

Inlaid Devotional Sculpture. In Nepal, where Hinduism intermingled with Buddhism, sculptors developed a metalwork style in which a traditional artistic use of polished stones became prevalent in devotional sculptures as well. Inlaid gems and semiprecious stones often enlivened their copper or bronze sculptures, which were almost always brightly gilded. Complex representations of deities, often multiarmed and adorned with celestial attributes, predominated, but some themes from early Buddhism were revived. In one particularly fine eighteenth-century example (FIG. A), Maya, the Mother of the Buddha, holds the legendary tree branch while the Buddha emerges from her side. The cast and **chased** (ornamented by hammering or incising the metal surface) details of the regal costume of Queen Maya, including fluttering scarves, elaborate jewelry, and a large crown, are studded with real jewels, pearls, and semiprecious stones. The tree, also, is richly inlaid, symbolizing the auspicious nature of the event. Both the tree and the figure rise from a pedestal shaped to suggest the blossoming lotus, a reference to the appearance of the Buddha's purity in the muddy pond of the material world.

***Tangka* Painting.** Buddhism was established relatively late in Tibet, but the region has since become almost wholly identified with the religion. With the rule of a lineage of Dalai Lamas established in the seventeenth century and continuing through to the twentieth century, and a related expansion of monasteries, the arts associated with Tantric Buddhism flourished. Wrathful manifestations of powerful deities were evoked in sculpted and painted forms, with the scroll-like *tangka* emerging as a major format. A nineteenth-century painting of Achala (FIG. B), one of a group of wrathful deities associated with truth, resolve, and the overcoming of obstacles, exemplifies this major aspect of Tibetan art. The deity exudes brilliant red flames while brandishing a sword and posing as if to strike. Following traditional practice, the artist—or artists, as such paintings may have employed highly specialized craftsmen—positions the terrifying figure on a lotus pedestal, establishing his ethereal nature. The background suggests the green hills and blue sky of the material world as well as the cosmic geometry envisioned in Tantric Buddhism. Repeated representations of the deity emphasize the efficacious function and conspicuous power of the image.

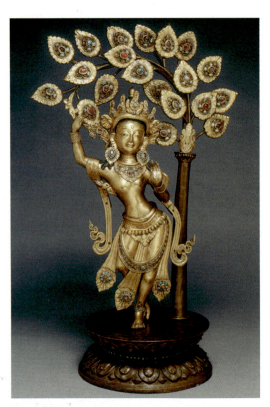

A. MAYA, MOTHER OF BUDDHA, HOLDING A TREE BRANCH
From Nepal. 18th century. Gilt bronze with inlaid precious stones, height 22″ (56 cm). Musée Guimet, Paris.

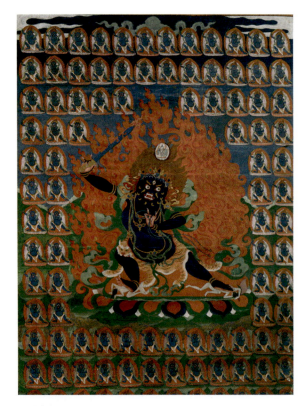

B. ACHALA
From Tibet. 19th century. Gouache on cotton, 33½ × 23⅔″ (85 × 60 cm). Musée Guimet, Paris.

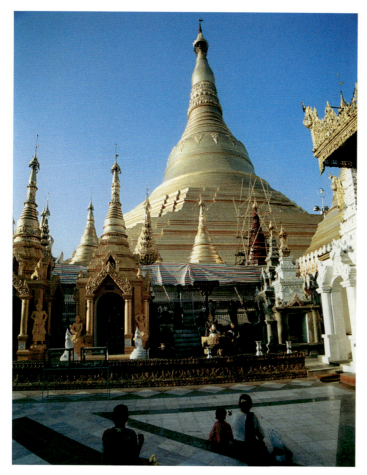

23-5 • SHWE-DAGON STUPA (PAGODA)
Yangon. 15th century. Construction at the site dates from at least the 14th century, with continuous replastering and redecoration to the present.

THE BUDDHIST AND HINDU INHERITANCE IN SOUTHEAST ASIA

India's Buddhist and Hindu traditions influenced Southeast Asia (discussed in Chapter 9), where they were absorbed by newly rising kingdoms in the regions now comprising Burma (Myanmar), Thailand, Cambodia, Vietnam, and Indonesia.

THERAVADA BUDDHISM IN BURMA AND THAILAND

In northern Burma, from the eleventh to the thirteenth century, rulers raised innumerable religious monuments—temples, monasteries, and stupas—in the Pagan Plain, following the Scriptures of Theravada Buddhism (also called Hinayana Buddhism, see Chapter 9). To the south arose the port city of Yangon (formerly known as Rangoon, called Dagon in antiquity), the nation's present-day capital. Established by Mon rulers (SEE FIG. 9–29) at least by the eleventh century, Yangon is site of the **SHWE-DAGON STUPA (FIG. 23–5)**, which enshrines relics of the Buddha. The modern structures of Shwe-dagon ("Golden Dagon") rise from an ancient core—fourteenth century or earlier—and reflect centuries of continual restoration and enhancement. The site

continues to be a center of Theravada devotion amid symbolic ornamentation—especially lotus elements symbolic of the Buddha's purity—and splendid decoration in gilding and precious stones supplied by pious contributions. Images of the Buddha, and sometimes his footprints alone, provide focal points for devotion.

In Thailand, the Sukhothai kingdom (mid thirteenth to late fourteenth century) also embraced Theravada Buddhism, although Hindu shrines were constructed as well in its capital city, Sukhothai (ancient name Sukhodaya). Artisans working under royal patrons developed a classic statement of Theravada ideals in bronze sculptures of the Buddha. Notable was their development of a free-standing walking Buddha. Especially evocative of the ascetic simplicity of Theravada Buddhism, however, are their many renditions of the Buddha Calling the Earth to Witness **(FIG. 23–6)**. Inspired by devotional texts and poetry, and further refined through reference to models from Sri Lanka, the iconographic and stylistic elements became notably formalized. The Buddha's cranial protuberance is interpreted as a flame of divine knowledge, as it was in southern India and Sri Lanka, and details of his ecclesiastical garb are reduced to a few elegant lines. The *mudras* (see page 304), or hand gestures, are quietly eloquent.

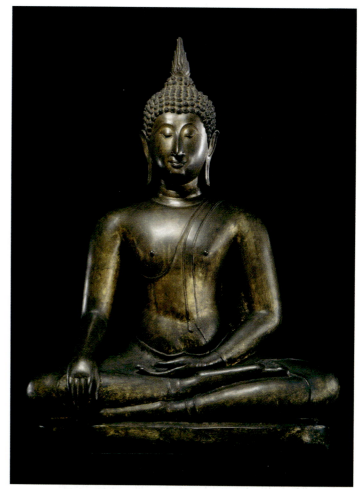

23-6 • SEATED SUKHOTAI BRONZE BUDDHA
Leaded bronze, height 35⅜" (90 cm). The Walters Art Museum, Baltimore. Bequest of A.B. Griswold, 1992. 54.2775

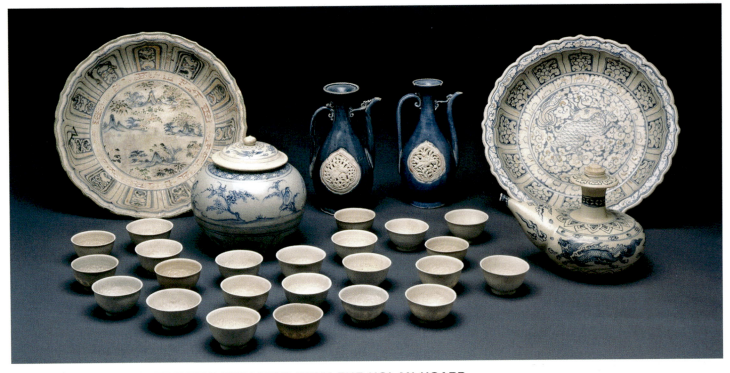

23-7 • GROUP OF VIETNAMESE CERAMICS FROM THE HOI AN HOARD
Late 15th to early 16th century, porcelain with underglaze blue decoration; barbed-rim dishes: (left) diameter 14″
(35.1 cm); (right) diameter 13¼″ (34.7 cm). Phoenix Art Museum. (2000.105–109)

More than 150,000 blue-and-white ceramic items were found in the hold of a sunken ship excavated in the late
1990s under commission from the Vietnamese government, which later sent many of the retrieved items for public
auction. The 23 small cups among the works shown here were found packed inside the jar.

VIETNAMESE CERAMICS

Both the Burmese and Thai kingdoms produced ceramics, often
inspired by stonewares and porcelains from China. Sukhothai
potters, for example, made green-glazed and brown-glazed wares,
called Sawankhalok wares. Even more widespread were the wares
of Vietnamese potters. For example, excavation of the Hoi An
"hoard" **(FIG. 23–7)**, actually the contents of a sunken ship laden
with ceramics for export, brought to light an impressive variety of
ceramic forms made by Vietnamese potters of the late fifteenth to
early sixteenth century. Painted in underglaze cobalt blue and
further embellished with overglaze enamels, these wares were
shipped throughout Southeast Asia and beyond, as far east as Japan
and as far west as England and the Netherlands.

INDONESIAN TRADITIONS

Indonesia, now the world's most populous Muslim country,
experienced a Hindu revival in the centuries following its Buddhist
period, which came to a close in the eighth or ninth century (see
Chapter 9). As a consequence, it has maintained unique traditions
that build upon the Hindu epics, especially the *Ramayana*. Islamic
monuments in Indonesia, like the Hindu and Buddhist ones, draw
from a rich and diverse repertoire of styles and motifs. The
MINARET MOSQUE of Kudus in central Java **(FIG. 23–8)** was built in
1549. The minaret serves as the tower from which Muslims are

called to worship five times daily, but the minaret's red brick,
general shape, and the niches that adorn its façade all recall Hindu
temples built in east Java about two centuries earlier. As in India,
Javanese artists worked in a consistent style, independent of
the religion of the patron. Their architecture did, of course,
accommodate the specific ritual functions of the building.

MUGHAL PERIOD

Islam first touched the South Asian subcontinent in the eighth
century, when Arab armies captured a small territory near the
Indus River. Later, beginning around 1000, Turkic factions from
central Asia, relatively recent converts to Islam, began military
campaigns into north India, at first purely for plunder, then
seeking territorial control. From 1193, various Turkic and Afghan
dynasties ruled portions of the subcontinent from the northern
city of Delhi. These sultanates, as they are known, constructed
forts, mausoleums, monuments, and mosques. Although these
early dynasties left their mark, it was the Mughal dynasty that
made the most inspired and lasting contribution to the art
of India.

The Mughals, too, came from central Asia. Muhammad Zahir-
ud-Din, known as Babur ("Lion" or "Panther"), was the first
Mughal emperor of India (r. 1526–30). He emphasized his Turkic

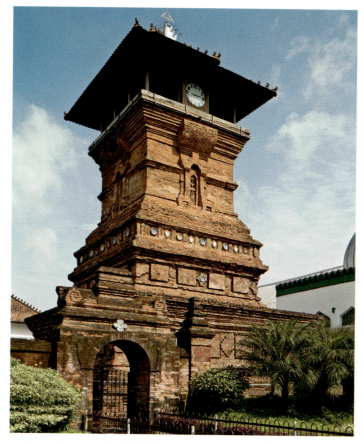

23-8 • MINARET MOSQUE
1549. Kudus, Java.

heritage, though he had equally impressive Mongol ancestry. After some initial conquests in central Asia, he amassed an empire stretching from Afghanistan to Delhi, which he conquered in 1526. Akbar (r. 1556–1605), the third ruler, extended Mughal control over most of north India, and under his two successors, Jahangir and Shah Jahan, northern India was generally unified by 1658. The Mughal Empire lasted until 1858, when the last Mughal emperor was deposed and exiled to Burma by the British.

MUGHAL ARCHITECTURE

Mughal architects were heir to a 300-year-old tradition of Islamic building in India. The Delhi sultans who preceded them had great forts housing government and court buildings. Their architects had introduced two fundamental Islamic structures, the mosque and the tomb, along with construction based on the arch and the dome. (Earlier Indian architecture had been based primarily on post-and-lintel construction.) They had also drawn freely on Indian architecture, borrowing both decorative and structural elements to create a variety of hybrid styles, and had especially benefited from the centuries-old Indian virtuosity in stonecarving and masonry. The Mughals followed in this tradition, synthesizing Indian, Persian, and central Asian elements for their forts, palaces, mosques, tombs, and cenotaphs (tombs or monuments to someone whose remains are actually somewhere else).

Akbar, an ambitious patron of architecture and city planning, constructed a new capital at a place he named Fatehpur Sikri ("City of Victory at Sikri"), celebrating his military conquests and the birth of his son Salim, who subsequently took on the throne name of Jahangir. The palatial and civic buildings, built primarily during Akbar's residence there from about 1572 to 1585, have drawn much admiration. There are two major components to Fatehpur Sikri: a religious section including the Jami Mosque and the administrative and residential section. Among the most extraordinary buildings in the administrative and residential section is the private audience hall (Diwan-i Khas) (see "A Closer Look," page 780). In the center of the hall is a tall pillar supporting a circular platform on which Akbar could sit as he received his nobles and dispensed justice. The structure recalls, perhaps consciously, the pillars erected by Ashoka (see Chapter 9) to promulgate his law.

THE TAJ MAHAL. Perhaps the most famous of all Indian Islamic structures, the Taj Mahal is sited on the bank of the Jamuna River at Agra, in northern India. Built between 1631 and 1648, it was commissioned as a mausoleum for his wife by the emperor Shah Jahan (r. 1628–58), who is believed to have taken a major part in overseeing its design and construction.

Visually, the Taj Mahal never fails to impress (SEE FIG. 23–1). As visitors enter through a monumental, hall-like gate, the tomb rises before them across a spacious garden set with long reflecting pools. Measuring some 1,000 by 1,900 feet, the enclosure is unobtrusively divided into quadrants planted with trees and flowers, and framed by broad walkways and stone inlaid in geometric patterns. In Shah Jahan's time, fruit trees and cypresses—symbolic of life and death, respectively—lined the walkways, and fountains played in the shallow pools. Truly, the senses were beguiled in this earthly evocation of paradise.

The garden in which the mausoleum is set is comprised of two parts divided by the Jamuna River. Thus while the structure appears to visitors to be set at the end of a garden, it is in fact in the center of a four-part garden, a traditional Mughal tomb setting used for earlier Mughal tombs. The tomb is flanked by two smaller structures not visible here, one a mosque and the other a hall designed in mirror image. They share a broad base with the tomb and serve visually as stabilizing elements. Like the entrance hall, they are made mostly of red sandstone, rendering even more startling the full glory of the tomb's white marble, a material previously reserved for the tombs of saints and so here implying an elevated religious stature for Shah Jahan and Mumtaz Mahal. The tomb is raised higher than these structures on its own marble platform. At each corner of the platform, a minaret defines the surrounding space. The minarets' three levels correspond to those of the tomb, creating a bond between them. Crowning each minaret is a **chattri** (pavilion). Traditional embellishments of Indian palaces, *chattris* quickly passed into the vocabulary of Indian Islamic architecture, where they appear prominently. Minarets occur in architecture throughout the Islamic world; from their heights, the faithful are called to prayer.

Luxury Arts

The decorative arts of India have been widely appreciated since the first century CE. An Indian ivory carving was found at Pompeii, while other Indian works of the time have been found along the Silk Route connecting China with Rome. For centuries Indian textiles have been made for export and copied in Europe for domestic consumption. Technically superb and crafted from precious materials, tableware, jewelry, furniture, and containers enhance the prestige of their owners and give visual pleasure as well. Metalwork and work in rock crystal, agate, and jade, carving in ivory, and intricate jewelry are all characteristic Indian arts. Because of the intrinsic value of their materials, however, pieces have been disassembled, melted down, and reworked, making the study of Indian luxury arts very difficult. Many pieces, like the carved ivory panel illustrated here, have no date or records of manufacture or ownership. And, like it, many such panels have been removed from a larger container or piece of furniture.

Carved in ivory against a golden ground, where openwork, stylized vines with spiky leaves weave an elegant arabesque, loving couples dally under the arcades of a palace courtyard, whose thin columns and cusped arches resemble the arcades of the palace of Tirumala Nayak (r. 1623–1659) in Madurai (present-day Tamil Nadu). Their huge eyes under heavy brows suggest the intensity of their gaze, and the artist's choice of the profile view shows off their long noses and sensuously thick lips. Their hair is tightly controlled; the men have huge buns, and the women long braids hanging down their backs. Are they divine lovers? After all, Krishna lived and loved on earth among the cowherd maidens. Or are we observing scenes of courtly romance?

The rich jewelry and well-fed look of the couples indicate a high station in life. Men as well as women have voluptuous figures—rounded buttocks and thighs, abdomens hanging over jeweled belts, and sharply indented slim waists that emphasize seductive breasts. Their smooth flesh contrasts with the diaphanous fabrics that swath their plump legs, and their long arms and elegant gestures seem designed to show off their rich jewelry—bracelets, armbands, necklaces, huge earrings, and ribbons. Such amorous couples symbolize harmony as well as fertility.

The erotic imagery suggests that the panel illustrated here might have adorned a container for personal belongings such as jewelry, perfume, or cosmetics. In any event, the ivory relief is a brilliant example of south Indian secular arts.

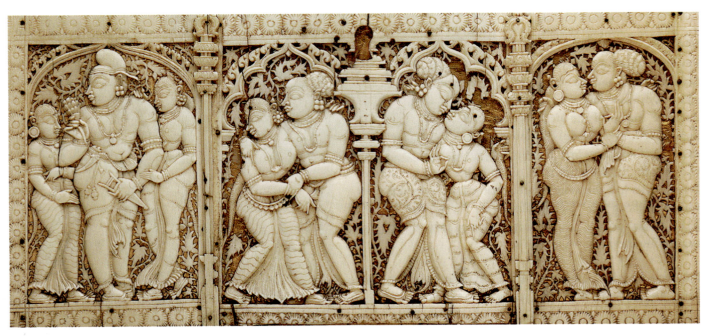

PANEL FROM A BOX
From Tamil Nadu, south India. Nayak dynasty, late 17th–18th century. Ivory backed with gilded paper, 6 × 12⅜ × ⅛″ (15.2 × 31.4 × 0.3 cm). Virginia Museum of Fine Arts.
The Arthur and Margaret Glasgow Fund. 80.171

established even before he became emperor. His focus on detail was much greater than that of his father. In his memoirs, he claimed:

> My liking for painting and my practice in judging it have arrived at such a point that when any work is brought before me, either of deceased artists or of those of the present day, without their names being told me I say on the spur of the moment that it is the work of such and such a man, and if there be a picture containing many portraits, and each face be the work of a different master, I can discover which face is the work of each of them. And if any other person has put in the eye and eyebrow of a face, I can perceive whose work the original face is and who has painted the eye and eyebrows.

Portraits become a major art under Jahangir. The portrait Jahangir commissioned of himself with the Safavid-dynasty Persian emperor Shah Abbas (FIG. 23–11) demonstrates his sense of his superiority: Jahangir is depicted much larger than Shah Abbas, who appears to bow deferentially to the Mughal emperor; Jahangir's head is centered in the halo; and he stands on the lion, whose body

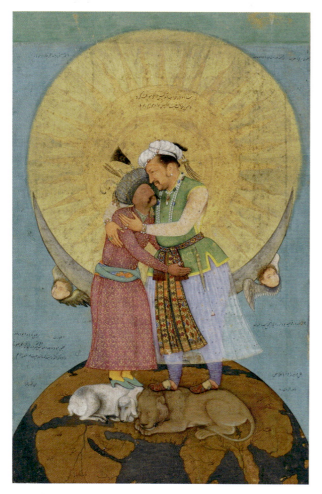

23-11 • Nadir al-Zaman (Abu'l Hasan) JAHANGIR AND SHAH ABBAS
From the St. Petersburg Album. Mughal period, c. 1618. Opaque watercolor, gold and ink on paper, 9⅜ × 6″ (23.8 × 15.4 cm). Freer Museum of Art, Smithsonian Institution, Washington, DC. Purchase, F1945.9. Freer Gallery, Washington

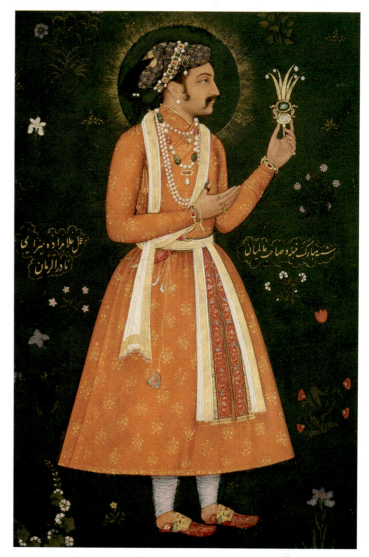

23-12 • Nadir al-Zaman (Abu'l Hasan) PRINCE KHURRAM, THE FUTURE SHAH JAHAN AT AGE 25
From the Minto Album. Mughal period, c. 1616–1617. Opaque watercolor, gold and ink on paper, 18⅛ × 4½″ (20.6 × 11.5 cm); page 15¼ × 10½″ (39 × 26.7 cm). Victoria & Albert Museum, London

spans a vast territory, including Shah Abbas's own Persia. We can only speculate on the target audience for this painting. Because it is small, it certainly would not be intended for Jahangir's subjects; a painting of this size could not be publicly displayed. But because we know that paintings were commonly sent by embassies from one kingdom to another, it may have been intended as a gift for Shah Abbas, one with a message of clear strength and superiority cloaked in the diplomatic language of cordiality.

Jahangir was succeeded by his son, Prince Khurram, who took the title Shah Jahan. Although Shah Jahan's greatest artistic achievements were in architecture, painting continued to flourish during his reign. A portrait of Prince Khurram bears an inscription indicating that he considered it "a very good likeness of me at age 25" (FIG. 23–12). Like all portraits of Shah Jahan, this one depicts him in profile, the view that has least likelihood of distortion. Holding an exquisite turban ornament, the prince stands quite type, this time with a perfection of proportion and a gentle, lyrical movement that complement the idealism of the setting. The scene embodies the sublime purity and grace of the divine, which, as in so much Indian art, is evoked into our human world to coexist with us as one.

INDIA'S ENGAGEMENT WITH THE WEST

By the time *Hour of Cowdust* was painted, India's regional rulers, both Hindu and Muslim, had reasserted themselves, and the vast Mughal Empire had shrunk to a small area around Delhi. At the same time, however, a new power, Britain, was making itself felt, inaugurating a markedly different period in Indian history.

BRITISH COLONIAL PERIOD

First under the mercantile interests of the British East India Company in the seventeenth and eighteenth centuries, and then under the direct control of the British government as a part of the British Empire in the nineteenth century, India was brought forcefully into contact with the West and its culture, a very different situation from its long-standing role in a world system that had included trade in both commodities and culture. The political concerns of the British Empire extended even to the arts, especially architecture. Over the course of the nineteenth century, the great cities of India, such as Calcutta (present-day Kolkata), Madras (Chennai), and Bombay (Mumbai), took on a European aspect as British architects built in the revivalist styles favored in England.

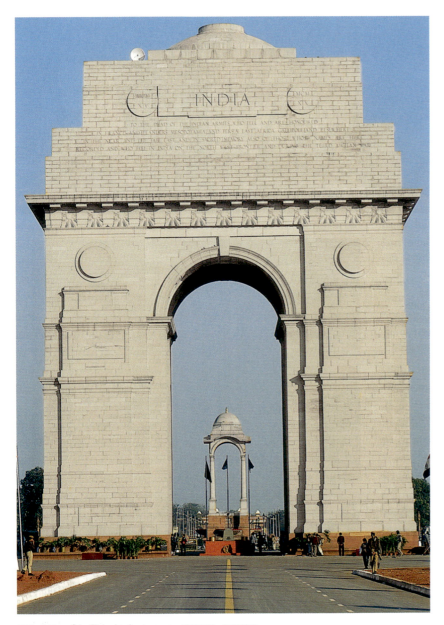

23–15 • Sir Edwin Lutyens INDIA GATE
Originally the All India War Memorial. New Delhi. British colonial period, 20th century.

NEW DELHI. In 1911, the British announced its intention to move the seat of government from Calcutta to a newly constructed Western-style capital city to be built at New Delhi, a move intended to capitalize on the long-standing association of Delhi with powerful rulers such as the Mughals. Two years later, Sir Edwin Lutyens (1869–1944) was appointed joint architect for New Delhi (with Herbert Baker), and was charged with laying out the new city and designing the Viceroy's House, the present-day Rashtrapati Bhavan (President's House). Drawing inspiration from Classical antiquity—as well as from more recent urban models, such as Paris and Washington, D.C.—Lutyens sited the Viceroy's House as a focal point along with the triumphal arch that he designed as the All India War Memorial, now called the **INDIA GATE (FIG. 23–15)**. In these works Lutyens sought to maintain the tradition of Classical architecture—he developed a "Delhi order" based on the Roman Doric—while incorporating massing, detail, and ornamentation derived from Indian architecture as well. The new capital was inaugurated in 1931.

MOTHER INDIA. Far prior to Britain's consolidation of imperial power in New Delhi a new spirit asserting Indian independence and pan-Asiatic solidarity was awakening. For example, working near Calcutta, the painter Abanindranath Tagore (1871–1951)—nephew of the poet Rabindranath Tagore (1861–1941), who went on to win the Nobel Prize for Literature in 1913—deliberately rejected the medium of oil painting and the academic realism of Western art. Like the Nihonga artists of Japan (SEE FIG. 25–15) with whom he was in contact, Tagore strove to create a style that reflected his ethnic origins. In **BHARAT MATA** (Mother India) he invents a nationalistic icon by using Hindu symbols while

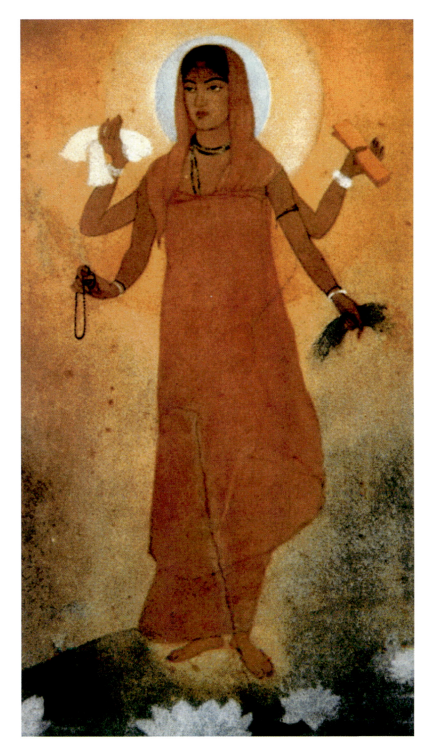

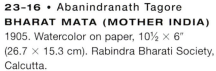

23–16 • Abanindranath Tagore
BHARAT MATA (MOTHER INDIA)
1905. Watercolor on paper, 10½ × 6″
(26.7 × 15.3 cm). Rabindra Bharati Society,
Calcutta.

also drawing upon the format and techniques of Mughal and Rajput painting **(FIG. 23–16)**.

THE MODERN PERIOD

In the wake of World War II, the imperial powers of Europe began to shed their colonial domains. The attainment of self-rule had been five long decades in the making, when finally—chastened by the nonviolent example of Mahatma Gandhi (1869–1948)—the British Empire relinquished its "Jewel in the Crown," which was partitioned to form two modern nations: India and Pakistan. After independence in 1947, the exuberant young nation welcomed a modern, internationalist approach to art and architecture.

JAWAHAR KALA KENDRA. Architect Charles Correa often draws on traditional Indian architectural forms. One example is his impressive **JAWAHAR KALA KENDRA**, a center for the visual and performing arts in Jaipur that was completed in 1992 **(FIG. 23–17)**. Like the original design of Jaipur, the building's design is based on a nine-square plan, and its elevation makes visual reference to the city's historic buildings. Correa's work is not confined to India, but

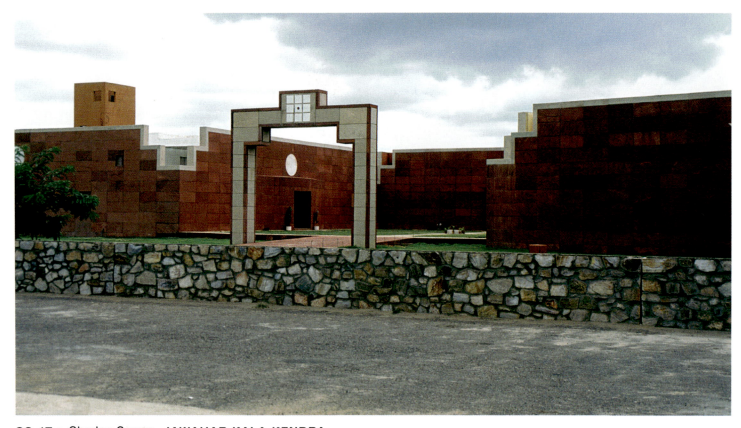

23-17 • Charles Correa JAWAHAR KALA KENDRA
1992. Jaipur. Like many of Correa's buildings, this arts center draws upon traditional Indian motifs and forms. Its many open spaces provide a feeling of connected space rather than individual rooms.

includes buildings in Europe and the United States, for example the Cognitive Sciences Complex at MIT completed in 2005.

TWO MODERN ARTISTS. Artists working after Indian independence have continued to study and work abroad, but often draw upon India's distinctive literary and religious traditions as well as regional and folk art traditions. One example is Manjit Bawa (b. 1941), who worked in Britain as a silkscreen artist before returning to India to settle in New Delhi. His distinctive canvases, painted meticulously in oil, juxtapose illusionistically modeled figures and animals against brilliantly colored backgrounds of flat, unmodulated color. The composite result, for example in **DHARMA AND THE GOD** (FIG. 23–18), brings a strikingly new interpretation to the heroic figures of Indian tradition.

With Anish Kapoor (b. 1954), as with so many artists living abroad, we must consider issues of identity. Although some of his work draws inspiration from his Indian origins, for example, his 1981 composition **AS IF TO CELEBRATE, I DISCOVERED A MOUNTAIN BLOOMING WITH RED FLOWERS (23–19)**, whose red and ocher mounds recall the vermilion and other pigments beautifully piled for sale outside Indian temples, other works make no reference to India. Kapoor represented Britain, where he now lives and works, at the Venice Biennale in 1990, further complicating the issue of his identity.

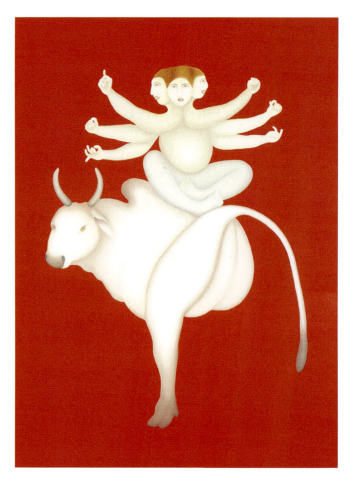

23-18 • Manjit Bawa DHARMA AND THE GOD
1984. Oil on canvas, 85 × 72¹⁵⁄₁₆″ (216 × 185.4 cm). Peabody Essex Museum, Salem, Massachusetts. The Davida and Chester Herwitz Collection

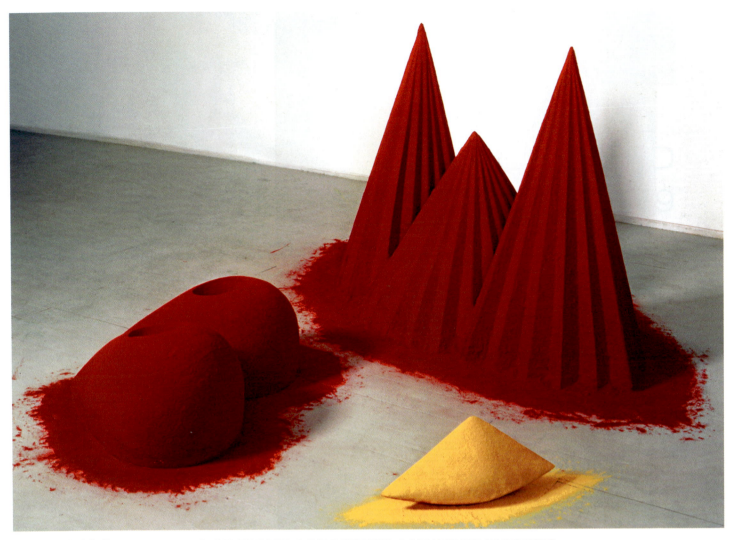

23–19 • Anish Kapoor AS IF TO CELEBRATE, I DISCOVERED A MOUNTAIN BLOOMING WITH RED FLOWERS
1981. Wood, cement, polystyrene and pigment, 3 elements, 38¼ (highest point) × 30 (widest point) × 63″ (97 × 76.2 × 160 cm); 13 × 28 × 32″ (33 × 71.1 × 81.3 cm); 8¼ × 6 × 18½″ (21 × 15.3 × 47 cm), overall dimensions variable. Arts Council Collection, South Bank Centre, London.

THINK ABOUT IT

23.1 Explain some of the ways that Islamic art and culture impacted that of the Indian subcontinent. Explain how the Taj Mahal demonstrates influence from building styles studied in Chapter 8, and indicate how it departs from prior styles on the Indian subcontinent.

23.2 Analyze the Shwe-Dagon Stupa (Pagoda) in Yangon, and determine how the structure incorporates influence from Indian buildings. In your answer, compare the stupa to at least one Indian building.

23.3 Analyze the form of the India Gate (SEE FIG. 23–15) and explain how the ancient Roman form of the triumphal arch (see, for example, the Arch of Titus (SEE FIG. 6–32) is used within a new Indian context.

23.4 Explain how the artist Anish Kapoor utilizes Indian themes in his work *As if to Celebrate, I Discovered a Mountain Blooming with Red Flowers* (SEE FIG. 23–19). What other ideas can you infer from this work?

23.5 From the works discussed in this chapter, select a two-dimensional religious artwork from each of two religions practiced in India. Compare and contrast both directly, determining similarities in regional style and technique as well as differences due to their varying religious contexts.

PRACTICE MORE: Compose answers to these questions, get flashcards for images and terms, and review chapter material with quizzes **www.myartslab.com**

Spring Dawn in the Han Palace ▶

Ming dynasty, 1500–1550. Section of a handscroll, ink and color on silk, 1' × 18'¹³⁄₁₆" (0.30 × 5.7 m). National Palace Museum, Taibei, Taiwan, Republic of China.

Two ladies unwrap a *qin*, the zither or lute that was the most respected of musical instruments.

A seated lady plays the *pipa*, an instrument introduced from Central Asia during the Tang dynasty.

Antique vessels of bronze, lacquer, and porcelain adorn the room and suggest the ladies' refined taste.

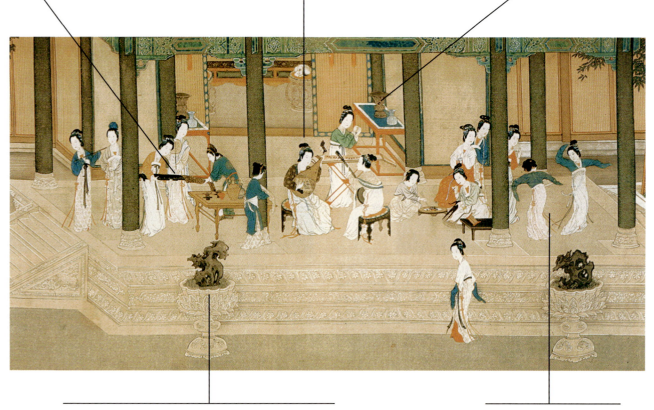

A tray landscape featuring an eroded rock provides a sculptural counterpart to landscape (mountain-and-water) painting and suggests a place where immortals might dwell.

Two ladies dance together letting their sleeves and sashes swirl.

SEE MORE: View the Closer Look feature for the detail of *Spring Dawn in the Han Palace* www.myartslab.com

background entirely. Qiu's graceful and elegant figures—although modeled after those in Tang works—are portrayed in a setting of palace buildings, engaging in such pastimes as chess, music, calligraphy, and painting. With its antique subject matter, refined technique, and flawless taste in color and composition, *Spring Dawn in the Han Palace* brought professional painting to a new high point (see "A Closer Look," above).

DECORATIVE ARTS

Qiu Ying painted to satisfy his patrons in Suzhou. The cities of the south were becoming wealthy, and newly rich merchants collected paintings, antiques, and art objects. The court, too, was prosperous and patronized the arts on a lavish scale. In such a setting, the decorative arts thrived.

MING BLUE-AND-WHITE WARES. The Ming became famous the world over for its exquisite ceramics, especially **porcelain** (see "The Secret of Porcelain," opposite). The imperial kilns in Jingdezhen, in Jiangxi Province, became the most renowned center for porcelain not only in all of China, but in all the world. Particularly noteworthy are the blue-and-white wares produced there during the ten-year reign of the ruler known as the Xuande

Marco Polo, it is said, was the one who named a new type of ceramic he found in China. Its translucent purity reminded him of the smooth whiteness of the cowry shell, *porcellana* in Italian. **Porcelain** is made from kaolin, an extremely refined white clay, and petuntse, a variety of the mineral feldspar. When properly combined and fired at a sufficiently high temperature, the two materials fuse into a glasslike, translucent ceramic that is far stronger than it looks.

Porcelaneous stoneware, fired at lower temperatures, was known in China by the seventh century, but true porcelain was perfected during the Song dynasty. To create blue-and-white porcelain such as the flask in FIGURE 24–7, blue pigment was made from cobalt oxide, finely

ground and mixed with water. The decoration was painted directly onto the unfired porcelain vessel, then a layer of clear glaze was applied over it. (In this technique, known as **underglaze** painting, the pattern is painted beneath the glaze.) After firing, the piece emerged from the kiln with a clear blue design set sharply against a snowy white background.

Entranced with the exquisite properties of porcelain, European potters tried for centuries to duplicate it. The technique was finally discovered in 1709 by Johann Friedrich Böttger in Dresden, Germany, who tried—but failed—to keep it a secret.

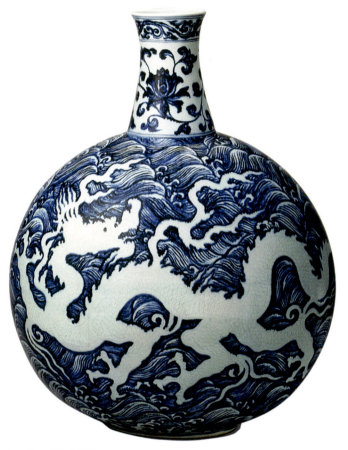

24-7 • FLASK
Ming dynasty, 1426–1435. Porcelain with decoration painted in underglaze cobalt blue. Collection of the Palace Museum, Beijing.

Dragons have featured prominently in Chinese folklore from earliest times—Neolithic examples have been found painted on pottery and carved in jade. In Bronze Age China, dragons came to be associated with powerful and sudden manifestations of nature, such as wind, thunder, and lightning. At the same time, dragons became associated with superior beings such as virtuous rulers and sages. With the emergence of China's first firmly established empire during the Han dynasty, the dragon was appropriated as an imperial symbol, and it remained so throughout Chinese history. Dragon sightings were duly recorded and considered auspicious. Yet even the Son of Heaven could not monopolize the dragon. During the Tang and Song dynasties the practice arose of painting pictures of dragons to pray for rain, and for Chan (Zen) Buddhists, the dragon was a symbol of sudden enlightenment.

Emperor (ruled 1426–1435), such as the **FLASK** in FIGURE **24–7**. The subtle shape, the refined yet vigorous decoration of dragons posturing above the sea, and the flawless glazing embody the high achievement of Ming artisans.

ARCHITECTURE AND CITY PLANNING

Centuries of warfare and destruction have left very few Chinese architectural monuments intact. The most important remaining example of traditional Chinese architecture is **THE FORBIDDEN CITY**, the imperial palace compound in Beijing, whose principal buildings were constructed during the Ming dynasty (**FIG. 24–8**).

THE FORBIDDEN CITY.   The basic plan of Beijing was the work of the Mongols, who laid out their capital city according to traditional Chinese principles. City planning began early in China—in the seventh century, in the case of Chang'an (present-day Xi'an), the capital of the Sui and Tang emperors. The walled city of Chang'an was laid out on a rectangular grid, with evenly spaced streets that ran north–south and east–west. At the northern end stood a walled imperial complex.

Beijing, too, was developed as a walled, rectangular city with streets laid out in a grid. The palace enclosure occupied the center of the northern part of the city, which was reserved for the Mongols. Chinese lived in the southern third of the city. Later, Ming and Qing emperors preserved this division, with officials living in the northern or Inner City and commoners living in the southern or Outer City. Under the third Ming emperor, Yongle (ruled 1403–1424), the Forbidden City was rebuilt as we see it today.

The approach to the Forbidden City was impressive. Visitors entered through the Meridian Gate, a monumental gate with side wings (SEE FIG. 24–8). Inside the Meridian Gate a broad courtyard is crossed by a bow-shaped waterway that is spanned by five arched marble bridges. At the opposite end of the courtyard is the Gate of Supreme Harmony, opening onto an even larger courtyard that houses three ceremonial halls raised on a broad platform. First is the Hall of Supreme Harmony, where, on the most important state occasions, the emperor was seated on his throne,

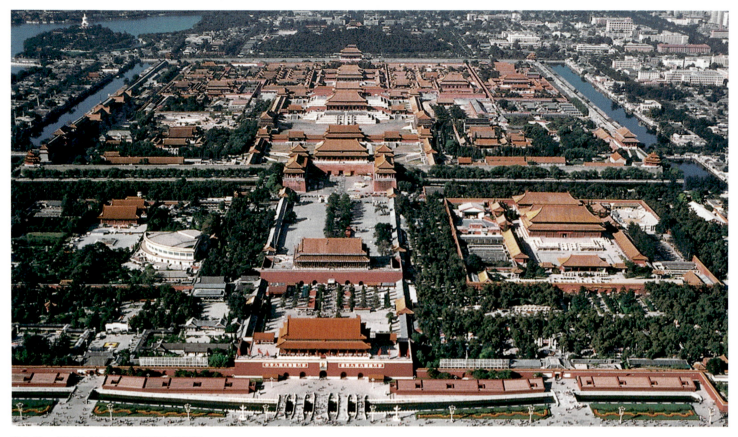

24-8 • THE FORBIDDEN CITY
Now the Palace Museum, Beijing. Mostly Ming dynasty.
View from the southwest.

SEE MORE: View a simulation about the Forbidden City
www.myartslab.com

facing south. Beyond is the smaller Hall of Central Harmony, then the Hall of Protecting Harmony. Behind these vast ceremonial spaces, still on the central axis, is the inner court, again with a progression of three buildings, this time more intimate in scale. In its balance and symmetry the plan of the Forbidden City reflects ancient Chinese beliefs about the harmony of the universe, and it emphasizes the emperor's role as the Son of Heaven, whose duty was to maintain the cosmic order from his throne in the middle of the world.

THE LITERATI AESTHETIC

In the south, particularly in the district of Suzhou, literati painting, associated with the educated men who served the court as government officials, remained the dominant trend. One of the major literati figures from the Ming period is Shen Zhou (1427–1509), who had no desire to enter government service and spent most of his life in Suzhou. He studied the Yuan painters avidly and tried to recapture their spirit in such works as *Poet on a Mountaintop* (see "*Poet on a Mountaintop*," page 802). Although the style of the painting recalls the freedom and simplicity of Ni Zan (SEE FIG. 24–3), the motif of a poet surveying the landscape from a mountain plateau is Shen's creation.

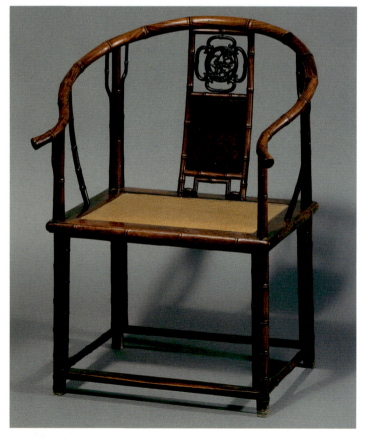

24-9 • ARMCHAIR
Ming dynasty, 16th–17th century. Huanghuali wood (hardwood), 39⅜ × 27¼ × 20″ (100 × 69.2 × 50.8 cm). The Nelson-Atkins Museum of Art, Kansas City, Missouri. Purchase, Nelson Trust (46-78/1)

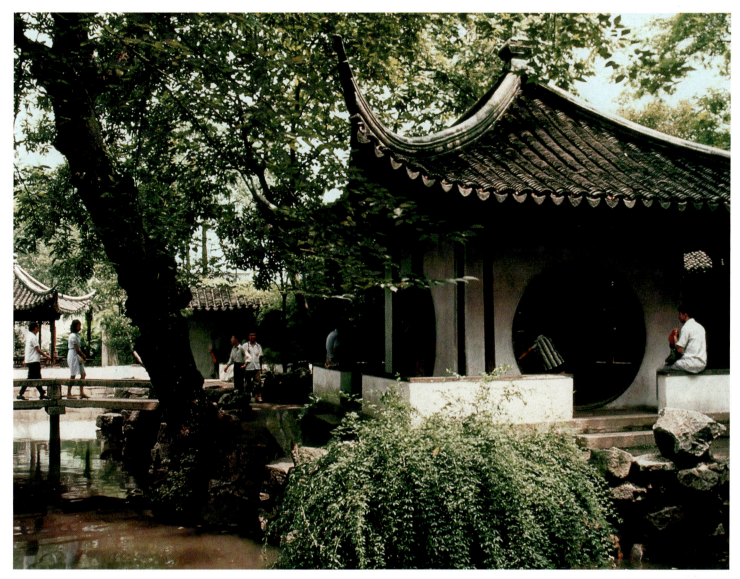

24-10 • GARDEN OF THE CESSATION OF OFFICIAL LIFE (ALSO KNOWN AS THE HUMBLE ADMINISTRATOR'S GARDEN)
Suzhou, Jiangsu. Ming dynasty, early 16th century.

Early in the sixteenth century, an official in Beijing, frustrated after serving in the capital for many years without promotion, returned home. Taking an ancient poem, "The Song of Leisurely Living," for his model, he began to build a garden. He called his retreat the Garden of the Cessation of Official Life to indicate that he had exchanged his career as a bureaucrat for a life of leisure. By leisure, he meant that he could now dedicate himself to calligraphy, poetry, and painting, the three arts dear to scholars in China.

LITERATI INFLUENCE ON FURNITURE, ARCHITECTURE, AND GARDEN DESIGN. The taste of the literati came to influence furniture and architecture, and especially the design of gardens. Chinese furniture made for domestic use reached the height of its development in the sixteenth and seventeenth centuries. Characteristic of Chinese furniture, the chair in **FIGURE 24–9** is constructed without the use of glue or nails. Instead, pieces fit together based on the principle of the **mortise-and-tenon** joint, in which a projecting element (tenon) on one piece fits snugly into a cavity (mortise) on another. Each piece of the chair is carved, as opposed to being bent or twisted, and the joints are crafted with great precision. The patterns of the wood grain provide subtle interest unmarred by any

painting or other embellishment. The style, like that of Chinese architecture, is one of simplicity, clarity, symmetry, and balance. The effect is formal and dignified but natural and simple—virtues central to the Chinese view of proper human conduct as well.

The art of landscape gardening also reached a high point during the Ming dynasty, as many literati surrounded their homes with gardens. The most famous gardens were created in the southern cities of the Yangzi Delta, especially in Suzhou. The largest surviving garden of the era is the **GARDEN OF THE CESSATION OF OFFICIAL LIFE (FIG. 24–10)**. Although modified and reconstructed many times through the centuries, it still reflects many of the basic ideas of the original Ming owner. About a third of the garden is

Poet on a Mountaintop

In earlier landscape paintings, human figures were typically shown dwarfed by the grandeur of nature. Travelers might be seen scuttling along a narrow path by a stream, while overhead towered mountains whose peaks conversed with the clouds and whose heights were inaccessible. Here, the poet has climbed the mountain and dominates the landscape. Even the clouds are beneath him. Before his gaze, a poem hangs in the air, as though he were projecting his thoughts.

The poem, composed by Shen Zhou himself, and written in his distinctive hand, reads:

White clouds like a scarf enfold the mountain's waist;
Stone steps hang in space—a long, narrow path.
Alone, leaning on my cane, I gaze intently at the scene,
And feel like answering the murmuring brook with the music of my flute.

(Translation by Jonathan Chaves, *The Chinese Painter as Poet*, New York, 2000, p. 46.)

Shen Zhou composed the poem and wrote the inscription at the time he painted the album. The style of the calligraphy, like the style of the painting, is informal, relaxed, and straightforward—qualities that were believed to reflect the artist's character and personality.

The painting reflects Ming philosophy, which held that the mind, not the physical world, was the basis for reality. With its perfect synthesis of poetry, calligraphy, and painting, and with its harmony of mind and landscape, *Poet on a Mountaintop* represents the essence of Ming literati painting.

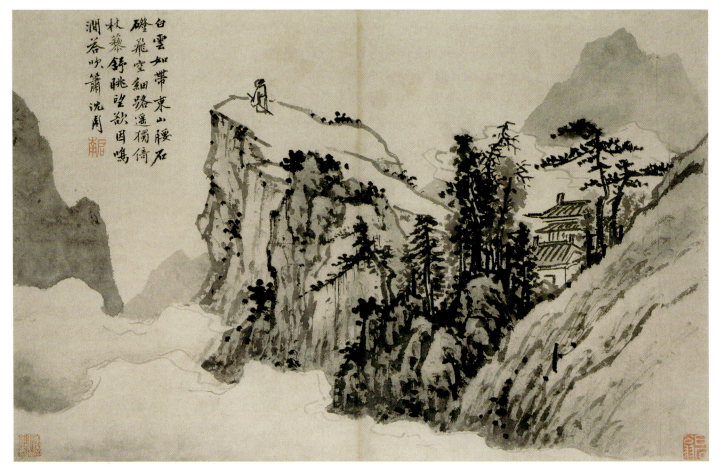

Shen Zhou **POET ON A MOUNTAINTOP**
Leaf from an album of landscapes; painting mounted as part of a handscroll. Ming dynasty, c. 1500.
Ink and color on paper, 15¼ × 23¾″ (40 × 60.2 cm). Nelson-Atkins Museum of Art, Kansas City, Missouri.
Purchase, Nelson Trust (46-51/2)

devoted to water through artificially created brooks and ponds. The landscape is dotted with pavilions, kiosks, libraries, studios, and corridors. Many of the buildings have poetic names, such as Rain Listening Pavilion and Bridge of the Small Flying Rainbow.

DONG QICHANG, LITERATI THEORIST. The ideas underlying literati painting found their most influential expression in the writings of Dong Qichang (1555–1636). A high official in the late Ming period, Dong Qichang embodied the literati tradition as poet, calligrapher, and painter. He developed a view of Chinese art history that divided painters into two opposing schools, northern and southern. The names have nothing to do with geography— a painter from the south might well be classed as northern—but reflect a parallel Dong drew with the northern and southern schools of Chan (Zen) Buddhism in China. The southern school of Chan, founded by the eccentric monk Huineng (638–713), was unorthodox, radical, and innovative; the northern school was traditional and conservative. Similarly, Dong's two schools of painters represented progressive and conservative traditions. In Dong's view the conservative northern school was dominated by professional painters whose academic, often decorative, style emphasized technical skill. In contrast, the progressive southern school preferred ink to color and free brushwork to meticulous detail. Its painters aimed for poetry and personal expression. In promoting this theory, Dong gave his unlimited sanction to literati painting, which he positioned as the culmination of the southern school, and he fundamentally influenced the way the Chinese viewed their own tradition.

Dong Qichang summarized his views on the proper training for literati painters in the famous statement "Read ten thousand books and walk ten thousand miles." By this he meant that one must first study the works of the great masters, then follow "heaven and earth," the world of nature. These studies prepared the way for greater self-expression through brush and ink, the goal of literati painting. Dong's views rested on an awareness that a painting of scenery and the actual scenery are two very different things. The excellence of a painting does not lie in its degree of resemblance to reality—that gap can never be bridged—but in its expressive power. The expressive language of painting is inherently abstract and lies in its nature as a construction of brushstrokes. For example, in a painting of a rock, the rock itself is not expressive; rather, the brushstrokes that suggest a rock are expressive.

With such thinking Dong brought painting close to the realm of calligraphy, which had long been considered the highest form of artistic expression in China. More than a thousand years before Dong's time, a body of critical terms and theories had evolved to discuss calligraphy in light of the formal and expressive properties of brushwork and composition. Dong introduced some of these terms—ideas such as opening and closing, rising and falling, and void and solid—to the criticism of painting.

Dong's theories are fully embodied in his painting **THE QING-BIAN MOUNTAINS (FIG. 24–11)**. According to his own inscription,

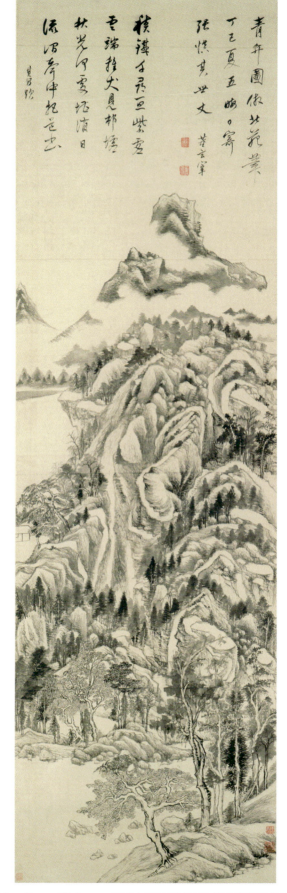

24–11 • Dong Qichang THE QINGBIAN MOUNTAINS
Ming dynasty, 1617. Hanging scroll, ink on paper, 21'8″ × 7'4⅜″ (6.72 × 2.25 m). Cleveland Museum of Art. Leonard C. Hanna, Jr., Fund

the painting was based on a work by the tenth-century artist Dong Yuan. Dong Qichang's style, however, is quite different from the styles of the masters he admired. Although there is some indication of foreground, middle ground, and distant mountains, the space is ambiguous, as if all the elements were compressed to the surface of the picture. With this flattening of space, the trees, rocks, and mountains become more readily legible in a second way, as semi-abstract forms made of brushstrokes.

Six trees arranged diagonally define the extreme foreground and announce themes that the rest of the painting repeats, varies, and develops. The tree on the left, with its outstretched branches and full foliage, is echoed first in the shape of another tree just across the river and again in a tree farther up and toward the left. The tallest tree of the foreground grouping anticipates the high peak that towers in the distance almost directly above it. The forms of the smaller foreground trees, especially the one with dark leaves,

are repeated in numerous variations across the painting. At the same time, the simple and ordinary-looking boulder in the foreground is transformed in the conglomeration of rocks, ridges, hills, and mountains above. This double reading, both abstract and representational, parallels the work's double nature as a painting of a landscape and an interpretation of a traditional landscape painting.

The influence of Dong Qichang on the development of Chinese painting of later periods cannot be overstated. Indeed, nearly all Chinese painters since the early seventeenth century have reflected his ideas in one way or another.

QING DYNASTY

In 1644, when the armies of the Manchu people to the northeast of China marched into Beijing, many Chinese reacted as though their civilization had come to an end. Yet, the Manchus had already

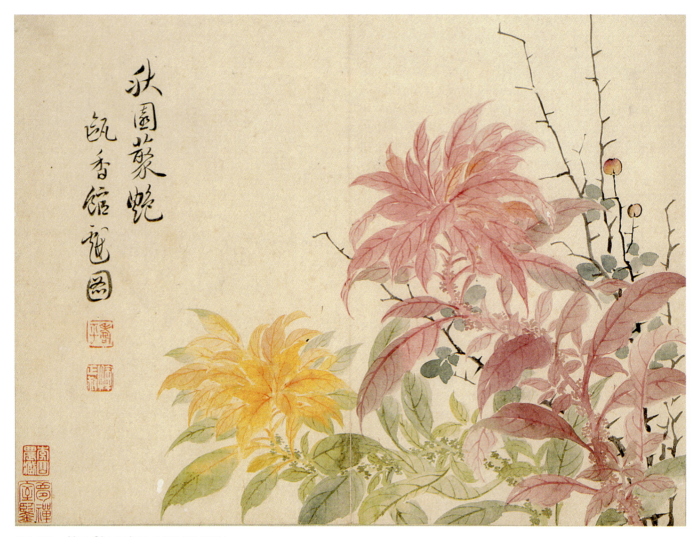

24-12 • Yun Shouping AMARANTH
Leaf from an album of flowers, bamboo, fruits, and vegetables. 1633–1690. Album of 10 leaves; ink and color on paper; each leaf 10 × 13″ (25.3 × 33.5 cm). Collection of Phoenix Art Museum. Gift of Marilyn and Roy Papp

The leaf is inscribed by the artist: "Autumn garden abounds in beauty, playfully painted by Ouxiangguan (Yun Shouping)."
Translation by Momoko Soma Welch.

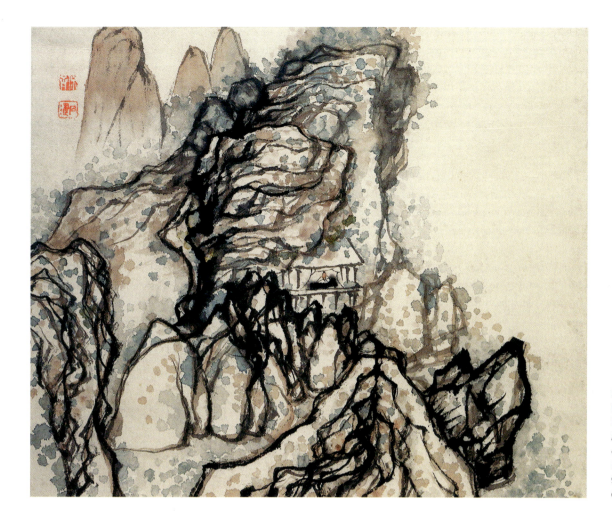

24–13 • Shitao
LANDSCAPE
Leaf from *An Album of Landscapes*. Qing dynasty, c. 1700. Ink and color on paper, 9½ × 11″ (24.1 × 28 cm). Collection C. C. Wang family

adopted many Chinese customs and institutions before their conquest. After gaining control of all of China, a process that took decades, they showed great respect for Chinese tradition. In art, all the major trends of the late Ming dynasty eventually continued into the Manchu, or Qing, dynasty (1644–1911).

ORTHODOX PAINTING

Literati painting had been established as the dominant tradition; it now became orthodox. Scholars followed Dong Qichang's recommendation and based their approach on the study of past masters, and they painted large numbers of works in the manner of Song and Yuan artists as a way of expressing their learning, technique, and taste.

The Qing emperors of the late seventeenth and eighteenth centuries were painters themselves. They collected literati painting, and their taste was shaped mainly by artists such as Wang Hui (SEE FIG. 24–1). Thus literati painting, long associated with reclusive scholars, ultimately became an academic style practiced at court. Imbued with values associated with scholarship and virtue, these paintings constituted the highest art form of the Qing court. The emperors also esteemed a style of bird-and-flower painting developed by Yun Shouping (1633–1690). Like the orthodox style of landscape painting, it was embraced by literati painters—many of them court officials themselves. The style, most often seen in

albums or fans, recalled aspects of Song- and Yuan-dynasty bird-and-flower painting, and artists cited their ancient models as a way to enrich both the meaning and the beauty of these small-format works. In a leaf from an album of flowers, bamboo, fruits and vegetables, which employs a variety of brush techniques (**FIG. 24–12**), Yun Shouping represents flowers of the autumn season.

INDIVIDUALIST PAINTING

The first few decades of Qing rule had been both traumatic and dangerous for those who were loyal—or worse, related—to the Ming. Some committed suicide, while others sought refuge in monasteries or wandered the countryside. Among them were several painters who expressed their anger, defiance, frustration, and melancholy in their art. They took Dong Qichang's idea of painting as an expression of the artist's personal feelings very seriously and cultivated highly original styles. These painters have become known as the individualists.

SHITAO. One of the individualists was Shitao (1642–1707), who was descended from the first Ming emperor and who took refuge in Buddhist temples when the dynasty fell. In his later life he brought his painting to the brink of abstraction in such works as **LANDSCAPE** (**FIG. 24–13**). A monk sits in a small hut, looking out onto mountains that seem to be in turmoil. Dots, used for centuries to indicate vegetation on rocks, here seem to have taken on a life of their own. The rocks also seem alive—about to swallow up the monk and his hut. Throughout his life Shitao continued to identify himself with the fallen Ming, and he felt that his secure world had turned to chaos with the Manchu conquest.

THE MODERN PERIOD

In the mid and late nineteenth century, China was shaken from centuries of complacency by a series of humiliating military defeats at the hands of Western powers and Japan. Only then did the government finally realize that these new rivals were not like the Mongols of the thirteenth century. China was no longer at the center of the world, a civilized country surrounded by "barbarians." Spiritual resistance was no longer sufficient to solve the problems brought on by change. New ideas from Japan and the West began to filter in, and the demand arose for political and cultural reforms. In 1911 the Qing dynasty was overthrown, ending 2,000 years of imperial rule, and China was reconceived as a republic.

During the first decades of the twentieth century Chinese artists traveled to Japan and Europe to study Western art. Returning to China, many sought to introduce the ideas and techniques they had learned, and they explored ways to synthesize the Chinese and the Western traditions. After the establishment of the present-day Communist government in 1949, individual artistic freedom was curtailed as the arts were pressed into the service of the state and its vision of a new social order. After 1979, however, cultural attitudes began to relax, and Chinese painters again pursued their own paths.

WU GUANZHONG.   One artist who emerged during the 1980s as a leader in Chinese painting is Wu Guanzhong (b. 1919). Combining his French artistic training and Chinese background, Wu Guanzhong developed a semiabstract style to depict scenes from the Chinese landscape. He made preliminary sketches on site, then, back in his studio, he developed these sketches into free interpretations based on his feeling and vision. An example of his work, PINE SPIRIT, depicts a scene in the Huang (Yellow) Mountains (FIG. 24–14). The technique, with its sweeping gestures of paint, is clearly linked to Abstract Expressionism, an influential Western movement of the post–World War II years (Chapter 32); yet the painting also claims a place in the long tradition of Chinese landscape as exemplified by such masters as Shitao.

Like all aspects of Chinese society, Chinese art has felt the strong impact of Western influence, and the question remains whether Chinese artists will absorb Western ideas without losing their traditional identity. Interestingly, landscape remains an important subject, as it has been for more than a thousand years, and calligraphy continues to play a vital role. Using the techniques and methods of the West, some of China's artists have joined an international avant-garde (see, for example, Wenda Gu in Chapter 32), while other painters still seek communion with nature through their ink brushstrokes as a means to come to terms with human life and the world.

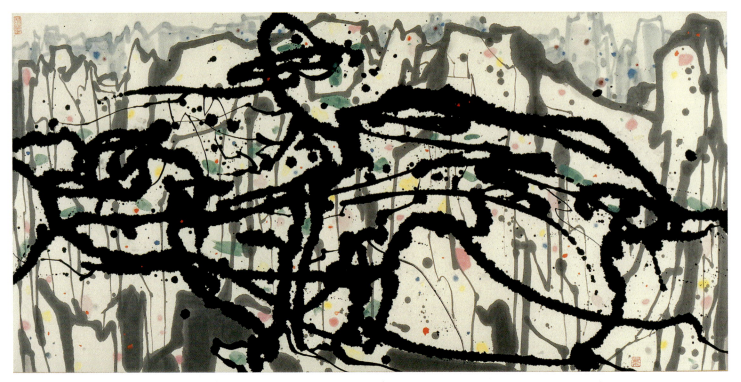

24-14 • Wu Guanzhong PINE SPIRIT
1984. Ink and color on paper, 2'3⅝" × 5'3½" (0.70 × 1.61 m). Spencer Museum of Art, The University of Kansas, Lawrence. Gift of the E. Rhodes and Leonard B. Carpenter Foundation

ARTS OF KOREA: THE JOSEON DYNASTY TO THE MODERN ERA

In 1392, General Yi Seonggye (1335–1408) overthrew the Goryeo dynasty (918–1392), establishing the Joseon dynasty (1392–1910), sometimes called the Yi dynasty. He first maintained his capital at Gaeseong, the old Goryeo capital, but moved it to Seoul in 1394, where it remained through the end of the dynasty. The Joseon regime rejected Buddhism, espousing Neo-Confucianism as the state philosophy. Taking Ming-dynasty China as its model, the new government patterned its bureaucracy on that of the Ming emperors, even adopting as its own such outward symbols of Ming imperial authority as blue-and-white porcelain. The early Joseon era was a period of cultural refinement and scientific achievement, during which Koreans invented Han'geul (the Korean alphabet) and movable type, not to mention the rain gauge, astrolabe, celestial globe, sundial, and water clock.

JOSEON CERAMICS

Like their Silla and Goryeo forebears (see Chapter 10), Joseon potters excelled in the manufacture of ceramics, taking their cue from contemporaneous Chinese wares, but seldom copying them directly.

BUNCHEONG CERAMICS. Descended from Goryeo celadons, Joseon-dynasty stonewares, known as *buncheong* wares, enjoyed widespread usage throughout the peninsula. Their decorative effect relies on the use of white slip that makes the humble stoneware resemble more expensive white porcelain. In fifteenth-century examples, the slip is often seen inlaid into repeating design elements stamped into the body.

Sixteenth-century *buncheong* wares are characteristically embellished with wonderfully fluid, calligraphic brushwork painted in iron-brown slip on a white slip ground. Most painted *buncheong* wares have stylized floral décor, but rare pieces, such as the charming wine bottle in **FIGURE 24–15**, feature pictorial decoration. In fresh, lively brushstrokes, a bird with outstretched wings grasps a fish that it has just caught in its talons; waves roll below, while two giant lotus blossoms frame the scene.

Japanese armies repeatedly invaded the Korean peninsula between 1592 and 1597, destroying many of the *buncheong* kilns, and essentially bringing the ware's production to a halt. Tradition holds that the Japanese took many *buncheong* potters home with them to produce *buncheong*-style wares, which were greatly admired by connoisseurs of the tea ceremony. In fact, the spontaneity of Korean *buncheong* pottery has inspired Japanese ceramics to this day.

PAINTED PORCELAIN. Korean potters produced porcelains with designs painted in underglaze cobalt blue as early as the fifteenth century, inspired by Chinese porcelains of the early Ming period (SEE FIG. 24–7). The Korean court dispatched artists from the royal painting academy to the porcelain kilns—located some 30 miles southeast of Seoul—to train porcelain decorators. As a result, from the fifteenth century onward, the painting on the best Korean porcelains closely approximated that on paper and silk, unlike in China, where ceramic decoration followed a path of its own with but scant reference to painting traditions.

In another unique development, Korean porcelains from the sixteenth and seventeenth centuries often feature designs painted in underglaze iron-brown rather than the cobalt blue customary in Ming porcelain. Also uniquely Korean are porcelain jars with bulging shoulders, slender bases, and short, vertical necks, which

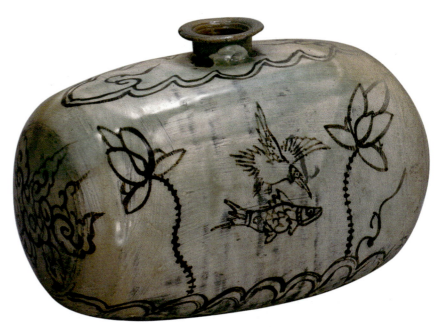

24-15 • HORIZONTAL WINE BOTTLE WITH DECORATION OF A BIRD CARRYING A NEWLY CAUGHT FISH
Korea. Joseon dynasty, 16th century. *Buncheong* ware: light gray stoneware with decoration painted in iron-brown slip on a white slip ground, 6¹⁄₁₀ × 9½″ (15.5 × 24.1 cm). Museum of Oriental Ceramics, Osaka, Japan. Gift of the Sumitomo Group (20773)

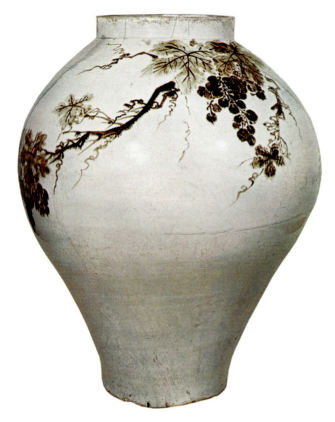

24-16 • BROAD-SHOULDERED JAR WITH DECORATION OF A FRUITING GRAPEVINE

Korea. Joseon dynasty, 17th century. Porcelain with decoration painted in underglaze iron-brown slip, height 22⅛″ (53.8 cm). Ewha Women's University Museum, Seoul, Republic of Korea.

Chinese potters invented porcelain during the Tang dynasty, probably in the eighth century. Generally fired in the range of 1300° to 1400° C, porcelain is a high-fired, white-bodied ceramic ware. Its unique feature is its translucency. Korean potters learned to make porcelain during the Goryeo dynasty, probably as early as the eleventh or twelfth century, though few Goryeo examples remain today. For many centuries, only the Chinese and Koreans were able to produce porcelains.

appeared by the seventeenth century and came to be the most characteristic ceramic shapes in the later Joseon period. Painted in underglaze iron-brown, the seventeenth-century jar shown in **FIGURE 24–16** depicts a fruiting grape branch around its shoulder. In typical Korean fashion, the design spreads over a surface unconstrained by borders, resulting in a balanced but asymmetrical design that incorporates the Korean taste for unornamented spaces.

JOSEON PAINTING

Korean secular painting came into its own during the Joseon dynasty. Continuing Goryeo traditions, early Joseon examples employ Chinese styles and formats, their range of subjects expanding from botanical motifs to include landscapes, figures, and a variety of animals.

Painted in 1447 by An Gyeon (b. 1418), **DREAM JOURNEY TO THE PEACH BLOSSOM LAND (FIG. 24–17)** is the earliest extant and dated Joseon secular painting. It illustrates a fanciful tale by China's revered nature poet Tao Qian (365–427), and recounts a dream about chancing upon a utopia secluded from the world for centuries while meandering among the peach blossoms of spring.

As with their Goryeo forebears, the monumental mountains and vast, panoramic vistas of such fifteenth-century Korean paintings, echo Northern Song painting styles. Chinese paintings of the Southern Song (1127–1279) and Ming periods (1368–1644) also influenced Korean painting of the fifteenth, sixteenth, and seventeenth centuries, though these styles never completely supplanted the imprint of the Northern Song masters.

THE SILHAK MOVEMENT. In the eighteenth century, a truly Korean style emerged, inspired by the *silhak* ("practical learning") movement, which emphasized the study of things Korean in addition to the Chinese classics. The impact of the movement is

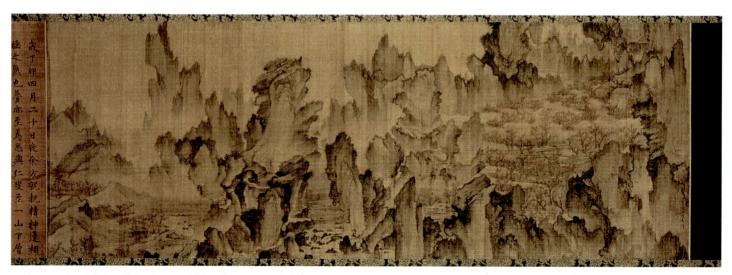

24-17 • An Gyeon DREAM JOURNEY TO THE PEACH BLOSSOM LAND
Korea. Joseon dynasty, 1447. Handscroll, ink and light colors on silk, 15¼ × 41¾″ (38.7 × 106.1 cm). Central Library, Tenri University, Tenri (near Nara), Japan.

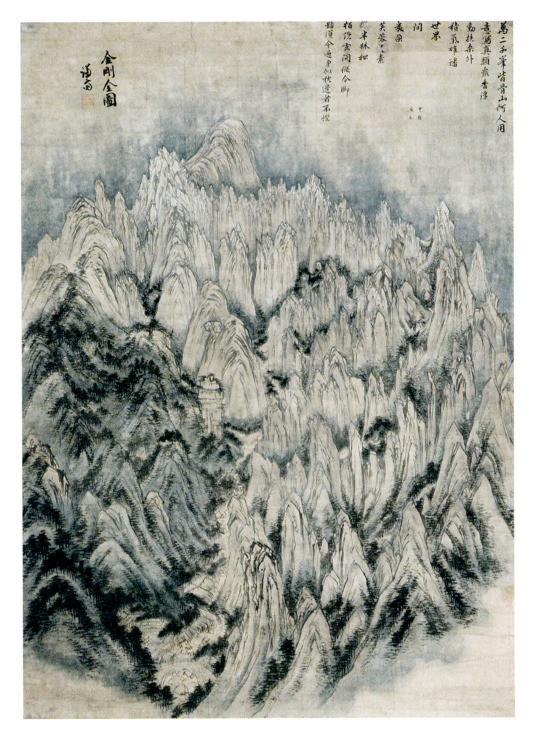

金剛全圖
謙齋

萬二千峯皆骨山何人用
意寫真類衆香浮
勇挟杳外
積氣雄蟠
世界
間
衆圖
炎圖
芙蓉之素
半林松
柏陰玄間継今脚
稿頂今逸爭如枕邊者不惺

甲寅
冬

24–18 • Jeong Seon
**PANORAMIC VIEW OF THE
DIAMOND MOUNTAINS
(GEUMGANG-SAN)**
Korean. Joseon Dynasty, 1734. Hanging
scroll, ink and colors on paper,
40⅝ × 37″ (130.1 × 94 cm). Lee'um,
Samsung Museum, Seoul, Republic
of Korea.

exemplified by the painter Jeong Seon (1676–1759), who chose well-known Korean vistas as the subjects of his paintings, rather than the Chinese themes favored by earlier artists. Among Jeong Seon's paintings are numerous representations of the Diamond Mountains (Geumgang-san), a celebrated range of craggy peaks along Korea's east coast. Painted in 1734, the scroll reproduced in **FIGURE 24–18** aptly captures the Diamond Mountains' needlelike peaks. The subject is Korean, and so is the energetic spirit and the intensely personal style, with its crystalline mountains, distant clouds of delicate ink wash, and individualistic brushwork.

Among figure painters, Sin Yunbok (b. 1758) is an important exemplar of the *silhak* attitude. Active in the late eighteenth and early nineteenth centuries, Sin typically depicted aristocratic figures in native Korean garb. The album leaf entitled **PICNIC AT THE LOTUS POND** (FIG. **24–19**) represents a group of Korean gentlemen enjoying themselves in the countryside on an autumn day in the company of several *gisaeng* (female entertainers). The figures are recognizably Korean—the women with their full coiffures, short jackets, and generous skirts, and the men with their beards, white robes, and wide-brimmed hats woven of horsehair and coated with black lacquer. The stringed instrument played by

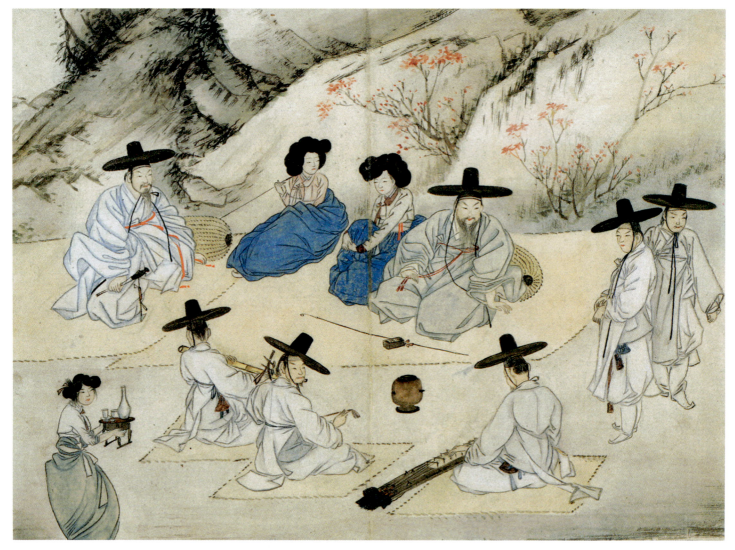

24–19 • Sin Yunbok PICNIC AT THE LOTUS POND
Leaf from an album of genre scenes. Korea. Joseon dynasty, late 18th century. Album of 30 leaves;
ink and colors on paper, 11⅛ × 13⅞″ (28.3 × 35.2 cm). Kansong Museum of Art, Seoul, Republic of Korea.

the gentleman seated at lower right is a *gayageum* (Korean zither), the most hallowed of all Korean musical instruments.

MODERN KOREA

Long known as "the Hermit Kingdom," the Joseon dynasty pursued a policy of isolationism, closing its borders to most of the world, except China, until 1876. Japan's annexation of Korea in 1910 brought the Joseon dynasty to a close, but effectively prolonged the country's seclusion from the outside world. The legacy of self-imposed isolation compounded by colonial occupation (1910–1945)—not to mention the harsh circumstances imposed by World War II (1939–1945), followed by the even worse conditions of the Korean War (1950–1953)—impeded Korea's artistic and cultural development during the first half of the twentieth century.

A MODERNIST PAINTER FROM KOREA.   Despite these privations, some modern influences did reach Korea indirectly via China and Japan, and beginning in the 1920s and 1930s a few Korean artists experimented with contemporary Western styles, typically painting in the manner of Cézanne or Gauguin, but sometimes trying abstract, nonrepresentational styles. Among these, Gim Hwangi (1913–1974) was influenced by Constructivism and geometric abstraction and would become one of twentieth-century Korea's influential painters. Like many Korean artists after the Korean War, Gim wanted to examine Western modernism at its source. He visited Paris in 1956 and then, from 1964 to 1974, lived and worked in New York, where he produced his best-known works. His painting **5-IV-71** presents a large pair of circular radiating patterns composed of small dots and squares in tones of blue, black, and gray **(FIG. 24–20)**. While appearing wholly Western in style, medium, concept, and even title—Gim Hwangi typically adopted the date of a work's creation as its title—*5-IV-71* also seems related to Asia's venerable tradition of monochrome **ink painting**, while suggesting a transcendence that seems Daoist or

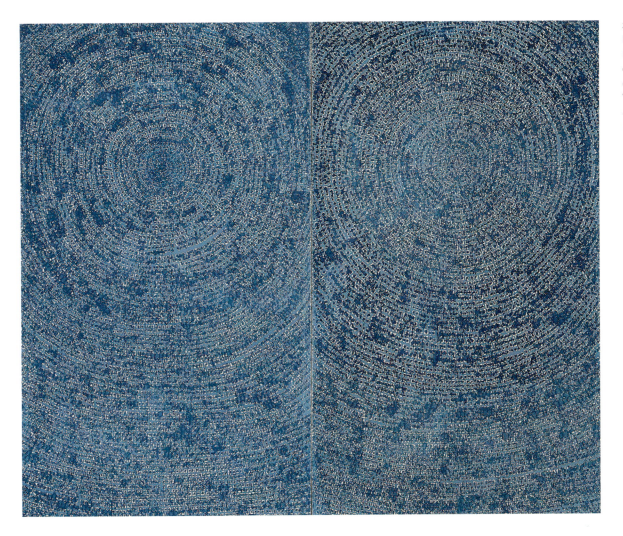

Buddhist in feeling. Given that the artist was Korean, that he learned the Chinese classics in his youth, that he studied art in Paris, and that he then worked in New York, it is possible that his painting embodies all of the above. Gim's painting illustrates the paradox that the modern artist faces while finding a distinctive, personal style: whether to paint in an updated version of a traditional style, in a wholly international style, in an international style with a distinctive local twist, or in an eclectic, hybrid style that incorporates both native and naturalized elements from diverse traditions. By addressing these questions, Gim Hwangi blazed a trail for subsequent Korean-born artists, such as the renowned video artist Nam June Paik (1932–2006), whose work can be seen in FIGURE 32–57.

THINK ABOUT IT

24.1 Explain the role played by one of the following three ways of thought prevalent in Chinese society—Daoism, Confucianism, and Buddhism—and discuss the implications that it had for the visual arts. Make specific reference to works from this chapter.

24.2 Examine a work commissioned by the court at Beijing and distinguish which of its features are typical of court art.

24.3 Discuss the place that calligraphy held within Chinese society and in relation to other arts. Then, explain why Dong Qichang's *The Qingbian Mountains* (SEE FIG. 24–11) has elicited comparison with the art of calligraphy.

24.4 Discuss the culture of the literati, including their values and their system of art patronage, and distinguish the formats of painting that they used.

24.5 Theorize reasons for the emergence of individualist painting in China, using works such as Shitao's *Landscape* (SEE FIG. 24–13) to support your argument.

PRACTICE MORE: Compose answers to these questions, get flashcards for images and terms, and review chapter material with quizzes **www.myartslab.com**

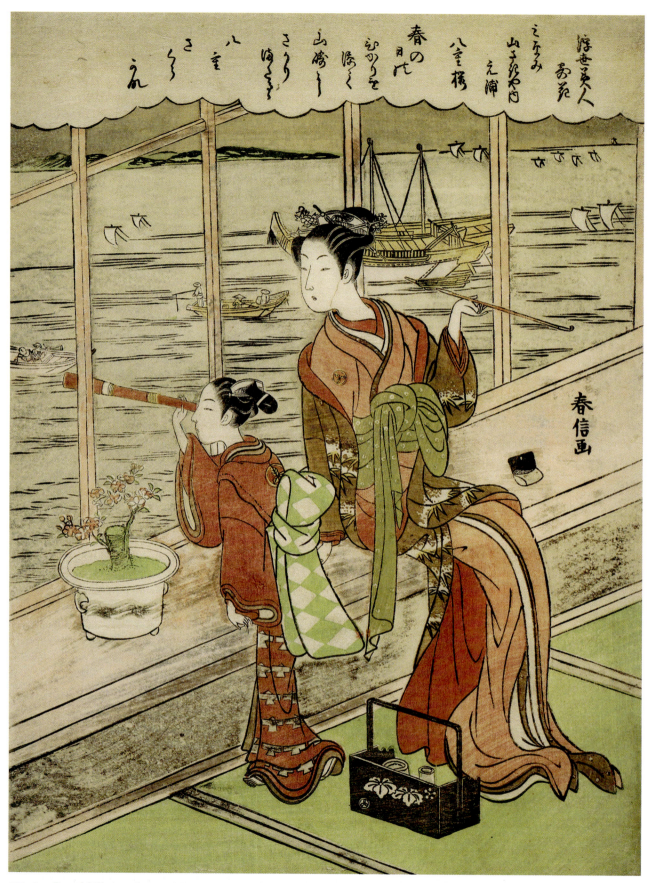

25-1 • Suzuki Harunobu THE FLOWERS OF BEAUTY IN THE FLOATING WORLD:
MOTOURA AND YAEZAKURA OF THE MINAMI YAMASAKIYA   Edo period, 1769.
Polychrome woodblock print on paper, 11⅜ × 8½″ (28.9 × 21.8 cm). Chicago Art Institute.
Clarence Buckingham Collection (1925.2116)

SEE MORE: View videos on *ukiyo-e* techniques **www.myartslab.com**

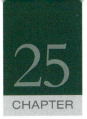

JAPANESE ART
AFTER 1333

Lounging at a window seat, a young woman pauses from smoking her pipe while the young girl at her side peers intently through a telescope at boats in a bay below (FIG. 25–1). The scene takes place in the city of Edo (now Tokyo) in the 1760s, during an era of peace and prosperity that started some 150 years earlier when the Tokugawa shoguns unified the nation. Edo was then the largest city in the world, with over 1 million inhabitants: samurai-bureaucrats and working-class townspeople. The commoners possessed a vibrant culture centered in urban entertainment districts, where geisha and courtesans (licenced prostitutes), such as the lady and her young trainee portrayed in this woodblock print, worked.

In the 1630s, the Tokugawa shogunate banned Japanese citizens from traveling abroad and restricted foreign access to the country. Nagasaki became Japan's sole international port, which only Koreans, Chinese, and Dutch could enter (and they could not travel freely around the country). The government did this to deter Christian missionaries and to assert authority over foreign powers. Not until 1853, when Commodore Matthew Perry of the United States forced Japan to open additional ports, did these policies change. Even so, foreign influences could not be prevented, as the tobacco pipe and telescope in this print testify.

The Japanese had first encountered Westerners—Portuguese traders—in the mid sixteenth century. The Dutch reached Japan by 1600 and brought tobacco and, soon after that, the telescope and other exotic optical devices, including spectacles, microscopes, other curious objects, and books, many illustrated. The Japanese people eagerly welcomed these foreign goods and imitated foreign customs, which conferred an air of sophistication on the user. Looking through the telescopes like the one in this print was a popular amusement of prostitutes and their customers. It also conveyed sexual overtones, because of its phallic shape, and suggests the ribald humor then in vogue. Novel optical devices, all readily available by the mid eighteenth century, offered a new way of seeing, and impacted the appearance of Japanese pictorial art. Yet Chinese influences in the arts still remained strong and spread throughout the population as never before, due to new efforts to educate the broader populace in Chinese studies. In varying degrees, the intermingling of diverse native and foreign artistic traditions has continued to shape the arts of Japan up to the present.

LEARN ABOUT IT

25.1 Evaluate the importance of Zen Buddhism to Japan's visual arts.

25.2 Compare art created in Kyoto to art made in the city of Edo during the Edo period.

25.3 Appraise the role and significance of crafts in Japanese artistic culture.

25.4 Recognize foreign influences on Japanese art in the Muromachi and Edo periods.

25.5 Understand the changing role of patronage in the development of Japanese art.

HEAR MORE: Listen to an audio file of your chapter **www.myartslab.com**

MUROMACHI PERIOD

By the year 1333, Japanese art had already developed a long and rich history (see "Foundations of Japanese Culture," page 817). Very early, a particularly Japanese sensitivity to artistic production had emerged, including a love of natural materials, fondness for representing elements of the natural world, and an overriding attention to fine craftsmanship. Aesthetically, Japanese arts had come to feature a taste for asymmetry, abstraction, brevity or boldness of expression, and humor—characteristics that continue to distinguish Japanese art, appearing and reappearing in ever-changing guises.

Late in the twelfth century, the authority of the emperor had been supplanted by rule by powerful and ambitious warriors (samurai) under the leadership of the shogun, the general-in-chief. But in 1333, Emperor Go-Daigo attempted to retake power. He failed and was forced into hiding in the mountains south of Kyoto where he set up a "southern court." Meanwhile, the shogunal family then in power, the Minamoto, was overthrown by warriors of the Ashikaga clan, who placed a rival to the upstart emperor on the throne in Kyoto, in a "northern court," and had him declare their clan head as shogun. They ruled the country from the Muromachi district in Kyoto, and finally vanquished the southern court emperors in 1392. The Muromachi period, also known as the Ashikaga era (1392–1573), formally began with this event.

The Muromachi period is marked by the ascendance of Zen Buddhism, introduced into Japan in the late twelfth century, whose austere ideals particularly appealed to the highly disciplined samurai. While Pure Land Buddhism, which had spread widely during the latter part of the Heian period (794–1185), remained popular, Zen (which means meditation) became the dominant cultural force in Japan among the ruling elite.

ZEN INK PAINTING

During the Muromachi period, brightly colored narrative handscrolls depicting native themes continued to be produced, but monochrome ink painting in black ink and its diluted grays—which had just been introduced to Japan from the continent at the end of the Kamakura period (1185–1333)—reigned supreme. Muromachi ink painting was heavily influenced by the aesthetics of Zen, but unlike earlier Zen paintings that had concentrated on depictions of important individuals associated with the Zen monastic tradition, many artists also began painting Chinese-style ink landscapes. Traditionally, the monk-artist Shubun (active c. 1418–1463) is regarded as Japan's first great master of the ink landscape. Unfortunately, no works survive that can be proven to be his. Two landscapes by Shubun's pupil Bunsei (active c. 1450–1460) have survived, however. The one shown in **FIGURE 25–2** is closely modeled on Korean ink landscape paintings that themselves copied Chinese Ming period models (such as FIG. 24–5). It contains a foreground consisting of a spit of rocky land with an overlapping series of motifs—a spiky pine tree, a craggy rock, a poet seated in a hermitage, and a brushwood fence

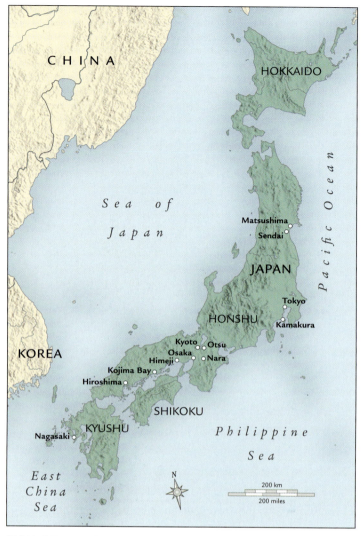

MAP 25-1 • JAPAN

Japan's wholehearted emulation of myriad aspects of Chinese culture began in the fifth century and was challenged by new influences from the West only in the mid nineteenth century after Western powers forced Japan to open its treaty ports to international trade.

surrounding a small garden of trees and bamboo. In the middle ground is space—emptiness, the void. We are expected to "read" the empty paper as representing water. Beyond the blank space, subtle tones of gray ink delineate a distant shore where fishing boats, a small hut, and two people stand. The two parts of the painting seem to echo each other across a vast expanse. The painting illustrates well the pure, lonely, and ultimately serene spirit of the Zen-influenced poetic landscape tradition.

SESSHU. Another of Shubun's pupils, Sesshu (1420–1506), outshone his master, and has come to be regarded as one of the greatest Japanese painters of all time. Although they completed training to become Zen monks, at the monastery, Shubun and his followers specialized in art rather than in religious ritual or teaching, unlike earlier Zen monk-painters for whom art production was just one facet of their lives. By Shubun's day, temples had formed their own

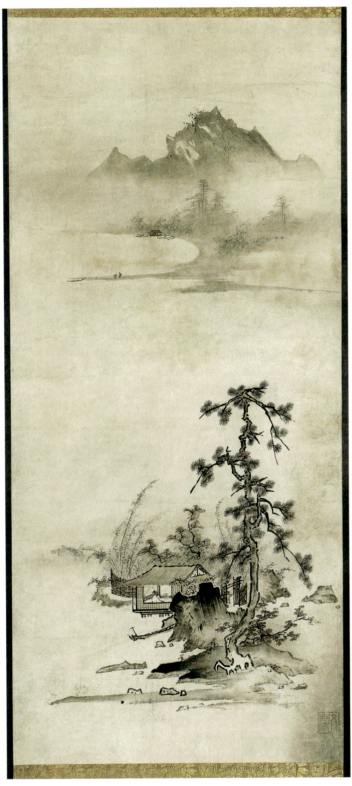

25-2 • Bunsei LANDSCAPE
Muromachi period, mid 15th century. Hanging scroll, ink and light colors on paper, 28¾ × 13″ (73.2 × 33 cm). Museum of Fine Arts, Boston. Special Chinese and Japanese Fund (05.203)

to head a small provincial Zen temple in western Japan, in his quest to concentrate on painting unencumbered by monastic duties and entanglements with the political elite. His new temple was patronized by a private and wealthy warrior clan that was engaged in trade with China. With funding from them, he had the opportunity to visit China in 1467 on a diplomatic mission. He traveled extensively there for three years, viewing the scenery, stopping at Zen (Chan in Chinese) monasteries, and studying Chinese paintings by professional artists rather than those by contemporary literati masters. When he returned from China, he remained in the provinces to avoid the turmoil in Kyoto, which was being devastated by civil warfare that would last for the next hundred years. Only a few paintings from Sesshu's years prior to his sojourn in China have recently come to light. These he painted in a style closer to Shubun and he signed them with another name. His paintings after his return demonstrate he consciously broke artistically with the refined landscape style of his teacher. These masterful paintings by Sesshu exhibit a bold, new spirit, evident in his **WINTER LANDSCAPE** **(FIG. 25–3)**. A cliff descending from the mist seems to cut the composition in two. Sharp, jagged brushstrokes delineate a series of

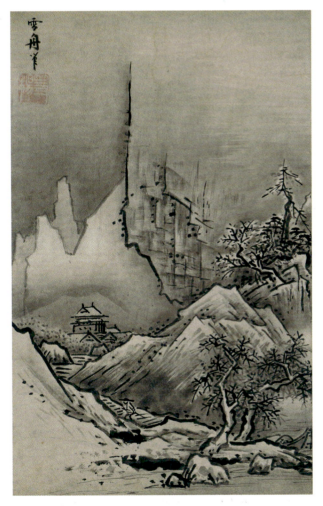

25-3 • Sesshu WINTER LANDSCAPE
Muromachi period, c. 1470s. Hanging scroll, ink on paper, 18¼ × 11½″ (46.3 × 29.3 cm). Collection of the Tokyo National Museum. National Treasure.

professional painting ateliers in order to meet demands for large numbers of paintings from warrior patrons. Sesshu trained as a Zen monk at Shokokuji, where Shubun had his studio. There, he worked in the painting atelier under Shubun for 20 years, but then left Kyoto

rocky hills, where a lone figure makes his way to a Zen monastery. Instead of a gradual recession into space, flat overlapping planes fracture the composition into crystalline facets. The white of the paper is left to indicate snow, while the sky is suggested by tones of gray. A few trees cling desperately to the rocky land, and the harsh chill of winter is boldly expressed.

THE ZEN DRY GARDEN

Zen monks led austere monastic lives in their quest for the attainment of enlightenment. In addition to daily meditation, they engaged in manual labor to provide for themselves and maintain their temple properties. Many Zen temples constructed dry landscape courtyard gardens, not for strolling in but for contemplative viewing. Cleaning and maintaining these gardens—pulling weeds, tweaking unruly shoots, and raking the gravel—was a kind of active meditation. It helped to keep their minds grounded.

The dry landscape gardens of Japan, *karesansui* ("dried-up mountains and water"), exist in perfect harmony with Zen Buddhism. The dry garden in front of the abbot's quarters in the Zen temple at Ryoanji is one of the most renowned Zen creations in Japan **(FIG. 25–4)**. A flat rectangle of raked gravel, about 29 by 70 feet, surrounds 15 stones of different sizes in islands of moss. The stones are set in asymmetrical groups of two, three, and five. Low, plaster-covered walls establish the garden's boundaries, but beyond the perimeter wall maple, pine, and cherry trees add color and texture to the scene. Called "borrowed scenery," these elements are a considered part of the design even though they grow outside the garden. The garden is celebrated for its severity and emptiness.

Dry gardens began to be built in the fifteenth and sixteenth centuries in Japan. By the sixteenth century, Chinese landscape painting influenced the gardens' composition, and miniature clipped plants and beautiful stones were arranged to resemble famous paintings. Especially fine and unusual stones were coveted and even carried off as war booty, such was the cultural value of these seemingly mundane objects.

The Ryoanji garden's design, as we see it today, probably dates from the mid seventeenth century. By the time the garden was created, such stone and gravel gardens had become highly intellectualized, abstract reflections of nature. This garden has been interpreted as representing islands in the sea, or mountain peaks rising above the clouds, perhaps even a swimming tigress with her cubs, or constellations of stars and planets. All or none of these interpretations may be equally satisfying—or irrelevant—to a monk seeking clarity of mind through contemplation.

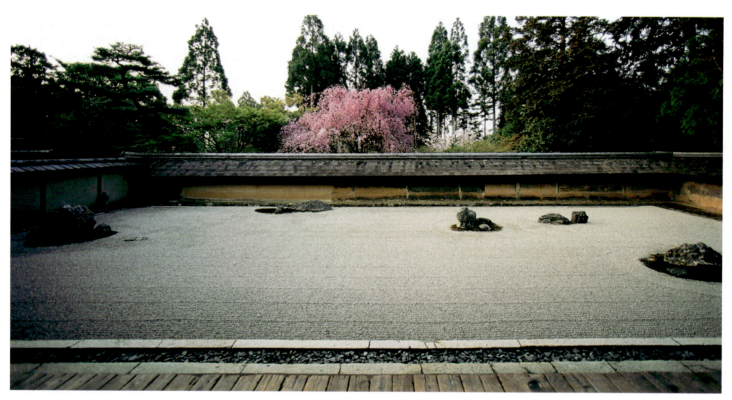

25-4 • ROCK GARDEN, RYOANJI, KYOTO
Muromachi period, c. 1480. Photographed spring 1993. Photograph by Michael S. Yamashita. UNESCO World Heritage Site, National Treasure.

The American composer John Cage once exclaimed that every stone at Ryoanji was in just the right place. He then said, "And every other place would also be just right." His remark is thoroughly Zen in spirit. There are many ways to experience Ryoanji. For example, we can imagine the rocks as having different visual "pulls" that relate them to one another. Yet there is also enough space between them to give each one a sense of self-sufficiency and permanence.

Foundations of Japanese Culture

With the end of the last Ice Age roughly 15,000 years ago, rising sea levels submerged the lowlands connecting Japan to the Asian landmass, creating the chain of islands we know today as Japan (MAP 25–1). Not long afterward, early Paleolithic cultures gave way to a Neolithic culture known as Jomon (c. 11,000–400 BCE) after its characteristic cord-marked pottery. During the Jomon period, a sophisticated hunter-gatherer culture developed. Agriculture supplemented hunting and gathering by around 5000 BCE, and rice cultivation began some 4,000 years later.

A fully settled agricultural society emerged during the Yayoi period (c. 400 BCE–300 CE), accompanied by hierarchical social organization and more centralized forms of government. As people learned to manufacture bronze and iron, use of those metals became widespread. Yayoi architecture, with its unpainted wood and thatched roofs, already showed the Japanese affinity for natural materials and clean lines, and the style of Yayoi granaries in particular persisted in the design of shrines in later centuries. The trend toward centralization continued during the Kofun period (c. 300–552 CE), an era characterized by the construction of large royal tombs, following the Korean practice. Veneration of leaders grew into the beginnings of the imperial system that has lasted to the present day.

The Asuka era (552–645 CE) began with a century of profound change as elements of Chinese civilization flooded into Japan, initially through the intermediary of Korea. The three most significant Chinese contributions to the developing Japanese culture were Buddhism (with its attendant art and architecture), a system of writing, and the structures of a centralized bureaucracy. The earliest extant Buddhist temple compound in Japan, Horyuji, which contains the oldest currently existing wooden buildings in the world, dates from this period.

The arrival of Buddhism also prompted some formalization of Shinto, the loose collection of indigenous Japanese beliefs and practices. Shinto is a religion that connects people to nature. Its rites are shamanistic and emphasize ceremonial purification. These include the invocation and appeasement of spirits, including those of the recently dead. Many Shinto deities are thought to inhabit various aspects of nature, such as particularly magnificent trees, rocks, and waterfalls, and living creatures such as deer. Shinto and Buddhism have in common an intense awareness of the transience of life, and as their goals are complementary—purification in the case of Shinto, enlightenment in the case of Buddhism—they have generally existed comfortably alongside each other to the present day.

The Nara period (645–794) takes its name from Japan's first permanently established imperial capital. During this time the founding works of Japanese literature were compiled and Buddhism became the most important force in Japanese culture. Its influence at court grew so great that in 794 the emperor moved the capital from Nara to Heian-kyo (present-day Kyoto), far from powerful monasteries.

During the Heian period (794–1185) an extremely refined court culture thrived, embodied today in an exquisite legacy of poetry, calligraphy, and painting. An efficient method for writing the Japanese language was developed, and with it a woman at the court wrote Japan's most celebrated fictional story, which some describe as the world's first novel: *The Tale of Genji*. Esoteric Buddhism, as hierarchical and intricate as the aristocratic world of the court, became popular.

The end of the Heian period was marked by civil warfare as regional warrior (samurai) clans were drawn into the factional conflicts at court. Pure Land Buddhism, with its simple message of salvation, offered consolation to many in troubled times. In 1185 the Minamoto clan defeated their arch rivals, the Taira, and their leader, Minamoto Yoritomo, assumed the position of shogun (general-in-chief). While paying respects to the emperor, Minamoto Yoritomo kept actual military and political power to himself, setting up his own capital in Kamakura. The Kamakura era (1185–1333) began a tradition of rule by shogun that lasted in various forms until 1868. It was also the time in which renewed contacts with China created the opportunity for Zen Buddhism, which was then flourishing in China (known there as Chan), to be introduced to Japan. By the end of the Kamakura period, numerous Zen monasteries had been founded in Kyoto and Kamakura, and Chinese and Japanese Chan/Zen monks were regularly visiting each others' countries.

MOMOYAMA PERIOD

The civil wars sweeping Japan laid bare the basic flaw in the Ashikaga system, which was that samurai were primarily loyal to their own feudal lord (*daimyo*), rather than to the central government. Battles between feudal clans grew more frequent, and it became clear that only a warrior powerful and bold enough to unite the entire country could control Japan. As the Muromachi period drew to a close, three leaders emerged who would change the course of Japanese history.

The first of these leaders was Oda Nobunaga (1534–1582), who marched his army into Kyoto in 1568 and overthrew the reigning Ashikaga shogun in 1573, initiating a new age of Japanese politics. A ruthless warrior, Nobunaga went so far as to destroy a Buddhist monastery because the monks refused to join his forces. Yet he was also a patron of the most rarefied and refined arts. Assassinated in the midst of one of his military campaigns, Nobunaga was succeeded by one of his generals, Toyotomi Hideyoshi (1537–1598), who soon gained complete power in Japan. He, too, patronized the arts when not leading his army, and he considered culture a vital adjunct to his rule. Hideyoshi, however, was overly ambitious. He believed that he could conquer both Korea and China, and he wasted much of his resources on two ill-fated invasions. A stable and long-lasting military regime

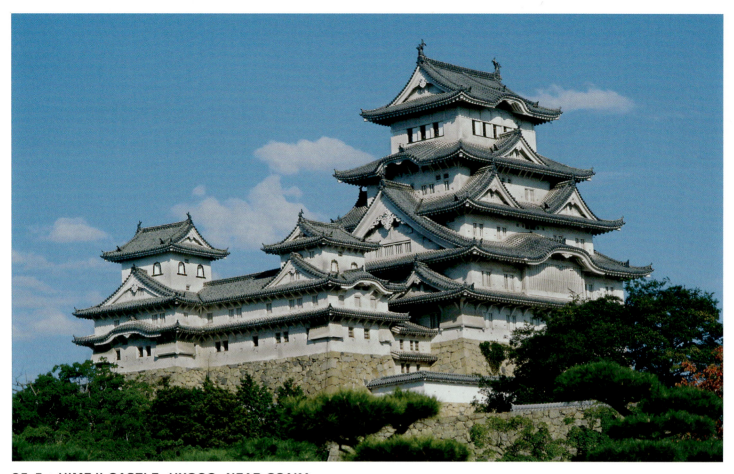

25-5 • HIMEJI CASTLE, HYOGO, NEAR OSAKA
Momoyama period, 1601–1609. Unesco World Heritage Site, National Treasure.

finally emerged soon after 1600 with the triumph of a third leader, Tokugawa Ieyasu (1543–1616), a former ally of Nobunaga who served as a senior retainer to Hideyoshi, and only asserted his power after Hideyoshi's death. But despite its turbulence, the era of Nobunaga and Hideyoshi, known as the Momoyama period (1573–1615), was one of the most creative eras in Japanese history.

Today the very word Momoyama conjures up images of bold warriors, luxurious palaces, screens shimmering with gold leaf, and, in contrast, rustic tea-ceremony ceramics. Europeans first made an impact in Japan at this time. After the arrival of a few wayward Portuguese explorers in 1543, traders and missionaries soon followed. It was only with the rise of Nobunaga, however, that Westerners were able to extend their activities beyond the ports of Kyushu, Japan's southernmost island. Nobunaga welcomed foreign traders, who brought him various products, the most influential of which were firearms.

ARCHITECTURE

European muskets and cannons quickly changed the nature of Japanese warfare and Japanese castle architecture. To protect castles from these new weapons, in the late sixteenth century they became heavily fortified garrisons. Some were eventually lost to warfare or torn down by victorious enemies, and others have been extensively altered over the years. One of the most beautiful of the few that have survived intact is Himeji, not far from the city of Osaka (FIG. 25–5). Rising high on a hill above the plains, Himeji has been given the name White Heron. To reach the upper fortress, visitors must follow angular paths beneath steep walls, climbing from one area to the next past stone ramparts and through narrow fortified gates, all the while feeling as though lost in a maze, with no sense of direction or progress. At the main building, a further climb up a series of narrow ladders leads to the uppermost chamber. There, the footsore visitor is rewarded with a stunning 360-degree view of the surrounding countryside.

DECORATIVE PAINTINGS FOR *SHOIN* ROOMS

Castles such as Himeji were sumptuously decorated, offering artists unprecedented opportunities to work on a grand scale. Interiors were divided into rooms by paper-covered sliding doors (**fusuma**), perfect canvases for large-scale murals. Free-standing folding screens (*byobu*) were also popular. Some had gold-leaf backgrounds, whose glistening surfaces not only conveyed light within the castle rooms but also displayed the wealth of the warrior leaders. Temples, too, commissioned large-scale paintings in these formats for grand reception rooms where the monks met with their wealthy warrior patrons (see "*Shoin* Design," opposite).

The Japanese tea ceremony and *shoin*-style interior residential architecture are undoubtedly the most significant and most enduring expressions of Japanese taste to emerge during the Momoyama period. **Shoin** combine a number of interior features in more-or-less standard ways, though no two rooms are ever the same. These features include wide verandas, walls divided by wood posts, floors covered with woven straw *tatami* mats, recessed panels in ceilings, sometimes painted and sometimes covered with reed matting, several shallow alcoves for prescribed purposes, *fusuma* (paper-covered sliding doors), and **shoji** screens—wood frames covered with translucent rice paper. The *shoin* illustrated here was built in 1601 as a guest hall, called Kojoin, at the Buddhist temple of Onjoji near Kyoto.

The *shoin* is a formal room for receiving important upper-class guests. With some variations due to differences in status, these rooms were designed for buildings used by samurai, aristocrats, and even well-to-do commoners. They are found in various types of buildings including private residences, living quarters at religious complexes (both Shinto shrines and Buddhist temples) and guesthouses or reception rooms at these places for use by high-ranking patrons, and at the finest houses of entertainment (such as seen in fig. 25–1) where geisha and courtesans entertained important guests. The owner of the building or the most important guest would be seated in front of the main alcove (*tokonoma*), which would contain a hanging scroll, an arrangement of flowers, or a large painted screen. Alongside that alcove was another that featured staggered shelves, often for displaying writing instruments. The veranda side of the room also contained a writing space fitted with a low writing desk.

The architectural harmony of a *shoin* is derived from standardization of its basic units, or modules. In Japanese carpentry, the common module of design and construction is the **bay**, reckoned as the distance from the center of one post to the center of another, which is governed in turn by the standard size of **tatami** floor mats. Although varying slightly from region to region, the size of a single *tatami* is about 3 by 6 feet. Room area in Japan is still expressed in terms of the number of *tatami* mats; for example, a room may be described as an eight-mat room.

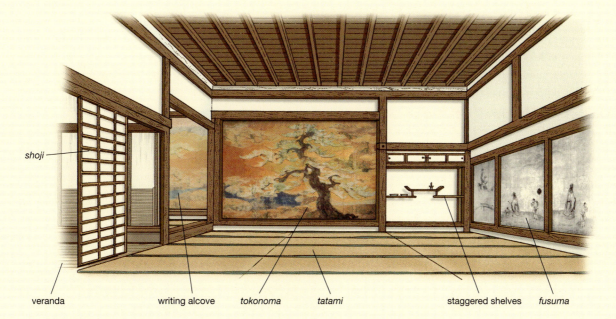

shoji

veranda   writing alcove   *tokonoma*   *tatami*   staggered shelves   *fusuma*

ARTIST'S RENDERING OF THE KOJOIN GUEST HOUSE AT ONJOJI
Otsu, Shiga prefecture. Momoyama period, 1601. National Treasure.

SEE MORE: View a simulation of *Shoin* Design **www.myartslab.com**

Daitokuji, a celebrated Zen monastery in Kyoto, has a number of subtemples for which Momoyama artists painted magnificent *fusuma*. One, the Jukoin, possesses *fusuma* by Kano Eitoku (1543–1590), one of the most brilliant painters from the hereditary lineage of professional artists known as the Kano school. Eitoku headed this school, which was founded by his grandfather. The Kano school painted for the highest ranking warriors from the sixteenth century through 1868. They perfected a new style that combined the Muromachi ink-painting tradition with brightly colored decorative subjects. **FIGURE 25–6** shows two of the three walls of **FUSUMA** panels at Jukoin painted by Eitoku when was in his mid twenties. To the left, the subject is the familiar Kano school theme of cranes and pines, both symbols of long life; to the right is a great gnarled plum tree, symbol of spring. The trees are so massive they seem to extend far beyond the panels. An island rounding both walls of the far corner provides a focus for the outreaching trees. Ingeniously, it

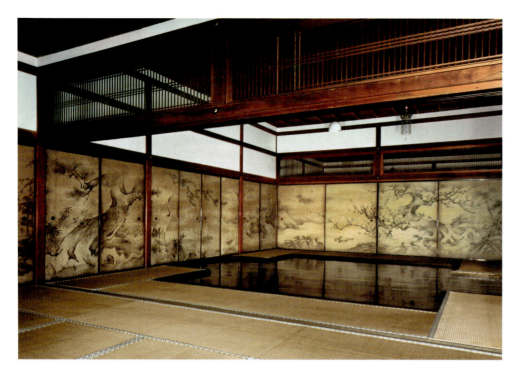

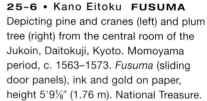

25-6 • Kano Eitoku FUSUMA
Depicting pine and cranes (left) and plum tree (right) from the central room of the Jukoin, Daitokuji, Kyoto. Momoyama period, c. 1563–1573. *Fusuma* (sliding door panels), ink and gold on paper, height 5′9⅛″ (1.76 m). National Treasure.

belongs to both compositions at the same time, thus uniting them into an organic whole. Eitoku's vigorous use of brush and ink, his powerfully jagged outlines, and his dramatic compositions recall the style of Sesshu, but the bold new sense of scale in his works is a defining characteristic of the Momoyama period.

THE TEA CEREMONY

Japanese art is never one-sided. Along with castles and their opulent interior decoration, there was an equal interest during the Momoyama period in the quiet, the restrained, and the natural. This was expressed primarily through the tea ceremony.

The term "tea ceremony," a phrase now in common use, does not convey the full meaning of *chanoyu*, the Japanese ritual drinking of tea, which has no counterpart in Western culture. Tea had been introduced to Japan in the ninth century. Then, it was molded into cakes and boiled. However, the advent of Zen brought to Japan a different way of preparing tea, with the leaves crushed into powder and then whisked in bowls with hot water. Zen monks used such tea as a mild stimulant to aid meditation. Others found it had medicinal properties.

SEN NO RIKYU.   The most famous tea master in Japanese history was Sen no Rikyu (1522–1591). He conceived of the tea ceremony as an intimate gathering in which a few people would enter a small rustic room, drink tea carefully prepared in front of them by their host, and quietly discuss the tea utensils or a Zen scroll hanging on the wall. He largely established the aesthetic of modesty, refinement, and rusticity that permitted the tearoom to serve as a respite from the busy and sometimes violent world outside. A traditional tearoom combines simple elegance and rusticity. It is made of natural materials such as bamboo and wood,

with mud walls, paper windows, and a floor covered with *tatami*. One tearoom that preserves Rikyu's design is named Taian **(FIG. 25–7)**. Built in 1582, it has a tiny door (guests must crawl to enter)

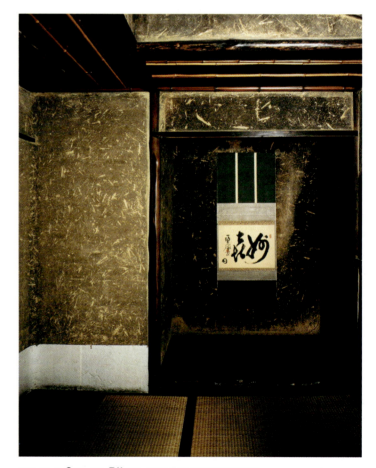

25-7 • Sen no Rikyu TAIAN TEAROOM
Myokian Temple, Kyoto. Momoyama period, 1582. National Treasure.

and miniature *tokonoma* for displaying a Zen scroll or a simple flower arrangement. At first glance, the room seems symmetrical. But a longer look reveals the disposition of the *tatami* does not match the spacing of the *tokonoma*, providing a subtle undercurrent of irregularity. The walls seem scratched and worn with age, but the *tatami* are replaced frequently to keep them clean and fresh. The mood is quiet; the light is muted and diffused through three small paper windows. Above all, there is a sense of spatial clarity. Nonessentials have been eliminated, so there is nothing to distract from focused attention. This tearoom aesthetic became an important element in Japanese culture.

THE TEA BOWL.   Every utensil connected with tea, including the water pot, the kettle, the bamboo spoon, the whisk, the tea caddy, and, above all, the tea bowl, came to be appreciated for its aesthetic quality, and many works of art were created for use in *chanoyu*.

The age-old Japanese admiration for the natural and the asymmetrical found full expression in tea ceramics. Korean-style rice bowls made for peasants were suddenly considered the epitome of refined taste, and tea masters urged potters to mimic their imperfect shapes. But not every misshapen bowl would be admired. A rarified appreciation of beauty developed that took into consideration such factors as how well a tea bowl fitted into the hands, how subtly the shape and texture of the bowl appealed to the eye, and who had previously used and admired it. For this purpose, the inscribed storage box became almost as important as the ceramic that fitted within it, and if a bowl had been given a name by a leading tea master, it was especially treasured by later generations.

One of the finest tea bowls extant is named Mount Fuji after Japan's most sacred peak **(FIG. 25–8)**. (Mount Fuji is depicted in FIGURE 25–12.) An example of **raku** ware—a hand-built, low-fired ceramic developed for use in the tea ceremony—the bowl was crafted by Hon'ami Koetsu (1558–1637), a leading cultural figure of his day. Koetsu was most famous as a calligrapher, but he was also a painter, poet, lacquer designer, sword connoisseur, and potter. With its small foot, straight sides, irregular shape, and crackled texture, this bowl exemplifies tea taste.

EDO PERIOD

When Tokugawa Ieyasu gained control of Japan, he forced the emperor to proclaim him shogun, a title neither Nobunaga nor Hideyoshi had held. His reign initiated the Edo period (1615–1868), named after the city that he founded (present-day Tokyo) as his capital. This period is alternatively known as the Tokugawa era. Under the rule of the Tokugawa family, peace and prosperity came at the price of a rigid and repressive bureaucracy. The problem of a potentially rebellious *daimyo* was solved by ordering all feudal lords to spend either half of each year, or every other year, in Edo, where their families were required to live. Zen Buddhism was supplanted as the prevailing intellectual force by a

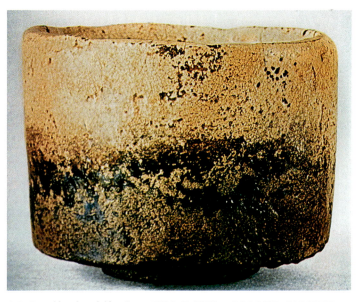

25-8 • Hon'ami Koetsu TEA BOWL, CALLED MOUNT FUJI
Momoyama-Edo period, early 17th century. *Raku* ware, height 3⅜″ (8.5 cm). Sakai Collection, Tokyo. National Treasure.

Connoisseurs developed a subtle vocabulary to discuss the aesthetics of tea. A favorite term was *sabi* ("loneliness"), which refers to the tranquility found when feeling alone. Other virtues were *wabi* ("poverty"), which suggests the artlessness of humble simplicity, and *shibui* ("bitter" or "astringent"), meaning elegant restraint. Tea bowls, such as this example, embody these aesthetics.

form of Neo-Confucianism, a philosophy formulated in Song-dynasty China that emphasized loyalty to the state, although the popularity of Buddhism among the commoner population surged at this time.

The shogunate officially divided Edo society into four classes. Samurai officials constituted the highest class, followed by farmers, artisans, and finally merchants. As time went on, however, merchants began to control the money supply, and in Japan's increasingly mercantile economy their accumulation of wealth soon exceeded that of the samurai, which helped, unofficially, to elevate their status. Reading and writing became widespread at all levels of society, and with literacy came intellectual curiosity and interest in the arts. All segments of the population—including samurai, merchants, townspeople, and rural peasants—were able to patronize artists. A rich cultural atmosphere developed unlike anything Japan had experienced before, in which artists worked in a wide variety of styles that appealed to these different groups of consumers.

RINPA SCHOOL PAINTING

During the Edo period, Edo was the shogun's city while life in Kyoto took its cues from the emperor and his court who resided there. Kyoto was also home to wealthy merchants, artists, and craftsmakers who served the needs of the courtiers and shared their interest in refined pursuits, such as the tea ceremony, and also their appreciation of art styles that recalled those perfected by aristocratic

The production of woodblock prints combined the expertise of three people: the artist, the carver, and the printer. Coordinating and funding the endeavor was a publisher, who commissioned the project and distributed the prints to stores or itinerant peddlers, who would sell them.

The artist supplied the master drawing for the print, executing its outlines with brush and ink on tissue paper. Colors might be indicated, but more often they were understood or decided on later. The drawing was passed on to the carver, who pasted it face down on a hardwood block, preferably cherrywood, so that the outlines showed through the paper in reverse. A light coating of oil might be brushed on to make the paper more transparent, allowing the drawing to stand out clearly. The carver then cut around the lines of the drawing with a sharp knife, always working in the same direction as the original brushstrokes. The rest of the block was chiseled away, leaving the outlines in relief. This block, which reproduced the master drawing, was called the **key block**. If the print was to be **polychrome**, having multiple colors, prints made from the key block were in turn pasted face down on blocks that would be used as guides for the carver of the color blocks. Each color generally required a separate block, although both sides of a block might be used for economy.

Once the blocks were completed, the printer took over. Paper for printing was covered lightly with animal glue (gelatin). Before printing, the paper was lightly moistened so that it would take ink and color well. Water-based ink or color was brushed over the block, and the paper placed on top and rubbed with a smooth, padded device called a *baren*, until the design was completely transferred. The key block was printed first, then the colors one by one. Each block was carved with two small marks called **registration marks**, in exactly the same place in the margins, outside of the image area—an L in one corner, and a straight line in another. By aligning the paper with these marks before letting it fall over the block, the printer ensured that the colors would be placed correctly within the outlines. One of the most characteristic effects of later Japanese prints is a grading of color from dark to pale. This was achieved by wiping some of the color from the block before printing, or by moistening the block and then applying the color gradually with an unevenly loaded brush—a brush loaded on one side with full-strength color and on the other with diluted color.

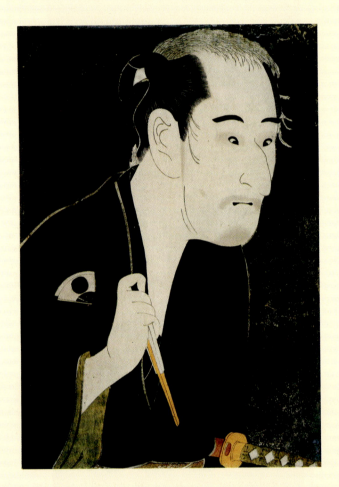

Toshusai Sharaku ONOE MATSUSUKE AS MATSUSHITA MIKINOSHIN

Edo period, 1794–95. Polychrome woodblock print, ink and colors on mica ground paper, 14³⁄₁₆ × 9¹¹⁄₁₆″ (36.1 × 24.6 cm). British Museum, London. (1909,0618,0.42)

Much as people today buy posters of their favorite sports, music, or movie stars, so, too, in the Edo period people clamored for images of their idols, actors of the popular form of drama known as Kabuki. The artist of this print was renowned for capturing the personality of his subjects. The actor has his eyes crossed, in what was a frozen, tension-filled moment in an action-packed play. The print has a shiny mica background, made of crushed shells, painstakingly applied by printers.

SEE MORE: View a video about the printmaking process of woodcut www.myartslab.com

models, Japanese aesthetics, and personal brushwork. The gentle rounded forms of the mountains intentionally recall the work of famous Chinese literati painters, and Taiga utilizes a stock landscape composition that separates foreground and background mountains with a watery expanse (SEE FIG. 25–2). However, he did not paint an imaginary Chinese scene but a personal vision of an actual Japanese place that he had visited—Kojima Bay—as a document accompanying the painting explains. Still, in deference to his admiration for Chinese literati, Taiga places two figures clad in Chinese robes on the right, midway up the mountain.

UKIYO-E: PICTURES OF THE FLOATING WORLD

Edo served as the shogun's capital as well as the center of a flourishing popular culture associated with tradespeople. Deeply Buddhist, commoners were acutely aware of the transience of life, symbolized, for example, by the cherry tree which blossoms so briefly. Putting a positive spin on this harsh realization, they sought to live by the mantra: Let's enjoy it to the full as long as it lasts. This they did to excess in the restaurants, theaters, bathhouses, and brothels of the city's pleasure quarters, named after the Buddhist phrase *ukiyo* ("floating world"). Every major city in Japan had these

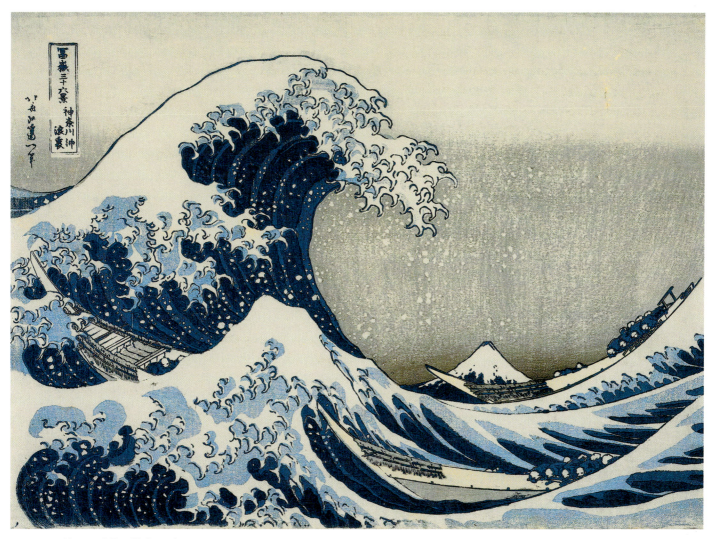

25-12 • Katsushika Hokusai THE GREAT WAVE
From *Thirty-Six Views of Mt. Fuji*. Edo period, c. 1831. Polychrome woodblock print on paper, 9⅞ × 14⅝"
(25 × 37.1 cm). Honolulu Academy of Arts, Honolulu, Hawaii. James A. Michener Collection (HAA 13, 695)

EXPLORE MORE: Gain insight from a primary source related to *The Great Wave* **www.myartslab.com**

quarters, and most were licensed by the government. But those of Edo were the largest and most famous. The heroes of the floating world were not famous samurai or aristocratic poets. Instead, swashbuckling Kabuki actors and beautiful courtesans were admired. These paragons of pleasure soon became immortalized in paintings and—because paintings were too expensive for common people—in woodblock prints known as *ukiyo-e* ("pictures of the floating world"; see "Japanese Woodblock Prints," opposite). Most prints were inexpensively produced by the hundreds and not considered serious fine art. Yet when first imported to Europe and America, they were immediately acclaimed and strongly influenced late nineteenth- and early twentieth-century Western art (see Chapter 30).

HARUNOBU. The first woodblock prints had no color, only black outlines. Soon artists added colors by hand to make them more resemble paintings. But to produce colored prints more rapidly they gradually devised a system to print colors using multiple blocks. The first artist to design prints that took advantage of this new technique,

known as **nishiki-e** ("brocade pictures"), was Suzuki Harunobu (1724–1770), famous for his images of courtesans (SEE FIG. 25–1).

HOKUSAI. During the first half of the nineteenth century, the heyday of popular travel, pictures of famous sights of Japan grew immensely popular. The two most famous *ukiyo-e* printmakers, Utagawa Hiroshige (1797–1858) and Katsushika Hokusai (1760–1849), specialized in this genre. Hiroshige's *Fifty-Three Stations of the Tokaido* and Hokusai's *Thirty-Six Views of Mt. Fuji* became the most successful sets of graphic art the world has known. The woodblocks were printed, and printed again, until they wore out. They were then recarved, and still more copies were printed. This process continued for decades, and thousands of prints from the two series are still extant.

THE GREAT WAVE (FIG. 25–12) is the most famous of the scenes from *Thirty-Six Views of Mt. Fuji*. The great wave rears up like a dragon with claws of foam, ready to crash down on the figures huddled in the boats below. Exactly at the point of imminent disaster, but far in the distance, rises Japan's most sacred peak, Mount Fuji, whose slopes, we suddenly realize, swing up like waves and whose snowy crown is like foam—comparisons the artist makes clear in the wave nearest us, caught just at the moment of greatest resemblance. In the late nineteenth century when Japonisme, or *japonism*, became the vogue in the West, Hokusai's art was greatly appreciated, even more so than it had been in Japan: The first book on the artist was published in France.

ZEN PAINTING: BUDDHIST ART FOR RURAL COMMONERS

Outside Japan's urban centers, art for commoners also flourished, much of it tied to their devotion to Buddhism. Deprived of the support of the samurai officials who now favored Confucianism, Buddhism nevertheless thrived during the Edo period through patronage from private individuals, many of them rural peasants. In the early eighteenth century, one of the great monks who preached in the countryside was the Zen master Hakuin Ekaku (1685–1769), born in a small village near Mount Fuji. After hearing a fire-and-brimstone sermon in his youth he resolved to become a monk and for years he traveled around Japan seeking out the strictest Zen teachers. He became the most important Zen master of the last 500 years, and invented many *koan* (questions posed to novices by Zen masters to guide their progression towards enlightenment during meditation), including the famous "What is the sound of one hand clapping?" He was also, in his later years, a self-taught painter and calligrapher, who freely gave away his scrolls to admirers (who included not only farmers but also artisans, merchants, and even samurai) as a way of spreading his religious message.

Hakuin's art differed from that of Muromachi period monk-painters like Bunsei and Sesshu (SEE FIGS. 25–2, 25–3). His work featured everyday Japanese subjects or Zen themes that conveyed his ideas in ways his humble followers could easily understand. He often painted Daruma (Bodhidharma in Sanskrit) (FIG. 25–13), the semilegendary Indian monk who founded Zen (see Chapter 11). Hundreds of Zen monks of the Edo period and later created simply brushed Zen ink paintings. Hakuin largely set the standards that subsequent Zen artists followed.

CRAFTS

The ingenuity and technical proficiency that contributed to the development of *ukiyo*-prints came about because of Japan's long history of fine crafts production. Textiles, ceramics, lacquer, woodwork, and metalwork were among the many crafts in which Japanese artisans excelled. In pre-modern Japan, unlike the West, no separate words distinguished fine arts (painting and sculpture) from crafts. (The Japanese word for fine art and corresponding modern Japanese language words for various types of craft were not coined until 1872.) This was largely because professional Japanese artist and crafts studios basically followed the same hereditary, hierarchical structure. A master artist directed all activity in a workshop of trainees, who gradually gained seniority through years of apprenticeship and innate talent. Sometimes, such as when a pupil was not chosen to succeed the master, he would go off and start his own studio. This teamwork approach to artistic production is characteristic of the way most traditional Japanese arts were created.

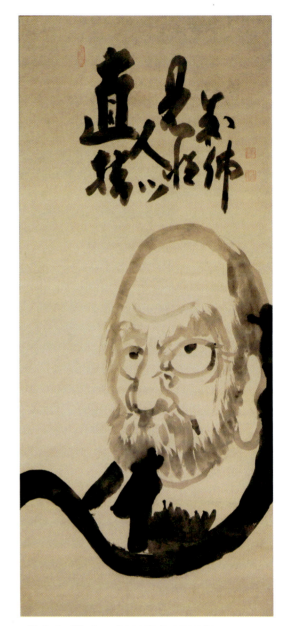

25-13 • Hakuin Ekaku GIANT DARUMA
Edo period, mid 18th century. Hanging scroll, ink on paper 4'3½" × 1'9¾" (130.8 × 55.2 cm). Manyo'an Collection, New Orleans 1973.2

As a self-taught amateur painter, Hakuin's painting style is the very antithesis of that of consummate professionals, such as painters of the Kano or Rinpa schools. The appeal of his art lies in its artless charm, humor, and astonishing force. Here Hakuin has portrayed the wide-eyed Daruma during his nine years of meditation in front of a temple wall in China. Intensity, concentration, and spiritual depth are conveyed by a minimal number of broad, forceful brushstrokes. The inscription is the ultimate Zen message, attributed to Daruma himself: "Pointing directly to the human heart, see your own nature and become Buddha."

A CLOSER LOOK

Kosode Robe ▸ With design of waves and floral bouquets. Edo period, second half of 18th century to early 19th century. White figured satin ground with silk and metallic thread embroidery, stencil tie-dyeing, brush painting; indigo blue dyed silk lining, height 64¾″ (163 cm), width 24½″ (61.5 cm) below sleeve, 50″ (127 cm) sleeve top. The Nelson-Atkins Museum of Art, Kansas City, Missouri. Gift of Mrs. Harold J. Owens (57-45)

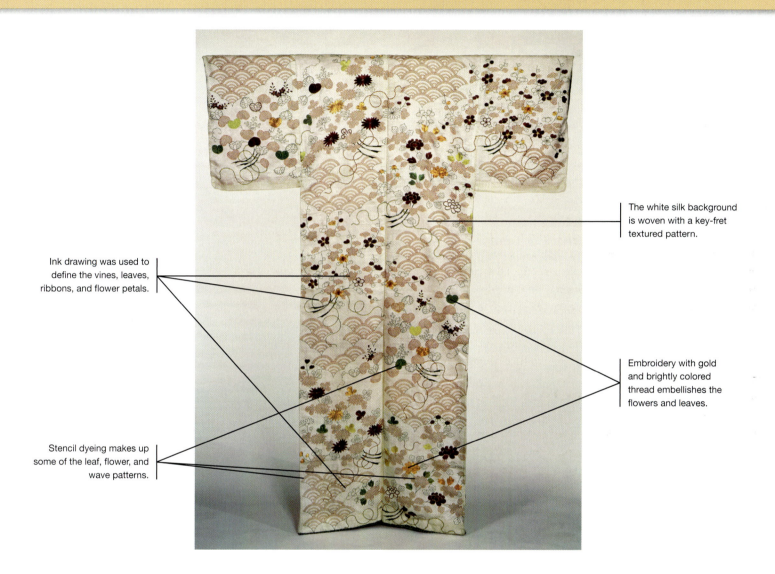

The white silk background is woven with a key-fret textured pattern.

Ink drawing was used to define the vines, leaves, ribbons, and flower petals.

Embroidery with gold and brightly colored thread embellishes the flowers and leaves.

Stencil dyeing makes up some of the leaf, flower, and wave patterns.

SEE MORE: View the Closer Look feature for *Kosode* Robe **www.myartslab.com**

KOSODE ROBES. The kimono is as much a symbol of Japanese culture as is the tea ceremony. Before the late nineteenth century, it was known as *kosode*. These loose, unstructured garments that wrap around the body and are cinched with a sash were the principal outer article of clothing of both men and women, beginning in the Muromachi period. *Kosode* ("small sleeves") refers to the vertical length of the sleeves (in contrast, young, unmarried women wore robes with long, flowing sleeves). Because of their fragility, few *kosode* prior to the Edo period

survive. But those from the eighteenth century reveal the opulent tastes of affluent merchant-class women of the day (see "A Closer Look," page 830). In the example shown, ribbons and flower bouquets float above abstract waves and scalloped-edged clouds in a playful, asymmetrical composition. Artisans used many techniques to create the rich interplay of textures and designs on this gorgeous robe, made in the country's premier textile center of Kyoto. Its design elements resemble those found in paintings of the period.

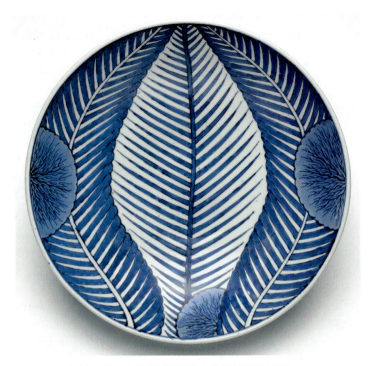

25-14 • LARGE PLATE WITH LEAF DESIGN
Edo period, early 18th century. Arita ware, *Ko*-Imari type. Porcelain with underglaze blue decoration, diameter 15⅜″ (39.1 cm). Nelson-Atkins Museum of Art, Kansas City. Purchase: Nelson Trust (63-4)

JAPANESE PORCELAIN. While the history of ceramic production dates to the earliest days of Japanese civilization, production of glazed, high-fired stoneware ceramics proliferated in Japan only from the sixteenth century, encouraged largely by the tea ceremony. The industry thrived in southern Japan, where, around 1600, influxes of more highly skilled Korean potters helped native artisans to learn new continental technologies that allowed them to manufacture porcelain for the first time. One town, Arita, became the center for the production of porcelain, created for export to the West and for domestic use. While tea ceremony aesthetics still favored rustic wares such as Koetsu's tea bowl (SEE FIG. 25–8), porcelain was more widely adopted for everyday use in response to a growing fashion for Chinese arts. Porcelains made in Arita are known by various names according to their dating and decorative schemes. Those ornamented exclusively with underglaze cobalt blue, the first porcelains made in Japan, are generally known as Imari, the name for the port city from which some of them were exported to Europe. However, the piece shown in **FIGURE 25–14** must have been made for domestic use, as the audaciously abstracted design would not have appealed to Europeans, who preferred more recognizable natural forms. Complementing the strong, vertical stylized leaves are small, half-round forms resembling chestnuts.

THE MODERN PERIOD

The tensions that resulted from Commodore Matthew Perry's forced opening of trade ports in Japan in 1853 precipitated the downfall of the Tokugawa shogunate. In 1868 the emperor was formally restored to power, an event known as the Meiji Restoration. The court soon moved from Kyoto to Edo, which was renamed Tokyo ("Eastern Capital"). After a period of intense industrialization in the first two decades after the Meiji Restoration, influential private individuals and government officials, sometimes working cooperatively, created new arts institutions including juried exhibitions, artists' associations, arts universities, and cultural heritage laws. These rekindled appreciation for the art of the past, encouraged

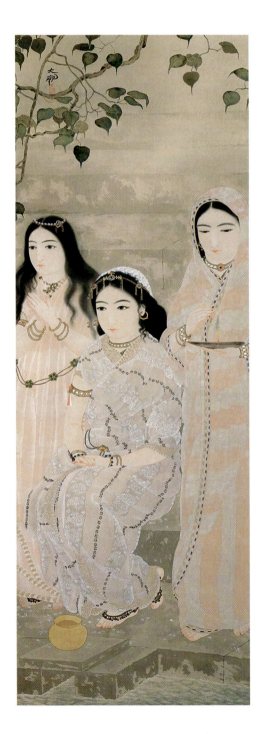

25-15 • Yokoyama Taikan FLOATING LIGHTS
Meiji period, 1909. One of a pair of hanging scrolls, ink, colors, and gold on silk, 56½ × 20½″ (143 × 52 cm). The Museum of Modern Art, Ibaraki.

perpetuation of artistic techniques threatened by adoption of Western ways, and stimulated new artistic production. Many of these arts institutions still exist today.

MEIJI-PERIOD NATIONALIST PAINTING

The Meiji period (1868–1912) marked a major change for Japan. Japanese society adapted various aspects of Western education, governmental systems, clothing, medicine, industrialization, and technology in efforts to modernize the nation. Teachers of sculpture and oil painting came from Italy, while adventurous Japanese artists traveled to Europe and America to study.

A MEIJI PAINTER. Ernest Fenollosa (1853–1908), an American who had recently graduated from Harvard, traveled to Japan in 1878 to teach philosophy and political economy at Tokyo University. Within a few years, he and a former student, Okakura Kakuzo (1862–1913), began urging artists to study traditional Japanese arts rather than to focus exclusively on Western art styles and media, but infuse them with a modern sensibility. Yokoyama Taikan (1868–1958) subsequently developed his personal style within the Nihonga (modern Japanese painting) genre promoted by Okakura. Encouraged by Okakura, who had gone there before him, Taikan visited India in 1903. He embraced Okakura's ideals of pan-Asian cultural nationalism, expressed in the first line of Okakura's book, *Ideals of the East* (1903), with the words "Asia is One." This outlook later contributed to fueling Japan's imperialist ambitions. Taikan's **FLOATING LIGHTS (FIG. 25–15)** was inspired by a visit to Calcutta, where he observed women engaged in divination on the banks of the Ganges. The naturalism of their semitransparent robes and the flowing water reveal his indebtedness to Western art. In contrast, the lightly applied colors, and graceful branches with delicate, mottled brushwork defining the leaves, recall techniques of Rinpa-school artists.

JAPAN AFTER WORLD WAR II

In the aftermath of World War II (1941–1945), Japan was a shambles, her great cities ruined. Nevertheless, under the U.S.-led Allied Occupation (1946–1952), the Japanese people immediately began rebuilding, unified by a sense of national purpose. Within ten years, Japan established nascent automobile, electronics, and consumer goods industries. Rail travel, begun in 1872, expanded and improved significantly after the war and by the time of the Tokyo Olympics in 1964 the capital had an extensive commuter rail system, and Japan was the world leader in city-to-city high-speed rail transit with its new Shinkansen (bullet train). As the rest of the world came to know Japan, foreign interest in its arts focused especially on the country's still thriving crafts traditions. Not only were these a source of national pride and identity, the skills and attitudes they fostered also served as the basis for Japan's national revival.

POSTWAR ARCHITECTURE. The Hiroshima Peace Memorial Museum and Park (FIG. 25–16) was one of the first monuments constructed after World War II. A memorial to those who perished on August 6, 1945, and an expression of prayers for world peace, it attests to the spirit of the Japanese people at this difficult juncture in history. Tange Kenzo (1913–2005), who would eventually become one of the masters of Modernist architecture, designed the complex after winning an open competition as a young, up-and-coming architect.

The building's design befits the solemnity of its function. Concrete piers raise its stripped concrete form 20 feet off the ground. The wood formwork of the concrete recalls the wooden forms of traditional Japanese architecture. But the use of concrete is also inspired by Le Corbusier's 1920s Modernist villas. Evenly spaced vertical concrete fins lining the façade afford light shade. They suggest both the regular spacing of elements present in modular *shoin* architecture (see "*Shoin* Design," page 819) and the values of Modernist architects who advocated that structure should

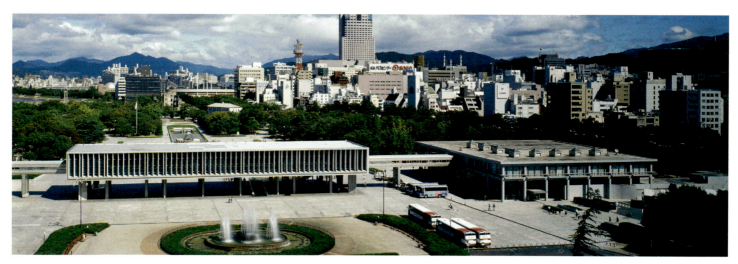

25-16 • Tange Kenzo HIROSHIMA PEACE MEMORIAL MUSEUM
Showa period, 1955. Main building (center) repaired in Heisei period, 1991. East building (right), the former Peace Memorial Hall, which first opened in 1955, was rebuilt in June 1994 and attached to the main building. Designated UNESCO World Heritage site in 1996.

This exquisite wooden box was crafted by Eri Sayoko (1945–2007). In 2002, the government designated her a Living National Treasure for her accomplishment in the art of cut-gold leaf (*kirikane*), traditionally used to decorate Buddhist sculpture and paintings (as in FIG. 11–15). The National Treasure designation originated in Japanese laws of 1897 that were intended to safeguard the nation's artistic heritage at a time when art was being bought by Western collectors but suffering neglect at home. In 1955 the government added provisions to honor living individuals who excel in traditional craft techniques with the title Living National Treasure. This historic preservation system is the most complex of its type in the world.

Eri was the third person awarded the title for cut-gold-leaf decoration and the first woman. In its encouragement of traditional crafts, the Living National Treasure system has greatly assisted women in gaining much-deserved recognition. In pre-modern Japan (encompassing the prehistoric era up to the start of the Meiji period in 1868), women mostly operated in the private sphere of the home where they created crafts for their own enjoyment or for devotional purposes. By the eighteenth century, this situation had begun to change, so that women could be poets, calligraphers, and painters; the wives or daughters of famous male artists gained the most recognition. Among the most famous was Gyokuran, wife of the literati painter Ike Taiga (SEE FIG. 25–11). However, the conservative nature of traditional Japanese crafts workshops meant women could not hold leadership positions in them, and until the postwar period they were seldom recognized for their achievements in crafts. Eri Sayoko flourished in the new climate, as one of the first women to work in the medium of cut-gold, which she took up via an unorthodox route.

Eri specialized in Japanese painting in high school and in design-dyeing in junior college. After marriage to a traditional Buddhist sculptor she started producing Buddhist paintings and began an apprenticeship with a master *kirikane* craftsman. She was so talented that after only three years she was able to exhibit her work professionally. Her art is informed by her deep study of the history of the technique, and her marvelous sensitivity for color betrays her training in dyeing. Eri's elegant, functional objects, typified by this box, are infused with modern sensibilities, although her designs have a basis in traditional *kirikane* patterns. Her art reveals that adherence to a craft tradition can still result in artistic originality.

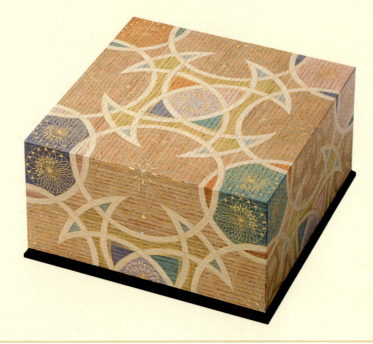

Eri Sayoko ORNAMENTAL BOX: DANCING IN THE COSMOS
Heisei period, 2006. Wood with polychrome and cut gold, height 33⅞" (86 cm), width 6½" (16.5 cm), depth 6½" (16.5 cm). Collection of Eri Kokei

dictate form. In this commission Tange infuses Modernist tendencies and materials with a Japanese sense of interval and refinement, characteristics also seen in the work of most younger contemporary Japanese architects active today.

POSTWAR CRAFTS. Throughout their history, the Japanese have displayed a heightened sensitivity toward the surface quality of things, for polish, for line, for exquisiteness and stylishness. Their appreciation of craft has continued to the present (see "Craftsmakers as Living National Treasures," above). Some crafts are made for use in the tea ceremony, which remains popular today. Others are produced as functional objects for use in the home, as high-fashion apparel, or simply as decoration. Many combine diverse influences, native and foreign, that the maker integrates uniquely, often using novel techniques invented to achieve the desired results. In this way, the traditions of fine crafts in Japan, among the signature achievements of Japanese culture, continue to be enriched.

A MODERN CERAMICIST. Perhaps because the arts of tea ceremony and flower arrangement both require ceramic vessels,

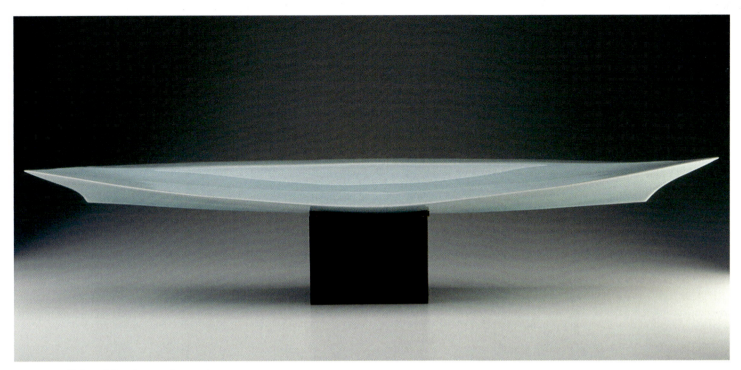

25–17 • Fukami Sueharu SKY II
Heisei period, c. 1990. Celadon-glazed porcelain with wood base 3 × 44⅛ × 9½″ (7.7 × 112.1 × 24.2 cm).
Helen Foresman Spencer Museum of Art, University of Kansas, Lawrence, Kansas.
Museum purchase: R. Charles and Mary Margaret Clevenger Fund (1992.0072)

the Japanese have a particular love for pottery. While some ceramicists continue to create *raku* tea bowls and other traditional wares, others experiment with new styles and innovative techniques.

Fukami Sueharu (b. 1947) is among the most innovative clay artists in Japan today. Yet his art has roots in the past—in his case, in Chinese porcelains with pale bluish-green glazes (*seihakuji*). Even so, his forms and fabrication methods, typified by his **SKY II**, are ultramodern (**FIG. 25–17**). He created the piece using a slip casting technique, in which he injected liquid clay into a mold using a high-pressure compressor. Although he sometimes makes functional pieces, mainly cylinders that could hold flower arrangements, *Sky II* shows his mastery of pure form. The title suggests sources of his abstract sculptural form: a wing or a blade of an aircraft slicing through the heavens. The pale blue sky-colored glaze enhances this allusion.

A plurality of artistic styles and media reflects Japan's long history and idiosyncratic worldview. While maintaining a strong sense of national identity, it has been able to absorb techniques and ideas from other lands, improve them, polish and refine them, and paradoxically make them its own. Deeply influenced by the Shinto and Buddhist religions, benefiting from a rich topography and mild climate, with citizens' lives revolving around a complex and hierarchical social structure, and reflecting a well-educated population curious about the rest of the world yet self-consciously different from it, the arts of Japan share common aesthetic principles that make them distinctively Japanese.

THINK ABOUT IT

25.1 Discuss the unique characteristics of Japanese Zen gardens, and explain how the rock garden at Ryoanji embodies the ideals of Zen Buddhism.

25.2 Explain how differences between pictorial styles of artists from the cities of Kyoto and Edo reflect the variations in the social status, and cultural and intellectual interests of the residents. Build your discussion upon a comparison of a painting or lacquer box by a Rinpa-school artist from Kyoto with a woodblock print that was made in Edo.

25.3 Discuss how the Japanese tea ceremony works and observe the role that craft arts play within it. Explore the unique aesthetics of the tearoom and craft arts associated with the ceremony, making reference to at least one work from this chapter.

25.4 Discuss Chinese influences on Japanese art styles and techniques in the Muromachi and Edo periods; for your answer, look back to Chapter 24 and draw specific comparisons between two works from each chapter.

25.5 Distinguish at least three different patron groups for Japanese arts and architecture in the Muromachi, Momoyama, and Edo periods. Discuss the kinds of arts and architecture each group preferred and how they were used by these patrons.

PRACTICE MORE: Compose answers to these questions, get flashcards for images and terms, and review chapter material with quizzes
www.myartslab.com

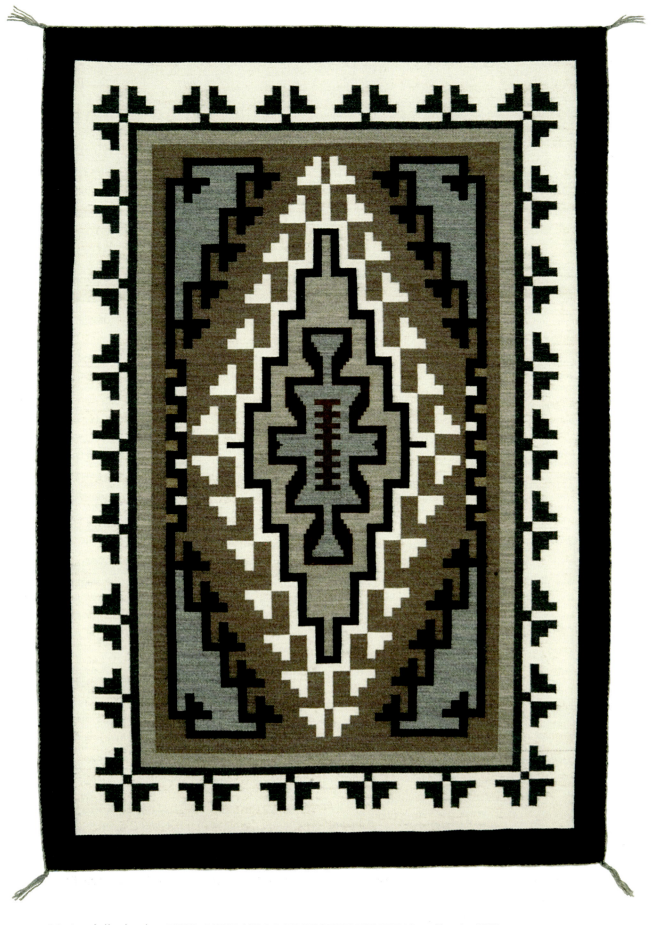

26-1 • Julia Jumbo TWO GREY HILLS TAPESTRY WEAVING   Navajo, 2003.
Handspun wool, 36 × 24½″ (91.2 × 62.1 cm). Wheelwright Museum of the American Indian,
Santa Fe, New Mexico.

ART OF THE AMERICAS AFTER 1300

According to Navajo mythology, the universe itself is a weaving, its fibers spun by Spider Woman out of sacred cosmic materials. Spider Woman taught the art of weaving to Changing Woman (a Mother Earth figure), and she in turn taught it to Navajo women, who continue to keep this art vital, seeing its continuation as a sacred responsibility. Early Navajo blankets were composed of simple horizontal stripes, but over time weavers have introduced more intricate patterns, and today Navajo rugs are woven in numerous distinctive styles.

The tapestry weaving in FIGURE 26–1 is designed in the Two Grey Hills style that developed during the early twentieth century around a trading post of that name in northwest New Mexico. Weavers who work in this style use the natural colors of undyed sheep's wool (only the black wool is sometimes dyed) to create dazzling geometric patterns. The artist Julia Jumbo (1928–2007), who learned to weave as a child, used her weavings to support her family. She raised her own sheep, and carded and spun her wool by hand before incorporating it into painstakingly made textiles. Jumbo is renowned for the clarity of her designs and the technical perfection of her fine weave. This outstanding work, created in 2003, attests to the vital and dynamic nature of Native American arts today.

When the first Europeans arrived, the Western Hemisphere was already inhabited from the Arctic Circle to Tierra del Fuego by peoples with long histories and rich cultural traditions (MAP 26–1). After 1492, when Christopher Columbus and his companions first sailed to the New World, the arrival of Europeans completely altered the destiny of the Americas. In Mesoamerica and South America the break with the past was sudden and violent: two great empires—the Aztec in Mexico and the Inca in South America—that had risen to prominence in the fifteenth century were rapidly destroyed. In North America the change took place more gradually, but the outcome was much the same. In both North and South America, natives succumbed to European diseases to which they had no immunity, especially smallpox, leading to massive population loss and social disruption. Over the next 400 years, many Native Americans were displaced from their ancestral homelands, and many present-day Native American ethnic groupings were formed by combinations of various survivor groups.

Despite all the disruption, during the past century the indigenous arts of the Americas have undergone a re-evaluation that has renewed the conception of what constitutes "American art." Native artists like Julia Jumbo continue to revive and reimagine indigenous traditions, revisit traditional outlooks, and restate their ancient customs and ideas in new ways. After being pushed to the brink of extinction, Native American cultures are experiencing a revival in both North and South America, as Native Americans assert themselves politically and insist on the connections between their history and the land.

LEARN ABOUT IT

26.1 Distinguish the styles, symbols, and techniques characteristic of Native American arts and crafts.

26.2 Explore the cultural developments and achievements of the Aztec and Inca empires.

26.3 Assess the role of portable and ephemeral media in the arts of the Americas.

26.4 Observe how indigenous arts have changed in the centuries since contact with Europe.

26.5 Explore the gender divisions in the production of the arts of the Americas.

HEAR MORE: Listen to an audio file of your chapter www.myartslab.com

THE AZTEC EMPIRE

In November 1519, the army of the Spanish soldier Hernán Cortés beheld for the first time the great Aztec capital of Tenochtitlan. The shimmering city, which seemed to be floating on the water, was built on an island in the middle of Lake Texcoco in the Valley of Mexico, and linked by broad causeways to the mainland. One of Cortés's companions later recalled the wonder the Spanish felt at that moment: "When we saw so many cities and villages built on the water and other great towns on dry land and that straight and level causeway going towards [Tenochtitlan], we were amazed … on account of the great towers and temples and buildings rising from the water, and all built of masonry. And some of our soldiers even asked whether the things that we saw were not a dream." (Bernal Díaz del Castillo, cited in Coe and Koontz 2005, p. 190.)

The Mexica people who lived in the remarkable city that Cortés found were then rulers of much of the land that later took their name, Mexico. Their rise to power had been recent and swift. Only 400 years earlier, according to their own legends, they had been a nomadic people living far north of the Valley of Mexico in a distant place called Aztlan. The term Aztec derives from the word Aztlan, and refers to all those living in Central Mexico who came from this mythical homeland, not just to the Mexica of Tenochtitlan.

The Mexica arrived in the Valley of Mexico in the thirteenth century. They eventually settled on an island in Lake Texcoco where they had seen an eagle perching on a prickly pear cactus (*nochtli*) growing out of a stone (*tetl*), a sign that their god Huitzilopochtli told them would mark the end of their wandering. They called the place Tenochtitlan. The city on the island was gradually expanded by reclaiming land from the lake, and serviced by a grid of artificial canals. In the fifteenth century, the Mexica—joined by allies in a triple alliance—began an aggressive campaign of expansion. The tribute they exacted from all over Mexico transformed Tenochtitlan into a glittering capital.

Aztec religion was based on a complex pantheon that combined Aztec deities with more ancient ones that had long been worshiped in central Mexico. According to Aztec belief, the gods had created the current era, or sun, at the ancient city of Teotihuacan in the Valley of Mexico (see Chapter 12). The continued existence of the world depended on human actions, including rituals of bloodletting and human sacrifice. Many Mesoamerican peoples believed that the world had been created multiple times before the present era. But while most Mesoamericans believed that they were living in the fourth era, or sun, the Mexica asserted that they lived in the fifth sun, a new era that coincided with the Aztec Empire. The Calendar Stone (see "A Closer Look," page 839) boldly makes this claim, using the dates of the destructions of the four previous eras to form the glyph that names the fifth sun, 4 Motion. The end of each period of 52 years in the Mesoamerican calendar was a particularly dangerous time that required a special fire-lighting ritual.

TENOCHTITLAN

An Aztec scribe drew an idealized representation of the city of Tenochtitlan and its sacred ceremonial precinct (**FIG. 26–2**) for the Spanish viceroy in 1545. It forms the first page of the *Codex Mendoza*. An eagle perched on a prickly pear cactus growing out of a stone—the symbol of the city—fills the center of the page. Waterways divide the city into four quarters, and indicate the lake surrounding the city. Early leaders of Tenochtitlan are shown sitting in the four quadrants. The victorious warriors at the bottom of the page represent Aztec conquests, and a count of years surrounds the entire scene. This image combines historical narration with idealized cartography, showing the city in the middle of the lake at the moment of its founding.

At the center of Tenochtitlan was the sacred precinct, a walled enclosure that contained dozens of temples and other buildings. The focal point of the sacred precinct was the Great Pyramid, a twin pyramid with paired temples on top: the one on the north dedicated to Tlaloc, an ancient rain god with a history extending

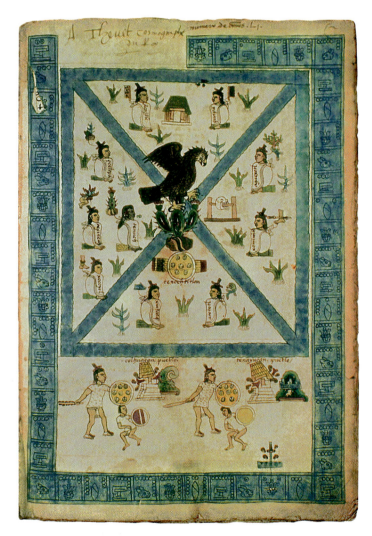

26-2 • THE FOUNDING OF TENOCHTITLAN
Page from *Codex Mendoza*. Mexico. Aztec, 1545. Ink and color on paper, 12⅜ × 8⁷⁄₁₆″ (21.5 × 31.5 cm). Bodleian Library, University of Oxford, England. MS. Arch Selden. A.1.fol. 2r

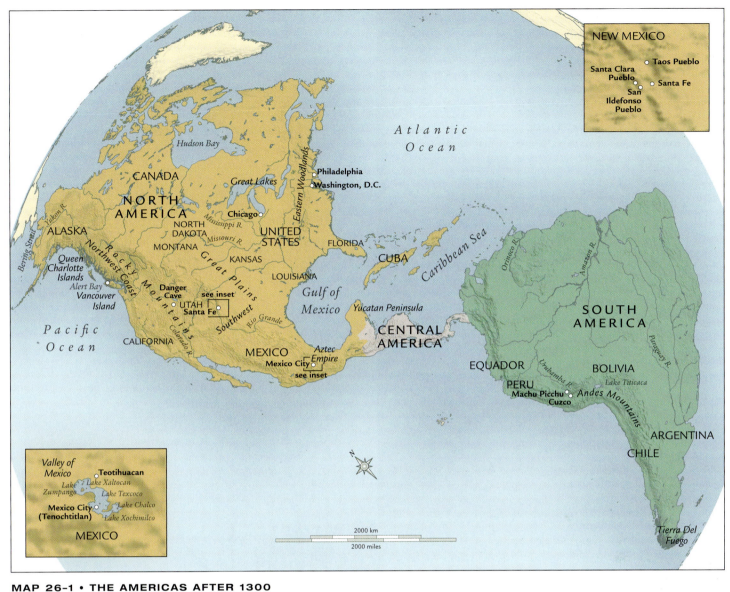

MAP 26–1 • THE AMERICAS AFTER 1300

Diverse cultures inhabited the Americas, each shaping a distinct artistic tradition.

back to Teotihuacan, and the one on the south dedicated to Huitzilopochtli, the solar god of the newly arrived Mexica tribe. Two steep staircases led up the west face of the pyramid from the plaza in front. Sacrificial victims climbed these stairs to the Temple of Huitzilopochtli, where priests threw them over a stone, quickly cut open their chests, and pulled out their still-throbbing hearts, a sacrifice that ensured the survival of the sun, the gods, and the Aztecs. The bodies were then rolled down the stairs and dismembered. Thousands of severed heads were said to have been kept on a skull rack in the plaza, represented in FIGURE 26–2 by the rack with a single skull to the right of the eagle.

During the winter rainy season the sun rose behind the Temple of Tlaloc, and during the dry season it rose behind the Temple of Huitzilopochtli. The double temple thus united two natural forces, sun and rain, or fire and water. During the spring and autumn equinoxes, the sun rose between the two temples.

SCULPTURE

Aztec sculpture was monumental, powerful, and often unsettling (see "A Closer Look," page 839). A particularly striking example is an imposing statue of Coatlicue, mother of the Mexica god Huitzilopochtli (FIG. 26–3). Coatlicue means "she of the serpent skirt," and this broad-shouldered figure with clawed feet has a skirt of twisted snakes. The statue may allude to the moment of Huitzilopochtli's birth: when Coatlicue conceived Huitzilopochtli from a ball of down, her other children—the stars and the moon—jealously conspired to kill her. As they attacked, Huitzilopochtli emerged from his mother's body fully grown and armed, drove off his half-brothers, and destroyed his half-sister, the moon goddess Coyolxauhqui. Coatlicue, however, did not survive the encounter. In this sculpture, she has been decapitated and a pair of serpents, symbols of gushing blood, rise from her neck to form her head. Their eyes are her eyes; their fangs, her tusks. Around her stump of

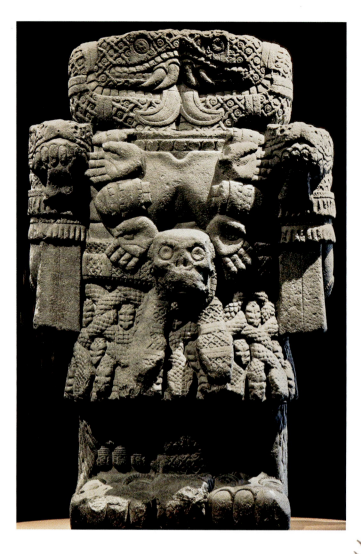

a neck hangs a necklace of human hands, hearts, and a dangling skull. Despite the surface intricacy, the statue's massive form creates an impression of solidity, and the entire sculpture leans forward, looming over the viewer. The colors with which it was originally painted would have heightened its dramatic impact.

FEATHERWORK

Indeed Aztec art was colorful. An idea of its iridescent splendor is captured in the feather headdress **(FIG. 26–4)** said to have been given by the Aztec emperor Moctezuma to Cortés, and thought to be the one listed in the inventory of treasures Cortés shipped to Charles V, the Habsburg emperor in Spain, in 1519. Featherwork was one of the glories of Mesoamerican art but very few of these extremely fragile artworks survive. The tropical feathers in this headdress exemplify the exotic tribute paid to the Aztecs; the long iridescent green feathers that make up most of the headdress are the exceedingly rare tail feathers of the quetzal bird—each male quetzal has only two such plumes. The feathers were gathered in small bunches, their quills reinforced with reed tubes, and then

**26-4 • FEATHER HEADDRESS
OF MOCTEZUMA**
Mexico. Aztec, before 1519.
Quetzal, blue cotinga, and other feathers
and gold on a fiber frame, 45⅝ × 68⅞″
(116 × 175 cm). Museum für
Völkerkunde, Vienna.

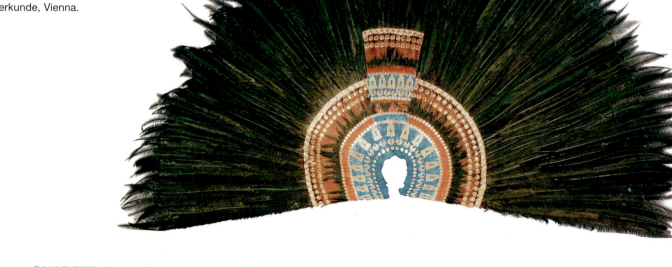

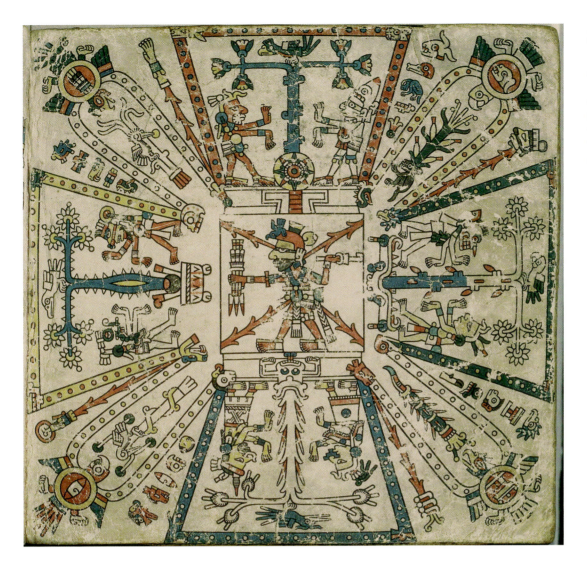

26-5 • A VIEW OF THE WORLD
Page from *Codex Fejervary-Mayer*. Mexico. Aztec or Mixtec, c. 1400–1519. Paint on animal hide, each page 6⅞ × 6⅞″ (17.5 × 17.5 cm), total length 13′3″ (4.04 m). The National Museums and Galleries on Merseyside, Liverpool, England.

sewn to the frame in overlapping layers, the joins concealed by small gold plaques. Featherworkers were esteemed craftspeople. After the Spanish invasion, they turned their exacting skills to "feather paintings" of Christian subjects.

MANUSCRIPTS

Aztec scribes also created brilliantly colored books: histories, maps, and divinatory almanacs. Instead of being bound on one side like European books, Mesoamerican books took the form of a screenfold, accordion-pleated so that each page was connected only to the two adjacent pages. This format allowed great flexibility: a book could be opened to show two pages, or unfolded to show six or eight pages simultaneously; different sections of the book could also be juxtaposed. A rare manuscript that survived the Spanish conquest provides a concise summary of Mesoamerican cosmology (FIG. 26–5). Mesoamerican peoples recognized five key directions: north, south, east, west, and center. At the center of the image is Xiuhtecutli, god of fire, time, and the calendar. Radiating from him are the four cardinal directions—each associated with a specific color, a deity, and a tree with a bird in its branches. Two hundred and sixty dots trace the eight-lobed path around the

central figure, referring to the 260-day Mesoamerican divinatory calendar; the 20 day signs of this calendar are also distributed throughout the image. By linking the 260-day calendar to the four directions, this image speaks eloquently of the unity of space and time in the Mesoamerican worldview.

The Aztec Empire was short-lived. Within two years of their arrival in Mexico, the Spanish conquistadors and their indigenous allies overran Tenochtitlan. They built their own capital, Mexico City, over its ruins and established their own cathedral on the site of Tenochtitlan's sacred precinct.

THE INCA EMPIRE

At the beginning of the sixteenth century the Inca Empire was one of the largest states in the world. It extended more than 2,600 miles along western South America, encompassing most of modern Peru, Ecuador, Bolivia, and northern Chile and reaching into present-day Argentina. Like the Aztec Empire, its rise was rapid and its destruction sudden.

The Incas called their empire the "Land of the Four Quarters." At its center was their capital, Cuzco, "the navel of

Calendar Stone ➤ Mexico. Aztec, c. 1500. Diameter 11'6¾" (3.6 m).
Museo Nacional de Antropología, Mexico City.

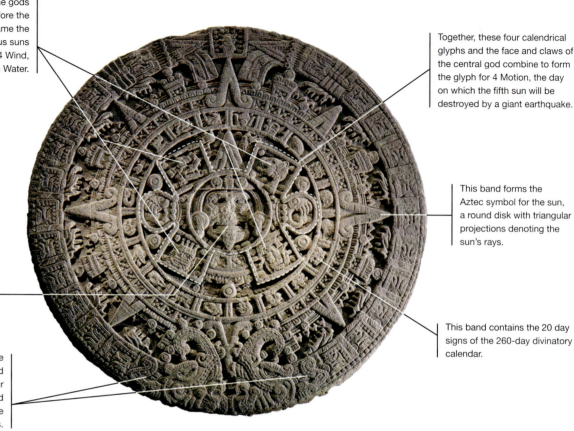

According to Mexica belief, the gods created the world four times before the present era. These cartouches name the days on which the four previous suns were destroyed: 4 Jaguar, 4 Wind, 4 Rain, and 4 Water.

Together, these four calendrical glyphs and the face and claws of the central god combine to form the glyph for 4 Motion, the day on which the fifth sun will be destroyed by a giant earthquake.

This central face combines elements of the sun god as the night sun in the underworld with the clawed hands and flint tongue of earth gods, symbolizing the night sun and the hungry earth.

This band forms the Aztec symbol for the sun, a round disk with triangular projections denoting the sun's rays.

Two fire serpents encircle the outer part of the disk. Stylized flames rise off their backs. Their heads meet at the bottom, and human faces emerge from the mouths of the serpents.

This band contains the 20 day signs of the 260-day divinatory calendar.

SEE MORE: View the Closer Look feature for the Calendar Stone **www.myartslab.com**

---

the world," located high in the Andes Mountains. The Inca state began as one of many small competing kingdoms that emerged in the highlands. In the fifteenth century the Incas began to expand, suddenly and rapidly, and had subdued most of their vast domain—through conquest, alliance, and intimidation—by 1500.

To hold this linguistically and ethnically diverse empire together, the Inca ("Inca" refers to both the ruler and the people) relied on religion, an efficient bureaucracy, and various forms of labor taxation, in which the payment was a set amount of time spent performing tasks for the state. In return the state provided gifts through local leaders and sponsored lavish ritual entertainments. Men might cultivate state lands, serve in the army, or work periodically on public works projects—building roads and terracing hillsides, for example—while women wove cloth as

tribute. No Andean civilization ever developed writing, but the Inca kept detailed accounts and historical records on knotted and colored cords (*quipu*).

To move their armies and speed transport and communication within the empire, the Incas built more than 23,000 miles of roads. These varied from 50-foot-wide thoroughfares to 3-foot-wide paths. Two main north–south roads, one along the coast and the other through the highlands, were linked by east–west roads. Travelers journeyed on foot, using llamas as pack animals. Stairways helped them negotiate steep mountain slopes, and rope suspension bridges allowed river gorge crossings. All along the roads, storehouses and lodgings—more than a thousand have been found—were spaced a day's journey apart. A relay system of runners could carry messages between Cuzco and the farthest reaches of the empire in about a week.

CUZCO

Cuzco, a capital of great splendor, was home to the Inca, ruler of the empire. Its urban plan was said to have been designed by the Inca Pachacuti (r. 1438–1471) in the shape of a puma, its head the fortress of Sacsahuaman, and its belly the giant plaza at the center of town. The city was divided into upper and lower parts, reflecting the dual organization of Inca society. Cuzco was the symbolic as well as the political center of the Inca Empire: everyone had to carry a burden when entering the city, and gold, silver, or textiles brought into the city could not afterward be removed from it.

Cuzco was a showcase of the finest Inca masonry, some of which can still be seen in the present-day city (see "Inca Masonry," page 842). Architecture was a major expressive form for the Inca, the very shape of individually worked stones conveying a powerful aesthetic impact (FIG. 26–6). In contrast to the massive walls, Inca buildings had gabled, thatched roofs. Doors, windows, and niches were trapezoid-shaped, narrower at the top than the bottom.

MACHU PICCHU

MACHU PICCHU, one of the most spectacular archaeological sites in the world, provides an excellent example of Inca architectural planning (FIG. 26–7). At 9,000 feet above sea level, it straddles a

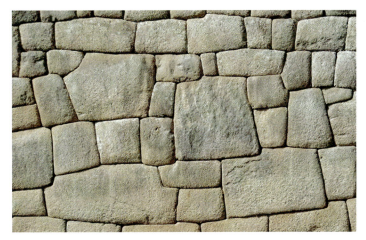

26-6 • INCA MASONRY, DETAIL OF A WALL AT MACHU PICCHU
Peru. Inca, 1450–1530.

26-7 • MACHU PICCHU
Peru. Inca, 1450–1530.

SEE MORE: View a video about Machu Picchu
www.myartslab.com

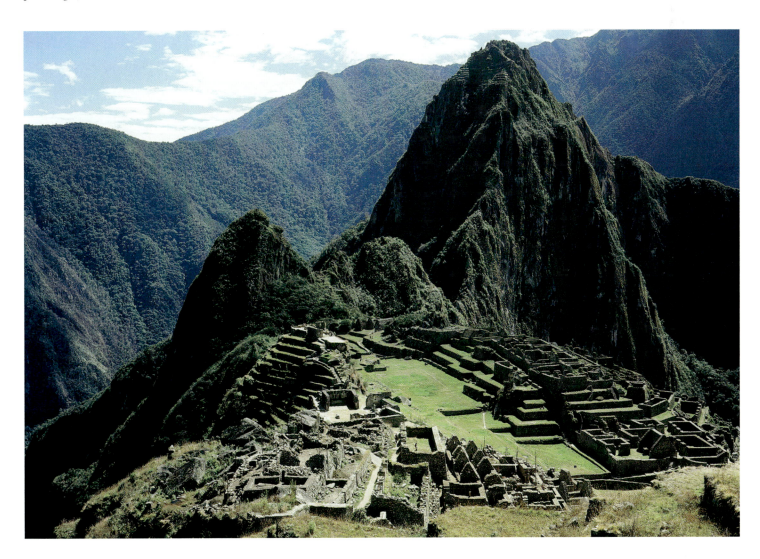

Working with the simplest of tools—mainly heavy stone hammers—and using no mortar, Inca builders created stonework of great refinement and durability: roads and bridges that linked the entire empire, terraces for growing crops, and structures both simple and elaborate. The effort expended on stone construction by the Inca was prodigious. Fine Inca masonry consisted of either rectangular blocks or irregular polygonal blocks (SEE FIG. 26–6). In both types, adjoining blocks were painstakingly shaped to fit tightly together without mortar. Their stone faces might be slightly beveled along their edges so that each block presented a "pillowed" shape expressing its identity, or walls might be smoothed into a continuous flowing surface in which the individual

blocks form a seamless whole. At a few Inca sites, the stones used in construction were boulder-size: up to 27 feet tall. In Cuzco, and elsewhere in the Inca empire, Inca masonry has survived earthquakes that have destroyed later structures.

At Machu Picchu (SEE FIGS. 26–6, 26–7), all buildings and terraces within its 3-square-mile extent were made of granite, the hard stone occurring at the site. Commoners' houses and some walls were constructed of irregular stones that were carefully fitted together, while fine polygonal or smoothed masonry distinguished palaces and temples.

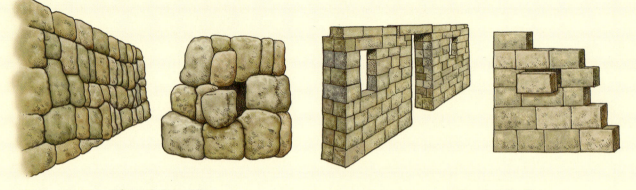

polygonal-stone wall   smooth-surfaced wall

SEE MORE: View a simulation about Inca masonry **www.myartslab.com**

ridge between two high peaks in the eastern slopes of the Andes and looks down on the Urubamba River. Stone buildings, today lacking only their thatched roofs, occupy terraces around central plazas, and narrow agricultural terraces descend into the valley. The site, near the eastern limits of the empire, was the royal estate of the Inca ruler Pachacuti. The court might retire to this warmer, lower-altitude palace when the Cuzco winter became too harsh to enjoy. Important diplomatic negotiations and ceremonial feasts may also have taken place at this country retreat. The entire complex is designed with great sensitivity to its surroundings, with walls and plazas framing stupendous vistas of the surrounding landscape, and carefully selected stones echoing the shapes of the mountains beyond.

TEXTILES

The production of fine textiles was already an important art in the Andes by the third millennium BCE (see Chapter 12). Among the

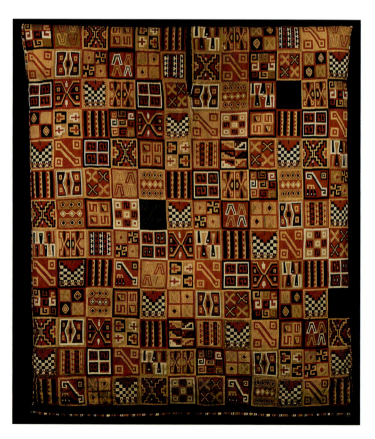

26–8 • TUNIC
Peru. Inca, c. 1500. Camelid fiber and cotton, 35⅞ × 30″
(91 × 76.5 cm). Dumbarton Oaks Research Library and Collections,
Pre-Columbian Collection, Washington, D.C.

Incas, textiles of cotton and camelid fibers (from llama, vicuña, and alpaca) were a primary form of wealth. One form of labor taxation required the manufacture of fibers and cloth, and textiles as well as agricultural products filled Inca storehouses. Cloth was deemed a fitting gift for the gods, so fine garments were draped around statues, and even burned as sacrificial offerings.

The patterns and designs on garments were not simply decorative but also carried symbolic messages, including indications of a person's ethnic identity and social rank. In the elaborate **TUNIC** in **FIGURE 26–8**, each square represents a miniature tunic. For example, tunics with checkerboard patterns were worn by military officers and royal escorts, and the four-part motifs may refer to the empire as the Land of the Four Quarters. The diagonal key motif is often found on tunics with horizontal border stripes but its meaning is not known. While we may not be sure what was meant in every case, patterns and colors appear to have been standardized like uniforms in order to convey information at a glance. Encompassing all these patterns associated with different ranks and statuses, this exquisitely woven tunic may have been a royal garment.

METALWORK

When they arrived in Peru in 1532, the Spanish were far less interested in Inca cloth than in their vast quantities of gold and silver. The Inca valued objects made of gold and silver not for their precious metal, but because they saw in them symbols of the sun and the moon. They are said to have called gold the "sweat of the sun" and silver the "tears of the moon." On the other hand, the Spanish exploration of the New World was propelled by feverish tales of native treasure. Whatever gold and silver objects the Spanish could obtain were melted down to enrich their royal coffers. Only a few small figures buried as offerings, like the little **LLAMA** shown in **FIGURE 26–9**, escaped the conquerors. The llama was thought to have a special connection with the sun, with rain, and with fertility, and a llama was sacrificed to the sun every morning in Cuzco. In this small silver figurine, the essential character of a llama is rendered with a few well-chosen details, but in keeping with the value that Andeans placed on textiles the blanket on its back is carefully described.

THE AFTERMATH OF THE SPANISH CONQUEST

Native American populations in Mexico and Peru declined sharply after the conquest because of the exploitative policies of the conquerors and the ravages of smallpox and other diseases that spread from Europe and against which the indigenous people had no immunity. This demographic collapse meant that the population of the Americas declined by as much as 90 percent in the century after contact with Europe. European missionaries suppressed local beliefs and practices and worked to spread Christianity throughout the Americas. Although increasing numbers of Europeans began to settle and dominate the land, native arts did not end with the Spanish conquest. Traditional arts,

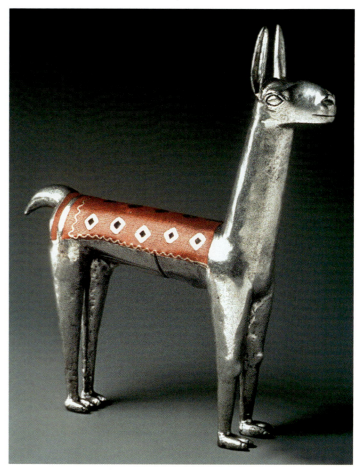

26-9 • LLAMA
From Bolivia or Peru, found near Lake Titicaca, Bolivia. Inca, 15th century. Cast silver with gold and cinnabar, 9 × 8½ × 1¾" (22.9 × 21.6 × 4.4 cm). American Museum of Natural History, New York.

including fine weaving, continue to this day, transforming and remaining vital as indigenous peoples adjust to a changing world.

NORTH AMERICA

In America north of Mexico, from the upper reaches of Canada and Alaska to the southern tip of Florida, many different peoples with widely varying cultures coexisted. Here, the Europeans came less as military men seeking riches to plunder than as families seeking land to farm. Unlike the Spaniards, they found no large cities with urban populations to resist them. However, although they imagined that the lands they settled were an untended wilderness, in fact nearly all of North America was populated and possessed by indigenous peoples. Over the next 400 years, by means of violence, bribery, and treaties, the English colonies and, in turn, the United States displaced nearly all Native Americans from their ancestral homelands. What indigenous art Euro-Americans encountered they viewed as a curiosity, not art.

Much Native American artwork was small, portable, fragile, and impermanent. In previous times these artworks were not

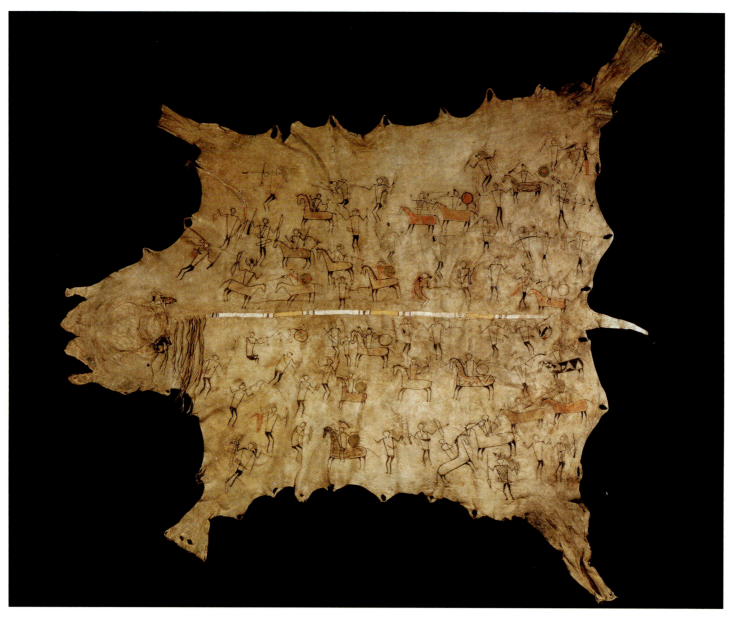

26-14 • BATTLE SCENE, HIDE PAINTING
North Dakota. Mandan, 1797–1800. Tanned buffalo hide, dyed porcupine quills, and black, red, green, yellow, and brown pigment, 7′10″ × 8′6″ (2.44 × 2.65 m). Peabody Museum of Archaeology, Harvard University, Cambridge, Massachusetts. 99-12-10/53121

This robe, collected in 1804 by Meriwether Lewis and William Clark on their expedition into western lands acquired by the United States in the Louisiana Purchase, is the earliest documented example of Plains painting. It was one of a number of Native American artworks that Lewis and Clark sent to President Thomas Jefferson. Jefferson displayed the robe in the entrance hall of his home at Monticello, Virginia.

The tipi leaned slightly into the prevailing west wind while the flap-covered door and smoke hole faced east, away from the wind. An inner lining covered the lower part of the walls and the perimeter of the floor to protect the occupants from drafts.

Tipis were the property and responsibility of women, who set them up at new encampments and lowered them when the group moved on. Blackfoot women could set up their huge tipis in less than an hour. Women quilled, beaded, and embroidered tipi linings, as well as backrests, clothing, and equipment. The patterns with which tipis were decorated, like their proportions and colors, varied from nation to nation, family to family, and individual to individual. In general, the bottom was covered with traditional motifs and the center section held personal images. When disassembled and packed to be dragged by a horse to another location, the tipi served as a platform for transporting other possessions. The Sioux arranged their tipis in two half-circles—one for the sky people and one for the earth people—divided along an east–west axis. When the Blackfoot people gathered in the summer for their ceremonial Sun Dance, their encampment contained hundreds of tipis in a circle a mile in circumference.

PLAINS INDIAN PAINTING. Plains men recorded their exploits in paintings on tipis and on buffalo-hide robes. The earliest documented painted buffalo-hide robe, presented to Lewis and

Clark during their transcontinental expedition, illustrates a battle fought in 1797 by the Mandan (of what is now North Dakota) and their allies against the Sioux (FIG. 26–14). The painter, trying to capture the full extent of a conflict in which five nations took part, shows a party of warriors in 22 separate episodes. The party is led by a man with a pipe and an elaborate eagle-feather headdress, and the warriors are armed with bows and arrows, lances, clubs, and flintlock rifles. Details of equipment and emblems of rank—headdresses, sashes, shields, feathered lances, powder horns for the rifles—are depicted carefully. Horses are shown in profile with stick legs, C-shaped hooves, and either clipped or flowing manes.

The figures stand out clearly against the light-colored background of the buffalo hide. The painter pressed lines into the hide, then filled in the forms with black, red, green, yellow, and brown pigments. A strip of colored porcupine quills runs down the spine of the buffalo hide. The robe would have been worn draped over the shoulders of the powerful warrior whose deeds it commemorates. As the wearer moved, the painted horses and warriors would seem to come alive, transforming the warrior into a living representation of his exploits.

Life on the Great Plains changed abruptly in 1869, when the transcontinental railway linking the east and west coasts of the United States was completed, providing easy access to Native American lands. Between 1871 and 1890, Euro-American hunters killed off most of the buffalo, and soon ranchers and then farmers moved into the Great Plains. The U.S. government forcibly moved the outnumbered and outgunned Native Americans to reservations, land considered worthless until the later discovery of oil and, in the case of the Black Hills, gold.

THE NORTHWEST COAST

From southern Alaska to northern California, the Pacific coast of North America is a region of unusually abundant resources. Its many rivers fill each year with salmon returning to spawn. Harvested and dried, the fish could sustain large populations throughout the year. The peoples of the Northwest Coast—among them the Tlingit, the Haida, and the Kwakwaka'wakw (formerly spelled Kwakiutl)—exploited this abundance to develop a complex and distinctive way of life in which the arts played a central role.

ANIMAL IMAGERY. Animals feature prominently in Northwest Coast art because each extended family group (clan) claimed descent from a mythic animal or animal-human ancestor, from whom the family derived its name and the right to use certain animals and spirits as totemic emblems, or crests. These emblems appear frequently in Northwest Coast art, notably in carved cedar house poles and the tall, free-standing poles (mortuary poles) erected to memorialize dead chiefs. Chiefs, who were males in the most direct line of

descent from the mythic ancestor, validated their status and garnered prestige for themselves and their families by holding ritual feasts known as potlatches, during which they gave valuable gifts to the invited guests. Shamans, who were sometimes also chiefs, mediated between the human and spirit worlds. Some shamans were female, giving them unique access to certain aspects of the spiritual world.

Northwest Coast peoples lived in large, elaborately decorated communal houses made of massive timbers and thick planks. Carved and painted partition screens separated the chief's quarters from the rest of the house. The Tlingit screen illustrated in FIGURE 26–15 came from the house of Chief Shakes of Wrangell (d. 1916), whose family crest was the grizzly bear. The image of a rearing

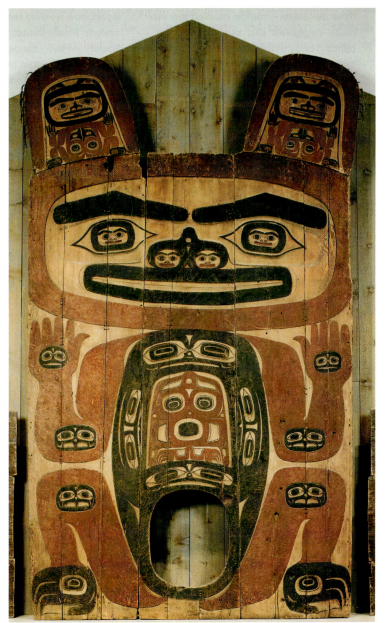

26-15 • GRIZZLY BEAR HOUSE-PARTITION SCREEN
The house of Chief Shakes of Wrangell, Canada. Tlingit people, c. 1840. Cedar, paint, and human hair, 15 × 8′ (4.57 × 2.74 m). Denver Art Museum, Denver, Colorado.

Navajo Night Chant

This chant accompanies the creation of a sand painting during a Navajo curing ceremony. It is sung toward the end of the ceremony and indicates the restoration of inner harmony and balance.

In beauty (happily) I walk.
With beauty before me I walk.
With beauty behind me I walk.
With beauty below me I walk.
With beauty above me I walk.
With beauty all around me I walk.
It is finished (again) in beauty.
It is finished in beauty.

(Cited in Washington Matthews, "The Night Chant: A Navaho Ceremony," in *Memoirs of the American Museum of Natural History*, Vol. 6. New York, 1902, p. 145.)

THE NAVAJOS. While some Navajo arts, like sand painting, have deep traditional roots, others have developed over the centuries of European contact. Navajo weaving (SEE FIG. 26–1) depends on the wool of sheep introduced by the Spaniards, and the designs and colors of Navajo blankets continue to evolve today in response to tourism and changing aesthetics. Similarly, jewelry made of turquoise and silver did not become an important Navajo art form until the mid nineteenth century. Traditionally, Navajo arts had strict gender divisions: women wove cloth, and men worked metal.

Sand painting, a traditional Navajo art, is the exclusive province of men. Sand paintings are made to the accompaniment of chants by shaman-singers in the course of healing and blessing ceremonies, and they have great sacred significance (see "Navajo Night Chant," above). The paintings depict mythic heroes and events; and as ritual art, they follow prescribed rules and patterns that ensure their power. To make them, the singer dribbles pulverized colored stones, pollen, flowers, and other natural colors over a hide or sand ground. The rituals are intended to cure by restoring harmony to the world. The paintings are not meant to be seen by the public and certainly not to be displayed in museums. They are meant to be destroyed by nightfall of the day on which they are made.

In 1919 a respected shaman-singer named Hosteen Klah (1867–1937) began to incorporate sand-painting images into weaving, breaking with the traditional prohibitions. Many Navajos took offense at Klah both for recording the sacred images and for doing so in what was traditionally a woman's art form. Klah had learned to weave from his mother and sister. The Navajo traditionally recognize at least three genders; Hosteen Klah was a *nadle*, or Navajo third-gender. Hence, he could learn both female and male arts; that is, he was trained both to weave and to heal. Hosteen Klah was not breaking artistic barriers in a conventional sense, but rather exemplifying the complexities of the traditional Navajo gender system. Klah's work was ultimately accepted because of his great skill and prestige.

The **WHIRLING LOG CEREMONY** sand painting, woven into tapestry **(FIG. 26–20)**, depicts part of the Navajo creation myth. The Holy People create the earth's surface and divide it into four parts. They create humans, and bring forth corn, beans, squash, and tobacco—the four sacred plants. A male-female pair of humans and

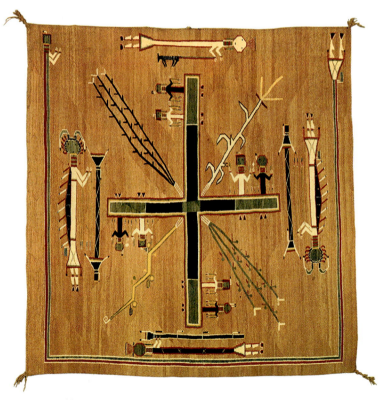

26-20 • Hosteen Klah WHIRLING LOG CEREMONY
Sand painting; tapestry by Mrs. Sam Manuelito. Navajo, c. 1925. Wool, 5′5″ × 5′10″ (1.69 × 1.82 m). Heard Museum, Phoenix, Arizona.

A NEW BEGINNING

While Native American art has long been displayed in anthropology and natural history museums, today the art of indigenous peoples is finally achieving full recognition by the art establishment (see "Craft or Art?," page 856). The Institute of American Indian Arts (IAIA), founded in 1962 in Santa Fe and attended by Native American students from all over North America, supports Native American aspirations in the arts today just as Dorothy Dunn's Studio School did in the 1930s. Staffed by Native American artists, the school encourages the incorporation of indigenous ideals in the arts without creating an official "style." As alumni achieved distinction and the IAIA museum in Santa Fe established a reputation for excellence, the institute has led Native American art into the mainstream of contemporary art (see Chapter 31).

To cite just one example, contemporary Native American artist Jaune Quick-to-See Smith (b. 1940) borrowed a well-known image by Leonardo da Vinci for her **THE RED MEAN (FIG. 26–21)**. She describes the work as a self-portrait, and indeed the center of the work has a bumper sticker that reads "Made in the U.S.A." above an identification number. The central figure quotes Leonardo's Vitruvian Man (see "The Vitruvian Man," page 637), but the message here is auto-biographical. Leonardo inscribed the human form within perfect geometric shapes to emphasize the perfection of the human body, while Smith put her silhouette inside the red X that signifies nuclear radiation. This image alludes both to the uranium mines found on some Indian reservations and to the fact that many have become temporary repositories for nuclear waste. The image's background is a collage of Native American tribal newspapers. Her self-portrait thus includes her ethnic identity and life on the reservation as well as

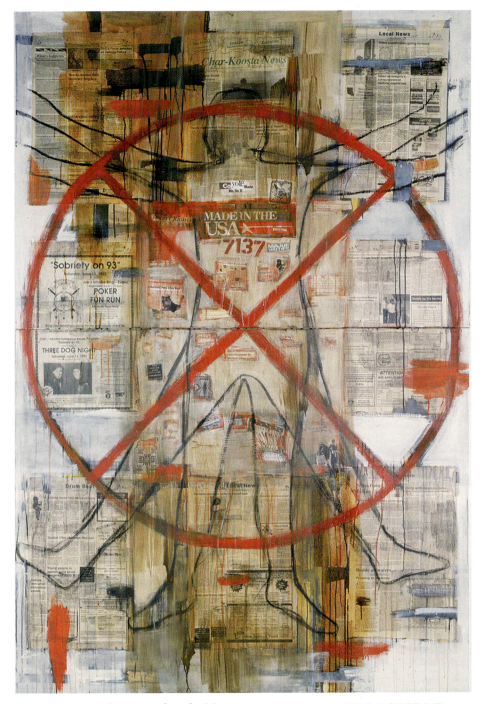

26–21 • Jaune Quick-to-See Smith THE RED MEAN: SELF PORTRAIT
1992. Acrylic, newspaper collage, and mixed media on canvas, 90 × 60" (228.6 × 154.4 cm). Smith College Museum of Art, Northampton, Massachusetts. Part gift from Janet Wright Ketcham, class of 1953, and part purchase from the Janet Wright Ketcham, class of 1953, Fund © Jaune Quick-to-See Smith

one of the sacred plants stand in each of the four quarters, defined by the central cross. The four Holy People (the elongated figures) surround the image, and the guardian figure of Rainbow Maiden frames the scene on three sides. Like all Navajo artists, Hosteen Klah hoped that the excellence of the work would make it pleasing to the spirits. Recently, shaman-singers have made permanent sand paintings on boards for sale, but they usually introduce slight errors in them to render the paintings ceremonially harmless.

the history of Western art.

Other artists, such as the Canadian Haida artist Bill Reid (1920–1998), have sought to sustain and revitalize traditional art in their work. Trained as a woodcarver, painter, and jeweler, Reid revived the art of carving totem poles and dugout canoes in the Haida homeland of Haida Gwaii—"Islands of the People"— known on maps today as the Queen Charlotte Islands. Late in life he began to create large-scale sculptures in bronze. With their

THE PEOPLING OF THE PACIFIC

On a map with the Pacific Ocean as its center, only the peripheries of the great landmasses of Asia and the Americas appear. Nearly one-third of the earth's surface is taken up by this vast expanse. Europeans arriving in Oceania in the late eighteenth and early nineteenth centuries noted four distinct but connected cultural-geographic areas: Australia, Melanesia, Micronesia, and Polynesia (MAP 27–1). Australia includes the continent, as well as the island of Tasmania to the southeast. Melanesia ("black islands," a reference to the dark skin color of its inhabitants) includes New Guinea and the string of islands that extend eastward from it as far as Fiji and New Caledonia. Micronesia ("small islands"), to the north of Melanesia, is a region of small islands and coral atolls. Polynesia ("many islands") is scattered over a huge, triangular region defined by New Zealand in the south, Rapa Nui (Easter Island) in the east, and the Hawaiian Islands to the north. The last region on earth to be inhabited by humans, Polynesia covers some 7.7 million square miles, of which fewer than 130,000 square miles are dry land—and most of that is New Zealand. With the exception of temperate New Zealand, with its marked seasons and snowcapped mountains, Oceania is in the tropics, that is, between the tropic of Cancer in the north and the tropic of Capricorn to the south.

Australia, Tasmania, and New Guinea formed a single continent during the last Ice Age, which began some 2.5 million years ago. About 50,000 years ago, when the sea level was some 330 feet lower than it is today, people moved to this continent from Southeast Asia, making at least part of the journey over open water.

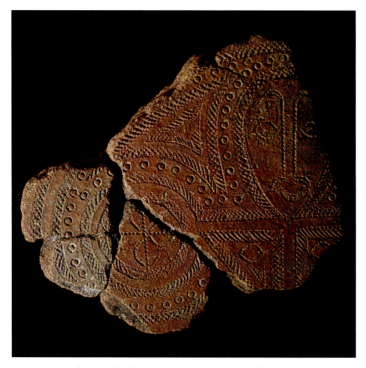

27-2 • FRAGMENTS OF A LARGE LAPITA JAR
Venumbo Reef, Santa Cruz Island, Solomon Islands. c. 1200–1100 BCE. Clay, height of human face motif approx. 1½" (4 cm).

Some 27,000 years ago humans were settled on the large islands north and east of New Guinea as far south as San Cristobal, but they ventured no farther for another 25,000 years. By about 4000 BCE—possibly as early as 7000 BCE—the people of Melanesia were raising pigs and cultivating taro, a plant with edible rootstocks. As the glaciers melted, the sea level rose, flooding low-lying coastal land. By around 4000 BCE a 70-mile-wide waterway, now called the Torres Strait, separated New Guinea from Australia, whose indigenous people continued their hunting and gathering way of life into the twentieth century.

The settling of the rest of the islands of Melanesia and the westernmost islands of Polynesia—Samoa and Tonga—coincided with the spread of the Lapita culture, named for a site in New Caledonia. The Lapita people were Austronesian speakers who probably migrated from Taiwan to Melanesia about 6,000 years ago. They spread throughout the islands of Melanesia beginning around 1500 BCE. They were farmers and fisherfolk who cultivated taro and yams, and brought with them dogs, pigs, and chickens, animals that these colonizers needed for food. They also carried with them the distinctive ceramics whose remnants today enable us to trace the extent of their travels. Lapita potters produced dishes, platters, bowls, and jars. Sometimes they covered their wares with a red slip, and they often decorated them with bands of incised and stamped patterns—dots, lines, and hatching—that may also have been used to decorate bark cloth and for tattooing. Most of the decoration was geometric, but some was figurative. The human face that appears in the example in FIGURE 27–2 is among the earliest representations of a human being, one of the most important subjects in Oceanic art. The Lapita people were skilled shipbuilders and navigators and engaged in inter-island trade. Over time the Lapita culture lost its widespread cohesion and evolved into various local forms. Its end is generally dated to the early centuries of the Common Era.

Polynesian culture emerged in the eastern Lapita region on the islands forming Tonga and Samoa. Just prior to the beginning of the first millennium CE, daring Polynesian seafarers, probably in double-hulled sailing canoes, began settling the scattered islands of Far Oceania and eastern Micronesia. Voyaging over open water, sometimes for thousands of miles, they reached Hawaii and Rapa Nui after about 500 CE and settled New Zealand around 800/900–1200 CE.

While this history of migrations across Melanesia to Polynesia and Micronesia allowed for cross-cultural borrowings, there are distinctions between these areas and within the regions as well. The islands that make up Micronesia, Melanesia, and Polynesia include both low-lying coral atolls and the tall tops of volcanic mountains that rise from the ocean floor. Raw materials available to residents of these islands vary greatly, and islander art and architecture utilize these materials in different ways. The soil of volcanic islands can be very rich and thus can support densely populated settlements with a local diversity of plants and animals. On the other hand, coral atolls do not generally have very good soil and thus cannot support

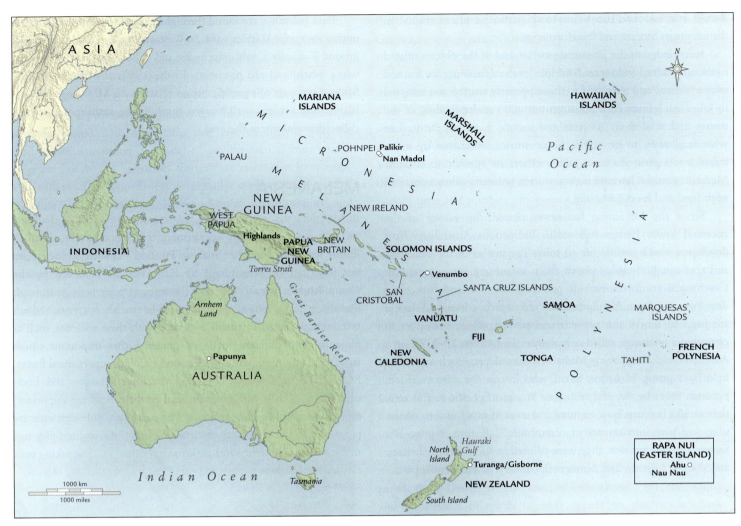

MAP 27–1 • PACIFIC CULTURAL-GEOGRAPHIC REGIONS

The Pacific cultures are found in four vast areas: Australia, Melanesia, Micronesia, and Polynesia.

large populations. In a like manner, volcanic islands can provide good stone for tools and building (as at Nan Madol, SEE FIG. 27–10), while coral is sharp but not particularly hard, and the strongest tools on a coral atoll are often those made from giant clam shells. Generally, the diversity of both plants and animals decreases from west to east among the Pacific islands.

The arts of this vast and diverse region display an enormous variety that is closely linked to each community's ritual and religious life. In this context, the visual arts were often just one strand in a rich weave that also included music, dance, and oral literature.

AUSTRALIA

The hunter-gatherers of Australia were closely attuned to the environments in which they lived until European settlers disrupted their way of life. Their only modification of the landscape was regular controlled burning of the underbrush, which encouraged new plant life and attracted animals. Their intimate knowledge of plants, animals, and water sources enabled them to survive and thrive in a wide range of challenging environments.

Indigenous Australian life is intimately connected with the concept of the Dreamtime, or the Dreaming. Not to be confused with our notions of sleep and dreams, the Dreaming refers to the period before humans existed. (The term, a translation from Arrente, one of the more than 250 languages spoken in Australia when Europeans arrived, was first used in the late nineteenth century to try to understand the indigenous worldview.) According to this complex belief system, the world began as a flat, featureless place. Ancestral Spirit Beings emerged from the earth or arrived from the sea, taking many different forms. The Spirit Beings had many adventures, and in crossing the continent they created all of its physical features: mountains, sand hills, creeks, and water holes. They also brought about the existence of animals, plants, and humans and created the ceremonies and sacred objects needed to ensure that they themselves were remembered, a system sometimes referred to as Aboriginal Laws. The Spirit Beings eventually returned to the earth or became literally one of its features. Thus, they are identified with specific places, which are honored as sacred sites. Indigenous Australians who practice this traditional religion believe that they are descended from the Spirit

Malagan also included rites to initiate young men and women into adulthood. After several months' training in seclusion in a ritual enclosure, they were presented to the public and carved and painted figures were given to them. The combined funerary and initiation ceremonies included feasts, masked dances, and the creation of a special house to display elaborately carved and painted sculptures **(FIG. 27–7)** that honored the dead. The display house illustrated, which dates to the early 1930s, is more than 14 feet wide and 12 deceased individuals are being honored. The carvings are large (the first on the left is nearly 6 feet in height) and take the form of horizontal friezes, standing figures, and poles containing several figures. They are visually complex, with tensions created between solid and pierced void, and between the two-dimensional painted patterns on three-dimensional sculptural forms. Kept secret until the final phase of the ceremonies, their unveiling was the climax of the festivities. After the ceremonies they were no longer considered ritually "active" and were destroyed or, since the late nineteenth century, sold to outsiders. *Malagan* figures are still being carved and ceremonies are held today.

NEW BRITAIN

TUBUAN MASK OF NEW BRITAIN. In the Papua New Guinea province of New Britain, which includes the Duke of York Islands, Tubuan masks represent the Tolai male secret society. This has different levels or grades of increasing knowledge and power, and wields both spiritual and social control, especially during the three months of ceremonies known as the "Time of the Tubuan."

Though initiation to the society is the main purpose of the ceremonies, the men of the village, who have achieved power through the accumulation of wealth, and in the past through bravery in war, use this period to call up the spirits represented by the masks, who have the authority to settle disputes, stop fights, punish lawbreakers, and force the payment of debts. Political power and authority are underscored and enhanced by their appearance, and in the past they had the power of life and death.

The masks represent both female and male spirits, though all the masks are danced by men. Local stories say women originally owned the masks and that they were stolen from them by men. The **TUBUAN MASK** (**FIG. 27–8**) represents the Mother, who gives birth to her children, the Duk Duk masks, which represent the new initiates into the society. With the appearance, first of the Mother masks, then of the Duk Duk masks, the initiates return to the village from the bush, where they have undergone intensive preparation to enter the society. The Tubuan mask has a distinctive, tall conical shape and prominent eyes formed by concentric white circles. The green leaf skirt is a very sacred part of the mask, which is made from painted bark cloth, various fibers, and feathers: Black feathers on top indicate a more powerful spirit than white feathers.

MICRONESIA

The majority of Micronesia's islands are small, low-lying coral atolls, but in the western region several are volcanic in origin. The eastern islands are more closely related culturally to Polynesia,

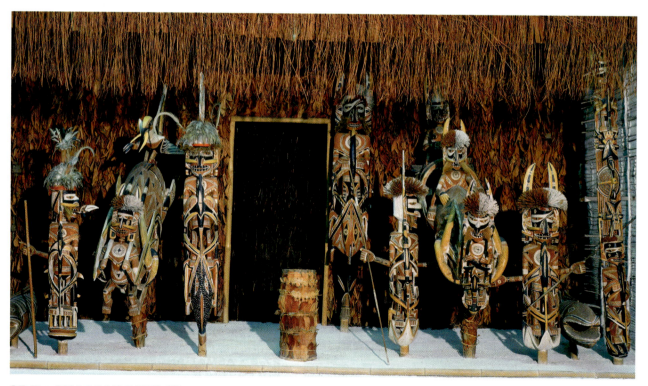

27-7 • *MALAGAN* DISPLAY
Medina village, New Ireland, Papua New Guinea. c. 1930. Height 82⅝″ (210 cm), width 137¾″ (350 cm).
Museum für Völkerkunde, Basel, Switzerland.

while those in the west show connections to Melanesia, especially in the men's houses found on Palau and Yap. The atolls—circular coral reefs surrounding lagoons where islands once stood—have a limited range of materials for creating objects of any kind. Micronesians are known especially for their navigational skills and their fine canoes. They also create textiles from banana and coconut fibers, bowls from turtle shells, and abstract human figures from wood, which is scarce. As in other parts of the Pacific, tattooing and the performative arts remain central to life.

WAPEPE NAVIGATION CHART.   Sailors from the Marshall Islands relied on celestial navigation (navigating by the sun and moon and stars) as well as a detailed understanding of the ocean currents and trade winds to travel from one island to another. To teach navigation to younger generations, elders traditionally used stick charts (*wapepe* or *mattang*)—maps that showed land, but also the path from one island to the next, the water a sailor would cross during his voyage.

In common use until the 1950s, the stick chart (FIG. 27–9) was a schematic diagram of the prevailing ocean currents and the characteristic wave patterns encountered between islands. The currents are represented by sticks held together by coconut fibers; the shells mark islands on the route. The arrangement of sticks around a shell indicates a zone of distinctive waves shaped by the effect of an island deflecting the prevailing wind. Such refracted waves enable a

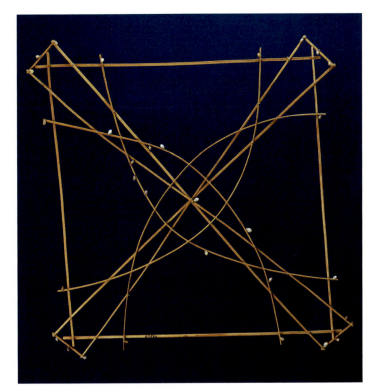

27-9 • *WAPEPE* NAVIGATION CHART
Marshall Islands. 19th century. Sticks, coconut fiber, shells, 29½ × 29½" (75 × 75 cm). Peabody Essex Museum, Salem.

navigator to sense the proximity of land without being able to see it, and to discern the least difficult course for making landfall. Although the *wapepe* is primarily functional, its combination of clarity, simplicity, and abstraction has an aesthetic impact.

NAN MADOL.   The basalt cliffs of the island of Pohnpei provided the building material for one of the largest and most remarkable stone architectural complexes in Oceania. Nan Madol, on its southeast coast, consists of 92 artificial islands set within a network of canals covering about 170 acres (MAP 27–2). Seawalls and breakwaters 15 feet high and 35 feet thick protect the area from the ocean. When it was populated, openings in the breakwaters gave canoes access to the ocean and allowed seawater to flow in and out with the tides, flushing clean the canals. While other similar complexes have been identified in Micronesia, Nan Madol is the largest and most impressive, reflecting the importance of the kings who ruled from the site. The artificial islands and the buildings atop them were built between the early thirteenth and seventeenth centuries, until the dynasty's political decline. The site had been abandoned by the time Europeans discovered it in the nineteenth century.

Nan Madol was an administrative and ceremonial center as well as, at one time, a home for as many as 1,000 people. The powerful kings drew upon this labor force to construct a monumental city. Both the buildings and the underlying islands are built of massive pieces of stone set in alternating layers of log-shaped stones and boulders of prismatic basalt. The largest of the

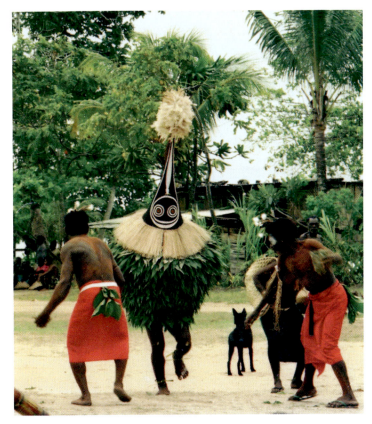

27-8 • TUBUAN MASK BEING DANCED
Tolai people, Duke of York Islands, New Britain, Papua New Guinea. c. 1990. Cloth, paint, fiber, feathers.

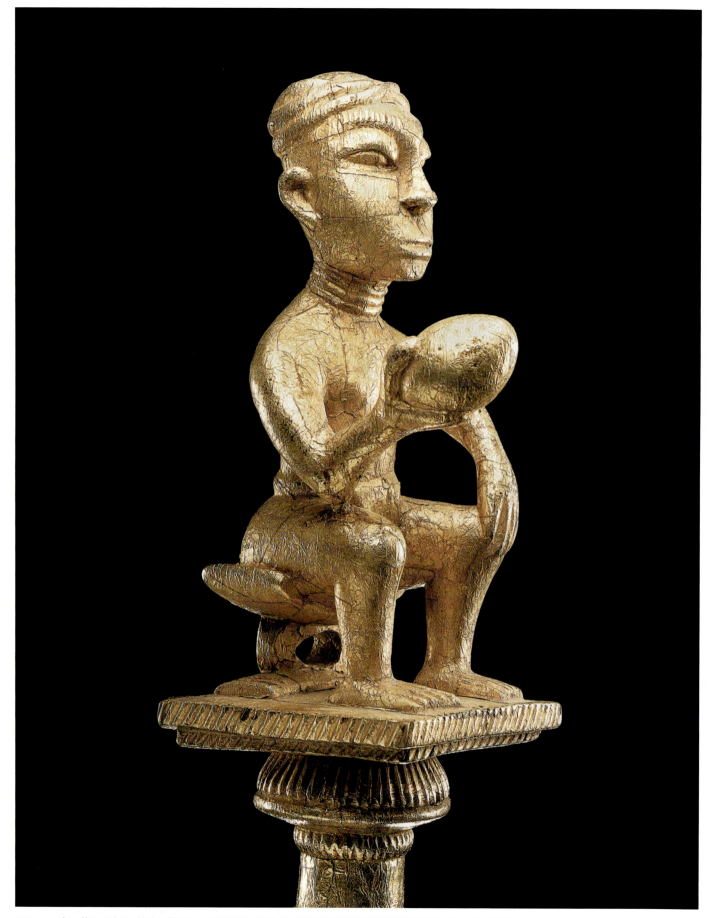

28-1 • Attributed to Kojo Bonsu **FINIAL OF A SPOKESPERSON'S STAFF (*OKYEAME POMA*)**
From Ghana. Ashanti culture, 1960s–1970s. Wood and gold, height 11¼″ (28.57 cm).
Sarah Da Vanzo Collection, Johannesburg, South Africa.

ART OF AFRICA IN THE MODERN ERA

Political power is like an egg, says an Ashanti proverb. Grasp it too tightly and it will shatter in your hand; hold it too loosely and it will slip from your fingers. Whenever the *okyeame* (spokesman) for one twentieth-century Ashanti ruler was conferring with that ruler or communicating the ruler's words to others, he held a staff with this symbolic caution on the use and abuse of power prominently displayed on the gold-leaf-covered finial **(FIG. 28–1)**. Since about 1900 these advisors have carried staffs of office such as the one pictured here. The carved figure at the top illustrates a story that may have multiple meanings when told by a witty owner. This staff was probably carved in the 1960s or 1970s by Kojo Bonsu. The son of Osei Bonsu (1900–1976), a famous carver, Kojo Bonsu lives in the Ashanti city of Kumasi and continues to carve prolifically.

A staff or scepter is a nearly universal symbol of authority and leadership. Today in many colleges and universities a ceremonial mace is still carried by the leader of an academic procession, and it is often placed in front of the speaker's lectern, as a symbol of the speaker's authority. The Ashanti spokesmen who carry their image-topped staffs are part of this widespread tradition.

Since the fifteenth century, when the first Europeans explored Africa, objects such as this staff have been shipped back to Western museums of natural history or ethnography, where they were catalogued as curious artifacts of "primitive cultures." Toward the end of the nineteenth century, however, changes in Western thinking about African culture gradually led more and more people to appreciate the inherent aesthetic qualities of these unfamiliar objects and at last to embrace them fully as art. In recent years the appreciation of traditional African arts have been further enhanced through the exploration of their meaning from the point of view of the people who made them.

If we are to understand African art such as this staff on its own terms, we must take it out of the glass case of the museum where we usually encounter it and imagine the artwork playing its vital role in a human community. Indeed, this is true of any work of art produced anywhere in the world. When we recognize in an artwork the true expression of values and beliefs, our imaginations cross a bridge to understanding.

LEARN ABOUT IT

28.1 Examine the role of the visual arts in the expression of power and authority by modern African leaders.

28.2 Summarize the role of the arts in divination to disclose the cause of misfortune in several African cultures.

28.3 Examine the role of African arts in its reaction to the colonial experience.

28.4 Contrast the ways in which African contemporary artists explore their search for an identity through their art.

28.5 Evaluate the role of masquerade in African rites of passage such as initiation and funeral rituals.

HEAR MORE: Listen to an audio file of your chapter **www.myartslab.com**

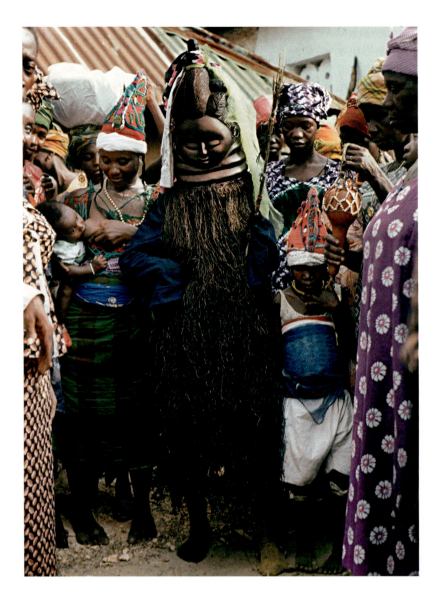

28-7 • TEMNE *NOWO* MASQUERADE
WITH ATTENDANTS
Sierra Leone. 1980.

the initiated. The white crescent at the top represents the quarter moon, under which the initiation is held. The white triangles below represent bull roarers—sacred sound-makers that are swung around the head on a long cord to recreate spirit voices. The large central X represents the scar that every initiated Bwa bears as a mark of devotion. The horizontal zigzags at the bottom represent the path of the ancestors and symbolize adherence to ancestral ways. That the path is difficult to follow is clearly conveyed. The curving red hook that projects in front of the face is said to represent the beak of the hornbill, a bird associated with the supernatural world and believed to be an intermediary between the living and the dead. The mask thus proudly announces the initiate's passage to adulthood while encoding secrets of initiation in abstract symbols of proper moral conduct.

INITIATION TO WOMANHOOD IN WEST AFRICA. Among the Mende, Temne, Vai, and Kpelle peoples of Sierra Leone, the initiation of girls into adulthood is organized by a society of older women called Sande or Bondo. The initiation culminates with a ritual bath in a river, after which the initiated return to the village.

At the ceremony, the Sande women wear black gloves and stockings, black costumes of shredded raffia fibers that cover the entire body, and black masks called *nowo* or *sowei* (FIG. 28–7).

With its glossy black surface, high forehead, elaborately plaited hairstyle decorated with combs, and refined facial features, the mask represents ideal female beauty. The mask is worn by a senior member of the women's Sande society whose responsibility it is to prepare Sande girls for their adult roles in society, including marriage and child rearing. The meanings of the mask are complex. It has been shown that the mask can be compared with the chrysalis of a certain African butterfly, with the creases at the base of the mask representing the segments of the chrysalis. Thus, the young woman entering adulthood is like a butterfly emerging from its cocoon. The comparison extends even further, for just as the butterfly feeds on the toxic sap of the milkweed to make itself poisonous to predatory birds, so the medicinal powers of the Sande society is believed to protect the young women from danger. The creases may additionally refer to the concentric waves that radiate outward as the initiate emerges from the river to take her place as a member of the adult community.

BWAMI ASSOCIATION AMONG THE LEGA. A ceremony of initiation may also accompany the achievement of other types of membership. Among the Lega people, who live in the dense forests between the headwaters of the Congo River and the great lakes of east Africa, the political system is based on a voluntary association called *bwami*, which comprises six levels or grades. Some 80 percent of all male Lega belong to *bwami*, and all aspire to the highest grade. Women can belong to *bwami* as well, although not at a higher grade than their husbands.

Promotion from one grade of *bwami* to the next takes many years. It is based not only on a candidate's character but also on his or her ability to pay the initiation fees, which increase dramatically with each grade. No candidate for any level of *bwami* can pay the fees without assistance: All must enlist the help of relatives to provide the necessary payment, which may include cowrie shells, goats, wild game, palm oil, clothing, and trade goods. Thus, the ambition to move from one level of *bwami* to the next encourages a harmonious community, for all must stay on good terms with other members of the community if they are to advance **(FIG. 28–8)**.

Bwami initiations into advanced grades are held in the plaza at the center of the community in the presence of all members.

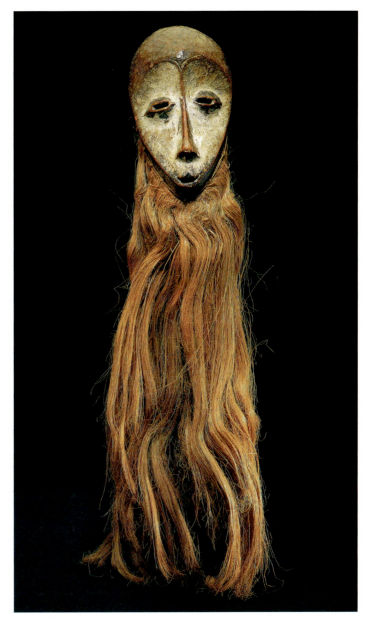

28-9 • BWAMI MASK (LUKWAKONGO)
From Democratic Republic of Congo. 20th century. Wood, plant fiber, and pigment, height 22¾" (57.5 cm). UCLA Fowler Museum of Cultural History, Los Angeles.

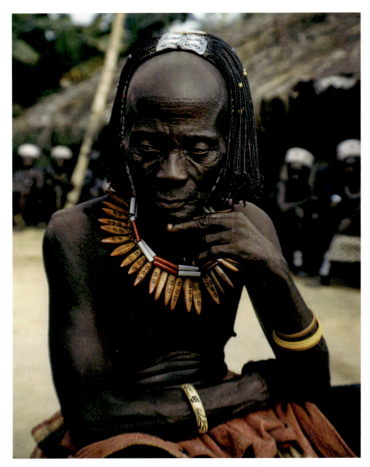

28-8 • LEGA TITLED-ELDER WEARING PRESTIGE HAT
From Democratic Republic of Congo, 1967. National Museum of African Art, Smithsonian Institution, Washington, D.C.
Eliot Elisofon Photographic Archive (EEPA EECL 2238)

Dances and songs are performed, and the values and ideals of the appropriate grade are explained through proverbs and sayings. These standards are illustrated by natural or crafted objects, which are presented to the initiate as signs of membership. At the highest two levels of *bwami*, such objects include exquisitely made small masks and sculpted figures.

The mask in **FIGURE 28–9** is associated with *yananio*, the second-highest grade of *bwami*. Typical of Lega masks, the head is fashioned as an oval into which is carved a concave, heart-shaped face with narrow, raised features. The masks are often colored white with clay and fitted with a long beard made of plant fibers. Too small to cover the face, they are displayed in other ways—held in the palm of a hand, for example, or attached to a thigh. Each

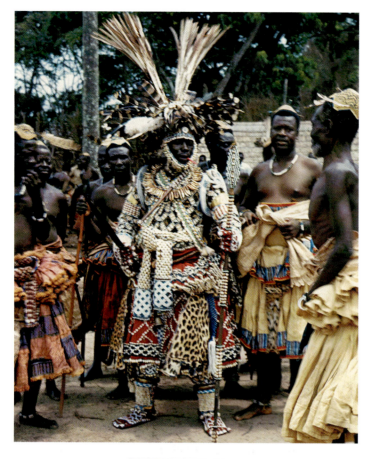

apoong) displays sumptuous adornment at his investiture. Each element of regalia signifies a prerogative of an individual's titled position relative to the position of others within a complicated system of titleholding. Naturally the most extravagant adornment is worn by the paramount ruler, as can be seen in the photograph taken by Eliot Elisofon of the Kuba *nyim* in 1971 (FIG. 28–15). Textile display is also an essential aspect of funeral rituals where textiles are worn at celebratory dances and displayed on the body of the deceased. The textiles are subsequently buried with the deceased, where the Kuba believe an individual remains for a period of time before being reborn.

YORUBA PALACE ART. The kings of the Yoruba people of Nigeria also manifested their authority and power through the large palaces in which they lived. In a typical palace plan, the principal rooms opened onto a veranda with elaborately carved posts facing a courtyard (FIG. 28–16). Elaborate carving also covered the palace doors. Among the most important Yoruba artists of the early twentieth century was Olowe of Ise (d. 1938), who

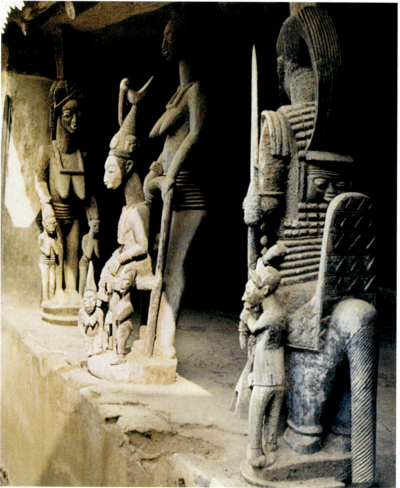

28-16 • VERANDA POSTS BY OLOWE OF ISE INSTALLED IN THE COURTYARD OF THE PALACE OF THE *OGAGA* OF IKERE
Nigeria, c. 1910–1914. Wood and pigment. Photograph taken in 1964.

EXPLORE MORE: Gain insight from a primary source related to Olowe of Ise's veranda posts www.myartslab.com

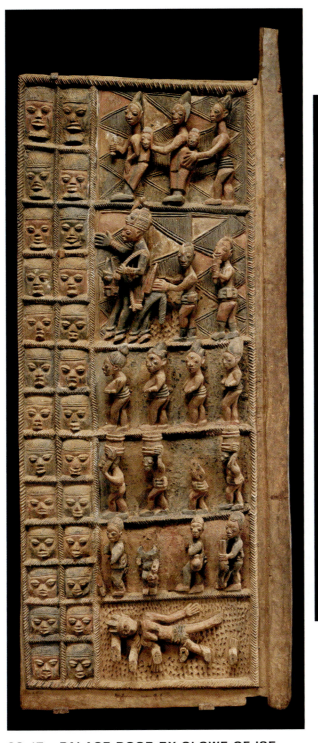

viewer. Their long necks and elaborate hairstyles make them appear even taller, unlike typical Yoruba sculpture which uses short, static figures. The figures are in such high relief that the upper portions are actually carved in the round. The figures move energetically against an underlying decorative pattern, and the entire surface of the doors was painted; only traces of the original colors remain.

This door panel commemorates the *arinjale* (king) of Ise receiving Major W.R. Reeve-Tucker, the first British traveling commissioner for the province, and his entourage. A separate door panel, in a private collection, presents the European entourage. In the second register of this panel, the *arinjale* is portrayed on horseback wearing a conical crown and accompanied by court messengers. A variety of other members of the court, including royal wives who are lifting their breasts (a gesture of generosity and affection performed by elder women), bearers carrying kegs of gunpowder, royal guards, and priests appear in other registers. The bottom register portrays a human sacrifice, with birds pecking at the corpse. Human sacrifice occurred rarely and was usually undertaken to ensure community survival. The two rows of heads on the left side of the panel may represent either ancestors of the *arinjale* or enemies taken in battle.

Olowe seems to have worked from the early 1900s until his death in 1938. Although he was famous throughout Yorubaland and called upon by patrons as distant as 60 miles from his home, few records of his activities remain, and only one European, Philip Allison, wrote of meeting him and watching him work. Allison described Olowe carving the iron-hard African oak "as easily as [he would] a calabash [gourd]."

28–17 • PALACE DOOR BY OLOWE OF ISE
From Ise Palace, Nigeria, Yoruba peoples. c. 1904–1910. Wood, pigment, height 81½″ × width 34⅝″ × depth 6¼″ (207 × 88 × 15.9 cm). National Museum of African Art, Smithsonian Institution, Washington, D.C. (88-13-1)

DEATH AND ANCESTORS

In the view of many African peoples, death is not an end but a transition—the leaving behind of one phase of life and the beginning of another. Just as ceremonies mark the initiation of young men and women into the community of adults, so too they mark the initiation of the newly dead into the community of spirits. Like the rites of initiation into adulthood, death begins with a separation from the community, in this case the community of the living. A period of isolation and trial follows, during which the newly dead spirit may, for example, journey to the land of ancestors. Finally, the deceased is reintegrated into a community, this time the community of ancestral spirits. The living who preserve the memory of the deceased may appeal to his or her spirit to intercede on their behalf with nature spirits or to prevent the spirits of the dead from using their powers to harm (see "Kuba Funerary Mask," pages 896–897).

carved doors and veranda posts for the rulers of the Ekiti–Yoruba kingdoms in southwestern Nigeria.

The door panel from the royal palace at Ise (**FIG. 28–17**) illustrates Olowe's artistry. Its asymmetrical composition combines narrative and symbolic scenes in horizontal rectangular panels. Tall figures carved in profile end in heads facing out to confront the

Kuba Funerary Mask

The Kuba people of the Democratic Republic of Congo perform funerary masquerades to honor deceased members of the men's initiation society and high-ranking individuals who belonged to the community council of elders.

In the southern Kuba region, funeral rites for initiated men are often accompanied by the appearance of one or more masquerade figures on the day of interment of the deceased. On these occasions initiation society members, family, and friends of the deceased celebrate the departed's life while mourning his death. In part, funeral rites are elaborate because of the belief that the spirit of the recently deceased (*mwendu*) may bring harm to his family or community if his achievements and status in life are not acknowledged at the funeral. The *mwendu* may be angered for a variety of reasons. Perhaps outstanding debts were not paid and the money or other goods were kept by a family member. Or the deceased had asked for something to be buried with him and this request was not honored. Disrespect is most often shown if the deceased is not given a proper burial, one equal to his rank in life. For an initiated man, a funeral masquerade is mandatory in this region, and members of the community-based men's initiation society show their solidarity with the deceased and his spirit by performing a masquerade at his funeral.

Among the most spectacular masquerades performed in the Kuba region is that of *Ngady mwaash*—the name means literally "female mask." The mask is carved from wood, and attached to a framework covered with cloth and decorated with beads and shells that forms the top, sides, and back of the head. Wooden ears, carved separately, are attached to the sides of the head. The face of the mask presents an exuberant blend of bold geometric patterns composed of contrasting areas of triangles and parallel lines. A triangular-shaped hat, identical to that worn by female diviners, is attached to the mask. The hat signifies that *Ngady mwaash* is invested with the power of nature spirits (*ngesh*) to whom Kuba diviners attribute their extraordinary powers.

The costume for *Ngady mwaash* is composed of a shirt and leggings made from animal hide or cloth, often extensively decorated with painted black-and-white triangles. Small wooden dowels attached to the front of the shirt represent breasts. Although wearing a woman's long embroidered skirt under a short decorated skirt affixed with a belt, *Ngady mwaash* is always performed by a man. Costume accessories include strands of beaded and shell-laden bandoliers that crisscross the

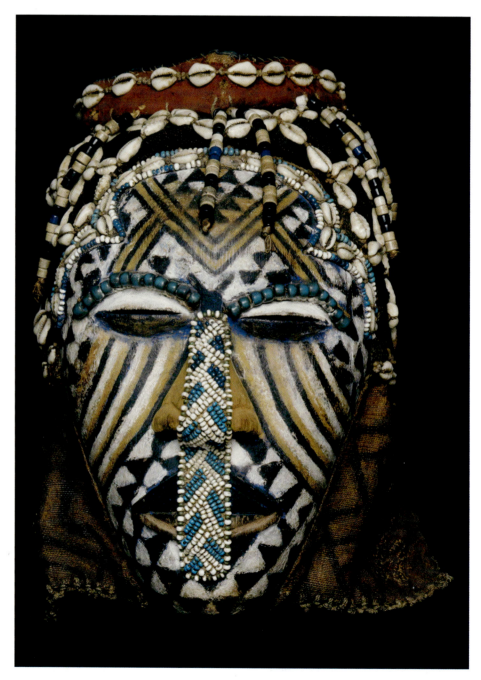

Ngady mwaash mask. Democratic Republic of Congo, Kuba peoples. Late 19th–mid 20th century. Wood, pigment glass beads, cowrie shells, fabric, thread, height 12½″ (31.8 cm). The Art Institute of Chicago. (1982.1505)

Bwoom masked dancer at the funeral of an initiated man. Democratic Republic of the Congo, Southern Kuba peoples. 1982.

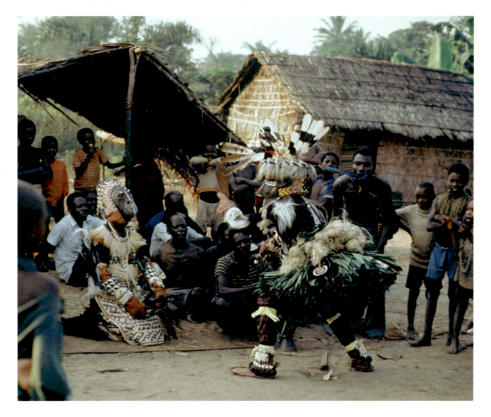

chest and decorated arm- and legbands. The mask, costume, and accessories, as well as the fly whisk that *Ngady mwaash* carries, represent wealth and high status.

The funeral masquerade performance is held near the residence of the man who has died, just prior to burial. The perimeter of the dance ground is lined with family, friends, and onlookers who have come to bid a final farewell to the deceased and witness the performance. *Ngady mwaash* takes turns performing with another masked figure designated as male, such as the masked figure *Bwoom*.

The individual character or persona of male and female masked figures is fully realized during performance. *Bwoom*, who carries a short sword, exudes power and restrained aggression. The dancer employs lunging movements and quick short jabs with his sword, causing onlookers to suspect that he may suddenly lose control and harm someone. This feeling of apprehension is a constituent part of the performance style of *Bwoom*, and is a principal reason why community members look forward to masquerade with such anticipation. In contrast, the performance style of *Ngady mwaash* is decidedly nonthreatening, with graceful movements as the dancer's body, legs, arms, and hands move in fluid gestures. The differences in the performance styles of male and female masquerade figures parallel the difference in the dance styles of men and women in Kuba culture. The men's initiation society, which organizes funeral masquerades, expresses its control and dominance of ritual affairs in part through the contrasting performance styles of *Bwoom* and *Ngady mwaash*.

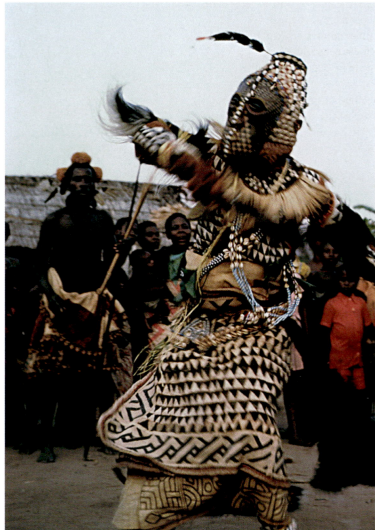

Ngady mwaash masked dancer at the funeral of an initiated man. Democratic Republic of the Congo, Southern Kuba peoples. 1982.

DOGON FUNERARY *DAMA*. Among the Dogon people of Mali, in west Africa, a collective funeral rite called *dama*, is held every 12 to 13 years **(FIG. 28–18)**. During *dama*, a variety of different masks perform to the sound of gunfire to drive the souls of the deceased from the village. Among the most common masks to perform is the *kanaga*, whose rectangular face supports a superstructure of planks that depict a woman, bird, or lizard with splayed legs.

For a deceased man, men from the community later engage in a mock battle on the roof of his home and participate in ritual hunts; for a deceased woman, the women of the community smash her cooking vessels on the threshold of her home. These portions of *dama* are reminders of human activities the deceased will no longer engage in. The *dama* may last as long as six days and include the performance of hundreds of masks. Because a *dama* is so costly, it is performed for several deceased elders at the same time. However, in certain Dogon communities frequented by tourists, *dama* performances have become more frequent as new masked characters are invented, including masks representing tourists holding wooden cameras or anthropologists holding notebooks in their hands. In response to tourists, Dogon mask-makers produce additional masks that are offered for sale at the conclusion of the performance.

FANG ANCESTOR GUARDIAN. The Fang, along with other peoples who live near the Atlantic coast from southern Cameroon through Rio Muni and into Gabon, shared a number of similar institutions and beliefs in which the skulls, bones, and relics of ancestors who had performed great deeds during their lifetimes were collected after burial and placed in a cylindrical bark container (*nsek-bieri*), which was preserved by the family. Deeds thus honored included being victorious in warfare, killing an elephant, being the first to trade with Europeans, bearing an especially large number of children, or founding a particular lineage or community. The bones and relics of deceased family members were thought to have special powers that could be drawn upon to aid the living with problems that confronted or threatened the family. Before colonial officials banned many ritual practices, ancestral spirits represented by the reliquaries were regularly consulted on problems with fertility—failure in conceiving and bringing to term children—or with hunting and farming, or before embarking on a commercial venture.

As a point of focus for mediation between the ancestors and the living, the Fang placed a wooden sculpture called a *bieri* on top of the container holding the relics. These sculptures functioned as

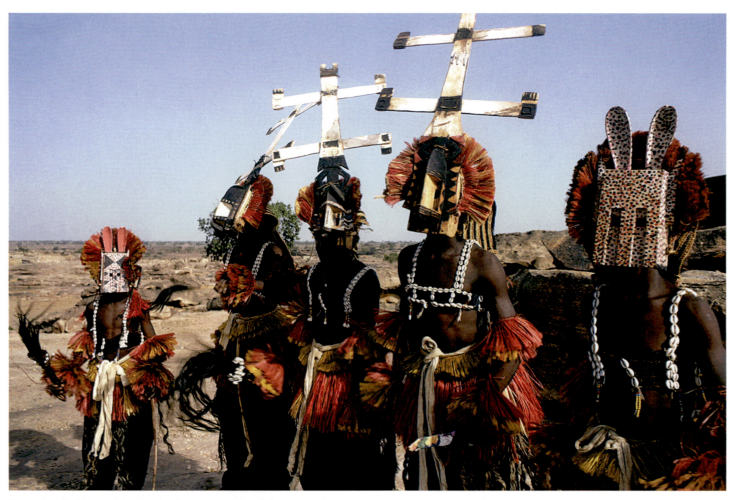

28-18 • *KANAGA* AND RABBIT MASQUERADE FIGURES AT *DAMA*
Mali. Dogon culture, 1959. National Museum of African Art, Smithsonian Institution, Washington, D.C. Eliot Elisofon Photographic Archives (EEPA 3502)

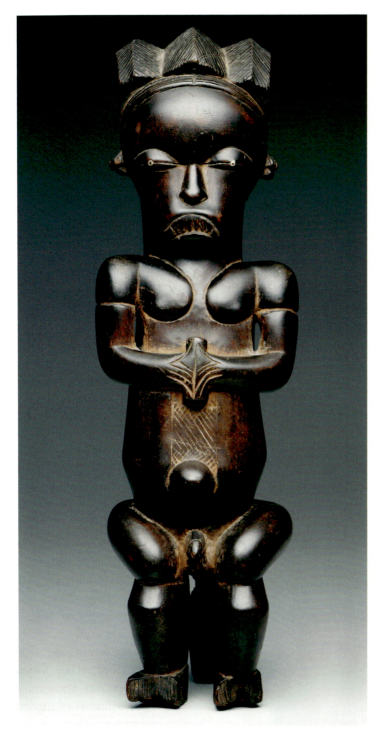

28–19 • RELIQUARY GUARDIAN (*EYEMA BIERI*)
From Gabon. Fang people, Mvai group, mid–late 19th century. Wood, metal, and shell, height 21¼" (53.97 cm). Dallas Museum of Art.
The Eugene and Margaret McDermott Art Fund, Inc. (2000.3.MCD)

points of contact for ancestral support and veneration and also as guardians to protect the relics from malevolent spirit forces (FIG. 28–19).

Bieri were carved in a number of different forms and styles, including large heads with long necks which were secured into the lid of the container; the container thus represents the body of the ancestors. Other *bieri* were created as full figures in a relatively

naturalistic style, with carefully arranged hairstyles, fully rounded torsos, and heavily muscled legs and arms. Both forms are today considered among the great masterpieces of African sculpture. Here, the figure's firmly set jaw and powerfully built, muscular body exudes a sense of authority and confidence. These powerfully realized sculptures were often enhanced by the frequent application of cleansing and purifying palm oil over an extended period of time. This has produced a rich, glossy black surface that may literally excrete oil.

An authority on Fang culture suggests that the Fang strive to achieve a balance between the opposing forces of chaos and order, male and female, pure and impure, powerful and weak. They value an attitude of quiet composure, of reflection and tranquility. These qualities are embodied in the symmetry of the *bieri*, which communicates the calm and wisdom of the ancestor while also instilling awe and fear in those not initiated into the Fang religion.

CONTEMPORARY ART

The photographs of rituals and ceremonies in this chapter show ways in which African traditional arts have continued during the modern era. All of the photographs are somewhat dated, yet even today performances are staged in which the traditional types of masks appear. Many African communities continue to recreate art forms according to their traditions. But Africa is ever-changing and, as new experiences pose new challenges and offer new opportunities, African art changes over time.

Perhaps the most obvious development in African art has been the adaptation of modern materials to traditional forms. Some Yoruba, for example, have used photographs and children's brightly colored, imported plastic dolls in place of the traditional *ere ibeji*, images of twins, shown in FIGURE 28–4. The Guro people of Côte d'Ivoire continue to commission delicate masks dressed with costly textiles and other materials, but they paint them with brilliantly colored oil-based enamel paints. The Baule create brightly painted versions of spirit-spouse figures dressed as businessmen or soccer players.

Throughout the colonial period and especially during the years following World War II, many African artists trained in the techniques of European art. In the postcolonial era, numerous African artists have studied in Europe and the United States, and many have become known internationally through exhibitions of their work in galleries and museums. Yet the diversity of influences on contemporary Africa makes it impossible to render a homogeneous view of what constitutes contemporary African art. As the art historian and curator Salah Hassan writes: "The development of a modern idiom in African art is closely linked to modern Africa's search for identity. Most contemporary works have apparent ties to traditional African folklore, belief systems and imagery. The only way to interpret or understand these works is in the light of the dual experience of colonialism and assimilation into Western culture in Africa. They reflect the search for a new identity."

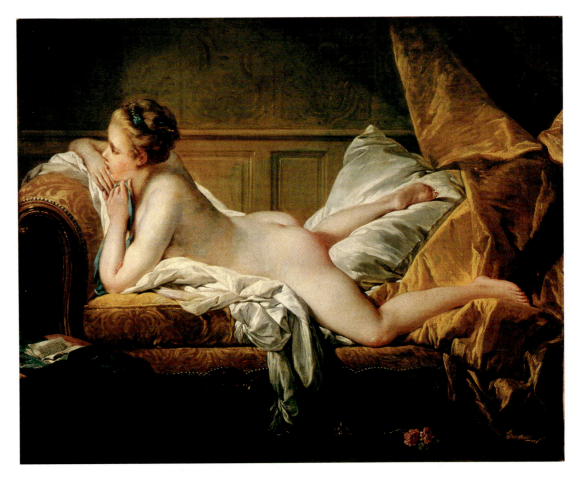

29-5 • François Boucher
**GIRL RECLINING:
LOUISE O'MURPHY**
1751. Oil on canvas,
28³/₄ × 23¹/₄″ (73 × 59 cm).
Wallfaf-Richartz Museum,
Cologne.

as his official examination canvas for admission to membership in the Royal Academy of Painting and Sculpture (see "Academies and Academy Exhibitions," page 924). Although there was no academic category to cover the painting, the academicians were so impressed by the canvas that they created a new category, the **fête galante**, or elegant outdoor entertainment, to describe this genre of painting.

BOUCHER.   The artist most closely associated with Parisian Rococo painting after Watteau's death is François Boucher (1703–1770). The son of a minor painter, Boucher in 1723 entered the workshop of an engraver where he was hired to reproduce Watteau's paintings for a collector, firmly establishing the future direction of his career.

After studying at the French Academy in Rome from 1727 to 1731, he settled in Paris and became an academician. Soon his life and career were intimately bound up with two women. The first was his artistically talented wife, Marie-Jeanne Buseau, who was a frequent model as well as a studio assistant to her husband. The other was Louis XV's mistress, Madame de Pompadour, who became his major patron and supporter. Pompadour was an amateur artist herself and took lessons in printmaking from Boucher. After he received his first royal commission in 1735, Boucher worked almost continuously on the decorations for the royal residences at Versailles and Fontainebleau. In 1755, he was

made chief inspector at the Gobelins tapestry manufactory, and provided designs for them as well as for the Sèvres porcelain and Beauvais tapestry manufactories. All these workshops produced both furnishings for the king and wares for sale on the open market by merchants such as Gersaint. Indeed, Boucher operated in a much more commercial market than artists in the previous century.

In 1765, Boucher became First Painter to the King. In this role he painted several portraits of Louis XV, scenes of daily life and mythological pictures, and a series of erotic works for private enjoyment often depicting the adventures of Venus. One such painting is **GIRL RECLINING: LOUISE O'MURPHY (FIG. 29–5)**. In this painting, the 18-year old Louise O'Murphy (whose identity is still debated by scholars), provocatively pink and completely nude, lies on her stomach on a couch. Her satiny pink and white clothing is strewn about beneath her, and pillows are scattered at her feet and on the floor; her hair is decorated with braids and a blue ribbon and a fallen pink rose lies on the floor. Louise's plump buttocks are displayed enticingly at the very center of the painting. There is little doubt about the subject of the painting; Boucher intended it to be overtly sensual. In contrast to Watteau's *fête galante*, in which nude gods, goddesses, and *putti* frolic around in unreal settings, the woman shown here is clearly human, contemporary, and lying in a very real Rococo room. Boucher's robust world of sensual pleasure recalls the style of Rubens (SEE FIG. 22–29), but Boucher has a lighter touch.

FRAGONARD. Another noteworthy master of French Rococo painting, Jean-Honoré Fragonard (1732–1806), studied with Boucher, who encouraged him to enter the competition for the Prix de Rome, the three- to five-year scholarship awarded to the top students in painting and sculpture graduating from the French Academy's art school. Fragonard won the prize in 1752 and spent the years 1756 to 1761 in Italy; however, it was not until 1765 that he was finally accepted as a member of the Royal Academy. He catered to the tastes of an aristocratic clientele, and, as a decorator of interiors, began to fill the vacuum left by Boucher's death in 1770.

Fragonard's **THE SWING** (FIG. 29–6) of 1767 was not part of an interior scheme. It was originally commissioned from painter Gabriel-François Doyen. Although the patron is unknown, Doyen's description reveals that the painting was clearly intended to be sensually explicit. He refused the commission, and gave it to

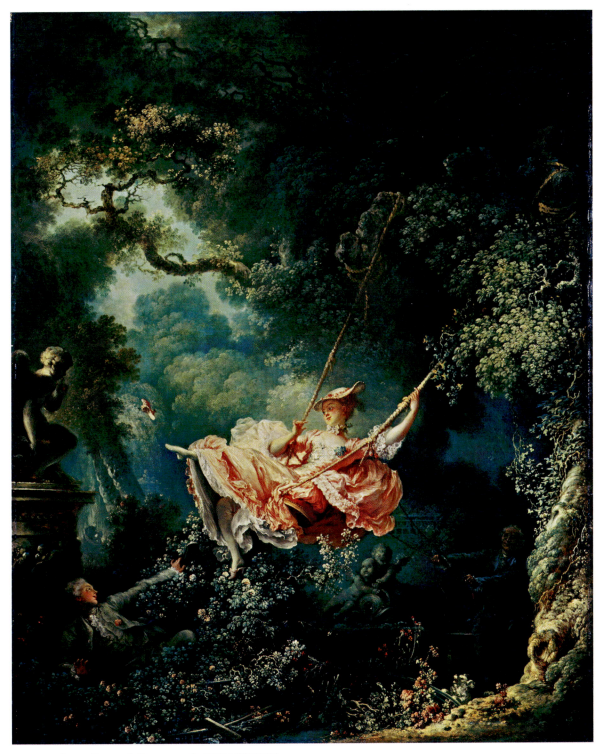

29-6 • Jean-Honoré Fragonard THE SWING
1766. Oil on canvas, 2′8⅝″ × 2′2″ (82.9 × 66 cm). The Wallace Collection, London.

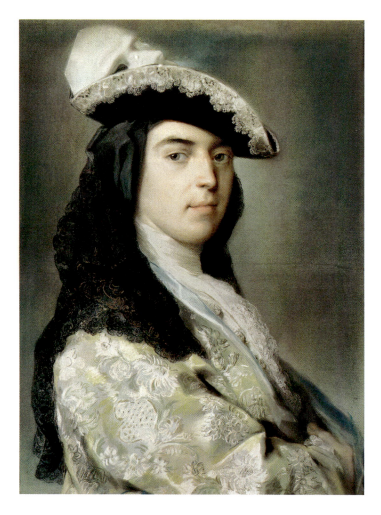

Pastel is a fast and versatile medium: Pastel crayons, made of pulverized pigment bound to a chalk base by weak gum water, can be used to sketch quickly and spontaneously, or they can be rubbed and blended on the surface of paper to produce a shiny and highly finished surface.

Carriera began her career designing lace patterns and painting miniature portraits on the ivory lids of snuffboxes before she graduated to pastel portraits. Her portraits were so widely admired that she was awarded honorary membership of Rome's Academy of Saint Luke in 1705, and was later admitted to the academies in Bologna and Florence. In 1720, she traveled to Paris, where she made a pastel portrait of the young Louis XV and was elected to the Royal Academy of Painting and Sculpture, despite the 1706 rule forbidding the further admission of women. Returning to Italy in 1721, she established herself in Venice as a portraitist of handsome young men such as the British aristocrat **CHARLES SACKVILLE, 2ND DUKE OF DORSET** (FIG. 29–10).

CANALETTO. A painted city view was by far the most prized souvenir of a stay in Venice. Two kinds of views were produced in Venice: the **capriccio** ("caprice," plural *capricci*), an imaginary

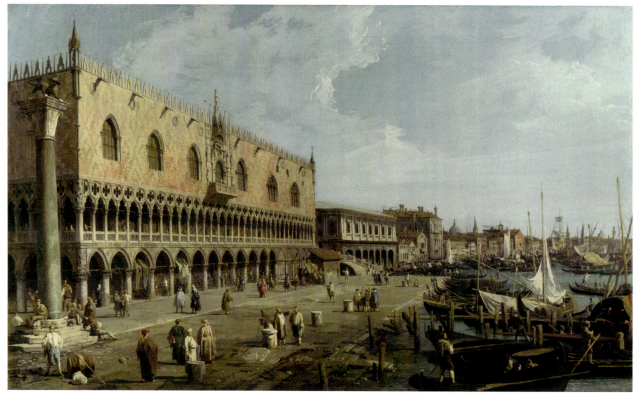

29-11 • Canaletto THE DOGE'S PALACE AND THE RIVA DEGLI SCHIAVONI
Late 1730s. Oil on canvas, 24⅛ × 39¼″ (61.3 × 99.8 cm). National Gallery, London. Wynn Ellis Bequest 1876 (NG 940)

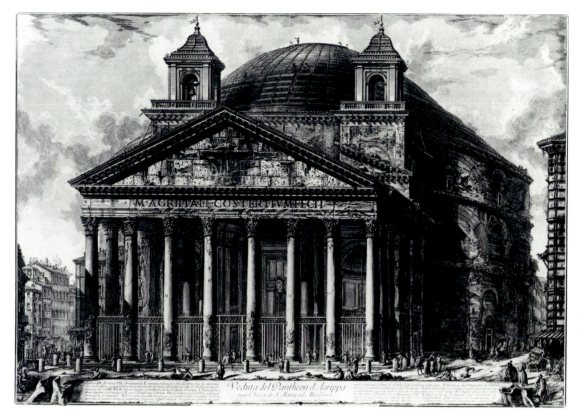

29-12 • Giovanni Battista Piranesi **VIEW OF THE PANTHEON, ROME**
From the Views of Rome series, first printed in 1756. Etching, 18⁹⁄₁₆ × 27⅛″ (47.2 × 69.7 cm). Kupferstich-kabinett, Staatliche Museen, Berlin.

landscape or cityscape in which the artist mixed actual structures, such as famous ruins, with imaginary ones to create attractive compositions; and the **veduta** ("view;" plural *vedute*), a more naturalistic rendering of famous views and buildings, well-known tourist attractions, and local color in the form of tiny figures of the Venetian people and visiting tourists. *Vedute* often encompassed panoramic views of famous landmarks, such as **THE DOGE'S PALACE AND THE RIVA DEGLI SCHIAVONI (FIG. 29–11)** by the Venetian artist Giovanni Antonio Canal, called Canaletto (1697–1768). It was thought that Canaletto used the camera obscura (see page 967) to render his *vedute* with exact topographical accuracy, but his drawings show that he seems to have worked freehand. In fact, his views are rarely topographically accurate and more often than not are composite images: It is a mark of his skill that Canaletto makes us want to believe that his *vedute* are "real." He painted and sold so many to British visitors that his dealer sent him to London from 1746 to 1755 to paint views of the English capital city for his British clients, who included several important aristocrats as well as King George III.

PIRANESI.   The city of Rome was also captured in *vedute* for the pleasure of tourists and armchair travelers, most notably by Giovanni Battista Piranesi (1720–1778). Trained in Venice as an architect, he moved to Rome and studied etching, eventually establishing a publishing house and becoming one of the century's most successful printmakers. Piranesi produced a large series of *vedute* of ancient Roman monuments and ruins. His **VIEW OF THE PANTHEON (FIG. 29–12)** is informed by a careful study of ancient

Roman architecture. Piranesi succeeds in breathing life into his images by creating grand, monumental scenes.

NEOCLASSICISM IN ROME

The intellectuals and artists who came to study and work in Rome often formed communities with a shared interest in Neoclassical ideals. A British coterie, for example, included Angelica Kauffmann (SEE FIG. 29–26), Benjamin West (SEE FIG. 29–27), and Gavin Hamilton, all of whom contributed to early Neoclassicism. Communities of artists from France and Germany were also established. One of the most influential communities of the period formed at the Villa Albani on the outskirts of Rome, under the sponsorship of Cardinal Alessandro Albani (1692–1779).

Cardinal Albani built his villa in 1760–1761 specifically to house and display his vast collection of antique sculpture, sarcophagi, intaglios (objects in which the design is carved out of the surface), cameos, and vases, and it became one of the most important stops on the Grand Tour. The villa was more than a museum: It was also a place to buy art and artifacts. Albani sold items to artists and tourists alike, to help satisfy the growing craze for antiquities; unfortunately, many were faked or heavily restored by artisans in the cardinal's employ.

In 1758 Albani hired Johann Joachim Winckelmann (1717–1768), the leading theoretician of Neoclassicism, as his secretary and librarian. The Prussian-born Winckelmann became an expert on Classical art while working in Dresden, where the French Rococo style that he deplored was still fashionable. In 1755, he published a pamphlet, *Thoughts on the Imitation of Greek*

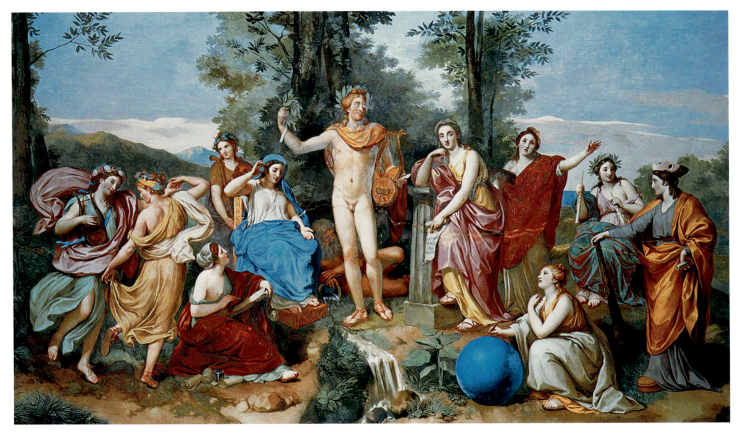

29-13 • Anton Raphael Mengs **PARNASSUS**
Ceiling fresco in the Villa Albani, Rome. 1761.

Works in Painting and Sculpture, in which he attacked the Rococo as decadent, arguing that modern artists could only claim their status as legitimate artists by imitating Greek art. Shortly afterward he went to work for Albani in Rome. In 1764, he published a second influential treatise, *The History of Ancient Art*, often considered one of the earliest art-historical studies. Here Winckelmann analyzed the history of art for the first time as a succession of period styles, an approach which later became the norm for art history books (including this one).

MENGS. Winckelmann's closest friend and colleague in Rome was a fellow German, Anton Raphael Mengs (1728–1779). In 1761 Cardinal Albani commissioned Mengs to create a painting for the ceiling of the great gallery in his new villa **(FIG. 29–13)**. To our eyes Mengs's **PARNASSUS** ceiling may seem stilted, but it is nevertheless significant as the first full expression of Neoclassicism in painting. The scene is taken from Classical mythology. Mount Parnassus in central Greece was where the ancients believed Apollo (god of poetry, music, and the arts) and the nine Muses (female personifications of artistic inspiration) resided. Mengs depicted Apollo standing at the center, almost nude and in the pose of the famous *Apollo Belvedere* in the Vatican collection; he holds a lyre and olive branch to represent artistic accomplishment. Around him are the Muses and their mother, Mnemosyne (Memory, leaning on a Doric column). Mengs arranged his figures in a roughly symmetrical, pyramidal

composition parallel to the picture plane, like the relief sculpture he had studied at Herculaneum. Winckelmann praised this work, claiming that it captured the "noble simplicity and calm grandeur" of ancient Greek sculpture. Shortly after completing this work Mengs left for Spain, where he served as court painter until 1777. Similarly, other artists from Rome moved around Europe, bringing Neoclassical ideas with them.

CANOVA. The theories of the Albani–Winckelmann circle were applied most vigorously by sculptors in Rome, who remained committed to Neoclassicism for almost 100 years. The leading Neoclassical sculptor of the late eighteenth and early nineteenth centuries was Antonio Canova (1757–1822). Born near Venice into a family of stonemasons, he settled in Rome in 1781, where he adopted the Neoclassical style under the guidance of the Scottish painter Gavin Hamilton and quickly became the most sought-after European sculptor of the period.

Canova specialized in two types of sculpture: grand public monuments for Europe's leaders, and erotic mythological subjects for the pleasure of private collectors. His **PAULINE BORGHESE AS VENUS (FIG. 29–14)** falls into the latter category, although it was commissioned by one of the most powerful rulers of Europe in the later eighteenth century, Emperor Napoleon of France (1769–1821). The subject is Napoleon's sister, Pauline, whom the emperor had arranged to marry Prince Camillo Borghese, a member of the

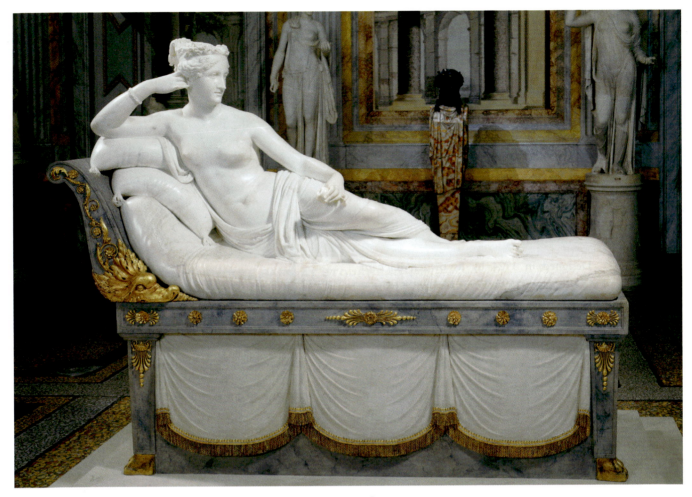

29-14 • Antonio Canova PAULINE BORGHESE AS VENUS
1808. Marble, length 6'7" (218.4 cm). Galleria Borghese, Rome.

famous Roman Borghese family. Pauline wished to be portrayed as Venus. She is shown semi-nude, reclining on a divan with the golden apple given to Venus by Paris, prince of Troy, as a sign that she was the fairest of the three major goddesses. The cushions and drapery seem impossibly real. The glistening white marble evokes the sensuality of Hellenistic sculpture, and the grey, white, and gold marble base brings a materiality to the sculpture above. Pauline's husband was displeased with the sculpture, which seemed to confirm rumors about his wife's questionable behavior, and installed the sculpture in a private room in the Villa Borghese, where it remains today.

NEOCLASSICISM AND EARLY ROMANTICISM IN BRITAIN

British tourists and artists in Italy were the leading supporters of early Neoclassicism, partly because of the burgeoning taste for revival styles at home. Nonetheless, the British interest in Classical revival styles was inflected slightly differently from Roman Neoclassicism. While Roman Neoclassicism looked to the past in order to revive a sense of moral and civic virtue, many later eighteenth-century British artists harnessed the concept of civic virtue to patriotism to create more Romantic works of art dedicated specifically to the British nation. It is in British art and literature that we find the beginnings of Romanticism.

Like Neoclassicism, Romanticism describes not only a style but also an attitude: It celebrates the individual and the subjective, while Neoclassicism celebrates the universal and the high-minded. Romanticism takes its name and many of its themes from the "romances"—novellas, stories, and poems written in Romance (Latin-derived) languages. The term "Romantic" suggests something fantastic or novelistic, perhaps set in a remote time or place, infused by a poetic, melancholic, or even terrifying spirit. One of the best examples of early Romanticism in literature is *The Sorrows of Young Werther* (1774) by Johann Wolfgang von Goethe (1749–1832), in which a sensitive, outcast young man fails at love and kills himself. This is a story about a troubled individual who loses his way; it does not recall ancient virtues or civic responsibility.

Neoclassicism and Romanticism existed side by side in the later eighteenth and early nineteenth centuries, the two ways of looking at the world each serving a purpose in society. Neoclassicism tended to be a more public art form, and Romanticism more individual and private. Sometimes Neoclassicism even functioned within Romanticism.

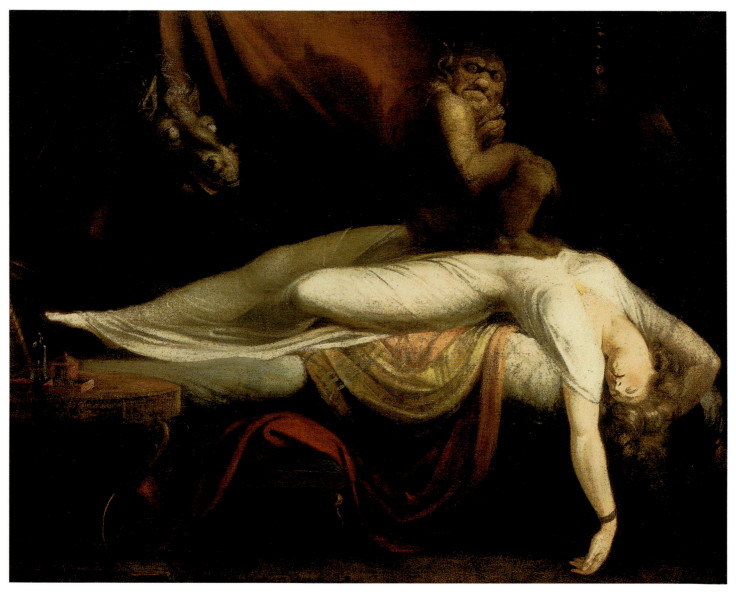

29-28 • John Henry Fuseli THE NIGHTMARE
1781. Oil on canvas, 39¾ × 49½" (101 × 127 cm). The Detroit Institute of Arts. Gift of Mr. and Mrs. Bert Smokler and Mr. and Mrs. Lawrence A. Fleischmann

Fuseli was not popular with the English critics. One writer said that his 1780 entry in the London Royal Academy exhibition "ought to be destroyed," and Horace Walpole called another painting in 1785 "shockingly mad, mad, mad, madder than ever." Even after achieving the highest official acknowledgment of his talents, Fuseli was called "the Wild Swiss" and "Painter to the Devil." But the public appreciated his work, and *The Nightmare*, exhibited at the Royal Academy in 1782, was repeated in at least three more versions and its imagery was disseminated through prints published by commercial engravers. One of these prints would later hang in the office of the Austrian psychoanalyst Sigmund Freud, who believed that dreams were manifestations of the dreamer's repressed desires.

Shakespeare, and Milton. His interest in the dark recesses of the human mind led him to paint supernatural and irrational subjects. In **THE NIGHTMARE (FIG. 29–28)**, he depicts a woman sprawled across a divan with her head thrown back. She is oppressed by a gruesome incubus (or *mara*, an evil spirit) crouching on her pelvis. According to legend, the incubus was believed to feed by stealing women and having sex with them; in her erotic dream the woman dreams that the incubus is about to feed upon her. In the background a horse with wild, phosphorescent eyes thrusts its head into the room through a curtain. The image communicates fear of

the unknown and unknowable, and sexuality without restraint. The painting was exhibited at the Royal Academy in 1782, and although not well received by Fuseli's peers, it clearly struck a chord with the public. He painted at least four versions of this subject and prints of it had a wide circulation.

Fuseli's friend William Blake (1757–1827), a highly original poet, painter, and printmaker, was also inspired by the dramatic aspect of Michelangelo's art. Trained as an engraver, he enrolled briefly at the Royal Academy, where he quickly rejected the teachings of Reynolds, believing that rules hinder rather than aid

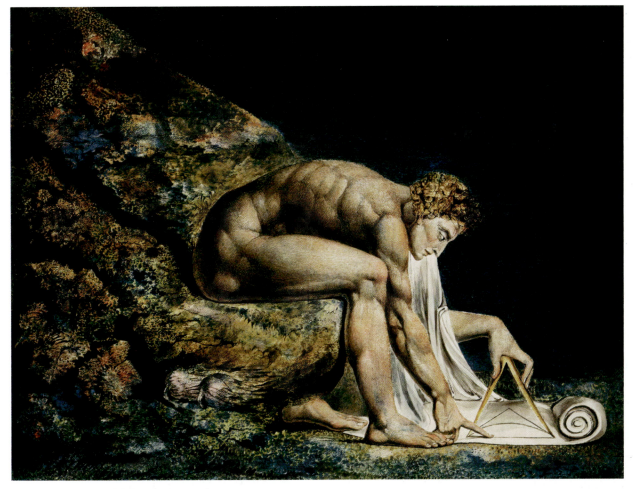

29-29 • William Blake NEWTON
1795–c. 1805. Color print finished in ink and watercolor, 18⅛ × 23⅝″ (46 × 60 cm). Tate, London.

creativity. He became a lifelong advocate of probing the unfettered imagination. For Blake, the imagination provided access to the higher realm of the spirit and reason was confined to the lower world of matter.

Blake was interested in probing the nature of good and evil, developing an idiosyncratic form of Christian belief, drawing on elements from the Bible, Greek mythology, and British legend. His "prophetic books," designed and printed in the mid 1790s, brought together painting and poetry to explore themes of spiritual crisis and redemption. Thematically related to the prophetic books are an independent series of 12 large color prints that he executed mostly in 1795, which may have some overarching theme; it is not obvious, however, what it is. These include the large print of **NEWTON (FIG. 29–29)**, the epitome of eighteenth-century rationalism, naked in a cave and obsessed with reducing the universe to a mathematical drawing with his compasses.

John Singleton Copley, whose portrait of the Mifflins is described above (SEE FIG. 29–1), moved from Boston to London after the Revolutionary War, never to return to his native country. In London, he established himself as a portraitist and painter of modern history in the vein of fellow American expatriate Benjamin West. Copley's most successful modern history painting

was **WATSON AND THE SHARK (FIG. 29–30)**, commissioned by Brook Watson, a wealthy London merchant and Tory politician, in 1778. Copley's painting dramatizes an episode of 1749, in which the 14-year-old Watson was attacked by a shark while swimming in Havana Harbor, and lost part of his right leg before being rescued by his comrades. Copley's pyramidal composition is made up of figures in a boat and the hapless Watson in the water with a highly imaginary shark set against the backdrop of the harbor. Several of the figures were inspired by Classical sources, but the scene portrayed is anything but Classical. In the foreground, the ferocious shark rushes on the helpless, naked Watson, while at the prow of the rescue boat a man raises his harpoon to attack the shark. At the left, two of Watson's shipmates strain to reach him while others in the boat look on in alarm. An African man, standing at the apex of the painting, holds a rope that curls over Watson's extended right arm, connecting him to the boat.

Some scholars have read the African figure as a servant waiting to hand the rope to his white master, but his inclusion has also been interpreted in more overtly political terms. The shark attack on Watson in Havana Harbor occurred while he was working in the transatlantic shipping trade, one aspect of which involved the shipment of slaves from Africa to the West Indies. At the time when

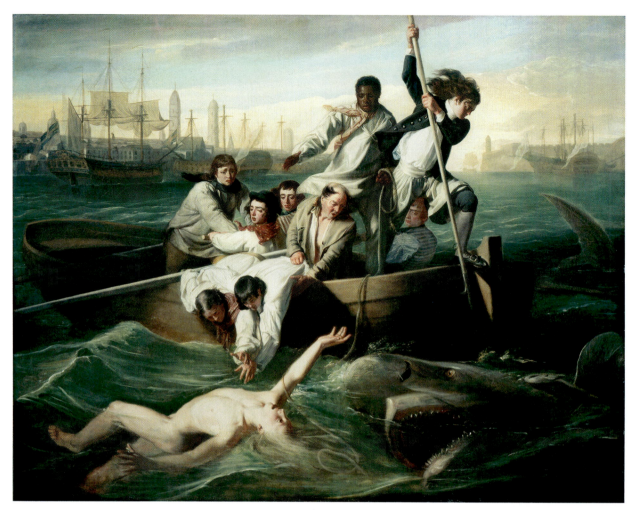

29-30 • John Singleton Copley WATSON AND THE SHARK
1778. Oil on canvas, 5'10¾" × 7'6½" (1.82 × 2.29 m). National Gallery of Art, Washington, D.C. Ferdinand Lammot Belin Fund

Watson commissioned this painting, debate was raging in the British Parliament over the interconnected issues of the Americans' recent Declaration of Independence and the slave trade. Several Tories, including Watson, opposed American independence, highlighting the hypocrisy of American calls for freedom from the British Crown while the colonists continued to deny freedom to African slaves. Indeed, during the Revolutionary War the British offered freedom to every runaway American slave who joined the British army or navy.

Copley's painting, its subject doubtless dictated by Watson, may therefore indicate Watson's sympathy for American slaves; or the figure may be included simply to indicate that the event took place in Havana. Copley was one of the first artists in the capital to exhibit his modern history paintings in public places around London, making money by charging admission fees and advertising his large paintings for sale. His sensational images and exhibitions took advantage of the spectacular displays of the *Phantasmagoria* (a sensational magic lantern display with smoke, mirrors, lights, and gauze "ghosts"), panoramas, dioramas, and the Eidophusikon (a miniature theater with special effects) of London in the early nineteenth century.

LATER EIGHTEENTH-CENTURY ART IN FRANCE

In late eighteenth-century France, the Rococo was replaced by Enlightenment ideas and by the gathering storm clouds of revolution. French art moved increasingly toward Neoclassicism. French architects held closer to Roman proportions and sensibility, while painters and sculptors increasingly embraced didactic Classicism and a plain Classical style.

ARCHITECTURE

French architects of the late eighteenth century generally considered Classicism not one of many alternative artistic styles but as the single, true style. Winckelmann's argument that "imitation of the ancients" was the key to good taste was taken to heart in France. The leading French Neoclassical architect was Jacques-Germain Soufflot (1713–1780), whose Church of Sainte-Geneviève (**FIG. 29–31**), known today as the **PANTHÉON**, is the most typical Neoclassical building in Paris. In it, Soufflot attempted to integrate three traditions: the Roman architecture he had seen on two trips to Italy; French and English Baroque Classicism; and the Palladian style

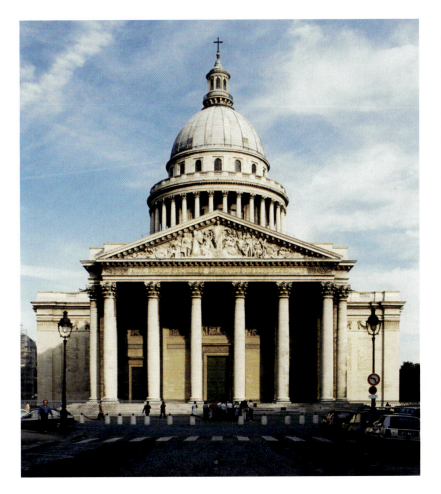

29-31 • Jacques-Germain Soufflot PANTHÉON (CHURCH OF SAINTE-GENEVIÈVE)
Paris. 1755–1792.

This building has an interesting history. Before it was completed, the Revolutionary government in control of Paris confiscated all religious properties to raise desperately needed public funds. Instead of selling Sainte-Geneviève, however, they voted in 1791 to make it the Temple of Fame for the burial of Heroes of Liberty. Under Napoleon I (r. 1799–1814), the building was resanctified as a Catholic church and was again used as such under King Louis-Philippe (r. 1830–1848) and Napoleon III (r. 1852–1870). Then it was permanently designated a nondenominational lay temple. In 1851, the building was used as a physics laboratory. Here the French physicist Jean-Bernard Foucault suspended his now-famous pendulum in the interior of the high crossing dome, and by measuring the path of the pendulum's swing proved his theory that the Earth rotated on its axis in a counterclockwise motion. In 1995, the ashes of Marie Curie, who had won the Nobel Prize in chemistry in 1911, were moved into this "memorial to the great men of France," making her the first woman to be enshrined there.

being revived at the time in England. The façade of the Panthéon, with its huge portico, is modeled on the proportions of ancient Roman temples. The dome, on the other hand, was inspired by seventeenth-century architecture, including Sir Christopher Wren's St. Paul's Cathedral in London (SEE FIG. 22–60), while the radical geometry of its central-plan Greek cross (FIG. 29–32)

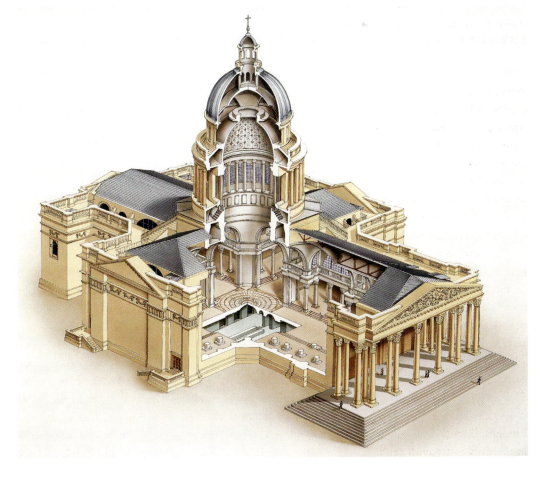

29-32 • PANTHÉON (CHURCH OF SAINTE-GENEVIÈVE), CUTAWAY ILLUSTRATION

SEE MORE: Click the Google Earth link for the Panthéon (Church of Sainte-Geneviève)
www.myartslab.com

owes as much to Burlington's Neo-Palladian Chiswick House (SEE FIG. 29–16) as it does to Christian tradition. The Pantheon, however, is not simply the sum of its parts. Its rational, ordered plan is constructed with rectangles, squares, and circles, while its relatively plain surfaces communicate severity and powerful simplicity.

PAINTING AND SCULPTURE

While French painters such as Boucher, Fragonard, and their followers continued to work in the Rococo style in the later decades of the eighteenth century, a strong reaction against the Rococo had set in by the 1760s. A leading detractor of the Rococo was Denis Diderot (1713–1784), whose 32-volume compendium of knowledge and skill, the *Encyclopédie* (produced in collaboration with Jean le Rond d'Alembert, 1717–1783) served as an archive of Enlightenment thought in France. In 1759, Diderot began to write reviews of the official Salon for a periodic newsletter for wealthy subscribers, and he is generally considered to be the founder of modern art criticism. Diderot believed that it was art's proper function to "inspire virtue and purify manners," a function that the Rococo was not designed to fulfill.

CHARDIN. Diderot greatly admired Jean-Siméon Chardin (1699–1779), an artist who as early as the 1730s began to create moralizing pictures in the tradition of seventeenth-century Dutch

genre painting by focusing on carefully structured but touching scenes of everyday middle-class life. **THE GOVERNESS** (FIG. 29–33), for instance, shows a finely dressed boy with books under his arm, being addressed by his governess as she prepares to brush his tricorn (three-cornered) hat. Scattered on the floor are a racquet, a shuttlecock, and playing cards, the childish pleasures that the boy leaves behind as he prepares to go to his studies and, ultimately, to a life of responsible adulthood. The work suggests the benevolent exercise of authority and willing submission to it.

GREUZE. Diderot reserved his highest praise for Jean-Baptiste Greuze (1725–1805), and his own plays of the late 1750s served as a source of inspiration for Greuze's painting. Diderot expanded the traditional range of theatrical works in Paris from mostly tragedy and comedy to include the *drame bourgeois*, the middle-class drama, and "middle tragedy," later called the "melodrama," both moralizing plays that communicated moral and civic lessons through simple, clear stories of ordinary life. Greuze's domestic genre paintings, such as **THE VILLAGE BRIDE** (FIG. 29–34), were visual counterparts to Diderot's *drame bourgeois* and 'middle tragedy'. In this painting, Greuze presents the action on a shallow, stagelike space under a dramatic spotlight. An elderly father reaches out to his affectionate family as he hands the dowry for his daughter to his new son-in-law; a notary records the event. The young couple link arms but are not overly familiar with one another; the bride is held by her mother and sister. In contrast to Hogarth's marriage contract (SEE FIG. 29–22), Greuze's painting demonstrates that virtue and poverty can coexist. This kind of highly emotional, theatrical, and moralizing genre scene was widely praised in Greuze's time, offering a counterpoint to early Neoclassical history painting in France.

VIGÉE-LEBRUN. While Greuze painted scenes of the poor and middle class, Marie-Louise-Élisabeth Vigée-Lebrun (1755–1842) became famous as Queen Marie Antoinette's favorite portrait painter. Vigée-Lebrun was also notable for her election into the French Royal Academy of Painting and Sculpture, which then made only four places available to women. In 1787, she painted **MARIE ANTOINETTE WITH HER**

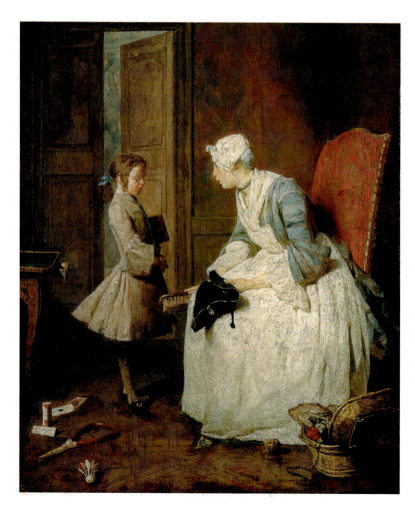

29-33 • Jean-Siméon Chardin THE GOVERNESS
1739. Oil on canvas, 18⅛ × 14¾″ (46 × 37.5 cm). National Gallery of Canada, Ottawa. Purchase, 1956

Chardin was one of the first French artists to treat the lives of women and children with sympathy and to portray the dignity of women's work in his images of young mothers, governesses, and kitchen maids. Shown at the Salon of 1739, *The Governess* was praised by contemporary critics, one of whom noted "the graciousness, sweetness, and restraint that the governess maintains in her discipline of the young man about his dirtiness, disorder, and neglect; his attention, shame, and remorse; all are expressed with great simplicity."

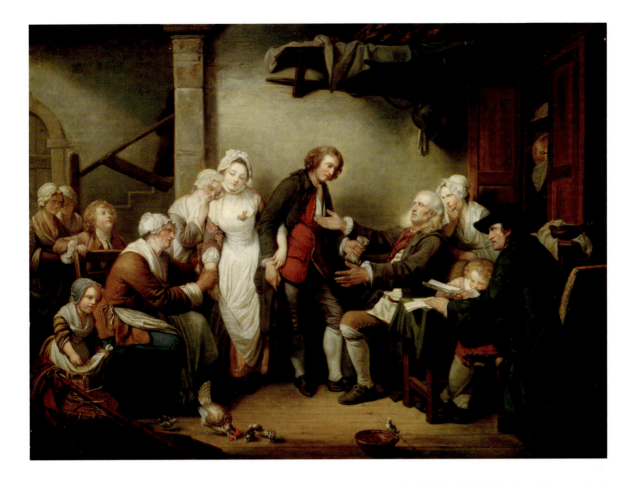

CHILDREN (FIG. 29–35). Drawing on the theme of the "good mother" seen earlier in Angelica Kauffmann's Neoclassical painting of Cornelia (SEE FIG. 29–26), Vigée-Lebrun portrays the queen as a kindly, stabilizing mother to try to counter public perceptions of her as selfish, extravagant, and immoral. The queen maintains her regal pose, as is appropriate, but her children are depicted more sympathetically: The princess leans affectionately against her mother's arm and the little dauphin, the heir to a throne he would never inherit, points to the empty cradle of a recently deceased sibling. The image alludes to the allegory of Abundance and is intended to assure peace and prosperity for France under the reign of her husband, Louis XVI, who came to the throne in 1774 but was executed, as was she, in 1792 during the Reign of Terror.

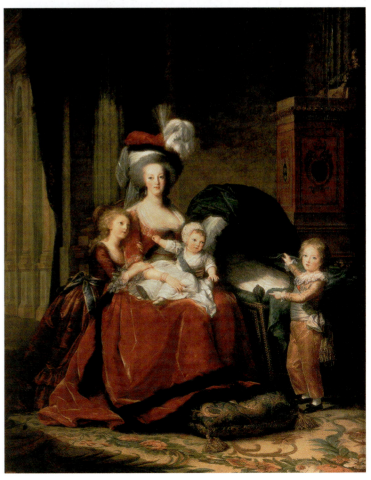

29-35 • Marie-Louise-Élisabeth Vigée-Lebrun
PORTRAIT OF MARIE ANTOINETTE WITH HER CHILDREN
1787. Oil on canvas, 9'1½" × 7'5⅝" (2.75 × 2.15 m). Musée National du Château de Versailles.

As the favorite painter to the queen, Vigée-Lebrun escaped from Paris with her daughter on the eve of the Revolution of 1789 and fled to Rome. After a very successful self-exile working in Italy, Austria, Russia, and England, the artist finally resettled in Paris in 1805 and again became popular with Parisian art patrons. Over her long career, she painted about 800 portraits in a vibrant style that changed very little over the decades.

DAVID. The most important French Neoclassical painter of the era was Jacques-Louis David (1748–1825), who dominated French art for over 20 years during the French Revolution and the subsequent reign of Napoleon. In 1774, he won the Prix de Rome and spent six years there, studying antique sculpture and learning the principles of Neoclassicism. After his return to Paris, he produced a series of severely plain Neoclassical paintings extolling the antique virtues of stoicism, masculinity, and patriotism.

Perhaps the most significant of these works was the **OATH OF THE HORATII** (FIG. 29–36) of 1784–1785. A royal commission, the work reflects the taste and values of Louis XVI, who along with his minister of the arts, Count d'Angiviller, was sympathetic to the Enlightenment. Like Diderot, d'Angiviller and the king believed that art should improve public morals. One of d'Angiviller's first official acts was to ban indecent nudity from the Salon of 1775 and commission a series of didactic history paintings. David's

commission for the *Oath of the Horatii* in 1784 was part of that general program.

The subject of the painting was inspired by the drama *Horace,* written by the great French playwright Pierre Corneille (1606–1684), which was in turn based on ancient Roman historical texts; the patriotic oath-taking incident depicted by David here, however, is not taken directly from these sources and seems to have been the artist's own invention. The scene is set in the seventh century BCE, at a time when Rome and its rival, Alba, a neighboring city-state, agreed to settle a border dispute and avert a war by holding a battle to the death between the three sons of Horace (the Horatii), representing Rome, and the three Curatii, representing Alba. In David's painting, the Horatii stand with arms outstretched toward their father, who reaches to them with the swords on which they pledge to fight and die for Rome. The power running through the outstretched fingers of young men to their father almost makes him

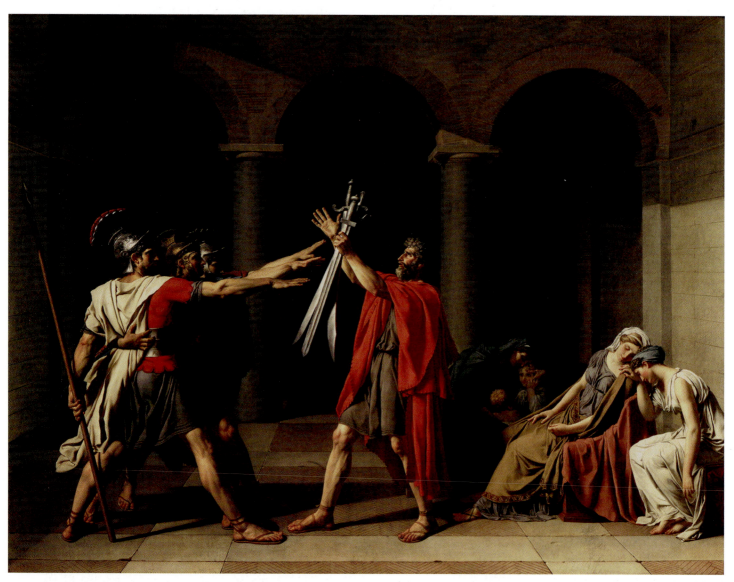

29–36 • Jacques-Louis David OATH OF THE HORATII
1784–1785. Oil on canvas, 10′8¼″ × 14′ (3.26 × 4.27 m). Musée du Louvre, Paris.

EXPLORE MORE: Gain insight from a primary source on Jacques-Louis David **www.myartslab.com**

step back. In contrast to the upright, muscular angularity of the men, the group of weeping women and frightened children are limp. They weep for the lives of both the Horatii and the Curatii. Sabina (in the center) is a sister of the Curatii, and also married to one of the Horatii; Camilla (at the far right) is sister to the Horatii and engaged to one of the Curatii. David's composition, which separates the men from the women and children spatially using framing background arches, dramatically contrasts the young men's stoic and willing self-sacrifice with the women's emotional collapse.

The emotional intensity of this history painting pushed French academy rules on decorum to the limit. Originally commissioned by the monarchy, it quickly and ironically became an emblem of the 1789 French Revolution. Its message of patriotism and sacrifice for the greater good effectively captured the mood of the leaders of the new French Republic established in 1792. As the revolutionaries abolished the monarchy and titles of nobility, took education out of the hands of the Church, and wrote a declaration of human rights, David joined the leftist Jacobin party and served very briefly as President of the National Convention in 1792 and as President of the Jacobin Club.

In 1793, David painted the death of the Jacobin leader, Jean-Paul Marat (FIG. 29–37). A radical journalist, Marat lived simply among the packing cases that he used as furniture, writing pamphlets urging the abolition of aristocratic privilege. Because he suffered from a painful skin ailment, he would often write while sitting in a medicinal bath. Charlotte Corday, a supporter of an opposition party, held Marat partly responsible for the 1792 riots in which hundreds of political prisoners judged sympathetic to the king were killed, and in retribution she stabbed Marat as he sat in his bath. David avoids the potential for sensationalism in the

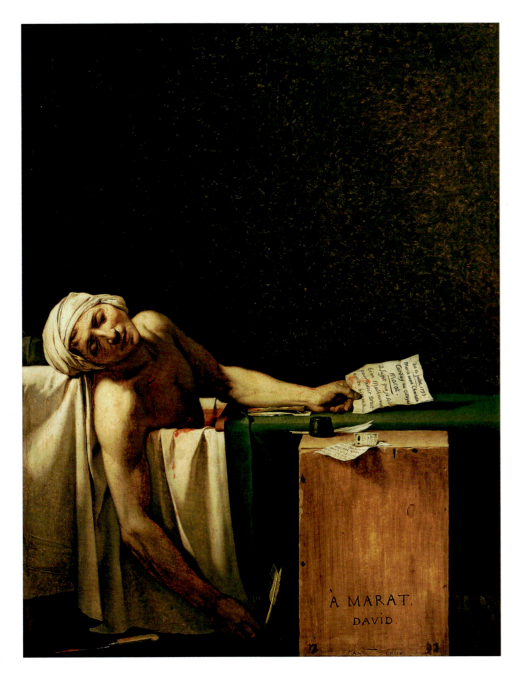

**29–37 • Jacobin-Louis David
DEATH OF MARAT**
1793. Oil on canvas, 5′5″ × 4′2½″ (1.65 × 1.28 m). Musées Royaux des Beaux-Arts de Belgique, Brussels.

In 1793, David was elected a deputy to the National Convention and was named propaganda minister and director of public festivals. Because he supported Robespierre and the Reign of Terror, he was twice imprisoned after its demise in 1794, albeit under lenient conditions that allowed him to continue painting.

paintings often explored dramatic subject matter taken from literature, current events, the natural world, or the artist's own imagination, with the goal of stimulating the viewer's sentiments and feelings. Romantic architecture experimented with the idea of matching a building's style to the personal needs, desires, and even fantasies of the patron.

NEOCLASSICISM AND ROMANTICISM IN FRANCE

Paris increasingly established itself as a major artistic center in the nineteenth century. The École des Beaux-Arts attracted students from all over Europe and the Americas, as did the **ateliers** (studios) of Parisian academic artists who offered private instruction. Artists competed fiercely for a spot in the Paris Salon, the annual exhibition that gradually opened to those who were not Academy members. Between 1800 and 1830, the academy system was the arbiter of artistic success in Paris. At the beginning of the nineteenth century there was a deep division between the *poussinistes* and *rubénistes* (see "Grading the Old Masters," page 764). The *poussinistes* argued that line, in the style of Poussin (SEE FIG. 22–54), created fundamental structure in a painting and should drive the work; the *rubénistes* argued that essential structure could be achieved more eloquently through a sophisticated use of rich, warm color, as demonstrated by Rubens (SEE FIG. 22–26). Similarly, the relative value of the *esquisse*, a preliminary sketch for a much larger work, was debated. Some argued that it was simply a tool for the larger, finished work, while others increasingly argued that the fast, impulsive expression of imagination captured in the *esquisse* made the finished painting seem dull and flat by comparison. This emphasis on expressiveness is seen in the blossoming of Romanticism in the period from 1815 to 1830.

THE GRAND MANNER PAINTINGS OF DAVID AND GROS. With the rise of Napoleon Bonaparte, Jacques-Louis David reestablished his dominant position in French painting. David saw in Napoleon the best hope for realizing France's Enlightenment-oriented political goals, and Napoleon saw in David a tested propagandist for revolutionary values. As Napoleon gained power and extended his rule across Europe, reforming law codes and abolishing aristocratic privilege, he commissioned David and his students to document his deeds.

David's glorification of Napoleon is already evident in his 1800 painting **NAPOLEON CROSSING THE SAINT-BERNARD** (or *Bonaparte Crossing the Alps*) **(FIG. 29–47)**. Napoleon is represented in the Grand Manner, with David using artistic license to imagine how Napoleon might have appeared as he led his troops over the Alps into Italy. He is shown exhorting

his troops to follow as he charges uphill on his rearing horse. His horse's flying mane and wild eyes, and his own swirling cape convey energy, impulse, and power. He charges past the heavy guns and troops in the background. When Napoleon fell from power in 1814, David went into exile in Brussels, where he died in 1825.

Antoine-Jean Gros (1771–1835) began working in David's studio as a teenager and eventually vied with his master for commissions from Napoleon. Gros traveled with Napoleon in Italy in 1797 and later became an official chronicler of his military campaigns. His painting **NAPOLEON IN THE PLAGUE HOUSE AT JAFFA (FIG. 29–48)** is also a representation of an actual event in the Grand Manner. During Napoleon's campaign against the Ottoman Turks in 1799, bubonic plague broke out among his troops. Napoleon decided to try to quiet the fears of the still-healthy soldiers by visiting the sick and dying, who were housed in a

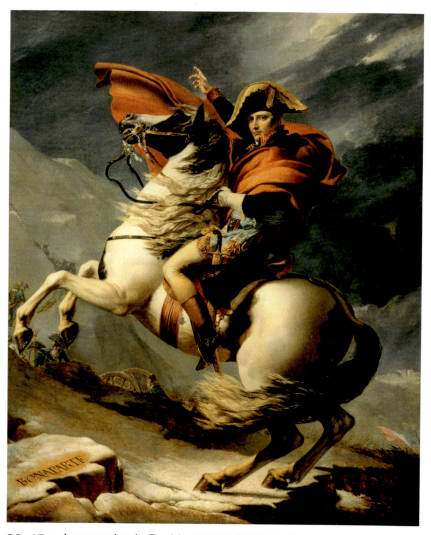

29-47 • Jacques-Louis David NAPOLEON CROSSING THE SAINT-BERNARD
1800–1801. Oil on canvas, 8′11″ × 7′7″ (2.7 × 2.3 m). Musée National du Château de la Malmaison, Rueil-Malmaison.

David flattered Napoleon by reminding the viewer of two other great generals from history who had led armies across the Alps—Charlemagne and Hannibal—by inscribing the names of all three in the rock in the lower left.

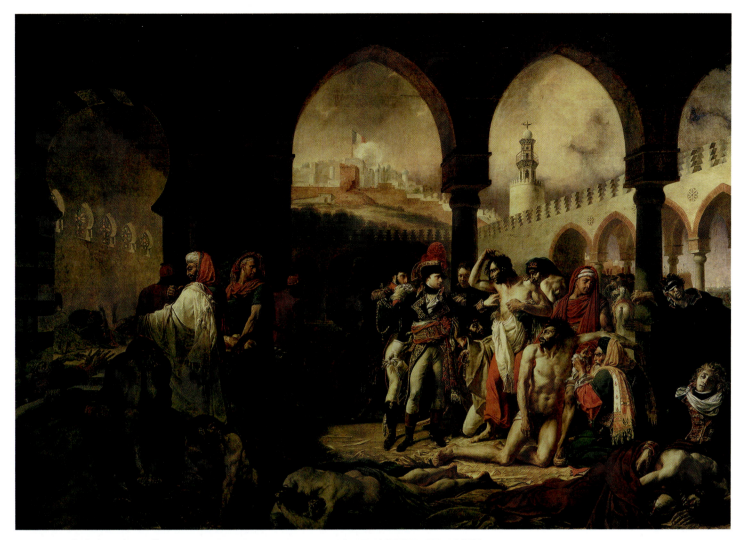

29-48 • Antoine-Jean Gros NAPOLEON IN THE PLAGUE HOUSE AT JAFFA
1804. Oil on canvas, 17′5″ × 23′7″ (5.32 × 7.2 m). Musée du Louvre, Paris.

converted mosque in the town of Jaffa (then part of the Ottoman Empire, and now in Israel). The format of Gros's painting—a shallow stage and a series of arcades behind the main protagonists—seems to have been inspired by David's *Oath of the Horatii*. But Gros's painting is quite different from David's: His color is more vibrant and his brushwork more spontaneous. The overall effect is Romantic, not simply because of the dramatic lighting and the wealth of details, both exotic and horrific, but also because the main action is meant to incite veneration of Napoleon the man more than republican virtue. At the center of the painting, surrounded by a small group of soldiers and a doctor, Napoleon reaches toward the sores of one of the victims in a pose that was meant to evoke Christ healing the sick with his touch. The huddled figures to the left remind us of the mouth of hell in Michelangelo's *Last Judgment* (SEE FIG. 20–34). At that time there was a rumor that shortly after Napoleon's visit to Jaffa, he ordered the remaining sick to be poisoned. Gros may have been aware of this rumor when he painted Napoleon as small and tentative compared to the Arab doctors and even the sick.

GÉRICAULT. Théodore Géricault (1791–1824) was a major early Romantic painter in Paris, although his career was cut short by his untimely death at age 32. After a brief stay in Rome in 1816–1817, where he discovered the art of Michelangelo, Géricault returned to Paris determined to paint a great modern history painting. He chose for his subject the scandalous and sensational shipwreck of the *Medusa* (see "*The Raft of the 'Medusa*,'" pages 946–947). In 1816, the *Medusa*, a ship carrying around 400 French colonists bound for Senegal, ran aground close to its destination. Its captain, an incompetent aristocrat commissioned by the newly restored monarchy of Louis XVIII, reserved all six lifeboats for himself, his officers, and several government representatives. The remaining 152 people were set adrift on a makeshift raft. When those on the raft were rescued 13 days later, only 15 had survived, some by living on human flesh. Since the captain had been a political appointee, the press used the horrific story to indict the monarchy for this and other atrocities in French-ruled Senegal. The moment in the story that Géricault chose to depict is one fraught with emotion, as the survivors on the raft experience both the fear that

The Raft of the "Medusa"

Théodore Géricault's monumental *The Raft of the "Medusa"* (FIG. A) fits the definition of a history painting in that it is a large (16 by 23 feet), multi-figured composition that represents an event in history. It may not qualify, however, on the basis of its function—to expose incompetence and a willful disregard for human life rather than to ennoble, educate, or remind viewers of their civic responsibility. The hero of this painting is also an unusual choice for a history painting; he is not an emperor or a king, or even an intellectual, but Jean Charles, a black man from French Senegal who showed endurance and emotional fortitude in the face of extreme peril.

The painting speaks powerfully through a composition that is arranged in a pyramid of bodies. The diagonal that begins in the lower left extends upwards to the waving figure of Jean Charles; the diagonal beginning with the dead man in the lower right extends through the mast and billowing sail, directs our attention to a huge wave. The painting captures the moment between hope of rescue and despair that the distant ship has not seen the survivors. The figures are emotionally suspended between hope of salvation and fear of imminent death. Significantly, the "hopeful" diagonal in Géricault's painting terminates in the vigorous figure of Jean Charles. By placing him at the top of the pyramid of survivors and giving him the power to save his comrades by signaling to the rescue ship, Géricault suggests metaphorically that freedom is often dependent on the most oppressed members of society.

Géricault prepared his painting carefully, using each of the prescribed steps for history painting in the French academic system. The work was the culmination of extensive study and experimentation. An early pen drawing (*The Sighting of the "Argus,"* FIG. B) depicts the survivors' hopeful response to the appearance of the rescue ship on the horizon at the extreme left. Their excitement is in contrast to the mournful scene of a man grieving over a dead youth on the right side of the raft. The drawing is quick, spontaneous and bursting with energy, like the *esquisse*. A later pen-and-wash drawing (FIG. C) reverses the composition, creates greater unity among the figures, and establishes the modeling of their bodies through light and shade. This is primarily a study of light and shade. Other

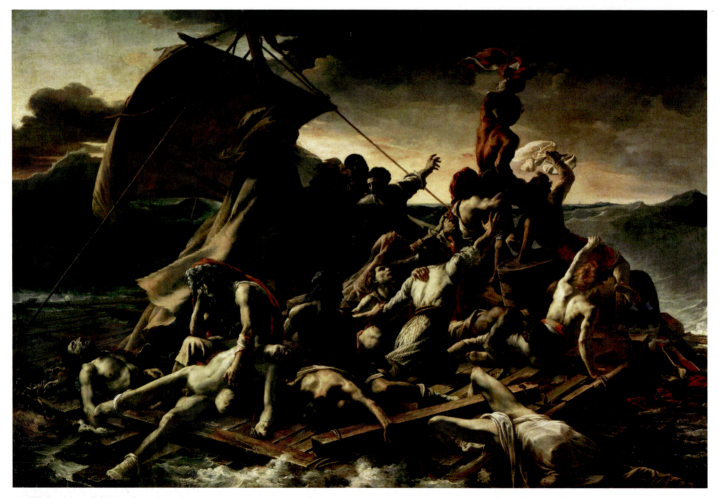

A. Théodore Géricault THE RAFT OF THE "MEDUSA"
1818–1819. Oil on canvas, 16′1″ × 23′6″ (4.9 × 7.16 m). Musée du Louvre, Paris.

studies would have focused on further analyses of the composition, arrangement of figures, and overall color scheme. The drawings look ahead to the final composition of the *The Raft of the "Medusa,"* but both still lack the figure of Jean Charles at the apex of the painting and the dead and dying figures at the extreme left and lower right, which fill out the composition's base.

Géricault also made separate studies of many of the figures, as well as of actual corpses, severed heads, and dissected limbs (FIG. D) supplied to him by friends who worked at a nearby hospital. For several months, according to Géricault's biographer, "his studio was a kind of morgue. He kept cadavers there until they were half-decomposed, and insisted on working in this charnel-house atmosphere…" However, he did not use cadavers for any specific figures in *The Raft of the "Medusa."* Rather, he traced the outline of his final composition onto its large canvas, and then painted each body directly from a living model, gradually building up his composition figure by figure. He drew from corpses and body parts in his studio to make sure that he understood the nature of death and its impact on the human form.

Indeed, Géricault did not describe the actual physical condition of the survivors on the raft: exhausted, emaciated, sunburned, and close to death. Instead, following the dictates of the Grand Manner, he gave his men athletic bodies and vigorous poses, evoking the work of Michelangelo and Rubens (Chapters 20 and 22). He did this to generalize and ennoble his subject, elevating it above the particulars of a specific shipwreck in the hope that it would speak to more fundamental human conflicts: humanity against nature, hope against despair, and life against death.

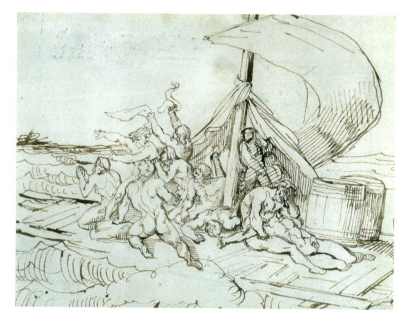

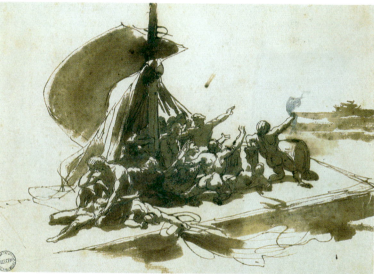

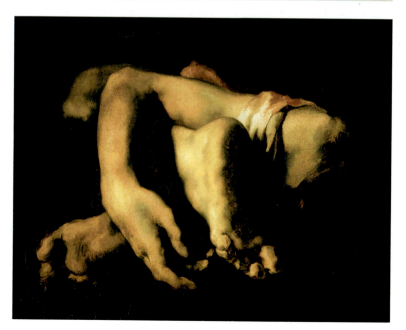

B. Théodore Géricault **THE SIGHTING OF THE "ARGUS"** (top)
1818. Pen and ink on paper, 13¾ × 16⅛″ (34.9 × 41 cm). Musée des Beaux-Arts, Lille.

C. Théodore Géricault **THE SIGHTING OF THE "ARGUS"** (middle)
1818. Pen and ink, sepia wash on paper, 8⅛ × 11¼″ (20.6 × 28.6 cm). Musée des Beaux-Arts, Rouen.

D. Théodore Géricault **STUDY OF HANDS AND FEET** (bottom)
1818–1819. Oil on canvas, 20½ × 25⅜″ (52 × 64 cm). Musée Fabre, Montpellier.

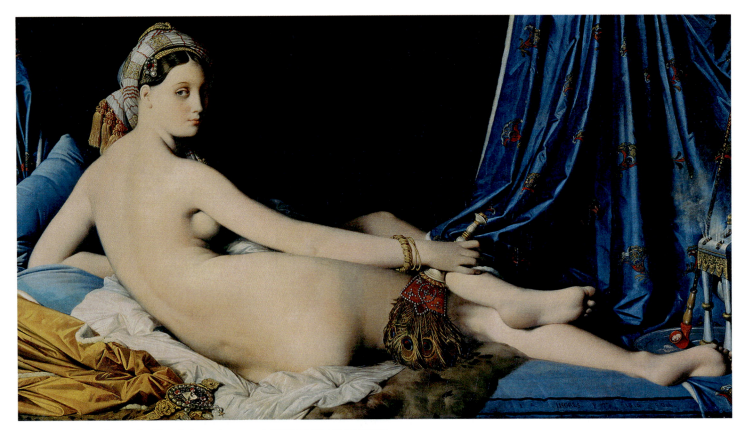

29-51 • Jean-Auguste-Dominique Ingres LARGE ODALISQUE
1814. Oil on canvas, approx. 35 × 64″ (88.9 × 162.5 m). Musée du Louvre, Paris.

During Napoleon's campaigns against the British in North Africa, the French discovered the exotic Near East. Upper-middle-class European men were particularly attracted to the institution of the harem, partly as a reaction against the egalitarian demands of women of their own class that had been unleashed by the French Revolution.

sculpture quickly became known simply as **THE MARSEILLAISE**, the name of the French national anthem written in 1792, the same year as the action depicted.

INGRES. Jean-Auguste-Dominique Ingres (1780–1867) served as director of the French Academy in Rome between 1835 and 1841. As a teacher and theorist, Ingres became one of the most influential artists of his time. His paintings offer another variant on the Romantic and Neoclassical, combining the precise drawing, formal idealization, Classical composition, and graceful lyricism of Raphael (SEE FIG. 20–6) with an interest in creating sensual and erotically charged images.

Although Ingres fervently desired to be accepted as a history painter, it was his paintings of female nudes and his portraits of women that made him famous. He painted numerous versions of the **odalisque**, an exoticized version of a female slave or concubine in a sultan's harem. In his **LARGE ODALISQUE (FIG. 29–51)**, the cool gaze of the odalisque is leveled at her master, while she twists her naked body in a sinuous, snakelike reclining pose, revealing a calculated eroticism. The cool blues of the divan and the curtain at the right heighten the effect of her cool, white skin and blue eyes; she is Ingres's and his patrons' fantasy of a "white" slave. The exotic details of her headdress, fan, and the

jeweled object in the foreground add to her languid sensuality. Ingres's commitment to academic line and formal structure was grounded in his Neoclassical training, but his fluid, attenuated female nudes are much more in the Romantic tradition.

Although Ingres complained that making portraits was a "considerable waste of time," his skill in rendering a physical likeness in a scintillating way and in mimicking the material qualities of clothing, hairstyles, and jewelry in paint was unparalleled. He painted many life-size and highly polished portraits, but he also produced—usually in just a day—exquisite, small portrait drawings that are extraordinarily fresh and lively. The charming **PORTRAIT OF MADAME DÉSIRÉ RAOUL-ROCHETTE (FIG. 29–52)** is a flattering yet credible interpretation of the relaxed and elegant sitter. With her gloved right hand, Madame Raoul-Rochette has removed her left-hand glove, drawing attention to her social status (traditionally, fine kid gloves were worn by members of the European upper class, who did not work with their hands) and her marital status (a wedding band is on her left hand). Her shiny taffeta dress, with its fashionably high waist and puffed sleeves, is rendered with deft yet light strokes that suggest rather than describe the fabric. Greater emphasis is given to her refined face and elaborate coiffure, which Ingres has drawn precisely and modeled with subtle handling of light and shade.

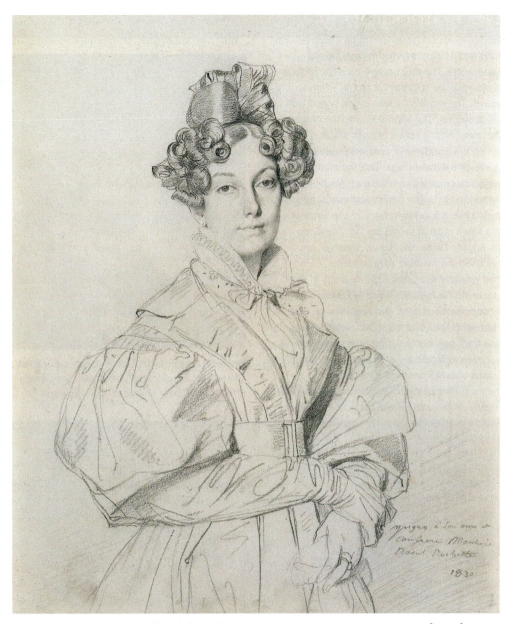

29–52 • Jean-Auguste-Dominique Ingres PORTRAIT OF MADAME DÉSIRÉ RAOUL-ROCHETTE

1830. Graphite on paper, 12⅝ × 9½″ (32.2 × 24.1 cm). Cleveland Museum of Art, Ohio.
Purchase from the J. H. Wade Fund (1927.437)

Madame Raoul-Rochette (1790–1878), née Antoinette-Claude Houdon, was the youngest daughter of the famous Neoclassical sculptor Jean-Antoine Houdon (SEE FIG. 29–40). In 1810, at age 20, she married Désiré Raoul-Rochette, a noted archaeologist, who later became the secretary of the Académie des Beaux-Arts (Academy of Fine Arts, founded in 1816 to replace the French Royal Academy of Painting and Sculpture) and a close friend of Ingres. Ingres's drawing of Madame Raoul-Rochette is inscribed to her husband, whose portrait Ingres also drew around the same time.

EXPLORE MORE: Gain insight from a primary source about Jean-Auguste-Dominique Ingres **www.myartslab.com**

DAUMIER. Honoré Daumier (1808–1879) came to Paris from Marseille in 1816. He studied drawing at the Académie Suisse, but he learned the technique of **lithography** (see page 952) as assistant to the lithographer Bélaird. He published his first lithograph in 1829, at age 21, in the weekly satirical magazine *La Silhouette*. In the wake of the 1830 revolution in Paris, Daumier began supplying pictures to *La Caricature*, an anti-monarchist, pro-republican magazine, and the equally partisan *Le Charivari*, the first daily newspaper illustrated with lithographs. In 1834, Daumier made a lithographic print of the atrocities on **RUE TRANSNONAIN** (FIG. 29–53). A government guard was shot and killed on this street during a demonstration by workers, and in response the guards

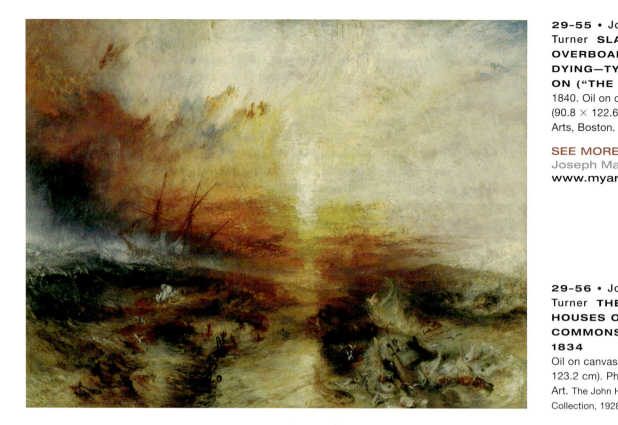

29-55 • Joseph Mallord William Turner **SLAVERS THROWING OVERBOARD THE DEAD AND DYING—TYPHOON COMING ON ("THE SLAVE SHIP")** 1840. Oil on canvas, 35¾ × 48¼" (90.8 × 122.6 cm). Museum of Fine Arts, Boston.

SEE MORE: View a video on Joseph Mallord William Turner www.myartslab.com

29-56 • Joseph Mallord William Turner **THE BURNING OF THE HOUSES OF LORDS AND COMMONS, 16TH OCTOBER 1834** Oil on canvas, 36¼ × 48½" (92.1 × 123.2 cm). Philadelphia Museum of Art. The John Howard McFadden Collection, 1928

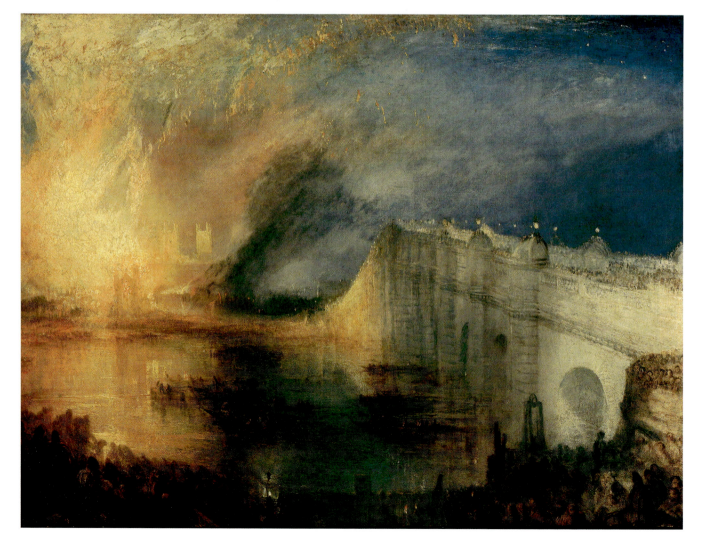

entered the Royal Academy in 1789, was elected a full academician at the unusually young age of 27, and later became a professor at the Royal Academy Schools. During the 1790s, Turner helped revolutionize the British watercolor tradition by rejecting careful underdrawing and topographic accuracy in favor of a freer application of paint and more generalized atmospheric effects. By the late 1790s, he was also exhibiting large-scale oil paintings of grand natural scenes and historical subjects. In his later work he sought to capture the **sublime**, a concept defined by philosopher Edmund Burke (1729–1797) as something that strikes awe and terror into the heart of the viewer. There is no real threat, however; the sublime is experienced vicariously and it is therefore thrilling and exciting.

Turner engages with contemporary social and political issues in his art on a sublime and cataclysmic scale. One of his later works, **SLAVERS THROWING OVERBOARD THE DEAD AND DYING —TYPHOON COMING ON ("THE SLAVE SHIP") (FIG. 29–55)**, depicts an event of genuine horror, based on an account in Thomas Clarkson's *The History of the Abolition of the Slave Trade* (1783), which was reprinted in 1840. Clarkson described the captain of a slave ship caught in the path of a typhoon. It was widely believed that insurance companies reimbursed for slaves lost at sea but not for those who died from sickness on board ship. In the foreground of Turner's painting, not readily recognizable and never quite legible, are the writhing bodies of slaves thrown overboard but still shackled together, fighting in vain for their lives. The fiery swirl of the sun, storm, and waves overwhelms these doomed souls.

Blazing color and light also dominate Turner's portrayal of **THE BURNING OF THE HOUSES OF LORDS AND COMMONS, 16TH OCTOBER 1834 (FIG. 29–56)**, which thrills with a sense of drama. We are not the only ones transfixed by the sight of a magnificent conflagration here: The foreground of the painting shows the south bank of the Thames packed with spectators. The fire was a national tragedy. London's ancient Houses of Parliament in Westminster Palace had witnessed some of the most important events in English history. The fire completely destroyed the House of Lords and left the House of Commons without a roof. Turner himself was witness to the scene and hurriedly made watercolor sketches; within a few months he had the large painting ready for exhibition. The brilliant light and color is the true theme of this painting, explaining why Turner was called "the painter of light."

COLE. Thomas Cole (1801–1848) was one of the first great professional landscape painters in the United States. Cole emigrated from England at age 17 and by 1820 was working as an itinerant portrait painter. With the help of a patron, he traveled in Europe between 1829 and 1832; upon his return to the United States he settled in New York and became a successful landscape painter. He frequently worked from observation when making sketches for his paintings, but, like most landscape painters of his generation, he produced his large finished works in the studio during the winter months.

In the mid 1830s, Cole painted **THE OXBOW (FIG. 29–57)** for exhibition at the National Academy of Design in New York. He

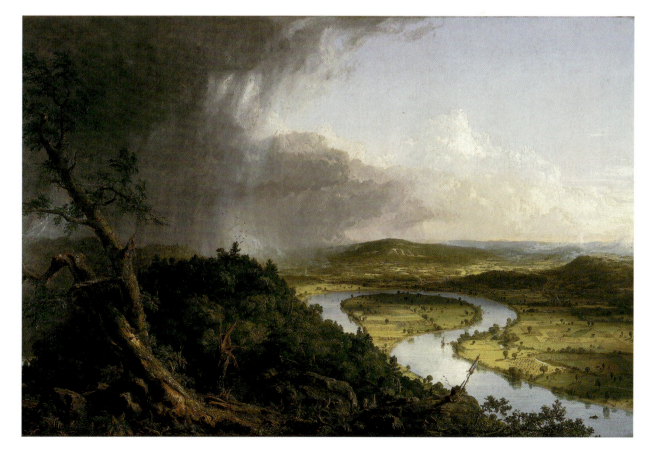

29-57 •
Thomas Cole
THE OXBOW
1836. Oil on canvas, 51½ × 76″ (1.31 × 1.94 m). Metropolitan Museum of Art, New York. Gift of Mrs. Russell Sage, 1908 (08.228)

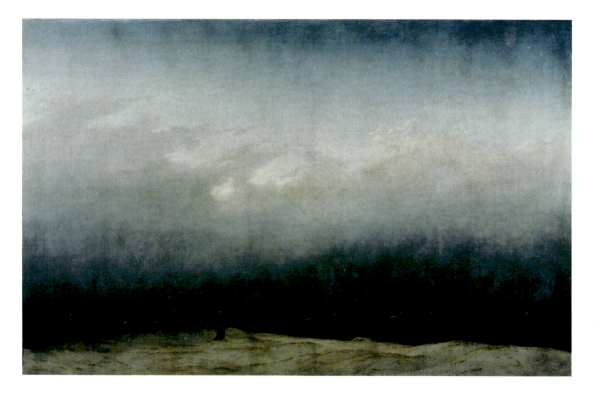

29-58 • Caspar David Friedrich **MONK BY THE SEA**
1809. Oil on canvas, 43 × 67¾″ (110 × 172 cm). Nationalgalerie, Berlin.

considered this one of his "view" paintings because it represents a specific place and time. Although most of his other view paintings were small, this one was for exhibition at the National Academy, so it is monumentally large. Its scale allows for a sweeping view of a spectacular oxbow bend in the Connecticut River from the top of Mount Holyoke in western Massachusetts. Cole wrote that the American landscape lacked the historic monuments that made European landscape interesting; there were no castles on the Hudson River of the kind found on the Rhine, and there were no ancient monuments in America of the kind found in Rome. On the other hand, he argued, America's natural wonders, such as this oxbow, should be viewed as America's natural "antiquities." The painting's title tells us that Cole depicts an actual spot, but, like other landscape painters who wished to impart a larger message about the course of history in their work, he composed the scene to convey the landscape's grandeur and significance, exaggerating the steepness of the mountain and setting the scene below a dramatic sky. Along a great sweeping arc produced by the dark clouds and the edge of the mountain, he contrasts the two sides of the American landscape: its dense, stormy wilderness and its congenial, pastoral valleys with settlements. The fading storm seems to suggest that the land is bountiful and ready to yield its fruits to civilization.

FRIEDRICH. In Germany, the Romantic landscape painter Caspar David Friedrich (1774–1840) considered landscape as a vehicle through which to achieve spiritual revelation. As a young man, he was influenced by the writings and teachings of Gotthard Kosegarten, a local Lutheran pastor and poet who taught that the divine was visible through a deep personal connection with nature. Kosegarten argued that just as God's book was the Bible, the

landscape was God's "Book of Nature." Friedrich studied at the Copenhagen Academy before settling in Dresden, where the poet Johann Wolfgang von Goethe encouraged him to make landscape the principal subject of his art. He sketched from nature but painted in the studio, synthesizing his sketches with his memories of and feelings about nature. In **MONK BY THE SEA** (FIG. 29–58), a long expanse of dark, moody beach is differentiated from the sky by no more than a vague horizon. The tiny figure of a monk contemplates the vastness and sublimity of the landscape from the edge of the water. The coastline is mysteriously quiet and fog has drawn a veil over most of the details of the landscape, creating a mood that is hushed and solemn.

Friedrich's landscape paintings were popular among members of the emerging nationalist movement in Germany after Napoleon's invasion in 1806. Interestingly, his work became less popular after Napoleon's defeat in 1815.

GOTHIC AND NEOCLASSICAL STYLES IN ARCHITECTURE

A mixture of Neoclassicism and Romanticism motivated architects in the early nineteenth century, many of whom worked in either mode, depending on the task at hand. Neoclassicism in architecture often imbued secular public buildings with a sense of grandeur and timelessness, while Romanticism evoked, for instance, the Gothic past with its associations of spirituality and community.

GOTHIC ARCHITECTURE. The British claimed the Gothic as part of their patrimony and erected a plethora of Gothic Revival buildings in the nineteenth century, among them the **HOUSES OF**

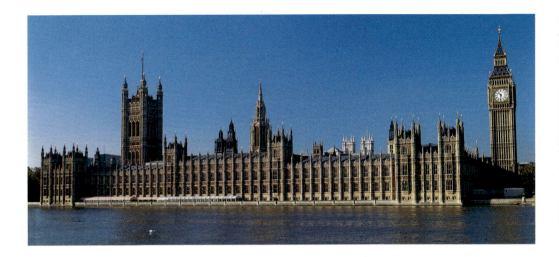

29-59 • Charles Barry and Augustus Welby Northmore Pugin **HOUSES OF PARLIAMENT, LONDON** 1836–1860. Royal Commission on the Historical Monuments of England, London.

Pugin published two influential books in 1836 and 1841, in which he argued that the Gothic style of Westminster Abbey was the embodiment of true English genius. In his view, the Greek and Roman Classical orders were stone replications of earlier wooden forms and therefore fell short of the true principles of stone construction.

PARLIAMENT (FIG. 29–59). After Westminster Palace had burned down in 1834, in the fire so memorably painted by Turner (SEE FIG. 29–56), the British government announced a competition for a new building to be designed in the English Perpendicular Gothic style, and to harmonize with the neighboring Westminster Abbey, the thirteenth-century church where English monarchs are crowned.

Charles Barry (1795–1860) and Augustus Welby Northmore Pugin (1812–1852) won the commission. Barry was responsible for the basic plan of the new building, whose symmetry suggests the balance of powers within the British parliamentary system; Pugin provided the intricate Gothic decoration laid over Barry's essentially Classical plan. The leading advocate of Gothic architecture in his era, Pugin published *Contrasts* in 1836, in which he compared the troubled modern era of materialism and mechanization unfavorably with the Middle Ages, which he represented as an idyllic epoch of deep spirituality and satisfying handcraft. For Pugin, Gothic was not a style but a principle, like Classicism. The Gothic, he insisted, embodied two "great rules" of architecture: "first, that there should be no features about a building which are not necessary for convenience, construction or propriety; second, that all ornament should consist of enrichment of the essential structure of the building."

In the nineteenth century, architects used the Gothic primarily for Roman Catholic and Anglican (Episcopalian in the United States) churches. The British-born American architect Richard Upjohn (1802–1878) designed many of the most important Gothic Revival churches in the United States, including **TRINITY CHURCH** in New York (FIG. 29–60). With its tall spire, long nave, and squared-off chancel, Trinity church quotes the early fourteenth-century British Gothic style particularly admired by Anglicans and Episcopalians. Every detail is rendered with historical accuracy, but the vaults are plaster, not masonry. The stained-glass windows above the altar were among the earliest of their kind in the United States.

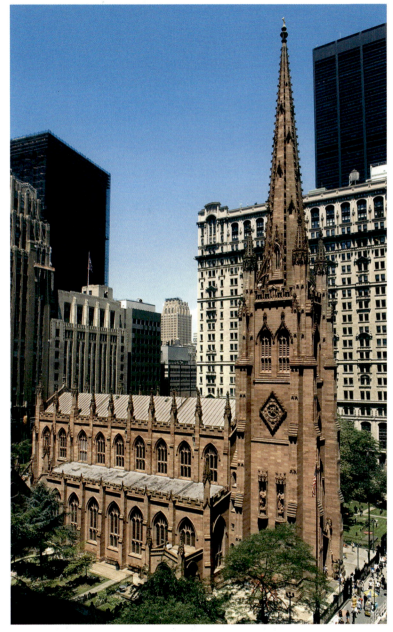

29-60 • Richard Upjohn **TRINITY CHURCH, NEW YORK CITY** 1839–1846.

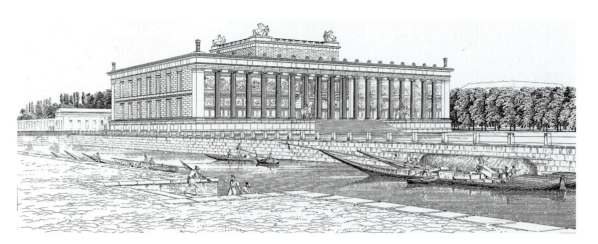

NEOCLASSICAL ARCHITECTURE. In several European capitals in the early nineteenth century, national museums were designed in the Neoclassical style, which positioned the new buildings as both temples of culture and displays of nationalism. Perhaps the most significant of these was the **ALTES MUSEUM** in Berlin, designed in 1822 by Karl Friedrich Schinkel (1781–1841) and built between 1824 and 1830 **(FIG. 29–61)**. The Altes Museum (Old Museum) was commissioned to display the royal art collection, and was thus built directly across from the Baroque royal palace on an island on the Spree River in the heart of Berlin. The museum's imposing façade consists of a screen of 18 Ionic columns raised on a platform with a central staircase. Attentive to the problem of lighting artworks on both the ground and the upper floors, Schinkel created interior courtyards on either side of a central rotunda.

Tall windows on the museum's outer walls provide natural illumination, and partition walls perpendicular to the windows eliminate glare on the varnished surfaces of the paintings on display.

Large public works in the Neoclassical style were also constructed in the United States. The most significant and symbolic Neoclassical building in Washington, D.C. is the **U.S. CAPITOL**, initially designed in 1792 by William Thornton (1759–1828), an amateur architect. His monumental plan featured a large dome over a temple front flanked by two wings to accommodate the House of Representatives and the Senate. In 1803, President Thomas Jefferson (1743–1826), also an amateur architect, hired a British-trained professional, Benjamin Henry Latrobe (1764–1820), to oversee the actual construction of the Capitol. Latrobe modified Thornton's design by adding a grand staircase and Corinthian colonnade on the

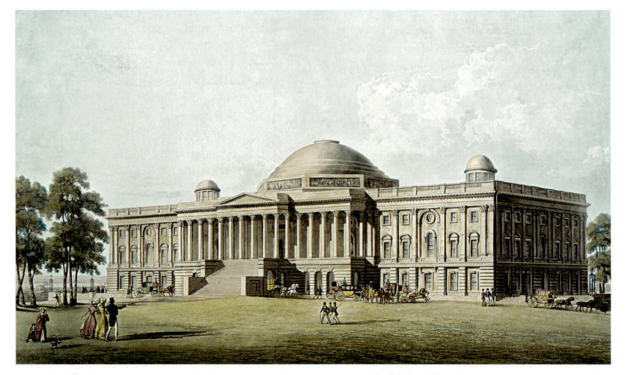

29–62 • Benjamin Henry Latrobe U.S. CAPITOL, WASHINGTON, D.C.
c. 1808. Engraving by T. Sutherland, 1825. New York Public Library. I. N. Phelps Stokes Collection, Myriam and Ira Wallach Division of Art, Prints, and Photographs

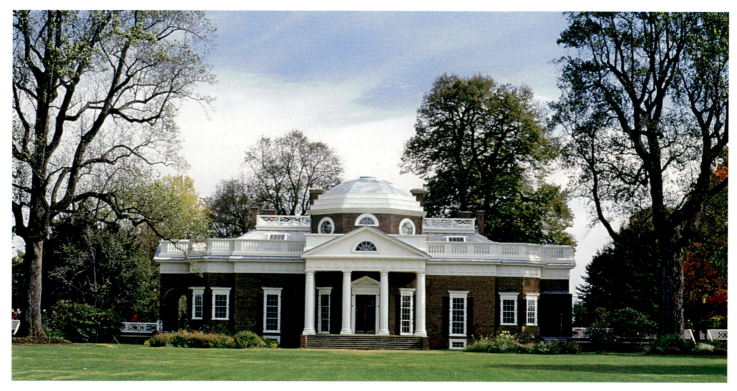

29–63 • Thomas Jefferson MONTICELLO
Charlottesville, Virginia. 1769–1782, 1796–1809.

SEE MORE: View multimedia features on Monticello **www.myartslab.com**

east front **(FIG. 29–62)**. After the British gutted the building in the war of 1812, Latrobe repaired the wings and designed a higher dome. Seeking new symbolic forms for the nation within the traditional Classical vocabulary, he also created a variation on the Corinthian order for the interior by substituting indigenous crops such as corn and tobacco for the Corinthian order's acanthus leaves. In 1817, he resigned his post. The reconstruction was completed under Charles Bulfinch (1763–1844), and another major renovation, resulting in a much larger dome, began in 1850.

Jefferson's designs for the mountaintop home he called **MONTICELLO** (Italian for "little mountain") near Charlottesville, Virginia, is an example of Neoclassical architecture in a private setting **(FIG. 29–63)**. Jefferson began the first phase of construction (1769–1782) when Virginia was still a British colony, and he based his design on the English Palladian style (see Chiswick House, FIG. 29–15). By 1796, however, he had become disenchanted with both the English and their architecture, and had come to admire French architecture while serving as the American minister in Paris. He then embarked upon a second building campaign at Monticello (1796–1809), enlarging the house and redesigning its brick and wood exterior so that its two stories appeared from the outside as one large story, in the manner then fashionable in Paris. The modern worlds of England, France, and America, as well as the ancient worlds of Greece and Rome, come together in this residence. In the second half of the nineteenth century, cultural borrowings would take on an even broader global scope.

THINK ABOUT IT

29.1 Summarize some of the key stylistic traits of French Rococo art and architecture, and explain how these traits relate to the social context of salon life. Then analyze one Rococo work from the chapter and explain how it is typical of the period style.

29.2 Write about how the Enlightenment interest in archaeology propelled the new movement of Neoclassicism in the eighteenth century.

29.3 Explain why artists as visually diverse as Delacroix and Friedrich can be classified under the category of Romanticism. Then evaluate the merits and pitfalls of "Romanticism" as a classifying term.

29.4 Discuss attitudes toward subject matter in the academies of Europe, particularly France and England. Explain what was included and excluded in the academic Grand Manner and why.

29.5 Write about the political climate during Francisco Goya's life, and then, through an analysis of his *Third of May, 1808* (FIG. 29–43), demonstrate how politics affected his art.

PRACTICE MORE: Compose answers to these questions, get flashcards for images and terms, and review chapter material with quizzes **www.myartslab.com**

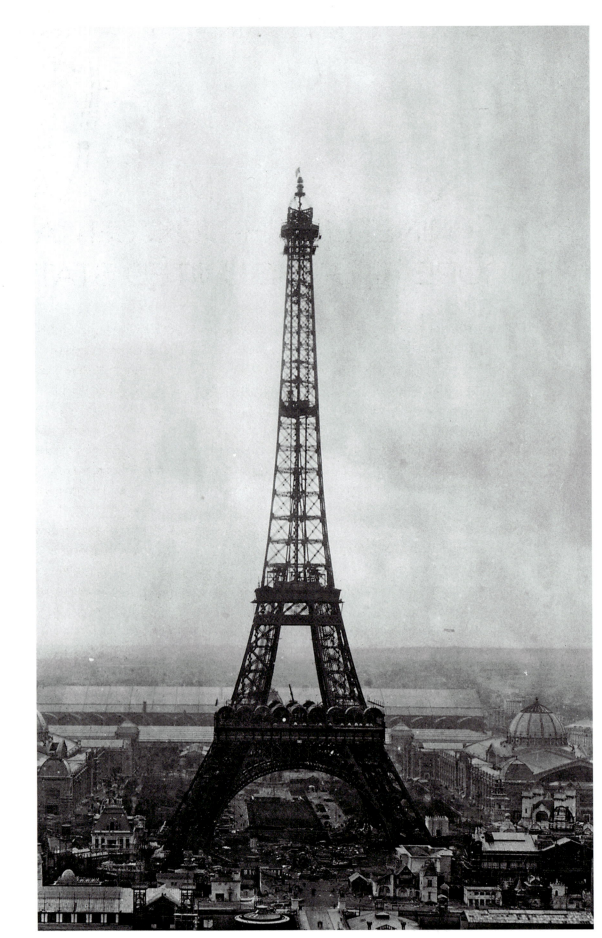

30-1 • Gustave Eiffel **EIFFEL TOWER** Paris. 1887–1889.

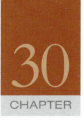
MID- TO LATE NINETEENTH-CENTURY ART IN EUROPE AND THE UNITED STATES

THE EIFFEL TOWER (FIG. 30–1) was designed and built by Gustave Eiffel (1832–1923) for the 1889 Universal Exposition in Paris. When completed, it stood 984 feet tall and was the tallest structure in the world, taller than the Egyptian pyramids or Gothic cathedrals. The Eiffel Tower served as the entrance to and was the main attraction of the Universal Exposition, one of more than 20 such international fairs staged throughout Europe and the United States in the second half of the nineteenth century. These events showcased and compared international industry, science, and the applied, decorative, and fine arts. An object of pride for the French nation, the Eiffel Tower was intended to demonstrate France's superior engineering, technological and industrial knowledge, and power. Although originally conceived as a temporary structure, it still stands today.

The initial response to the Eiffel Tower was mixed. In 1887, a group of 47 writers, musicians, and artists wrote to Le Temps protesting "the erection … of the useless and monstrous Eiffel Tower," which they described as "a black and gigantic factory chimney." Gustave Eiffel, however, said, "I believe the tower will have its own beauty," and that it "will show that we [the French] are not simply an amusing people, but also the country of engineers." Indeed, when completed, the Eiffel Tower quickly became an international symbol of advanced thought and modernity among artists, and was admired by the public as a wondrous spectacle. The great French theorist Roland Barthes described it in 1979 as the "universal symbol of Paris."

The tower was one of the city's most photographed structures in 1889, its immensity dwarfing the tiny buildings below. Copies of photographs taken by professional and commercial photographers were sold to thousands of tourists visiting the Universal Exposition. This photograph, from late March 1889, shows the tower still under construction but almost complete; the bottom two tiers with the fairgrounds below show evidence of rapid last-minute construction.

LEARN ABOUT IT

30.1 Evaluate the role played by academic art and architecture in the art world of the late nineteenth century.

30.2 Examine the early experiments that led to the emergence of photography as a new art form.

30.3 Analyze the ways in which the movement toward realism in art reflected the social and political concerns of the nineteenth century.

30.4 Investigate the origins of Impressionism and describe its form and content.

30.5 Compare and contrast the several manifestations of Post-Impressionism.

HEAR MORE: Listen to an audio file of your chapter www.myartslab.com

EUROPE AND THE UNITED STATES IN THE MID TO LATE NINETEENTH CENTURY

The technological, economic, and social transformations set in motion by the Industrial Revolution intensified in the nineteenth century. Increasing demands for coal and iron necessitated improvements in mining, metallurgy, and transportation. Likewise, the development of the locomotive and steamship facilitated the shipment of raw materials and merchandise, made passenger travel easier, and encouraged the growth of cities (SEE MAP 30–1). These changes also set in motion a vast population migration, as the rural poor moved to cities to find work in factories, mines, and mechanical manufacturing. Industrialists and entrepreneurs enjoyed new levels of wealth and prosperity in this system, but conditions for workers—many of them women and children—were often abysmal. Although new government regulations led to some improvements, socialist movements condemned the exploitation of workers by capitalist factory owners and advocated communal or state ownership of the means of production and distribution.

In 1848, workers' revolts broke out in several European capitals. In that year also, Karl Marx and Friedrich Engels published the *Communist Manifesto*, which predicted the violent overthrow of the bourgeoisie (middle class) by the proletariat (working class), the abolition of private property, and the creation of a classless society. At the same time, the Americans Lucretia Mott and Elizabeth Cady Stanton organized the country's first women's rights convention, in Seneca Falls, New York. They called for the equality of women and men before the law, property rights for married women, the acceptance of women into institutions of higher education, the admission of women to all trades and professions, equal pay for equal work, and women's suffrage.

The nineteenth century also witnessed the rise of imperialism. In order to create new markets for their products and to secure access to cheap raw materials and cheap labor, European nations established numerous new colonies by dividing up most of Africa and nearly a third of Asia. Colonial rule frequently suppressed indigenous cultures while exploiting the economic development of colonized areas.

Scientific discoveries led to the telegraph, telephone, and radio. By the end of the nineteenth century, electricity powered lighting, motors, trams, and railways in most European and American cities. Developments in chemistry created many new products, such as aspirin, disinfectants, photographic chemicals, and more effective explosives. The new material of steel, an alloy of iron and carbon, was lighter, harder, and more malleable than iron, and replaced it in heavy construction and transportation. In medicine and public health, Louis Pasteur's purification of beverages through heat (pasteurization) and the development of vaccines, sterilization, and antiseptics led to a dramatic decline in mortality rates all over the Western world.

Some scientific discoveries challenged traditional religious beliefs and affected social philosophy. Geologists concluded that the Earth was far older than the estimated 6,000 years sometimes claimed by biblical literalists. In 1859, Charles Darwin proposed that life evolved through natural selection. Religious conservatives attacked Darwin's account, which seemed to deny divine creation and even the existence of God. Some of his more extreme supporters, however, suggested that the "survival of the fittest" had advanced the human race, with certain types of people—particularly the Anglo-Saxon upper classes—achieving the pinnacle of social evolution. "Social Darwinism" provided a rationalization for the poor conditions of the working class and a justification for colonizing the "underdeveloped" parts of the world.

In the arts, industrialists, merchants, professionals, the middle classes, some governments, and national academies of art became new sources of patronage. Large annual exhibitions in European and American cultural centers took on increasing importance as a means for artists to show their work, win prizes, attract buyers, and gain commissions. Cheap illustrated newspapers and magazines published art criticism that influenced the reception and production of art, both making and breaking artistic careers, and commercial art dealers emerged as important brokers of art and taste.

The second half of the nineteenth century saw vast changes in how art was conceptualized and created. Some artists became committed political or social activists as industrialization and social unrest continued, while others retreated into their own imagination. Some responded to the ways in which photography transformed vision and perception, many setting themselves up as photographers, while other artists emulated the new medium's clarity in their own work. Still others investigated the difference between photography's detailed but superficial description of visual reality and a deeper, more human reality as a source of inspiration, and others explored the artistic potential of photography's sometimes visually unbalanced compositions, its tendency to compress the illusion of depth and assert its flatness, its lack of an even focus across the picture plane or sometimes the reverse, or even the inability of early photography to "see" red and green equally, causing blank areas of white and black in a photograph. Thus, by the late nineteenth century, while many artists were exploring the reliability of observed reality, others were venturing into the realm of abstraction.

FRENCH ACADEMIC ARCHITECTURE AND ART

The Académie des Beaux-Arts (founded in 1816 to replace the disbanded Royal Academy of Painting and Sculpture) and its official art school, the École des Beaux-Arts, continued to exert a powerful influence over the visual arts in France during the nineteenth century. Academic artists controlled the Salon juries, and major public commissions routinely went to academic architects, painters,

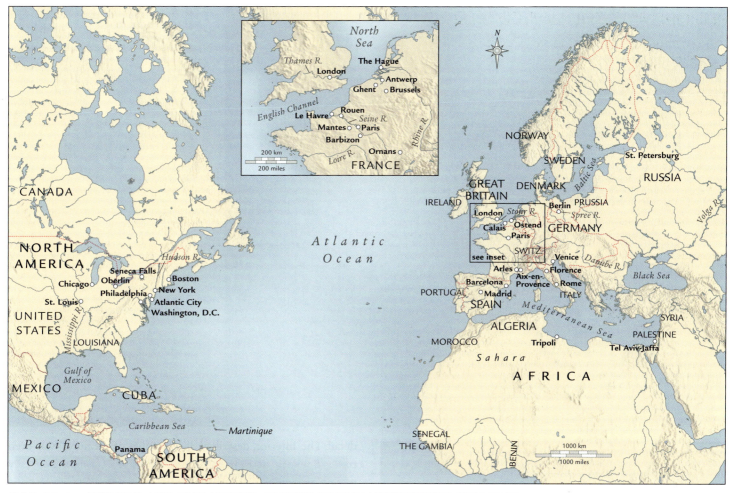

MAP 30-1 • EUROPE AND THE UNITED STATES IN THE NINETEENTH CENTURY

In the nineteenth century, Europe and the United States became increasingly industrialized and many European nations established colonial possessions around the world. Paris was firmly established as the center of the Western art world.

and sculptors. Artists and architects from Europe and the United States came to Paris to study the conventions of academic art.

Academic art and architecture frequently depended upon motifs drawn from historic models—a practice called **historicism**. Elaborating on earlier Neoclassical and Romantic revivals, historicist art and architecture encompassed the sweep of history. Historicists often combined allusions to several different historical periods in a single work. Some academic artists catered to the public taste for exotic sights with Orientalist paintings (see "Orientalism," page 966). These works also combined disparate elements, borrowing from Egyptian, Turkish and Indian cultures to create an imaginary Middle Eastern world.

ACADEMIC ARCHITECTURE

In 1848, after rioting over living conditions erupted in French cities, Napoleon III launched sweeping new reforms. The riots devastated Paris's central neighborhoods, and Georges-Eugène Haussmann (1809–1891) was engaged to redraw the street grid and rebuild the city. Haussmann's ideal was to impose a new rational plan of broad avenues, parks, and open public places upon the medieval heart of Paris. He demolished entire neighborhoods of narrow, winding, medieval streets, summarily evicting the poor from their slums, and replaced them with grand new buildings erected along wide, straight, tree-lined avenues that were suitable for horse-drawn carriages and strolling pedestrians.

The **OPÉRA** (FIG. 30–2), a new city opera house designed by Charles Garnier (1825–1898) and now one of the major Parisian landmarks, was built at an intersection of Haussmann's grand avenues. Accessible from all directions, the Opéra was designed with transportation and vehicular traffic in mind, and with a modern cast-iron internal frame; yet in other respects it is a masterpiece of historicism based mostly on the Baroque style, revived here to recall an earlier period of greatness in France. The massive façade, featuring a row of paired columns over an arcade, was intended to recall the seventeenth-century wing of the Louvre, an association meant to suggest the continuity of the French nation and to flatter Emperor Napoleon III by comparing him favorably with King Louis XIV. The building's primary function—as a place of entertainment for Napoleon III, his entourage, and the French social elite—accounts for its luxurious

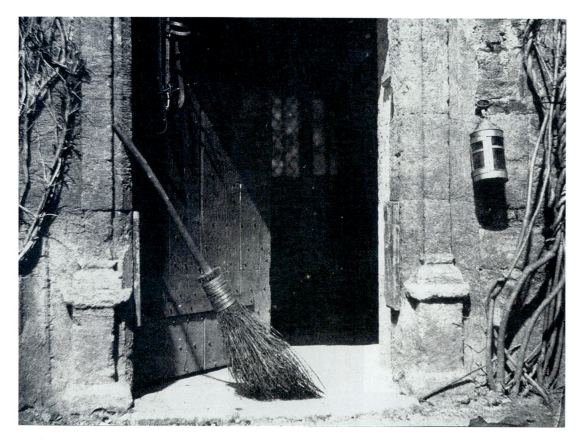

30-8 • Henry Fox Talbot
THE OPEN DOOR
1843. Salt-paper print from a calotype negative. Science Museum, London. Fox Talbot Collection

number of positive images inexpensively. But the **calotype**, as he later called it, produced a soft, fuzzy image. When he heard of Daguerre's announcement, Talbot rushed to make his own announcement and patent his process. The term for these processes—photography, derived from the Greek for "drawing with light"—was coined by Herschel.

The emerging technology of photography was quickly put to use for making a visual record for contemporary audiences and future generations. Early on, however, photographers also experimented with the expressive possibilities of the new medium and worked to create striking compositions. Between 1844 and 1846, Talbot published a book in six parts entitled *The Pencil of Nature*, illustrated entirely with salt-paper prints made from calotype negatives. Most of the photographs were of idyllic rural scenery or carefully arranged still lifes; they were presented as works of art rather than documents of a precisely observed reality. Talbot realized that the imprecision of his process could not compete with the commercial potential of the daguerreotype, and so rather than trying to do so, he chose to view photography in visual and artistic terms. In **THE OPEN DOOR** (FIG. 30–8), for example, shadows create a repeating pattern of diagonal lines that contrast with the vertical lines of the architecture. The photograph expresses nostalgia for a rural way of life that was fast disappearing in industrial England.

Other early photographers worked on assignment and chose the photographic process that best suited their final product. In 1851, the French government decided to commission photographs of the major architectural monuments of France, in part because so

much of ancient France had been destroyed during the Revolution. Édouard-Denis Baldus (1813–1882) was one of several photographers assigned to make photographs for the Mission Héliographique through the Commission des Monuments Historiques. He relied on many techniques, including calotypes, wet-plate/collodion negatives, albumen prints, and heliogravure. Since the photographs had to be reproduced for publication, he was unable to use daguerreotypes. Ironically, despite intense competitive national pride over the French and English versions of photography, some of the best calotypes were made in France and some of the best daguerreotypes in England and the United States. This albumen print by Baldus, **HOUSE WITH STAIRCASE** (FIG. 30–9) is one of 11 photographs that he took for his famous folio *Vues de Paris en Photographie*.

American photographers used wet-plate glass negative and albumen paper print processes to document the momentous events of the Civil War (1861–1865). Timothy O'Sullivan (c. 1840–1882) was a "camera operator" for Matthew Brady (1822–1896) at the beginning of the conflict, and, working with Alexander Gardner (1821–1882), he made war photographs that were distributed widely. **THE HOME OF THE REBEL SHARPSHOOTER** (FIG. 30–10) was taken after the Battle of Gettysburg in July 1863. The technical difficulties were considerable. Wet-plate technology required that the glass plate used to make the negative be coated with a sticky substance holding the light-sensitive chemicals; if the plate dried, the photograph could not be taken. Likewise, if dust contaminated the plate, the image would also be ruined. Long

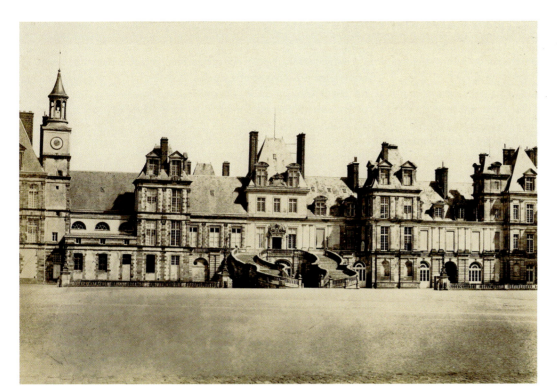

30-9 • Édouard-Denis Baldus
HOUSE WITH STAIRCASE
1858. Albumen print, 7⅜ × 10⅝″
(18.7 × 27 cm). #39 from 11
albumen prints from *Vues de Paris
en Photographie*, Fine Arts
Museums of San Francisco.

exposure times made action photographs impossible, so early war photographs were taken in camp or in the aftermath of battle. O'Sullivan's image seems to show a rebel sharpshooter who has been killed in his look-out. But this rock formation was in the middle of the battlefield, and had neither the height nor the view needed for a sharpshooter. In fact, the photographer dragged the dead body to the site and posed it; and the rifle propped against the wall was O'Sullivan's. The staging of this photograph raises questions about visual fact and fiction. Like a painting, a photograph is composed to create a picture, but photography promises a kind of factuality that we do not expect from painting. Interestingly, the manipulation of this photograph did not concern nineteenth-century viewers, who understood clearly photography's inability to record the visual world without bias.

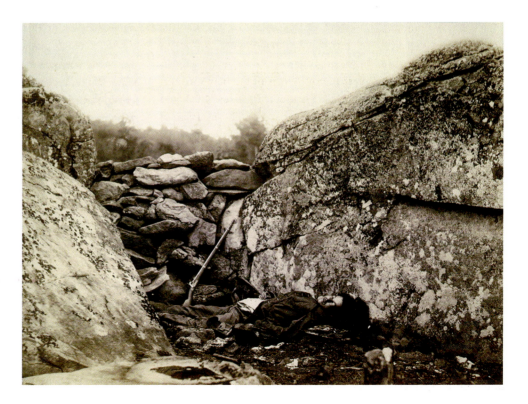

30-10 • Timothy O'Sullivan
**THE HOME OF THE REBEL
SHARPSHOOTER: BATTLE
FIELD AT GETTYSBURG**
1863. Albumen print. Library of Congress,
Washington, D.C.

A camera is essentially a lightproof box with a hole, called an aperture, which is usually adjustable in size and regulates the amount of light that strikes the film. The aperture is covered with a lens, to focus the image on the film, and a shutter, a hinged flap that opens for a controlled amount of time in order to regulate the length of time the film is exposed to light—usually a small fraction of a second. Modern cameras with viewfinders and small single-lens reflex cameras are generally used at eye level, permitting the photographer to see virtually the same image that will be captured on film.

In modern black-and-white chemical photography, silver halide crystals (silver combined with iodine, chlorine, or other halogens) are suspended in a gelatin base to make an emulsion that coats the film; in early photography, before the invention of plastic, a glass plate was coated with a variety of emulsions. When the shutter is open, light reflected off objects enters the camera and strikes the film, exposing it. Pale objects reflect more light than dark ones. The silver in the emulsion collects most densely where it is exposed to the most light, producing a "negative" image on the film. Later, when the film is placed in a chemical bath (developed), the silver deposits turn black, as if tarnishing. The more light the film receives, the denser the black tone created. A positive image is created from a negative in the darkroom, where the film negative is placed over a sheet of paper that, like the film, has also been treated to be light-sensitive. Light is then directed through the negative onto the paper to create a positive image. Multiple positive prints can be generated from a single negative.

Today this chemical process has been largely replaced by digital photography, which records images as digital information files that can be manipulated on computers rather than in darkrooms. The potential of this new photographic medium is being exploited in contemporary art (see pages 1127–1128).

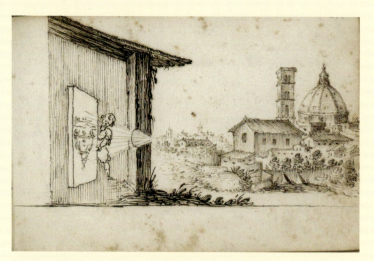

ILLUSTRATION OF A CAMERA OBSCURA
From "Sketchbook on Military Art, including Geometry, Fortifications, Artillery, Mechanics, and Pyrotechnics." Possibly Italian. 17th century. 275 l., illus. (part col.), 4⅝ × 6⅜" (12 × 16 cm). Library of Congress. Rosenwald 363, Rosenwald Collection

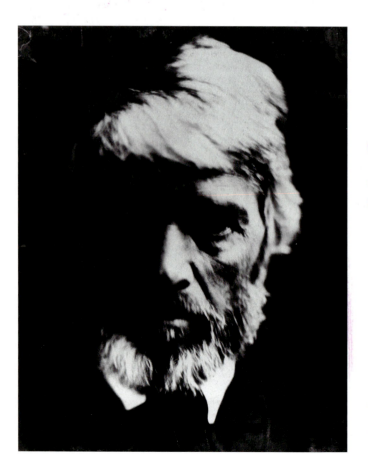

One of the most creative early photographers was Julia Margaret Cameron (1815–1879), who received her first camera as a gift from her daughters when she was 49. Her principal subjects were the great men and women of British arts, letters, and sciences, many of whom had long been family friends. Cameron's approach was experimental and radical. Like many of her portraits, that of the famous British historian THOMAS CARLYLE is deliberately slightly out of focus (FIG. 30–11): Cameron consciously rejected the sharp focus of commercial portrait photography, which she felt accentuated the merely physical attributes and neglected the inner character of the subject. By blurring the details, she sought to call attention to the light that suffused her subjects and to their thoughtful expressions. In her autobiography, Cameron said: "When I have had such men before my camera my whole soul has endeavored to do its duty towards them in recording faithfully the greatness of the inner as well as the features of the outer man."

30–11 • Julia Margaret Cameron PORTRAIT OF THOMAS CARLYLE
1867. Silver print, 10 × 8" (25.4 × 20.3 cm). The Royal Photographic Society, Collection at National Museum of Photography, Film, and Television, England.

THE BEGINNINGS OF THE AVANT-GARDE: REALISM AND BEYOND

In reaction to the rigidity of academic training, some French artists began to consider themselves members of an **avant-garde**, meaning "advance guard" or "vanguard." The term was coined by the French military during the Napoleonic era to designate the forward units of an advancing army that scouted territory that the main force would soon occupy. Avant-garde artists saw themselves as working in advance of an increasingly bourgeois society. The term was first mentioned in connection with art around 1825 in the political programs of French utopian socialists. Henri de Saint-Simon (1760–1825) suggested that in order to transform modern industrialized society into an ideal state, it would be necessary to gather together an avant-garde of intellectuals, scientists, and artists to lead France into the future.

In 1831, the architect Eugène Viollet-le-Duc applied the term to the artists of Paris in the aftermath of the revolution of 1830. Viollet-le-Duc vehemently opposed the French academic system of architectural training. His concept of the avant-garde called for a small elite of independent radical thinkers, artists, and architects to break away from the Académie des Beaux-Arts and the norms of society in order to forge new thoughts, ideas, and ways of looking at the world and art. He foresaw that this life would require the sacrifice of artists' reputations and sales of their work. Most avant-garde artists were neither as radical nor as extreme as Viollet-le-Duc, and, as we have seen, the relationship between the Académie des Beaux-Arts and the avant-garde was complex. Nonetheless, the idea was embraced by a number of artists who have come to characterize the period.

REALISM AND REVOLUTION

In the modern world of Paris at mid-century—a world plagued by violence, social unrest, overcrowding, and poverty—the grand, abstract themes of academic art seemed irrelevant to those thinkers who would come to represent the avant-garde. Rising food prices, high unemployment, political disenfranchisement, and government inaction led to a popular rebellion and the overthrow of the July Monarchy by a coalition of socialists, anarchists, and workers (see page 949), but conflicts among the reformers led to another uprising, in which more than 10,000 of the working poor were killed or injured in their struggle against the new government's forces. Against this social and political backdrop a new intellectual movement, known as Realism, originated in the novels of Émile Zola, Charles Dickens, Honoré de Balzac, and others who wrote about the lives of the urban lower classes. Realism in art was less of a style than a commitment to paint the modern world honestly, without turning away from the brutal truths of life for many ordinary people.

COURBET. Gustave Courbet (1819–1877) was one of the first artists to call himself "avant-garde" or "Realist." A big, blustery man, he was, in his own words, "not only a Socialist but a democrat and a Republican: in a word, a supporter of the whole Revolution." Born and raised near the Swiss border in the French town of Ornans, he moved to Paris in 1839. The street fighting in Paris in 1848 radicalized him and was a catalyst for two large canvases that have come to be regarded as the defining works of Realism. In 1849, he painted the first of these, THE STONE BREAKERS (FIG. 30–12).

At over 5 feet high and 8 feet wide, *The Stone Breakers* depicted a young boy and an old man crushing rock to produce

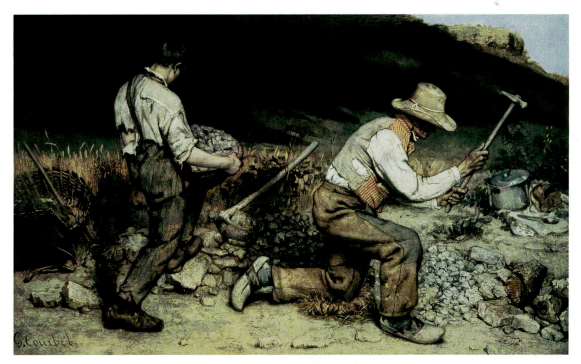

30-12 • Gustave Courbet THE STONE BREAKERS
1849. Oil on canvas, 5′3″ × 8′6″ (1.6 × 2.59 m). Formerly Gemäldegalerie, Dresden. Destroyed in World War II.

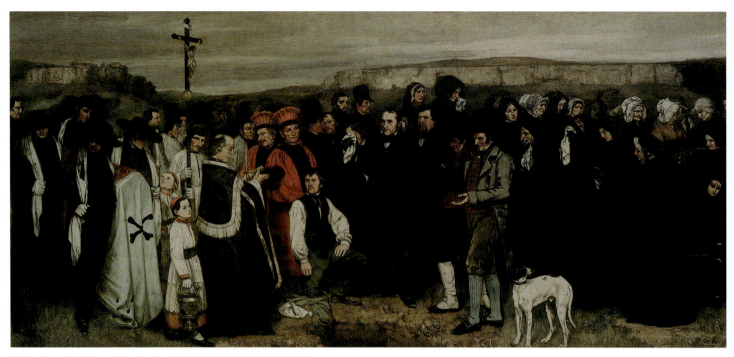

30–13 • Gustave Courbet **A BURIAL AT ORNANS**
1849. Oil on canvas, 10′3½″ × 21′9″ (3.1 × 6.6 m). Musée d'Orsay, Paris.

A Burial at Ornans was inspired by the 1848 funeral of Courbet's maternal grandfather, Jean-Antoine Oudot, a veteran of the Revolution of 1789. The painting is not meant as a record of that particular funeral, however, since Oudot is shown alive in profile at the extreme left of the canvas, his image adapted by Courbet from an earlier portrait. The two men to the right of the open grave, dressed not in contemporary but in late eighteenth-century clothing, are also revolutionaries of Oudot's generation. Their proximity to the grave suggests that one of their peers is being buried. Courbet's picture may be interpreted as linking the revolutions of 1789 and 1848, both of which sought to advance the cause of democracy in France.

the gravel used for roadbeds: the lowliest, most backbreaking form of work. Stonebreakers represent the disenfranchised peasants on whose backs modern life was being built. The younger figure strains to lift a large basket of rocks to the side of the road. Although he wears a tattered shirt and trousers, his boots are of modern make. The older man, almost broken by the work, pounds the rocks as he kneels. He wears the more traditional clothing of a peasant, including traditional wooden clogs. The boy represents a grim future, while the man signifies an increasingly obsolete rural past. Both are faceless laborers. Courbet described the inspiration for this painting:

> [N]ear Maisières [in the vicinity of Ornans], I stopped to consider two men breaking stones on the highway. It's rare to meet the most complete expression of poverty, so an idea for a picture came to me on the spot. I made an appointment with them at my studio for the next day … . On the one side is an old man, seventy … . On the other side is a young fellow … in his filthy tattered shirt … . Alas, in labor such as this, one's life begins that way, and it ends the same way.

Two things are clear from this description: Courbet intended to make a political statement, and he invited the men back to his studio so that he could study them more carefully, following academic methods.

By rendering labor on the scale of a history painting, Courbet intended to provoke. In academic art, monumental canvases on this scale were reserved for heroic subjects; by his work, Courbet suggests that even the lowest in society could be venerated as heroes. Instead of the usual highly finished academic style and inspiring message, his canvas reveals the brutality of modern life, his rough use of paint, dull, dark colors, awkward poses, and stilted composition making the scene feel realistic, gloomy, and degrading. In 1865, his friend, the anarchist philosopher Pierre-Joseph Proudhon (1809–1865), described *The Stone Breakers* as the first socialist picture ever painted, "an irony of our industrial civilization, which continually invents wonderful machines to perform all kinds of labor … yet is unable to liberate man from the most backbreaking toil." Courbet himself described the work as a depiction of "injustice."

Courbet began to paint **A BURIAL AT ORNANS (FIG. 30–13)** immediately after *The Stone Breakers*. Also exhibited at the 1850–1851 Salon, it is a vast painting, measuring roughly 10 by 21 feet, and depicts a burial on a life-size scale. A crush of people attend the graveside service. In the center, the gravedigger kneels over the gaping hole in the ground; to the left the clergy seem distracted and bored, perhaps reflecting the indifference of the institutional order of France after the 1848 revolution; to the right, the huddle of rural mourners, Courbet's heroes of modern life, weep in various states of grief, while in the highlighted foreground, closest to viewers, a bored altar boy and a distracted dog focus attention away from the central activity of the assembled crowd. Although painted on a scale befitting the funeral of a hero, Courbet's depiction has none of the idealization of traditional history painting; instead, it shows all the awkward, blundering numbness of a real funeral, with an emphasis on its brutal, physical reality. When shown at the Salon, the painting was attacked by critics who objected to the elevation of a provincial funeral to the scale of history painting, to Courbet's disrespect for the rules of academic composition, and even to the lack of any suggestion of the afterlife. Courbet had submitted his work to the Salon knowing that it would be denounced, however. He purposefully challenged the prescribed subjects, style, and finish of academic painting to establish his avant-garde position and to create controversy, which he embraced. When the 1854 Salon was cancelled and some of his works were refused for the International Exposition of 1855, Courbet had a temporary building constructed on rented land near the fair's Pavilion of Art and installed a show of his own works that he called the "Pavilion of Realism," clearly asserting his independence from the Salon as many other artists would also do later.

MILLET.   Similar claims of political radicalism were made about Jean-François Millet (1814–1875), although he denied them. Millet grew up on a farm but lived and worked in Paris between 1837 and 1848. He was awarded a state commission (with stipend) for his part in the 1848 revolution, allowing him to move to Barbizon, just south of Paris where he painted the hardships of the rural poor.

Among the best known of Millet's works is **THE GLEANERS** (**FIG. 30–14**), which shows three women gathering stray grain from the ground after harvest time. Despite its warm colors, the scene is one of extreme poverty. Gleaning was a form of relief offered to the rural poor by landowners, although it required hours of backbreaking work to collect enough wheat to make a single

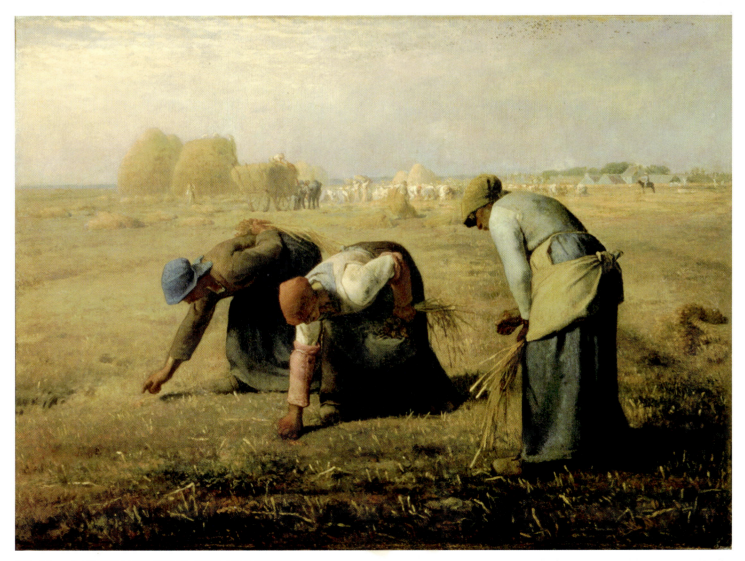

30–14 • Jean-François Millet THE GLEANERS
1857. Oil on canvas, 33 × 44″ (83.8 × 111.8 cm). Musée d'Orsay, Paris.

The Mass Dissemination of Art

Just as contemporary artists can distribute photographic reproductions of their work, in the eighteenth century, artists used engraving or etching to reproduce their work for distribution to a larger audience.

Works of art that won prizes or created controversy were often engraved for reproduction. Artists generally hired specialists to render their work in print form, and sold prints at bookstores or magazine stands. J. M. W. Turner used a team of engravers to capture the delicate tonal shadings of his works. An engraved copper plate could be printed upward of 100 times before the repeated pressing took its toll on image quality. In the later nineteenth century, artists increasingly used steel engraving, wood engraving, and lithography for printing. Those more durable surfaces could print up to 10,000 copies of an image without much loss of quality, though only a few artists experienced such demand.

One of the canniest self-marketers of the century was Alexandre Cabanel. After Napoleon III bought *The Birth of Venus*, the artist sold the reproduction rights to the art dealer Adolphe Goupil, who in turn hired other artists (in this case Adolphe Jourdan) to create at least two smaller-scale copies of the work (one of which is FIG. 30–4). After the original artist had approved the copies and signed them, the dealer used these as models for engravers who cut the steel plates. The dealer then sold the smaller versions of the work.

Another example of a work that was widely reproduced is Frederic Church's *Heart of the Andes* (1859), which was so popular in New York and London that it had to be protected by a rope; the painting was sold for $10,000, at that date the highest price ever paid for a painting by an American artist.

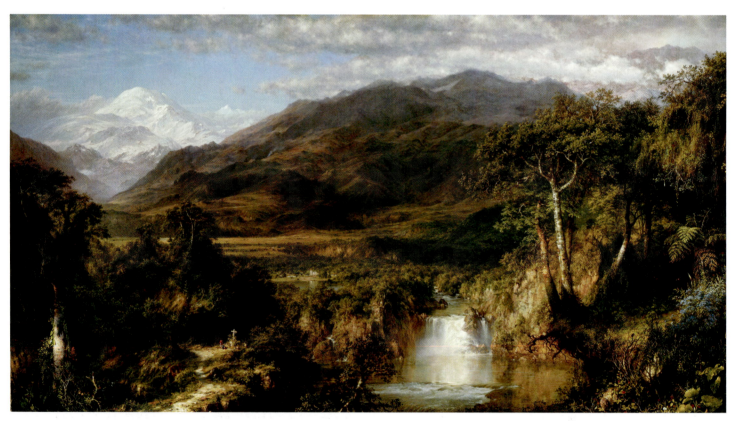

Frederic Church **HEART OF THE ANDES**
1859. Oil on canvas, 66⅛ × 119¼" (168 × 302.9 cm). Metropolitan Museum of Art, New York. Bequest of Margaret E. Dows, 1909

loaf of bread. Two women are bent over to reach the tiny stalks of grain remaining on the ground. A third woman straightens to ease her back. When Millet exhibited the painting in 1857, critics noted its implicit social criticism and described the work as "Realist."

COROT.   Another, more romantic and less political approach to depicting rural life can be seen in the paintings of Jean-Baptiste-Camille Corot (1796–1875). Corot painted historical landscapes early in his career, but steadily moved toward more "naturalistic"

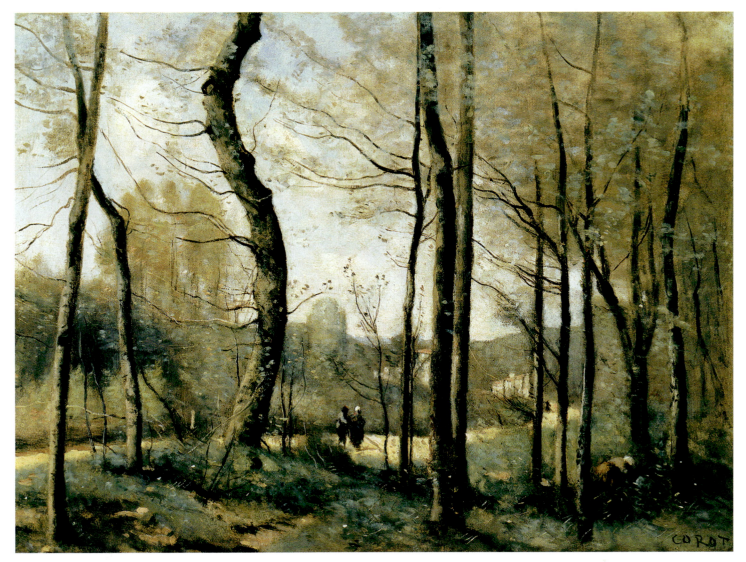

30–15 • Jean-Baptiste-Camille Corot **FIRST LEAVES, NEAR MANTES**
c. 1855. Oil on canvas, 13⅜ × 18⅛″ (34 × 46 cm). Carnegie Museum of Art, Pittsburgh, Pennsylvania.

and intimate scenes of rural France. **FIRST LEAVES, NEAR MANTES** (FIG. 30–15) depicts a scene infused with the soft mist of early spring in the woods. Corot's feathery brushwork representing the soft, new foliage contrasts with the stark, vertical tree trunks and branches, and, together with the fresh green of the new undergrowth, creates a perfectly balanced sense of a clear spring day. A man and woman pause to talk on the road winding from left to right through the painting, while a woman labors in the woods at the lower right. Corot invites us to imagine ourselves in the picture and feel the crisp, bright air. These images of peaceful country life held great appeal for Parisians who had experienced the chaos of the 1848 revolution and who lived in an increasingly crowded, noisy, and fast-paced metropolis.

BONHEUR.   Among the period's most popular painters of farm life was Rosa Bonheur (1822–1899), who was raised in Paris but was drawn to the countryside. Bonheur's success in what was then a male domain owed much to the socialist convictions of

her parents, who belonged to a radical utopian sect, founded by the Comte de Saint-Simon (1760–1825), that believed not only in the equality of women but also in a future female Messiah. Bonheur's father, a drawing teacher, provided most of her artistic training.

Bonheur dedicated herself to realistic depictions of modern farm animals, which were becoming increasingly obsolete as technology and industrialization transformed farming. She studied her subjects intensely by reading zoology books and making detailed studies in stockyards and slaughterhouses. (To gain access to these all-male preserves, she received police permission to dress in men's clothing.) Her professional breakthrough came at the Salon of 1848, where she showed eight paintings and won a first-class medal. **THE HORSE FAIR** (FIG. 30–16), painted in 1853, was based on a horse market near Salpêtrière, but was also partly inspired by the Parthenon marbles in London and by the art of Géricault. The scene portrays the display of splendid Percheron horses by their grooms, some walking obediently in their circle,

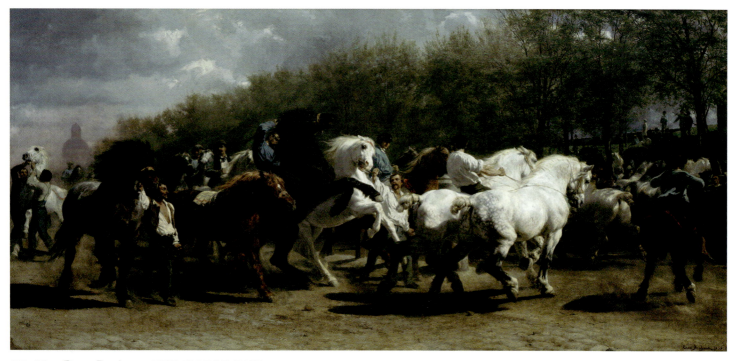

30–16 • Rosa Bonheur **THE HORSE FAIR**
1853–1855. Oil on canvas, 8'¼" × 16'7½". Metropolitan Museum of Art, New York.

EXPLORE MORE: Gain insight from a primary source on Rosa Bonheur **www.myartslab.com**

others rearing up, not yet quite broken. *The Horse Fair* has been interpreted by some scholars as a commentary on the lack of rights for women in the 1850s, but it was not read that way at the time. Although a monumental painting (at more than 8 by 16 feet) of farm animals, normally lower-ranking subjects, it was highly praised at the 1848 Salon. When the painting later toured throughout Britain and the United States, members of the public paid to see it. It was widely disseminated in print form on both sides of the Atlantic, and was purchased for the new Metropolitan Museum of Art in New York in 1889. Bonheur became so famous working within the Salon system that in 1865 she received France's highest award, membership in the Legion of Honor, becoming the first woman to be awarded its Grand Cross.

THE PAINTER OF MODERN LIFE: MANET

Along with the concept of the avant-garde, the second great concept that shaped art in France at this time was the idea of modernity. The experience of modernity—of constant change and renewal—is linked to the dynamic nature of city life. The themes of the modern city and of political engagement with modern life in an industrialized world are key to understanding the development of painting and literature in France in the second half of the nineteenth century.

Poet and essayist Charles Baudelaire argued that, in order to speak for their time and place, artists' work had to be infused with the idea of modernity. Modernity called for modern urban subjects and a new approach to seeing and representing the visual world—a break with the past in order to better comprehend and

comment on the present. Especially after the invention of photography, art was expected to offer new ways of representing reality. One who rose to the challenge was the French painter Édouard Manet (1832–1883).

LE DÉJEUNER SUR L'HERBE.   At mid-century, the Académie des Beaux-Arts increasingly opened Salon exhibitions to non-academic artists, resulting in a surge in the number of works submitted to, and inevitably rejected by, the Salon jury. In 1863, the jury turned down nearly 3,000 works, leading to a storm of protest. In response, Napoleon III tried to mediate the dispute by ordering an exhibition of the refused work called the *Salon des Refusés* ("Salon of the Rejected Ones"). Featured in it was Manet's painting **LE DÉJEUNER SUR L'HERBE (THE LUNCHEON ON THE GRASS) (FIG. 30–17).** A well-born Parisian who had studied in the early 1850s with the independent artist Thomas Couture (1815–1879), Manet had by the early 1860s developed a strong commitment to Realism, largely as a result of his friendship with the poet Baudelaire who called for a "Painter of Modern Life." Manet's *Le Déjeuner sur l'Herbe* invokes Baudelaire's spirit, and in doing so scandalized contemporary viewers all the way up to Napoleon III himself. Ironically, the resulting *succès de scandale* ("success from scandal") helped establish Manet's career as a radical artist.

The most scandalous aspect of the painting was the "immorality" of Manet's theme: a suburban picnic featuring two fully dressed bourgeois gentlemen (in fact, Manet's brother, wearing the hat of a student, and his brother-in-law), a naked woman to the front left, and another scantily dressed woman in the background. Manet's

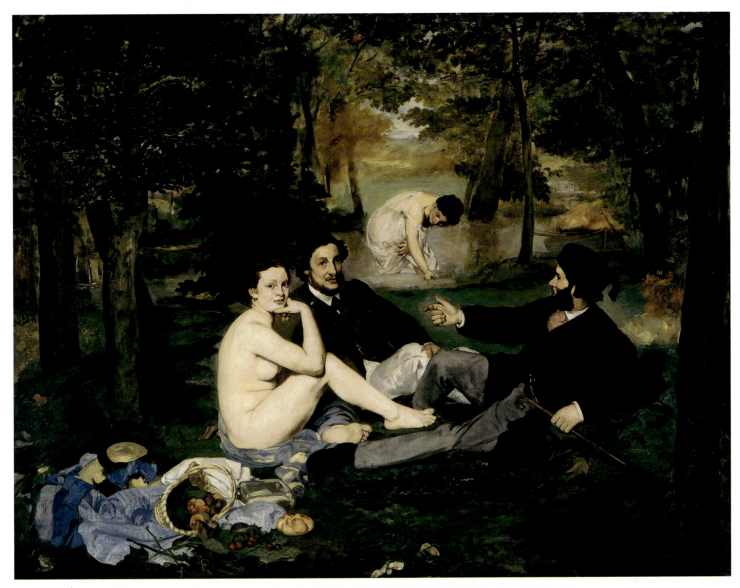

30-17 • Édouard Manet LE DÉJEUNER SUR L'HERBE (THE LUNCHEON ON THE GRASS)
1863. Oil on canvas, 7′ × 8′8″ (2.13 × 2.64 m). Musée d'Orsay, Paris.

audience assumed that these women were prostitutes, and the men their customers. Equally shocking were its references to important works of art of the past, which Académie des Beaux-Arts artists were expected to make, combined with its crude, unvarnished modernity. In contrast, one of the paintings that gathered most renown at the official Salon in that year was Alexandre Cabanel's *Birth of Venus* (SEE FIG. 30–4), which, because it presented nudity in a conventionally acceptable, Classical environment, was favorably reviewed and quickly entered the collection of Napoleon III.

Manet apparently conceived of *Le Déjeuner sur l'Herbe* as a modern version of a Venetian Renaissance painting in the Louvre, the *Pastoral Concert*, then believed to be by Giorgione but now attributed to both Titian and Giorgione or to Titian exclusively (SEE FIG. 20–22). Manet's composition also refers to a Marcantonio Raimondi engraving of Raphael's *The Judgment of Paris*—itself based on Classical reliefs of river gods and nymphs. Manet's modern interpretation of the scene, however, combined with his

modern style, was intentionally provocative. The stark lighting of his nude, the cool colors, the flat, cutout quality of his figures who seem as if they are set against a painted backdrop, all suggest the seamier side of city life. Presenting this under a flimsy guise of academic art underlined Manet's subversiveness.

OLYMPIA. Shortly after completing *Le Déjeuner sur l'Herbe*, Manet painted **OLYMPIA (FIG. 30–18)**, its title alluding to a socially ambitious prostitute of the same name in a novel and play by Alexandre Dumas the Younger. Like *Le Déjeuner sur l'Herbe*, Manet's *Olympia* was based on a Venetian Renaissance source, Titian's "*Venus*" of Urbino (SEE FIG. 20–24), which Manet had earlier copied in Florence. At first, his painting appears to pay homage to Titian's in its subject matter (at that time believed to be a Venetian courtesan) and composition. However, Manet made his modern counterpart the very antithesis of Titian's. Titian's female is curvaceous and softly rounded, Manet's is angular and flattened;

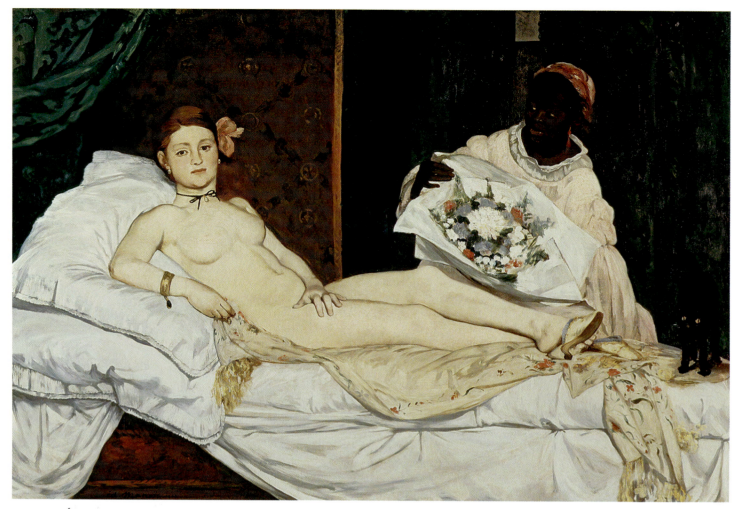

30-18 • Édouard Manet OLYMPIA
1863. Oil on canvas, 4′3″ × 6′2¼″ (1.31 × 1.91 m). Musée du Louvre, Paris.

Titian's colors are warm and rich, Manet's are cold and harsh, like a photograph; Titian's Venus looks coyly at the male spectator, Manet's Olympia appears coldly indifferent. Our relationship with Olympia is underscored by the reaction of her cat, which—unlike the sleeping dog in the Titian—arches its back at us. Finally, instead of looking up at us, Olympia gazes down at us, indicating that she is in the position of power and that we are subordinate, akin to the black servant at the foot of the bed who brings her a bouquet of flowers. In reversing the Titian, Manet overturns the entire tradition of the accommodating female nude. Not surprisingly, conservative critics vilified *Olympia* when it was exhibited at the Salon of 1865.

Manet generally submitted his work to every Salon, but when several were rejected in 1867, he did as Courbet had done in 1855: He asserted his independence by renting a hall nearby and staging his own show. This made Manet the unofficial leader of a group of progressive artists and writers who gathered at the Café Guerbois in the Montmartre district of Paris. Among the artists who frequented the café were Degas, Monet, Pissarro, and Renoir, all of whom would soon exhibit together as the Impressionists and follow Manet's lead in challenging academic conventions.

LATER WORKS. Manet worked closely with all of these artists and frequently painted themes similar to the Impressionists, even occasionally employing a lighter Impressionist palette of colors, but always retaining his previous dedication to the portrayal of modern urban life. In 1874, for instance, he painted **BOATING** (FIG. 30–19) in which two figures sit in a boat on a sunny summer day. The man, a *canotier* or lower-class boatman, is dressed in the standard uniform of white round-neck shirt and pants with a flat straw hat (boater). He has the helm of the boat. The young girl with him sits uneasily in the boat, neither comfortable in her position nor in her dress. The fact that she has no chaperone hints at impropriety. Despite the apparent Impressionist subject and colors, there is a gritty urban realism to Manet's painting that is in stark contrast to Morrisot's more idyllic and upper-class *Summer's Day* (SEE FIG. 30–30).

Manet's *A Bar at the Folies-Bergère* (see "A Closer Look," page 980) returns to the complex theme of gender and class relations in modern urban life. Here is a hard-working young girl serving drinks at a bar in the famous nightclub. She has an unfashionably ruddy face and hands scrubbed raw. In the glittering light created by the electric bulbs and mirrors of the café-concert frequented by Manet and his compatriots she seems stiff and distant. She

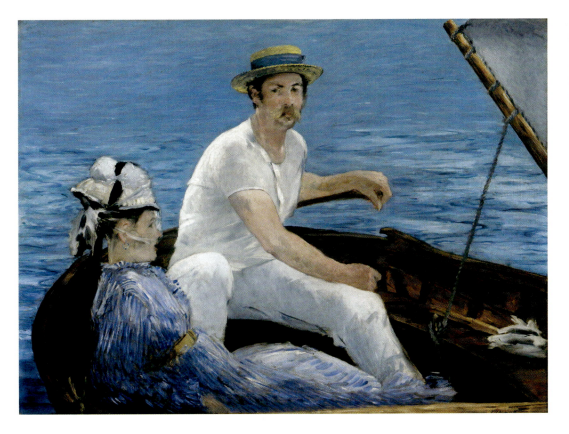

30–19 • Édouard Manet
BOATING
1874. Oil on canvas, 38¼ × 51¼″
(97.2 × 130.2 cm).
Metropolitan Museum of Art,
New York. H. O. Havemeyer
Collection, 1929

refuses to meet the gaze of her client. The barmaid is at once detached from the scene and part of it, one of the many items on display for purchase. This image is about sexualized looking and the barmaid's uneasy reflection in the mirror, which seems to acknowledge that both her class and gender expose her to visual and even sexual consumption.

RESPONSES TO REALISM BEYOND FRANCE

Artists of other nations embraced their own forms of realism in the period after 1850 as the social effects of urbanization and industrialization began to be felt in their countries. While these artists did not label themselves as Realists like their contemporaries in France, they did share their interest in presenting an unflinching look at grim reality and the difficult lives of the working poor.

REALISM IN RUSSIA: THE WANDERERS. In Russia, a variant on French Realism developed in relation to a new concern for the peasantry. In 1861, the tsar abolished serfdom, emancipating Russia's peasants from the virtual slavery they had endured on the large estates of the aristocracy. Two years later, a group of painters inspired by the emancipation declared allegiance both to the peasant cause and to freedom from the St. Petersburg Academy of Art, which had controlled Russian art since 1754. Rejecting what they considered the escapist aesthetics of the Academy, the members of the group dedicated themselves to a socially useful realism. Committed to bringing art to the people in traveling exhibitions, they called themselves "The Wanderers." By the late 1870s, members of the group, like their counterparts in music and

literature, had also joined a nationalist movement to reassert what they considered to be an authentic Russian culture rooted in the traditions of the peasantry, rejecting the Western European customs that had long predominated among the Russian aristocracy.

Ilya Repin (1844–1930), who attended the St. Petersburg Academy and won a scholarship to study in Paris, joined the Wanderers in 1878 after his return to Russia. He painted a series of works illustrating the social injustices then prevailing in his homeland, including **BARGEHAULERS ON THE VOLGA** (**FIG. 30–20**), which features a wretched group of peasants condemned to the brutal work of pulling ships up the Volga River. To heighten our sympathy for these workers, Repin placed a youth in the center of the group, a young man who will soon be as worn out as his companions unless something is done to rescue him. Thus the painting is a call to action.

REALISM IN THE UNITED STATES. Realism was not a term used in the United States, but there were several kinds of realism in American art. Thomas Eakins (1844–1916), for instance, made a series of uncompromising paintings that were criticized for their controversial subject matter. Born in Philadelphia, Eakins trained at the Pennsylvania Academy of the Fine Arts, but since he regarded the training in anatomy as not rigorous enough—lacking realism, as he might have put it—he supplemented his training at the Jefferson Medical College nearby. He later studied at the École des Beaux-Arts in Paris and then spent six months in Spain, where he encountered the profound realism of Baroque artists Jusepe de Ribera and Diego Velázquez (SEE FIGS. 22–19, 22–21). After he returned

A Bar at the Folies-Bergère

by **Édouard Manet, 1881–1882. Oil on canvas. 37¾ × 51¼″ (95.9 × 130 cm).** Courtauld Gallery, London. P.1934.SC.234

In the late nineteenth century, the café-concert was frequented by avant-garde artists such as Degas, Seurat, and Manet. The Folies-Bergère was one of the largest of these café-concerts in Paris, offering circuses, musicals, and vaudeville acts. Note the legs of a trapeze artist who is part of the spectacle to the upper left.

Reflected in the mirror are members of the elegant crowd who have come to the performances at the Folies-Bergère. The men are dressed in top hats and the women in rich costumes. Though their opera glasses they observe lazily the many glittering spectacles performed for their benefit as the electric light dances off the crystal chandelier behind the young girl's head.

The barmaid looks out of the painting at us as if we are her next customer, but she stands stiffly and formally, neither acknowledging nor smiling at us; her sleeves are rolled up and she seems weary from her work. On the other hand, she seems to lean forward to engage in conversation with the top-hatted client in her mirror reflection, suggesting either Manet's intention to create an ambiguous narrative or a curved mirror.

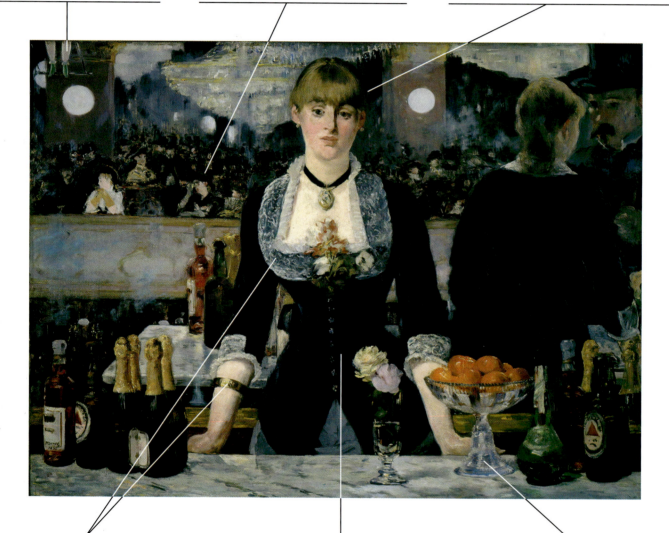

The bangles and lace at the barmaid's wrists and neck suggest a rise in the availability of consumption goods in the shops and department stores of the modern city, perhaps implying that the barmaid, who displays herself like the luscious oranges to the right, is also available for purchase.

Manet presents the Folies-Bergère as a place where the enjoyments of alcohol, the circus and vaudeville, and even sexual transactions take place. The weary girl stands at the bar, barely differentiated from her background, like one of so many glittering objects on display, to be consumed both visually and sexually.

On the marble bar-top Manet has spread a glorious still life of liquor bottles, tangerines, and flowers to entice the customer.

SEE MORE: View the Closer Look feature for *A Bar at the Folies-Bergère* www.myartslab.com

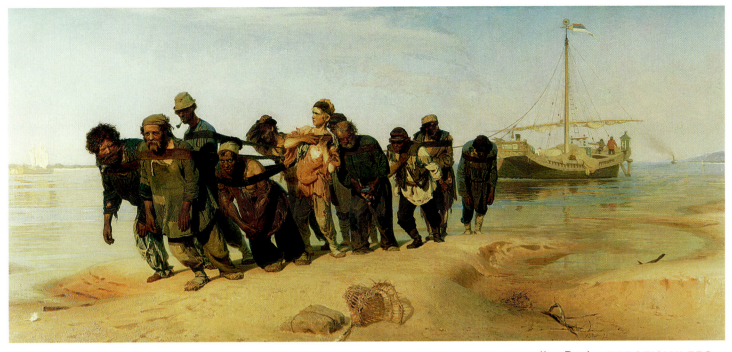

30-20 • Ilya Repin **BARGEHAULERS ON THE VOLGA**
1870–1873. Oil on canvas, 4′3¾″ × 9′3″ (1.3 × 2.81 m). State Russian Museum, St. Petersburg.

to Philadelphia in 1870, he specialized in frank portraits and scenes of everyday life whose lack of conventional charm generated little popular interest. But he was a charismatic teacher, and was soon appointed director of the Pennsylvania Academy.

THE GROSS CLINIC (FIG. 30–21) was one of Eakins's most controversial paintings. Although created specifically for the 1876 Philadelphia centennial show, it was rejected for the fine-art exhibition and relegated to the display area for scientific and medical inquiry. The painting shows Dr. Samuel David Gross performing an operation that he pioneered, as

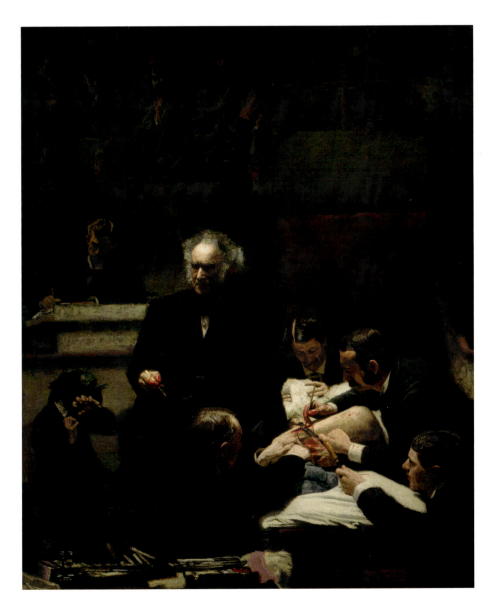

30-21 • Thomas Eakins **THE GROSS CLINIC**
1875. Oil on canvas, 8′ × 6′5″ (2.44 × 1.98 m). Philadelphia Museum of Art, Pennsylvania.

Eakins, who taught anatomy and figure drawing at the Pennsylvania Academy of the Fine Arts, disapproved of the academic technique of drawing from plaster casts. In 1879, he said, "At best, they are only imitations, and an imitation of an imitation cannot have so much life as an imitation of nature itself." He added, "The Greeks did not study the antique … the draped figures in the Parthenon pediment were modeled from life, undoubtedly."

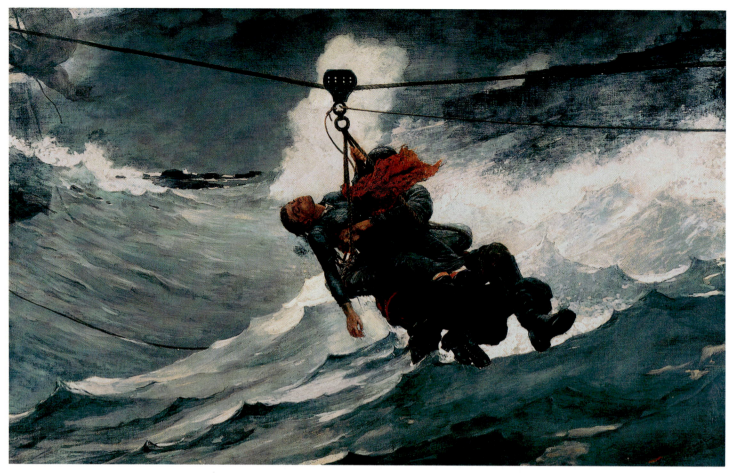

30–22 • Winslow Homer THE LIFE LINE
1884. Oil on canvas, 28¾ × 44⅝″ (73 × 113.3 cm). Philadelphia Museum of Art, Pennsylvania. The George W. Elkins Collection

In the early sketches for this work, the man's face was visible. The decision to cover it focuses more attention not only on the victim, but also on the true hero, the mechanical apparatus known as the "breeches buoy."

he pauses to lecture to students taking notes in the background. The figures assisting the surgery are highlighted, but the rest of the operating theater is in deep shadow. Dr. Gross is dressed in street clothes, typical surgical attire before sterile procedure was introduced, and as he pauses he reveals his bloody hand. The stockinged feet of the patient, a young boy, are visible; his mother shields her eyes in horror. In the mid nineteenth century, surgeons were regarded with fear, especially teaching surgeons who frequently thought of the poor as objects on which to practice; for the poor, a visit to the hospital frequently meant death. Eakins captures the sinister aspect of Gross's fearsome skill. But the dramatic light that evokes both Rembrandt and the Spanish Baroque is significant because it illuminates the forehead of the doctor, thus acknowledging the intellect of this brilliant surgeon.

Winslow Homer (1836–1910) also painted with an unadorned realism later in his life. Born in Boston, he began his career as a 21-year-old freelance illustrator for popular periodicals such as *Harper's Weekly*, which sent him to cover the Civil War in 1862. In 1867, after a ten-month sojourn in France, he returned to make painted versions of the nostalgic rural scenes that had figured

in his illustrations for magazines. He developed a commitment to depicting the working poor after he spent 1881–1882 in a tiny English fishing village on the rugged North Sea coast. Moved by the hard lives and strength of character of the people there, he turned from idyllic subjects to themes of heroic struggle against natural adversity. In England, he was particularly impressed by the "breeches buoy," a mechanical apparatus used for rescue at sea. During the summer of 1883, he made sketches of one imported by the lifesaving crew in Atlantic City, New Jersey. The following year he painted **THE LIFE LINE** (FIG. 30–22), which depicts a coastguard saving a shipwrecked woman with the use of a breeches buoy—a testament not simply to valor but also to ingenuity.

The sculptor Edmonia Lewis (1845–c. 1911) was born in New York State to a Chippewa mother and an African-American father; she was orphaned at the age of 4, and raised by her mother's family. As a teenager, with the help of abolitionists, she attended Oberlin College, the first college in the United States to grant degrees to women, and then moved to Boston. Her highly successful busts and medallions of abolitionist leaders and Civil War heroes financed her move to Rome in 1867.

Galvanized by the struggle for equality of newly freed slaves, Lewis created **FOREVER FREE** (FIG. 30–23) as a memorial to the Emancipation Proclamation. Although it retains Neoclassical forms, this sculpture addresses a modern issue—the end of slavery in America. The standing African-American man raises his hand with the broken shackles still attached; next to him a woman kneels and prays in thanks. This sculpture not only celebrates emancipation, but also subtly reflects white attitudes towards women and people of color. Lewis creates her female as less racialized and more submissive than her male counterpart so that

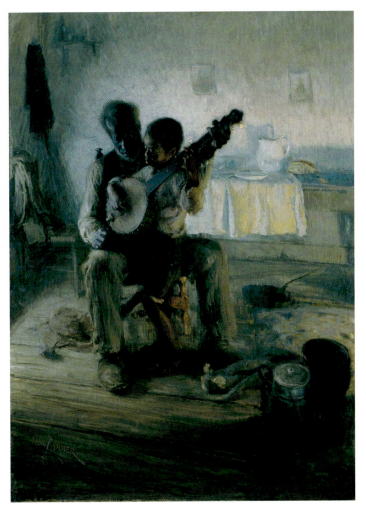

30-24 • Henry Ossawa Tanner THE BANJO LESSON
1893. Oil on canvas, 49 × 35½″ (124.4 × 90 cm). Hampton University Museum, Virginia.

the figure would better reflect the concept of ideal womanhood and be more appealing to white audiences.

Henry Ossawa Tanner (1859–1937) was the most successful African-American painter of the late nineteenth and early twentieth centuries. The son of a bishop in the African Methodist Episcopal Church, Tanner grew up in Philadelphia, sporadically studied art with Thomas Eakins at the Pennsylvania Academy of the Fine Arts between 1879 and 1885, and then worked as a photographer and drawing teacher in Atlanta. In 1891, he moved to Paris to further his academic training. In the early 1890s, Tanner began making paintings with African-American themes, as he put it, to paint the "serious and pathetic side of life." Tanner's **THE BANJO LESSON** (FIG. 30–24) shows an elderly man teaching a young boy seated on his lap to play the banjo. Both are serious and intent. Their poverty fades as they concentrate together. Mutuality, respect, patience, and attention connect the man and child. Although the banjo player was a common derogatory caricature of African-Americans, Tanner takes up the theme and transforms it into a subject of dignity and pride. He turned to biblical painting after a trip to Palestine in 1897.

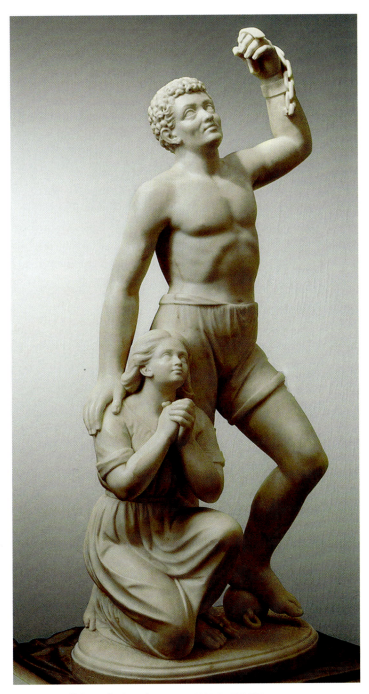

30-23 • Edmonia Lewis FOREVER FREE
1867. Marble, 41¼ × 22 × 17″ (104.8 × 55 × 43.2 cm). Howard University Art Gallery, Washington, D.C.

IMPRESSIONISM

The generation of French painters maturing around 1870 also painted modern urban subjects, but from a perspective very different from that of Manet and the Realists. These artists painted the upper middle class at leisure in the countryside and in the city, and although several members of this group painted rural scenes, their point of view tended to be that of a city person.

In April 1874, a group of artists, including Paul Cézanne, Edgar Degas, Claude Monet, Berthe Morisot, Camille Pissarro, and Pierre-Auguste Renoir, exhibited together in Paris under the title of the Société Anonyme des Artistes Peintres, Sculpteurs, Graveurs, etc. (Anonymous Corporation of Artist-Painters, Sculptors, Engravers, etc.). Pissarro organized the group along the lines advocated by anarchists such as Proudhon, who urged citizens to band together into self-supporting grass-roots organizations, rather than relying on state-sanctioned institutions. Pissarro envisioned the Société as a mutual aid group for artists who opposed the state-funded Salons. While the Impressionists are the best remembered of its members today, at the time the group included artists working in several styles. All 30 participants agreed not to submit anything that year to the Salon, which had in the past often rejected their work. This exhibition was a declaration of independence from the Académie and a bid to gain the public's attention directly.

While their exhibition received some positive reviews, one critic, Louis Leroy, writing in the satirical journal *Charivari*, seized upon the title of Monet's painting *Impression: Sunrise* (SEE FIG. 30–26), and dubbed the entire exhibition "impressionist." Leroy sought to ridicule the fast, open brushstrokes and unfinished look of some of the paintings, but Monet and his colleagues liked the name and kept it as it aptly described their aim to render the fleeting moment in paint. Seven more Impressionist exhibitions were held between 1876 and 1886, with the membership of the group varying slightly on each occasion; only Pissarro participated in all eight shows. The relative success of these exhibitions prompted other artists to organize their own alternatives to the Salon, and by 1900 the independent exhibition and gallery system had all but replaced the Salon system in Paris. This in turn brought to an end the Académie des Beaux-Arts' control over the display of art and thus centrally determined artistic "standards" effectively ended.

THE LANDSCAPE

Claude Monet (1840–1926) was a leading exponent of Impressionism. Born in Paris but raised in the port city of Le Havre, he trained briefly with an academic teacher but soon established his own studio. His friend Charles-François Daubigny urged him to "be faithful to his impression" and suggested that he create a floating studio on a boat and paint *en plein air* (outdoors). Monet's early works depict a side of modernity that the Realists did not show. Like other Impressionists, he was more interested in creating a modern painting style than in producing biting social commentary, although his thematic focus was also modern life. The Impressionists celebrated the semi-rural pleasures of outings to the suburbs

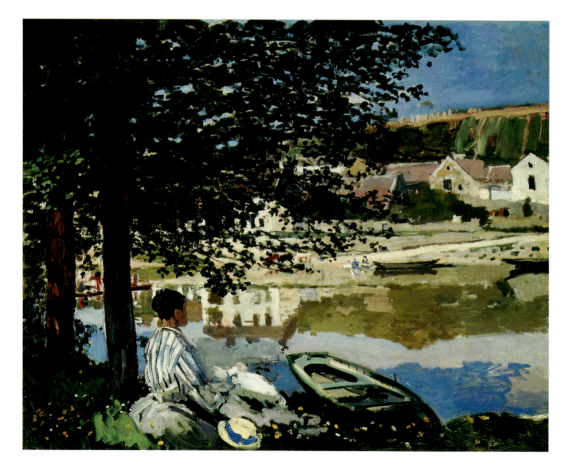

**30-25 • Claude Monet
ON THE BANK OF THE
SEINE, BENNECOURT**
1868. Oil on canvas, 32 × 39⅔″
(81.5 × 100.7 cm). Art Institute of
Chicago. Potter Palmer Collection,
1922.427

EXPLORE MORE: Gain
insight from a primary
source on Claude Monet
www.myartslab.com

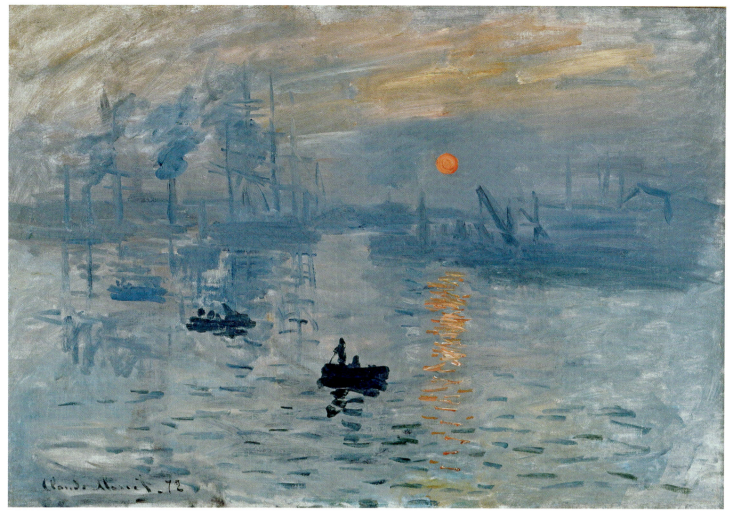

30-26 • Claude Monet IMPRESSION: SUNRISE
1872. Oil on canvas, 19 × 24⅜″ (48 × 63 cm). Musée Marmottan, Paris.

afforded by the Paris train system. Few early works depict locations far from Paris; most feature the Parisian middle and upper middle classes out walking, boating, and visiting the fashionable new parks in the city or at places just outside of town.

Many of Monet's early works include shimmering expanses of water, such as **ON THE BANK OF THE SEINE, BENNECOURT (FIG. 30–25)**, a scene of a young woman in summer, sitting under trees on a riverbank, a small row boat on the river in front of her. At first we think this is a country scene; on closer inspection, however, we see a landing and several buildings on the far bank, and other boats on the water. It is quite a crowded scene, but the intense brightness of Monet's colors makes the first impression one of pure sunlight. (One critic even complained that the painting made his eyes hurt.) To achieve this effect, Monet dispensed entirely with underpainting as taught by the Académie des Beaux-Arts, instead applying flat expanses of pure color directly onto the canvas, unmixed and straight from the tube. The invention of the collapsible metal paint tube in 1841 led to the manufacture of ready-to-use oil colors that painters could conveniently pack and take with them. No longer confined to grinding colors in a studio,

artists like Monet could now paint anywhere. Eschewing the tedium of the academic program for painting, Monet sought to capture the play of light quickly, before it changed. This was a new, modern landscape. As he said: "The Romantics have had their day."

In the summer of 1870, the Franco-Prussian War broke out and Monet fled to London, where he spent time with Pissarro and his future art dealer, Paul Durand-Ruel. The disastrous loss of the major industrial regions of Alsace and Lorraine to Prussia at the end of the war had an equally disastrous impact on the French economy. In Paris, for two months between March and May 1871, the working classes rose up and established the Commune, a working-class city government, the suppression of which led to an estimated 20,000 dead and 7,500 imprisoned. The horror rocked Paris and made people fearful. Courbet was imprisoned for a short time and, in artists' circles, the fear of being branded as an enemy of the state sent a chill through everyone. After 1871, overt political commentary in French art diminished, and the challenge of the avant-garde was expressed increasingly as a rebellion in style.

In 1873, just after returning to Paris, Monet painted **IMPRESSION: SUNRISE (FIG. 30–26)**, a view of the sun rising in

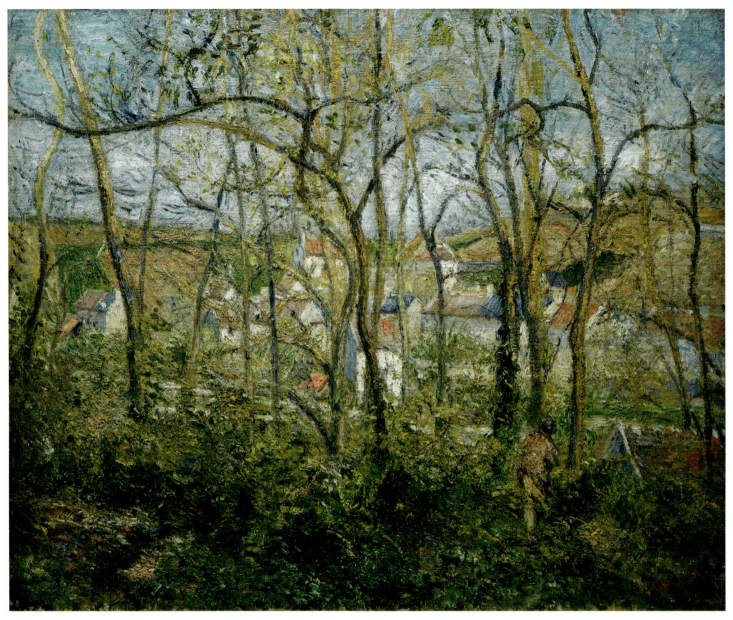

30–27 • Camille Pissarro WOODED LANDSCAPE AT L'HERMITAGE, PONTOISE
1878. Oil on canvas, 18⅝₁₆ × 22¹⁄₁₆″ (46.5 × 56 cm). Nelson-Atkins Museum of Art, Kansas City, Missouri. Gift of Dr. and Mrs. Nicholas S. Pickard

the morning fog over the harbor at Le Havre. The painting is rendered almost entirely as color alone. The foreground is eliminated and the horizon line disappears among steamships and docks in the background; forms and atmosphere are shimmering shapes in color. We find our bearings in this painting slowly, but once we do, we "feel" the scene with our eyes. Monet registers the intensity and shifting forms of a first sketch and renders it as the final work of art. The criticism leveled against his paintings was that they were not "finished." The American painter Lilla Cabot Perry, who befriended Monet in his later years, recalled him telling her:

> When you go out to paint, try to forget what objects you have before you—a tree, a house, a field, or whatever. Merely think, Here is a little square of blue, here an oblong of pink,

here a streak of yellow, and paint it just as it looks to you, the exact color and shape, until it gives your own naive impression of the scene before you.

Monet's friend and fellow artist Camille Pissarro (1830–1903) offered a new image of the landscape in a style similar to Monet's. He painted scenes where the urban meets the rural; some of his paintings portray the rural landscape alone, but many show urban visitors to the countryside or small towns or factories embedded in the land as the city encroaches upon them. Born in the Dutch West Indies to French parents and raised near Paris, Pissarro studied art in Paris during the 1850s and early 1860s. In 1870, while he and Monet lived in London, Pissarro embraced the ideas that would later become known as Impressionism. The two artists worked together in England, trying to capture what Pissarro described as "plein air light and fugitive effects." The impact on both painters was a lightening of color intensity and hue, and a loosening of brushstroke.

Following his return to France, Pissarro settled in Pontoise, a small, hilly village northwest of Paris where he worked for most of the 1870s in an Impressionist style, using high-keyed color and short brushstrokes to capture fleeting qualities of light and atmosphere. In the late 1870s, his painting became more visually complex and the colors darkened again. His **WOODED LANDSCAPE AT L'HERMITAGE, PONTOISE (FIG. 30–27)**, for instance, has a foreground composition of trees that screens the view of a rural path and village behind, flattening space and even partly masking the figure at the lower right. Pissarro applies his paint thickly here, with a multitude of short, multi-directional brushstrokes.

THE FIGURE

In contrast, the Impressionist painter Pierre-Auguste Renoir (1841–1919) focused most of his attention on figure painting,

producing mostly images of the upper middle class at leisure. When he met Monet at the École des Beaux-Arts in 1862, he was in fact working as a figure painter. Monet encouraged him to lighten his palette and to paint outdoors, and by the mid 1870s Renoir was combining a spontaneous handling of natural light with animated figural compositions. In his **MOULIN DE LA GALETTE (FIG. 30–28)**, for example, Renoir depicts crowds dancing in dappled sunlight that falls through the trees. The Moulin de la Galette (the "Pancake Mill"), in the Montmartre section of Paris, was an old-fashioned Sunday afternoon dance hall, which opened its outdoor courtyard during good weather. In this painting, Renoir has glamorized the working-class clientele of the dance hall by placing his artist friends and their models in their midst. These attractive people are shown in attitudes of relaxed congeniality, smiling, dancing, and chatting. He underscores the innocence of their flirtations by including children in the painting in the lower left, while emphasizing the ease of their relations through the relaxed informality of the scene. The overall mood is knit together by sunlight falling through the

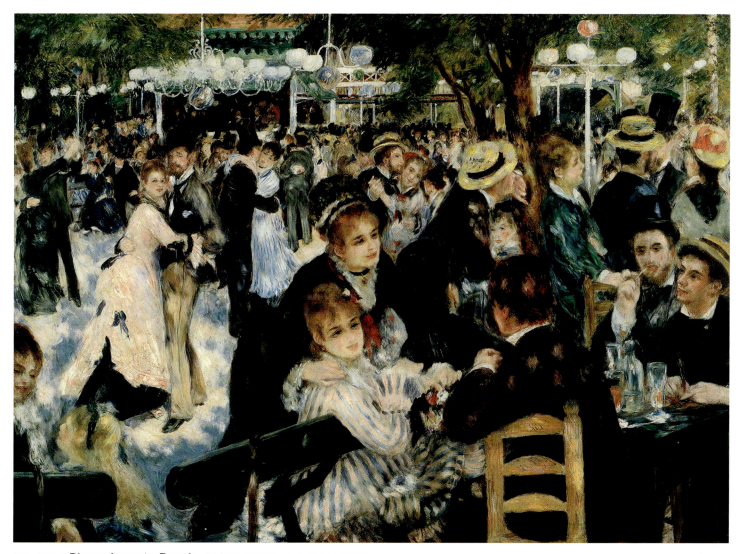

30–28 • Pierre-Auguste Renoir MOULIN DE LA GALETTE
1876. Oil on canvas, 4'3½" × 5'9" (1.31 × 1.75 m). Musée d'Orsay, Paris.

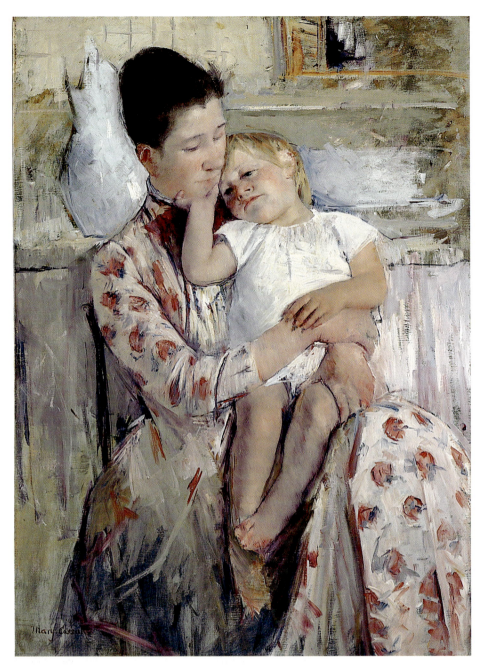

30-29 • Mary Cassatt MOTHER AND CHILD
c. 1890. Oil on canvas, 35½ × 25⅜" (90.2 × 64.5 cm). Wichita Art Museum, Kansas.

academic training, eventually settling in France. The realism of the figure paintings she exhibited at the Salons of the early and mid 1870s attracted the attention of Degas, who invited her to participate in the fourth Impressionist exhibition in 1879. Although she, like Degas, remained a studio painter and printmaker, her distaste for what she called the "tyranny" of the Salon jury system made her one of the group's staunchest supporters.

Cassatt focused her artistic career on the world she knew best: the domestic and social life of upper-middle-class women. Around 1890 she painted **MOTHER AND CHILD (FIG. 30–29)**, one of many representations of the theme in her career. The painting shows the intimate contact between a mother and child after a bath and just before the child falls asleep. The drowsy face and flushed cheeks of the child and the weight of its limbs have a natural quality to them, even though the space occupied by the figures seems flattened. The solidly modeled forms of the hands and faces contrast with the strong, broad, and unfinished quality of the brushstrokes of the lower part of the mother's dress and the background. Cassatt elevates this small vignette of modern life into a homage to motherhood. Though she lived as an expatriate, Cassatt retained her connections in the United States, and when her friends and relatives came to visit she encouraged them to buy art by the Impressionists, thus creating a market for their work in the United States even before one developed in France.

The French artist Berthe Morisot (1841–1895) also defied societal conventions to become a professional painter, and her work also took as its main subject the female figure. Morisot and her sister, Edma, copied paintings in the Louvre and studied with several teachers, including Corot, in the late 1850s and early 1860s. The sisters exhibited their art in the five Salons between 1864 and 1868, the year they met Manet. In 1869, Edma married and gave up painting to devote herself to domestic duties, but Berthe continued painting, even after her 1874 marriage to Manet's brother, Eugène, and the birth of their daughter in 1879. Morisot sent nine paintings to the first exhibition of the Impressionists in 1874 and showed her work in all but one of their subsequent shows.

As a respectable bourgeois lady, Berthe Morisot was not free to prowl the city looking for modern subjects, and, like Cassatt's,

trees and Renoir's soft brushwork weaving blues and purples through the crowd and around the canvas. This idyllic image of a carefree time and place encapsulates Renoir's idea of the essence of art: "For me a picture should be a pleasant thing, joyful and pretty—yes pretty! There are quite enough unpleasant things in life without the need for us to manufacture more."

The American expatriate Mary Cassatt (1844–1926; SEE FIG. 30–32) also exhibited her work with the Impressionists and, like Renoir, became highly skilled in compositions that focused on the figure. Born near Pittsburgh to a well-to-do family, she studied at the Pennsylvania Academy of the Fine Arts in Philadelphia between 1861 and 1865, and then moved to Paris for further

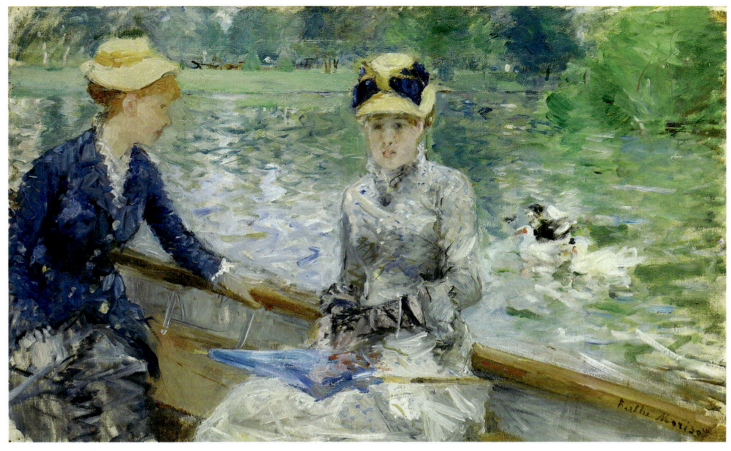

30–30 • Berthe Morisot **SUMMER'S DAY**
1879. Oil on canvas, 17¹³⁄₁₆ × 29⁵⁄₁₆″ (45.7 × 75.2 cm). National Gallery, London. Lane Bequest, 1917

her painting was confined to depictions of women's lives, a subject she knew well. In the 1870s, she painted in an increasingly fluid and painterly style, flattening her picture plane and making her brushwork more visible. In her oil painting **SUMMER'S DAY (FIG. 30–30)**, Morisot shows two elegant young ladies on a pleasant outing on the lake of the fashionable Bois du Boulogne. Unlike the figures in Manet's *Boating* (SEE FIG. 30–19), Morisot's women are properly accompanied by each other, and their ferry is steered by an unseen boatman who is at their behest. First exhibited in the fifth Impressionist exhibition in 1880, *Summer's Day* explores the formal side of Impressionism: Its brushstrokes and colors are skillfully handled. While Morisot was unable to comment on modern city life in ways her brother-in-law might, she nevertheless painted intensely modern pictures.

MODERN LIFE

Subjects of urban work and leisure also attracted Edgar Degas (1834–1917), although his vision is closer to Realism in its social commentary. Instead of painting out of doors, Degas composed his pictures in the studio from working drawings and photographs. He received rigorous academic training at the École des Beaux-Arts in the mid 1850s and subsequently spent three years in Italy studying the Old Masters. Assured compositional structure and intensity of line were hallmarks of his art throughout his career.

The son of a Parisian banker, Degas's painting themes and style were closer to Manet's than to the Impressionists'. In the 1870s, he began painting the modern life of the city: the racetrack, the music hall, and the opera, often focusing on those working to provide the entertainment rather than on their audience. He became the painter of the Paris ballet in the 1870s and 1880s at a time when it was in decline. Degas did not draw or paint actual dancers in rehearsal; rather, he hired dancers, often very young "ballet rats," to come to his studio to pose for him. His ballet paintings and pastels contain acerbic social commentary. **THE REHEARSAL ON STAGE (FIG. 30–31)**, for example, is a contrived scene, not an actual event. Many dancers' poses are uncharacteristic of the actual ballet but are included to show how the life of a dancer is tiresome, involving tedious hours of work. In this pastel, several young dancers look bored or exhausted, and to the far right sit two gentleman visitors who, the artist may be suggesting, pay to see the girls practice. The composition is set in a raked space, as if viewed from a box close to the stage. The abrupt foreshortening is emphasized by the dark scrolls of the double basses that jut up from the lower left. The angular viewpoint may derive from Japanese prints, which Degas collected, while the cropping of figures on the left suggests photography, which he also practiced. The Realist novelist Edmond de Goncourt (1822–1896), a friend of Degas, described him as capturing "the soul of modern life."

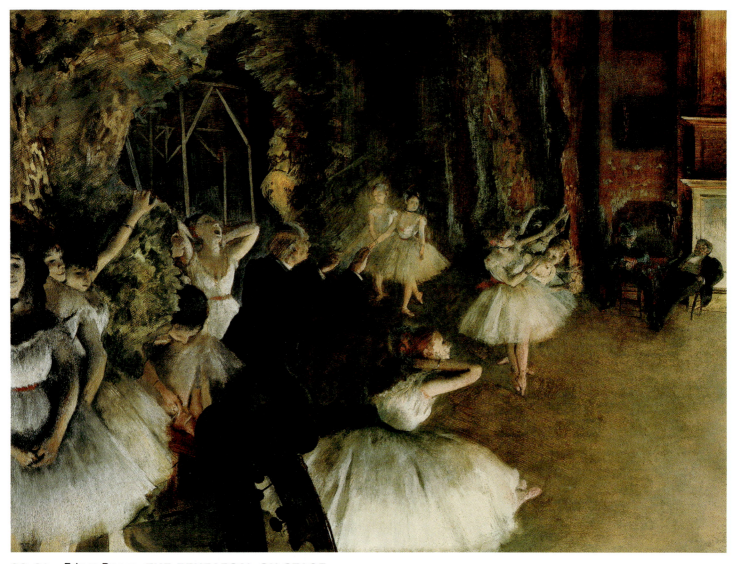

30–31 • Edgar Degas THE REHEARSAL ON STAGE
c. 1874. Pastel over brush-and-ink drawing on thin, cream-colored wove paper, laid on bristol board, mounted on canvas, 21⅜ × 28¾″ (54.3 × 73 cm). Metropolitan Museum of Art, New York. Bequest of Mrs. H. O. Havemeyer Collection, Gift of Horace Havemeyer, 1929 (29.160.26)

In the right background of Degas's picture sit two well-dressed, middle-aged men, who enjoy their intimacy with the dancers at informal rehearsal. Because ballerinas generally came from lower-class families and exhibited their scantily clad bodies in public—something prohibited for "respectable" bourgeois women—they were widely assumed to be sexually available, and they often attracted the attentions of wealthy men willing to support them in exchange for sexual favors. Thus several of Degas's ballet pictures also include one or more of the dancers' mothers, who would accompany their daughters to rehearsals and performances in order to safeguard their virtue.

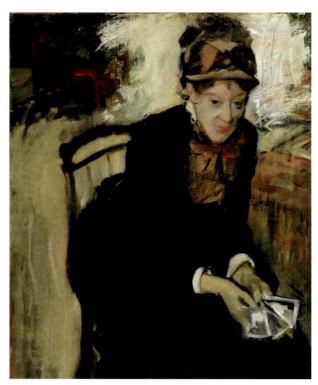

30–32 • Edgar Degas PORTRAIT OF MARY CASSATT
1880–1884. Oil on canvas, 28⅛ × 23⅛″ (71.4 × 58.7 cm). National Portrait Gallery, Smithsonian Institution, Washington, D.C.

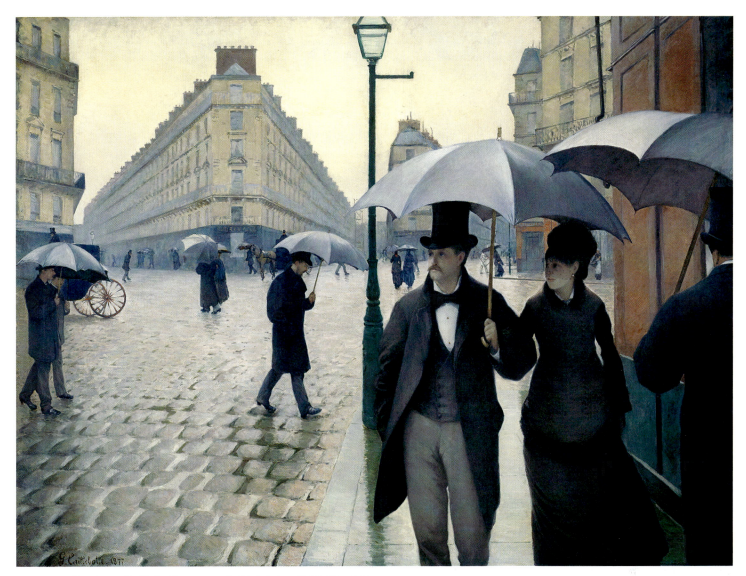

30–33 • Gustave Caillebotte **PARIS STREET, RAINY DAY**
1877. Oil on canvas, 83½ × 108¾" (212.2 × 276.2 cm). Art Institute of Chicago. Part of the Charles H. and
Mary F. S. Worcester Fund

Degas's **PORTRAIT OF MARY CASSATT (FIG. 30–32)** is very different from his ballet pictures. It shows Cassatt as an uncharacteristically strong, intense, and intelligent woman for her time. She leans forward in her chair as if to engage the viewer in conversation in the midst of playing cards. Cassatt carved out a career for herself painting in a radical style and earned the respect of artists like Degas at a time when such professionalism in women was frowned upon. In this portrait Degas shows Cassatt's sharp intellect, something he rarely revealed in other paintings of women.

Gustave Caillebotte (1848–1894), another friend of Degas, was involved in organizing several Impressionist exhibitions; he also purchased the work of his friends, amassing a large collection of paintings. He studied with an academic teacher privately and qualified for the École des Beaux-Arts, but never attended. Caillebotte was fascinated by the streets of Paris, especially Haussmann's modernized street plan, and his subjects and compositions characteristically represent modern life. His **PARIS STREET, RAINY DAY (FIG. 30–33)** has an unconventional, almost telescopic composition that tilts the perspective. The street itself seems to be the subject of this painting; the people are huddled under umbrellas or pushed to the sides of the composition. The figure to the far right is even cropped in half, as in a photograph, and the couple strolling toward us are squeezed between him and the lamppost.

LATE NINETEENTH-CENTURY ART AND THE BEGINNINGS OF MODERNISM

The Realists and Impressionists continued to contribute to avant-garde art until the late nineteenth century, but by the mid 1880s they had relinquished their dominance to a younger generation of artists. The period after Impressionism seems less unified and less directed, involving artists from several different nations taking art in many new visual directions. This generation of artists increasingly defined avant-garde art in terms of visual experimentation, working to develop the precise manner of painting appropriate to their message. Some reinterpreted art as an expression of an interior world of the imagination, while others reconstructed the world around them in paint using new visual languages.

These artists included French Post-Impressionists, who explored inner ways of expressing the outer world, sometimes escaping from the city to the countryside or even to far-flung places; late nineteenth-century French sculptors, who studied the passionate physicality of the human form; British artists, inspired by medieval history in both painting and design; Symbolist artists, who retreated into fantastical and sometimes horrifying worlds of the imagination; Art Nouveau artists, who rejected the rational order of the industrial world to create images and designs ruled by the writhing, moving asymmetrical shapes of growing plants; and even landscape designers, who recast the urban cityscape into a rambling natural landscape.

At the end of the century and late in his life, Paul Cézanne (see pages 1007–1009) altered this course by returning to an intense visual study of the world around him, scrutinizing it like a specimen on a dissecting table and urging younger artists to consider new ways of creating meaning in painting. In 1906, the year Cézanne died, a retrospective exhibition of his life's work in Paris revealed his methods to the next generation of artists, the creators of Modernism.

POST-IMPRESSIONISM

The English critic Roger Fry coined the term "Post-Impressionism" in 1910 to describe a diverse group of painters whose work he had collected for an exhibition. He acknowledged that these artists did not share a unified style or approach to art, but they all used Impressionism as a springboard for their individual expressions of modernity in art.

SEURAT. Georges Seurat (1859–1891) was born in Paris and trained at the École des Beaux-Arts. He was dedicated to the clarity of structure that he found in Classical relief sculpture, and to

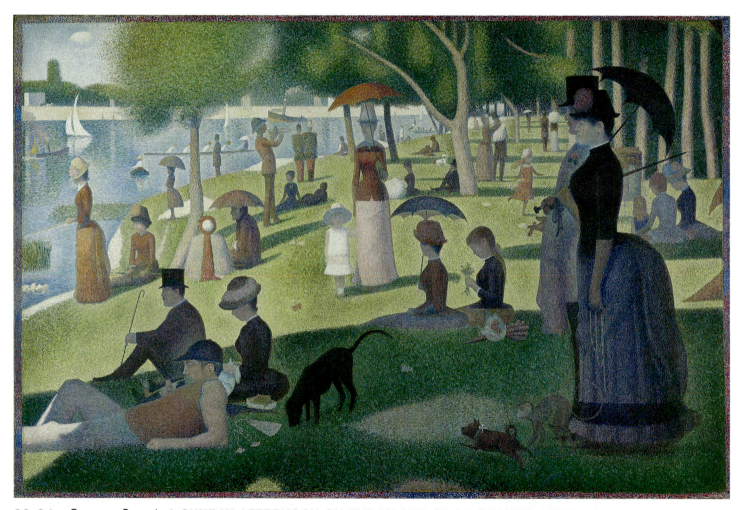

30-34 • Georges Seurat A SUNDAY AFTERNOON ON THE ISLAND OF LA GRANDE JATTE
1884–1886. Oil on canvas, 6′9½″ × 10′1¼″ (207 × 308 cm). Art Institute of Chicago. Helen Birch Bartlett Memorial Collection

the seemingly systematic but actually quite emotive use of color suggested by optics and color theory. He was particularly interested in the "law of the simultaneous contrast of colors" formulated by Michel-Eugène Chevreul in the 1820s. Chevreul observed that adjacent objects not only cast reflections of their own color onto their neighbors, but also create in them the effect of their **complementary color**. Thus, when a blue object is set next to a yellow one, the eye will detect in the blue object a trace of purple, the complement of yellow, and in the yellow object a trace of orange, the complement of blue.

Seurat explored how color hues and tones adjacent to one another create this visual effect of a third color. He studied carefully which hues could be combined, and in what proportions, to produce the effect of a particular color. His goal was to find ways to create retinal vibrations that enlivened the painted surface. He painted in distinctive short, multi-directional strokes of almost pure color, in what came to be known by the various names of "Divisionism" (the term preferred by Seurat), "Pointillism," and "Neo-Impressionism." In theory, these juxtaposed small strokes of color would merge in the viewer's eye to produce the impression of other colors. When perceived from a certain distance they would appear more luminous and intense than the same colors seen separately, while on close observation Seurat's strokes and colors would remain distinct and separate, creating an almost abstract arrangement of color and shape.

Seurat's monumental painting **A SUNDAY AFTERNOON ON THE ISLAND OF LA GRANDE JATTE** (FIG. 30–34) was first exhibited at the eighth and final Impressionist exhibition in 1886. He presented this large canvas as a "demonstration" piece to prove his worth as an artist and to advertise his smaller works. The painting contained 11 colors, with the purest hue of each that he could find. He laid these out in a single row on his palette, while creating a second, upper row of the same colors mixed with white and a third lower row mixed with black. He painted the entire canvas using this range of colors. When viewed from a distance of about 9 feet, the painting reads as figures in a park rendered in many colors and tones; but when viewed from a distance of 3 feet, the individual marks of color become more distinct and the forms begin to dissolve into abstraction.

The painting represents a sunny Sunday afternoon, the newly designated official day off for French working families to spend time together. The park, on the island of the Grande Jatte, just west of Paris, was accessible by train. There was a social hierarchy in Parisian parks in the late nineteenth century; the Bois du Boulogne (SEE FIG. 30–30) was an upper-middle-class park in an area of grand avenues, whereas the Grande Jatte faced a lower-class industrial area across the river. The figures represent a range of lower-middle-class "types" that would have been easily recognizable to the nineteenth-century viewer, such as the strolling man and his companion to the right, usually identified as a *boulevardier* (or citified dandy) and a *cocotte* (a single woman of the demi-monde), or the *canotier* (working-class oarsman) to the left.

VAN GOGH.   Among the artists to experiment with Divisionism, Impressionism and modernity was the Dutch painter Vincent van Gogh (1853–1890), who transformed his artistic sources into a highly expressive personal style. The oldest son of a Protestant minister, Van Gogh worked as an art dealer, a teacher, and an evangelist before deciding in 1880 to become an artist. After brief periods of study in Brussels, The Hague, and Antwerp, in 1886 he moved to Paris, where he discovered the Parisian avant-garde. Van Gogh adapted Seurat's Divisionism, for instance, by applying brilliantly colored paint in multi-directional strokes of **impasto** (thick applications of paint) to give his pictures a turbulent emotional energy and a palpable surface texture.

Van Gogh was a socialist who believed that modern life, with its constant social change and focus on progress and success, alienated people from one other and from themselves (see "Modern Artists and World Cultures: Japonisme," pages 994–995). His own paintings are efforts to communicate his emotional state and establish a connection between artist and viewer, thereby overcoming the emotional barrenness that he felt modern society created. In a prolific output over only ten years, he produced paintings that would contribute significantly to the later emergence of Expressionism, in which the artist's emotional intensity overrides fidelity to the actual appearance of things. Van Gogh described his working method in a letter to his brother:

> I should like to paint the portrait of an artist friend who dreams great dreams, who works as the nightingale sings, because it is his nature. This man will be fair-haired. I should like to put my appreciation, the love I have for him, into the picture. So I will paint him as he is, as faithfully as I can— to begin with. But that is not the end of the picture. To finish it, I shall be an obstinate colorist. I shall exaggerate the fairness of the hair, arrive at tones of orange, chrome, pale yellow. Behind the head—instead of painting the ordinary wall of the shabby apartment, I shall paint infinity, I shall do a simple background of the richest, most intense blue that I can contrive, and by this simple combination, the shining fair head against this rich blue background, I shall obtain a mysterious effect, like a star in the deep blue sky.

One of the most famous examples of this approach is **THE STARRY NIGHT** (FIG. 30–35), painted from careful observation and the artist's imagination. Above the quiet town, the sky pulsates with celestial rhythms and blazes with exploding stars. Contemplating life and death in a letter, Van Gogh wrote: "Just as we take the train to get to Tarascon or Rouen, we take death to reach a star." This idea is rendered visible in this painting by the cypress tree, a traditional symbol of both death and eternal life, which rises dramatically to link the terrestrial and celestial realms. The brightest star in the sky is actually a planet, Venus, which is associated with love. It is possible that the picture's extraordinary energy also expresses Van Gogh's euphoric hope of gaining in death the love that had eluded him in life. The painting is a riot of

Modern Artists and World Cultures: Japonisme

In 1887, Vincent van Gogh painted *Japonaiserie: Flowering Plum Tree*. He was deeply affected by recently imported examples of Japanese art and prints, which he appreciated for their "exotic" visual effects. Japan was opened to Western trade and diplomacy in 1853, after a lengthy isolation, and in 1855 trade agreements permitted the regular exchange of goods with Japan. Among the first Japanese art objects to come to Paris was a sketchbook entitled *Manga* by Hokusai (1760–1849), which was eagerly passed around by Parisian artists. Several of them began to collect Japanese objects; the 1867 Paris International Exposition mounted the first show of Japanese prints in Europe; and immediately thereafter, Japanese lacquers, fans, bronzes, hanging scrolls, kimonos, ceramics, illustrated books, and **ukiyo-e** (prints of the "floating world," the realm of geishas and popular entertainment) began to appear for sale in specialty shops, art galleries, and even some department stores in Paris. The French obsession with Japan reached such a level by 1872 that the art critic Philippe Burty named the phenomenon **Japonisme**.

Vincent van Gogh admired the design and handcrafted quality of Japanese prints, which he both owned and copied. His *Japonaiserie: Flowering Plum Tree* is largely copied from Hiroshige's woodblock print *Plum Orchard, Kameido*. Van Gogh makes use of the same flattened tree with its asymmetrical branches, thin, shooting twigs, and tiny blossoms in his foreground; the same smaller trees in the middle ground; and the same railing in the background, behind which can be seen several figures and a small hut. Van Gogh has also appropriated Hiroshige's color scheme and flattened picture plane, as well as his banners of text. But he also made significant changes in his adaptation. He flattened the scene more extremely than Hiroshige had done. His grass is a uniform blanket of green, the flat gray trees with hard black outlines are flat and undifferentiated, and it is not clear whether the yellow blossoms are in front of or behind the thickly painted red sky. Indeed, Hiroshige's print suggests greater spatial depth than Van Gogh's imitation. Van Gogh also frames his painting with a bold, rather crudely painted orange frame with pseudo-Japanese characters scrawled around it, as if to accentuate the "primitiveness" of the image and its source. Van Gogh knew little about Japanese culture and less about the Japanese painting or printmaking tradition. He uses the Hiroshige print as a prompt in order to conjure up what he saw as a simpler, more "primitive" culture than his own, at a time when other artists, such as Paul Gauguin traveled the world in search of "primitive" cultures to inspire their art.

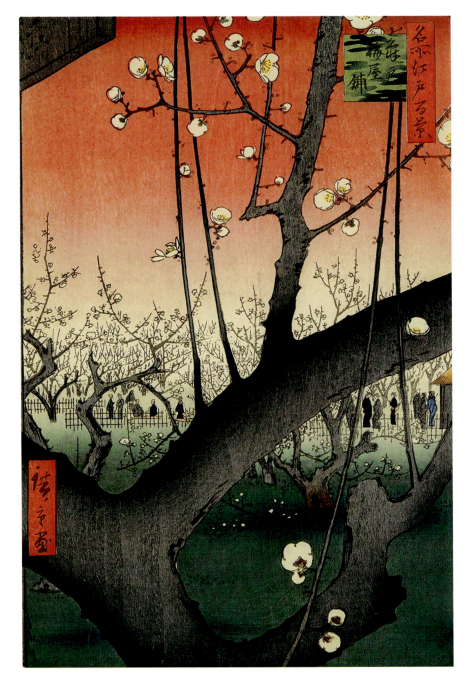

Hiroshige **PLUM ORCHARD, KAMEIDO**
1857. From *One Hundred Famous Views of Edo*. Woodblock print, 13¼ × 8⅝" (33.6 × 47 cm). Brooklyn Museum, New York.

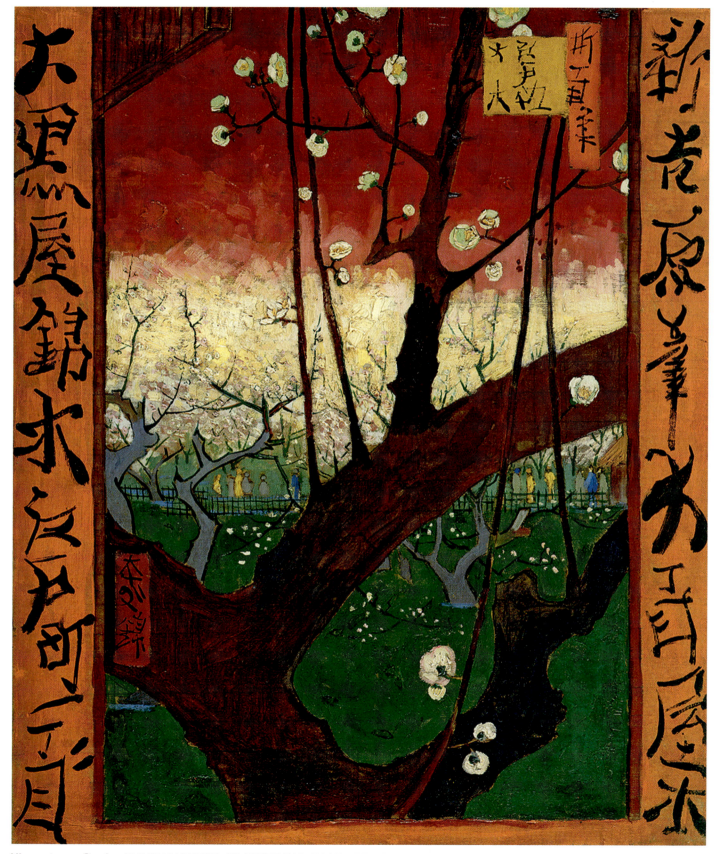

Vincent van Gogh JAPONAISERIE: FLOWERING PLUM TREE
1887. Oil on canvas, 21½ × 18″ (54.6 × 45.7 cm). Vincent van Gogh Museum, Amsterdam.

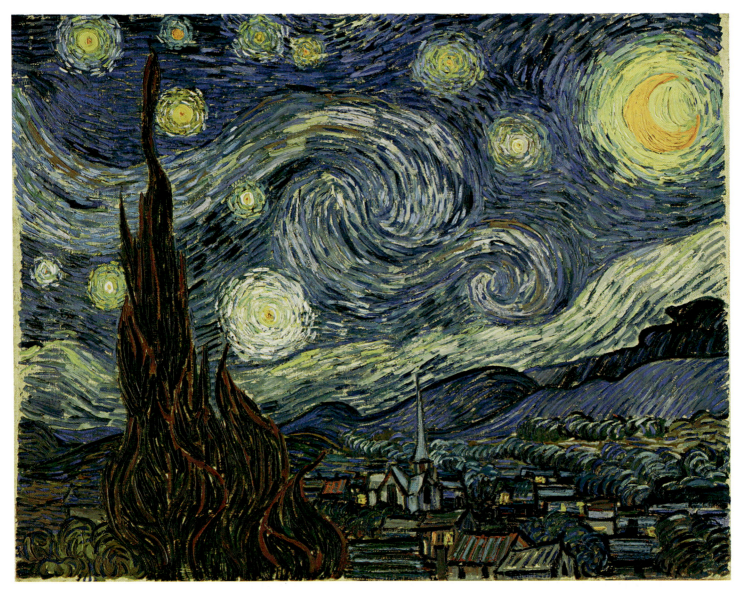

30-35 • Vincent van Gogh THE STARRY NIGHT
1889. Oil on canvas, 28¾ × 36¼″ (73 × 93 cm). Museum of Modern Art, New York.
Acquired through the Lillie P. Bliss Bequest (472.1941)

brushwork, as rail-like strokes of intense color writhe across its surface. Van Gogh's brushwork is immediate, expressive, and intense. During the last year and a half of his life, he experienced repeated psychological crises that lasted for days or weeks. While they were raging, he wanted to hurt himself, heard loud noises in his head, and could not paint. The stress and burden of these attacks led him to the asylum where he painted *The Starry Night*, and eventually to suicide in July 1890.

GAUGUIN.   In painting from imagination as much as from nature in *The Starry Night*, Van Gogh may have been following the advice of his friend Paul Gauguin (1848–1903), who once counseled another artist: "Don't paint from nature too much. Art is an abstraction. Derive this abstraction from nature while dreaming before it, and think more of the creation that will result." Gauguin's

art abstracts from nature like Van Gogh's, and it laid foundations for even more abstracted art in the twentieth century. Born in Paris to a Peruvian mother and a radical French journalist father, Gauguin lived in Peru until age 7. During the 1870s and early 1880s, he enjoyed a comfortable bourgeois life as a stockbroker, painting in his spare time under the tutelage of Pissarro. Between 1880 and 1886, he exhibited in the final four Impressionist exhibitions. In 1883, he lost his job during a stock market crash; three years later he abandoned his wife and five children to pursue a full-time painting career. Gauguin knew firsthand the business culture of his time and came to despise it, writing disparagingly to a friend of "the European struggle for money." Believing that escape to a more "primitive" place would bring with it the simpler pleasures of life, Gauguin lived for extended periods in the French province of Brittany between 1886 and

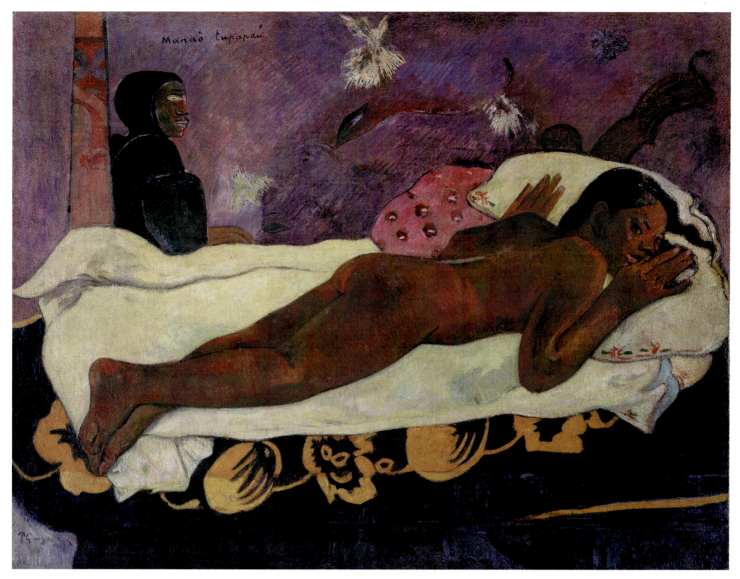

30-36 • Paul Gauguin **MANAO TUPAPAU (SPIRIT OF THE DEAD WATCHING)**
1892. Oil on burlap mounted on canvas, 28⅝ × 36⅜″ (73 × 92 cm). Collection Albright-Knox Art Gallery, Buffalo, NY.
A. Conger Goodyear Collection, 1965.

EXPLORE MORE: Gain insight from a primary source on Paul Gauguin www.myartslab.com

1891, traveled to Panama and Martinique in 1887, spent two months in Arles with Van Gogh in 1888, and then in 1891 sailed for Tahiti, a French colony in the South Pacific. After a final sojourn in France in 1893–1895, Gauguin returned to the Pacific, where he died in 1903.

Gauguin's art was inspired by sources as varied as medieval stained glass, folk art, and Japanese prints; he sought to paint in a "primitive" way employing the so-called "decorative" qualities of folk art such as brilliantly colored flat shapes, an anti-naturalist use of color, and thick, black outlines to feign "primitiveness." Gauguin called his style "synthetism," because he believed it synthesized observation and the artist's feelings about a subject in an abstracted application of line, shape, space, and color.

MANAO TUPAPAU (THE SPIRIT OF THE DEAD KEEP WATCH) (FIG. 30–36) portrays a thickly outlined, androgynous nude figure lying prone on a bed, close to sleep. In the background the spirit of the dead watches over the figure. Gauguin implicitly suggests that this painting represents a scene from Tahitian religion, but there is no evidence that this is the case. The painting is not intended to be naturalistic or realistic, evoking a mood rather than representing a specific scene. Like many of Gauguin's works, this painting shows the late nineteenth-century desire to "get away" from the oppressive life of the city, and to get back to so-called "primitive" versions of culture.

LATE NINETEENTH-CENTURY ART IN BRITAIN

In the 1840s, Britain also encountered social and political upheaval. The depression of the "hungry forties," the Irish Potato Famine, and the Chartist Riots threatened social stability in England. Artists in Britain at mid century painted scenes of religious, medieval, or moral exemplars using a tight realistic style that was quite different from French Realism.

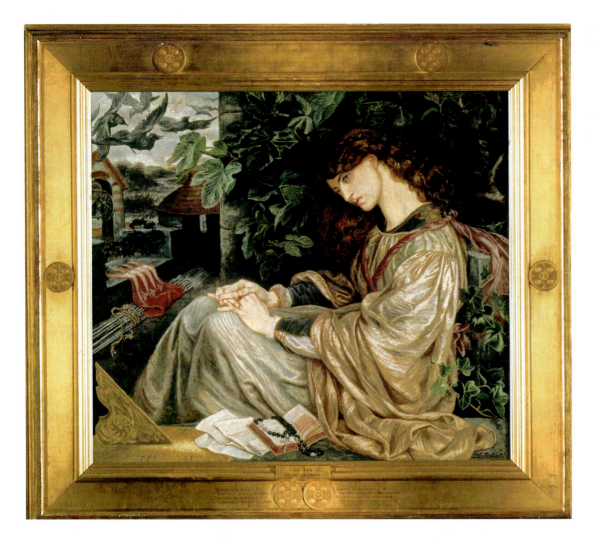

ROSSETTI AND THE PRE-RAPHAELITES. In 1848, seven young London artists formed the Pre-Raphaelite Brotherhood in response to what they considered the misguided practices of contemporary British art. Instead of the "Raphaelesque" conventions taught at the Royal Academy, the Pre-Raphaelites looked back to the Middle Ages and early Renaissance (before Raphael) for a beauty and spirituality that they found lacking in their own time. The Pre-Raphaelites invoked what they imagined was the more moralistic and "real" art of this earlier time.

Dante Gabriel Rossetti (1828–1882) was a leading member and spokesperson of the Pre-Raphaelite Brotherhood, although his art grew increasingly visionary in later years. His painting **LA PIA DE' TOLOMEI** (FIG. 30–37) illustrates a scene from Dante's

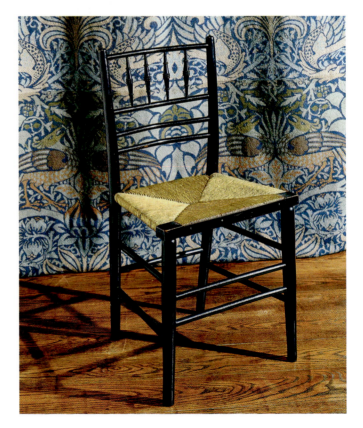

30-38 • FOREGROUND: Philip Webb SINGLE CHAIR FROM THE SUSSEX RANGE
In production from c. 1865. Ebonized wood with rush seat, 33 × 16½ × 14″ (83.8 × 42 × 35.6 cm).

BACKGROUND: William Morris "PEACOCK AND DRAGON" CURTAIN
1878. Handloomed jacquard-woven woolen twill, 12′10½″ × 11′5⅝″ (3.96 × 3.53 m). Chair and curtain manufactured by Morris & Company. The William Morris Gallery, London Borough of Waltham Forest.

Art on Trial in 1877

This is a partial transcript of Whistler's testimony at the libel trial that he initiated against the art critic John Ruskin. Whistler's responses often provoked laughter, and the judge at one point threatened to clear the courtroom.

Q: What is your definition of a Nocturne?

A: I have, perhaps, meant rather to indicate an artistic interest alone in the work, divesting the picture from any outside sort of interest which might have been otherwise attached to it. It is an arrangement of line, form, and color first … The *Nocturne in Black and Gold* [SEE FIG. 30–39] is a night piece, and represents the fireworks at Cremorne.

Q: Not a view of Cremorne?

A: If it were called a view of Cremorne, it would certainly bring about nothing but disappointment on the part of beholders. It is an artistic arrangement. It was marked 200 guineas …

Q: I suppose you are willing to admit that your pictures exhibit some eccentricities; you have been told that over and over again?

A: Yes, very often.

Q: You send them to the gallery to invite the admiration of the public?

A: That would be such a vast absurdity on my part that I don't think I could.

Q: Did it take you much time to paint the *Nocturne in Black and Gold*? How soon did you knock it off?

A: I knocked it off in possibly a couple of days; one day to do the work, and another to finish it.

Q: And that was the labor for which you asked 200 guineas?

A: No, it was for the knowledge gained through a lifetime.

The judge ruled in Whistler's favor; Ruskin had indeed libeled him. But he awarded Whistler damages of only one farthing. Since in those days the person who brought the suit had to pay all the court costs, the case ended up bankrupting the artist.

Purgatory in which La Pia (the Pious One), wrongly accused of infidelity and locked up by her husband, is dying. The rosary and prayer book at her side refer to her piety, while the sundial and ravens suggest the passage of time and her impending death. La Pia's continuing love for her husband is represented by his letters, which lie under her prayer book. The luxuriant fig leaves that surround her are traditionally associated with shame, and they seem to suck her into themselves. They have no source in Dante, but are relevant to Rossetti: Jane Burden, his model for this and many other paintings as well as his lover, was the wife of his friend William Morris. La Pia twists at her wedding ring in the painting. It is hard to believe that this painting about La Pia's imprisonment for adultery is not also about Rossetti and Jane Burden.

MORRIS AND THE ARTS AND CRAFTS MOVEMENT.   Other British artists drew inspiration from the medieval past as a panacea for modern life in London. William Morris (1834–1896) worked briefly as a painter under the influence of the Pre-Raphaelites before turning his attention to interior design and decoration. Morris's interest in crafts developed in the context of a widespread reaction against the shoddy design of industrially produced goods. Unable to find satisfactory furnishings for his new home after his marriage in 1859, Morris designed and constructed them himself, with the help of friends, later founding a decorating firm to produce a full range of medieval-inspired objects. Although many of the furnishings offered by Morris & Company were expensive, one-of-a-kind items, others, such as the rush-seated chair illustrated here (**FIG. 30–38**), were inexpensive and simple,

intended as a handcrafted alternative to machine-made furniture. Concerned with creating a "total" environment, Morris and his colleagues designed not only furniture but also stained glass, tiles, wallpaper, and fabrics, such as the "Peacock and Dragon" curtain seen in the background of FIGURE 30–38.

Morris inspired what became known as the Arts and Crafts Movement. He rebelled against the idea that art was a highly specialized product made for a small elite, and he hoped to usher in a new era of art for the people. He said in lectures: "I do not want art for a few, any more than education for a few, or freedom for a few." A socialist, Morris opposed mass production and the deadening impact of factory life on the industrial worker. He argued that when laborers made handcrafted objects, they had the satisfaction of being involved in the entire process of creation and thus produced honest and beautiful things. He was inspired by the romance of the medieval craft tradition, ignoring its harsh realities.

WHISTLER.   The American expatriate James Abbott McNeill Whistler (1834–1903) also focused his attention on the rooms and walls where art was hung, but he did so more to satisfy elitist tastes for beauty for its own sake. He also became embroiled in several artistic controversies that laid the groundwork for the art of the next century. After flunking out of West Point in the early 1850s, Whistler studied art in Paris, where he was briefly influenced by Courbet's Realism; the two artists painted several seascapes together. He settled in London in 1859, after which his art began to take on a more "decorative" quality that he called "aesthetic"

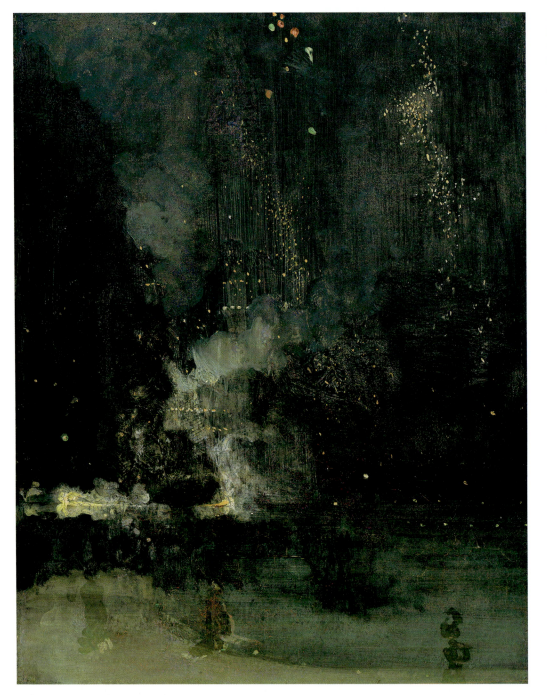

30-39 • James Abbott McNeill Whistler **NOCTURNE IN BLACK AND GOLD, THE FALLING ROCKET**
1875. Oil on panel, 23¾ × 18⅜″ (60.2 × 46.7 cm). Detroit Institute of Arts, Detroit, Michigan. 46.309

EXPLORE MORE: Gain insight from a primary source about James Abbott McNeill Whistler's *Nocturne in Black and Gold, The Falling Rocket*
www.myartslab.com

and which increasingly diverged from observed reality. He believed that the arrangement of a room (or a painting) could be aesthetically pleasing in itself, without reference to the outside world. He was among the first artists to hang art in a single horizontal row on a wall, rather than "stacked" in Salon style. He even occasionally designed exhibition rooms for his art, with the aim of creating a total harmony of objects and space.

Whistler's ideas about art were revolutionary. He was among the first artists to conceive of his paintings as abstractions from rather than representations of observed reality, and he was among the first to collect Japanese art, fascinated by its "decorative" (see page 997) line, color, and shape, although he understood little about its meaning or intent. By the middle of the 1860s, Whistler began to

entitle his works "Symphonies" and "Arrangements," suggesting that their themes resided in their compositions rather than their subject matter. He painted several landscapes with the musical title "Nocturne," and when he exhibited some of these in 1877, he drew the scorn of England's leading art critic, John Ruskin (1819–1900), a supporter of the Pre-Raphaelites and their moralistic intentions. Decrying Whistler's work as carelessly lacking in finish and purpose, Ruskin's review asked how an artist could "demand 200 guineas for flinging a pot of paint in the public's face."

The most controversial painting in Whistler's 1877 exhibition was **NOCTURNE IN BLACK AND GOLD, THE FALLING ROCKET (FIG. 30–39)**, and Ruskin's objections to it precipitated one of the most notorious court dramas in art history. Painted in restricted tonalities, at first glance the work appears completely abstract. In fact, the painting is a night scene depicting a fireworks show over a lake at Cremorne Gardens in London, with viewers vaguely discernible along the lake's edge in the foreground. The term "Nocturne" was taken from the titles of piano compositions by the Romantic composer Frederic Chopin: Whistler wanted to evoke an association between the abstract qualities of art and music. After reading Ruskin's review, Whistler sued the critic for libel (see "Art on Trial in 1877," page 999). He deliberately turned the courtroom into a public forum in which both to defend and advertise his art. On the witness stand, he defended his view that art has no higher purpose than creating visual delight, claiming that paintings need not have a subject matter. While Whistler never made a completely abstract painting, his theories were integral to the development of abstract art in the next century.

SYMBOLISM

The move toward abstraction can also be seen in Symbolism, an international movement in art and literature that comprised a loose affiliation of artists making works addressing the irrational fears, desires, and impulses of the human mind. A fascination with the dark recesses of the mind emerged over the last decades of the nineteenth century, encompassing photographic and scientific examinations of the nature of insanity, as well as a popular interest in the spirit world of mediums. Some Symbolist artists sought escape from modern life in irrational worlds of unrestrained emotion as described by authors such as Edgar Allan Poe (1809–1849), whose terrifying stories of the supernatural were popular across Europe. It is not coincidental that Sigmund Freud (1856–1939), who compared artistic creation to the process of dreaming, wrote his pioneering *The Interpretation of Dreams* (1900) during this period.

The Symbolists rejected the values of rationalism and material progress that dominated modern Western culture, choosing instead to explore the nonmaterial realms of emotion, imagination, and spirituality. Ultimately the Symbolists sought a deeper and more mysterious reality than the one encountered in everyday life, which they conveyed through strange and ambiguous subject matter and stylized forms that suggest hidden and elusive meanings. They transformed appearances in order to give pictorial form to psychic experience, and they often compared their works to dreams.

Symbolism in painting closely paralleled a similar movement among poets and writers who also abjured materialism and who retreated into fantasy worlds conjured from their imaginations. For example, Joris-Karl Huysmans's novel *À Rebours* (*Against the Grain*), published in 1884, has a single character, an aristocrat named Des Esseintes, who locked himself away from the world because "Imagination could easily be substituted for the vulgar realities of things." Claiming that nature was irrelevant, Des Esseintes mused: "Nature has had her day" and "wearied aesthetes" should take refuge in artworks "steeped in ancient dreams or antique corruptions, far removed from the manner of our present day."

MOREAU. A visionlike atmosphere pervades the later work of Gustave Moreau (1826–1898), an older academic artist whom the Symbolists regarded as a precursor. The Symbolists particularly admired Moreau's renditions of the biblical Salome, the young Judaean princess who, at the instigation of her mother, Herodias, performed an erotic dance before her stepfather, Herod, and demanded as reward the head of John the Baptist (Mark 6:21–28). In **THE APPARITION** (**FIG. 30–40**), exhibited at the Salon of 1876, the seductive Salome confronts a vision of the saint's severed head,

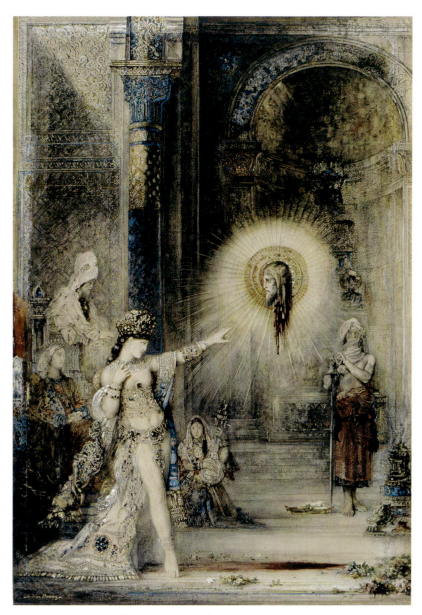

30–40 • Gustave Moreau THE APPARITION
1874–1876. Watercolor on paper, 41⁵⁄₁₆ × 28³⁄₁₆″ (106 × 72.2 cm). Musée du Louvre, Paris.

which hovers open-eyed in midair, dripping blood yet also radiating holy light. Moreau depicted this sensual and macabre scene and its exotic setting in linear detail, with touches of jewel-like color to create an atmosphere of voluptuous decadence that amplifies Salome's role as *femme fatale* who uses her sensuality to destroy her male victim.

The Symbolists, like many smaller groups of artists in the late nineteenth century, staged independent art exhibitions; they were not interested in the approbation of the general public. Unlike the Impressionists, for instance, who hired halls, printed programs, and charged a small admission fee for their exhibitions, the Symbolists mounted more modest shows. During the 1889 Universal Exposition, they hung some works in a café a few blocks away from the grounds, with the result that the exhibition went almost unnoticed by the press.

MUNCH. Symbolism originated in France but had a profound impact on the avant-garde in other countries, where it frequently took on Expressionist tendencies. In Norway, Edvard Munch (1863–1944) produced a body of work that shows the terrifying workings of an anguished mind. THE SCREAM (FIG. 30–41) is the stuff of nightmares and horror movies; its harsh swirling colors and lines throw us wildly around the painting, but bring us right back to where we started, trapped between going forward into an unknown horror and going back into a known one. Munch described how the painting began: "One evening I was walking along a path; the city was on one side,

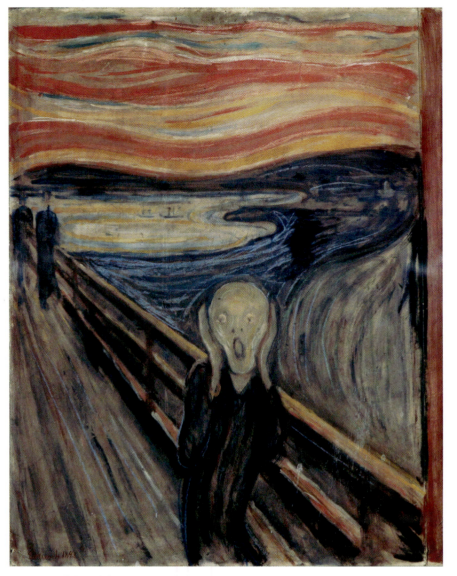

30-41 • Edvard Munch **THE SCREAM**
1893. Tempera and casein on cardboard, 36 × 29″ (91.3 × 73.7 cm). Nasjonalgalleriet, Oslo.

and the fjord below. I was tired and ill … . I sensed a shriek passing through nature … . I painted this picture, painted the clouds as actual blood." A silent scream echoes throughout the painting.

ENSOR. The Belgian painter and printmaker James Ensor (1860–1949) brought together Symbolist and Expressionist tendencies in equally terrifying paintings. He studied for four years at the Brussels Academy, but spent the rest of his life in the nearby coastal resort town of Ostend. THE INTRIGUE (FIG. 30–42) shows a tightly packed group of people bustling and jostling towards us. Their faces are covered with blank, sometimes eyeless masks modeled on the grotesque papier-mâché masks that his family sold for the pre-Lenten carnival, a major holiday in Ostend. These disturbing faces create a mindless

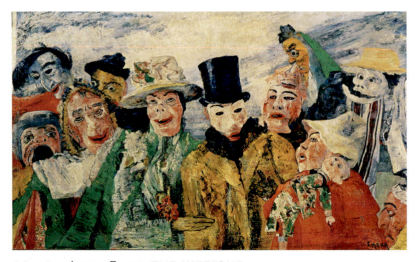

30-42 • James Ensor **THE INTRIGUE**
1890. Oil on canvas, 35½ × 59″ (90.3 × 150 cm). Koninklijk Museum voor Schone Kunsten, Antwerp.

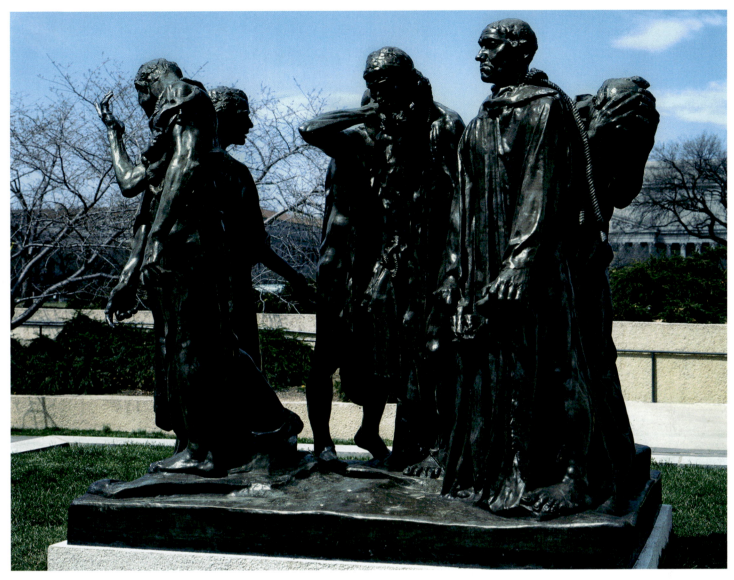

30–43 • Auguste Rodin THE BURGHERS OF CALAIS
1884–1889. Bronze, 6′10½″ × 7′11″ × 6′6″ (2.1 × 2.4 × 2 m). Hirshhorn Museum and Sculpture Garden,
Smithsonian Institution, Washington, D.C. Gift of Joseph H. Hirshhorn, 1966

crowd that seems to move menacingly upon us. Ensor's acidic colors and deliberately crude handling increase the sense of danger. The threat posed by this picture, however, is located firmly in the mind.

LATE NINETEENTH-CENTURY FRENCH SCULPTURE

A defiance of conventional expectations and an interest in emotional expressiveness also characterize the work of late nineteenth-century Europe's most successful and influential sculptor, Auguste Rodin (1840–1917), and his contemporary Camille Claudel (1864–1943). Born in Paris and trained as a decorative craftworker, Rodin failed on three occasions to gain entrance to the École des Beaux-Arts and consequently spent the first 20 years of his career as an assistant to other sculptors and decorators. After a trip to Italy in 1875, where he saw the sculpture of Donatello and Michelangelo, Rodin developed a style of vigorously modeled figures in unconventional,

even awkward poses, which was simultaneously scorned by academic critics and admired by the general public.

Rodin's status as a major sculptor was confirmed in 1884, when he won a competition to create **THE BURGHERS OF CALAIS** (**FIG. 30–43**), commissioned to commemorate an event from the Hundred Years War. In 1347, Edward III of England offered to spare the besieged city of Calais if six leading citizens (or burghers)—dressed only in sackcloth with rope halters and carrying the keys to the city—surrendered themselves to him for execution. Rodin shows the six volunteers preparing to give themselves over to what they assume will be their deaths. Rodin defies academic conventions: Instead of elevating the hostages as heroes, he brings them down off their pedestal and places them at eye level. Instead of noble resignation, they show anguish and despair. Entirely unidealized, these awkward figures are restless, agitated, and distressed. Their exaggerated expressions, lengthened

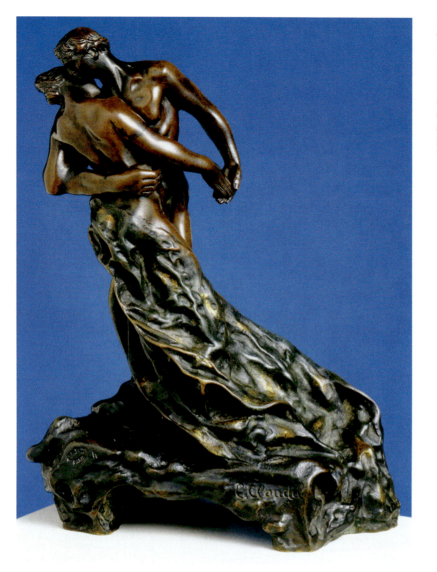

30–44 • Camille Claudel
THE WALTZ
1892–1905. Bronze, height 9⅞″ (25 cm).
Neue Pinakothek, Munich.

French composer Claude Debussy,
a close friend of Claudel, displayed a cast
of this sculpture on his piano. Debussy
acknowledged the influence of art and
literature on his musical innovations.

arms, enlarged hands and feet, and heavy cloaks accentuate their burden; they seem unable to take another step. The discomfort and raw emotional power of this sculpture were not what the commissioners at Calais expected. Nevertheless, Rodin's ability to stylize human physicality for expressive purposes transformed late nineteenth-century sculpture and paved the way for subsequent sculptural abstractions.

Camille Claudel (1864–1943) was an assistant in Rodin's studio while he worked on *The Burghers of Calais*. Claudel studied sculpture from 1879 to 1883, before becoming Rodin's student. She also became his mistress; their often-stormy relationship lasted 15 years. Most often remembered for her dramatic life story, Claudel enjoyed independent professional success but suffered a breakdown that sent her to a mental hospital for the last 30 years of her life.

One of Claudel's most celebrated works is **THE WALTZ (FIG. 30–44)**, of which she produced several versions in various sizes between 1892 and 1905. The sculpture depicts a dancing couple, both nude, although the woman's lower body is covered with long, flowing drapery. In Claudel's original conception, the figures were

entirely nude; she was forced to add the drapery after an inspector from the Ministry of Fine Arts declared their sensuality unacceptable, and recommended that her state commission for a marble version of the work be revoked. The subject of the waltz alone was controversial at this time because of the close contact demanded of dancers. Claudel added enough drapery to persuade the inspector to reinstate the commission, but she never finished it. She did, however, modify *The Waltz*, casting it in bronze as a tabletop sculpture. In this version, the spiral flow of the cloth creates the illusion of rapturous movement as the dancers twirl together, nearly losing their balance.

ART NOUVEAU

The swirling mass of drapery in Claudel's *The Waltz* has a stylistic affinity with Art Nouveau (French for "new art"), a movement launched in the early 1890s that permeated all aspects of European art, architecture, and design for more than a decade. Like the contemporary Symbolists, the practitioners of Art Nouveau largely rejected the values of modern industrial society and sought new aesthetic forms that combined a pre-industrial sense of beauty with fresh asymmetrical designs. They drew particular inspiration like his reliance on a refined decorative line, derived in part from English reformers such as William Morris.

GAUDÍ. The application of graceful linear arabesques to all aspects of design, evident in the entry hall of the Tassel House, began a vogue that spread across Europe. In Spain, where the style was called *Modernismo*, the major practitioner was the Catalan architect Antonio Gaudí i Cornet (1852–1926). Gaudí integrated natural forms into the design of buildings and parks that are still revolutionary in their dynamic freedom of line.

In 1904, the wealthy industrialist Josep Batlló commissioned Gaudí to design a private residence to surpass the lavish houses of other prominent families in Barcelona. Gaudí retained the underlying structure of the building that existed in the space for Batlló's new home, but completely transformed the façade and interior spaces. The façade **(FIG. 30–46)** is a dreamlike fantasy of undulating sandstone sculptures and multicolored glass and tile

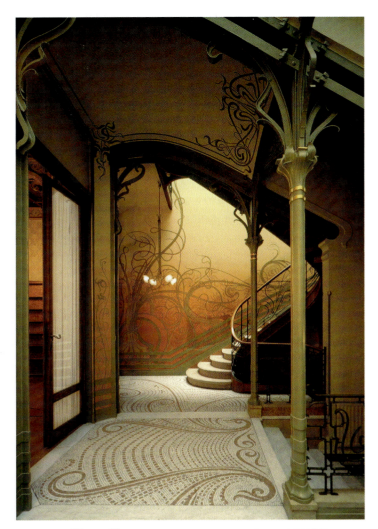

30-45 • Victor Horta **STAIRWAY, TASSEL HOUSE**
Brussels. 1892–1893.

from nature, especially from organisms such as vines, snakes, flowers, and winged insects, whose delicate and sinuous forms were adapted to their graceful and attenuated linear designs. Following a commitment to organic principles, practitioners of Art Nouveau also sought to harmonize all aspects of design into a beautiful whole, as found in nature itself.

HORTA. The artist most responsible for developing the Art Nouveau style in architecture was the Belgian Victor Horta (1861–1947). Trained at the academies in Ghent and Brussels, Horta worked in the office of a Neoclassical architect in Brussels for six years before opening his own practice in 1890. In 1892, he received his first important commission, a private residence in Brussels for a Professor Tassel. The result, especially the house's entry hall and staircase **(FIG. 30–45)**, was strikingly original. The ironwork, wall decoration, and floor tiles were all designed in an intricate series of long, graceful curves. Although Horta's sources are still debated, he was apparently impressed by the stylized linear designs of the English Arts and Crafts Movement of the 1880s. His concern for integrating the various arts into a more unified whole,

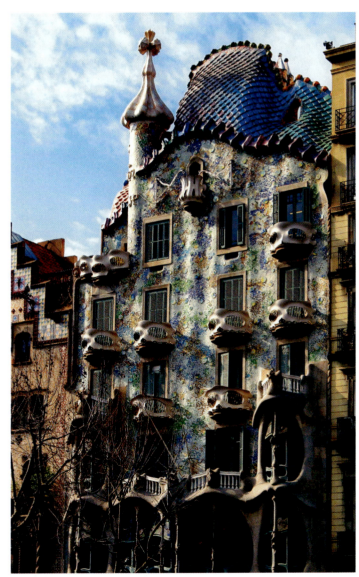

30-46 • Antonio Gaudí **CASA BATLLÒ**
43 Passeig de Gracia, Barcelona. 1900–1907.

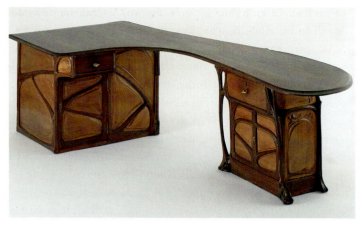

30-47 • Hector Guimard DESK
c. 1899 (remodeled after 1909). Olive wood with ash panels, 28¾ × 47¾″ (73 × 121 cm). Museum of Modern Art, New York.
Gift of Madame Hector Guimard

district of Paris that housed the most bohemian of the avant-garde artists. In the late 1880s, Toulouse-Lautrec dedicated himself to depicting the nightlife of Montmartre, and the cafés, theaters, dance halls, and brothels that he himself frequented.

Toulouse-Lautrec made roughly 30 posters between 1891 and 1901 for several of the more famous nightspots, advertising their most popular dancers. One of his most famous features the notoriously limber café dancer **JANE AVRIL** performing the infamous can-can **(FIG. 30–48)**. Toulouse-Lautrec places Avril on a stage that zooms into the background, with the hand and face of a double-bass player, part of the instrument, and pages of music framing the lower right of the poster. The bold foreshortening and prominent placement of the bass recall the compositions of Degas (SEE FIG. 30–31), but the overall feeling of the image is quite different. Toulouse-Lautrec's image emphasizes Avril's sexuality in order to draw in the crowds, while Degas's pastels reveal visual

surfaces that mix the Islamic, Gothic, and Baroque visual traditions of Barcelona in imaginative ways. The gaping lower-story windows are the source of the building's nickname, the "house of yawns," while the use of what look like giant human tibia for upright supports led to its other nickname, the "house of bones." The roof resembles a recumbent dragon with overlapping tiles as scales. A fanciful turret rises at its edge, recalling the sword of St. George—patron of Catalonia—plunged into the back of his legendary foe. Gaudí's highly personal alternative to academic historicism and modern industrialization in urban buildings such as this reflects his affinity with Iberian traditions as well as his concern to provide imaginative organic surroundings to enrich the lives of city dwellers.

GUIMARD. In France, Art Nouveau was also sometimes known as the *Style Guimard* after its leading French practitioner, Hector Guimard (1867–1942). Guimard worked in an eclectic manner during the early 1890s, but in 1895 he met and was influenced by Horta. He went on to design the famous Art Nouveau-style entrances for the Paris Métro (subway) and devoted considerable effort to interior design and furnishings, such as this **DESK** that he made for himself **(FIG. 30–47)**: Instead of a static and stable object, Guimard handcrafted an asymmetrical, organic entity that seems to undulate and grow.

TOULOUSE-LAUTREC. Henri de Toulouse-Lautrec (1864–1901) was born into an aristocratic family in the south of France. He had a genetic disorder and suffered several childhood accidents that halted his growth and left him physically disabled. He moved to Paris in 1882, where he had private academic training and then discovered the work of Degas, which changed his artistic perspective. He also discovered Montmartre, the low-class entertainment

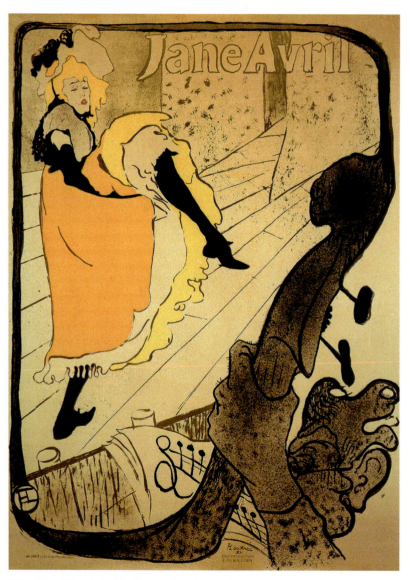

30-48 • Henri de Toulouse-Lautrec JANE AVRIL
1893. Lithograph, 50½ × 37″ (129 × 94 cm).
San Diego Museum of Art.
Gift of the Baldwin M. Baldwin Foundation (1987.32)

beauty in the roughest raw material. Toulouse-Lautrec outlines his forms, flattens his space, and suppresses modeling to accommodate the cheap colored lithographic printing technique he used, which afforded only three or four colors. His curving lines and the hand-drawn lettering are also distinctively Art Nouveau.

CÉZANNE AND THE BEGINNINGS OF MODERNISM

No artist had a greater impact on the next generation of Modern painters than Paul Cézanne (1839–1906). The son of a prosperous banker in the southern French city of Aix-en-Provence, Cézanne studied art first in Aix and then in Paris, where he participated in the circle of Realist artists around Manet. His early pictures, somber in color and coarsely painted, often depicted Romantic themes of drama and violence, and were consistently rejected by the Salon.

In the early 1870s, Cézanne changed his style under the influence of Pissarro. He adopted a bright palette and broken brushwork, and began painting landscapes. Like the Impressionists, with whom he exhibited in 1874 and 1877, Cézanne dedicated himself to the study of what he called the "sensations" of nature. Unlike the Impressionists, however, he did not seek to capture transitory effects of light and atmosphere; instead, he created highly structured paintings of an ordered nature through a methodical application of color that merged drawing and modeling into a single process. His professed aim was to "make of Impressionism something solid and durable, like the art of the museums."

Cézanne's dedicated pursuit of this goal is evident in his repeated paintings of MONT SAINTE-VICTOIRE, a mountain close to his home in Aix, which he depicted in hundreds of drawings and about 30 oil paintings between the 1880s and his death in 1906. The view here (FIG. 30–49) presents the mountain rising above the Arc Valley, which is dotted with buildings and trees, and crossed at the far right by a railroad viaduct. Framing the scene to the left is an evergreen tree, which echoes the contours of the mountains, creating visual harmony between the two principal elements of the

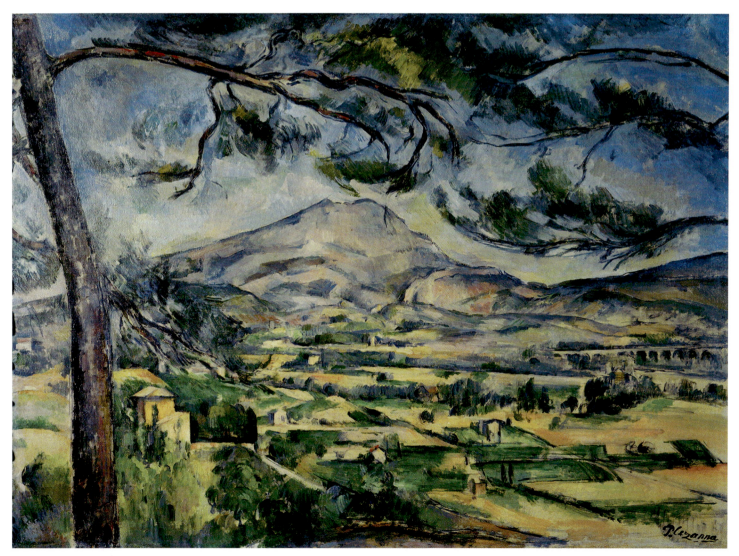

30-49 • Paul Cézanne **MONT SAINTE-VICTOIRE**
c. 1885–1887. Oil on canvas, 25½ × 32" (64.8 × 92.3 cm). Courtauld Institute of Art Gallery, London. P.1934.SC.55

SEE MORE: View a video about Paul Cézanne's *Mont Sainte-Victoire* www.myartslab.com

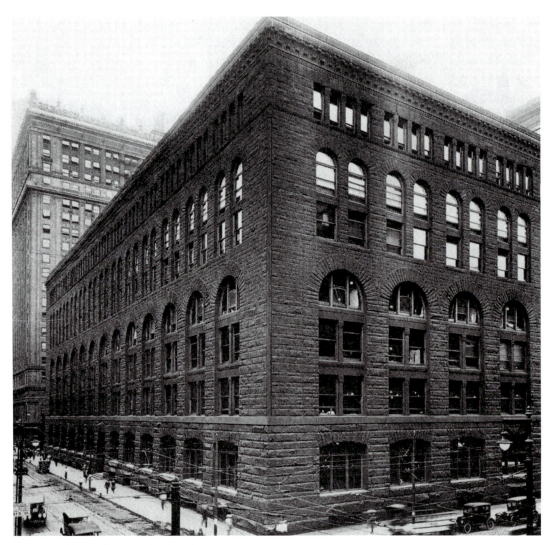

30-54 • Henry Hobson Richardson **MARSHALL FIELD WHOLESALE STORE**
Chicago. 1885–1887. Demolished c. 1935.

The World's Columbian Exposition was intended to be a model of the ideal American city—clean, spacious, carefully planned, and Classically styled—in contrast to the soot and overcrowding of most unplanned American cities. Frederick Law Olmsted, the designer of New York City's Central Park (see "The City Park," page 1014), was responsible for the landscape design of the exposition. He converted the marshy lakefront into a series of lagoons, canals, ponds, and islands, some laid out formally, as in the White City, and others informally, as in the "Midway," containing the busy conglomerate of pavilions of "less civilized" nations. Between these two parts stood a ferris wheel, which provided a spectacular view of the fair and the city. After the fair, most of its buildings were demolished, but Olmsted's landscaping has remained.

RICHARDSON.   The second American architect to study at the École des Beaux-Arts was Henry Hobson Richardson (1838–1886). Born in Louisiana and educated at Harvard, Richardson returned from Paris in 1865 to settle in New York. He designed architecture in a variety of revival styles and became famous for a robust, rusticated style known as Richardsonian Romanesque. In 1885, he designed the **MARSHALL FIELD WHOLESALE STORE** in Chicago (FIG. 30–54). The design drew on the heavy, blocklike shapes and imposing scale of Italian Renaissance palazzos such as the Medici-Riccardi palace in Florence (SEE FIG. 19–5), and occupied most of a city block. The rough stone facing, the arched windows, and the decorated cornice all evoke historical architectural antecedents. Even so, Richardson's eclecticism resulted in a readily identifiable personal style.

Plain and sturdy, Richardson's building was a revelation to the young architects of Chicago then engaged in rebuilding the city after the disastrous fire of 1871. About the same time, new technology for producing steel, a strong, cheap alloy of iron, created new structural opportunities for architects. William Le Baron Jenney (1832–1907) built the first steel-skeleton building in Chicago; his lead was quickly followed by younger architects, known as the Chicago School. The rapidly rising cost of urban land made tall buildings desirable; structural steel and the electric elevator, first manufactured in 1889, made them possible.

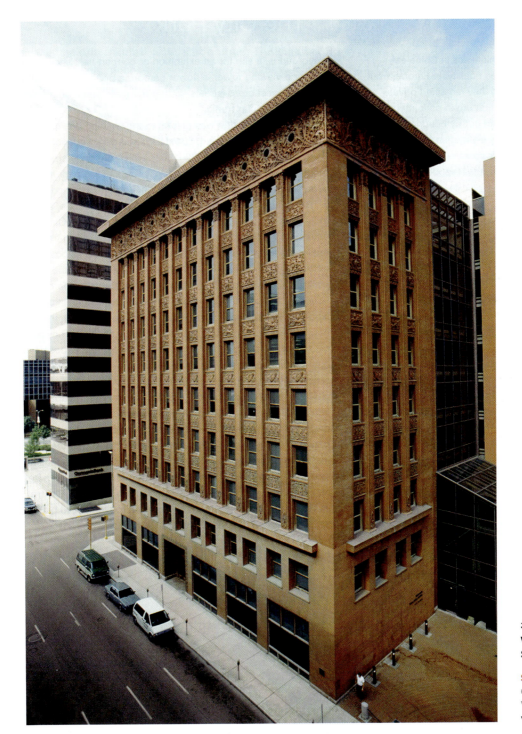

30–55 • Louis Sullivan
WAINWRIGHT BUILDING
St. Louis, Missouri. 1890–1891.

SEE MORE: Click the
Google Earth link for the
Wainwright Building
www.myartslab.com

SULLIVAN. Equipped with new structural materials and improved passenger elevators, driven by new economic considerations, and inspired by Richardson's departure from Beaux-Arts historicism, the Chicago School architects produced a new kind of building—the skyscraper—and a new style of architecture. An example of their work, and evidence of its rapid spread throughout the Midwest, is Louis Sullivan's **WAINWRIGHT BUILDING** in St. Louis, Missouri (FIG. 30–55). The Boston-born Sullivan (1856–1924) studied for a year at the Massachusetts Institute of Technology (MIT), home of the United States' first formal architecture program, and for an equally brief period at the École des

Beaux-Arts in Paris, where he developed a distaste for historicism. He settled in Chicago in 1875, partly because of the building boom there that had followed the fire of 1871, and in 1883 he entered into a partnership with the Danish-born engineer Dankmar Adler (1844–1900).

Sullivan's first major skyscraper, the Wainwright Building, has a U-shaped plan that provides an interior light-well for the illumination of inside offices. The ground floor, designed to house shops, has wide plate-glass windows for the display of merchandise. The second story, or mezzanine, also features large windows for the illumination of the shop offices. Above the mezzanine rise seven

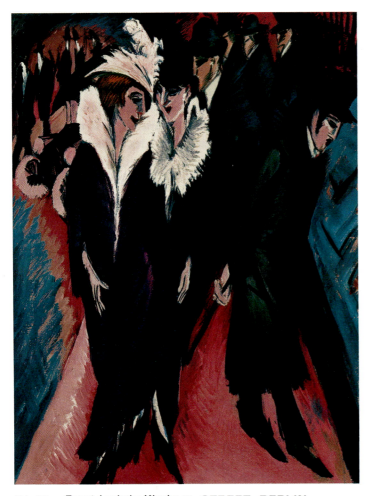

31-13 • Ernst Ludwig Kirchner STREET, BERLIN
1913. Oil on canvas, 47½ × 35⅞" (120.6 × 91 cm). Museum of Modern Art, New York. Purchase (274.39)

especially Berlin, are powerfully critical of urban existence. In Ernst Ludwig Kirchner's **STREET, BERLIN (FIG. 31–13)**, two prostitutes—their profession advertised by their large feathered hats and fur-trimmed coats—strut past well-dressed bourgeois men whom they view as potential clients. They seem to have deliberately embarrassed the man to their left, smirking as he hurriedly refocuses his attention on the shop window to the right. The women and men appear as artificial and dehumanized figures, with masklike faces and stiff gestures. Their bodies crowd together, but they are psychologically distant from one another. The harsh biting colors, tilted perspective, and piercingly sharp brushstrokes make this a disturbing Expressionistic image of urban degeneracy and alienation.

INDEPENDENT EXPRESSIONISTS

Beyond the members of The Bridge, many other artists in Germany and Austria worked in an Expressionist mode before World War I. One, Käthe Kollwitz (1867–1945), was committed to working-class causes and pursued social change primarily through printmaking because of this cheap and easily disseminable medium's potential to reach a wide audience. Between 1902 and 1908, she produced a series of seven etchings showing the

sixteenth-century German Peasants' War. **THE OUTBREAK (FIG. 31–14)**, a lesson in the power of group action, portrays the ugly fury of the peasants as they charge forward armed only with farm tools, bent on revenge against their oppressors for years of abuse. The faces of the two figures at the front of the charge are particularly grotesque while the leader, Black Anna—whom Kollwitz modeled on herself—signals the attack with a gesture that is inhumanly fierce. Her arms silhouetted against the sky, and the crowded mass of workers with their farm tools, form a passionate picture of political revolt.

Like Kollwitz, Paula Modersohn-Becker (1876–1907) studied at the Berlin School of Art for Women. In 1898, she moved to Worpswede, an artists' retreat in rural northern Germany. Dissatisfied with the Worpswede artists' naturalistic approach to rural life, after 1900 she made four trips to Paris to view recent developments in Post-Impressionist painting. Although obviously informed by the "primitivizing" tendencies of other artists such as Gauguin (SEE FIG. 30–36) toward women at the time, her physically small and yet monumental **SELF-PORTRAIT WITH AN AMBER NECKLACE (FIG. 31–15)** subverts those same tendencies. Modersohn-Becker appears as a kind of earth mother, surrounded by plants and with flowers in her hair and hands, but she also has a powerful, human presence. Modersohn-Becker looks out of the canvas at us, calmly returning our gaze and establishing her humanity. While painted in the manner of other Modernists, this tender self-portrait reveals an artist of strong independent ideas and a woman of sharp intelligence.

In contrast to Modersohn-Becker's gentle self-portrait, **SELF-PORTRAIT NUDE (FIG. 31–16)** of 1911 by the Austrian artist Egon Schiele (1890–1918) conveys physical and psychological torment. Schiele's father died insane from untreated syphilis when the artist

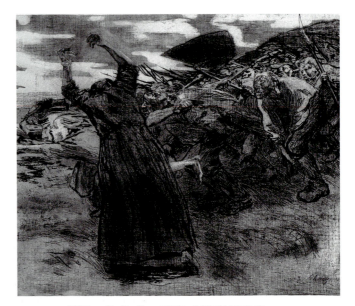

31-14 • Käthe Kollwitz THE OUTBREAK
From the *Peasants' War* series. 1903. Etching, 20 × 23⅓" (50.7 × 59.2 cm). Kupferstichkabinett, Staatliche Museen zu Berlin, Preussischer Kulturbesitz. Kunstmuseum, Switzerland (1748)

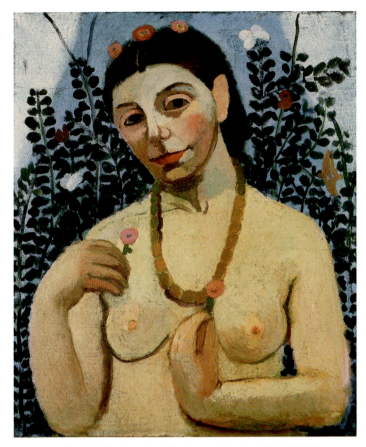

31-15 • Paula Modersohn-Becker SELF-PORTRAIT WITH AN AMBER NECKLACE
1906. Oil on canvas, 24 × 19¾" (61 × 50 cm).
Öffentliche Kunstsammlung Basel.

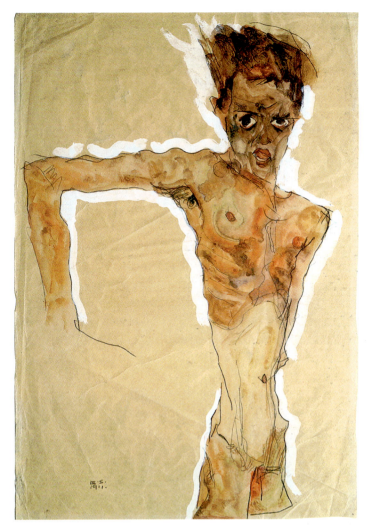

31-16 • Egon Schiele SELF-PORTRAIT NUDE
1911. Gouache and pencil on paper, 20¼ × 13¾" (51.4 × 35 cm).
Metropolitan Museum of Art, New York. Bequest of Scofield Thayer, 1982
(1984.433.298)

was just 14, and as a result Schiele had a tendency to conflate suffering and sexuality throughout his life. In many drawings and watercolors, Schiele portrays women in demeaning, sexually explicit poses that emphasize their animal nature, and in his self-portraits the artist turns the same harsh gaze upon himself, revealing deep ambivalence toward sexuality and the body in his art and his life. In *Self-Portrait Nude*, he stares out of the picture with anguish, his emaciated body stretched and displayed in a halo of harsh light. Mutilated and impotent, he has neither right hand nor genitals. The missing body parts have been interpreted in Freudian fashion as the artist's symbolic self-punishment for indulgence in masturbation, then commonly believed to lead to insanity.

SPIRITUALISM OF THE BLUE RIDER

Formed in Munich by the Russian artist Vassily Kandinsky (1866–1944) and the German artist Franz Marc (1880–1916), Der Blaue Reiter ("The Blue Rider") was named for a popular image of a blue knight, the St. George on the city emblem of Moscow. Just as St. George had been a spiritual leader in society, so The Blue Rider aspired to offer spiritual leadership in the arts. Its first exhibition was held in December 1911 and included the work of 14 artists working in a wide range of styles, from realism to radical abstraction.

By 1911, Marc was mostly painting animals rather than humans. He had a spiritual affinity to animals, which he felt were more "primitive" and thus purer than humans, enjoying a more spiritual relationship with nature. He rendered them in big, bold forms painted in almost-primary colors. In **THE LARGE BLUE HORSES (FIG. 31–17)**, the animals merge into a homogenous unit. Their sweeping contours reflect the harmony of their collective existence and echo the curved lines of the hills behind them, suggesting that they are also in harmony with their surroundings. The blue of the horses alludes to St. George and to the spirituality of the natural world.

Born into a wealthy family in Moscow, Kandinsky initially trained as a lawyer, but after visiting exhibitions of Modern art in Germany and taking private art lessons, he gave up the legal profession, moved to Munich, and established himself as an artist. His early works make frequent reference to Russian folk culture, which he admired for its "primitivism."

Kandinsky may have been a synesthete—i.e. someone who "hears" colors and "sees" sound. Whether he was or not, his art is

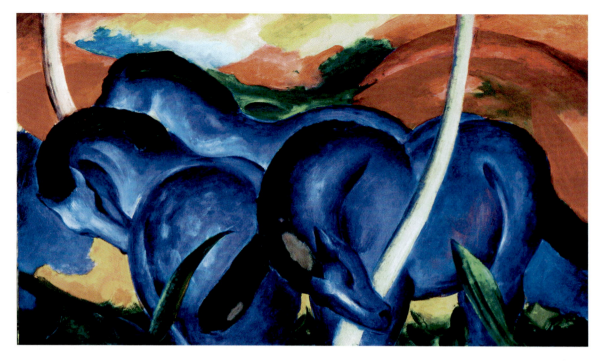

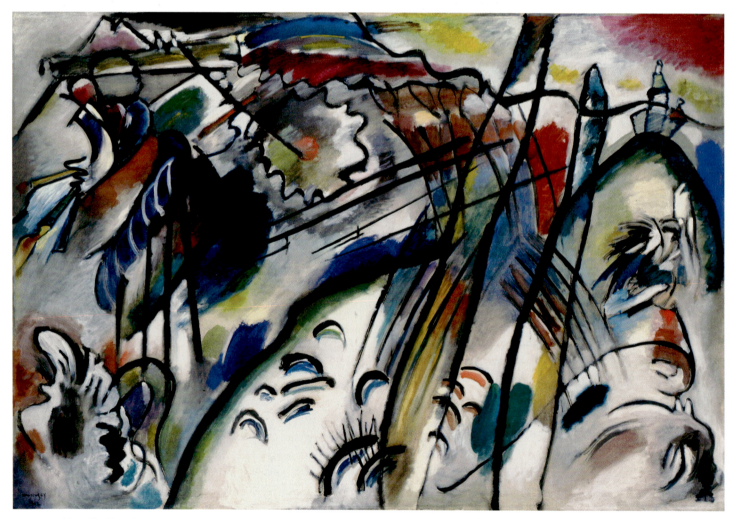

31–18 • Vassily Kandinsky IMPROVISATION 28 (SECOND VERSION)
1912. Oil on canvas, 43⅞″ × 63⅞″ (111.4 × 162.2 cm). Guggenheim Museum, New York. Gift, Solomon R. Guggenheim. 37.239

EXPLORE MORE: Gain insight from a primary source by Vassily Kandinsky www.myartslab.com

clearly that of an artist for whom sound and color were inextricably linked. His early study of the work of Whistler (SEE FIG. 30–39) convinced him that the arts of painting and music were related: Just as a composer organizes sound, so a painter organizes color and form. Kandinsky was particularly interested in the music of the Austrian composer Arnold Schoenberg, who around 1910 introduced a momentous change in musical history. All Western music since antiquity was previously based on the arrangement of notes into scales, or modes (such as today's common major and minor), and composers chose the scale they worked in for expressive reasons. Particularly since the Baroque period, each note in any given scale had a role to play, and these roles operated in a clear hierarchy that served to reinforce what became known as the "tonal center," a kind of home base or place of repose in the musical composition. Schoenberg eliminated the tonal center and treated all tones equally, denying the listener any place of repose and instead prolonging the tension (and thus, he felt, the expression) of his music indefinitely. Kandinsky contacted the composer and was delighted to find out that he also painted in an Expressionist style. Kandinsky believed that if music could exist without a tonal center, could art exist without subject matter?

Kandinsky was thus one of the first artists to investigate the theoretical possibility of purely abstract painting. He gave his works musical titles, such as "Composition" and "Improvisation," and aspired to make paintings that responded to his inner state rather than an external stimulus and which would be entirely autonomous, making no reference to the visible world. In 1912, he painted a series of works, including **IMPROVISATION 28 (FIG. 31–18)**, that he claimed was the first truly abstract art. In these, Kandinsky's colors leap and dance, with different colors expressing different emotions. For Kandinsky, painting was a utopian spiritual force. He believed that art's traditional focus on accurate rendering of the physical world was a basically materialistic quest. Art should not depend so much on mere physical reality. He hoped that his paintings would lead humanity toward a deeper awareness of spirituality and the inner world. Rather than searching for correspondence between the painting and the world where none is intended, the artist asks us to look at the painting as if we were hearing a symphony, responding instinctively and spontaneously to this or that passage, and then to the total experience. Kandinsky further explained the musical analogy in his book *Concerning the Spiritual in Art*: "Color directly influences the soul. Color is the keyboard, the eyes are the hammers, the soul is the piano with many strings. The artist is the hand that plays, touching one key or another purposively, to cause vibrations in the soul."

Despite Kandinsky's noble aspirations, however, works such as *Improvisation 28* are not entirely abstract. They often retain a vestige of the landscape—Kandinsky found references to nature the hardest to transcend—as well as suggestions of horses, boats, and oars. But these half-recognized forms increasingly act in his works as a kind of punctuation mark to increase or decrease our speed, or raise or lower our emotions, as our eyes fly around his canvases.

EXTENSIONS OF CUBISM

As Cubism emerged from the studios of Braque and Picasso, it was clear to the art world that they had altered the artistic discourse irrevocably. Cubism's way of viewing the world resonated with artists all over Europe, in Russia, and even in the United States. These artists interpreted Cubism in their own ways, significantly broadening and extending its visual message beyond the ideas and objects of Picasso and Braque.

FRANCE. Robert Delaunay (1885–1941) and his wife, the Ukrainian-born Sonia Delaunay-Terk (b. Sonia Stern, 1885–1979), took the relatively monochromatic and relatively static forms of Cubism in a new direction. Delaunay's early work was inflected with Fauvist color; he also had a deep interest in communicating spirituality through color and participated in Blue Rider exhibitions. In 1910, he began to fuse this intense interest in color with Cubist forms to create paintings celebrating the modern city and modern technology. In **HOMAGE TO BLÉRIOT (FIG. 31–19)**, Delaunay pays tribute to Louis Blériot, the French pilot who in 1909 became the first person to fly across the English Channel, by

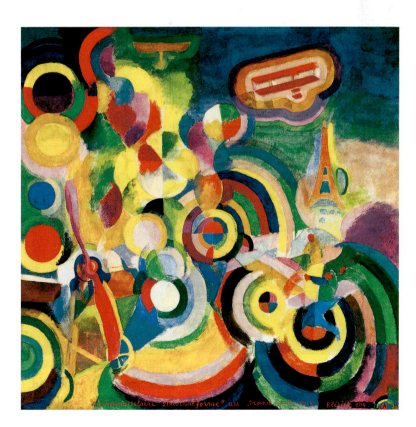

31–19 • Robert Delaunay HOMAGE TO BLÉRIOT
1914. Tempera on canvas, 8'2½" × 8'3" (2.5 × 2.51 m). Öffentliche Kunstsammlung Basel, Kunstmuseum, Basel, Switzerland. Emanuel Hoffman Foundation

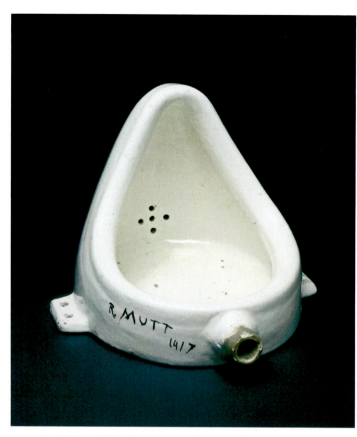

31-30 • Marcel Duchamp FOUNTAIN
1917. Porcelain plumbing fixture and enamel paint, height 24⅝"
(62.5 cm). Photograph by Alfred Stieglitz. Philadelphia Museum of Art,
Pennsylvania. Louise and Walter Arensberg Collection (1998-74-1)

SEE MORE: View a video on Marcel Duchamp
www.myartslab.com

stripped away before the essence of art disappears? Since Whistler's famous court case (see "Art on Trial in 1877," page 999), most avant-garde artists would have responded that a work of art need be neither descriptive nor well-crafted but, before 1917, none would have argued, as Duchamp does in this piece, that "art" might be primarily conceptual. For centuries, artists regularly employed studio assistants to craft parts, if not all, of the art objects that they designed. In some ways Duchamp translated that practice into modern terms by arguing that art objects might not only be crafted (in part) by others, but that the objects of art could actually be manufactured for the artist in the mass-produced world. In a clever twist of logic, Duchamp simultaneously makes a commentary on consumption, modernity, and the irrationality of the modern age by arguing that the "readymade" work of art, as a manufactured object, simply bypasses the craft tradition. Duchamp translated this idea into physical form in *Fountain*.

Fountain is one of the most transgressive works of art in Western history. It is still funny, mad, and obscene; it refers openly to bathroom functions, to humanity's most degraded functions and vulnerable states, and it challenges every assumption made about the nature of art. When *Fountain* was rejected, as Duchamp anticipated it would be, the artist resigned from the Society in mock horror, and

published an unsigned editorial in a Dada journal detailing what he described as the scandal of the R. Mutt case. He wrote: "The only works of art America has given are her plumbing and bridges," adding, "Whether Mr. Mutt with his own hands made the fountain or not has no importance. He CHOSE it. He took an ordinary article of life, placed it so that its useful significance disappeared under the new title and point of view—created a new thought for that object."

After Duchamp returned to Paris, he challenged the French art world with a piece that he entitled **L.H.O.O.Q. (FIG. 31–31)**, and that he described as a "modified readymade." In 1911, Leonardo's famous *Mona Lisa* (SEE FIG. 20–5) was stolen from the Louvre and it took two years to recover it. While missing, however, the painting became even more famous than when it had actually been on public display, being widely and badly reproduced on postcards, posters, and in advertising. Duchamp chose to comment on the nature of fame and on the degraded image of the *Mona Lisa* in *L.H.O.O.Q.* In 1919, he purchased a cheap postcard reproduction of the *Mona Lisa* and drew a mustache and beard on her famously

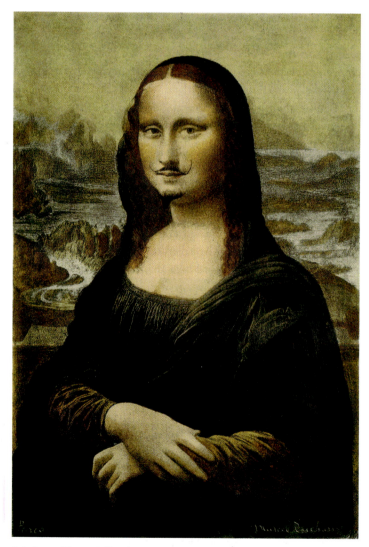

31-31 • Marcel Duchamp L.H.O.O.Q.
1919. Pencil on reproduction of Leonardo da Vinci's *Mona Lisa*.
7¾ × 4¾" (19.7 × 12.1 cm). Philadelphia Museum of Art, Pennsylvania.
Louise and Walter Arensberg Collection

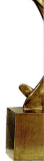

enigmatic face. In doing so he turned a sacred cultural artifact into an object of crude ridicule. The letters that he scrawled across the bottom of the card, "L.H.O.O.Q.," when read aloud sound phonetically similar to the French slang phrase *elle a chaud au cul*, politely translated as "she's hot for it," thus adding a crude sexual innuendo to the already cheapened image. Like *Fountain*, this work challenges preconceived notions about morality or virtue being a basis for art and introduces disgust as a viable artistic subject. Indeed, as one of Dada's founders said: "Dada was born of disgust."

Duchamp made only a few readymades. In fact, he created very little art at all after about 1922, when he devoted himself mostly to chess. When asked about his occupation, he described himself as a "retired artist," but his ideas have been among the most influential on art produced since 1960.

BERLIN DADA. Early in 1917, Hugo Ball and the Romanian-born poet Tristan Tzara (1896–1963) organized the Galerie Dada. Tzara also edited the magazine *Dada*, which quickly attracted the attention of like-minded artists and writers in several European capitals and in the United States. The movement spread farther when expatriate members of Hugo Ball's circle in Switzerland returned to their homelands after the war. Richard Huelsenbeck (1892–1974), for instance, took Dada to Germany, where he helped found the Club Dada in Berlin in April 1918.

Dada pursued a slightly different agenda and took on different forms in each of its major centers. A distinctive feature of Berlin Dada was its agitprop agenda. It also produced an unusually large amount of visual art—especially collage and **photomontage** (photographic collage)—compared to the more literary forms of Dada elsewhere.

Kurt Schwitters (1887–1948), for instance, who met Huelsenbeck and other Dadaists in 1919, used discarded rail tickets, postage stamps, ration coupons, beer labels, and other street detritus to create visual poetry. Schwitters termed his two- and three-dimensional works of art, made out of the wasted ephemera of the industrial world, *Merzbilder*. *Merz* was Schwitters's term for the refuse he collected; *Bild* is German for "picture." In his "Merz Pictures," Schwitters's collaged together fragments of newspaper and other printed material with drawn or painted images. He wrote that garbage demanded equal rights with painting. In **MERZBILD 5B** (**FIG. 31–32**), Schwitters has collaged printed fragments from the street with newspaper scraps to comment on the postwar disorder of defeated Germany. One fragment describes the brutal overthrow of the short-lived socialist republic in Bremen.

Hannah Höch (1889–1978) produced even more pointed political photomontages. Between 1916 and 1926, she worked for Verlang, Berlin's largest publishing house, designing decorative

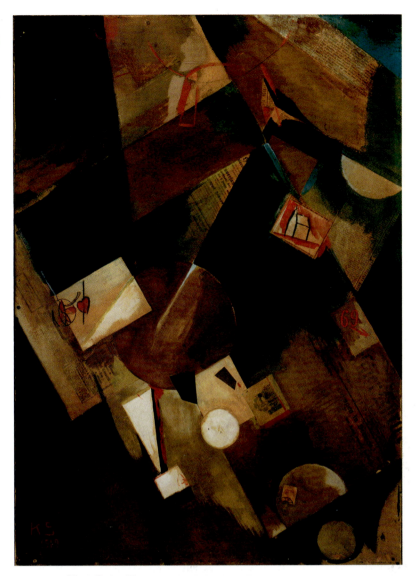

31–32 • Kurt Schwitters MERZBILD 5B (PICTURE-RED-HEART-CHURCH)
April 26, 1919. Collage, tempera, and crayon on cardboard, 32⅞ × 23¾" (83.4 × 60.3 cm). Guggenheim Museum, New York. 52.1325

patterns and writing articles on crafts for a women's magazine. Höch considered herself part of the women's movement in the 1920s. She disapproved of contemporary mass-media representations of women and had to fight for her place as the sole woman among the Berlin Dada group, one of whom described her contribution disparagingly as merely conjuring up beer and sandwiches. In **CUT WITH THE DADA KITCHEN KNIFE THROUGH THE LAST WEIMAR BEER-BELLY CULTURAL EPOCH IN GERMANY (FIG. 31–33)**, Höch collages images and words from the popular press, political posters, and photographs to create a complex and angry critique of the Weimar Republic in 1919. She shows women physically cutting apart the beer-bloated German establishment in this photomontage and includes portraits of androgynous Dada characters, such as herself and several other Berlin Dada artists, along with Marx and Lenin. It is tempting to wonder which side she really thinks her fellow Dadaists stand on.

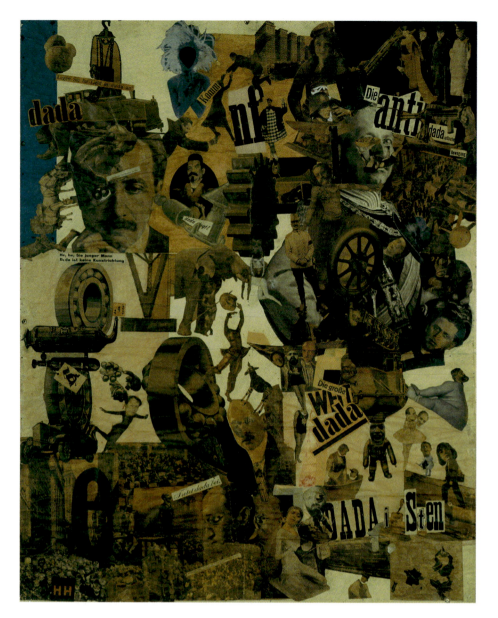

31–33 • Hannah Höch **CUT WITH THE DADA KITCHEN KNIFE THROUGH THE LAST WEIMAR BEER-BELLY CULTURAL EPOCH IN GERMANY**
1919. Collage, 44⅞ × 35⅜″ (114 × 90 cm). Nationalgalerie, Staatliche Museen zu Berlin, Berlin.

EXPLORE MORE: Gain insight from a primary source on Hannah Höch
www.myartslab.com

MODERNIST TENDENCIES IN AMERICA

When avant-garde Modern art was first widely exhibited in the United States, it received a cool welcome. While some American artists did work in abstract or Modern ways, most preferred to work in a more naturalistic manner, at least until around 1915.

THE ASHCAN SCHOOL

In the first decade of the twentieth century, a vigorous realist movement coalesced in New York City around the charismatic painter and teacher Robert Henri (1865–1929), who rejected the idyllic Impressionist imagery of the previous generation in America. Henri told his students: "Paint what you see. Paint what is real to you." In 1908, he organized an exhibition of artists called The Eight, four of whom trained and worked as newspaper illustrators and whose exhibition introduced scenes of gritty urban life in New York City to American art. Five of The Eight, who painted the street life of the immigrant poor specifically, were dubbed the Ashcan School.

Henri greatly admired Manet's paintings of modern life and the art of the Spanish Baroque. He traveled to Spain where, in 1906, he painted **LA REINA MORA (FIG. 31–34).** "La Reina Mora" (the Moorish Queen) was the stage name of Milagros Morena, a well-known Andalusian dancer. In the painting Moreno stands proudly in a red-flowered costume with a fringed skirt, a luxurious silver-white shawl, and pink satin dancing shoes, wearing several rings on her fingers, a golden bracelet around one wrist, and two decorative necklaces around her neck. Her jet-black hair is dressed with ribbons or flowers. Morena's face is covered with a whitish makeup that is in contrast to the darker skin of her neck and arms, making her strong black eyebrows, deep dark eyes, rouged cheeks, and red lips stand out dramatically.

STIEGLITZ AND THE "291" GALLERY

The chief proponent of European Modern art in the United States was the photographer Alfred Stieglitz (1864–1946), who in the years before World War I organized several small exhibitions

In his own photographs, Stieglitz tried to compose poetic images of romanticized urban scenes. In **THE FLATIRON BUILDING** (**FIG. 31–35**), the tree trunk to the right is echoed by branches in the grove farther back, and in the wedge-shaped Flatiron Building to the rear. An arc of chairs and a low wall behind seem to encircle the trees. The entire scene is suffused with a misty wintery atmosphere, which the artist created by manipulating his viewpoint, exposure, and possibly both the negative and positive images.

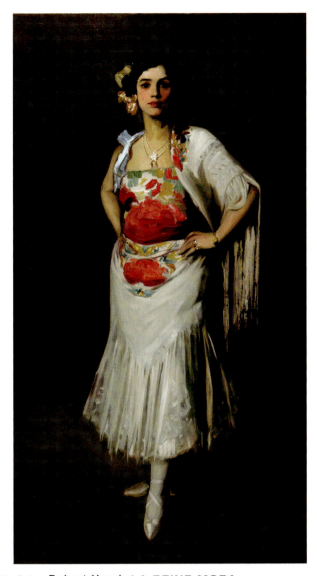

31-34 • Robert Henri **LA REINE MORA**
1906. Oil on canvas, 78 × 42¹⁄₁₆″ (198 × 107 cm). Museum purchase from the Jere Abbott Acquisitions Fund, Colby Museum of Art.

featuring the art of major Modernists at a tiny gallery at 291 Fifth Avenue, known simply as 291. Stieglitz, like Kahnweiler in Paris, supported many of the early American Modernist painters and photographers in New York. As a photographer himself, he sought to establish the legitimacy of photography as a fine art with these exhibitions.

Born in New Jersey to a wealthy German immigrant family, Stieglitz studied photography in the 1880s at the Technische Hochschule in Berlin, quickly recognizing photography's artistic potential. In 1890, he began to photograph New York City street scenes. He promoted his views through an organization called the Photo-Secession, founded in 1902, and two years later opened the 291 gallery. By 1910, this gallery had become a focal point for both photographers and artists, with Stieglitz giving shows (sometimes their first) to artists such as Arthur Dove, John Marin, and Georgia O'Keeffe, and bringing to America the art of European artists such as Kandinsky, Braque, Cézanne, and Rodin.

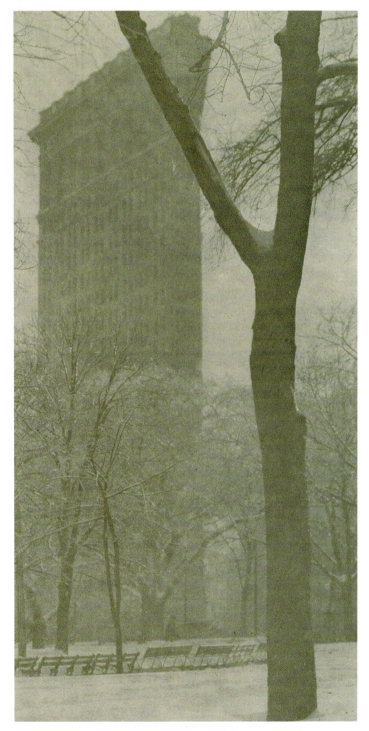

31-35 • Alfred Stieglitz **THE FLATIRON BUILDING**
1903. Photogravure, 6¹¹⁄₁₆ × 3⁵⁄₁₆″ (17 × 8.4 cm) mounted. Metropolitan Museum of Art, New York. Gift of J. B. Neumann, 1958 (58.577.37)

Portrait of a German Officer

by Marsden Hartley, 1914. Oil on canvas, 68¼ × 41⅜" (1.78 × 1.05 m). Metropolitan Museum of Art, New York. The Alfred Stieglitz Collection, 1949 (49.70.42)

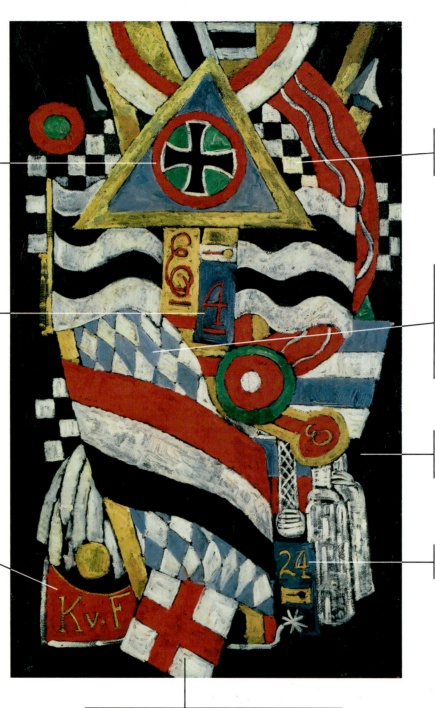

Symbolic references to Freyburg include epaulettes, lance tips, and the Iron Cross he was awarded the day before he was killed.

His regiment number ("4") is shown at the center of the abstracted chest along with a red cursive "E," which stands for "Edmund" (Hartley's given name). This places Hartley over Freyburg's heart.

Hartley identifies his subject with his initials ("Kv.F") in gold on red.

The black-and-white checkerboard patterns evoke Freyburg's love of chess.

The blue-and-white diamond pattern comes from the Bavarian flag; the red, white, and black bands constitute the flag of the German Empire, adopted in 1871; and the black-and-white stripes are those of the historic flag of Prussia.

The funereal black background heightens the intensity of the foreground colors.

The young man's age ("24") is noted in gold on blue.

While living in Berlin in 1914, Hartley fell in love with a young Prussian lieutenant, Karl von Freyburg, whom Hartley described as "in every way a perfect being—physically, spiritually, and mentally." Freyburg's death in World War I devastated Hartley, who memorialized his fallen lover in this symbolic portrait.

SEE MORE: View the Closer Look feature for *Portrait of a German Officer* www.myartslab.com

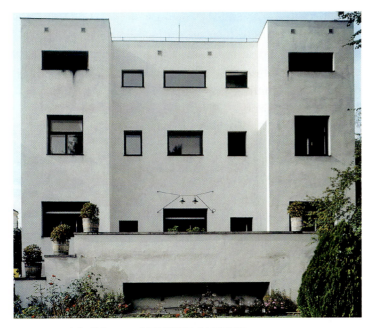

31-39 • Adolf Loos STEINER HOUSE
Vienna. 1910.

EUROPEAN MODERNISM

In Europe, a stripped-down and severely geometric style of Modern architecture developed, partly in reaction to the natural organic lines of Art Nouveau. In Vienna, Adolf Loos (1870–1933), one of the pioneers of European architectural Modernism, insisted in his 1913 essay "Ornament and Crime" that "The evolution of a culture is synonymous with the removal of ornament from utilitarian objects." For Loos, ornament was a sign of cultural degeneracy. Thus

his **STEINER HOUSE** (FIG. 31–39) is a stucco-covered, reinforced concrete construction without decorative embellishment. Loos argued that the exterior's only function was to provide protection from the elements; the placement of the plain rectangular windows, for instance, was ostensibly determined by interior needs.

The most important French Modern architect was Le Corbusier, who established several important precepts that influenced architects for the next half-century. His **VILLA SAVOYE** (FIG. 31–40), a private home outside Paris, is an icon of the International Style (see "The International Style," page 1057) that also reflects his Purist ideals in its rectilinear design and lack of ornamentation. It is also one of the best expressions of Le Corbusier's **domino construction** system, first elaborated in 1914, in which slabs of ferroconcrete (concrete reinforced with steel bars) rest on six free-standing steel posts, placed at the positions of the six dots on a domino playing piece. Over the next decade Le Corbusier further explored the possibilities of the domino system and in 1926 published "The Five Points of a New Architecture," in which he proposed raising houses above the ground on **pilotis** (free-standing posts); using flat roofs as terraces; using movable partition walls slotted between supports on the interior and **curtain walls** (nonloadbearing exterior walls) to allow greater design flexibility; and using ribbon windows (windows that run the length of the wall). All of these became features of Modern architecture. Le Corbusier described the Villa Savoye as "a machine for living in," meaning that it was designed as rationally as a car or a machine. He also developed designs for mass-produced standardized housing as many architects did after World War I to help rebuild Europe's destroyed infrastructure.

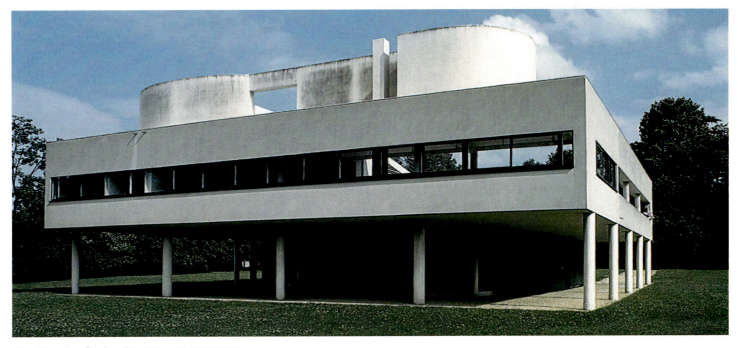

31-40 • Le Corbusier VILLA SAVOYE
Poissy-sur-Seine, France. 1929–1930.

EXPLORE MORE: Click the Google Earth link for Villa Savoye www.myartslab.com

AMERICAN MODERN ARCHITECTURE

CONNECTION TO THE LAND. Frank Lloyd Wright (1867–1959) was not only America's most important Modernist architect, he was also one of the most influential architects in the world in the early twentieth century. After briefly studying engineering at the University of Wisconsin, Wright apprenticed to a Chicago architect, then spent five years with the firm of Dankmar Adler and Louis Sullivan (SEE FIG. 30–55), eventually becoming their chief drafter. In 1893, Wright established his own office, specializing in domestic architecture. Around 1900, he and several other architects in the Oak Park suburb of Chicago began to design low, horizontal houses with flat roofs and heavy overhangs that echoed the flat plains of the prairie in the Midwest. This group of architects was known as the Prairie School.

The FREDERICK C. ROBIE HOUSE (FIG. 31–41) is one of Wright's early masterpieces in the Prairie Style. It was designed around a central chimney (to radiate heat throughout the house in the bitter Chicago winter), and features a low, flat overhanging roof (to shade against the summer sun) with open porches for sleeping outside in the cool of summer nights. The roof is dramatically cantilevered on both sides of the chimney. The windows are arranged in low bands around the house; many are stained glass, creating a colored screen between the interior of the house and the outside world while also inviting the viewer to look through the windows into the garden beyond.

The horizontal emphasis continues inside. The main living level is one long space divided into living and dining areas by a free-standing fireplace. There are no dividing walls. Wright visited the Japanese exhibit at the 1893 Chicago World's Fair and was deeply influenced by the aesthetics of Japanese architecture, particularly its use of space and screenlike windows (see "Shoin Design," page 819). Wright's homes frequently featured built-in closets and bookcases, and he hid heating and lighting fixtures when possible. He also designed and arranged the furniture for his interiors (FIG. 32–42). Here, the chairs are machine-cut in modern geometric designs, while their high backs huddle around the table to create the intimate effect of a room within a room. Wright integrated lights and flower holders into the posts closest to the table's corners so that there would be no need for lights or flowers on the table.

Wright had an uneasy relationship with European Modernist architecture. Although he routinely used new building materials such as concrete, glass, and steel, he also tried to create a more natural sensibility by connecting his buildings to their sites using brick, wood, or local stone. He was uninterested in the machine aesthetic of Le Corbusier.

FALLINGWATER (FIG. 31–43) in rural Pennsylvania is perhaps the best-known expression of Wright's conviction that buildings should not simply sit *on* the landscape but exist *in* it. Fallingwater was commissioned by Edgar Kaufmann, a Pittsburgh department

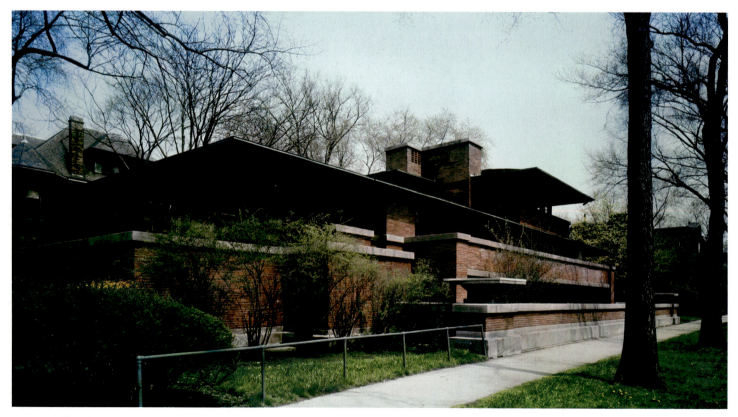

31-41 • Frank Lloyd Wright FREDERICK C. ROBIE HOUSE
Chicago. 1906–1909.

EXPLORE MORE: Click the Google Earth link for the Robie House www.myartslab.com

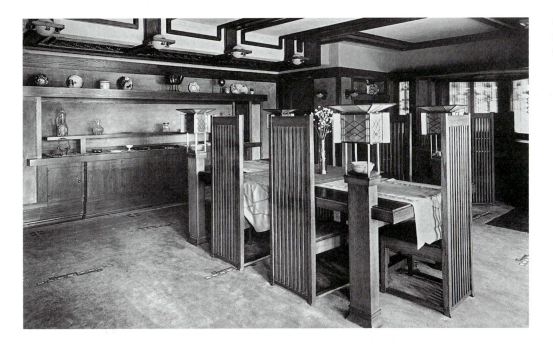

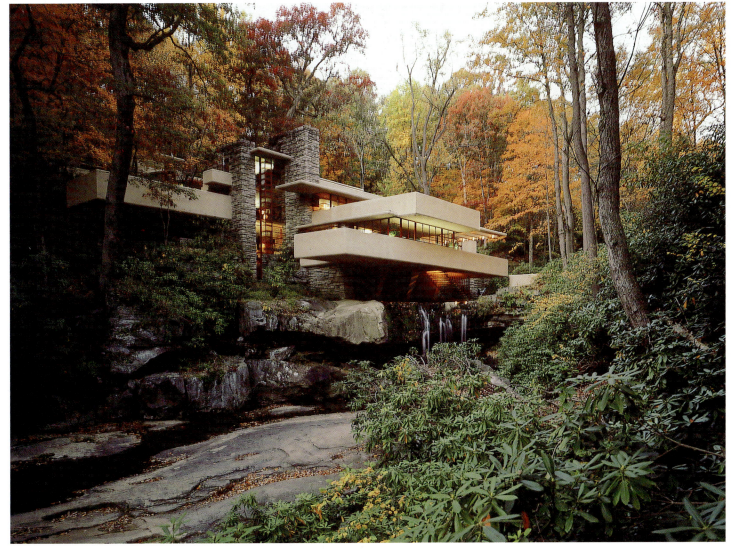

31–43 • Frank Lloyd Wright **EDGAR KAUFMANN HOUSE, FALLINGWATER**
Mill Run, Pennsylvania. 1937.

SEE MORE: View an animated video of Fallingwater www.myartslab.com

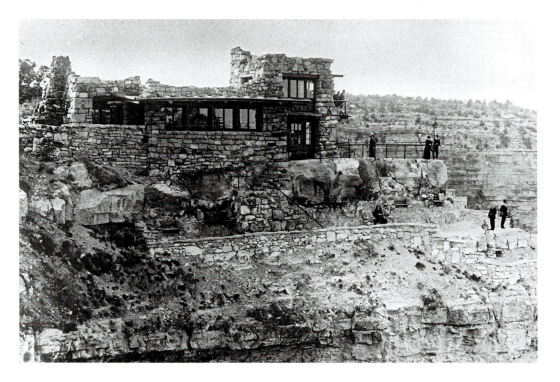

store owner, to replace a family summer cottage on the site of a waterfall and a pool where his children played. To Kaufmann's surprise, Wright decided to build the new house right into the cliff and over the pool, allowing the waterfall to flow around and under the house. A large boulder where the family had sunbathed in the summers was used for the central hearthstone of the fireplace. In a dramatic move that engineers questioned (with reason, as subsequent history has shown), Wright used cantilevers to extend a series of broad concrete terraces out from the cliff to parallel the huge slabs of rock below. The terraces are all poured concrete, but Wright painted them a soft earth tone; he made use of local wood and stone wherever possible. Wright preferred to design rural or suburban structures and disliked the inner city. When asked what could be done to improve city architecture, Wright responded: "Tear it down."

Mary Colter (1869–1958) also expressed a strong connection to the land in her architecture. Born in Pittsburgh and educated at the California School of Design in San Francisco, she spent much of her career as an architect and decorator for the Fred Harvey Company, which operated luxury hotels throughout the Southwest. Colter was an avid student of Native American art, especially the architecture of the Hopi and Pueblo peoples, and her buildings quoted liberally from those traditions. She designed several visitor facilities at Grand Canyon National Park, of which **LOOKOUT STUDIO** (**FIG. 31–44**) is one of the most dramatic. The building perches on the edge of the chasm; its foundation is the natural rock of the canyon, and its walls are built from stones quarried nearby. The roofline is deliberately irregular to echo the surrounding canyon wall. Inside, Colter used exposed logs for many of the structural supports and ceiling, in homage to Hopi architecture. The only concession to modernity is a liberal use of

glass windows and a cement floor. Colter's work on hotels and railroad stations throughout the region helped to establish the distinctive Southwest style.

THE AMERICAN SKYSCRAPER. After 1900, New York City assumed a lead over Chicago in the development of the skyscraper, whose soaring height was made possible by the use of the steel-frame skeleton for structural support (see "The Skyscraper," page 1050). New York clients rejected the more utilitarian Chicago style of Louis Sullivan and others, preferring the historicizing approach then still popular on the east coast. The **WOOLWORTH BUILDING** (**FIG. 31–45**), designed by the Minnesota-based firm of Cass Gilbert (1859–1934), was the world's tallest building at 792 feet and 55 floors when first completed. Its Gothic-style external details, inspired by the soaring towers of late medieval churches, gave the building a strong visual personality. Because of its Gothic style, Gilbert called it his "Cathedral of Commerce."

ART BETWEEN THE WARS IN EUROPE

World War I had a devastating effect on Europe's artists and architects. Many artists responded to the destruction and loss of a generation of young men by criticizing the European tradition, while others sought to rebuild. Either way, much of the art created between 1919 and 1939 addressed the needs and concerns of society directly.

UTILITARIAN ART FORMS IN RUSSIA

In the 1917 Russian Revolution, the radical socialist Bolsheviks overthrew the tsar, withdrew Russia from the world war, and turned inward to fight a civil war that lasted until 1920 and led to

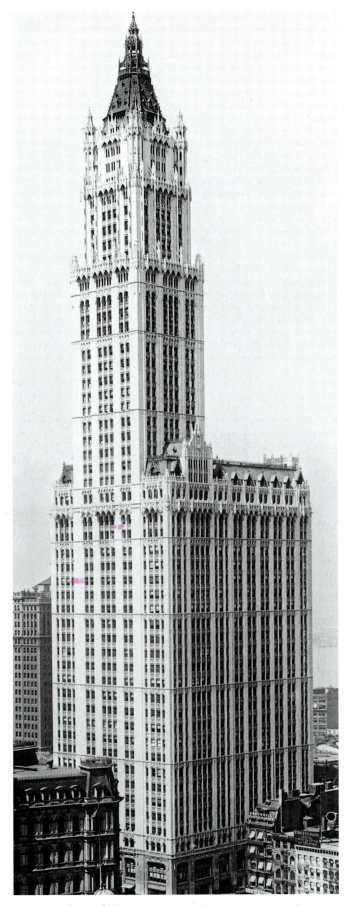

the establishment of the U.S.S.R. (Union of Soviet Socialist Republics). Most Russian avant-garde artists enthusiastically supported the Bolsheviks and were initially supported by them.

CONSTRUCTIVISM. The case of Aleksandr Rodchenko (1891–1956) is fairly representative. An early associate of Malevich (SEE FIG. 31–25), Rodchenko used drafting tools to make abstract drawings. He exhibited as a Suprematist in 1921 when he showed three large, flat, monochromatic panels painted red, yellow, and blue, which he titled *Last Painting* (now lost). After this, he renounced painting as a basically selfish activity and condemned self-expression as weak and socially irresponsible.

Also in 1921, Rodchenko helped to establish the Constructivists, a post-revolutionary group of artists dedicated to working collectively for the good of the state who described themselves as workers who literally "constructed" art for the people. Rodchenko was convinced that self-expression in art did not contribute enough to society, so after 1921 he worked as a photographer producing posters, books, textiles, and theater sets to promote communism.

In 1925, Rodchenko designed a model workers' club for the Soviet Pavilion at the Paris International Exposition of Modern Decorative and Industrial Arts (FIG. 31–46). Rodchenko designed the club for ease of use and simplicity of construction; the furniture was made of wood because Soviet industry was best equipped for mass production in wood. The high, straight backs of the chairs were meant to promote a physical and moral posture of uprightness among the workers.

Another artist active in early Soviet Russia was El Lissitzky (1890–1941), who, after the Revolution, was invited to teach architecture and graphic arts at the Vitebsk School of Fine Arts where Malevich also taught. By 1919, Lissitzky was both teaching and using a Constructivist vocabulary for propaganda posters and

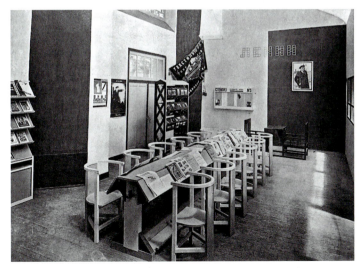

31-45 • Cass Gilbert WOOLWORTH BUILDING
New York. 1911–1913. Collection of the New York Historical Society, New York

31-46 • Aleksandr Rodchenko WORKERS' CLUB
Exhibited at the International Exposition of Modern Decorative and Industrial Arts, Paris. 1925. Rodchenko-Stepanova Archive, Moscow

The development of the skyscraper design and aesthetic depended on several things: The use of metal beams and girders for the structural-support skeleton; the separation of the building-support structure from the enclosing wall layer (the cladding); the use of fireproof materials and measures; the use of elevators; and the overall integration of plumbing, central heating, artificial lighting, and ventilation systems. The first generation of skyscrapers, built between about 1880 and 1900, were concentrated in the Midwest, chiefly in Chicago and St. Louis (SEE FIG. 30–55). Second-generation skyscrapers, mostly with over 20 stories, date from after 1895 and are found more frequently in New York. The first tall buildings were free-standing towers, sometimes with a base, such as the Woolworth Building of 1911–1913 (SEE FIG. 31–45). New York City's Building Zone Resolution of 1916 introduced mandatory setbacks—decreases in girth as the building rose—to ensure light and ventilation to adjacent sites. Built in 1931, the 1,250-foot setback form of the Empire State Building, diagrammed here, has a streamlined design. The Art Deco exterior cladding (see inset below) conceals the structural elements and mechanisms such as elevators that make its great height possible. The Empire State Building was the tallest building in the world when it was built and its distinctive profile ensures that it remains one of the most recognizable even today.

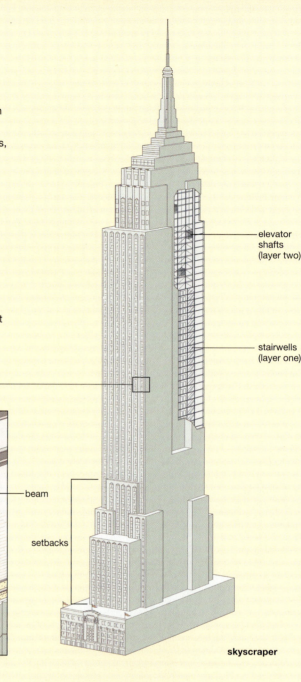

elevator shafts (layer two)

stairwells (layer one)

beam

setbacks

skyscraper

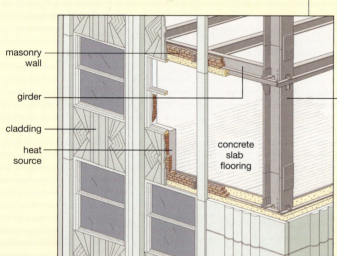

masonry wall

girder

cladding

heat source

concrete slab flooring

SEE MORE: View a simulation of skyscraper construction **www.myartslab.com**

for work that he called the Proun (pronounced "pro-oon"), thought to be an acronym for the Russian *proekt utverzhdenya novogo* ("project for the affirmation of the new"). Although most Prouns were paintings or prints, a few were installed in specific sites (**FIG. 31–47**) to create a total environment. Lissitzky rejected painting as too personal and imprecise, preferring to "construct" Prouns for the collective using the less personal instruments of mechanical drawing. Like many other Soviet artists of the late 1920s, Lissitzky also turned to more socially engaged projects such

as architectural design, typography, photography, and photomontage for publication.

SOCIALIST REALISM. In the mid 1920s, Soviet artists increasingly rejected abstraction in favor of a more universally accessible, and thus more politically useful, Socialist Realism that was ultimately established as official Soviet art. Many of Russia's pioneering Modernists and Constructivists, including Rodchenko, made the change willingly because they were already committed to the

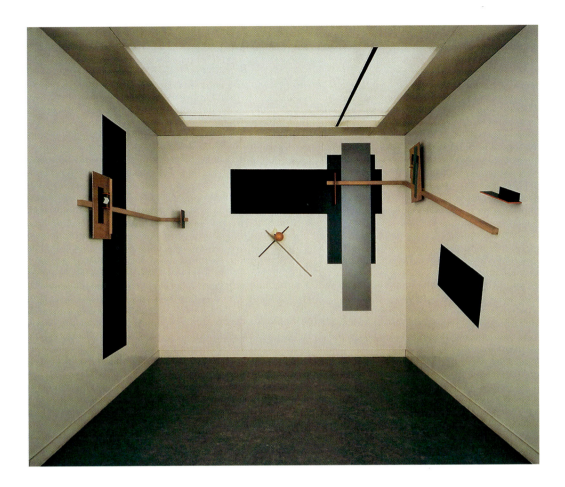

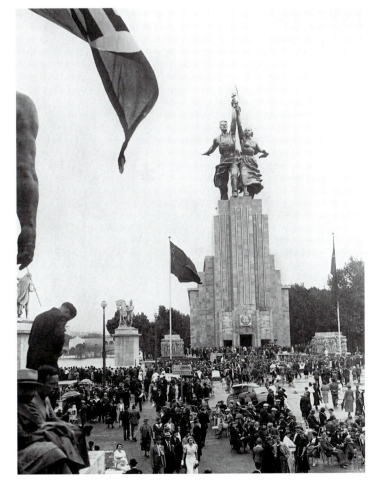

national cause, but others, who refused to change, were fired from public positions and lost public support.

The move to Socialist Realism was led by the Association of Artists of Revolutionary Russia (AKhRR), founded in 1922 to depict Russian workers, peasants, revolutionary activists, and the Red Army. AKhRR sought to document the history of the U.S.S.R. by promoting its leaders and goals. Artists were commissioned to create public paintings and sculptures as well as posters for mass distribution; their subjects were heroic or inspirational people and themes, and their style was an easily readable realism.

Vera Mukhina (1889–1953) was a member of AKhRR and is best known for her 78-foot-tall stainless-steel sculpture of a **WORKER AND COLLECTIVE FARM WOMAN (FIG. 31–48)** made for the Soviet Pavilion at the Paris Universal Exposition of 1937. The sculpture shows a powerfully built male factory worker and an equally powerful female farm laborer with their hammer and sickle held high in the air, reflecting the same tools as appeared on the Soviet flag. The figures are portrayed as equals, partners in their common cause, striding purposefully into the future with determined faces set and their windblown clothing billowing behind them.

31–48 • Vera Mukhina **WORKER AND COLLECTIVE FARM WOMAN**
Sculpture for the Soviet Pavilion, Paris Universal Exposition. 1937. Stainless steel, height approx. 78′ (23.8 m).

RATIONALISM IN THE NETHERLANDS

In the Netherlands after World War I, abstraction took a different turn than in the U.S.S.R. The Dutch artist Piet Mondrian (1872–1944) encountered Cubism on a trip to Paris in 1912 where he began to abstract animals, trees, and landscapes, searching for their "essential" form. After his return to the Netherlands, he met Theo van Doesburg (1883–1931) who, in 1917, started a magazine named *De Stijl* (*The Style*) that became a focal point for Dutch artists, architects, and designers after the war. In the magazine, Van Doesburg argued that there are two kinds of beauty: sensual or subjective beauty, and a higher, rational, and universal beauty and that De Stijl (note the term translates as "*The* Style" rather than "*A* Style") artists should aspire to create the latter kind of beauty. Mondrian adhered to De Stijl's rational, universal beauty by eliminating everything sensual or subjective from his paintings, but he also followed M. H. J. Schoenmaekers's ideas about Theosophy, as expressed in his 1915 book *New Image of the World*. Schoenmaekers argued that an inner visual construction of nature consisted of a balance between opposing forces, such as heat and cold, male and female, order and disorder, and that artists might represent this inner construction in abstract paintings by using only horizontal and vertical lines and primary colors.

Mondrian's later paintings seem to be visual embodiments of both Schoenmaekers's theory and De Stijl's artistic ideas. In **COMPOSITION WITH YELLOW, RED, AND BLUE (FIG. 31–49)**, for example, Mondrian uses three primary colors (red, yellow, and blue), three neutrals (white, gray, and black), and a grid of horizontal and vertical lines in his search for the essence of higher beauty and the balance of forces. Mondrian's opposing lines and colors balance a harmony of opposites that he called a "dynamic equilibrium" and which he achieved by carefully plotting an arrangement of colors, shapes, and visual weights grouped asymmetrically around the edges of a canvas, with the center acting as a blank white fulcrum. Mondrian hoped that De Stijl would have applications in the real world and would help to create an entirely new visual environment for living, designed according to the rules of a "universal beauty" that, when perfectly balanced, would both balance and purify the world. Mondrian said that he hoped to be the world's last artist, because, while art brought humanity to everyday life, when "universal beauty" infused all aspects of life, there would no longer be a need for art.

The architect and designer Gerrit Rietveld (1888–1964) applied Mondrian's principles of dynamic equilibrium and De Stijl's theories to architecture to create one of the most important examples of the International Style (see "The International Style,"

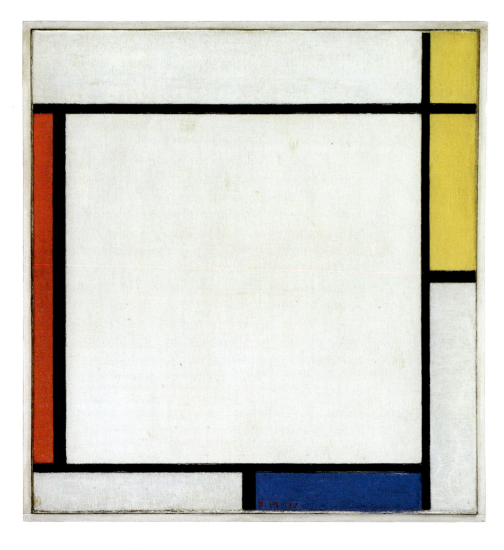

31-49 • Piet Mondrian
COMPOSITION WITH YELLOW, RED, AND BLUE, 1927
1927. Oil on canvas, 14⅞ × 13¾" (37.8 × 34.9 cm). The Menil Collection, Houston.
© 2010 Mondrian/Holtzman Trust c/o HCR International, Virginia 20186 USA

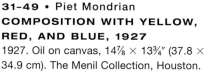

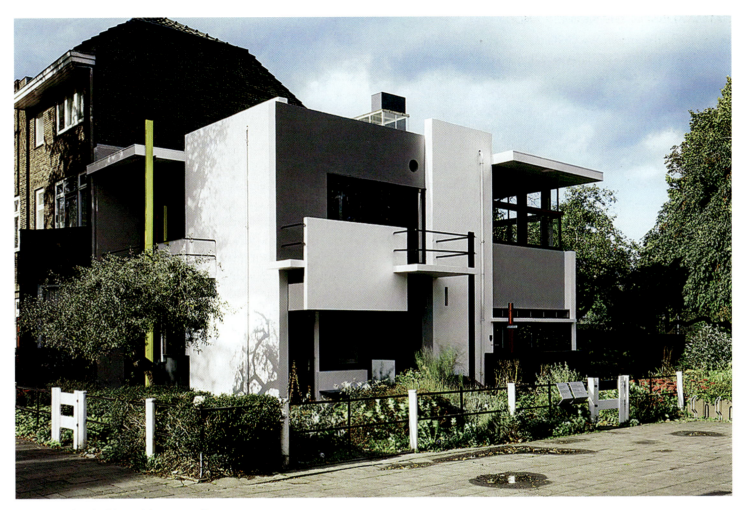

31–50 • Gerrit Rietveld **SCHRÖDER HOUSE**
Utrecht, the Netherlands. 1925.

EXPLORE MORE: Click the Google Earth link for the Schröder House
www.myartslab.com

page 1057). The radically asymmetrical exterior of the **SCHRÖDER HOUSE** in Utrecht (**FIG. 31–50**) is composed of interlocking gray and white planes of varying sizes, combined with horizontal and vertical accents in primary colors and black. The **"RED-BLUE" CHAIR** (**FIG. 31–51**) echoes the arrangement in the interior, where sliding partitions allow modifications in the spaces used for sleeping, working, and entertaining. The patron of the house, Truus Schröder-Schröder, wanted a home that suggested an elegant austerity, with basic necessities sleekly integrated into a balanced and restrained whole.

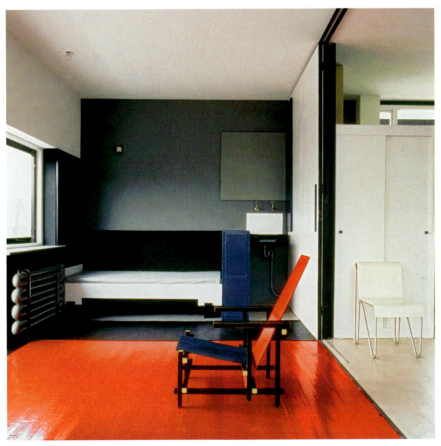

31–51 • Gerrit Rietveld **INTERIOR, SCHRÖDER HOUSE, WITH "RED-BLUE" CHAIR**
1925.

BAUHAUS ART IN GERMANY

In Germany, the creators of the Bauhaus ("House of Building"), which had been founded by Walter Gropius (1883–1969) in Weimar in 1919, found the strict geometric shapes and lines of Purism and De Stijl too rigid and argued that a true German architecture and design should emerge organically. At the Bauhaus, Gropius brought together German architects, designers, and craft workers whose collective creative energy could be harnessed to create an integrated system of design and production based on German traditions and styles. Gropius believed that he could revive the spirit of collaboration of the medieval building guilds (*Bauhütten*) that had erected Germany's cathedrals.

Although Gropius's "Bauhaus Manifesto" of 1919 declared that "the ultimate goal of all artistic activity is the building," the Bauhaus offered no formal training in architecture until 1927. Gropius's students were allowed to begin architectural training only after they completed a mandatory foundation course and received full training in design and crafts in the Bauhaus workshops. These included pottery, metalwork, textiles, stained glass, furniture, wood carving, and wall paintings. In 1922, Gropius also added a new emphasis on industrial design and the next year hired the Hungarian-born László Moholy-Nagy (1895–1946) to reorient the workshops toward more functional design suitable for mass production.

In 1925, when the Bauhaus moved to Dessau, Gropius designed its new building. Although the structure openly acknowledges its reinforced concrete, steel, and glass materials, there is also a balanced asymmetry to its three large cubic areas that was intended

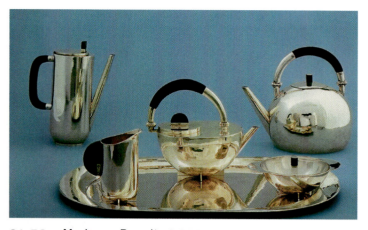

31-53 • Marianne Brandt COFFEE AND TEA SERVICE
1924. Silver and ebony, with Plexiglas cover for sugar bowl. Bauhaus Archiv, Berlin.

to convey the dynamism of modern life (**FIG. 31–52**). A glass-panel wall wraps around two sides of the workshop wing of the building to provide natural light for the workshops inside, while a parapet below demonstrates how modern engineering methods could create light, airy spaces. Both Moholy-Nagy and Gropius left the Bauhaus in 1928. The school eventually moved to Berlin in 1932, but lasted only one more year before the new German chancellor, Adolf Hitler, forced its closure (see "Suppression of the Avant-Garde in Nazi Germany," page 1055). Hitler opposed Modern art on two grounds: First, it was cosmopolitan and not nationalistic enough; second, he believed it to be overly influenced by Jews. The first was a matter of opinion; the second was patently untrue.

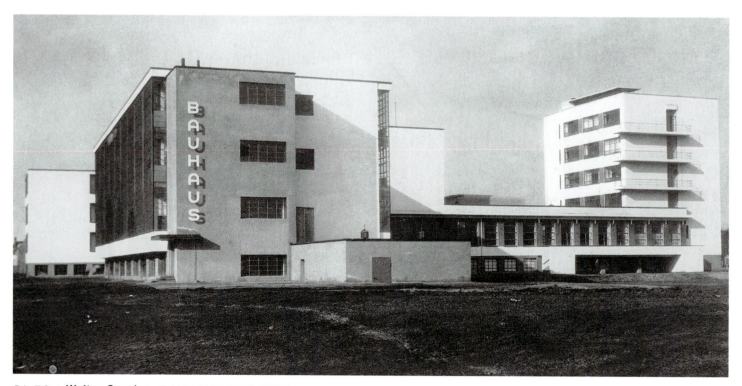

31-52 • Walter Gropius BAUHAUS BUILDING
Dessau, Germany. 1925–1926. View from northwest.

Suppression of the Avant-Garde in Nazi Germany

In the 1930s, the avant-garde was increasingly disparaged by Hitler and the rising Nazi Party. This led to a concerted effort to suppress it. One of the principal targets was the Bauhaus. Through much of the 1920s, classes there were taught by important artists such as Paul Klee, Vassily Kandinsky, Josef Albers, and Ludwig Mies van der Rohe. But they struggled against an increasingly hostile and reactionary political climate. As early as 1924, conservatives accused the Bauhaus of being not only educationally unsound but also politically subversive. To avoid having the school shut down by the opposition, Gropius moved it to Dessau in 1925, at the invitation of Dessau's liberal mayor, but he left office soon after the relocation and his successors faced increasing political pressure to close the school as it was a prime center of Modernist practice. The Bauhaus was forced to move again in 1932, this time to Berlin.

After Adolf Hitler came to power in 1933, the Nazi Party mounted an even more aggressive campaign against Modern art. In his youth Hitler had been a mediocre landscape painter, and he developed an intense hatred of the avant-garde. During the first year of his regime, the Bauhaus was forced to close permanently. A number of the artists, designers, and architects who had been on its faculty—including Albers, Gropius, and Mies—fled to the United States.

The Nazis also attacked German Expressionist artists, whose often-intense depictions of German politics and the economic crisis after the war criticized the state and whose frequent caricatures of German facial features and body types undermined Nazi attempts to redraw Germans as idealized Aryans. Expressionist and avant-garde art was removed from museums and confiscated, and artists were forbidden to buy paint or canvas and were subjected to public intimidation.

In 1937, the Nazi leadership organized an exhibition of what they termed "Degenerate Art" in an attempt to ridicule the banned Modern art and erase its makers. The Nazis described the avant-garde and Modernism as sick and degenerate, presenting the confiscated paintings and sculptures as specimens of pathology and scrawling slogans and derisive commentaries on the walls of the exhibition (see illustration). Ironically, the exhibition of 650 paintings, sculptures, prints, and books confiscated from German museums and artists was viewed by as many as 2 million people in four months in Munich, and by another 1 million on its three-year tour of German cities.

Large numbers of confiscated works that were supposed to be destroyed were looted by Nazi officials and sold in Switzerland in exchange for foreign currency. The ownership of much of the surviving art is still in question. Many artists fled to neighboring countries or the United States, but some, such as Ernst Ludwig Kirchner, whose *Street, Berlin* (SEE FIG. 31–13) was included in the "Degenerate Art" exhibit, were driven to suicide by their loss. Even the work of artists sympathetic to the Nazi position was not safe. Emil Nolde (SEE FIG. 31–12), who joined the Nazi Party in 1932, also had his art confiscated.

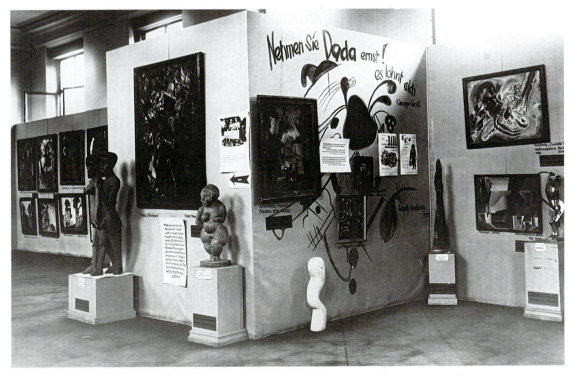

THE DADA WALL IN ROOM 3 OF THE "DEGENERATE ART" ("ENTARTETE KUNST") EXHIBITION
Munich. 1937.

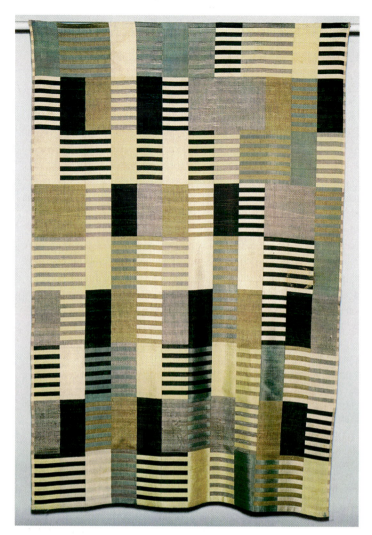

31-54 • Anni Albers WALL HANGING
1926. Silk, two-ply weave, 5'11⅝" × 3'11⅝" (1.83 × 1.22 m).
Busch-Reisinger Museum, Harvard University, Cambridge,
Massachusetts. Association Fund

Marianne Brandt's (1893–1983) elegant tea and coffee service (FIG. 31–53), handcrafted in silver, is an example of the collaboration between design and industry at the Bauhaus. This set was a prototype for mass production in cheaper metals such as nickel silver. After the Bauhaus moved to Dessau, Brandt also designed lighting fixtures and table lamps for mass production, earning much-needed revenue for the school. After Moholy-Nagy and Gropius's departure, Brandt took over the metal workshop for a year before she too left, in 1929. As a woman in the otherwise all-male metal workshop, Brandt made an exceptional contribution to the Bauhaus.

Although it was claimed that women were admitted to the Bauhaus on an equal basis with men, Gropius opposed their education as architects and channeled them into what he considered the more gender-appropriate workshops of pottery and textiles. Berlin-born Anni Albers (b. Annelise Fleischmann, 1899–1994) arrived at the school in 1922 and married the Bauhaus graduate and professor Josef Albers (1888–1976) in 1925. Obliged to enter the textiles workshop rather than the painting studio, Anni Albers made "pictorial" weavings and wall hangings (FIG. 31–54) that were so innovative they actually replaced paintings on the walls of several modern buildings. Her decentralized, rectilinear designs make reference to the aesthetics of De Stijl, but differ in their open acknowledgment of the natural process of weaving. Albers's goal was "to let threads be articulate … and find a form for themselves to no other end than their own orchestration."

SURREALISM AND THE MIND

At the same time in France in the early 1930s, a group of artists and writers took a very different approach to Modernism in a revolt against logic and reason. The Surrealists embraced the irrational, disorderly, aberrant, and even violent social interventions. Surrealism emerged initially as an offshoot of Dada from the mind of the poet André Breton (1896–1966). Breton trained in medicine and psychiatry and served in a neurological hospital during World War I where he used Freudian analysis on shell-shocked soldiers. By 1924, Breton, still drawn to the vagaries of the human mind, published the "Manifesto of Surrealism" in which he interpreted Freud's theory that the human mind is a battleground where the irrational forces of the unconscious mind wage a constant war against the rational, orderly, and oppressive forces of the conscious mind. Breton wanted to explore humanity's most base, irrational, and forbidden sexual desires, fantasies, and violent instincts by freeing the conscious mind from reason. As Breton wrote in 1934, "we still live under the rule of logic." Thus, he and other Surrealists developed strategies to liberate the unconscious using dream analysis, free association, automatic writing, word games, and hypnotic trances. Surrealists studied acts of "criminal madness" and the "female mind" in particular, believing the latter to be weaker and more irrational than the male mind. Breton believed that the only way to improve the war-sick society of the 1920s was to discover the more intense "surreality" that lay beyond rational constraint.

AUTOMATISM. Surrealist artists employed a variety of techniques, including **automatism**, to release the mind from conscious control and to produce surprising new juxtapositions of imagery and forms. Max Ernst (1891–1976), a self-taught German artist who collaborated in Dada in Cologne and later joined Breton's circle in Paris, was particularly inventive in his use of automatism. In 1925, Ernst developed the automatist technique of **frottage**, in which he rubbed a pencil or crayon over a piece of paper placed on a textured surface. The resulting image stimulated Ernst's imagination. As he gazed at it, he began to see fantastic creatures, plants, and landscapes that he articulated more clearly with additional drawing. Ernst adapted frottage to painting, calling this new technique **grattage**. He created images by scraping layers of paint over a canvas laid over a textured surface, and then "revealing" the imagery he saw in the paint with additional painting. **THE HORDE** (FIG. 31–55) shows a nightmarish scene of

After World War I, increased exchanges between Modern architects led to the development of a common formal language, transcending national boundaries, which came to be known as the International Style. The term gained wide currency as a result of a 1932 exhibition at the Museum of Modern Art in New York, "The International Style: Architecture Since 1922," organized by the architectural historian Henry-Russell Hitchcock and the architect and curator Philip Johnson. Hitchcock and Johnson identified three fundamental principles of the style.

The first was "the conception of architecture as volume rather than mass." The use of a structural skeleton of steel and ferroconcrete made it possible to eliminate loadbearing walls on both the exterior and interior. The building could then be wrapped in a skin of glass, metal, or masonry, creating the effect of enclosed space (volume) rather than dense material (mass). Interiors featured open, free-flowing plans providing maximum flexibility in the use of space.

The second was "regularity rather than symmetry as the chief means of ordering design." Regular distribution of structural supports and the use of standard building parts promoted rectangular regularity rather than the balanced axial symmetry of Classical architecture. The avoidance of Classical balance also encouraged an asymmetrical disposition of the building's components, such as doors and windows.

The third was the rejection of "arbitrary applied decoration." The new architecture depended on the intrinsic elegance of its materials and the formal arrangement of its elements to produce harmonious aesthetic effects. In sum, the most extreme International Style building would be an unadorned glass box.

According to Hitchcock and Johnson, the International Style originated in the Netherlands (in De Stijl), France (in Purism), and Germany (at the Bauhaus). After the exhibition and publication of the catalog listing the characteristics of the International Style in 1932, it spread to the United States.

The first concentrated manifestation of the International Style was in 1927 at the Deutscher Werkbund's Weissenhofsiedlung exhibition in Stuttgart, Germany, directed by Ludwig Mies van der Rohe (1886–1969), an architect who, like Gropius, was associated with the Bauhaus in Germany. The purpose of this semipermanent show was to present a range of model homes that used new technologies and made no reference to historical styles. The buildings in the exhibition featured flat roofs, plain walls, off-center openings, and rectilinear designs by Mies, Gropius, Le Corbusier, and others.

The conceptual clarity of the International Style allowed it to remain vital until the 1970s, especially in the United States, where many of its original European architects, such as Mies and Gropius, who had escaped Hitler and the rise of Nazism in Germany in the 1930s, practiced.

---

wooden-looking monsters who advance against some unseen opponent. Like much of Ernst's other work of the period, this frightening image seems to evoke the horrors of World War I that Ernst had experienced firsthand in the German army.

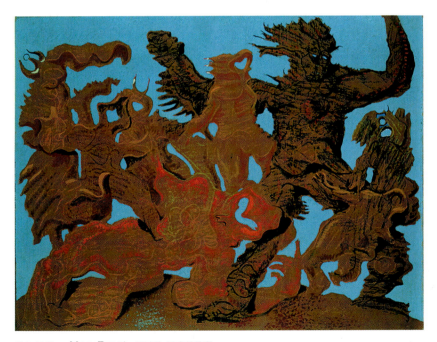

31–55 • Max Ernst THE HORDE
1927. Oil on canvas, 44⅞ × 57½″ (114 × 146.1 cm).
Stedelijk Museum, Amsterdam.

UNEXPECTED JUXTAPOSITIONS. The paintings of Salvador Dalí (1904–1989) include more recognizable figures and forms but they also reveal the visual wonders of a subconscious mind run wild. Dalí trained at the San Fernando Academy of Fine Arts in Madrid, where he mastered the traditional methods of illusionistic representation, and traveled to Paris in 1928, where he met the Surrealists. Dalí's contribution to Surrealist theory was the "paranoid-critical method," in which he cultivated the paranoid's ability to misread, mangle, and misconstrue ordinary appearances, thus liberating himself from the shackles of conventional thought. Dalí then painted what he had imagined.

Dalí's paintings generally deal with a few key themes: sexuality, violence, and putrefaction. In the **BIRTH OF LIQUID DESIRES** (FIG. 31–56), we see a large yellow **biomorphic** form (an organic shape resembling a living organism) that looks like a monster's face, a painter's palette, or a woman's body as the backdrop for four figures. A woman in white embraces a hermaphroditic figure who stands with one foot in a bowl that is being filled with liquid by a third figure, partially hidden, while a fourth figure enters a cavernous hole to the left. On a thick black cloud above the scene the question is posed: "Consign: to waste the total slate?" Dalí claimed that he arrived at his

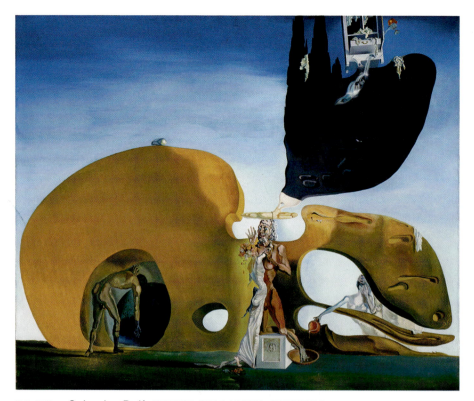

31-56 • Salvador Dalí BIRTH OF LIQUID DESIRES
1931–1932. Oil and collage on canvas, 37⅞ × 44¼″ (96.1 × 112.3 cm). Guggenheim Museum, New York. Peggy Guggenheim Collection. 76.2553 PG 100

surreality. One of the most disturbingly exquisite and mockingly humorous examples is **OBJECT (LUNCHEON IN FUR) (FIG. 31–57)**, by the Swiss artist Meret Oppenheim (1913–1985). Oppenheim was one of the few women invited to participate in the Surrealist movement. Surrealists generally treated women as their muses or as objects of study, but not their equals: Picasso even claimed to have "given" Oppenheim the idea for this sculpture. *Object* consists of an actual cup, saucer, and spoon covered with the fur of a Chinese gazelle (chosen for its resemblance in texture to pubic hair). It transposes two objects (a tea setting and gazelle fur) from their ordinary reality, recontextualizes them in an irrational new surreality, and transforms them into an uncanny object that is simultaneously desirous and deeply disturbing.

BIOMORPHIC ABSTRACTION. The Catalan artist Joan Miró (1893–1983) exhibited regularly with the Surrealists but never formally joined the movement. Miró's biomorphic abstraction is also intended to free the mind from rationality, but in a more benign manner. His **COMPOSITION (FIG. 31–58)** of 1933 is populated by curving biomorphic primal or mythic shapes and forms that are arranged by chance, and seem to emerge from the artist's mind uncensored, like doodles, to dance gleefully around the canvas. The Surrealists used the free association of doodling to relax the conscious mind and allow images to bubble up from the unconscious. Miró reportedly doodled on his canvases before working up in paint the shapes and forms revealed there. His forms do seem to take shape before our eyes, but their identity is always in flux. Miró was also fascinated by children's art, which he thought of as spontaneous

imagery by writing down his nightmares and merely painting what his paranoid-critical mind had conjured up. Dalí's images are thus, as Breton advocated, "the true process of thought, free from the exercise of reason and from any aesthetic or moral purpose." They defy rational interpretation although they trigger fear, anxiety, and even regression in our empathetic minds.

Dalí's strangely compelling art also draws on the Surrealist interest in unexpected juxtapositions of disparate realities. Surrealists argued that by juxtaposing several disparate ordinary objects in strange new contexts artists could create an uncanny

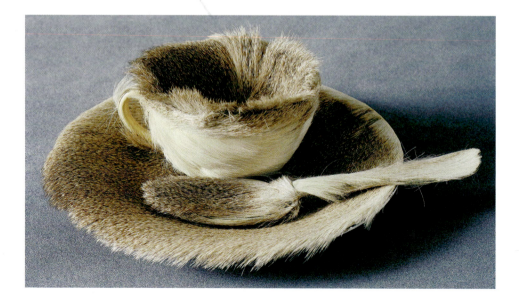

31-57 • Meret Oppenheim OBJECT (LUNCHEON IN FUR)
1936. Fur-covered cup, diameter 4⅜″ (10.9 cm); fur-covered saucer, diameter 9⅜″ (23.7 cm); fur-covered spoon, length 8″ (20.2 cm); overall height, 2⅞″ (7.3 cm). Museum of Modern Art, New York.

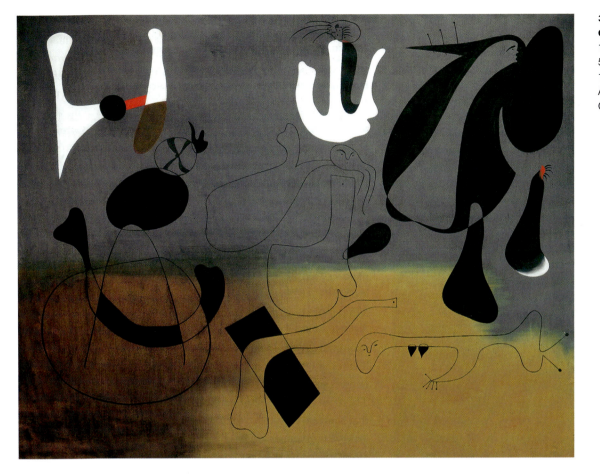

31–58 • Joan Miró
COMPOSITION
1933. Oil on canvas,
51¼ × 63½″ (130.2 ×
161.3 cm). Wadsworth
Athenaeum, Hartford,
Connecticut.

and expressive and, although he was a well-trained artist himself, he said that he wished he could learn to paint with the freedom of a child.

If Miró's paintings suggest movement, the American artist Alexander Calder (1898–1976) actually made biomorphic forms move. Calder trained as an engineer and took some art classes before traveling to Paris in 1926. Although not an official member of the movement, his sculpture was particularly admired by the Surrealists, with whom he exhibited on occasion. Calder came from a family of monumental sculptors, so it is not surprising that he reacted against his heritage by exploring the use of light new industrial materials in his sculpture. Like other sculptors of his generation, he explored negative space, removed sculpture from its pedestal, and hung it from the ceiling. The movement in Calder's art is not driven by motors; his sculptures are brushed into movement by air currents that make his unstable balanced forms bob and dip independently and seemingly randomly. Calder's metal sculptures, which are attached to wire arms and hung from the ceiling, are termed **mobiles. LOBSTER TRAP AND FISH TAIL** (FIG. 31–59) is composed of delicately balanced flat biomorphic forms and wire. At first it seems to be abstract, but the title works on our imagination to help us find the lobster trap and fish tail as they bob and spin

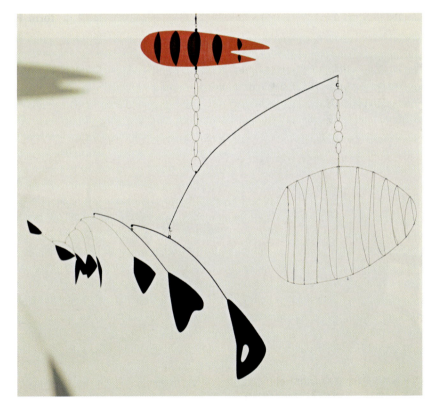

31-59 • Alexander Calder **LOBSTER TRAP AND FISH TAIL**
1939. Painted steel wire and sheet aluminum, approx. 8′6″ × 9′6″
(2.6 × 2.9 m). Museum of Modern Art, New York.
Commissioned by the Advisory Committee for the Stairwell of the Museum
(590.139.a–d)

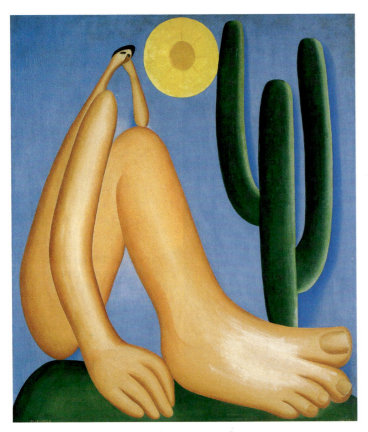

31–71 • Tarsila do Amaral ABAPORÚ (THE ONE WHO EATS)
1928. Oil on canvas, 34 × 29″ (86.4 × 73.7 cm). Museo de Arte Latinoamericano, Buenos Aires. *Courtesy of Guilherme Augusto do Amaral/Malba-Coleccion Constantini, Buenos Aires*

used to declare their artistic independence from Europe. Modern Art Week brought avant-garde poets, dancers, and musicians as well as visual artists to São Paulo and took on a distinctly confrontational character. Poets derided their elders in poetry, dancers enacted modern versions of traditional dances, and composer Hector Villa-Lobos (1887–1959) appeared on stage in a bathrobe and slippers to play new music based on Afro-Brazilian rhythms.

In 1928, the São Paulo poet Oswald de Andrade, one of Modern Art Week's organizers, wrote the *Anthropophagic Manifesto* proposing a tongue-in-cheek if radical solution to Brazil's seeming dependence on European culture. He suggested that Brazilians should imitate the ancient Brazilians' response to Portuguese explorers arriving on their shore: Eat them. He mockingly described this relationship as anthropophagic or cannibalistic and proposed that Brazilians should gobble up European culture, digest it, let it strengthen their Brazilianness, and then get rid of it.

The painter who most closely embodies this irreverent attitude is Tarsila do Amaral (1887–1974), a daughter of the coffee-planting aristocracy who studied in Europe with Fernand Léger (SEE FIG. 31–21), among others. Her painting **ABAPORÚ (THE ONE WHO EATS) (FIG. 31–71)** shows an appreciation of the art of Léger

ancient god, while the European Frida holds a forceps: A blood vessel connects the god to the forceps through the hearts of the two Fridas. Kahlo suffered a broken pelvis in an accident at 17, and endured a lifetime of surgical interventions—this work alludes to her constant pain, as well as to the Aztec custom of human sacrifice by heart removal. The significance of Kahlo's art, apart from its memorable self-expression, lies in its investigation of larger issues of Mexican identity. This painting addresses issues of mixed heritage in Mexico, sexuality, and gender identity within the context of Kahlo's own life.

BRAZIL

Other Latin American art was dominated by the academic tradition in the nineteenth century; several nations had thriving academies, large art communities, and significant numbers of artists traveling to Paris to study. By 1914, artists in many Latin American countries had begun to paint national themes in their own versions of Impressionism. After the war, artists who studied abroad also brought home ideas drawn from Modern art and the European avant-garde which they translated into a specifically Latin American vision. For instance in 1922, as Brazil marked the centenary of its independence from Portugal, the avant-garde in São Paulo celebrated with Modern Art Week, an event Brazilian artists

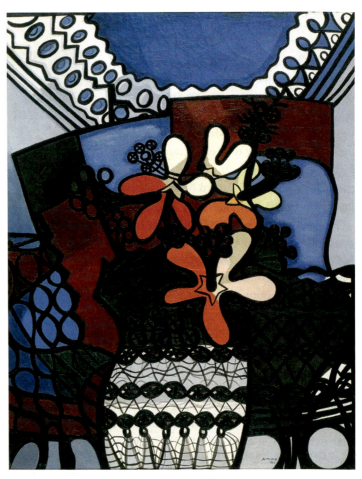

31–72 • Amelia Peláez MARPACÍFICO (HIBISCUS)
1943. Oil on canvas, 45½ × 35″ (115.6 × 88.9 cm). Art Museum of the Americas, Washington, D.C. *Gift of IBM*

and Brancusi (SEE FIGS. 31–27, 31–28), which Tarsila collected. But she has cleverly inserted several "tropical" clichés into her own work in the abstracted forms of a cactus and a lemon-slice sun. The subject is Andrade's irreverent cannibal who sits in an almost caricatural Brazilian landscape, as if to say: If Brazilians are caricatured abroad as cannibals, then let us act like cannibals. As Andrade wrote in one of his manifestos: "Carnival in Rio is the religious outpouring of our race. Richard Wagner yields to the samba. Barbaric but ours. We have a dual heritage: The jungle and the school."

CUBA

Cuba's 1920s avant-garde was one of the most interdisciplinary, consisting of anthropologists, poets, composers, and even a few scientists, who gathered in Havana and called themselves "The Minority." They issued a manifesto in 1927 repudiating government corruption, "Yankee imperialism," and dictatorship on any continent. "Minority" artists, they urged, should pursue a new, popular, Modern art rooted in Cuban soil.

Amelia Peláez (1896–1968) left Cuba for Paris shortly after this manifesto was issued. When she returned home, she joined the anthropologist Lydia Cabrera to study Cuban popular and folk arts. Her paintings focus on the woman's realm—the domestic interior—and national identity, as in **MARPACÍFICO (HIBISCUS) (FIG. 31–72)**. The overall language of this work is Cubist, as seen in the flattened overlapping forms and compressed pictorial space, but it shows a mirror, a tabletop, and local hibiscus flowers embroidered in paint with heavy black outlines and pure color that would be instantly recognizable in Cuba as representing the flat fan-shaped stained-glass windows that decorate many Cuban homes.

POSTWAR ART IN EUROPE AND THE AMERICAS

FIGURAL RESPONSES AND *ART INFORMEL* IN EUROPE

The horrors of World War II surpassed even those of World War I. The human loss was almost too profound and grotesque to comprehend. Between loss of life in action, those killed in work camps and death camps (concentration camps), those lost to starvation, and those lost in the bombing of civilian targets, more than 30 million people died and a further estimated 40 million people were displaced. The unimaginable horror of the concentration camps and the awful impact of the dropping of nuclear bombs shook humanity to its core. Winston Churchill described the extent of the catastrophe: "What is Europe now? A rubble heap, a charnel house, a breeding ground of pestilence and hate."

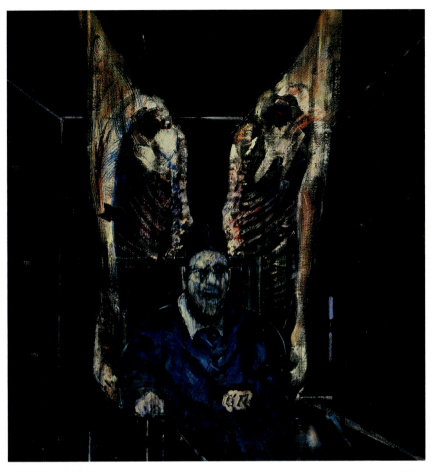

31–73 • Francis Bacon HEAD SURROUNDED BY SIDES OF BEEF
1954. Oil on canvas, 50¾ × 48″ (129 × 122 cm). Art Institute of Chicago. Harriott A. Fox Fund

Most European artists in the immediate postwar period used their art to try to come to terms with what they had experienced, many debating about how best to do this: Some artists worked figuratively while others painted abstractions.

In England, Francis Bacon (1909–1992) used his canvases to capture the horrors that haunted him. Bacon was self-taught and produced very few pictures until the 1940s. He served as an air-raid warden during World War II and saw the bloody impact of the bombing of civilians in London firsthand. In **HEAD SURROUNDED BY SIDES OF BEEF (FIG. 31–73)**, Bacon shows the imperious Pope Innocent X reduced to an anguished and insubstantial man howling in a black void as two bloody sides of beef enclose him in a claustrophobic box that contains his frightful screams and amplifies his terror. The painting was directly inspired by Diego Velázquez's portrait of Pope Innocent X (1650) and by Rembrandt paintings of dripping meat. Bacon wrote of his art: "I hope to make the best human cry in painting … to remake the violence of reality itself."

One of the most distinctive postwar European art movements was *Art Informel* ("formless art"), which was also called *tachisme* (*tache* is French for "spot" or "stain"). *Art Informel* was promoted by the French critic Michel Tapié (1909–1987) who suggested that art should express an authentic concept of postwar humanity through simple, honest marks.

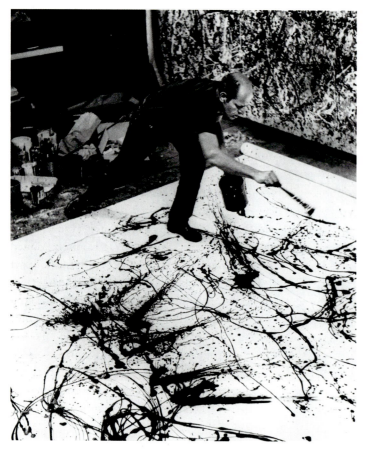

31–79 • Hans Namuth PHOTOGRAPH OF JACKSON POLLOCK PAINTING
The Springs, New York. 1950.

SEE MORE: View a video of Jackson Pollock painting
www.myartslab.com

renovated barn, where he placed his canvases on the floor so that he could reach into them from all four sides. The German expatriate artist Hans Hofmann (1880–1966) had poured and dripped paint before Pollock, but Pollock's unrestrained gestures transformed the idea of painting and the way that artists viewed the canvas. Pollock painted by moving around and within the canvas, dripping and scoring commercial-grade enamel paint (rather than specialist artist's paint) onto it using sticks and trowels. Pollock's urgent arcs and whorls of paint have been described as chaotic, but he saw them as labyrinths that led the viewer along complex paths and into an organic calligraphic web of natural and biomorphic forms. Pollock's all-over composition lacks hierarchical arrangement; it has multiple moving focal points and it denies perspectival space. Yet, as the paint travels around the canvas in arcs and ellipses, it never escapes the edges of the canvas. There is also a top and a bottom: Turn the image upside down and it appears "wrong." Like a coiled spring, the painting seems full of anxious energy that is ready to explode at any moment.

Autumn Rhythm is heroic in scale: It is almost 9 feet tall by 17 feet wide and it engulfs the viewer's entire field of vision. According to Lee Krasner, Pollock was a "jazz addict" who spent many hours listening to the explosively improvised bebop of Charlie Parker and Dizzy Gillespie. Pollock was also interested in Native American art, which he associated with his western roots and which enjoyed widespread coverage in popular and art magazines in the 1930s. Pollock was particularly struck by the images and processes of Navajo sand painters who demonstrated their work at the Natural History Museum in New York. And, of course, he drew on Jung's theories of the collective unconscious. But Pollock was not merely

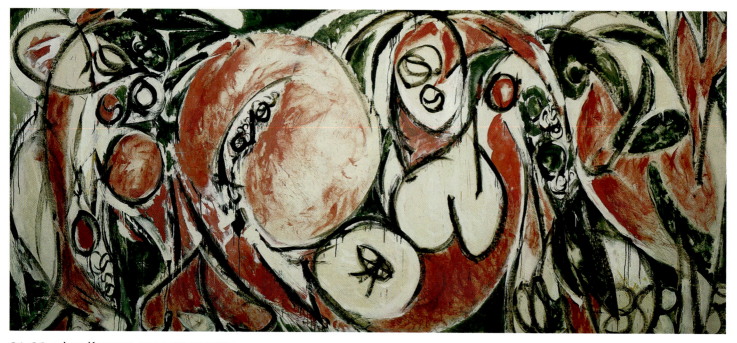

31–80 • Lee Krasner THE SEASONS
1957. Oil on canvas, 7'8¾" × 16'11¾" (2.36 × 5.18 m). Whitney Museum of American Art, New York. Purchased with funds from Frances and Sydney Lewis (by exchange), the Mrs. Percy Uris Purchase Fund, and the Painting and Sculpture Committee (87.7)

the sum of his parts. His paintings communicate on a grand, modern, but primal level. In a radio interview, he said that he was creating for "the age of the airplane, the atom bomb, and the radio."

OTHER ACTION PAINTERS. Lee Krasner (1908–1984) studied in New York with Hans Hofmann and produced fully nonrepresentational paintings with all-over compositions several years before Pollock. She moved in with Pollock in 1942 and virtually stopped painting in order to take care of him. They moved to Long Island in 1945, where she set up a small studio in a guest bedroom and produced small, tight, gestural paintings. After Pollock's death in an automobile crash in 1956, Krasner took over his studio and produced a series of large, dazzling gestural paintings that marked her re-emergence into the mainstream art world. Works such as **THE SEASONS (FIG. 31–80)** feature bold, sweeping curves that

express not only a new sense of liberation but also her powerful identification with the forces of nature in bursting, rounded forms and springlike colors. Krasner said that "Painting, for me, when it really 'happens' is as miraculous as any natural phenomenon."

In contrast, Willem de Kooning (1904–1997) wrote that "Art never seems to make me peaceful or pure." An immigrant from the Netherlands, de Kooning was friendly with several Modern artists including Elaine Marie Fried, whom he married. His view of the world was never simple or certain. He remarked: "I work out of doubt." De Kooning's painting was always highly structured and controlled. He made careful under-drawings, and painted and scraped several layers of paint in the process of creating a single canvas. His gestural strokes appear spontaneous but they are, in fact, the result of hours of experiment and failure. De Kooning painted strokes, scraped them off, and repeated the process until the exact

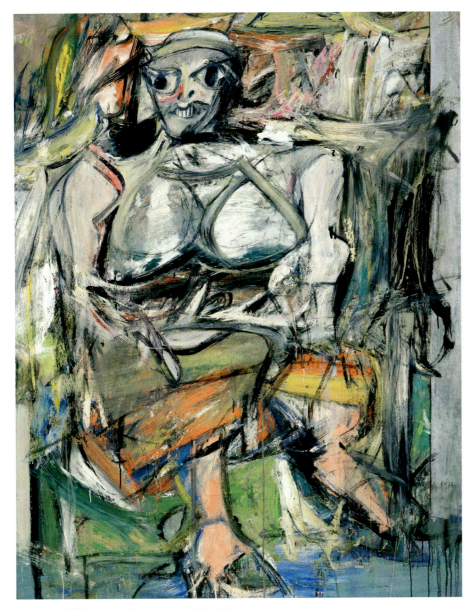

31–81 • Willem de Kooning WOMAN I
1950–1952. Oil on canvas, 75⅞ × 58″ (192.7 × 147.3 cm). Museum of Modern Art, New York.

mark he wanted emerged. In 1953, de Kooning shocked the art world by moving away from pure abstraction with a series of figurative paintings of women. **WOMAN I (FIG. 31–81)** took the artist two years to complete and de Kooning's wife Elaine estimated that he scraped and repainted it about 200 times. It portrays a figure who seems at once grotesque and rapacious, and the image is both hostile and sexist. It is powerfully sexual, full of implied violence, and intensely passionate. De Kooning described his "Woman" paintings as images of great fertility goddesses like the *Woman from Willendorf* (SEE FIG. 1–7), or as a composite of stereotypes taken from the media and film.

Abstract Expressionism spread quickly to Canada. In his native Montreal, the French Canadian painter Jean-Paul Riopelle (1923–2002) worked with Les Automatistes (The Automatists), a group of artists using the Surrealist technique of automatism to create abstract paintings. In 1947, Riopelle moved to Paris and, in the early 1950s, began to squeeze paint directly onto the canvas and spread it with a palette knife to create an all-over painting of bright swatches of color that are suggestive of broken shards of stained glass traversed by a network of spidery lines, as in **KNIGHT WATCH (FIG. 31–82)**.

Helen Frankenthaler (b. 1928) visited Pollock's studio in 1951 and went on to create a more lyrical version of Action painting that had a significant impact on later artists. Like Pollock, she worked on the floor, but she poured paint onto the unprimed canvas in thin washes so that it soaked into the fabric rather than sitting on its surface. Frankenthaler

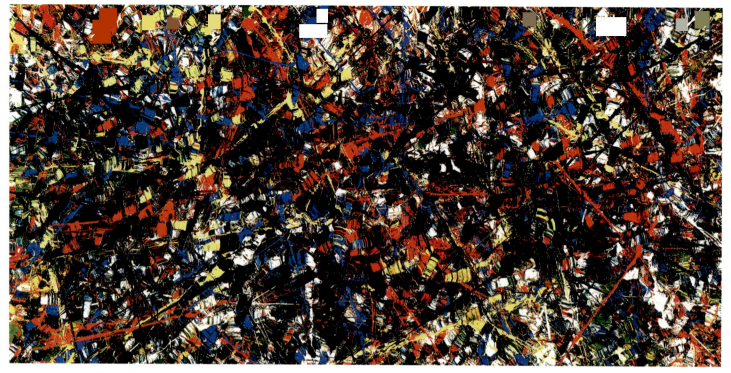

31–82 • Jean-Paul Riopelle **KNIGHT WATCH**
1953. Oil on canvas, 38 × 76⅝″ (96.6 × 194.8 cm). National Gallery of Canada, Ottawa, Ontario.

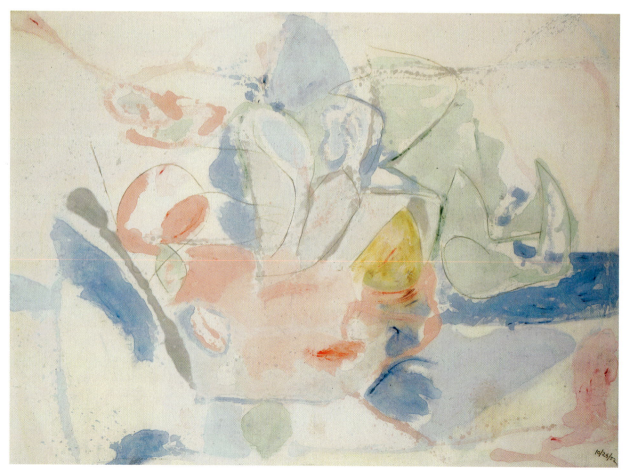

31–83 • Helen Frankenthaler **MOUNTAINS AND SEA**
1952. Oil and charcoal on canvas, 7′2¾″ × 9′8¼″ (2.2 × 2.95 m). Collection of the artist on extended loan to the
National Gallery of Art, Washington, D.C.

described her process as starting with an aesthetic question or image and evolving as the process of painting took over as a self-expressive act. She described her working method: "I will sometimes start a picture feeling, What will happen if I work with three blues … ? And very often midway through the picture I have to change the basis of the experience. Or I add and add to the canvas…. When I say gesture, my gesture, I mean what my mark is. I think there is something now that I am still working out in paint; it is a struggle for me to both discard and retain what is gestural and personal." In **MOUNTAINS AND SEA** (FIG. 31–83), Franken-thaler poured several colors onto the canvas and outlined selected forms in charcoal. The result reminded her of the coast of Nova Scotia where she frequently went to sketch.

COLOR FIELD PAINTING

New York School artists used abstract means to express various kinds of emotional states, not all of them as urgent or improvisatory as those of the Action painters. The Color Field painters moved in a different direction, painting large, flat areas of color to evoke more transcendent, contemplative moods in paint.

Mark Rothko (1903–1970) had very little formal art training but by 1940 was already producing paintings that were deeply influenced by the European Surrealists and by Jung's archetypal imagery. By the mid-1940s, Rothko began to paint very large canvases with rectangular shapes arranged in a vertical format in which he allowed his colors to bleed into one another. These canvases, such as **LAVENDER AND MULBERRY** (FIG. 31–84), are

31–84 • Mark Rothko LAVENDER AND MULBERRY
1959. Oil on paper mounted on fiberboard, 37¾ × 24¾″ (95.9 × 62.8 cm). Hirshhorn Museum and Sculpture Garden, Smithsonian Institution, Washington, D.C.
Gift of Joseph H. Hirshhorn 1966

The Dinner Party

Judy Chicago's **THE DINNER PARTY** is a large, complex, mixed-media installation dedicated to hundreds of women and women artists rescued from anonymity by early feminist artists and historians. It took five years of collaborative effort to make, and it drew on the assistance of hundreds of female and several male volunteers working as ceramists, needleworkers, and china painters. *The Dinner Party* is composed of a large, triangular table, each side stretching 48 feet; Chicago conceived of the equilateral triangle as a symbol of both the feminine and the equalized world sought by feminism. The table rests on a triangular platform of 2,300 triangular porcelain tiles comprising the "Heritage Floor" that bears the names of 999 notable women from myth, legend, and history. Along each side of the table are 13 place settings representing famous women—13 being the number of men at the Last Supper as well as the number of

witches in a coven. The 39 women thus honored by individual place settings include the mythical, such as the goddess Ishtar and the Amazon, and historical personages such as the Egyptian queen Hatshepsut, the Roman scholar Hypatia, the medieval French queen Eleanor of Aquitaine, the author Christine de Pizan (see page 531), the Italian Renaissance noblewoman Isabella d'Este (see page 658), the Italian Baroque painter Artemisia Gentileschi (SEE FIG. 22–14), the eighteenth-century English feminist writer Mary Wollstonecraft, the nineteenth-century American abolitionist Sojourner Truth, and the twentieth-century American painter Georgia O'Keeffe (shown here).

Each larger-than-life place setting includes a 14-inch-wide painted porcelain plate, ceramic flatware, a ceramic chalice with a gold interior, and an embroidered napkin, sitting upon an elaborately ornamented runner. The runners are

decorated using stitching and weaving techniques and motifs appropriate to the time and place in which each woman lived. Most of the plates feature abstract designs based on female genitalia because, as Chicago said, "that is all [these women] had in common…. They were from different periods, classes, ethnicities, geographies, experiences, but what kept them within the same confined historical space" was their biological sex. The empty plates represent the fact that they "had been swallowed up and obscured by history instead of being recognized and honored."

The prominent place accorded to china painting and needlework in *The Dinner Party* both celebrates traditional women's crafts and argues for their place in the pantheon of "high art," while at the same time informing the viewer about some of the unrecognized contributions that women have made to history.

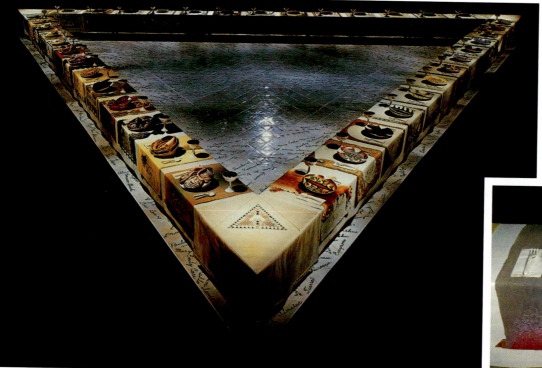

Judy Chicago THE DINNER PARTY
1974–1979. Overall installation view. White tile floor inscribed in gold with 999 women's names; triangular table with painted porcelain, sculpted porcelain plates, and needlework, each side 48 × 42 × 3′ (14.6 × 12.8 × 1 m). Brooklyn Museum of Art, New York.
Gift of the Elizabeth A. Sackler Foundation (2002.10)

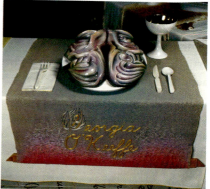

Georgia O'Keeffe
Place setting, detail of *The Dinner Party*.

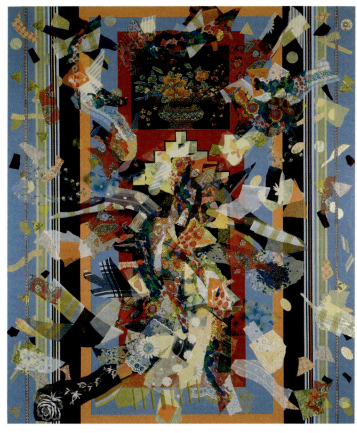

32-20 • Miriam Schapiro PERSONAL APPEARANCE #3
1973. Acrylic and fabric on canvas, 60 × 50″ (152.4 × 127 cm).
Private collection.

of female genitalia to challenge the male-dominated art world and to validate the female body and experience. In 1970, she established a feminist studio art course at Fresno State College (now California State University, Fresno) and the next year moved to Los Angeles to join the painter Miriam Schapiro (b. 1923) in establishing a Feminist Art Program at the new California Institute of the Arts (CalArts). At this time she also began to make *The Dinner Party*, one of the largest and best-known feminist artworks of the decade (see "*The Dinner Party*," opposite).

In 1971–1972, Chicago, Schapiro, and 21 of their female students created *Womanhouse*, a collaborative art environment located in a run-down Hollywood mansion which the artists renovated and filled with feminist installations. In collaboration with Sherry Brody, Schapiro also created *Dollhouse*, a mixed-media construction of several miniature rooms adorned with richly patterned fabrics. She subsequently began to incorporate pieces of fabric into her acrylic paintings, developing a type of work she called **femmage** (from "female" and "collage"). Schapiro's femmages, such as **PERSONAL APPEARANCE #3 (FIG. 32–20)**, celebrate traditional women's crafts. Schapiro later returned to New York to lead the Pattern and Decoration movement, a group of both female and male artists who merged the aesthetics of abstraction with ornamental motifs derived from women's craft, folk art, and art beyond the Western tradition in a nonhierarchical manner.

MENDIETA. Ana Mendieta (1948–1985) was born in Cuba but was sent to Iowa in 1961 as part of "Operation Peter Pan," which relocated 14,000 unaccompanied Cuban children after the 1959 revolution brought Fidel Castro and communism to power in Cuba. Mendieta never fully recovered from the trauma of her removal: A sense of personal dislocation haunted her and a desire to leave her bodily imprint on the earth drove her art. Mendieta used ritualistic actions in performances that connected her to the earth. She was inspired by both *santería*, the African-Cuban religion (SEE FIG. 31–75), and the work of Beuys (SEE FIG. 32–15). Mendieta produced more than 200 body works called "Silhouettes" in which she explored ways to "plant" herself in the earth. She recorded these performances in photographs and on film. The **TREE OF LIFE** series **(FIG. 32–21)** was created in Iowa, where she studied and lived. This photograph shows Mendieta with arms upraised like an earth goddess, pressed against a tree and covered in mud, as if to invite the tree to absorb her and connect her to her "maternal source." Like many of Mendieta's other works, this piece celebrates the notion that women have a deeper identification with nature than do men.

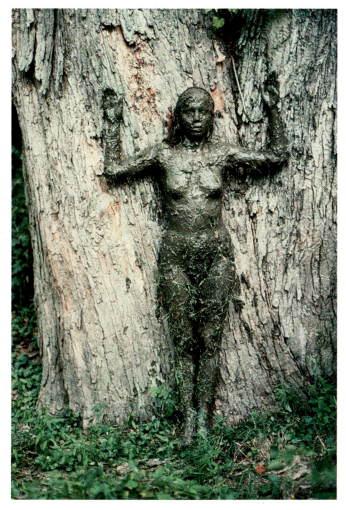

32-21 • Ana Mendieta UNTITLED, FROM THE TREE OF LIFE SERIES
1977. Color photograph, 20 × 13¼″ (50.8 × 33.7 cm). Courtesy of Galerie Lelong, New York and the estate of Ana Mendieta.

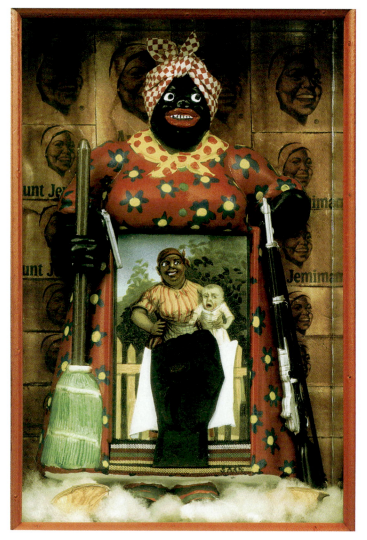

32-22 • Betye Saar THE LIBERATION OF AUNT JEMIMA

1972. Mixed media, 11¾ × 11⅞ × 2¾" (29.8 × 30.3 × 7 cm), Berkeley Art Museum, University of California. Purchased with the aid of funds from the National Endowment for the Arts (selected by The Committee for the Acquisition of Afro-American Art)

SAAR. African-American sculptor Betye Saar (b. 1926) makes works of art about race in America that are both militantly feminist and racially activist. For **THE LIBERATION OF AUNT JEMIMA (FIG. 32–22)**, Saar created a collage out of appropriated two- and three-dimensional images of the derogatory stereotype of a cheerfully servile "mammy," here transformed into a militant black feminist. The larger "mammy" figure is actually a notepad holder, to which Saar has attached another picture of a "mammy" holding a crying white child; in front of that is a large clenched black fist, the symbol of Black Power. In place of a pencil the main "mammy" holds a broom and a rifle. The rifle and fist contrast sharply with the repeated images of a smiling Aunt Jemima in the background. Saar's **appropriation** (taking material from one source and using it, unaltered, in another) of contrasting images from popular culture subverts and critiques the servile black female stereotype by both liberating her and threatening the viewer.

EARTHWORKS AND SITE-SPECIFIC SCULPTURE

In the early 1970s, as Process artists reintroduced the handcrafted into art, another group of artists began working with the earth as a medium to be manipulated, crafted, and changed. Earth artists used the land as their canvas. They made art outdoors, frequently manipulating raw materials found at the site to create **earthworks** that are usually **site-specific** (designed for a specific location). Some of these artists created vast sculptures that altered the landscape permanently, while others made ambitious works that only temporarily changed a place. Some Earth art is located in remote locations and is directly accessible to only a few people, while other examples have been made available to many. Earth art, like Performance and Conceptual art, is often intended to be noncommodifiable but it is frequently recorded in photographs and on film, with the result that these images become collectable objects. Earth art should not be confused with Environmental art: The former uses the land (or city) as a place on which to make art, whereas the latter seeks to draw attention to an imperiled natural environment.

SMITHSON. Robert Smithson (1938–1973) created **SPIRAL JETTY** (FIG. 32–23), one of the most significant earthworks, in 1970. This is a 1,500-foot spiraling earthen jetty that extends into the Great Salt Lake in Utah. To Smithson, the Great Salt Lake represented both a primordial ocean that cultivated life and a dead sea that killed it. Smithson liked the way that skeletons of abandoned oil rigs along the lake's shore looked like dinosaur bones; his jetty was supposed to remind viewers of the remains of ancient civilizations. Smithson also incorporated one of the few living organisms found in the otherwise dead lake into his work: an alga that turns a reddish color under certain conditions. Smithson's *Spiral Jetty* is one vehicle wide: To create the jetty, earth was hauled out into the lake in a huge land-moving truck.

Smithson used the spiral because it is an essential shape in nature and has been used in human art for millennia. The spiral curls and uncurls, endlessly suggesting growth and decay, creation and destruction. Smithson ordered that no maintenance be done on *Spiral Jetty*; he wanted the sculpture to be governed by the natural elements over time. The work was intended to illustrate the "ongoing dialectic" in nature between constructive and destructive forces. The jetty is now covered with crystallized salt; it remains visible today and can be seen on Google Earth.

CHRISTO AND JEANNE-CLAUDE. The most visible site-specific artists in America were Christo Javacheff (b. 1935) and Jeanne-Claude de Guillebon (1935–2009). Christo and Jeanne-Claude, as they were known, embarked on vast projects (both rural and urban) that sometimes took many years of planning to realize. In 1958, Christo emigrated from Bulgaria to Paris, where he met Jeanne-Claude; they moved to New York together in 1964. Their work was political and interventionist, frequently commenting on capitalism and consumer culture by wrapping or packaging buildings or large swatches of land in fabric: They "wrapped" the

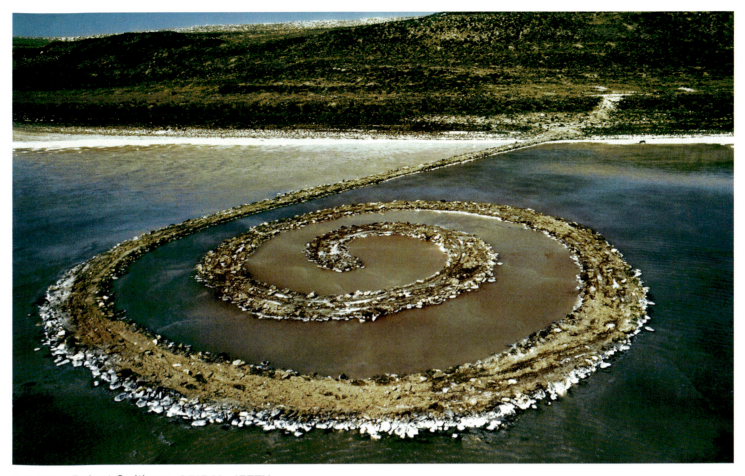

32-23 • Robert Smithson **SPIRAL JETTY**
1970. Mud, precipitated salt crystals, rocks, and water, length 1,500 × width 15′ (457 × 4.5 m). Great Salt Lake, Utah.
Collection: DIA Center for the Arts, New York

EXPLORE MORE: Click the Google Earth link for Spiral Jetty **www.myartslab.com**

Reichstag in Berlin and 1 million square feet of Australian coastline, for instance. In each case the process of planning and battling bureaucracies was part of the art, frequently taking years to complete. By contrast, the wrapping itself usually took only a few weeks and the completed project was in place for even less time. Christo and Jeanne-Claude funded each new project from the sale of books, Christo's original artworks like drawings, collages, and other ephemera relating to the preceding projects. In February 2005, Christo and Jeanne-Claude installed **THE GATES, CENTRAL PARK, NEW YORK, 1979-2005 (FIG. 32–24)**. This project took 26 years to realize, during which time the artists battled their way through various New York bureaucracies, meeting many obstacles and making changes to the work along the way. They finally installed 7,503 saffron-colored nylon panels on "gates" along 23 miles of pathway in Central Park. The brightly colored flapping panels enlivened the frigid February landscape and were an enormous public success. The installation lasted for only 16 days.

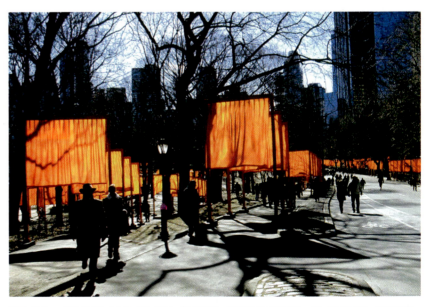

32-24 • Christo and Jeanne-Claude **THE GATES, CENTRAL PARK, NEW YORK CITY, 1979-2005**
1979–2005.

SEE MORE: View an interactive map of Christo's and Jeanne-Claude's *The Gates* **www.myartslab.com**

Controversies Over Public Funding for the Arts

Should public money help pay for art that some taxpayers believe to be offensive and indecent? This question started a political battle in 1989–1990 after controversial works of art by Robert Mapplethorpe (1946–1989) and Andres Serrano (b. 1950) went on public display in exhibitions funded in part by the National Endowment for the Arts (NEA), an agency of the Federal government. The ensuing debate pitted artists and museum administrators against political and religious figures. This battle over artists' rights and responsibilities is now referred to as the "Culture Wars."

Serrano's PISS CHRIST was at the center of the debate. Serrano did not use public money directly to create this work, but the Southeastern Center for Contemporary Art (SECCA), which exhibited *Piss Christ* in a group exhibition, was a recipient of NEA funds. The Reverend Donald Wildmon, leader of the American Family Association, described *Piss Christ* as "hate-filled, bigoted, anti-Christian, and obscene," and told his many followers to flood Congress and the NEA with letters protesting the misuse of public funds. This resulted in several high-profile conservative Republican politicians joining his attack.

At the same time, the traveling exhibition "The Perfect Moment," a retrospective of the work of photographer Mapplethorpe, who had recently died from AIDS, was canceled by the Corcoran Gallery of Art in Washington, D.C., for fear that the show's content might cause offense. "The Perfect Moment" had been organized by the Institute of Contemporary Art (ICA) in Philadelphia, was NEA-funded, and included several homoerotic and sadomasochistic images. When it was shown in Cincinnati, the museum director was arrested. Additionally, four artists known as the "NEA Four" (Karen Finley, John Fleck, Holly Hughes, and Tim Miller), who made lesbian, gay, or radical feminist art, had their grants rescinded amid a flurry of debate. Congress slashed NEA funding by $45,000: the amount of Serrano's $15,000 SECCA grant, plus the ICA's $30,000 grant for the Mapplethorpe show. The NEA Four sued and won back their grants, but a so-called "obscenity clause" was added to NEA regulations requiring jurors to consider the "general standards of decency and respect for the diverse beliefs and values of the American public" when making awards.

During the next five years, the NEA was largely restructured by the Republican-controlled House of Representatives, some of whose members wanted to eliminate the agency altogether. In 1996, Congress reduced the NEA's budget by 40 percent.

Controversies over public funding continued, however. In 1999, the Brooklyn Museum of Art exhibited "Sensation: Young British Artists from the Saatchi Collection," causing another major controversy over public funding and offensive art. The Brooklyn Museum kept the show open in direct defiance of a threat from Mayor Rudolph Giuliani to eliminate city funding and evict the museum from its city-owned building if it persisted in showing art that he considered "sick" and "disgusting." Giuliani and Catholic leaders took particular offense at Chris Ofili's *The Holy Virgin Mary* (SEE FIG. 32–45). When the Brooklyn Museum of Art still refused to cancel the show, Giuliani withheld the city's monthly maintenance payment to the museum of $497,554 and filed a suit in the state court to revoke its lease. In response, the museum filed for an injunction against Giuliani's actions on the grounds that they violated the First Amendment and the United States District Court for the Eastern District of New York eventually barred Giuliani from punishing or retaliating against the museum in any way for mounting the exhibition. Guiliani had argued that Ofili's art fostered religious intolerance, but the court ruled that the government has "no legitimate interest in protecting any or all religions from views distasteful to them," adding that taxpayers "subsidize all manner of views with which they do not agree" and even those "they abhor."

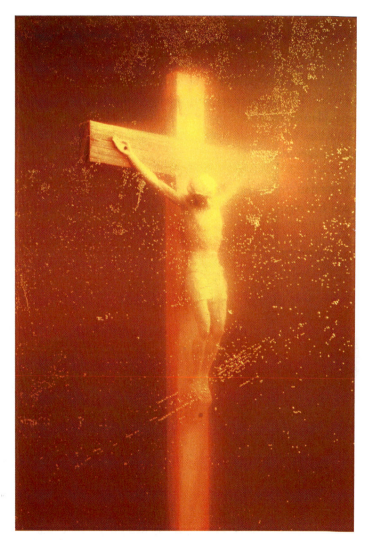

Andres Serrano **PISS CHRIST**
1989. Cibachrome print mounted on Plexiglas,
23½ × 16″ (59.7 × 40.6 cm).

and how easily they can be destroyed. As the other houses around it were demolished, Whiteread sprayed concrete on the inner walls of her house to make a cast of the space within it. Then she dismantled the house. The white concrete left behind outlined a ghostly trace of the space within the house that had once been someone's home. The publicity surrounding Whiteread's *House* brought to the fore several critical issues in British society, including homelessness, the costs and benefits of urban renewal, and the place of the working class in society. Whiteread's piece demonstrates how a work of visual art can articulate controversial issues in ways that are impossible using other means of communication. Whiteread intended *House* to make a political statement about "the state of housing in England; the ludicrous policy of knocking down homes like this and building badly designed tower blocks which themselves have to be knocked down after 20 years."

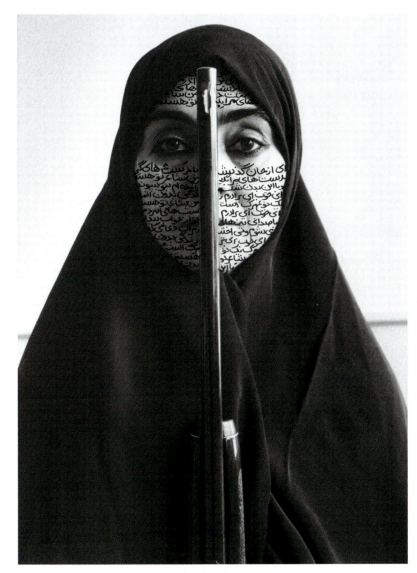

32-51 • Shirin Neshat REBELLIOUS SILENCE
1994. Black-and-white RC print and ink (photo taken by C. Preston), 11 × 14" (27.9 × 35.6 cm). Barbara Gladstone Gallery, New York.

EXPLORE MORE: Gain insight from a primary source by Shirin Neshat www.myartslab.com

POSTCOLONIAL DISCOURSE

With increased migration and the expansion of global communications and economies, questions of personal, political, cultural, and national identity also emerged in the 1990s. Postcolonial artists began to explore issues of contested identity and the identity struggle of postcolonial peoples, and to investigate the dissonance produced by transnational (mis)communication between colonizers and the postcolonized. Many of these artists, such as Shirin Neshat and Rasheed Araeen, speak with unfamiliar but forthright and significant new artistic voices.

NESHAT. In **REBELLIOUS SILENCE** (FIG. 32–51) from her 1994 "Women of Allah" series of photographs, Shirin Neshat (b. 1957) explores how Iranian women are stereotyped by the West. Her photographs and videos assert that Islamic women's identities are more varied and complex than is frequently perceived. Each of Neshat's "Women of Allah" photographs portrays both a part of an Iranian woman's body, such as her hands or her feet, overwritten with Farsi text and with a weapon. In *Rebellious Silence*, the woman wears the traditional chador but her face is visible, written over with calligraphy and with a rifle barrel bisecting it vertically. The calligraphy and rifle barrel seem to protect her from the viewer, but they also create a sense of incomprehensibility or foreignness that prompts us to try to categorize her. Likewise, although the woman wears a chador, she looks directly and defiantly out of the photograph at us, meeting our gaze and returning it. She challenges us to acknowledge her as an individual, in this case a strong and beautiful woman; but the image simultaneously and paradoxically prompts us to see her as a stereotypical Iranian woman in a chador more than as an individual. Neshat's photograph asks us to confront our prejudices while also raising questions about women's power and feminism in contemporary Iran.

ARAEEN. Rasheed Araeen (b. 1935) is from Pakistan and lives in London. He founded the journal *Black Phoenix* in 1978, which in 1989 became *Third Text*, a leading journal on postcolonial art, culture, and ethnicity. In 1985–1986, Araeen made **GREEN PAINTING IV** (FIG. 32–52), a work comprised of nine equal-sized panels. The five central panels contain photographs of the head of a young bull prepared for ritual sacrifice with garlands around its neck and framed by Urdu text. The other four panels are painted a flat green—the primary color in the Pakistani flag, an important color in Islam, and a color that Araeen associates with youthful rawness and flexibility, like a green twig. Yet the central panels also appear to form a crucifix. Araeen has said that his pictures are not just superimpositions of Western and Pakistani cultures, but are images that speak about "cutting and

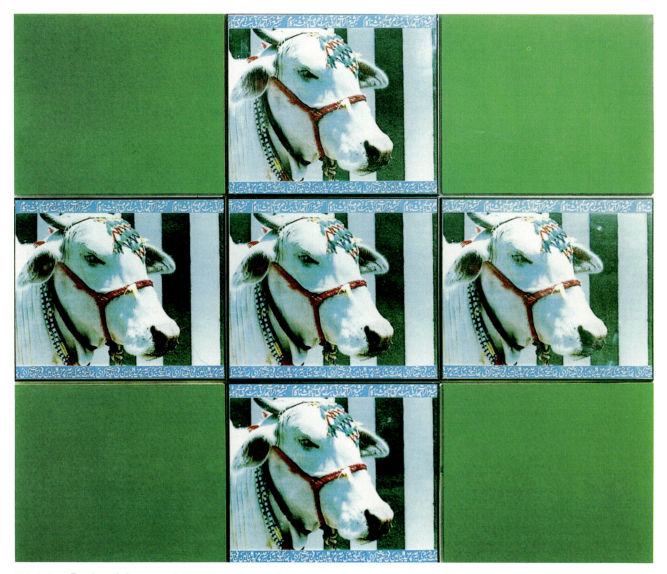

32-52 • Rasheed Araeen GREEN PAINTING IV
1985–1986. Five color photographs with Urdu text and acrylic on four
plywood panels, 5′9″ × 6′10″ (1.75 × 2.08 m). Collection of the artist.

rupturing," that investigate postcolonial dissonance and mis-
communication. He argues that when someone British or
American sees the cross in his art, for instance, they almost
invariably read Pakistani culture through a Christian lens, thereby
distorting, misinterpreting, and stereotyping the "other." Araeen's
art demands a more nuanced understanding of cultures on their
own terms and according to their own visual languages.

SEARLE. Berni Searle (b. 1964) explores her South African
identity in the wake of Apartheid in her art. In the **COLOR ME**
series **(FIG. 32–53)**, she photographs her head and torso covered in
powdered pigment that changes her skin color from red to yellow
to brown to white. Searle asks us to see that race and identity are
not as simple as skin pigmentation, and that superficial or skin-
deep characteristics do not define a person. The fragility and
impermanence of the pigmentation also underscore the instability
of stereotypes and the complexity of real identity.

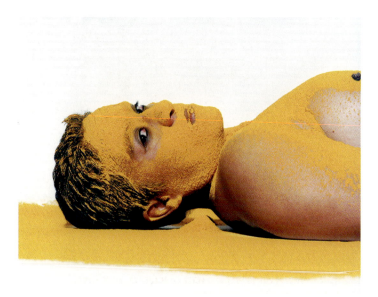

32-53 • Berni Searle
UNTITLED FROM COLOR ME SERIES
1998. Michael Stevenson Gallery, Cape Town.

HIGH TECH AND DECONSTRUCTIVIST ARCHITECTURE

Architecture and architectural practice was transformed in the 1980s and 1990s by computer-aided design (CAD) programs with 3-D graphics. These programs enabled architects to design structures virtually, to calculate engineering stresses faster and more precisely, to experiment with new ways to use advanced building technologies and materials, and to imagine new ways of composing a building's mass.

HIGH TECH ARCHITECTURE. High Tech architects broke out of the restrictive shape of the Modernist "glass box" (SEE FIG. 32–25) to experiment with dramatically designed engineering marvels. These buildings are characterized by a spectacular use of new technologies, materials, equipment, and components, and frequently by their visible display of service systems such as heating and power.

The **HONG KONG & SHANGHAI BANK (FIG. 32–54)** by the British architect Norman Foster (b. 1935) is among the most spectacular examples of High Tech architecture. Foster was invited to spare no expense in designing this futuristic 47-story skyscraper. The loadbearing steel skeleton, composed of giant masts and girders, is on the exterior. The individual stories hang from it, making possible the uninterrupted rows of windows that fill the building with natural light. In addition, the banking hall in the lower part of the building has a ten-story atrium space that is flooded with daylight refracted into it by motorized "sunscoops" at the top of the structure that are programmed to track the sun's rays and channel them into the building. The sole concession Foster makes to tradition in this design is his placement of two bronze lions flanking the public entrance. These were taken from the bank's previous headquarters; touching the lions before entering the bank is believed to bring good luck.

DECONSTRUCTIVIST ARCHITECTURE. Deconstructivist architecture, a more theory-based architecture than High Tech, emerged in the early 1990s. Deconstructivist architects deliberately disturb traditional architectural assumptions about harmony, unity, and stability to create "decentered," skewed, and distorted designs. Several Deconstructivist architects admire the aesthetic of Russian Suprematists and Constructivists (SEE FIGS. 31–26, 31–46), which they frequently combine with the principles of Deconstruction as developed by the French philosopher Jacques Derrida (1930–2004). Derridean Deconstruction asserts that no written text possesses a single, intrinsic meaning. For Derrida, meaning is always "intertextual," thus a product of one text's relationship to other texts: It is always "decentered," "dispersed," or "diffused" through an infinite web of "signs," which themselves have unstable meanings. Deconstructivist architecture is likewise intertextual, in that it plays with meaning by mixing diverse architectural features, forms, and contexts, and is decentered in its diffusion as well as in its perceived instability of both meaning and form.

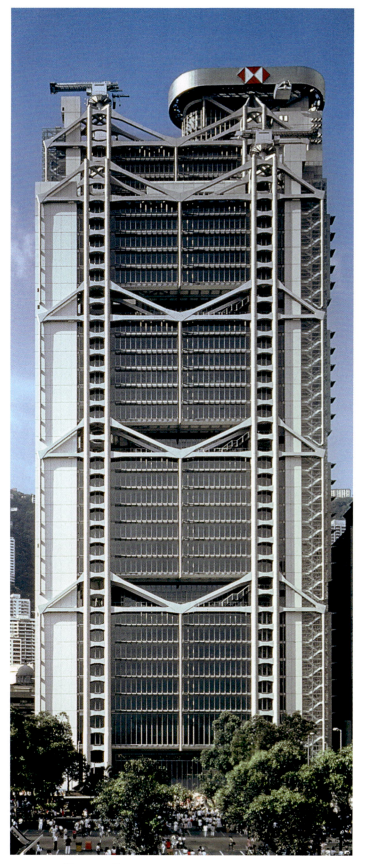

32-54 • Norman Foster **HONG KONG & SHANGHAI BANK**
Hong Kong. 1986.

SEE MORE: View a simulation about the Hong Kong & Shanghai Bank www.myartslab.com

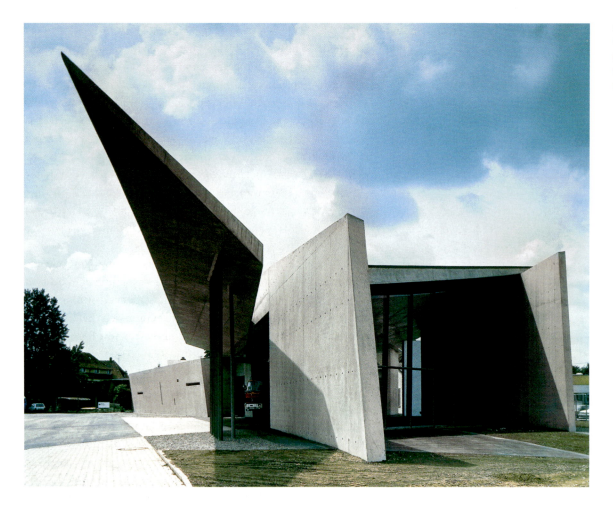

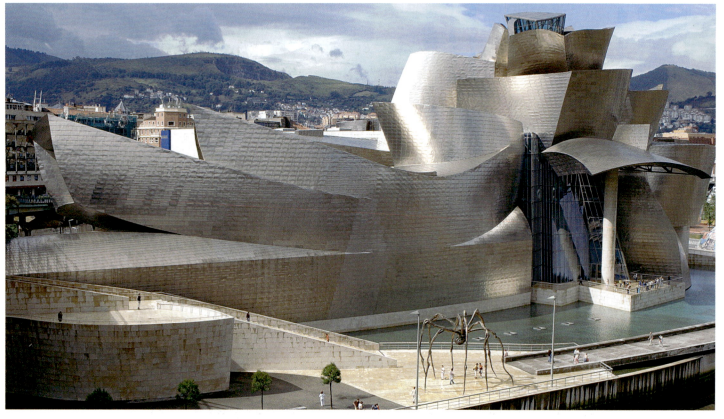

32-56 • Frank O. Gehry **GUGGENHEIM MUSEUM**
Bilbao, Spain. 1993–1997.

A good example of Deconstructivist architecture is the **VITRA FIRE STATION** in Weil-am-Rhein, Germany (FIG. 32–55) by the Baghdad-born architect Zaha Hadid (b. 1950), who studied in London and established her practice there in 1979. Formally influenced by the paintings of Kasimir Malevich (SEE FIG. 31–25), the Vitra Fire Station features reinforced concrete walls that lean into one another, meet at unexpected angles, and jut out dramatically into space, denying a sense of visual unity but creating a feeling of immediacy, speed, and dynamism appropriate to the building's function.

The Toronto-born, California-based Frank O. Gehry (b. 1929) also creates unstable and Deconstructivist building masses and curved winglike shapes that extend far beyond the building's mass. One of his most spectacular designs is the **GUGGENHEIM MUSEUM** in Bilbao, Spain (FIG. 32–56). In the 1990s, art-museum designs became more and more spectacular as the museum increasingly came to define the visual landscape of cities. Gehry developed this asymmetrical design using a CATIA CAD program that enabled him to create a powerfully organic, sculptural structure. The complex steel skeleton is covered by a thin skin of silvery titanium that shimmers gold or silver depending on the time of day and the weather conditions. From the north the building resembles a living organism, while from other angles it looks like a giant ship, referencing the industry on which Bilbao has traditionally depended and thereby identifying the museum with the city. Despite the sculptural beauty of the museum, however, the interior is a notoriously difficult space in which to display art.

VIDEO AND FILM

In the last decades of the twentieth century, the rapid development and increasingly widespread availability of hand-held video cameras created a new medium for artists. Video artists rejected traditional forms and meanings to make art that was deliberately nonprecious, often using the video image to address the place and prevalence of television in our culture. Today Video art is even more prevalent because of the explosion in digital and visual imagery. In fact, most contemporary Video art is digitally produced, while innovations in projecting video and DVD images on large screens (or on any surface) have transformed how and where Video art is projected and to a certain extent its subject.

PAIK. One of the pioneers of Video art was the Korean-born Nam June Paik (1931–2006), who made experimental music in the late 1950s and early 1960s under the influence of John Cage. He began working with modified television sets in 1963, and began making Video art in 1965, the same year that Sony released the first portable video camera. Paik predicted that just "as collage technique replaced oil paint, the cathode ray [television] tube will replace the canvas." Later, he worked with live, recorded, and computer-generated images displayed on video monitors of varying sizes, which he often combined into works of art such as **ELECTRONIC SUPERHIGHWAY: CONTINENTAL U.S.** (FIG. 32–57), a site-specific sculpture created for the Holly Solomon Gallery in New York. This featured a neon outline map of the United States set against a wall of dozens of computer-controlled video monitors

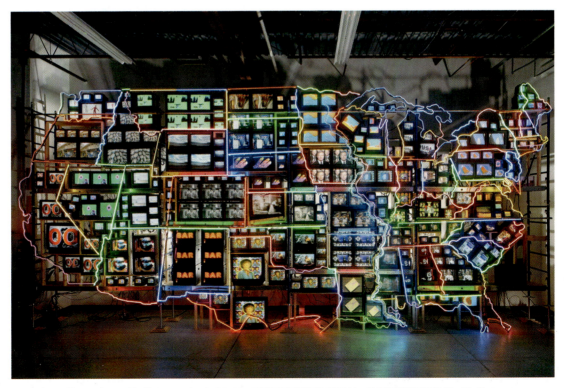

32-57 • Nam June Paik ELECTRONIC SUPERHIGHWAY: CONTINENTAL U.S.
1995. Forty-seven-channel closed-circuit video installation with 313 monitors, neon, steel structure, color, and sound, approx. 15 × 32 × 4' (4.57 × 9.75 × 1.2 m). Courtesy Holly Solomon Gallery, New York.

displaying rapidly changing soundtracked images that reflected each state's culture and history. The work addresses both the prevalence and power of the mixed messages transmitted by television in our society. The monitor for New York State projected a closed-circuit live video feed of gallery visitors, who were thus transformed from passive spectators into active participants in the piece as the monitor constructed their media identity in front of them as they watched.

VIOLA.   In 1996, the California video artist Bill Viola (b. 1951) created **THE CROSSING** (FIG. **32–58)** which consists of a double projection of two brilliantly colored videos on opposite sides of a 16-foot screen. On one side, Viola projects a video loop of a silhouette of a man who slowly emerges from the background to fill the entire screen. As he does this, a drop of water starts to fall, growing in size as the man moves forward slowly until at last a deluge washes him away. The soundtrack meanwhile goes from a small dripping noise to a torrential roar. On the reverse screen, a similar scenario unfolds, except that this time the man appears in the background with tiny flames licking at his feet that grow into a wild conflagration that finally engulfs him. This side also has a soundtrack of the sound of the fire growing in intensity. But Viola's piece is about the way that vision informs perception, and there is in fact only one soundtrack—we simply perceive it differently according to whatever image we are watching. This video is profoundly sensory but also meditative; its elemental symbolism is informed by Viola's spirituality and intense study of world religions.

GLOBALISM: INTO THE NEW MILLENNIUM

In the last decade, the growth in international art exhibitions and art fairs has created new opportunities for artists, dealers, and collectors to meet and network in ways that, until quite recently, would have been considered impossible, or unproductive. Until recently the only truly international fora for new art were the Venice Biennale (established in 1903 and held every two years) and Documenta, in Kassel, West Germany (established in 1955 and held roughly every five years). Today there are at least 30 international biennial exhibitions around the world, as well as many more vast international art fairs: Art Basel in Switzerland, Art Basel Miami in Miami Beach, the Frieze Art Fair in London, the Armory Show in New York, and the Fiore Internationale d'Art Contemporain (FIAC) in Paris, to mention just a few. Finally, the Internet has allowed visual access to art globally. We can find information on practically any exhibited art, and much that is not exhibited, on

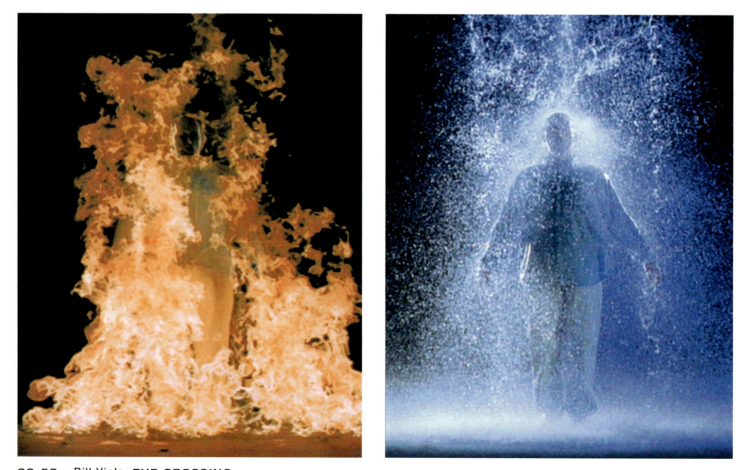

32-58 • Bill Viola THE CROSSING
1996. Video/sound installation with two channels of color video projection onto screens 16′ (4.88 m) high. Private collection.

our laptops. This new globalism has forced artists to question not just how their own identities but also how those of others are formed, and to realize that neither identity nor art is as simple or as univalent as it might have seemed as recently as in the 1990s.

Art in the new millennium seems to be heading in several directions simultaneously, constantly shifting and recalibrating new perspectives and concerns as part of an increasingly complicated global discourse. The art of our own times may be the most difficult to classify and analyze, but it has increasingly focused on global issues, raising questions about national identities, ethnic or racial identities, colonial and postcolonial identities, human rights, global economic, political, and natural environments, the widening divide between the rich and poor nations of the world, and technological change in every aspect of our lives. Today's artists are actively engaged in society at all levels and their art frequently reflects their ambition to be agents of change in troubling and unstable times.

ART AND TECHNOLOGY

STUDIO CRAFTS. Dale Chihuly (b. 1941) has been producing major public sculptures in glass for 30 years, but his creations are as fresh today as they were in 1975. Chihuly's sculptures are both technologically innovative and experimental. **THE SUN** (FIG. 32–59), a multi-part blown-glass sculpture using the latest glass-making techniques, shows Chihuly's profound interest in natural forms and global energies. The sun bursts forth in a multitude of twisting, wriggling, spiraling forms as if the unremittingly intense light of Phoenix has taken physical shape and come to life. Brilliantly liquid, visually thrilling, and accessible, Chihuly's sculptures suggest a deeper connection with nature, inviting contemplation, meditation, and an awareness of global environmentalism.

DIGITAL PHOTOGRAPHY SINCE 2000. Photography has always been a malleable and mutable medium. Even in the nineteenth century photographs were manipulated to create fictional imagery out of what appeared to be a factual visual record. It is often difficult and time-consuming to manipulate a chemical-mechanical process, however, and it was only with the development of digital technology that manipulation became a fast, easy, and standard way to create photographic images.

The Canadian artist Jeff Wall (b. 1946) uses multiple digital photographs and elaborate stage sets to create large complex photographic narratives that he considers analogous to the history paintings of the nineteenth century, and which he exhibits as gloriously colored transparencies mounted in light boxes—the format frequently used in modern advertising in public places.

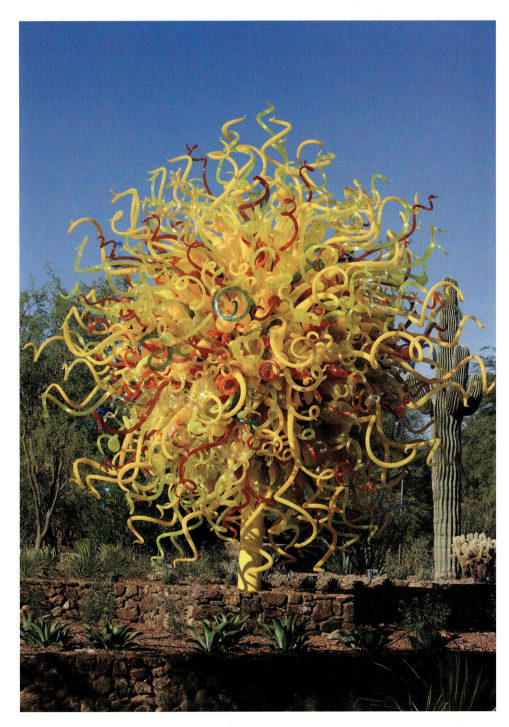

32–59 • Dale Chihuly THE SUN
2008. Desert Botanical Garden, Phoenix, Arizona. Installed November 22, 2008– May 31, 2009.

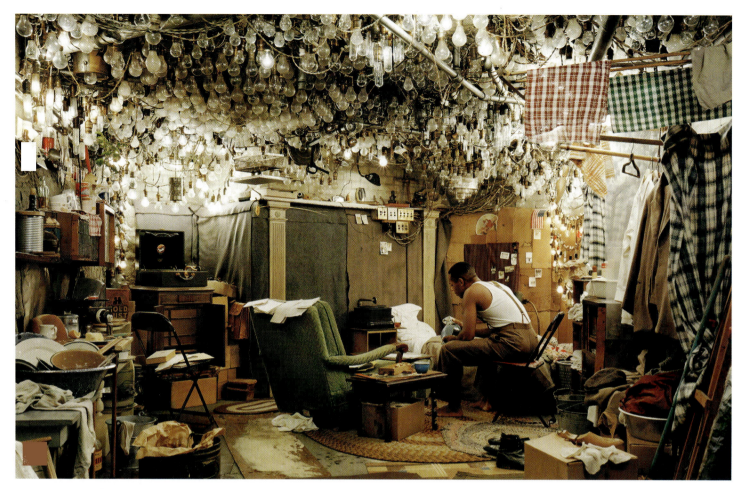

32-60 • Jeff Wall **AFTER "INVISIBLE MAN" BY RALPH ELLISON, THE PREFACE**
1999–2001. Transparency in lightbox, 68½ × 98⅝" (174 × 250.5 cm).

EXPLORE MORE: Gain insight from a primary source related to Jeff Wall www.myartslab.com

Wall creates his photographs like a movie director, carefully designing the sets and posing his actors. He takes multiple photographs that he then combines digitally to create one final transparency. **AFTER "INVISIBLE MAN" BY RALPH ELLISON, THE PREFACE** (FIG. 32–60) is an elaborate composition for which Wall spent 18 months designing and constructing the sets and three weeks actually taking photographs. The image illustrates a passage from Ralph Ellison's 1951 novel about an African-American man's search for fulfillment that ends in disillusionment and retreat. Wall shows us the cellar room, "warm and full of light," to which Ellison's character retreats and which is heated and lit by 1,369 light bulbs powered by electricity stolen from the power company. For Ellison, these lights seem to illuminate the sad truth of the character's existence.

INSTALLATION ART. Tony Oursler's 2009 exhibition at Metro Pictures raises issues about how the average American constructs his or her identity in the digital age. The installation (art installed in a specific space for which it was made) included several oversized sculptural versions of the things that we cannot seem to live without today: an enormous cell phone entitled **MULTIPLEXED** (FIG. 32–61), a giant five-dollar bill, a "forest of smoldering cigarettes," an arrangement of oversized self-help books, and a Genie bottle containing a video of the artist himself. Oursler's exhibition is a clever updating of Pop art's critique of consumer society, making sly references to Warhol, Oldenburg, and even Lichtenstein (SEE FIGS. 32–10, 32–11, 32–12). Objects come to life by means of superimposed animated video projections that make the cigarettes seem to burn, "Abe" Lincoln to pull faces, Oursler himself to try to escape his bottle, and the cell phone (in this illustration) to spew forth, as the press release states, "disjointed snippets of conversations." Oursler asks us to consider how the world of technology, constantly bombarding us with images, creates an intense visual overload and frames our concept of identity.

ART AND IDENTITIES

The artists featured in this final section investigate their individual and group identities—a growing and ever-more complex concern in the new millennium—in a wide range of ways, breaking down traditional distinctions between medium and message in the process, and dissolving boundaries to create art that is as interesting, exciting, difficult, and confusing as the world itself is today.

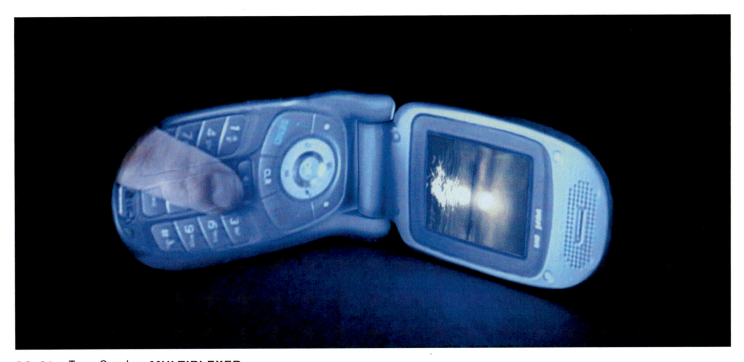

32–61 • Tony Oursler MULTIPLEXED
2008. Fiberglass, 37 × 33 × 17" (94 × 83.8 × 43.2 cm).
MetroPicture (MP 574)

BARNEY.   Between 1994 and 2002, Matthew Barney (b. 1967) created a now legendary series of films entitled *The Cremaster Cycle* in which he developed an arcane sexual mythology. The cycle is premised on the concept of gender mutability, questioning gender assignation and roles throughout. The cremaster muscle for which the series is named controls the ascent and descent of the testes, usually in response to changes in temperature but also in response to fear or sexual arousal, and it also determines sexual differentiation in the human embryo. Barney uses a diagrammatic representation of the cremaster muscle as his visual emblem throughout the series.

Each film has its own complex narrative and catalog of multilayered symbols. *Cremaster 3* (2002) describes the construction of the Chrysler Building in New York and features Richard Serra (SEE FIG. 32–42) as the architect. A segment of the film is set in the Guggenheim Museum's rotunda (SEE FIG. 32–27). Barney, playing Serra's apprentice and dressed in a peach-colored kilt and gagged, must accomplish a series of tasks to assert his supremacy over Serra. As in a video game, Barney scales the walls of the Guggenheim rotunda to complete a task on each level before gaining enlightenment. Along the way he is challenged by a line of Rockettes dressed as Masonic lambs, by warring punk-rock bands, by a leopard woman (played by Aimee Mullins), and finally by Serra. The settings and costumes are lavish, and the epic plot is baroquely interconnected. In **MAHABYN (FIG. 32–62)**, Barney and the leopard woman transform into Masons—they are shown here in modified Masonic costume.

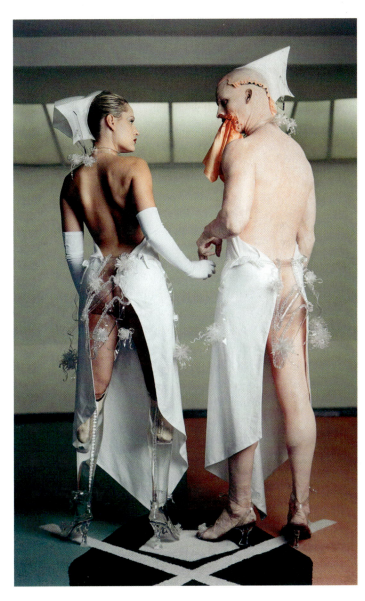

32–62 • Matthew Barney CREMASTER 3: MAHABYN
2002. 46½ × 54 × 1½" (118 × 137 × 3.8 cm). Guggenheim Museum, New York.

The entire filmic cycle addresses the crisis of identity experienced by white, middle-class heterosexual male artists in America in an era seemingly dominated by identity politics.

BEECROFT.   Vanessa Beecroft also set her **VB35** (FIG. 32–63) in the Guggenheim Museum's rotunda and also uses performance to examine gender roles, although she explores perceptions of the female body and femininity. Unlike Barney, she does not appear in her work. Many of Beecroft's performances refer obliquely to her own battle with anorexia. The artist numbers her performances—*vb35* is her 35th piece—and in it she questions both the nature of today's distorted concept of feminine beauty and voyeuristic looking. For the performance, Beecroft hired 15 professional fashion models, each of whom was fashionably thin, tall, and white. The models were directed to stand in a loose group, facing forward. Ten wore high heels and designer bikinis, while five wore nothing but high heels. They stood staring blankly ahead while the audience was permitted to observe them from the foyer or the ramp of the museum, thus acquiescing in the gaze that objectified them. The event was "invitation only" so the atmosphere was charged with

exclusivity, but Beecroft complicated this piece by heightening the tension in two ways: First, the group of professional models whose business it is to be looked at commanded the museum; and second, the audience was instructed to behave in very precise ways—they were not allowed to speak to the models, make eye contact with them, or invade their physical or emotional space in any way. This strategy cleverly inverted the normal relationship between looker and looked-at. A sexual charge filled the air, but ironically the models claimed control. Viewers found that they were intimidated and discomforted: They felt as though they had been caught in the act of looking illicitly. As one critic put it: "we found ourselves confronted by the cool authority of the art's nakedness, and we had no role to play … so we drifted and loitered."

GU.   Wenda Gu (b. 1955) dedicates his art to bringing people together. Trained in traditional ink painting at China's National Academy of Fine Arts, he emigrated to the United States in 1987 and began an ongoing global project entitled the "United Nations Series" in 1992. Each "monument" in this series is made from human hair collected from barbershops and hair salons worldwide

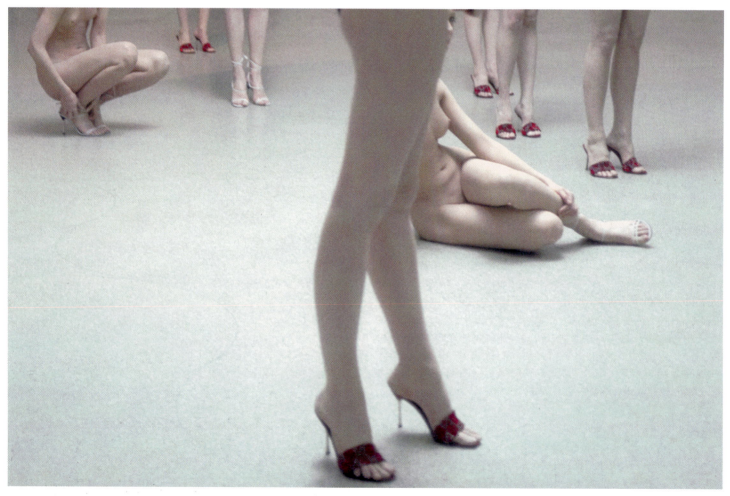

32-63 • Vanessa Beecroft **VB35**
1998. Performance.

EXPLORE MORE: Gain insight from a primary source by Vanessa Beecroft **www.myartslab.com**

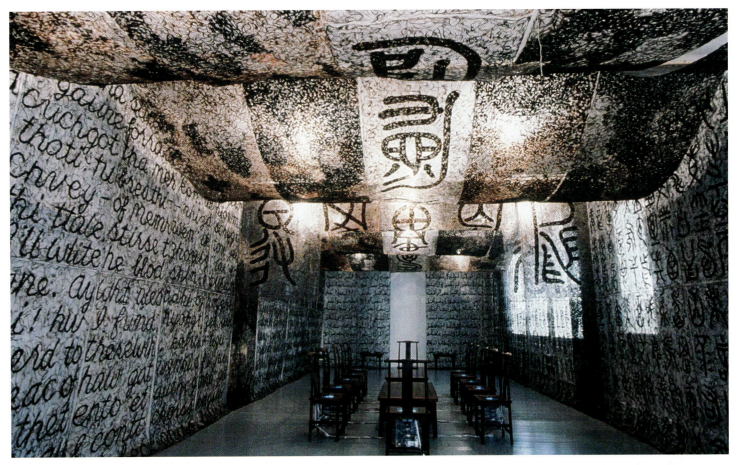

32-64 • Wenda Gu UNITED NATIONS SERIES: TEMPLE OF HEAVEN
1998. Installation with screens of human hair, wooden chairs and tables, and video. Commissioned by the Asia Society. Collection of the artist.

and which Gu presses into bricks or weaves into carpets and curtains covered with ideograms of his own invention. **UNITED NATIONS SERIES: TEMPLE OF HEAVEN** (FIG. 32–64) contains hair from many different nations and blended scripts based on Chinese, English, Hindi, and Arabic characters that "evoke the limitations of human knowledge." Gu also creates "national" monuments—examples have been installed in Poland, Israel, and Taiwan, among other places—made from hair collected in, and addressing issues specific to, that particular country. The "transnational" monuments from the "United Nations Series," on the other hand, address more global themes, using hair blended from several different countries to suggest a "brave new racial identity" for the new millennium.

OSPINA. In his series **COLOMBIA LAND** (FIG. 32–65), the Colombian artist Nadín Ospina (b. 1960) uses Lego figures, blown up in photographs and sculptures to gargantuan size, to caricature stereotypical images of Colombia as a nation of drug lords and violence. *Colombia Land* is a funny but also sinister parody of a Legoland theme park. In this piece, Ospina mimics a typical *National Geographic* cover by placing a Lego bandit with an automatic weapon, bands of ammunition slung across his chest, and

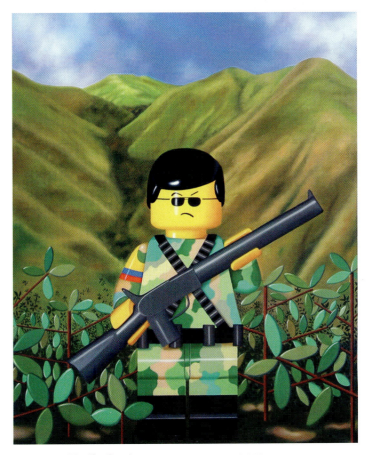

32-65 • Nadín Ospina COLOMBIA LAND
2004. Centro Cultural de la Universidad de Salamanca, Bogotá.

dark glasses hiding his eyes, amid a crop of drugs. Such a figure would be threatening were he not transformed into a child's toy. Ospina describes Colombia as "an art and culture hijacked by violence," and his art explores the cultural colonization of Colombia by Western European and American popular culture as well as Colombia's own complicated self-perceptions.

HAMMONS. A socially minded artist strongly committed to working in the public realm, David Hammons (b. 1943) is an out-spoken critic of the gallery system in America, lamenting the lack of challenging content and representation of African Americans in exhibitions. He has described the art world as being "like Novocain. It used to wake you up but now it puts you to sleep." Hammons argues that only art that intervenes in and transacts with society is uncontaminated by commerce and still jolts people awake. In **UNTITLED** (FIG. 32–66), the artist creates a witty but biting satire on the still ambiguous place of African Americans in American society. Hammons originally created this flag in 1990 for the Studio Museum, Harlem, in response to a controversy concerning the flying of the Confederate flag on public buildings in some states. It has since been installed in several other museums, including the Museum of Modern Art in New York in 2000. The colors in Hammons's flag are those of the Pan-African or Universal Negro Improvement Association and African Communities League flag, which was created in 1920 by African Americans to symbolize the "Rights of Negro Peoples of the World." The red stands for the blood that unites all people of African descent and that was spilled in the quest for liberation; the black stands for the symbolic nation of black people; and the green stands for the verdant lands of Africa. The piece makes a poignant and pointed comment about race in America.

SHONIBARE. Yinka Shonibare (b. 1962) is a British-Nigerian artist based in London. His art examines how identity is informed, perceived, and constructed through the twists and turns of colonial history, as well as class, race, and self-perception. **HOW TO BLOW UP TWO HEADS AT ONCE (LADIES)** (FIG. 32–67) is a life-size sculpture of two headless women whose skin color, and thus on a superficial level whose race, is indeterminate. Although the figures have women's bodies, they seem to have masculine hands. They face off against one another in a dueling pose with nineteenth-century flintlock pistols drawn and pointed at each other's absent heads. They wear what appear to be nineteenth-century costumes, but their brightly colored dresses are made of a Dutch wax fabric that is usually associated with West African nations. The complexities of the history and use of the fabric, and the way that Shonibare uses it, give us some idea of the multiple and eliding meanings in this sculpture. This brilliantly colored and patterned fabric, worn by millions of Africans today, originally came from Indonesia, was imported and copied by Dutch colonists in Africa, was manufactured in bulk in cotton mills in Manchester, England, and was then exported to West Africa, where it was copied, modified, transformed, and now possessed by West African cultures. Ironically, Shonibare buys the fabric for his sculptures at London's

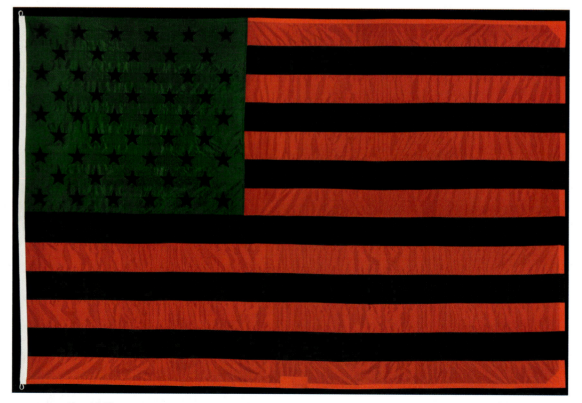

32-66 • David Hammons UNTITLED
2004. Studio Museum, Harlem. Nylon, 6 × 10′ (1.82 × 3 m). Gift of the artist (04.2.19)

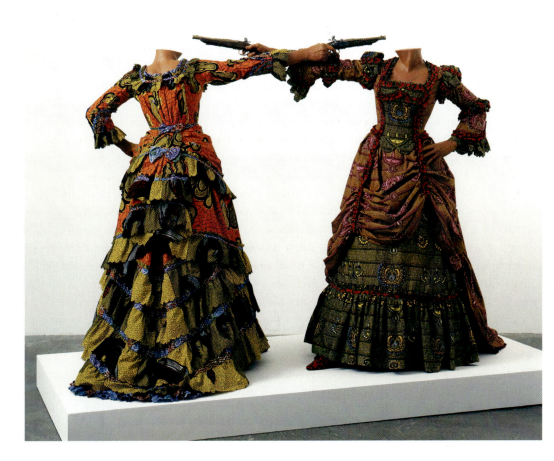

32-67 • Yinka Shonibare, MBE

HOW TO BLOW UP TWO HEADS AT ONCE (LADIES) 2006. Two fiberglass mannequins, two prop guns, Dutch, wax printed cotton textile, shoes, leather riding boots, plinth, 93½ × 63 × 48″ (237 × 160 × 122 cm). Museum purchase with funds provided by Wellesley College Friends of Art, 2007.124.1-2

Brixton market. Shonibare challenges our perceptions about issues of race, postcolonialism, property, ownership, violence, and class. His work, although witty and ironic, is also acerbic as it shows us the tangled web of forces that construct identity.

SIERRA.   Santiago Sierra (b. 1966), a Spanish artist who lives in Mexico City, addresses race, ethnicity, and the capitalist exploitation of the poor in his interventionist artworks. At the 49th Venice Biennale in 2001, Sierra created a very visible commentary on the luxurious indulgence and elitist atmosphere of the exhibition and on the relative invisibility of both poverty and race there. For this piece, Sierra paid 133 non-European men to dye their naturally black hair blond and to make themselves visible around Venice for the duration of the exhibition **(FIG. 32–68)**. The shocking white hair on dark-skinned men made them very visible and placed a group of individuals who normally melt into the background of society front and center, persistently reminding viewers of both their presence and their relative poverty—the only reason their hair was blond was because they needed the money.

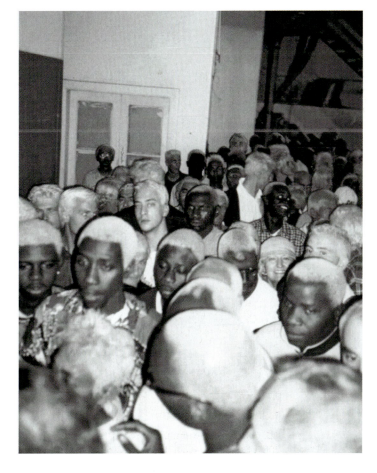

32-68 • Santiago Sierra **133 PEOPLE PAID TO HAVE THEIR HAIR DYED BLOND**
2001. 49th Venice Biennale

Sierra paid 133 non-European men to dye their hair blond. In the exhibition, he presented video footage of the dyeing process.

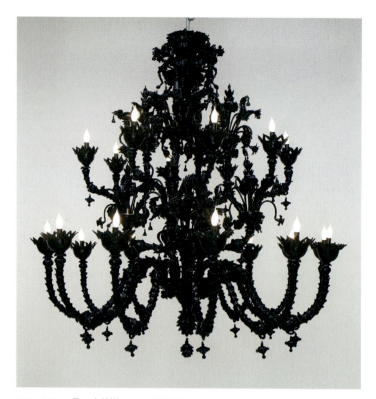

32–69 • Fred Wilson CHANDELIER MORI
2003. United States Pavilion, 50th Venice Biennale.

WILSON. In the 1990s, artists increasingly began to critique the constructed narratives of the traditional museum exhibition. The museum was acknowledged as a place in which curators, who make decisions about what to show and how to arrange works in an exhibition, create history rather than revealing it and, in the process, frequently reveal their own prejudices. Fred Wilson (b. 1954) is best known for *Mining the Museum* (1992), a brilliant interventionist piece in which he inverted and subverted the Baltimore Historical Society's collection. Wilson "mined" the museum's storage area and found that, while the objects on show were mostly about white history, there were numerous objects relating to African-American history in the vaults. He "inserted" many of these into the main museum display, including some horrific objects used to restrain African-American slaves, thereby upsetting and reshaping the story told in the original exhibition.

In 2003, Wilson represented the United States at the Venice Biennale with *Speak of Me As I Am*, a multi-part installation that focused on the history of Africans in Venice. This included several black sculptures made with Murano glass, a kind of glass made in Venice for centuries, set in a black-and-white tiled room with "graffiti" on the walls consisting of excerpts from African-American slave narratives and a video installation of Shakespeare's *Othello* being screened backwards. The title of the work, *Speak of*

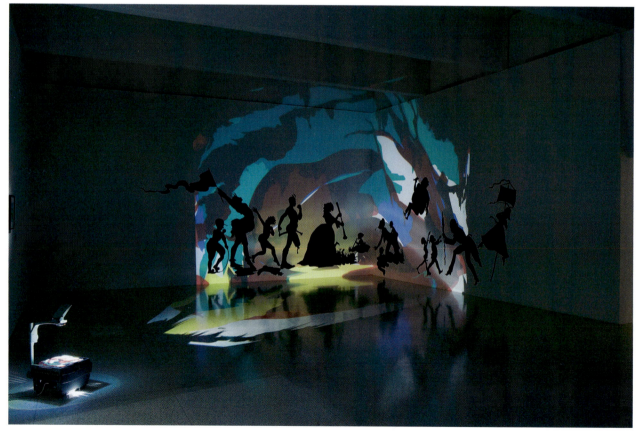

32–70 • Kara Walker DARKYTOWN REBELLION
2001. Cut paper and projection on wall, 14 × 37' (4.3 × 11.3 m) overall. Musée d'Art Moderne Grand-Duc Jean, Luxembourg.

SEE MORE: View a video about Kara Walker www.myartslab.com

Me As I Am, is taken from words spoken by Othello, the "Moor," in Shakespeare's play. **CHANDELIER MORI (FIG. 32–69)**, the chandelier from Wilson's installation, is also made from Murano glass but, unlike the brilliantly glittering Venetian glass chandeliers seen around the city, this one emphasizes blackness. The title suggests the *memento mori* or *vanitas* painting that reminds viewers that death comes to all of us, drawing attention to the fact that the commerce of Venice was built on the back of African labor and at the cost of African lives.

WALKER. It is fitting to end this book with some of the most challenging and provocative art made in America today. The art of Kara Walker (b. 1969) hits raw nerves, shocks, and horrifies. Walker makes her work by cutting large-scale silhouettes of figures out of black construction paper, waxing them to the walls of galleries, and illuminating them with projected light. In **DARKYTOWN REBELLION (FIG. 32–70)**, a scene showing a slave revolt and massacre, the walls of the gallery are covered by black-silhouetted figures that tell an unfolding tale of horror. The room swirls with beautifully colored white, black, pink, green, blue, and yellow projected lights and shadows dancing on the walls. As we walk around the space looking at the figures, we step in front of the projector and our own shadows are cast on the walls, placing us uncomfortably close to or actually in the narrative. Walker's stories and caricatural figures are drawn variously from slave narratives, minstrel shows, advertising memorabilia, and even from Harlequin romance novels, blending fiction and fact to evoke a history of oppression and terrible violence—she does not balk at portraying unpleasant or painful bodily functions either, such as excretion, vomiting, and childbirth. Walker's characters are black and white stereotypes. She contrasts the tight, cramped features of her white characters with the stereotypical black features of her African Americans. She even refers to some of her characters as "nigger wenches" or "pickaninnies."

Walker plays on white fears of miscegenation and insecurities about racial purity. She pushes so far over the border of the acceptable that visiting one of her installations can be a terrifying and disruptive experience. Her figures disturb us intensely because of what they make us do. As silhouettes, they are all black, which means that we cannot identify their race by skin color. In order to read the narrative, however, we need to differentiate the characters and so have to look for other visual markers of race, making us draw upon an entire history of ugly stereotypes in the process. We are forced to examine the figures for thin or big lips, flat or curly hair, elegant or raggedy clothes. In this way Walker catches us in the act of being racist, making clear that she is speaking to us personally, not to some theoretical racist, and that racism is neither theoretical nor a thing of the past. As Walker has said: "It's interesting that as soon as you start telling the story of racism you start reliving it." She might also have said that when you experience her cycloramas, you become part of them.

Walker shows us that identity is not nearly as clear-cut as we would like to think. We are all complicated beings, constantly negotiating and renegotiating our place in the world, changing and reinventing ourselves. Kara Walker's art is not pleasant, but it changes us by altering our perception of the world. It makes us confront a world that we do not want to believe exists, and shows us that the work of visual artists—past, present, and future—can reveal things about the time and place in which it was created and about the world we inhabit in ways that are beyond the reach of any other form of communication.

THINK ABOUT IT

32.1 Discuss the emergence of Pop art in the 1950s and 1960s in the work of artists such as Richard Hamilton and Andy Warhol. Explain how and why Pop reacted to Abstract Expressionism.

32.2 Write about the importance of the dematerialized object in the art of postwar United States. Then discuss how representational art regained importance in later years, particularly after 1980, and explain the new forms that representation took.

32.3 Distinguish the three waves of feminism and assess their impact on the visual arts.

32.4 Analyze how contemporary American artists have used their art to address social and political issues surrounding race. Select and discuss the work of at least two artists from the chapter such as David Hammons, Kerry James Marshall, Kara Walker, or Fred Wilson.

32.5 Explain how globalism has impacted the visual arts and discuss how artists use contemporary strategies to speak to issues in their local cultures. Analyze one such artwork from the chapter.

PRACTICE MORE: Compose answers to these questions, get flashcards for images and terms, and review chapter material with quizzes
www.myartslab.com

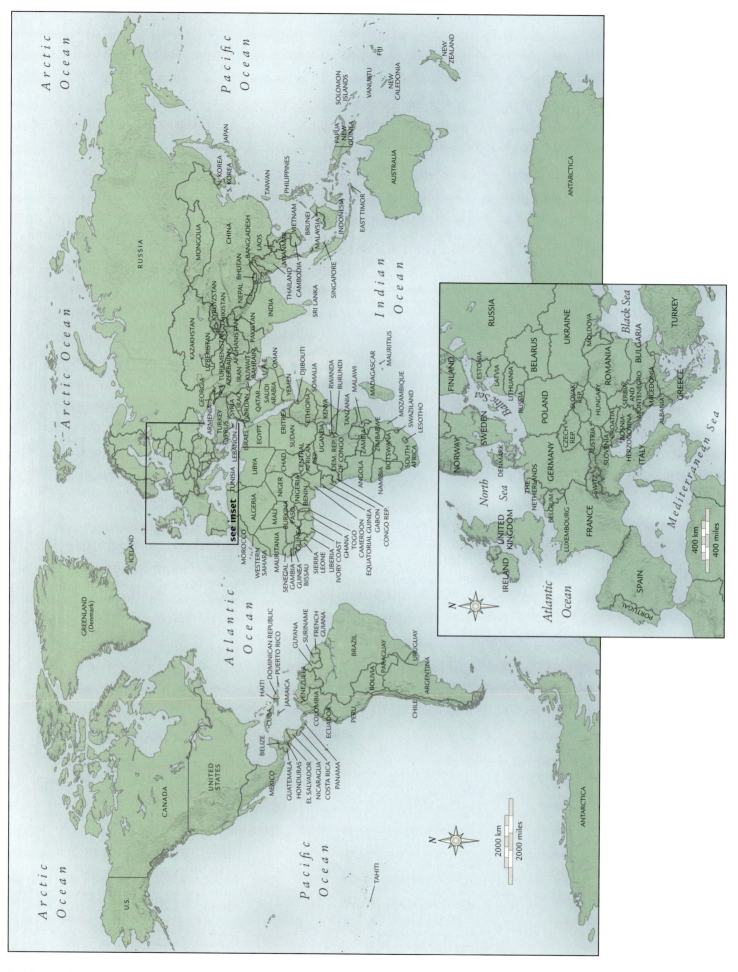

Arctic Ocean

Pacific Ocean

Arctic Ocean

Arctic Ocean

RUSSIA

MONGOLIA

CHINA

N. KOREA
S. KOREA
JAPAN
TAIWAN

PHILIPPINES

SOLOMON ISLANDS
VANUATU
FIJI
NEW CALEDONIA
NEW ZEALAND

PAPUA NEW GUINEA

AUSTRALIA

ANTARCTICA

KAZAKHSTAN

UZBEKISTAN
TURKMENISTAN
KYRGYZSTAN
TAJIKISTAN

NEPAL BHUTAN
BANGLADESH
MYANMAR
LAOS
THAILAND
CAMBODIA
VIETNAM
BRUNEI
MALAYSIA
SINGAPORE
INDONESIA
EAST TIMOR

INDIA

SRI LANKA

GEORGIA
ARMENIA
TURKEY
CYPRUS
AZERBAIJAN
IRAN AFGHANISTAN
PAKISTAN

ISRAEL
LEBANON
SYRIA
IRAQ
JORDAN
KUWAIT
QATAR
BAHRAIN
U.A.E.
SAUDI ARABIA
OMAN
YEMEN

Indian Ocean

DJIBOUTI
SOMALIA
RWANDA
BURUNDI
MALAWI
MADAGASCAR
MAURITIUS

TUNISIA
MOROCCO
WESTERN SAHARA
ALGERIA
LIBYA
EGYPT
MALI
NIGER
CHAD
SUDAN
ERITREA
ETHIOPIA
UGANDA
KENYA
TANZANIA
ZAMBIA
ZIMBABWE
MOZAMBIQUE
SWAZILAND
LESOTHO

MAURITANIA
SENEGAL
GAMBIA
GUINEA-BISSAU
GUINEA
SIERRA LEONE
LIBERIA
IVORY COAST
GHANA
TOGO
BENIN
BURKINA FASO
NIGERIA
CAMEROON
EQUATORIAL GUINEA
GABON
CONGO REP.
CENTRAL AFRICAN REP.
DEM. REP. OF CONGO
ANGOLA
NAMIBIA
BOTSWANA
SOUTH AFRICA

see inset

ICELAND

GREENLAND (Denmark)

Atlantic Ocean

GUYANA
SURINAME
FRENCH GUIANA
VENEZUELA
COLOMBIA
ECUADOR
PERU
BRAZIL
BOLIVIA
PARAGUAY
URUGUAY
ARGENTINA
CHILE

HAITI
CUBA
JAMAICA
DOMINICAN REPUBLIC
PUERTO RICO

BELIZE
MEXICO
GUATEMALA
HONDURAS
EL SALVADOR
NICARAGUA
COSTA RICA
PANAMA

UNITED STATES

CANADA

U.S.

Pacific Ocean

TAHITI

N

2000 km
2000 miles

ANTARCTICA

RUSSIA
UKRAINE
MOLDOVA
Black Sea
TURKEY

FINLAND
ESTONIA
LATVIA
LITHUANIA
RUSSIA
BELARUS
POLAND
SLOVAK REP.
HUNGARY
ROMANIA
BULGARIA
GREECE
MACEDONIA
ALBANIA
SERBIA AND MONTENEGRO

NORWAY
SWEDEN
DENMARK
North Sea
Baltic Sea
THE NETHERLANDS
GERMANY
CZECH REP.
AUSTRIA
SLOVENIA
CROATIA
BOSNIA-HERZEGOVINA
ITALY

IRELAND
UNITED KINGDOM
BELGIUM
LUXEMBOURG
FRANCE
SWITZ.

Atlantic Ocean

SPAIN
PORTUGAL

Mediterranean Sea

N

400 km
400 miles

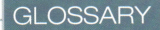

abacus (p. 108)   The flat slab at the top of a **capital**, directly under the **entablature**.

abbey church (p. 239)   An abbey is a religious community headed by an abbot or abbess. An abbey church often has an especially large choir to provide space for the monks or nuns.

absolute dating (p. 12)   A method of assigning a precise historical date to periods and objects, based on known and recorded events in the region, as well as technically extracted physical evidence (such as carbon-14 disintegration). See also **radiometric dating, relative dating**.

abstract, abstraction (p. 8)   Any art that does not represent observed aspects of nature or transforms visible forms into a stylized image. Also: the **formal** qualities of this process.

academy (p. 924)   A place of study, the word coming from the Greek name of a garden near Athens where Plato and, later, Platonic philosophers held discussions. Academies of fine arts, such as the Academy of Drawing or the Royal Academy of Painting, were created to foster the arts by teaching, by discussion, by exhibitions, and occasionally by financial aid.

acanthus (p. 110)   A Mediterranean plant whose leaves are reproduced in architectural ornament used on **moldings, friezes**, and **Corinthian capitals**.

acropolis (p. 129)   The citadel of an ancient Greek city, located at its highest point and housing temples, a treasury, and sometimes a royal palace. The most famous is the Acropolis in Athens.

acroterion (acroteria) (p. 110)   An ornament at the corner or peak of a roof.

adobe (p. 393)   Sun-baked blocks made of clay mixed with straw. Also: the buildings made with this material.

aedicula (p. 609)   A decorative architectural frame, usually found around a niche, door, or window. An aedicula is made up of a **pediment** and **entablature** supported by **columns** or **pilasters**.

agora (p. 138)   An open space in a Greek town used as a central gathering place or market. See also **forum**.

aisle (p. 228)   Passage or open corridor of a church, hall, or other building that parallels the main space, usually on both sides, and is delineated by a row, or **arcade**, of **columns** or **piers**. Called side aisles when they flank the **nave** of a church.

album (p. 795)   A book consisting of a series of painting or prints (album leaves) mounted into book form.

allegory (p. 625)   In a work of art, an image (or images) that symbolizes an idea, concept, or principle, often moral or religious.

alloy (p. 23)   A mixture of metals; different metals melted together.

amalaka (p. 301)   In Hindu architecture, the circular or square-shaped element on top of a spire (**shikhara**), often crowned with a **finial**, symbolizing the cosmos.

ambulatory (p. 228)   The passage (walkway) around the **apse** in a **basilican** church or around the central space in a **central-plan building**.

amphora (p. 101)   An ancient Greek jar for storing oil or wine, with an egg-shaped body and two curved handles.

aniconic (p. 262)   A symbolic representation without images of human figures, very often found in Islamic art.

animal interlace or style (p. 427)   Decoration made of interwoven animals or serpents, often found in Celtic and early medieval Northern European art.

ankh (p. 51)   A looped cross signifying life, used by ancient Egyptians.

appropriation (p. 1102)   Term used to describe the practice of some postmodern artists of adopting images in their entirety from other works of art or from visual culture for use in their own art. The act of recontextualizing the appropriated image allows the artist to critique both it and the time and place in which it was created.

apse, apsidal (p. 192)   A large semicircular or polygonal (and usually **vaulted**) niche protruding from the end wall of a building. In the Christian church, it contains the altar. Apsidal is an adjective describing the condition of having such a space.

arabesque (p. 263)   A type of linear surface decoration based on foliage and **calligraphic** forms, usually characterized by flowing lines and swirling shapes.

arcade (p. 172)   A series of **arches**, carried by **columns** or **piers** and supporting a common wall or **lintel**. In a **blind arcade**, the arches and supports are **engaged** (attached to the wall) and have a decorative function.

arch (p. 271)   In architecture, a curved structural element that spans an open space. Built from wedge-shaped stone blocks called **voussoirs**, which, when placed together and held at the top by a trapezoidal **keystone**, form an effective space-spanning and weight-bearing unit. Requires **buttresses** at each side to contain the outward **thrust** caused by the weight of the structure. **Corbel arch** (p. 16): an arch or **vault** formed by **courses** of stones, each of which projects beyond the lower course until the space is enclosed; usually finished with a **capstone**. **Horseshoe arch** (p. 268): an arch of more than a half-circle; typical of western Islamic architecture. **Round arch** (p. 271): arch that displaces most of its weight, or downward thrust along its curving sides, transmitting that weight to adjacent supporting uprights (door or window jambs, columns, or piers). Ogival arch: a pointed arch created by S-curves. Relieving arch: an arch built into a heavy wall just above a **post-and-lintel** structure (such as a gate, door, or window) to help support the wall above by transferring the load to the side walls. **Transverse arch** (p. 457): an arch that connects the wall **piers** on both sides of an interior space, up and over a stone vault.

Archaic smile (p. 114)   The curved lips of an ancient Greek statue, usually interpreted as a way of animating facial features.

architrave (p. 108)   The bottom element in an **entablature**, beneath the **frieze** and the **cornice**.

archivolt (p. 473)   A **molded** band framing an **arch**, or a series of stone blocks that rest directly on the **columns**.

ashlar (p. 99)   Highly finished, precisely cut block of stone. When laid in even courses, ashlar masonry creates a uniform face with fine joints. Often used as a facing on the visible exterior of a building, especially as a veneer for the **façade**. Also called **dressed stone**.

assemblage (p. 1026)   Artwork created by gathering and manipulating two- and/or three-dimensional found objects.

astragal (p. 110)   A thin convex decorative **molding**, often found on Classical **entablatures**, and usually decorated with a continuous row of beadlike circles.

atelier (p. 944)   The studio or workshop of a master artist or craftsperson, often including junior associates and apprentices.

atmospheric perspective (p. 562)   See **perspective**.

atrial cross (p. 941)   The cross placed in the **atrium** of a church. In Colonial America, used to mark a gathering and teaching place.

atrium (p. 160)   An unroofed interior courtyard or room in a Roman house, sometimes having a pool or garden, sometimes surrounded by **columns**. Also: the open courtyard in front of a Christian church; or an entrance area in modern architecture.

automatism (p. 1056)   A technique whereby the usual intellectual control of the artist over his or her brush or pencil is foregone. The artist's aim is to allow the subconscious to create the artwork without rational interference.

avant-garde (p. 971)   Term derived from the French military word meaning "before the group," or "vanguard." Avant-garde denotes those artists or concepts of a strikingly new, experimental, or radical nature for their time.

axis (p. xxxii)   An implied line around which the elements of a picture are organized.

axis-mundi (p. 297)   A concept of an "axis of the world," which marks sacred sites and denotes a link between the human and celestial realms. For example, in Buddhist art, the *axis mundi* can be marked by monumental freestanding decorative **pillars**.

bailey (p. 473)   The outermost walled courtyard of a castle.

baldachin (p. 467)   A canopy (whether suspended from the ceiling, projecting from a wall, or supported by **columns**) placed over an honorific or sacred space such as a throne or church altar.

bar tracery (p. 507)   See **tracery**.

barbarian (p. 151)   A term used by the ancient Greeks and Romans to label all foreigners outside their cultural orbit (e.g., Celts, Goths, Vikings). The word derives from an imitation of what the "barblings" of their language sounded like to those who could not understand it.

bargeboards (p. 870)   Boards covering the rafters at the gable end of a building; bargeboards are often carved or painted.

barrel vault (p. 188)   See **vault**.

base (p. 110)   Any support. Also: masonry supporting a statue or the shaft of a **column**.

basilica (p. 192)   A large rectangular building. Often built with a **clerestory**, side **aisles** separated from the center **nave** by **colonnades**, and an **apse** at one or both ends. Roman centers for administration, later adapted to Christian church use.

battered (p. 418)   An architectural design whereby walls are sloped inward toward the top to increase stability.

bay (p. 172)   A unit of space defined by architectural elements such as **columns, piers**, and walls.

beehive tomb (p. 98)   A **corbel-vaulted** tomb, conical in shape like a beehive, and covered by an earthen mound.

Benday dots (p. 1093)   In modern printing and typesetting, the individual dots that, together with many others, make up lettering and images. Often machine- or computer-generated, the dots are very small and closely spaced to give the effect of density and richness of tone.

bi (p. 333)   A jade disk with a hole in the center.

bilum (p. 863)   Netted bags made mainly by women throughout the central highlands of New Guinea. The bags can be used for everyday purposes or even to carry the bones of the recently deceased as a sign of mourning.

biomorphic (p. 1057)   A term used in the early twentieth century to denote the biologically or organically inspired shapes and forms that were routinely included in abstracted Modern art.

black-figure (p. 105)   A style or technique of ancient Greek pottery in which black figures are painted on a red clay ground. See also **red-figure**.

blackware (p. 853)   A **ceramic** technique that produces pottery with a primarily black surface with **matte** and glossy patterns on the surface.

blind arcade (p. 780)   See **arcade**.

bodhisattva (p. 297)   In Buddhism, a being who has attained enlightenment but chooses to remain in this world in order to help others advance spiritually. Also defined as a potential Buddha.

Book of Hours (p. 547)   A private prayer book, containing a calendar, services for the canonical hours, and sometimes special prayers.

boss (p. 554)   A decorative knoblike element that can be found in many places, such as at the intersection of a Gothic **rib vault** or in the buttonlike projections of metalwork.

bracket, bracketing (p. 335)   An architectural element that projects from a wall to support a horizontal part of a building, such as beams or the eaves of a roof.

buon fresco (p. 87)   See **fresco**.

burin (p. 590)   A metal instrument used in **engraving** to cut lines into the metal plate. The sharp end of the burin is trimmed to give a diamond-shaped cutting point, while the other end is finished with a wooden handle that fits into the engraver's palm.

buttress, buttressing p. 172)   A projecting support built against an external wall, usually to counteract the lateral **thrust** of a **vault** or **arch** within. In Gothic architecture, a **flying buttress** is an arched bridge above the **aisle** roof that extends from the upper **nave** wall, where the lateral thrust of the main vault is greatest, down to a solid **pier**.

cairn (p.17)   A pile of stones or earth and stones that served both as a prehistoric burial site and as a marker of underground tombs.

calligraphy (p. 279)   Handwriting as an art form.

calotype (p. 968)   The first photographic process utilizing negatives and paper positives. It was invented by William Henry Fox Talbot in the late 1830s.

calyx krater (p. 118)   See **krater**.

came (cames) (p. 497)   A lead strip used in the making of leaded or **stained-glass windows**. Cames have an indented groove on the sides into which the separate pieces of glass are fitted to hold the composition together.

cameo (p. 178)   Gemstone, clay, glass, or shell having layers of color, carved in **low relief** to create an image and ground of different colors.

camera obscura (p. 967)   An early cameralike device used in the Renaissance and later for recording images of nature. Made from a dark box (or room) with a hole in one side (sometimes fitted with a lens), the camera obscura operates when bright light shines through the hole, casting an upside-down image of an object outside onto the inside wall of the box.

canon of proportions (p. 65)   A set of ideal mathematical ratios in art based on measurements, as in the proportional relationships among the basic elements of the human body.

canopic jar (p. 56)   Special jars used to store the major organs of a body before embalming, found in ancient Egyptian culture.

capital (p. 110)   The sculpted block that tops a **column**. According to the **conventions** of the **orders**, capitals include different decorative elements. See **order**. A **historiated capital** is one displaying a figural composition of a **narrative** scene.

capriccio (p. 912)   A painting or print of a fantastic, imaginary landscape, usually with architecture.

capstone (p. 99)   The final, topmost stone in a **corbel arch** or **vault**, which joins the sides and completes the structure.

cartoon (p. 497)   A full-scale drawing used to transfer or guide a design onto a surface (such as a wall, canvas, panel, or **tapestry**) to be painted, carved, or woven.

cartouche (p. 189)   A frame for a **hieroglyphic** inscription formed by a rope design surrounding an oval space. Used to signify a sacred or honored name. Also: in architecture, a decorative device or plaque, usually with a plain center used for inscriptions or epitaphs.

caryatid (p. 107)   A sculpture of a draped female figure acting as a **column** supporting an **entablature**.

cassone (cassoni) (p. 616)   An Italian dowry chest often highly decorated with carvings, paintings, **inlaid** designs, and gilt embellishments.

catacomb (p. 219)   A subterranean burial ground consisting of tunnels on different levels, having niches for urns and **sarcophagi** and often incorporating rooms (**cubiculae**).

cathedral (p. 222)   The principal Christian church in a diocese, the bishop's administrative center and housing his throne (*cathedra*).

celadon (p. 352)   A high-fired, transparent glaze of pale bluish-green hue whose principal coloring agent is an oxide of iron. In China and Korea, such glazes typically were applied over a pale gray **stoneware** body, though Chinese potters sometimes applied them over **porcelain** bodies during the Ming (1368–1644) and Qing (1644–1911) dynasties. Chinese potters invented celadon glazes and initiated the continuous production of celadon-glazed wares as early as the third century CE.

cella (p. 108)   The principal interior room at the center of a Greek or Roman temple within which the cult statue was usually housed. Also called the **naos**.

celt (p. 377)   A smooth, oblong stone or metal object, shaped like an axe-head.

cenotaph (p. 771)   A funerary monument commemorating an individual or group buried elsewhere.

centering (p. 172)   A temporary structure that supports a masonry **arch** and **vault** or **dome** during construction until the mortar is fully dried and the masonry is self-sustaining.

central-plan building (p. 228)   Any structure designed with a primary central space surrounded by symmetrical areas on each side. For example, a **rotunda** or a Greek-cross plan (equal-armed cross).

ceramics (p. 22)   A general term covering all types of wares made from fired clay, including **porcelain** and **terra cotta**.

chacmool (p. 390)   In Mayan sculpture, a half-reclining figure probably representing an offering bearer.

chaitya (p. 302)   A type of Buddhist temple found in India. Built in the form of a hall or **basilica**, a *chaitya* hall is highly decorated with sculpture and usually is carved from a cave or natural rock location. It houses a sacred shrine or **stupa** for worship.

chamfer (p. 780)   The slanted surface produced when an angle is trimmed or beveled, common in building and metalwork.

chasing (p. 776)   Ornamentation made on metal by **incising** or hammering the surface.

château (châteaux) (p. 691)   A French country house or residential castle. A *château fort*, is a military castle incorporating defensive works such as towers and battlements.

chattri (chattris) (p. 779)   A decorative pavilion with an umbrella-shaped **dome** in Indian architecture.

chevron (p. 350)   A decorative or heraldic motif of repeated Vs; a zigzag pattern.

chiaroscuro (p. 634)   An Italian word designating the contrast of dark and light in a painting, drawing, or print. *Chiaroscuro* creates spatial depth and volumetric forms through gradations in the intensity of light and shadow.

cista (cistae) (p. 166)   **Cylindrical** containers used by wealthy women as a case for toiletry articles such as a mirror.

clerestory (p. 58)   The topmost zone of a wall with windows in a **basilica** extending above the aisle roofs. Provides direct light into the central interior space (the **nave**).

cloister (p. 442)   An open space within a monastery, surrounded by an **arcaded** or colonnaded walkway, often having a fountain and garden. The most important monastic buildings (e.g., dormitory, refectory) open off of it. Since members of a cloistered order do not leave the monastery or interact with outsiders, the cloister represents the center of their enclosed world.

codex (codices) (p. 243)   A book, or a group of **manuscript** pages (folios), held together by stitching or other binding on one side.

coffer (p. 197)   A recessed decorative panel that is used to reduce the weight of and to decorate ceilings or **vaults**. The use of coffers is called coffering.

coiling (p. 845)   A technique in basketry. In coiled baskets a spiraling structure is held in place by another material.

collage (p. 1026)   A composition made of cut and pasted scraps of materials, sometimes with lines or forms added by the artist.

colonnade (p. 69)   A row of **columns**, supporting a straight **lintel** (as in a **porch** or **portico**) or a series of **arches** (an **arcade**).

colophon (p. 432)   The data placed at the end of a book listing the book's author, publisher, **illuminator**, and other information related to its production. In East Asian **handscrolls**, the inscriptions which follow the painting are also called colophons.

column (p. 110)   An architectural element used for support and/or decoration. Consists of a rounded or polygonal vertical **shaft** placed on a **base** and topped by a decorative **capital**. In Classical architecture, built in accordance with the rules of one of the architectural **orders**. Columns can be free-standing or attached to a background wall (**engaged**).

combine (p. 1085)   Combinations of painting and sculpture using nontraditional art materials.

complementary color (p. 993)   The primary and secondary colors across from each other on the color wheel (red and green, blue and orange, yellow and purple). When juxtaposed, the intensity of both colors increases. When mixed together, they negate each other to make a neutral gray-brown.

composite order (p. 163)   See **order**.

composite pose or **image** (p. 9)   Combining different viewpoints within a single representation of a subject.

composition (p. xxix)   The overall arrangement, organizing design, or structure of a work of art.

conch (p. 234)   A half-**dome**.

cong (p. 328)   A square or octagonal jade tube with a cylindrical hole in the center. A symbol of the earth, it was used for ritual worship and astronomical observations in ancient China.

connoisseurship (p. 741)   A term derived from the French word connoisseur, meaning "an expert," and signifying the study and evaluation of art based primarily on **formal**, visual, and stylistic analysis. A connoisseur studies the style and technique of an object to assess its relative quality and identify its maker through visual comparison with other works of secure authorship. See also **contextualism**; **formalism**.

contrapposto (p. 121)   An Italian term meaning "set against," used to describe the pose that results from setting parts of the body in opposition to each other around a central **axis**.

convention (p. 51)   A traditional way of representing forms.

corbel, corbeling (p. 16)   An early roofing and arching technique in which each **course** of stone projects slightly beyond the previous layer (a corbel) until the uppermost corbels meet. Results in a high, almost pointed **arch** or **vault**.

corbeled vault (p. 99)   See **vault**.

Corinthian order (p. 108)   See **order**.

cornice (p. 110)   The uppermost section of a Classical **entablature**. More generally, a horizontally projecting element found at the top of a building wall or **pedestal**. A raking cornice is formed by the junction of two slanted cornices, most often found in **pediments**.

course (p. 99)   A horizontal layer of stone used in building.

crenellation (p. 44)   Alternating higher and lower sections along the top of a defensive wall, giving a stepped appearance and forming a permanent shield for defenders on top of a fortified building.

crocket (p. 585)   A stylized leaf used as decoration along the outer angle of spires, pinnacles, gables, and around **capitals** in Gothic architecture.

cruciform (p. 232)   A term describing anything that is cross-shaped, as in the cruciform plan of a church.

cubiculum (cubicula) (p. 224)   A small private room for burials in the **catacombs**.

cuneiform (p. 28)   An early form of writing with wedge-shaped marks impressed into wet clay with a **stylus**, primarily used by ancient Mesopotamians.

curtain wall (p. 1045)   A wall in a building that does not support any of the weight of the structure.

cyclopean construction (p. 93)   A method of building using huge blocks of rough-hewn stone. Any large-scale, monumental building project that impresses by sheer size. Named after the Cyclopes (sing. Cyclops) one-eyed giants of legendary strength in Greek myths.

cylinder seal (p. 32)   A small cylindrical stone decorated with **incised** patterns. When rolled across soft clay or wax, the resulting raised pattern or design (**relief**) served in Mesopotamian and Indus Valley cultures as an identifying signature.

dado (dadoes) (p. 163)   The lower part of a wall, differentiated in some way (by a molding or different coloring or paneling) from the upper section.

daguerreotype (p. 967)   An early photographic process that makes a positive print on a light-sensitized copperplate; invented and marketed in 1839 by Louis-Jacques-Mandé Daguerre.

demotic writing (p. 77)   The simplified form of ancient Egyptian **hieratic writing**, used primarily for administrative and private texts.

dendrochronology (p. xxxvi)   The dating of wood based on the patterns of the growth rings.

desert varnish (p. 400)   In southwestern North America, a substance that turned cliff faces into dark surfaces. Neolithic artists would draw images by scraping through the dark surface.

diptych (p. 215)   Two panels of equal size (usually decorated with paintings or **reliefs**) hinged together.

dogu (p. 356)   Small human figurines made in Japan during the Jomon period. Shaped from clay, the figures have exaggerated expressions and are in contorted poses. They were probably used in religious rituals.

dolmen (p. 17)   A prehistoric structure made up of two or more large upright stones supporting a large, flat, horizontal slab or slabs.

dome (p. 188)   A rounded **vault**, usually over a circular space. Consists of curved masonry and can vary in shape from hemispherical to bulbous to ovoidal. May use a supporting vertical wall (**drum**), from which the vault springs, and may be crowned by an open space (**oculus**) and/or an exterior **lantern**. When a dome is built over a square space, an intermediate element is required to make the transition to a circular drum. There are two systems: A dome on **pendentives** (spherical triangles) incorporates **arched**, sloping intermediate sections of wall that carry the weight and **thrust** of the dome to

heavily **buttressed** supporting **piers**. A dome on **squinches** uses an arch built into the wall (squinch) in the upper corners of the space to carry the weight of the dome across the corners of the square space below. A half-dome or **conch** may cover a semicircular space.

domino construction (p. 1045)   System of building construction introduced by the architect Le Corbusier in which reinforced concrete floor slabs are floated on six free-standing posts placed as if at the positions of the six dots on a domino playing piece.

Doric order (p. 108)   See **order**.

dressed stone (p. 85)   See **ashlar**.

drillwork (p. 190)   The technique of using a drill for the creation of certain effects in sculpture.

drum (p. 110)   The wall that supports a **dome**. Also: a segment of the circular **shaft** of a **column**.

drypoint (p. 748)   An **intaglio** printmaking process by which a metal (usually copper) plate is directly inscribed with a pointed instrument (**stylus**). The resulting design of scratched lines is inked, wiped, and printed. Also: the print made by this process.

earthenware (p. 22)   A low-fired, opaque **ceramic** ware that is fired in the range of 800 to 900 degrees Celsius. Earthenware employs humble clays that are naturally heat resistant; the finished wares remain porous after firing unless glazed. Earthenware occurs in a range of earth-toned colors, from white and tan to gray and black, with tan predominating.

earthwork (p. 1102)   Usually very large scale, outdoor artwork that is produced by altering the natural environment.

echinus (p. 110)   A cushionlike circular element found below the **abacus** of a **Doric capital**. Also: a similarly shaped molding (usually with egg-and-dart motifs) underneath the **volutes** of an Ionic capital.

electronic spin resonance (p. 12)   Method that uses magnetic field and microwave irradiation to date material such as tooth enamel and its surrounding soil.

elevation (p. 108)   The arrangement, proportions, and details of any vertical side or face of a building. Also: an architectural drawing showing an exterior or interior wall of a building.

emblema (emblemata) (p. 202)   In a **mosaic**, the elaborate central motif on a floor, usually a self-contained unit done in a more refined manner, with smaller **tesserae** of both marble and semiprecious stones.

embroidery (p. 484)   Stitches applied on top of an already-woven fabric ground.

encaustic (p. 79)   A painting medium using pigments mixed with hot wax.

engaged column (p. 173)   A column attached to a wall. See also **column**.

engraving (p. 590)   An **intaglio** printmaking process of inscribing an image, design, or letters onto a metal or wood surface from which a print is made. An engraving is usually drawn with a sharp implement (**burin**) directly onto the surface of the plate. Also: the print made from this process.

entablature (p. 108)   In the Classical **orders**, the horizontal elements above the **columns** and **capitals**. The entablature consists of, from bottom to top, an **architrave**, a **frieze**, and a **cornice**.

entasis (p. 108)   A slight swelling of the **shaft** of a Greek **column**. The optical illusion of entasis makes the column appear from afar to be straight.

etching (p. 748)   An **intaglio** printmaking process in which a metal plate is coated with acid-resistant resin and then inscribed with a **stylus** in a design, revealing the plate below. The plate is then immersed in acid, and the design of exposed metal is eaten away by the acid. The resin is removed, leaving the design etched permanently into the metal and the plate ready to be inked, wiped, and printed.

Eucharist (p. 222)   The central rite of the Christian Church, from the Greek word "thanksgiving." Also known as the Mass or Holy Communion, it is based on the Last Supper. According to traditional Catholic Christian belief, consecrated bread and wine become the body and blood of Christ; in Protestant belief, bread and wine symbolize the body and blood.

exedra (exedrae) (p. 199)   In architecture, a semicircular niche. On a small scale, often used as decoration, whereas larger exedrae can form interior spaces (such as an **apse**).

expressionism (p. 151)   Terms describing a work of art in which forms are created primarily to evoke subjective emotions rather than a rational response.

façade (p. 52)   The face or front wall of a building.

faience (p. 87)   Type of **ceramic** covered with colorful, opaque glazes that form a smooth, impermeable surface. First developed in ancient Egypt.

fang ding (p. 328)   A square or rectangular bronze vessel with four legs. The *fang ding* was used for ritual offerings in ancient China during the Shang dynasty.

femmage (p. 1101)   From "female" and "**collage**," the incorporation of fabric into painting.

fête galante (p. 908)   A subject in painting depicting well-dressed people at leisure in a park or country setting. It is most often associated with eighteenth-century French Rococo painting.

filigree (p. 87)   Delicate, lacelike ornamental work.

fillet (p. 110)   The flat ridge between the carved out **flutes** of a **column shaft**. See also fluting.

finial (p. 308)   A knoblike architectural decoration usually found at the top point of a spire, pinnacle, canopy, or gable. Also found on furniture; also the ornamental top of a staff.

flutes, fluted (p. 110)   In architecture, evenly spaced, rounded parallel vertical grooves incised on **shafts** of **columns** or columnar elements (such as **pilasters**).

flying buttress (p. 496)   See **buttress**.

flying gallop (p. 87)   Animals posed off the ground with legs fully extended backwards and forwards to signify that they are running.

foreshortening (p. 119)   The illusion created on a flat surface in which figures and objects appear to recede or project sharply into space. Accomplished according to the rules of perspective.

formal analysis (p. xxix)   An exploration of the visual character that artists bring to their works through the expressive use of elements such as line, form, color, and light, and through its overall structure or composition.

Formalism, formalist (p. 1073)   An approach to the understanding, appreciation, and valuation of art based almost solely on considerations of form. This approach tends to regard an artwork as independent of its time and place of making. In the 1940s, Formalism was most ardently proposed by critic Clement Greenberg. See also **connoisseurship**.

forum (p. 178)   A Roman town center; site of temples and administrative buildings and used as a market or gathering area for the citizens.

four-iwan mosque (p. 271)   See **iwan** and **mosque**.

fresco (p. 87)   A painting technique in which water-based pigments are applied to a surface of wet plaster (called **buon fresco**). The color is absorbed by the plaster, becoming a permanent part of the wall. **Fresco secco** is created by painting on dried plaster, and the color may flake off. Murals made by both these techniques are called frescoes.

fresco secco (p. 87)   See **fresco**.

frieze (p. 108)   The middle element of an **entablature**, between the **architrave** and the cornice. Usually decorated with sculpture, painting, or moldings. Also: any continuous flat band with **relief sculpture** or painted decorations.

frottage (p. 1056) A design produced by laying a piece of paper over a textured surface and rubbing with charcoal or other soft medium.

fusuma (p. 818) Sliding doors covered with paper, used in traditional Japanese construction. *Fusuma* are often highly decorated with paintings and colored backgrounds.

gallery (p. 236) In church architecture, the story found above the side **aisles** of a church, usually open to and overlooking the **nave**. Also: in secular architecture, a long room, usually above the ground floor in a private house or a public building used for entertaining, exhibiting pictures, or promenading. Also: a building or hall in which art is displayed or sold. Also: *galleria*.

garbhagriha (p. 301) From the Sanskrit word meaning "womb chamber," a small room or shrine in a Hindu temple containing a holy image.

genre painting (p. 712) A term used to loosely categorize paintings depicting scenes of everyday life, including (among others) domestic interiors, parties, inn scenes, and street scenes.

geoglyphs (p. 392) Earthen designs on a colossal scale, often created in a landscape as if to be seen from an aerial viewpoint.

gesso (p. 544) A ground made from glue, gypsum, and/or chalk forming the ground of a wood panel or the priming layer of a canvas. Provides a smooth surface for painting.

gilding (p. 87) The application of paper-thin **gold leaf** or gold pigment on an object made from another medium (for example, a sculpture or painting). Usually used as a decorative finishing detail.

giornata (giornate) (p. 537) Adopted from the Italian term meaning "a day's work," a giornata is the section of a **fresco** plastered and painted in a single day.

gold leaf (p. 47) Paper-thin sheets of hammered gold that are used in **gilding**. In some cases (such as Byzantine **icons**), also used as a ground for paintings.

gold foil (p. 87) A thin sheet of gold.

gopura (p. 775) The towering gateway to an Indian Hindu temple complex. A temple complex can have several different *gopuras*.

Grand Manner (p. 922) An elevated style of painting popular in the eighteenth century in which the artist looked to the ancients and to the Renaissance for inspiration; for portraits as well as history painting, the artist would adopt the poses, compositions, and attitudes of Renaissance and antique models.

Grand Tour (p. 911) Popular during the eighteenth and nineteenth centuries, an extended tour of cultural sites in France and Italy intended to finish the education of a young upper-class person primarily from Britain or North America.

granulation (p. 87) A technique of decoration in which metal granules, or tiny metal balls, are fused onto a metal surface.

graphic arts (p. xxiv) A term referring to those arts that are drawn or printed and that utilize paper as primary support.

grattage (p. 1056) A pattern created by scraping off layers of paint from a canvas laid over a textured surface. See also **frottage**.

grid (p. 64) A system of regularly spaced horizontally and vertically crossed lines that gives regularity to an architectural plan or to the composition of a work of art. Also: in painting, a grid is used to allow designs to be enlarged or transferred easily.

grisaille (p. 538) A style of monochromatic painting in shades of gray. Also: a painting made in this style.

groin vault (p. 188) See **vault**.

grozing (p. 497) In **stained-glass** windows, chipping away at the edges of a piece of glass to achieve the precise shape needed for inclusion in the composition.

hall church (p. 518) A church with a **nave** and **aisles** of the same height, giving the impression of a large, open hall.

handscroll (p. 337) A long, narrow, horizontal painting or text (or combination thereof) common in Chinese and Japanese art and of a size intended for individual use. A handscroll is stored wrapped tightly around a wooden pin and is unrolled for viewing or reading.

hanging scroll (p. 795) In Chinese and Japanese art, a vertical painting or text mounted within sections of silk. At the top is a semicircular rod; at the bottom is a round dowel. Hanging scrolls are kept rolled and tied except for special occasions, when they are hung for display, contemplation, or commemoration.

haniwa (p. 356) Pottery forms, including cylinders, buildings, and human figures, that were placed on top of Japanese tombs or burial mounds.

Happening (p. 1085) An art form developed by Allan Kaprow in the 1960s incorporating performance, theater, and visual images. A Happening was organized without a specific narrative or intent; with audience participation, the event proceeded according to chance and individual improvisation.

hemicycle (p. 508) A semicircular interior space or structure.

henge (p. 18) A circular area enclosed by stones or wood posts set up by Neolithic peoples. It is usually bounded by a ditch and raised embankment.

hieratic scale (p. 27) The use of different sizes for powerful or holy figures and for ordinary people to indicate relative importance. The larger the figure, the greater the importance.

hieroglyph (p. 52) Picture writing; words and ideas rendered in the form of pictorial symbols.

high relief (p. 304) See **relief sculpture**.

historiated capital (p. 479) See **capital**.

historicism (p. 963) The strong consciousness of and attention to the institutions, themes, styles, and forms of the past, made accessible by historical research, textual study, and archaeology.

history paintings (p. 924) Paintings based on historical, mythological, or biblical narratives. Once considered the noblest form of art, history paintings generally convey a high moral or intellectual idea and are often painted in a grand pictorial style.

horizon line A horizontal "line" formed by the implied meeting point of earth and sky. In **linear perspective**, the **vanishing point** or points are located on this "line."

horseshoe arch (p. 268) See **arch**.

hue (p. xxii) Pure color. The saturation or intensity of the hue depends on the purity of the color. Its value depends on its lightness or darkness.

hydria (p. 139) A large ancient Greek and Roman jar with three handles (horizontal ones at both sides and one vertical at the back), used for storing water.

hypostyle hall (p. 66) A large interior room characterized by many closely spaced columns that support its roof.

icon (p. 237) An image representing a sacred figure or event in the Byzantine, and later in the Orthodox, Church. Icons were venerated by the faithful, who believed them to have miraculous powers to transmit messages to God.

iconic image (p. 224) A picture that expresses or embodies an intangible concept or idea.

iconoclasm (p. 245) The banning or destruction of images, especially **icons** and religious art. Iconoclasm in eighth- and ninth-century Byzantium and sixteenth- and seventeenth-century Protestant territories arose from differing beliefs about the power, meaning, function, and purpose of imagery in religion.

iconography (p. xxxiii) Identifying and studying the subject matter and conventional motifs or symbols in works of art.

iconology (p. xxxv) Interpreting works of art as embodiments of cultural situation by placing them within broad social, political, religious, and intellectual contexts.

iconophile (p. 246) From the Greek for "lovers of images." In Byzantine art, iconophiles advocated for the continued use of **iconic images** in art.

iconostasis (p. 245) The partition screen in a Byzantine or Orthodox church between the **sanctuary** (where the Mass is performed) and the body of the church (where the congregation assembles). The iconostasis displays **icons**.

idealization (p. xxiv) A process in art through which artists strive to make their forms and figures attain perfection, based on pervading cultural values and/or their own personal ideals.

ideograph (p. 331) A written character or symbol representing an idea or object. Many Chinese characters are ideographs.

ignudi (p. 645) Heroic figures of nude young men.

illumination (p. 425) A painting on paper or parchment used as an illustration and/or decoration in **manuscripts** or **albums**. Usually richly colored, often supplemented by gold and other precious materials. The artists are referred to as illuminators. Also: the technique of decorating manuscripts with such paintings.

impasto (p. 748) Thick applications of pigment that give a painting a palpable surface texture.

impost block (p. 600) A block, serving to concentrate the weight above, imposed between the **capital** of a **column** and the springing of an **arch** above.

incising (p. 32) A technique in which a design or inscription is cut into a hard surface with a sharp instrument. Such a surface is said to be incised.

ink painting (p. 810) A monochromatic style of painting developed in China using black ink with gray washes.

inlay (p. 30) To set pieces of a material or materials into a surface to form a design. Also: material used in or decoration formed by this technique.

installation (p. 1087) Contemporary art created for a specific site, especially a gallery or outdoor area, that creates a complete and controlled environment.

intaglio (p. 590) Term used for a technique in which the design is carved out of the surface of an object, such as an **engraved seal** stone. In the **graphic arts**, intaglio includes **engraving**, **etching**, and **drypoint**—all processes in which ink transfers to paper from **incised**, ink-filled lines cut into a metal plate.

intarsia (p. 617) Decoration formed through wood **inlay**.

intuitive perspective (p. 184) See **perspective**.

Ionic order (p. 108) See **order**.

iwan (p. 71) A large, **vaulted** chamber in a **mosque** with a monumental **arched** opening on one side.

jamb (p. 473) In architecture, the vertical element found on both sides of an opening in a wall, and supporting an **arch** or **lintel**.

japonisme (p. 994) A style in French and American nineteenth-century art that was highly influenced by Japanese art, especially prints.

jasperware (p. 917) A fine-grained, unglazed, white **ceramic** developed by Josiah Wedgwood, often colored by metallic oxides with the raised designs remaining white.

jataka tales (p. 300) In Buddhism, stories associated with the previous lives of Shakyamuni, the historical Buddha.

joggled voussoirs (p. 272) Interlocking **voussoirs** in an **arch** or **lintel**, often of contrasting materials for colorful effect.

joined-block sculpture (p. 367) A method of constructing large-scale wooden sculpture developed in

Japan. The entire work is constructed from smaller hollow blocks, each individually carved, and assembled when complete. The joined-block technique allowed the production of larger sculpture, as the multiple joints alleviate the problems of drying and cracking found with sculpture carved from a single block.

kantharos (p. 117)   A type of Greek vase or goblet with two large handles and a wide mouth.

keep (p. 473)   The innermost and strongest structure or central tower of a medieval castle, sometimes used as living quarters, as well as for defense. Also called a donjon.

kente (p. 892)   A woven cloth made by the Ashanti peoples of Africa. Kente cloth is woven in long, narrow pieces in complex and colorful patterns, which are then sewn together.

key block (p. 826)   A key block is the master block in the production of a colored **woodblock print**, which requires different blocks for each color. The key block is a flat piece of wood upon which the outlines for the entire design of the print were first drawn on its surface and then all but these outlines were carved away with a knife. These outlines serve as a guide for the accurate **registration** or alignment of the other blocks needed to add colors to specific parts of a print.

keystone (p. 172)   The topmost **voussoir** at the center of an **arch**, and the last block to be placed. The pressure of this block holds the arch together. Often of a larger size and/or decorated.

kiln (p. 22)   An oven designed to produce enough heat for the baking, or firing, of clay.

kiva (p. 398)   A ceremonial enclosure, usually wholly or partly underground, used for ritual purposes by modern Pueblo peoples and Ancestral Puebloans. *Kivas* may be round or square, made of **adobe** or stone, and they usually feature a hearth and a small indentation in the floor behind it.

kondo (p. 360)   The main hall inside a Japanese Buddhist temple where the images of Buddha are housed.

korambo (p. 863)   A ceremonial or spirit house in Pacific cultures, reserved for the men of a village and used as a meeting place as well as to hide religious artifacts from the uninitiated.

kore (kourai) (p. 114)   An Archaic Greek statue of a young woman.

koru (p. 870)   A design depicting a curling stalk with a bulb at the end that resembles a young tree fern, and often found in Maori art.

kouros (kouroi) (p. 114)   An Archaic Greek statue of a young man or boy.

kowhaiwhai (p. 870)   Painted curvilinear patterns often found in Maori art.

krater (p. 99)   An ancient Greek vessel for mixing wine and water, with many subtypes that each have a distinctive shape. **Calyx krater**: a bell-shaped vessel with handles near the base that resemble a flower calyx. **Volute krater**: a type of krater with handles shaped like scrolls.

Kufic (p. 272)   An ornamental, angular Arabic script.

kylix (p. 124)   A shallow Greek cup, used for drinking, with a wide mouth and small handles near the rim.

lacquer (p. 22)   A type of hard, glossy surface varnish used on objects in East Asian cultures, made from the sap of the Asian sumac or from shellac, a resinous secretion from the lac insect. Lacquer can be layered and manipulated or combined with pigments and other materials for various decorative effects.

lakshana (p. 303)   Term used to designate the thirty-two marks of the historical Buddha. The *lakshana* include, among others, the Buddha's golden body, his long arms, the wheel impressed on his palms and the soles of his feet, and his elongated earlobes.

lamassu (p. 42)   Supernatural guardian-protector of ancient Near Eastern palaces and throne rooms, often represented sculpturally as a combination of the bearded head of a man, powerful body of a lion or bull, wings of an eagle, and the horned headdress of a god, usually possessing five legs.

lancet (p. 502)   A tall, narrow window crowned by a sharply pointed **arch**, typically found in Gothic architecture.

lantern (p. 458)   A turretlike structure situated on a roof, **vault**, or **dome**, with windows that allow light into the space below.

leythos (lekythoi) (p. 141)   A slim Greek oil vase with one handle and a narrow mouth.

linear perspective (p. 593)   See **perspective**.

linga shrine (p. 310)   A place of worship centered on an object or representation in the form of a phallus (the lingam), which symbolizes the power of the Hindu god Shiva.

lintel (p. 473)   A horizontal element of any material carried by two or more vertical supports to form an opening.

literati (p. 337)   The English word used for the Chinese *wenren* or the Japanese *bunjin*, referring to well educated artists who enjoyed literature, **calligraphy**, and painting as a pastime. Their paintings are termed **literati painting**.

literati painting (p. 791)   A style of painting that reflects the taste of the educated class of East Asian intellectuals and scholars. Aspects include an appreciation for the antique, small scale, and an intimate connection between maker and audience.

lithography (p. 951)   Process of making a print (lithograph) from a design drawn on a flat stone block with greasy crayon. Ink is applied to the wet stone and adheres only to the greasy areas of the design.

loggia (p. 532)   Italian term for a covered open-air **gallery**. Often used as a corridor between buildings or around a courtyard, loggias usually have **arcades** or **colonnades**.

logosyllabic (p. 385)   A writing system consisting of both logograms (symbols that represent words) and phonetic signs (symbols that represent sounds, in this case syllables). Cuneiform, Maya, and Japanese are examples of logosyllabic scripts.

longitudinal-plan building (p. 228)   Any structure designed with a rectangular shape. If a cross-shaped building, the main arm of the building would be longer then any arms that cross it. For example, **basilicas** or Latin-cross plan churches.

lost-wax casting (p. 413)   A method of casting metal, such as bronze, by a process in which a wax mold is covered with clay and plaster, then fired, melting the wax and leaving a hollow form. Molten metal is then poured into the hollow space and slowly cooled. When the hardened clay and plaster exterior shell is removed, a solid metal form remains to be smoothed and polished.

low relief (p. 39)   See **relief sculpture**.

lunette (p. 223)   A semicircular wall area, framed by an **arch** over a door or window. Can be either plain or decorated.

lusterware (p. 277)   **Ceramic** pottery decorated with metallic glazes.

madrasa (p. 271)   An Islamic institution of higher learning, where teaching is focused on theology and law.

maenad (p. 104)   In ancient Greece, a female devotee of the wine god Dionysos who participated in orgiastic rituals. She is often depicted with swirling drapery to indicate wild movement or dance. (Also called a Bacchante, after Bacchus, the Roman name of Dionysos.)

majolica (p. 571)   Pottery painted with a tin glaze that, when fired, gives a lustrous and colorful surface.

mandala (p. 299)   An image of the cosmos represented by an arrangement of circles or concentric geometric shapes containing diagrams or images. Used for meditation and contemplation by Buddhists.

mandapa (p. 301)   In a Hindu temple, an open hall dedicated to ritual worship.

mandorla (p. 474)   Light encircling, or emanating from, the entire figure of a sacred person.

manuscript (p. 242)   A handwritten book or document.

maqsura (p. 268)   An enclosure in a Muslim **mosque**, near the **mihrab**, designated for dignitaries.

martyrium (martyria) (p. 237)   In Christian architecture, a church, chapel, or shrine built over the grave of a martyr or the site of a great miracle.

mastaba (p. 53)   A flat-topped, one-story structure with slanted walls over an ancient Egyptian underground tomb.

matte (p. 571)   Term describing a smooth surface that is without shine or luster.

mausoleum (p. 177)   A monumental building used as a tomb. Named after the tomb of Mausolos erected at Halikarnassos around 350 BCE.

medallion (p. 225)   Any round ornament or decoration. Also: a large medal.

megalith (p. 17)   A large stone used in prehistoric building. Megalithic architecture employs such stones.

megaron (p. 93)   The main hall of a Mycenaean palace or grand house, having a columnar **porch** and a room with central fireplace surrounded by four **columns**.

memento mori (p. 907)   From Latin for "remember that you must die." An object, such as a skull or extinguished candle, typically found in a **vanitas** image, symbolizing the transience of life.

memory image (p. 8)   An image that relies on the generic shapes and relationships that readily spring to mind at the mention of an object.

menorah (p. 219)   A Jewish lamp-stand with seven or nine branches; the nine-branched menorah is used during the celebration of Hanukkah. Representations of the seven-branched menorah, once used in the Temple of Jerusalem, became a symbol of Judaism.

metope (p. 110)   The carved or painted rectangular panel between the **triglyphs** of a **Doric frieze**.

mihrab (p. 261)   A recess or niche that distinguishes the wall oriented toward Mecca (**qibla**) in a **mosque**.

millefiori (p. 428)   A term derived from the Italian for "a thousand flowers" that refers to a glass-making technique in which rods of differently-colored glass are fused in a long bundle that is subsequently sliced to produce disks or beads with small-scale, multicolor patterns.

minaret (p. 267)   A tower on or near a **mosque**, varying extensively in form throughout the Islamic world, from which the faithful are called to prayer five times a day.

minbar (p. 261)   A high platform or pulpit in a **mosque**.

miniature (p. 243)   Anything small. In painting, miniatures may be illustrations within **albums** or **manuscripts** or intimate portraits.

mirador (p. 275)   In Spanish and Islamic palace architecture, a very large window or room with windows, and sometimes balconies, providing views to interior courtyards or the exterior landscape.

mithuna (p. 302)   The amorous male and female couples in Buddhist sculpture, usually found at the entrance to a sacred building. The *mithuna* symbolize the harmony and fertility of life.

moai (p. 859)   Statues found in Polynesia, carved from tufa, a yellowish brown volcanic stone, and depicting the human form. Nearly 1,000 of these statues have been found on the island of Rapa Nui but their significance has been a matter of speculation.

mobile (p. 1059)   A sculpture made with parts suspended in such a way that they move in a current of air.

modeling (p. xxix) In painting, the process of creating the illusion of three-dimensionality on a two-dimensional surface by use of light and shade. In sculpture, the process of molding a three-dimensional form out of a malleable substance.

module (p. 341) A segment or portion of a repeated design. Also: a basic building block.

molding (p. 315) A shaped or sculpted strip with varying contours and patterns. Used as decoration on architecture, furniture, frames, and other objects.

mortise-and-tenon (p. 19) A method of joining two elements. A projecting pin (tenon) on one element fits snugly into a hole designed for it (mortise) on the other. Such joints are very strong and flexible.

mosaic (p. 146) Images formed by small colored stone or glass pieces (**tesserae**), affixed to a hard, stable surface.

mosque (p. 261) An edifice used for communal Islamic worship.

Mozarabic (p. 433) An eclectic style practiced in Christian medieval Spain while much of the Iberian peninsula was ruled by Muslim dynasties.

mudra (p. 304) A symbolic hand gesture in Buddhist art that denotes certain behaviors, actions, or feelings.

mullion (p. 507) A slender vertical element or colonnette that divides a window into subsidiary sections.

muqarna (p. 275) Small nichelike components stacked in tiers to fill the transition between differing vertical and horizontal planes.

naos (p. 236) The principal room in a temple or church. In ancient architecture, the **cella**. In a Byzantine church, the **nave** and **sanctuary**.

narrative image (p. 224) A picture that recounts an event drawn from a story, either factual (e.g., biographical) or fictional.

narthex (p. 222) The vestibule or entrance **porch** of a church.

nave (p. 192) The central space of a **basilica**, two or three stories high and usually flanked by aisles.

necking (p. 110) The molding at the top of the **shaft** of the **column**.

necropolis (p. 53) A large cemetery or burial area; literally a "city of the dead."

negative space (p. 120) Empty space, surrounded and shaped so that it acquires a sense of form or volume.

nemes headdress (p. 51) The royal headdress of Egypt.

niello (p. 87) A metal technique in which a black sulfur alloy is rubbed into fine lines **engraved** into metal (usually gold or silver). When heated, the **alloy** becomes fused with the surrounding metal and provides contrasting detail.

nishiki-e (p. 813) A multicolored and ornate Japanese print.

oculus (p. 188) In architecture, a circular opening. Oculi are usually found either as windows or at the apex of a **dome**. When at the top of a dome, an oculus is either open to the sky or covered by a decorative exterior **lantern**.

odalisque (p. 950) Turkish word for "harem slave girl" or "concubine."

ogee (p. 551) An S-shaped curve. See **arch**.

oinochoe (p. 128) A Greek jug used for wine.

olpe (p. 105) Any Greek vase or jug without a spout.

one-point perspective See **perspective**.

orant (p. 222) The representation of a standing figure praying with outstretched and upraised arms.

oratory (p. 232) A small chapel.

order (p. 110) A system of proportions in Classical architecture that includes every aspect of the building's plan, elevation, and decorative system. **Composite**: a combination of the **Ionic** and the **Corinthian** orders.

The **capital** combines **acanthus** leaves with **volute** scrolls. **Corinthian**: the most ornate of the orders, the Corinthian includes a **base**, a **fluted column shaft** with a capital elaborately decorated with acanthus leaf carvings. Its **entablature** consists of an **architrave** decorated with **moldings**, a **frieze** often containing sculptured **reliefs**, and a **cornice** with dentils. **Doric**: the column shaft of the Doric order can be fluted or smooth-surfaced and has no base. The Doric capital consists of an undecorated **echinus** and **abacus**. The Doric entablature has a plain architrave, a frieze with **metopes** and **triglyphs**, and a simple cornice. **Ionic**: the column of the Ionic order has a base, a fluted shaft, and a capital decorated with volutes. The Ionic entablature consists of an architrave of three panels and moldings, a frieze usually containing sculpted relief ornament, and a cornice with dentils. **Tuscan**: a variation of Doric characterized by a smooth-surfaced column shaft with a base, a plain architrave, and an undecorated frieze. A colossal order is any of the above built on a large scale, rising through several stories in height and often raised from the ground by a **pedestal**.

orientalism (p. 966) The fascination with Middle Eastern cultures.

orthogonal (p. 140) Any line running back into the represented space of a picture perpendicular to the imagined picture plane. In **linear perspective**, all orthogonals converge at a single **vanishing point** in the picture and are the basis for a **grid** that maps out the internal space of the image. An orthogonal plan is any plan for a building or city that is based exclusively on right angles, such as the grid plan of many major cities.

pagoda (p. 341) An East Asian **reliquary** tower built with successively smaller, repeated stories. Each story is usually marked by an elaborate projecting roof.

painterly (p. xxiv) A style of painting which emphasizes the techniques and surface effects of brushwork (also color, light, and shade).

palace complex (p. 41) A group of buildings used for living and governing by a ruler and his or her supporters, usually fortified.

palazzo (p. 600) Italian term for palace, used for any large urban dwelling.

palmette (p. 139) A fan-shaped ornament with radiating leaves.

panel painting Any painting executed on a wood support. The wood is usually planed to provide a smooth surface. A panel can consist of several boards joined together.

parapet (p. 138) A low wall at the edge of a balcony, bridge, roof, or other place from which there is a steep drop, built for safety. A parapet walk is the passageway, usually open, immediately behind the uppermost exterior wall or battlement of a fortified building.

parchment (p. 243) A writing surface made from treated skins of animals. Very fine parchment is known as **vellum**.

parish church (p. 239) Church where local residents attend regular services.

parterre (p. 760) An ornamental, highly regimented flowerbed. An element of the ornate gardens of seventeenth-century palaces and **châteaux**.

passage grave (p. 17) A prehistoric tomb under a **cairn**, reached by a long, narrow, slab-lined access passageway or passageways.

pastel (p. 912) Dry pigment, chalk, and gum in stick or crayon form. Also: a work of art made with pastels.

pedestal (p. 107) A platform or **base** supporting a sculpture or other monument. Also: the block found below the base of a Classical **column** (or **colonnade**), serving to raise the entire element off the ground.

pediment (p. 108) A triangular gable found over major architectural elements such as Classical Greek **porticoes**, windows, or doors. Formed by an **entablature** and the ends of a sloping roof or a raking **cornice**. A similar architectural element is often used decoratively

above a door or window, sometimes with a curved upper **molding**. A broken pediment is a variation on the traditional pediment, with an open space at the center of the topmost angle and/or the horizontal cornice.

pendentive (p. 236) The concave triangular section of a **vault** that forms the transition between a square or polygonal space and the circular **base** of a **dome**.

peplos (p. 115) A loose outer garment worn by women of ancient Greece. A cloth rectangle fastened on the shoulders and belted below the bust or at the waist.

Performance art (p. 1085) An artwork based on a live, sometimes theatrical performance by the artist.

peristyle (p. 66) A surrounding **colonnade** in Greek architecture. A peristyle building is surrounded on the exterior by a colonnade. Also: a peristyle court is an open colonnaded courtyard, often having a pool and garden.

perspective (p. 184) A system for representing three-dimensional space on a two-dimensional surface. **Atmospheric perspective**: A method of rendering the effect of spatial distance by subtle variations in color and clarity of representation. **Intuitive perspective**: A method of giving the impression of recession by visual instinct, not by the use of an overall system or program. Oblique perspective: An intuitive spatial system in which a building or room is placed with one corner in the picture plane, and the other parts of the structure recede to an imaginary vanishing point on its other side. Oblique perspective is not a comprehensive, mathematical system. **One-point** and multiple-point perspective (also called **linear**, scientific or mathematical perspective): A method of creating the illusion of three-dimensional space on a two-dimensional surface by delineating a horizon line and multiple **orthogonal** lines. These recede to meet at one or more points on the horizon (called **vanishing points**), giving the appearance of spatial depth. Called scientific or mathematical because its use requires some knowledge of geometry and mathematics, as well as optics. Reverse perspective: A Byzantine perspective theory in which the orthogonals or rays of sight do not converge on a vanishing point in the picture, but are thought to originate in the viewer's eye in front of the picture. Thus, in reverse perspective the image is constructed with orthogonals that diverge, giving a slightly tipped aspect to objects.

photomontage (p. 1039) A photographic work created from many smaller photographs arranged (and often overlapping) in a composition, which is then rephotographed.

pictograph (p. 331) A highly stylized depiction serving as a symbol for a person or object. Also: a type of writing utilizing such symbols.

picture plane (p. 573) The theoretical plane corresponding with the actual surface of a painting, separating the spatial world evoked in the painting from the spatial world occupied by the viewer.

picture stone (p. 436) A medieval northern European memorial stone covered with figural decoration. See also **rune stone**.

picturesque (p. 917) A term describing the taste for the familiar, the pleasant, and the agreeable, popular in the eighteenth and nineteenth centuries in Europe. Originally used to describe the "picture like" qualities of some landscape scenes. When contrasted with the **sublime**, the picturesque stood for the interesting but ordinary domestic landscape.

piece-mold casting (p. 328) A casting technique in which the mold consists of several sections that are connected during the pouring of molten metal, usually bronze. After the cast form has hardened, the pieces of the mold are disassembled, leaving the completed object.

pier (p. 266) A masonry support made up of many stones, or rubble and concrete (in contrast to a column **shaft** which is formed from a single stone or a series of **drums**), often square or rectangular in plan, and capable of carrying very heavy architectural loads.

pietà (p. 231)   A devotional subject in Christian religious art. After the Crucifixion the body of Jesus was laid across the lap of his grieving mother, Mary. When others are present the subject is called the Lamentation.

pietra dura (p. 781)   Italian for "hard stone." Semiprecious stones selected for color, variation, and cut in shapes to form ornamental designs such as flowers or fruit.

pietra serena (p. 600)   A gray Tuscan limestone used in Florence.

pilaster (p. 160)   An **engaged column**-like element that is rectangular in format and used for decoration in architecture.

pilgrimage church (p. 239)   A site that attracts visitors wishing to venerate **relics** as well as attend services.

pillar (p. 219)   In architecture, any large, free-standing vertical element. Usually functions as an important weight-bearing unit in buildings.

pilotis (p. 1045)   Free-standing posts.

pinnacle (p. 499)   In Gothic architecture, a steep pyramid decorating the top of another element such as a **buttress**. Also: the highest point.

plate tracery (p. 502)   See **tracery**.

plinth (p. 163)   The slablike base or **pedestal** of a **column**, statue, wall, building, or piece of furniture.

pluralism (p. 1106)   A social structure or goal that allows members of diverse ethnic, racial, or other groups to exist peacefully within the society while continuing to practice the customs of their own divergent cultures, thus providing to artists a variety of valid contemporary styles.

podium (p. 138)   A raised platform that acts as the foundation for a building, or as a platform for a speaker.

polychrome, polychromy (p. 521)   The multi-colored painting decoration applied to any part of a building, sculpture, or piece of furniture.

polyptych (p. 564)   An altarpiece constructed from multiple panels, sometimes with hinges to allow for movable wings.

porcelain (p. 22)   A high-fired, vitrified, translucent, white **ceramic** ware that employs two specific clays— kaolin and petuntse—and is fired in the range of 1,300 to 1,400 degrees Celsius. The relatively high proportion of silica in the body clays renders the finished porcelains translucent. Like **stonewares**, porcelains are glazed to enhance their aesthetic appeal and to aid in keeping them clean. By definition, porcelain is white, though it may be covered with a glaze of bright color or subtle hue. Chinese potters were the first in the world to produce porcelain, which they were able to make as early as the eighth century.

porch (p. 108)   The covered entrance on the exterior of a building. With a row of **columns** or **colonnade**, also called a **portico**.

portal (p. 39)   A grand entrance, door, or gate, usually to an important public building, and often decorated with sculpture.

portico (p. 62)   In architecture, a projecting roof or porch supported by **columns**, often marking an entrance. See also **porch**.

post-and-lintel (p. 16)   An architectural system of construction with two or more vertical elements (posts) supporting a horizontal element (**lintel**).

potassium-argon dating (p. 12)   Technique used to measure the decay of a radioactive potassium isotope into a stable isotope of argon, and inert gas.

potsherd (p. 22)   A broken piece of **ceramic** ware.

poupou (p. 871)   A house panel, often carved with designs and found in Pacific cultures.

Prairie Style (p. 1046)   Style developed by a group of midwestern architects who worked together using the aesthetic of the Prairie and indigenous prairie plants for landscape design to design mostly domestic homes and small public buildings mostly in the midwest.

predella (p. 548)   The base of an altarpiece, often decorated with small scenes that are related in subject to that of the main panel or panels.

primitivism (p. 1022)   The borrowing of subjects or forms usually from non-European or prehistoric sources by Western artists. Originally practiced by Western artists as an attempt to infuse their work with the naturalistic and expressive qualities attributed to other cultures, especially colonized cultures.

pronaos (p. 108)   The enclosed vestibule of a Greek or Roman temple, found in front of the **cella** and marked by a row of **columns** at the entrance.

proscenium (p. 150)   The stage of an ancient Greek or Roman theater. In modern theater, the area of the stage in front of the curtain. Also: the framing **arch** that separates a stage from the audience.

psalter (p. 253)   In Jewish and Christian scripture, a book containing the psalms, or songs, attributed to King David.

psykter (p. 127)   A Greek vessel with an extended bottom allowing it to float in a larger krater; used to chill wine.

putto (putti) (p. 229)   A plump, naked little boy, often winged. In Classical art, called a cupid; in Christian art, a cherub.

pylon (p. 66)   A massive gateway formed by a pair of tapering walls of oblong shape. Erected by ancient Egyptians to mark the entrance to a temple complex.

qibla (p. 267)   The **mosque** wall oriented toward Mecca indicated by the **mihrab**.

quatrefoil (p. 503)   A four-lobed decorative pattern common in Gothic art and architecture.

quillwork (p. 845)   A Native American decorative craft technique. The quills of porcupines and bird feathers are dyed and attached to materials in patterns.

radiometric dating (p. 12)   A method of dating pre-historic works of art made from organic materials, based on the rate of degeneration of radiocarbons in these materials. See also **relative dating**, **absolute dating**.

raigo (p. 372)   A painted image that depicts the Amida Buddha and other Buddhist deities welcoming the soul of a dying worshiper to paradise.

raku (p. 821)   A type of **ceramic** pottery made by hand, coated with a thick, dark glaze, and fired at a low heat. The resulting vessels are irregularly shaped and glazed, and are highly prized for use in the Japanese tea ceremony.

readymade (p. 1037)   An object from popular or material culture presented without further manipulation as an artwork by the artist.

red-figure (p. 118)   A style and technique of ancient Greek vase painting characterized by red clay-colored figures on a black background. (The figures are reserved against a painted ground and details are drawn, not engraved, as in **black-figure style**.)

register (p. 30)   A device used in systems of spatial definition. In painting, a register indicates the use of differing groundlines to differentiate layers of space within an image. In sculpture, the placement of self-contained bands of **reliefs** in a vertical arrangement. See **registration marks**.

registration marks (p. 826)   In Japanese **woodblock printing**, these were two marks carved on the blocks to indicate proper alignment of the paper during the printing process. In multicolor printing, which used a separate block for each color, these marks were essential for achieving the proper position or registration of the colors.

relative dating (p. 12)   See **radiometric dating**.

relic (p. 239)   A venerated object associated with a saint or martyr.

relief sculpture (p. 5)   A three-dimensional image or design whose flat background surface is carved away to a

certain depth, setting off the figure. Called **high** or **low (bas) relief** depending upon the extent of projection of the image from the background. Called **sunken relief** when the image is carved below the original surface of the background, which is not cut away.

reliquary (p. 299)   A container, often made of precious materials, used as a repository to protect and display sacred **relics**.

repoussé (p. 87)   A technique of hammering metal from the back to create a protruding image. Elaborate **reliefs** are created with wooden armatures against which the metal sheets are pressed and hammered.

rhyton (p. 88)   A vessel in the shape of a figure or an animal, used for drinking or pouring liquids on special occasions.

rib vault (p. 495)   See **vault**.

ridgepole (p. 16)   A longitudinal timber at the apex of a roof that supports the upper ends of the rafters.

roof comb (p. 386)   In a Mayan building, a masonry wall along the apex of a roof that is built above the level of the roof proper. Roof combs support the highly decorated false façades that rise above the height of the building at the front.

rosettes (p. 105)   A round or oval ornament resembling a rose.

rotunda (p. 197)   Any building (or part thereof) constructed in a circular (or sometimes polygonal) shape, usually producing a large open space crowned by a **dome**.

round arch (p. 172)   See **arch**.

roundel (p. 160)   Any element with a circular format, often placed as a decoration on the exterior of architecture.

rune stone (p. 436)   A stone used in early medieval northern Europe as a commemorative monument, which is carved or inscribed with runes, a writing system used by early Germanic peoples.

rustication (p. 600)   In building, the rough, irregular, and unfinished effect deliberately given to the exterior facing of a stone edifice. Rusticated stones are often large and used for decorative emphasis around doors or windows, or across the entire lower floors of a building. Also, masonry construction with conspicuous, often beveled joints.

salon (p. 905)   A large room for entertaining guests; a periodic social or intellectual gathering, often of prominent people; a hall or **gallery** for exhibiting works of art.

sanctuary (p. 102)   A sacred or holy enclosure used for worship. In ancient Greece and Rome, consisted of one or more temples and an altar. In Christian architecture, the space around the altar in a church called the chancel or presbytery.

sarcophagus (p. 49)   A stone coffin. Often rectangular and decorated with **relief sculpture**.

scarab (p. 51)   In Egypt, a stylized dung beetle associated with the sun and the god Amun.

scarification (p. 403)   Ornamental decoration applied to the surface of the body by cutting the skin for cultural and/or aesthetic reasons.

school of artists (p. 281)   An art historical term describing a group of artists, usually working at the same time and sharing similar styles, influences, and ideals. The artists in a particular school may not necessarily be directly associated with one another, unlike those in a workshop or **atelier**.

scribe (p. 242)   A writer; a person who copies texts.

scriptorium (scriptoria) (p. 242)   A room in a monastery for writing or copying **manuscripts**.

scroll painting (p. 243)   A painting executed on a rolled support. Rollers at each end permit the horizontal scroll to be unrolled as it is studied or the vertical scroll to be hung for contemplation or decoration.

sculpture in the round (p. 5)   Three-dimensional sculpture that is carved free of any background or block.

seals (p. 338)   Personal emblems usually carved of stone in **intaglio** or **relief** and used to stamp a name or legend onto paper or silk. In China, they traditionally employ the archaic characters appropriately known as "seal script," of the Zhou or Qin. Cut in stone, a seal may state a formal given name, or it may state any of the numerous personal names that China's painters and writers adopted throughout their lives. A treasured work of art often bears not only the seal of its maker but also those of collectors and admirers through the centuries. In the Chinese view, these do not disfigure the work but add another layer of interest.

serdab (p. 53)   In Egyptian tombs, the small room in which the *ka* statue was placed.

sfumato (p. 634)   Italian term meaning "smoky," soft, and mellow. In painting, the effect of haze in an image. Resembling the color of the atmosphere at dusk, *sfumato* gives a smoky effect.

sgraffito (p. 602)   Decoration made by **incising** or cutting away a surface layer of material to reveal a different color beneath.

shaft (p. 110)   The main vertical section of a **column** between the **capital** and the **base**, usually circular in cross section.

shaft grave (p. 98)   A deep pit used for burial.

shikhara (p. 301)   In the architecture of northern India, a conical (or pyramidal) spire found atop a Hindu temple and often crowned with an **amalaka**.

shoin (p. 819)   A term used to describe the various features found in the most formal room of upper-class Japanese residential architecture.

shoji (p. 819)   A standing Japanese screen covered in translucent rice paper and used in interiors.

siapo (p. 874)   A type of **tapa** cloth found in Samoa and still used as an important gift for ceremonial occasions.

silkscreen printing (p. 1091)   A technique of printing in which paint or ink is pressed through a stencil and specially prepared cloth to produce a previously designed image. Also called serigraphy.

sinopia (sinopie) (p. 537)   Italian word taken from "Sinope," the ancient city in Asia Minor that was famous for its red-brick pigment. In **fresco** paintings, a full-sized, preliminary sketch done in this color on the first rough coat of plaster or *arriccio*.

site-specific sculpture (p. 1102)   A sculpture commissioned and/or designed for a particular location.

slip (p. 120)   A mixture of clay and water applied to a ceramic object as a final decorative coat. Also: a solution that binds different parts of a vessel together, such as the handle and the main body.

spandrel (p. 172)   The area of wall adjoining the exterior curve of an **arch** between its springing and the **keystone**, or the area between two arches, as in an **arcade**.

spolia (p. 465)   Latin for "hide stripped from an animal." Term used for fragments of older architecture or sculpture reused in a secondary context.

springing (p. 172)   The point at which the curve of an **arch** or **vault** meets with and rises from its support.

squinch (p. 236)   An **arch** or **lintel** built across the upper corners of a square space, allowing a circular or polygonal dome to be more securely set above the walls.

stained glass (p. 464)   Molten glass stained with color using metallic oxides. Stained glass is most often used in windows, for which small pieces of different colors are precisely cut and assembled into a design, held together by lead **cames**. Additional details may be added with vitreous paint.

stave church (p. 436)   A Scandinavian wooden structure with four huge timbers (staves) at its core.

stele (stelae) (p. 27)   A stone slab placed vertically and decorated with inscriptions or reliefs. Used as a grave marker or memorial.

stereobate (p. 110)   A foundation upon which a Classical temple stands.

still life (p. xxxv)   A type of painting that has as its subject inanimate objects (such as food, dishes, fruit, or flowers).

stoa (p. 107)   In Greek architecture, a long roofed walk-way, usually having **columns** on one long side and a wall on the other.

stoneware (p. 22)   A high-fired, vitrified, but opaque **ceramic** ware that is fired in the range of 1,100 to 1,200 degrees Celsius. At that temperature, particles of silica in the clay bodies fuse together so that the finished vessels are impervious to liquids, even without glaze. Stoneware pieces are glazed to enhance their aesthetic appeal and to aid in keeping them clean (since unglazed ceramics are easily soiled). Stoneware occurs in a range of earth-toned colors, from white and tan to gray and black, with light gray predominating. Chinese potters were the first in the world to produce stoneware, which they were able to make as early as the Shang dynasty.

stringcourse (p. 499)   A continuous horizontal band, such as a **molding**, decorating the face of a wall.

studiolo (p. 617)   A room for private conversation and the collection of fine books and art objects. Also known as a study.

stupa (p. 298)   In Buddhist architecture, a bell-shaped or pyramidal religious monument, made of piled earth or stone, and containing sacred **relics**.

stylobate (p. 110)   In Classical architecture, the stone foundation on which a temple **colonnade** stands.

stylus (p. 28)   An instrument with a pointed end (used for writing and printmaking), which makes a delicate line or scratch. Also: a special writing tool for **cuneiform** writing with one pointed end and one triangular.

sublime (p. 955)   djective describing a concept, thing, or state of greatness or vastness with high spiritual, moral, intellectual or emotional value; or something awe-inspiring. The sublime was a goal to which many nineteenth-century artists aspired in their artworks.

sunken relief (p. 71)   See **relief sculpture**.

symposium (p. 118)   An elite gathering of wealthy and powerful men in ancient Greece that focused principally on wine, music, poetry, conversation, games, and love making.

syncretism (p. 222)   A process whereby artists assimilate images and ideas from other traditions or cultures and give them new meanings.

taotie (p. 328)   A mask with a dragon or animal-like face common as a decorative motif in Chinese art.

tapa (p. 874)   A type of cloth used for various pur-poses in Pacific cultures, made from tree bark stripped and beaten, and often bearing subtle designs from the mallets used to work the bark.

tapestry (p. 484)   Multicolored pictorial or decorative weaving meant to be hung on a wall or placed on furniture. Pictorial or decorative motifs are woven directly into the fabric of the cloth itself.

tatami (p. 819)   Mats of woven straw used in Japanese houses as a floor covering.

tempera (p. 141)   A painting medium made by blending egg yolks with water, pigments, and occasionally other materials, such as glue.

tenebrism (p. 724)   The use of strong **chiaroscuro** and artificially illuminated areas to create a dramatic contrast of light and dark in a painting.

terra cotta (p. 114)   A medium made from clay fired over a low heat and sometimes left unglazed. Also: the orange-brown color typical of this medium.

tessera (tesserae) (p. 146)   The small piece of stone, glass, or other object that is pieced together with many others to create a **mosaic**.

tetrarchy (p. 204)   Four-man rule, as in the late Roman Empire, when four emperors shared power.

thatch (p. 17)   Plant material such as reeds or straw tied over a framework of poles.

thermo-luminescence dating (p. 12)   A technique that measures the irradiation of the crystal structure of material such as flint or pottery and the soil in which it is found, determined by luminescence produced when a sample is heated.

tholos (p. 138)   A small, round building. Sometimes built underground, as in a Mycenaean tomb.

tholos tomb (p. 98)   See **tholos**.

thrust (p. 172)   The outward pressure caused by the weight of a **vault** and supported by **buttressing**. See **arch**.

tierceron (p. 554)   In vault construction, a secondary rib that arcs from a **springing** point to the rib that runs lengthwise through the **vault**, called the ridge rib.

tondo (p. 128)   A painting or **relief sculpture** of circular shape.

torana (p. 300)   In Indian architecture, an ornamented gateway **arch** in a temple, usually leading to the **stupa**.

torc (p. 151)   A circular neck ring worn by Celtic warriors.

toron (p. 417)   In West African **mosque** architecture, the wooden beams that project from the walls. Torons are used as support for the scaffolding erected annually for the replastering of the building.

tracery (p. 502)   Stonework or woodwork applied to wall surfaces or filling the open space of windows. In **plate tracery**, openings are cut through the wall. In **bar tracery**, **mullions** divide the space into vertical segments and form decorative patterns at the top of the opening or panel.

transept (p. 228)   The arm of a **cruciform** church, perpendicular to the **nave**. The point where the nave and transept cross is called the crossing. Beyond the crossing lies the **sanctuary**, whether apse, choir, or chevet.

transverse arch (p. 457)   An **arch** that connects the wall **piers** on both sides of an interior space, up and over a stone **vault**.

trefoil (p. 294)   An ornamental design made up of three rounded lobes placed adjacent to one another.

triforium (p. 502)   The element of the interior elevation of a church, found directly below the **clerestory** and consisting of a series of **arched** openings. The triforium can be made up of openings from a narrow wall passageway, or it can be attached directly to the wall.

triglyph (p. 110)   Rectangular block between the **metopes** of a **Doric frieze**. Identified by the three carved vertical grooves, which approximate the appearance of the end of a wooden beam.

triptych (p. 564)   An artwork made up of three panels. The panels may be hinged together so the side segments (wings) fold over the central area.

trompe l'oeil (p. 617)   A manner of representation in which the appearance of natural space and objects is re-created with the express intention of fooling the eye of the viewer, who may be convinced that the subject actually exists as three-dimensional reality.

trumeau (p. 473)   A **column**, **pier**, or post found at the center of a large **portal** or doorway, supporting the **lintel**.

tugra (p. 284)   A **calligraphic** imperial monogram used in Ottoman courts.

tukutuku (p. 871)   Lattice panels created by women from the Maori culture and used in architecture.

Tuscan order (p. 161)   See **order**.

twining (p. 845)   A basketry technique in which short rods are sewn together vertically. The panels are then joined together to form a vessel.

tympanum (p. 473) In Classical architecture, the vertical panel of the **pediment**. In medieval and later architecture, the area over a door enclosed by an **arch** and a **lintel**, often decorated with sculpture or **mosaic**.

ukiyo-e (p. 994) A Japanese term for a type of popular art that was favored from the sixteenth century, particularly in the form of color **woodblock prints**. *Ukiyo-e* prints often depicted the world of the common people in Japan, such as courtesans and actors, as well as landscapes and myths.

undercutting (p. 214) A technique in sculpture by which the material is cut back under the edges so that the remaining form projects strongly forward, casting deep shadows.

underglaze (p. 799) Color or decoration applied to a ceramic piece before glazing.

upeti (p. 874) A carved wooden design tablet, used to create patterns in cloth by dragging the fabric across it, and found in Pacific cultures.

urna (p. 303) In Buddhist art, the curl of hair on the forehead that is a characteristic mark of a buddha. The *urna* is a symbol of divine wisdom.

ushnisha (p. 303) In Asian art, a round turban or tiara symbolizing royalty and, when worn by a buddha, enlightenment.

vanishing point (p. 608) In a **perspective** system, the point on the **horizon line** at which orthogonals meet. A complex system can have multiple vanishing points.

vanitas (p. 751) An image, especially popular in Europe during the seventeenth century, in which all the objects symbolize the transience of life. *Vanitas* paintings are usually of still lifes or genre subjects.

vault (p. 17) An arched masonry structure that spans an interior space. **Barrel** or tunnel vault: an elongated or continuous semicircular vault, shaped like a half-cylinder.

Corbeled vault: a vault made by projecting **courses** of stone. **Groin** or cross vault: a vault created by the intersection of two barrel vaults of equal size which creates four side compartments of identical size and shape. Quadrant or half-barrel vault: as the name suggests a half-barrel vault. **Rib vault**: ribs (extra masonry) demarcate the junctions of a groin vault. Ribs may function to reinforce the groins or may be purely decorative. See also **corbeling**.

veduta (p. 913) Italian for "vista" or "view." Paintings, drawings, or prints often of expansive city scenes or of harbors.

vellum (p. 243) A fine animal skin prepared for writing and painting. See also **parchment**.

verism (p. 170) style in which artists concern themselves with describing the exterior likeness of an object or person, usually by rendering its visible details in a finely executed, meticulous manner.

vihara (p. 301) From the Sanskrit term meaning "for wanderers." A *vihara* is, in general, a Buddhist monastery in India. It also signifies monks' cells and gathering places in such a monastery.

volute (p. 110) A spiral scroll, as seen on an **Ionic capital**.

votive figure (p. 31) An image created as a devotional offering to a god or other deity.

voussoir (p. 172) The oblong, wedge-shaped stone blocks used to build an arch. The topmost voussoir is called a **keystone**.

warp (p. 286) The vertical threads in a weaver's loom. Warp threads make up a fixed framework that provides the structure for the entire piece of cloth, and are thus often thicker than weft threads. See also **weft**.

wattle and daub (p. 17) A wall construction method combining upright branches, woven with twigs (wattles) and plastered or filled with clay or mud (daub).

weft (p. 286) The horizontal threads in a woven piece of cloth. Weft threads are woven at right angles to and through the warp threads to make up the bulk of the decorative pattern. In carpets, the weft is often completely covered or formed by the rows of trimmed knots that form the carpet's soft surface. See also **warp**.

westwork (p. 439) The monumental, west-facing entrance section of a Carolignian, Ottonian, or Romanesque church. The exterior consists of multiple stories between two towers; the interior includes an entrance vestibule, a chapel, and a series of **galleries** overlooking the nave.

white-ground (p. 141) A type of ancient Greek pottery in which the background color of the object was painted with a **slip** that turns white in the firing process. Figures and details were added by painting on or **incising** into this slip. White-ground wares were popular in the Classical period as funerary objects.

woodblock print (p. 589) A print made from one or more carved wooden blocks. In Japan, woodblock prints were made using multiple blocks carved in **relief**, usually with a block for each color in the finished print. See also **woodcut**.

woodcut (p. 590) A type of print made by carving a design into a wooden block. The ink is applied to the block with a roller. As the ink remains only on the raised areas between the carved-away lines, these carved-away areas and lines provide the white areas of the print. Also: the process by which the woodcut is made.

yaksha, yakshi (p. 296) The male (*yaksha*) and female (*yakshi*) nature spirits that act as agents of the Hindu gods. Their sculpted images are often found on Hindu temples and other sacred places, particularly at the entrances.

ziggurat (p. 28) In Mesopotamia, a tall stepped tower of earthen materials, often supporting a shrine.

Susan V. Craig, updated by Carrie L. McDade

This bibliography is composed of books in English that are appropriate "further reading" titles. Most items on this list are available in good libraries, whether college, university, or public institutions. Recently published works have been emphasized so that the research information would be current. There are three classifications of listings: general surveys and art history reference tools, including journals and Internet directories; surveys of large periods that encompass multiple chapters (ancient art in the Western tradition, European medieval art, European Renaissance through eighteenth-century art, modern art in the West, Asian art, and African and Oceanic art, and art of the Americas); and books for individual Chapters 1 through 32.

General Art History Surveys and Reference Tools

Adams, Laurie Schneider. *Art across Time*. 4th ed. New York: McGraw-Hill, 2011.

Barnet, Sylvan. *A Short Guide to Writing about Art*. 10th ed. Upper Saddle River, NJ: Pearson/Prentice Hall, 2010.

Bony, Anne. *Design: History, Main Trends, Main Figures*. Edinburgh: Chambers, 2005.

Boström, Antonia. *Encyclopedia of Sculpture*. 3 vols. New York: Fitzroy Dearborn, 2004.

Broude, Norma, and Mary D. Garrard, eds. *Feminism and Art History: Questioning the Litany*. Icon Editions. New York: Harper & Row, 1982.

Chadwick, Whitney. *Women, Art, and Society*. 4th ed. New York: Thames & Hudson, 2007.

Chilvers, Ian, ed. *The Oxford Dictionary of Art*. 4th ed. New York: Oxford Univ. Press, 2009.

Curl, James Stevens. *A Dictionary of Architecture and Landscape Architecture*. 2nd ed. Oxford: Oxford Univ. Press, 2006.

Davies, Penelope J. E., et al. *Janson's History of Art: The Western Tradition*. 8th ed. Upper Saddle River, NJ: Prentice Hall, 2010.

The Dictionary of Art. Ed. Jane Turner. 34 vols. New York: Grove's Dictionaries, 1996.

Encyclopedia of World Art. 17 vols. New York: McGraw-Hill, 1959–84.

Frank, Patrick, Duane Preble, and Sarah Preble. *Prebles' Artforms*. 10th ed. Upper Saddle River, NJ: Pearson/Prentice Hall, 2008.

Gaze, Delia, ed. *Dictionary of Women Artists*. 2 vols. London: Fitzroy Dearborn, 1997.

Griffiths, Antony. *Prints and Printmaking: An Introduction to the History and Techniques*. 2nd ed. London: British Museum Press, 1996.

Hadden, Peggy. *The Quotable Artist*. New York: Allworth Press, 2002.

Hall, James. *Dictionary of Subjects and Symbols in Art*. 2nd ed. Boulder, CO: Westview Press, 2008.

Holt, Elizabeth Gilmore, ed. *A Documentary History of Art*. 3 vols. New Haven: Yale Univ. Press, 1986.

Honour, Hugh, and John Fleming. *The Visual Arts: A History*. 7th ed. rev. Upper Saddle River, NJ: Pearson/Prentice Hall, 2010.

Johnson, Paul. *Art: A New History*. New York: HarperCollins, 2003.

Kemp, Martin, ed. *The Oxford History of Western Art*. Oxford: Oxford Univ. Press, 2000.

Kleiner, Fred S. *Gardner's Art through the Ages*. Enhanced 13th ed. Belmont, CA: Thomson/Wadsworth, 2011.

Kostof, Spiro. *A History of Architecture: Settings and Rituals*. 2nd ed. Revised. Greg Castillo. New York: Oxford Univ. Press, 1995.

Mackenzie, Lynn. *Non-Western Art: A Brief Guide*. 2nd ed. Upper Saddle River, NJ: Pearson/Prentice Hall, 2001.

Marmor, Max, and Alex Ross, eds. *Guide to the Literature of Art History 2*. Chicago: American Library Association, 2005.

Onians, John, ed. *Atlas of World Art*. New York: Oxford Univ. Press, 2004.

Sayre, Henry M. *Writing about Art*. 6th ed. Upper Saddle River, NJ: Pearson/Prentice Hall, 2009.

Sed-Rajna, Gabrielle. *Jewish Art*. Trans. Sara Friedman and Mira Reich. New York: Abrams, 1997.

Slatkin, Wendy. *Women Artists in History: From Antiquity to the Present*. 4th ed. Upper Saddle River, NJ: Pearson/Prentice Hall, 2001.

Sutton, Ian. *Western Architecture: From Ancient Greece to the Present*. World of Art. New York: Thames & Hudson, 1999.

Trachtenberg, Marvin, and Isabelle Hyman. *Architecture, from Prehistory to Postmodernity*. 2nd ed. Upper Saddle River, NJ: Pearson/Prentice Hall, 2002.

Watkin, David. *A History of Western Architecture*. 4th ed. New York: Watson-Guptill, 2005.

Art History Journals: A Select List of Current Titles

African Arts. Quarterly. Los Angeles: Univ. of California at Los Angeles, James S. Coleman African Studies Center, 1967–.

American Art: The Journal of the Smithsonian American Art Museum. 3/year. Chicago: Univ. of Chicago Press, 1987–.

American Indian Art Magazine. Quarterly. Scottsdale, AZ: American Indian Art Inc., 1975–.

American Journal of Archaeology. Quarterly. Boston: Archaeological Institute of America, 1885–.

Antiquity: A Periodical of Archaeology. Quarterly. Cambridge: Antiquity Publications Ltd., 1927–.

Apollo: The International Magazine of the Arts. Monthly. London: Apollo Magazine Ltd., 1925–.

Architectural History. Annually. Farnham, UK: Society of Architectural Historians of Great Britain, 1958–.

Archives of American Art Journal. Quarterly. Washington, DC: Archives of American Art, Smithsonian Institution, 1960–.

Archives of Asian Art. Annually. New York: Asia Society, 1945–.

Ars Orientalis: The Arts of Asia, Southeast Asia, and Islam. Annually. Ann Arbor: Univ. of Michigan Dept. of Art History, 1954–.

Art Bulletin. Quarterly. New York: College Art Association, 1913–.

Art History: Journal of the Association of Art Historians. 5/year. Oxford: Blackwell Publishing Ltd., 1978–.

Art in America. Monthly. New York: Brant Publications Inc., 1913–.

Art Journal. Quarterly. New York: College Art Association, 1960–.

Art Nexus. Quarterly. Bogata, Colombia: Arte en Colombia Ltda, 1976–.

Art Papers Magazine. Bimonthly. Atlanta: Atlanta Art Papers Inc., 1976–.

Artforum International. 10/year. New York: Artforum International Magazine Inc., 1962–.

Artnews. 11/year. New York: Artnews LLC, 1902–.

Bulletin of the Metropolitan Museum of Art. Quarterly. New York: Metropolitan Museum of Art, 1905–.

Burlington Magazine. Monthly. London: Burlington Magazine Publications Ltd., 1903–.

Dumbarton Oaks Papers. Annually. Locust Valley, NY: J. J. Augustin Inc., 1940–.

Flash Art International. Bimonthly. Trevi, Italy: Giancarlo Politi Editore, 1980–.

Gesta. Semiannually. New York: International Center of Medieval Art, 1963–.

History of Photography. Quarterly. Abingdon, UK: Taylor & Francis Ltd., 1976–.

International Review of African American Art. Quarterly. Hampton, VA: International Review of African American Art, 1976–.

Journal of Design History. Quarterly. Oxford: Oxford Univ. Press, 1988–.

Journal of Egyptian Archaeology. Annually. London: Egypt Exploration Society, 1914–.

Journal of Hellenic Studies. Annually. London: Society for the Promotion of Hellenic Studies, 1880–.

Journal of Roman Archaeology. Annually. Portsmouth, RI: Journal of Roman Archaeology LLC, 1988–.

Journal of the Society of Architectural Historians. Quarterly. Chicago: Society of Architectural Historians, 1940–.

Journal of the Warburg and Courtauld Institutes. Annually. London: Warburg Institute, 1937–.

Leonardo: Art, Science and Technology. 6/year. Cambridge, MA: MIT Press, 1968–.

Marg. Quarterly. Mumbai, India: Scientific Publishers, 1946–.

Master Drawings. Quarterly. New York: Master Drawings Association, 1963–.

October. Cambridge, MA: MIT Press, 1976–.

Oxford Art Journal. 3/year. Oxford: Oxford Univ. Press, 1978–.

Parkett. 3/year. Zürich, Switzerland: Parkett Verlag AG, 1984–.

Print Quarterly. Quarterly. London: Print Quarterly Publications, 1984–.

Simiolus: Netherlands Quarterly for the History of Art. Quarterly. Apeldoorn, Netherlands: Stichting voor Nederlandse Kunsthistorische Publicaties, 1966–.

Woman's Art Journal. Semiannually. Philadelphia: Old City Publishing Inc., 1980–.

Internet Directories for Art History Information: A Selected List

ARCHITECTURE AND BUILDING,
http://www.library.unlv.edu/arch/rsrce/webresources/
A directory of architecture websites collected by Jeanne Brown at the Univ. of Nevada at Las Vegas. Topical lists include architecture, building and construction, design, history, housing, planning, preservation, and landscape architecture. Most entries include a brief annotation and the last date the link was accessed by the compiler.

ART HISTORY RESOURCES ON THE WEB,
http://witcombe.sbc.edu/ARTHLinks.html
Authored by Professor Christopher L. C. E. Witcombe of Sweet Briar College in Virginia, since 1995, the site includes an impressive number of links for various art historical eras as well as links to research resources, museums, and galleries. The content is frequently updated.

ART IN FLUX: A DIRECTORY OF RESOURCES FOR RESEARCH IN CONTEMPORARY ART,
http://www.boisestate.edu/art/artinflux/intro.html
Cheryl K. Shurtleff of Boise State Univ. in Idaho, has authored this directory, which includes sites selected according to their relevance to the study of national or international contemporary art and artists. The subsections include artists, museums, theory, reference, and links.

ARTCYCLOPEDIA: THE GUIDE TO GREAT ART ON THE INTERNET
http://www.artcyclopedia.com
With more than 2,100 art sites and 75,000 links, this is one of the most comprehensive web directories for artists and art topics. The primary search is by artist's name but access is also available by title of artwork, artistic movement, museums and galleries, nationality, period, and medium.

MOTHER OF ALL ART AND ART HISTORY LINKS PAGES
http://umich.edu/~motherha
Maintained by the Dept. of the History of Art at the Univ. of Michigan, this directory covers art history departments, art museums, fine arts schools and departments as well as links to research resources. Each entry includes annotations.

VOICE OF THE SHUTTLE,
http://vos.ucsb.edu
Sponsored by Univ. of California, Santa Barbara, this directory includes more than 70 pages of links to humanities and humanities-related resources on the Internet. The structured guide includes specific subsections on architecture, on art (modern and contemporary), and on art history. Links usually include a one-sentence explanation and the resource is frequently updated with new information.

ARTBABBLE
http://www.artbabble.org/
An online community created by staff at the Indianapolis Museum of Art to showcase art-based video content, including interviews with artists and curators, original documentaries, and art installation videos. Partners and contributors to the project include Art21, Los Angeles County Museum of Art, The Museum of Modern Art, The New York Public Library, San Francisco Museum of Modern Art, and Smithsonian American Art Museum.

YAHOO! ARTS>ART HISTORY,
http://dir.yahoo.com/Arts/Art_History/
Another extensive directory of art links organized into subdivisions with one of the most extensive being "Periods and

Movements." Links include the name of the site as well as a few words of explanation.

Ancient Art in the Western Tradition, General

Amiet, Pierre. *Art in the Ancient World: A Handbook of Styles and Forms*. New York: Rizzoli, 1981.

Beard, Mary, and John Henderson. *Classical Art: From Greece to Rome*. Oxford History of Art. Oxford: Oxford Univ. Press, 2001.

Boardman, John. *Oxford History of Classical Art*. New York: Oxford Univ. Press, 2001.

Chitham, Robert. *The Classical Orders of Architecture*. 2nd ed. Boston: Elsevier/Architectural Press, 2005.

Ehrich, Robert W., ed. *Chronologies in Old World Archaeology*. 3rd ed. 2 vols. Chicago: Univ. of Chicago Press, 1992.

Gerster, Georg. *The Past from Above: Aerial Photographs of Archaeological Sites*. Ed. Charlotte Trümpler. Trans. Stewart Spencer. Los Angeles: J. Paul Getty Museum, 2005.

Groenewegen-Frankfort, H. A., and Bernard Ashmole. *Art of the Ancient World: Painting, Pottery, Sculpture, Architecture from Egypt, Mesopotamia, Crete, Greece, and Rome*. Library of Art History. Upper Saddle River, NJ: Prentice Hall, 1972.

Haywood, John. *The Penguin Historical Atlas of Ancient Civilizations*. New York: Penguin, 2005.

Milleker, Elizabeth J., ed. *The Year One: Art of the Ancient World East and West*. New York: Metropolitan Museum of Art, 2000.

Nagle, D. Brendan. *The Ancient World: A Social and Cultural History*. 7th ed. Upper Saddle River, NJ: Pearson/Prentice Hall, 2010.

Saggs, H. W. F. *Civilization before Greece and Rome*. New Haven: Yale Univ. Press, 1989.

Smith, William Stevenson. *Interconnections in the Ancient Near East: A Study of the Relationships between the Arts of Egypt, the Aegean, and Western Asia*. New Haven: Yale Univ. Press, 1965.

Tadgell, Christopher. *Imperial Form: From Achaemenid Iran to Augustan Rome*. New York: Whitney Library of Design, 1998.

———. *Origins: Egypt, West Asia and the Aegean*. New York: Whitney Library of Design, 1998.

Trigger, Bruce G. *Understanding Early Civilizations: A Comparative Study*. New York: Cambridge Univ. Press, 2003.

Woodford, Susan. *The Art of Greece and Rome*. 2nd ed. New York: Cambridge Univ. Press, 2004.

European Medieval Art, General

Backman, Clifford R. *The Worlds of Medieval Europe*. 2nd ed. New York: Oxford Univ. Press, 2009.

Bennett, Adelaide Louise, et al. *Medieval Mastery: Book Illumination from Charlemagne to Charles the Bold: 800–1475*. Trans. Lee Preedy and Greta Arblaster-Holmer. Turnhout: Brepols, 2002.

Benton, Janetta R. *Art of the Middle Ages*. World of Art. New York: Thames & Hudson, 2002.

Binski, Paul. *Painters*. Medieval Craftsmen. London: British Museum Press, 1991.

Brown, Sarah, and David O'Connor. *Glass-painters*. Medieval Craftsmen. London: British Museum Press, 1991.

Calkins, Robert G. *Medieval Architecture in Western Europe: From a.d. 300 to 1500*. New York: Oxford Univ. Press, 1998.

Cherry, John F. *Goldsmiths*. Medieval Craftsmen. London: British Museum Press, 1992.

Clark, William W. *The Medieval Cathedrals*. Westport, CT: Greenwood Press, 2006.

Coldstream, Nicola. *Masons and Sculptors*. Medieval Craftsmen. London: British Museum Press, 1991.

———. *Medieval Architecture*. Oxford History of Art. Oxford: Oxford Univ. Press, 2002.

De Hamel, Christopher. *Scribes and Illuminators*. Medieval Craftsmen. London: British Museum Press, 1992.

Duby, Georges. *Art and Society in the Middle Ages*. Trans. Jean Birrell. Malden, MA: Blackwell, 2000.

Fossier, Robert, ed. *The Cambridge Illustrated History of the Middle Ages*. Trans. Janet Sondheimer and Sarah Hanbury Tenison. 3 vols. Cambridge: Cambridge Univ. Press, 1986–97.

Hürlimann, Martin, and Jean Bony. *French Cathedrals*. Rev. & enlarged ed. London: Thames & Hudson, 1967.

Jotischky, Andrew, and Caroline Susan Hull. *The Penguin Historical Atlas of the Medieval World*. New York: Penguin, 2005.

Kenyon, John. *Medieval Fortifications*. Leicester: Leicester Univ. Press, 1990.

Pfaffenbichler, Matthias. *Armourers*. Medieval Craftsmen. London: British Museum Press, 1992.

Rebold Benton, Janetta. *Art of the Middle Ages*. World of Art. New York: Thames & Hudson, 2002.

Rudolph, Conran, ed. *A Companion to Medieval Art*. Blackwell Companions to Art History. Oxford: Blackwell, 2006.

Sekules, Veronica. *Medieval Art*. Oxford History of Art. New York: Oxford Univ. Press, 2001.

Snyder, James, Henry Luttikhuizen, and Dorothy Verkerk. *Art of the Middle Ages*. 2nd ed. Upper Saddle River, NJ: Pearson/Prentice Hall, 2006.

Staniland, Kay. *Embroiderers*. Medieval Craftsmen. London: British Museum Press, 1991.

Stokstad, Marilyn. *Medieval Art*. 2nd ed. Boulder, CO: Westview Press, 2004.

———. *Medieval Castles*. Greenwood Guides to Historic Events of the Medieval World. Westport, CT: Greenwood Press, 2005.

European Renaissance through Eighteenth-Century Art, General

Black, C. F., et al. *Cultural Atlas of the Renaissance*. New York: Prentice Hall, 1993.

Blunt, Anthony. *Art and Architecture in France, 1500–1700*. 5th ed. Revised. Richard Beresford. Pelican History of Art. New Haven: Yale Univ. Press, 1999.

Brown, Jonathan. *Painting in Spain: 1500–1700*. Pelican History of Art. New Haven: Yale Univ. Press, 1998.

Cole, Bruce. *Studies in the History of Italian Art, 1250–1550*. London: Pindar Press, 1996.

Graham-Dixon, Andrew. *Renaissance*. Berkeley: Univ. of California Press, 1999.

Harbison, Craig. *The Mirror of the Artist: Northern Renaissance Art in Its Historical Context*. Perspectives. New York: Abrams, 1995.

Harris, Ann Sutherland. *Seventeenth-Century Art & Architecture*. 2nd ed. Upper Saddle River, NJ: Pearson/Prentice Hall, 2008.

Harrison, Charles, Paul Wood, and Jason Gaiger. *Art in Theory 1648–1815: An Anthology of Changing Ideas*. Oxford: Blackwell, 2000.

Hartt, Frederick, and David G. Wilkins. *History of Italian Renaissance Art: Painting, Sculpture, Architecture*. 7th ed. Upper Saddle River, NJ: Pearson/Prentice Hall, 2011.

Jestaz, Bertrand. *The Art of the Renaissance*. Trans. I. Mark Paris. New York: Abrams, 1994.

Minor, Vernon Hyde. *Baroque & Rococo: Art & Culture*. New York: Abrams, 1999.

Paoletti, John T., and Gary M. Radke. *Art in Renaissance Italy*. 3rd ed. Upper Saddle River, NJ: Pearson/Prentice Hall, 2005.

Smith, Jeffrey Chipps. *The Northern Renaissance*. Art & Ideas. London and New York: Phaidon Press, 2004.

Stechow, Wolfgang. *Northern Renaissance, 1400–1600: Sources and Documents*. Upper Saddle River, NJ: Pearson/Prentice Hall, 1966.

Summerson, John. *Architecture in Britain, 1530–1830*. 9th ed. Pelican History of Art. New Haven: Yale Univ. Press, 1993.

Waterhouse, Ellis K. *Painting in Britain, 1530 to 1790*. 5th ed. Pelican History of Art. New Haven: Yale Univ. Press, 1994.

Whinney, Margaret Dickens. *Sculpture in Britain: 1530–1830*. 2nd ed. Revised. John Physick. Pelican History of Art. London: Penguin, 1988.

Modern Art in the West, General

Arnason, H. H. *History of Modern Art: Painting, Sculpture, Architecture, Photography*. 6th ed. Upper Saddle River, NJ: Pearson/Prentice Hall, 2009.

Ballantyne, Andrew, ed. *Architectures: Modernism and After*. New Interventions in Art History, 3. Malden, MA: Blackwell, 2004.

Barnitz, Jacqueline. *Twentieth-Century Art of Latin America*. Austin: Univ. of Texas Press, 2001.

Bjelajac, David. *American Art: A Cultural History*. Rev. and expanded ed. Upper Saddle River, NJ: Pearson/Prentice Hall, 2005.

Bowness, Alan. *Modern European Art*. World of Art. New York: Thames & Hudson, 1995.

Brettell, Richard R. *Modern Art, 1851–1929: Capitalism and Representation*. Oxford History of Art. Oxford: Oxford Univ. Press, 1999.

Chipp, Herschel B. *Theories of Modern Art: A Source Book by Artists and Critics*. California Studies in the History of Art, 11. Berkeley: Univ. of California Press, 1984.

Clarke, Graham. *The Photograph*. Oxford History of Art. Oxford: Oxford Univ. Press, 1997.

Craven, David. *Art and Revolution in Latin America, 1910–1990*. New Haven: Yale Univ. Press, 2002.

Craven, Wayne. *American Art: History and Culture*. 2nd ed. Boston: McGraw-Hill, 2003.

Doordan, Dennis P. *Twentieth-Century Architecture*. New York: Abrams, 2002.

Doss, Erika. *Twentieth-Century American Art*. Oxford History of Art. Oxford: Oxford Univ. Press, 2002.

Edwards, Steve, and Paul Wood, eds. *Art of the Avant-Gardes*. Art of the 20th Century. New Haven: Yale Univ. Press, 2004.

Foster, Hal, et al. *Art Since 1900: Modernism, Antimodernism, Postmodernism*. New York: Thames & Hudson, 2004.

Gaiger, Jason, ed. *Frameworks for Modern Art*. Art of the 20th Century. New Haven: Yale Univ. Press, 2003.

———, and Paul Wood, eds. *Art of the Twentieth Century: A Reader*. New Haven: Yale Univ. Press, 2003

Hamilton, George Heard. *Painting and Sculpture in Europe, 1880–1940*. 6th ed. Pelican History of Art. New Haven: Yale Univ. Press, 1993.

Hammacher, A. M. *Modern Sculpture: Tradition and Innovation*. Enl. ed. New York: Abrams, 1988.

Harris, Ann Sutherland, and Linda Nochlin. *Women Artists: 1550–1950*. Los Angeles: Los Angeles County Museum of Art, 1976.

Harrison, Charles, and Paul Wood, eds. *Art in Theory: 1900–2000: An Anthology of Changing Ideas*. 2nd ed. Malden, MA: Blackwell, 2003.

Hunter, Sam, John Jacobus, and Daniel Wheeler. *Modern Art: Painting, Sculpture, Architecture, Photography*. 3rd rev. & exp. ed. Upper Saddle River, NJ: Pearson/Prentice Hall, 2004.

Krauss, Rosalind E. *Passages in Modern Sculpture*. Cambridge, MA: MIT Press, 1977.

Mancini, JoAnne Marie. *Pre-Modernism: Art-World Change and American Culture from the Civil War to the Armory Show*. Princeton: Princeton Univ. Press, 2005.

Marien, Mary Warner. *Photography: A Cultural History*. 3rd ed. Upper Saddle River, NJ: Pearson/Prentice Hall, 2011.

Meecham, Pam, and Julie Sheldon. *Modern Art: A Critical Introduction*. 2nd ed. New York: Routledge, 2005.

Newlands, Anne. *Canadian Art: From Its Beginnings to 2000*. Willowdale, Ont.: Firefly Books, 2000.

Phaidon Atlas of Contemporary World Architecture. London: Phaidon Press, 2004.

Powell, Richard J. *Black Art: A Cultural History*. 2nd ed. World of Art. New York: Thames & Hudson, 2003.

Rosenblum, Naomi. *A World History of Photography*. 4th ed. New York: Abbeville Press, 2007.

Ruhrberg, Karl. *Art of the 20th Century*. Ed. Ingo F. Walther. 2 vols. New York: Taschen, 1998.

Scully, Vincent Joseph. *Modern Architecture and Other Essays*. Princeton: Princeton Univ. Press, 2003.

Stiles, Kristine, and Peter Selz. *Theories and Documents of Contemporary Art: A Sourcebook of Artists' Writings*. California Studies in the History of Art, 35. Berkeley: Univ. of California Press, 1996.

Tafuri, Manfredo. *Modern Architecture*. History of World Architecture. 2 vols. New York: Electa/Rizzoli, 1986.

Traba, Marta. *Art of Latin America, 1900–1980*. Washington, DC: Inter-American Development Bank, 1994.

Upton, Dell. *Architecture in the United States*. Oxford History of Art. Oxford: Oxford Univ. Press, 1998.

Wood, Paul, ed. *Varieties of Modernism*. Art of the 20th Century. New Haven: Yale Univ. Press, 2004.

Woodham, Jonathan M. *Twentieth Century Design*. Oxford History of Art. Oxford: Oxford Univ. Press, 1997.

Asian Art, General

Addiss, Stephen, Gerald Groemer, and J. Thomas Rimer, eds. *Traditional Japanese Arts and Culture: An Illustrated Sourcebook*. Honolulu: Univ. of Hawai'i Press, 2006.

Barnhart, Richard M. *Three Thousand Years of Chinese Painting*. New Haven: Yale Univ. Press, 1997.

Blunden, Caroline, and Mark Elvin. *Cultural Atlas of China*. 2nd ed. New York: Checkmark Books, 1998.

Brown, Kerry, ed. *Sikh Art and Literature*. New York: Routledge in collaboration with the Sikh Foundation, 1999.

Chang, Léon Long-Yien, and Peter Miller. *Four Thousand Years of Chinese Calligraphy*. Chicago: Univ. of Chicago Press, 1990.

Chang, Yang-mo. *Arts of Korea*. Ed. Judith G. Smith. New York: Metropolitan Museum of Art, 1998.

Clark, John. *Modern Asian Art*. Honolulu: Univ. of Hawai'i Press, 1998.

Clunas, Craig. *Art in China*. 2nd ed. Oxford History of Art. Oxford: Oxford Univ. Press, 2009.

Coaldrake, William H. *Architecture and Authority in Japan*. London: Routledge, 1996.

Cohen, Warren I. *East Asian Art and American Culture: A Study in International Relations*. New York: Columbia Univ. Press, 1992.

Collcutt, Martin, Marius Jansen, and Isao Kumakura. *Cultural Atlas of Japan*. New York: Facts on File, 1988.

Craven, Roy C. *Indian Art: A Concise History*. Rev. ed. World of Art. New York: Thames & Hudson, 1997.
Dehejia, Vidya. *Indian Art. Art & Ideas*. London: Phaidon Press, 1997.
Fisher, Robert E. *Buddhist Art and Architecture*. World of Art. New York: Thames & Hudson, 1993.
Fu, Xinian. *Chinese Architecture*. Ed. & exp., Nancy S. Steinhardt. New Haven: Yale Univ. Press, 2002.
Hearn, Maxwell K., and Judith G. Smith, eds. *Arts of the Sung and Yüan: Papers Prepared for an International Symposium*. New York: Dept. of Asian Art, Metropolitan Museum of Art, 1996.
Heibonsha Survey of Japanese Art. 31 vols. New York: Weatherhill, 1972–80.
Hertz, Betti-Sue. *Past in Reverse: Contemporary Art of East Asia*. San Diego: San Diego Museum of Art, 2004.
Japanese Arts Library. 15 vols. New York: Kodansha International, 1977–87.
Kerlogue, Fiona. *Arts of Southeast Asia*. World of Art. New York: Thames & Hudson, 2004.
Khanna, Balraj, and George Michell. *Human and Divine: 2000 Years of Indian Sculpture*. London: Hayward Gallery, 2000.
Lee, Sherman E. *A History of Far Eastern Art*. 5th ed. Ed. Naomi Noble Richards. New York: Abrams, 1994.
———. *China, 5000 Years: Innovation and Transformation in the Arts*. New York: Solomon R. Guggenheim Museum, 1998.
Liu, Cary Y., and Dora C.Y. Ching, eds. *Arts of the Sung and Yüan: Ritual, Ethnicity, and Style in Painting*. Princeton: Art Museum, Princeton Univ., 1999.
McArthur, Meher. *The Arts of Asia: Materials, Techniques, Styles*. New York: Thames & Hudson, 2005.
———. *Reading Buddhist Art: An Illustrated Guide to Buddhist Signs and Symbols*. New York: Thames & Hudson, 2002.
Mason, Penelope. *History of Japanese Art*. 2nd ed. Upper Saddle River, NJ: Pearson/Prentice Hall, 2005.
Michell, George. *Hindu Art and Architecture*. World of Art. London: Thames & Hudson, 2000.
———. *The Penguin Guide to the Monuments of India*. 2 vols. New York: Viking, 1989.
Mitter, Partha. *Indian Art*. Oxford History of Art. Oxford: Oxford Univ. Press, 2001.
Murase, Miyeko. *Bridge of Dreams: The Mary Griggs Burke Collection of Japanese Art*. New York: Metropolitan Museum of Art, 2000.
Nickel, Lukas, ed. *Return of the Buddha: The Qingzhou Discoveries*. London: Royal Academy of Arts, 2002.
Pak, Youngsook, and Roderick Whitfield. *Buddhist Sculpture*. Handbook of Korean Art. London: Laurence King, 2003.
Sullivan, Michael. *The Arts of China*. 5th ed., rev. & exp. Berkeley: Univ. of California Press, 2008.
Thorp, Robert L., and Richard Ellis Vinograd. *Chinese Art & Culture*. New York: Abrams, 2001.
Topsfield, Andrew, ed. *In the Realm of Gods and Kings: Arts of India*. London: Philip Wilson, 2004.
Tucker, Jonathan. *The Silk Road: Art and History*. Chicago: Art Media Resources, 2003.
Tregear, Mary. *Chinese Art*. Rev. ed. World of Art. New York: Thames & Hudson, 1997.
Vainker S. J. *Chinese Pottery and Porcelain: From Prehistory to the Present*. New York: Braziller, 1991.

African and Oceanic Art and Art of the Americas, General

Anderson, Richard L., and Karen L. Field, eds. *Art in Small-Scale Societies: Contemporary Readings*. Upper Saddle River, NJ: Pearson/Prentice Hall, 1993.
Bacquart, Jean-Baptiste. *The Tribal Arts of Africa*. New York: Thames & Hudson, 1998.
Bassani, Ezio, ed. *Arts of Africa: 7000 Years of African Art*. Milan: Skira, 2005.
Benson, Elizabeth P. *Retratos: 2,000 Years of Latin American Portraits*. San Antonio, TX: San Antonio Museum of Art, 2004.
Berlo, Janet Catherine, and Lee Anne Wilson. *Arts of Africa, Oceania, and the Americas: Selected Readings*. Upper Saddle River, NJ: Prentice Hall, 1993.
Calloway, Colin G. *First Peoples: A Documentary Survey of American Indian History*. 3rd ed. Boston: Bedford/St. Martin's, 2008.
Coote, Jeremy, and Anthony Shelton, eds. *Anthropology, Art, and Aesthetics*. New York: Oxford Univ. Press, 1992.
Drewal, Henry, and John Pemberton III. *Yoruba: Nine Centuries of African Art and Thought*. New York: Center for African Art, 1989.
Evans, Susan Toby. *Ancient Mexico & Central America: Archaeology and Culture History*. 2nd ed. New York: Thames & Hudson, 2008.
———, and David L. Webster, eds. *Archaeology of Ancient Mexico and Central America: An Encyclopedia*. New York: Garland, 2001.
———, and Joanne Pillsbury, eds. *Palaces of the Ancient New World: A Symposium at Dumbarton Oaks, 10th and 11th October, 1998*. Washington, DC: Dumbarton Oaks Research Library and Collection, 2004.
Geoffroy-Schneiter, Bérénice. *Tribal Arts*. New York: Vendome Press, 2000.
Hiller, Susan, ed. & compiled. *The Myth of Primitivism: Perspectives on Art*. London: Routledge, 1991.
Mack, John, ed. *Africa, Arts and Cultures*. London: British Museum Press, 2000.
Mexico: Splendors of Thirty Centuries. New York: Metropolitan Museum of Art, 1990.
Nunley, John W., and Cara McCarty. *Masks: Faces of Culture*. New York: Abrams in assoc. with the Saint Louis Art Museum, 1999.
Perani, Judith, and Fred T. Smith. *The Visual Arts of Africa: Gender, Power, and Life Cycle Rituals*. Upper Saddle River, NJ: Pearson/Prentice Hall, 1998.
Phillips, Tom, ed. *Africa: The Art of a Continent*. New York: Prestel, 1995.
Price, Sally. *Primitive Art in Civilized Places*. 2nd ed. Chicago: Univ. of Chicago Press, 2001.
Rabineau, Phyllis. *Feather Arts: Beauty, Wealth, and Spirit from Five Continents*. Chicago: Field Museum of Natural History, 1979.
Schuster, Carl, and Edmund Carpenter. *Patterns that Connect: Social Symbolism in Ancient & Tribal Art*. New York: Abrams, 1996.
Scott, John F. *Latin American Art: Ancient to Modern*. Gainesville: Univ. Press of Florida, 1999.
Stepan, Peter. *Africa*. Trans. John Gabriel and Elizabeth Schwaiger. London: Prestel, 2001.
Visonà, Monica Blackmun, et al. *A History of Art in Africa*. 2nd ed. Upper Saddle River, NJ: Pearson/Prentice Hall, 2008.

Introduction

Acton, Mary. *Learning to Look at Paintings*. 2nd ed. New York: Routledge, 2009.
Arnold, Dana. *Art History: A Very Short Introduction*. Oxford and New York: Oxford Univ. Press, 2004.
Baxandall, Michael. *Patterns of Intention: On the Historical Explanation of Pictures*. New Haven: Yale Univ. Press, 1985.
Clearwater, Bonnie. *The Rothko Book*. London: Tate Publishing, 2006.
Decoteau, Pamela Hibbs. *Clara Peeters, 1594–ca. 1640 and the Development of Still-Life Painting in Northern Europe*. Lingen: Luca Verlag, 1992.
Geertz, Clifford. *"Art as a Cultural System."* Modern Language Notes 91 (1976): 1473–1499.
Hochstrasser, Julie Berger. *Still Life and Trade in the Dutch Golden Age*. New Haven: Yale Univ. Press, 2007.
Holstein, Jonathan. *The Pieced Quilt: An American Design Tradition*. New York: Galahad Books, 1973.
Jolly, Penny Howell. *"Rogier van der Weyden's Escorial and Philadelphia Crucifixions and Their Relation to Fra Angelico at San Marco."* Oud Holland 95 (1981): 113–126.
Mainardi, Patricia. *"Quilts: The Great American Art."* The Feminist Art Journal 2/1 (1973): 1, 18–23.
Miller, Angela L., et al. *American Encounters: Art, History, and Cultural Identity*. Upper Saddle River, NJ: Pearson/Prentice Hall, 2008.
Minor, Vernon Hyde. *Art History's History*. Upper Saddle River, NJ: Pearson/Prentice Hall, 2001.
Nelson, Robert S., and Richard Shiff, eds. *Critical Terms for Art History*. 2nd ed. Chicago: Univ. of Chicago Press, 2003.
Panofsky, Erwin. *Studies in Iconology: Humanistic Themes in the Art of the Renaissance*. New York: Oxford Univ. Press, 1939.
______. *Meaning in the Visual Arts*. Phoenix ed. Chicago: Univ. of Chicago Press, 1982.
Preziosi, Donald, ed. *The Art of Art History: A Critical Anthology*. 2nd ed. Oxford and New York: Oxford Univ. Press, 2009.
Rothko, Mark. *Writings on Art*. Ed. Miguel López-Remiro. New Haven: Yale Univ. Press, 2006.
Rothko, Mark. *The Artist's Reality: Philosophies of Art*. Ed. Christopher Rothko. New Haven: Yale Univ. Press, 2004.
Schapiro, Meyer. *"The Apples of Cézanne: An Essay on the Meaning of Still Life."* Art News Annual 34 (1968): 34–53. Reprinted in Modern Art 19th & 20th Centuries: Selected Papers 2, London: Chatto & Windus, 1978.
Sowers, Robert. *Rethinking the Forms of Visual Expression*. Berkeley: Univ. of California Press, 1990.
Taylor, Joshua. *Learning to Look: A Handbook for the Visual Arts*. 2nd ed. Chicago: Chicago Univ. Press, 1981.
Tucker, Mark. *"Rogier van der Weyden's 'Philadelphia Crucifixion.'"* Burlington Magazine 139 (1997): 676–683.
Wang, Fangyu, et al, eds. *Master of the Lotus Garden: The Life and Art of Bada Shanren (1626–1705)*. New Haven: Yale Univ. Press, 1990.

Chapter 1 Prehistoric Art

Aujoulat, Norbert. *Lascaux: Movement, Space, and Time*. New York: Abrams, 2005.
Bahn Paul G. *The Cambridge Illustrated History of Prehistoric Art*. Cambridge Illustrated History. Cambridge: Cambridge Univ. Press, 1998.
Bataille, Georges. *The Cradle of Humanity: Prehistoric Art and Culture*. Ed. Stuart Kendall. Trans. Michelle Kendall and Stuart Kendall. New York: Zone Books, 2005.
Berghaus, Gunter. *New Perspectives on Prehistoric Art*. Westport, CT: Praeger, 2004.
Chippindale, Christopher. *Stonehenge Complete*. 3rd ed. New York: Thames & Hudson, 2004.
Clottes, Jean. *Chauvet Cave: The Art of Earliest Times*. Salt Lake City: Univ. of Utah Press, 2003.
———. *World Rock Art*. Trans. Guy Bennett. Los Angeles: Getty Conservation Institute, 2002.
———, and J. David Lewis-Williams. *The Shamans of Prehistory: Trance and Magic in the Painted Caves*. Trans. Sophie Hawkes. New York: Abrams, 1998.
Connah, Graham. *African Civilizations: An Archaeological Perspective*. 2nd ed. Cambridge: Cambridge Univ. Press, 2001.
Coulson, David, and Alec Campbell. *African Rock Art: Painting and Engravings on Stone*. New York: Abrams, 2001.
Cunliffe, Barry W, ed. *The Oxford Illustrated History of Prehistoric Europe*. New York: Oxford Univ. Press, 2001.
Forte, Maurizio, and Alberto Siliotti. *Virtual Archaeology: Re-Creating Ancient Worlds*. New York: Abrams, 1997.
Freeman, Leslie G. *Altamira Revisited and Other Essays on Early Art*. Chicago: Institute for Prehistoric Investigation, 1987.
Garlake, Peter S. *The Hunter's Vision: The Prehistoric Art of Zimbabwe*. Seattle: Univ. of Washington Press, 1995.
Gowlett, John A. J. *Ascent to Civilization: The Archaeology of Early Humans*. 2nd ed. New York: McGraw-Hill, 1993.
Guthrie, R. Dale. *The Nature of Paleolithic Art*. Chicago: Univ. of Chicago Press, 2005.
Jope, E. M. *Early Celtic art in the British Isles*. 2 vols. New York: Oxford Univ. Press, 2000.
Kenrick, Douglas M. *Jomon of Japan: The World's Oldest Pottery*. New York: Kegan Paul, 1995.
Leakey, Richard E., and Roger Lewin. *Origins Reconsidered: In Search of What Makes Us Human*. New York: Doubleday, 1992.
Le Quellec, Jean-Loïc. *Rock Art in Africa: Mythology and Legend*. Trans. Paul Bahn. Paris: Flammarion, 2004.
Leroi-Gourhan, André. *The Dawn of European Art: An Introduction to Paleolithic Cave Painting*. Trans. Sara Champion. Cambridge: Cambridge Univ. Press, 1982.
Lewis-Williams, J. David. *The Mind in the Cave: Consciousness and the Origins of Art*. New York: Thames & Hudson, 2002.
Megaw, Ruth, and Vincent Megaw. *Celtic Art: From Its Beginnings to the Book of Kells*. Rev. & expanded ed. New York: Thames & Hudson, 2001.
O'Kelly, Michael J. *Newgrange: Archaeology, Art, and Legend*. New Aspects of Antiquity. London: Thames & Hudson, 1982.
Price, T. Douglas. *Images of the Past*. 5th ed. Boston: McGraw-Hill, 2008.
Renfrew, Colin, ed. *The Megalithic Monuments of Western Europe*. London: Thames & Hudson, 1983.
Sandars, N. K. *Prehistoric Art in Europe*. 2nd ed. Pelican History of Art. New Haven: Yale Univ. Press, 1992.
Sura Ramos, Pedro A. *The Cave of Altamira*. Gen. Ed. Antonio Beltran. New York: Abrams, 1999.
Sieveking, Ann. *The Cave Artists*. Ancient People and Places, vol. 93. London: Thames & Hudson, 1979.
White, Randall. *Prehistoric Art: The Symbolic Journey of Mankind*. New York: Abrams, 2003.

Chapter 2 Art of the Ancient Near East

Akurgal, Ekrem. *Ancient Civilizations and Ruins of Turkey: From Prehistoric Times until the End of the Roman Empire*. 5th ed. London: Kegan Paul, 2002.
Aruz, Joan, et al, eds. *Beyond Babylon: Art, Trade, and Diplomacy in the Second Millennium B.C.* New Haven: Yale Univ. Press, and Metropolitan Museum of Art, 2008.
———, ed. *Art of the First Cities: The Third Millennium b.c. from the Mediterranean to the Indus*. New York: Metropolitan Museum of Art, 2003.
Bahrani, Zainab. *The Graven Image: Representation in Babylonia and Assyria*. Archaeology, Culture, and Society Series. Philadelphia: Univ. of Pennsylvania Press, 2003.

Boardman, John. *Persia and the West: An Archaeological Investigation of the Genesis of Achaemenid Art*. New York: Thames & Hudson, 2000.
Bottero, Jean. *Everyday Life in Ancient Mesopotamia*. Trans. Antonia Nevill. Baltimore, MD.: Johns Hopkins Univ. Press, 2001.
Charvat, Petr. *Mesopotamia before History*. Rev. & updated ed. New York: Routledge, 2002.
Crawford, Harriet. *Sumer and the Sumerians*. 2nd ed. New York: Cambridge Univ. Press, 2004.
Curtis, John, and Nigel Tallis, eds. *Forgotten Empire: The World of Ancient Persia*. Berkeley: Univ. of California Press, 2005.
Ferrier, R. W., ed. *The Arts of Persia*. New Haven: Yale Univ. Press, 1989.
Frankfort, Henri. *The Art and Architecture of the Ancient Orient*. 5th ed. Pelican History of Art. New Haven: Yale Univ. Press, 1996.
Haywood, John. *Ancient Civilizations of the Near East and Mediterranean*. London: Cassell, 1997.
Meyers, Eric M., ed. *The Oxford Encyclopedia of Archaeology in the Near East*. 5 vols. New York: Oxford Univ. Press, 1997.
Moorey, P. R. S. *Idols of the People: Miniature Images of Clay in the Ancient Near East*. The Schweich Lectures of the British Academy; 2001. New York: Oxford Univ. Press, 2003.
Polk, Milbry, and Angela M. H. Schuster. *The Looting of the Iraq Museum, Baghdad: The Lost Legacy of Ancient Mesopotamia*. New York: Abrams, 2005.
Reade, Julian. *Assyrian Sculpture*. Cambridge, MA: Harvard Univ. Press, 1999.
Roaf, Michael. *Cultural Atlas of Mesopotamia and the Ancient Near East*. New York: Facts on File, 1990.
Winter, Irene. *"Sex, Rhetoric, and the Public Monument: The Alluring Body of the Male Ruler."* In *Sexuality in Ancient Art*, edited by Natalie Kampen and Bettina A. Bergmann. Cambridge: Cambridge Univ. Press, 1996: 11–26.
Roux, Georges. *Ancient Iraq*. 3rd ed. London: Penguin, 1992.
Zettler, Richard L., and Lee Horne, ed. *Treasures from the Royal Tombs of Ur*. Philadelphia: Univ. of Pennsylvania, Museum of Archaeology and Anthropology, 1998.

Chapter 3 Art of Ancient Egypt

Arnold, Dieter. *Temples of the Last Pharaohs*. New York: Oxford Univ. Press, 1999.
Baines, John, and Jaromír Málek. *Cultural Atlas of Ancient Egypt*. Rev. ed. New York: Facts on File, 2000.
Brier, Bob. *Egyptian Mummies: Unraveling the Secrets of an Ancient Art*. New York: Morrow, 1994.
Egyptian Art in the Age of the Pyramids. New York: Metropolitan Museum of Art, 1999.
The Egyptian Book of the Dead: The Book of Going Forth by Day: Being the Papyrus of Ani (Royal Scribe of the Divine Offerings). 2nd rev. ed. Trans. Raymond O. Faulkner. San Francisco: Chronicle, 2008.
Freed, Rita E. Sue D'Auria, and Yvonne J. Markowitz. *Pharaohs of the Sun: Akhenaten, Nefertiti, Tutankhamen*. Boston: Museum of Fine Arts in assoc. with Bulfinch Press/Little, Brown, 1999.
Hawass, Zahi A. *Tutankhamun and the Golden Age of the Pharaohs*. Washington, DC: National Geographic, 2005.
Johnson, Paul. *The Civilization of Ancient Egypt*. Updated ed. New York: HarperCollins, 1999.
Kozloff, Arielle P. *Egypt's Dazzling Sun: Amenhotep III and His World*. Cleveland: Cleveland Museum of Art, 1992.
Lehner, Mark. *The Complete Pyramids*. New York: Thames & Hudson, 2008.
Love Songs of the New Kingdom. Trans. John L. Foster. New York: Scribner, 1974; Austin: Univ. of Texas Press, 1992.
Málek, Jaromir. *Egypt: 4,000 Years of Art*. London: Phaidon Press, 2003.
Pemberton, Delia. *Ancient Egypt*. Architectural Guides for Travelers. San Francisco: Chronicle, 1992.
Robins, Gay. *The Art of Ancient Egypt*. Rev. ed. Cambridge, MA: Harvard Univ. Press, 2008.
Roehrig, Catharine H., Renee Dreyfus, and Cathleen A. Keller. *Hatshepsut, from Queen to Pharaoh*. New York: Metropolitan Museum of Art, 2005.
Russmann, Edna R. *Egyptian Sculpture: Cairo and Luxor*. Austin: Univ. of Texas Press, 1989.
Smith, Craig B. *How the Great Pyramid Was Built*. Washington, DC: Smithsonian Books, 2004.
Smith, William Stevenson. *The Art and Architecture of Ancient Egypt*. 3rd ed. Revised. William Kelly Simpson. Pelican History of Art. New Haven: Yale Univ. Press, 1998.
Strouhal, Eugen. *Life of the Ancient Egyptians*. Trans. Deryck Viney. Norman: Univ. of Oklahoma Press, 1992.
Strudwick, Nigel, and Helen Studwick. *Thebes in Egypt: A Guide to the Tombs and Temples of Ancient Luxor*. Ithaca, NY: Cornell Univ. Press, 1999.
Thomas, Thelma K. *Late Antique Egyptian Funerary Sculpture: Images for this World and for the Next*. Princeton: Princeton Univ. Press, 2000.
Tiradritti, Francesco. *Ancient Egypt: Art, Architecture and History*. Trans. Phil Goddard. London: British Museum Press, 2002.
The Treasures of Ancient Egypt: From the Egyptian Museum in Cairo, New York: Rizzoli, 2003.
Wilkinson, Richard H. *The Complete Temples of Ancient Egypt*. New York: Thames & Hudson, 2000.
———. *Reading Egyptian Art: A Hieroglyphic Guide to Ancient Egyptian Painting and Sculpture*. London: Thames & Hudson, 1992.
Winstone, H.V. F. *Howard Carter and the Discovery of the Tomb of Tutankhamen*. Rev. ed. Manchester: Barzan, 2006.
Ziegler, Cristiane, ed. *The Pharaohs*. New York: Rizzoli, 2002.
Zivie-Coche, Christiane. *Sphinx: History of a Monument*. Trans. David Lorton. Ithaca, NY: Cornell Univ. Press, 2002.

Chapter 4 Art of the Ancient Aegean

Castleden, Rodney. *The Knossos Labyrinth: A New View of the "Palace of Minos" at Knossos*. London: Routledge, 1990.
———. Mycenaeans. New York: Routledge, 2005.
Demargne, Pierre. *The Birth of Greek Art*. Trans. Stuart Gilbert and James Emmons. Arts of Mankind, vol. 6. New York: Golden, 1964.
Doumas, Christos. *The Wall-Paintings of Thera*. 2nd ed. Trans. Alex Doumas. Athens: Kapon Editions, 1999.
Fitton, J. Lesley. *Cycladic Art*. 2nd ed. London: British Museum Press, 1999.
Getz-Gentle, Pat. *Personal Styles in Early Cycladic Sculpture*. Madison: Univ. of Wisconsin Press, 2001.
Hamilakis, Yannis. ed. *Labyrinth Revisited: Rethinking "Minoan" Archaeology*. Oxford: Oxbow, 2002.
Hendrix, Elizabeth. *"Painted Ladies of the Early Bronze Age,"* The Metropolitan Museum of Art Bulletin, New Series, 55/3 (Winter 1997–1998): 4–15.
Higgins, Reynold A. *Minoan and Mycenean Art*. New. ed. World of Art. New York: Thames & Hudson, 1997.
Hitchcock, Louise. *Minoan Architecture: A Contextual Analysis*. Studies in Mediterranean Archaeology and Literature, Pocket-Book, 155. Jonsered: P. Åströms Förlag, 2000.
Hoffman, Gail L. *"Painted Ladies: Early Cycladic II Mourning Figures?"* American Journal of Archaeology, 106/4 (October 2002): 525–550.
Immerwahr, Sara Anderson. *Aegean Painting in the Bronze Age*. University Park: Pennsylvania State Univ. Press, 1990.
Preziosi, Donald, and Louise Hitchcock. *Aegean Art and Architecture*. Oxford History of Art. Oxford: Oxford Univ. Press, 1999.
Shelmerdine, Cynthia W., ed. *The Cambridge Companion to the Aegean Bronze Age*. New York: Cambridge Univ. Press, 2008.

Chapter 5 Art of Ancient Greece

Barletta, Barbara A. *The Origins of the Greek Architectural Orders*. New York: Cambridge Univ. Press, 2001.
Beard, Mary. *The Parthenon*. Cambridge, MA: Harvard Univ. Press, 2003.
Belozerskaya, Marina, and Kenneth D.S. Lapatin. *Ancient Greece: Art, Architecture, and History*. Los Angeles: J. Paul Getty Museum, 2004.
Boardman, John. *Early Greek Vase Painting: 11th–6th Centuries b.c.: A Handbook*. World of Art. London: Thames & Hudson, 1998.
———. *Greek Sculpture: The Archaic Period: A Handbook*. World of Art. London: Thames & Hudson, 1991.
———. *Greek Sculpture: The Classical Period: A Handbook*. London: Thames & Hudson, 1985.
———. *Greek Sculpture: The Late Classical Period and Sculpture in Colonies and Overseas*. World of Art. New York: Thames & Hudson, 1995.
———. *The History of Greek Vases: Potters, Painters, and Pictures*. New York: Thames & Hudson, 2001.
Burn, Lucilla. *Hellenistic Art: From Alexander the Great to Augustus*. Los Angeles: J. Paul Getty Museum, 2004.
Clark, Andrew J., Maya Elston, Mary Louise Hart. *Understanding Greek Vases: A Guide to Terms, Styles, and Techniques*. Los Angeles: J. Paul Getty Museum, 2002.
De Grummond, Nancy T. and Brunilde S. Ridgway. *From Pergamon to Sperlonga: Sculpture in Context*. Berkeley: Univ. of California Press, 2000.
Donohue, A. A. *Greek Sculpture and the Problem of Description*. New York: Cambridge Univ. Press, 2005.
Fullerton, Mark D. *Greek Art*. Cambridge: Cambridge Univ. Press, 2000.
Hard, Robin. *The Routledge Handbook of Greek Mythology: Based on H.J. Rose's "Handbook of Greek Mythology."* 7th ed. London: Routledge, 2008.
Hurwit, Jeffrey M. *The Acropolis in the Age of Pericles*. New York: Cambridge Univ. Press, 2004.
Karakasi, Katerina. *Archaic Korai*. Los Angeles: J. Paul Getty Museum, 2003.
Lawrence, A. W. *Greek Architecture*. 5th ed. Revised. R. A. Tomlinson. Pelican History of Art. New Haven: Yale Univ. Press, 1996.
Martin, Roland. *Greek Architecture: Architecture of Crete, Greece, and the Greek World*. History of World Architecture. New York: Electa/Rizzoli, 1988.
Neils, Jenifer. *The British Museum Concise Introduction to Ancient Greece*. Ann Arbor: Univ. of Michigan, 2008.
Osborne, Robin. *Archaic and Classical Greek Art*. Oxford History of Art. Oxford: Oxford Univ. Press, 1998.
Palagia, Olga, ed. *Greek Sculpture: Function, Materials, and Techniques in the Archaic and Classical Periods*. New York: Cambridge Univ. Press, 2006.
———, and J. J. Pollitt, eds. *Personal Styles in Greek Sculpture*. Yale Classical Studies, vol. 30. Cambridge: Cambridge Univ. Press, 1996.
Pedley, John Griffiths. *Greek Art and Archaeology*. 4th ed. Upper Saddle River, NJ: Pearson/Prentice Hall, 2007.
Pollitt, J. J. *Art and Experience in Classical Greece*. Cambridge: Cambridge Univ. Press, 1972; reprinted 1999.
———. *The Art of Ancient Greece: Sources and Documents*. 2nd ed. rev. Cambridge: Cambridge Univ. Press, 2001.
Ridgway, Brunilde Sismondo. *The Archaic Style in Greek Sculpture*. 2nd ed. Chicago: Ares, 1993.
———. *Fifth Century Styles in Greek Sculpture*. Princeton: Princeton Univ. Press, 1981.
———. *Fourth Century Styles in Greek Sculpture*. Wisconsin Studies in Classics. Madison: Univ. of Wisconsin Press, 1997.
———. *Hellenistic Sculpture 1: The Styles of ca. 331–200 b.c.* Wisconsin Studies in Classics. Madison: Univ. of Wisconsin Press, 1990.
Stafford, Emma J. *Life, Myth, and Art in Ancient Greece*. Los Angeles: J. Paul Getty Museum, 2004.
Stewart, Andrew F. *Greek Sculpture: An Exploration*. 2 vols. New Haven: Yale Univ. Press, 1990.
Whitley, James. *The Archaeology of Ancient Greece*. New York: Cambridge Univ. Press, 2001.

Chapter 6 Etruscan and Roman Art

Bianchi Bandinelli, Ranuccio. *Rome: The Centre of Power: Roman Art to a.d. 200*. Trans. Peter Green. Arts of Mankind, 15. London: Thames & Hudson, 1971.
———. *Rome: The Late Empire: Roman Art a.d. 200–400*. Trans. Peter Green. Arts of Mankind, 17. New York: Braziller, 1971.
Borrelli, Federica. *The Etruscans: Art, Architecture, and History*. Ed. Stefano Peccatori and Stefano Zuffi. Trans. Thomas Michael Hartmann. Los Angeles: J. Paul Getty Museum, 2004.
Brendel, Otto J. *Prolegomena to the Study of Roman Art*. New Haven, Yale Univ. Press, 1979.
———. *Etruscan Art*. 2nd ed. Pelican History of Art. New Haven: Yale Univ. Press, 1995.
Conlin, Diane Atnally. *The Artists of the Ara Pacis: The Process of Hellenization in Roman Relief Sculpture*. Studies in the History of Greece & Rome. Chapel Hill: Univ. of North Carolina Press, 1997.
Cornell, Tim, and John Matthews. *Atlas of the Roman World*. New York: Facts on File, 1982.
D'Ambra, Eve. *Roman Art*. Cambridge: Cambridge Univ. Press, 1998.
Elsner, Jas. *Imperial Rome and Christian Triumph: The Art of the Roman Empire a.d. 100–450*. Oxford History of Art. Oxford: Oxford Univ. Press, 1998.
Gabucci, Ada. *Ancient Rome: Art, Architecture, and History*. Eds. Stefano Peccatori and Stephano Zuffi. Trans. T. M. Hartman. Los Angeles: J. Paul Getty Museum, 2002.
Haynes, Sybille. *Etruscan Civilization: A Cultural History*. Los Angeles: J. Paul Getty Museum, 2000.
Holloway, R. Ross. *Constantine & Rome*. New Haven: Yale Univ. Press, 2004.
Kleiner, Fred. S. *A History of Roman Art*. Belmont, CA: Thomson/Wadsworth, 2007.
MacDonald, William L. *The Architecture of the Roman Empire: An Introductory Study*. Rev. ed. 2 vols. Yale Publications in the History of Art, 17, 35. New Haven: Yale Univ. Press, 1982.
———. *The Pantheon: Design, Meaning, and Progeny*. New foreword. John Pinto. Cambridge, MA: Harvard Univ. Press, 2002.

Mattusch, Carol C. *Pompeii and the Roman Villa: Art and Culture around the Bay of Naples*. Washington, D.C. National Gallery of Art, 2008.

Mazzoleni, Donatella. *Domus: Wall Painting in the Roman House*. Los Angeles: J. Paul Getty Museum, 2004.

Packer, James E. *The Forum of Trajan in Rome: A Study of the Monuments in Brief*. Berkeley: Univ. of California Press, 2001.

Pollitt, J. J. *The Art of Rome, c. 753 b.c.–337 a.d.: Sources and Documents*. Upper Saddle River, NJ: Pearson/Prentice Hall, 1966.

Polybius. *The Histories*. Trans. W.R. Paton. 6 vols. Loeb Classical Library. Cambridge, MA: Harvard Univ. Press, 2000.

Ramage, Nancy H., and Andrew Ramage. *Roman Art: Romulus to Constantine*. 5th ed. Upper Saddle River, NJ: Pearson/Prentice Hall, 2009.

Spivey, Nigel. *Etruscan Art*. World of Art. New York: Thames & Hudson, 1997.

Stamper, John W. *The Architecture of Roman Temples: The Republic to the Middle Empire*. New York: Cambridge Univ. Press, 2005.

Stewart, Peter. *Statues in Roman Society: Representation and Response*. Oxford Studies in Ancient Culture and Representation. New York: Oxford Univ. Press, 2003.

Strong, Donald. *Roman Art*. 2nd ed. rev. & annotated. Ed. Roger Ling. Pelican History of Art. New Haven: Yale Univ. Press, 1995.

Ward-Perkins, J. B. *Roman Architecture*. History of World Architecture. New York: Electa/Rizzoli, 1988.

———. *Roman Imperial Architecture*. Pelican History of Art. New Haven: Yale Univ. Press, 1981.

Wilson Jones, Mark. *Principles of Roman Architecture*. New Haven: Yale Univ. Press, 2000.

Chapter 7 Jewish, Early Christian, and Byzantine Art

Age of Spirituality: Late Antique and Early Christian Art, Third to Seventh Century. New York: Metropolitan Museum of Art, 1979.

Beckwith, John. *Early Christian and Byzantine Art*. 2nd ed. Pelican History of Art. New Haven: Yale Univ. Press, 1979.

Bleiberg, Edward, ed. *Tree of Paradise: Jewish Mosaics from the Roman Empire*. Brooklyn:

Brooklyn Museum, 2005.

Cioffarelli, Ada. *Guide to the Catacombs of Rome and Its Surroundings*. Rome: Bonsignori, 2000.

Cormack, Robin, and Maria Vassilaki, eds. *Byzantium, 330–1453*. London: Royal Academy of Arts, 2008.

Cutler, Anthony. *The Hand of the Master: Craftsmanship, Ivory, and Society in Byzantium 9th–11th Centuries*. Princeton: Princeton Univ. Press, 1994.

Durand, Jannic. *Byzantine Art*. Paris: Terrail, 1999.

Eastmond, Antony, and Liz James, eds. *Icon and Word : The Power of Images in Byzantium: Studies Presented to Robin Cormack*. Burlington, VT: Ashgate, 2003.

Evans, Helen C., ed. *Byzantium: Faith and Power (1261–1557)*. New York: Metropolitan Museum of Art, 2004.

———, and William D. Wixom, eds. *The Glory of Byzantium: Art and Culture of the Middle Byzantine era, a.d. 843–1261*. New York: Abrams, 1997.

Fine, Steven. *Art and Judaism in the Greco–Roman World: Toward a New Jewish Archaeology*. New York: Cambridge Univ. Press, 2005.

Freely, John. *Byzantine Monuments of Istanbul*. Cambridge: New York: Cambridge Univ. Press, 2004.

Grabar, André. *Byzantine Painting: Historical and Critical Study*. Trans. Stuart Gilbert. New York: Rizzoli, 1979.

Hachlili, Rachel. *Ancient Mosaic Pavements: Themes, Issues, and Trends*. Leiden: Brill, 2009.

Jensen, Robin Margaret. *Understanding Early Christian Art*. New York: Routledge, 2000.

Kitzinger, Ernst. *The Art of Byzantium and the Medieval West: Selected Studies*. Ed. W. Eugene Kleinbauer. Bloomington: Indiana Univ. Press, 1976.

———. *Byzantine Art in the Making: Main Lines of Stylistic Development in Mediterranean Art, 3rd–7th Century*. Cambridge, MA: Harvard Univ. Press, 1977.

Kleinbauer, W. Eugene. *Hagia Sophia*. London: Scala, 2004.

Krautheimer, Richard, and Slobodan Curcic. *Early Christian and Byzantine Architecture*. 4th ed. Pelican History of Art. New Haven: Yale Univ. Press, 1992.

Levine, Lee I., and Zeev Weiss, eds. *From Dura to Sepphoris: Studies in Jewish Art and Society in Late Antiquity*. Journal of Roman Archaeology: Supplementary Series, no. 40. Portsmouth, R.I.: Journal of Roman Archaeology, 2000.

Lowden, John. *Early Christian and Byzantine Art*. Art & Ideas. London: Phaidon Press, 1997.

Maguire, Henry. *The Icons of Their Bodies: Saints and Their Images in Byzantium*. Princeton: Princeton Univ. Press, 1996.

Mainstone, Rowland J. *Hagia Sophia: Architecture, Structure and Liturgy of Justinian's Great Church*. 2nd ed. New York: Thames & Hudson, 2001.

Mango, Cyril. *Art of the Byzantine Empire, 312–1453: Sources and Documents*. Upper Saddle River, NJ: Pearson/Prentice Hall, 1972.

Mathew, Gervase. *Byzantine Aesthetics*. London: John Murray, 1963.

Mathews, Thomas F. *Byzantium: From Antiquity to the Renaissance*. Perspectives. New York: Abrams, 1998.

———. *The Clash of Gods: A Reinterpretation of Early Christian Art*. Rev. ed. Princeton: Princeton Univ. Press, 1999.

Olin, Margaret. *The Nation without Art: Examining Modern Discourses on Jewish Art*. Lincoln: Univ. of Nebraska Press, 2001.

Olsson, Birger, and Magnus Zetterholm, eds. *The Ancient Synagogue from Its Origins until 200 c.e.: Papers Presented at an International Conference at Lund University, October 14–17, 2001*. Coniectanea Biblica: New Testament Series, 39. Stockholm: Almqvist & Wiksell International, 2003.

Ousterhout, Robert. *Master Builders of Byzantium*. Princeton: Princeton Univ. Press, 1999.

Rodley, Lyn. *Byzantine Art and Architecture: An Introduction*. Cambridge: Cambridge Univ. Press, 1994.

Rutgers, Leonard V. *Subterranean Rome: In Search of the Roots of Christianity in the Catacombs of the Eternal City*. Leuven: Peeters, 2000.

Sed-Rajna, Gabrielle. *Jewish Art*. Trans. Sara Friedman and Mira Reich. New York: Abrams, 1997.

Spier, Jeffrey, ed. *Picturing the Bible: The Earliest Christian Art*. New Haven: Yale Univ. Press, 2007.

Tadgell, Christopher. *Imperial Space: Rome, Constantinople and the Early Church*. New York: Whitney Library of Design, 1998.

Vio, Ettore. *St. Mark's: The Art and Architecture of Church and State in Venice*. New York: Riverside Book, 2003.

Webb, Matilda. *The Churches and Catacombs of Early Christian Rome: A Comprehensive Guide*. Brighton, UK: Sussex Academic Press, 2001.

Weitzmann, Kurt. *Late Antique and Early Christian Book Illumination*. New York: Braziller, 1977.

———. *Place of Book Illumination in Byzantine Art*. Princeton: Art Museum, Princeton Univ., 1975.

Wharton, Annabel Jane. *Refiguring the Post-Classical City: Dura Europos, Jerash, Jerusalem and Ravenna*. Cambridge: Cambridge Univ. Press, 1995.

White, L. Michael. *The Social Origins of Christian Architecture*. 2 vols. Baltimore, MD: Johns Hopkins Univ. Press, 1990.

Chapter 8 Islamic Art

Al-Faruqi, Isma'il R., and Lois Ibsen Al Faruqi. *Cultural Atlas of Islam*. New York: Macmillan, 1986.

Atil, Esin. *The Age of Sultan Suleyman the Magnificent*. Washington, DC: National Gallery of Art, 1987.

Baker, Patricia L. *Islam and the Religious Arts*. London: Continuum, 2004.

Barry, Michael A. *Figurative Art in Medieval Islam and the Riddle of Bihzâd of Herât (1465–1535)*. Paris: Flammarion, 2004.

Blair, Sheila S., and Jonathan Bloom. *The Art and Architecture of Islam 1250–1800*. Pelican History of Art. New Haven: Yale Univ. Press, 1995.

Denny, Walter B. *Iznik: The Artistry of Ottoman Ceramics*. New York: Thames & Hudson, 2004.

Dodds, Jerrilynn D., ed. *Al-Andalus: The Art of Islamic Spain*. New York: Metropolitan Museum of Art, 1992.

Ecker, Heather. *Caliphs and Kings: The Art and Influence of Islamic Spain*. Washington, DC: Arthur M. Sackler Gallery, Smithsonian Institution, 2004.

Ettinghausen, Richard, Oleg Grabar, and Marilyn Jenkins-Madina. *Islamic Art and Architecture, 650–1250*. 2nd ed. Pelican History of Art. New Haven: Yale Univ. Press, 2001.

Frishman, Martin, and Hasan-Uddin Khan. *The Mosque: History, Architectural Development and Regional Diversity*. London: Thames & Hudson, 1994.

Grabar, Oleg. *The Formation of Islamic Art*. Rev. and enlarged. New Haven: Yale Univ. Press, 1987.

———. *The Great Mosque of Isfahan*. New York: New York Univ. Press, 1990.

———. *Islamic Visual Culture, 1100–1800*. Burlington, VT: Ashgate, 2006.

———. *Mostly Miniatures: An Introduction to Persian Painting*. Princeton: Princeton Univ. Press, 2000.

———, Mohammad Al-Asad, Abeer Audeh, and Said Nuseibeh. *The Shape of the Holy: Early Islamic Jerusalem*. Princeton: Princeton Univ. Press, 1996.

Hillenbrand, Robert. *Islamic Art and Architecture*. World of Art. London: Thames & Hudson, 1999.

Irwin, Robert. *The Alhambra*. Cambridge, MA: Harvard Univ. Press, 2004.

Khalili, Nasser D. *Visions of Splendour in Islamic Art and Culture*. London: Worth Press, 2008.

Komaroff, Linda, and Stefano Carboni, eds. *The Legacy of Genghis Khan: Courtly Art and Culture in Western Asia, 1256–1353*. New York: Metropolitan Museum of Art, 2002.

Lentz, Thomas W., and Glenn D. Lowry. *Timur and the Princely Vision: Persian Art and Culture in the Fifteenth Century*. Los Angeles: Los Angeles County Museum of Art, 1989.

Necipolu, Gülru. *The Age of Sinan: Architectural Culture in the Ottoman Empire*. Princeton: Princeton Univ. Press, 2005.

Petruccioli, Attilio, and Khalil K. Pirani, eds. *Understanding Islamic Architecture*. New York: Routledge Curzon, 2002.

Roxburgh, David J., ed. *Turks: A Journey of a Thousand Years, 600–1600*. London: Royal Academy of Arts, 2005.

Sims, Eleanor, B. I. Marshak, and Ernst J. Grube. *Peerless Images: Persian Painting and Its Sources*. New Haven: Yale Univ. Press, 2002.

Stanley, Tim, Mariam Rosser-Owen, and Stephen Vernoit. *Palace and Mosque: Islamic Art from the Middle East*. London: V&A Publications, 2004.

Stierlin, Henri. *Islamic Art and Architecture*. New York: Thames & Hudson, 2002.

Tadgell, Christopher. *Four Caliphates: The Formation and Development of the Islamic Tradition*. London: Ellipsis, 1998.

Ward, R. M. *Islamic Metalwork*. New York: Thames & Hudson, 1993.

Watson, Oliver. *Ceramics from Islamic Lands*. New York: Thames & Hudson in assoc. with the al-Sabah Collection, Dar al-Athar al-Islamiyyah, Kuwait National Museum, 2004.

Chapter 9 Art of South and Southeast Asia before 1200

Atherton, Cynthia Packert. *The Sculpture of Early Medieval Rajasthan*. Studies in Asian Art and Archaeology, vol. 21. New York: Brill, 1997.

Behl, Benoy K. *The Ajanta Caves: Artistic Wonder of Ancient Buddhist India*. New York: Abrams, 1998.

Behrendt, Kurt A. *The Buddhist Architecture of Gandhara*. Handbook of Oriental Studies: Section Two: India, vol. 17. Boston: Brill, 2004.

Chakrabarti, Dilip K. *India, an Archaeological History: Palaeolithic Beginnings to Early Historic Foundations*. 2nd ed. New York: Oxford Univ. Press, 2009.

Craven, Roy C. *Indian Art: A Concise History*. Rev. ed. World of Art. New York: Thames & Hudson, 1997.

Czuma, Stanislaw J. *Kushan Sculpture: Images from Early India*. Cleveland: Cleveland Museum of Art, 1985.

Dehejia, Vidya. *Art of the Imperial Cholas*. New York: Columbia Univ. Press, 1990.

———. *The Sensuous and the Sacred: Chola Bronzes from South India*. New York: American Federation of Arts, 2002.

Dessai, Vishakha N., and Darielle Mason, eds. *Gods, Guardians, and Lovers: Temple Sculptures from North India, a.d. 700–1200*. New York: Asia Society Galleries, 1993.

Dhavalikar, Madhukar Keshav. *Ellora*. New York: Oxford Univ. Press, 2003.

Girard-Geslan, Maud. *Art of Southeast Asia*. Trans. J. A. Underwood. New York: Abrams, Inc., 1998.

Heller, Amy. *Early Himalayan Art*. Oxford: Ashmolean Museum, 2008.

Huntington, Susan L. *The Art of Ancient India: Buddhist, Hindu, Jain*. New York: Weatherhill, 1985.

———. *Leaves from the Bodhi Tree: The Art of Pala India (8th–12th Centuries) and Its International Legacy*. Dayton, OH: Dayton Art Institute, 1990.

Hutt, Michael. *Nepal: A Guide to the Art and Architecture of the Kathmandu Valley*. Boston: Shambhala, 1995.

Knox, Robert. *Amaravati: Buddhist Sculpture from the Great Stupa*. London: British Museum Press, 1992.

Khanna, Sucharita. *Dancing Divinities in Indian Art: 8th–12th Century a.d.* Delhi: Sharada Pub. House, 1999.

Kramrisch, Stella. *The Art of Nepal*. New York: Abrams, 1964.

———. *The Presence of Siva*. Princeton: Princeton Univ. Press, 1981.

Meister, Michael, ed. *Encyclopedia of Indian Temple Architecture*. 2 vols. in 7. Philadelphia: Univ. of Pennsylvania Press, 1983.

Michell, George. *Elephanta*. Bombay: India Book House, 2002.

———. *Hindu Art and Architecture*. World of Art. London: Thames & Hudson, 2000.

Mitter, Partha. *Indian Art*. Oxford History of Art. Oxford: Oxford Univ. Press, 2001.

Neumayer, Erwin. *Lines on Stone: The Prehistoric Rock Art of India.* New Delhi: Manohar, 1993.

Pal, Pratapaditya, ed. *The Ideal Image: The Gupta Sculptural Tradition and Its Influence.* New York: Asia Society, 1978.

Poster, Amy G. *From Indian Earth: 4,000 Years of Terracotta Art.* Brooklyn, NY: Brooklyn Museum, 1986.

Skelton, Robert, and Mark Francis. *Arts of Bengal: The Heritage of Bangladesh and Eastern India.* London: Whitechapel Art Gallery, 1979.

Stierlin, Henri. *Hindu India: From Khajuraho to the Temple City of Madurai.* Taschen's World Architecture. New York: Taschen, 1998.

Tadgell, Christopher. *India and South-East Asia: The Buddhist and Hindu Tradition.* New York: Whitney Library of Design, 1998.

Williams, Joanna G. *Art of Gupta India, Empire and Province.* Princeton: Princeton Univ. Press, 1982.

Chapter 10 Chinese and Korean Art before 1279

Ciarla, Roberto, ed. *The Eternal Army: The Terracotta Soldiers of the First Chinese Emperor.* Vercelli: White Star, 2005.

Fong, Wen, ed. *Beyond Representation: Chinese Painting and Calligraphy, 8th–14th Century.* Princeton Monographs in Art and Archaeology, 48. New York: Metropolitan Museum of Art, 1992.

Fraser, Sarah Elizabeth. *Performing the Visual: The Practice of Buddhist Wall Painting in China and Central Asia, 618–960.* Stanford, CA: Stanford Univ. Press, 2004.

James, Jean M. *A Guide to the Tomb and Shrine Art of the Han Dynasty 206 b.c.–a.d. 220.* Chinese Studies, 2. Lewiston, NY: Mellen Press, 1996.

Karetzky, Patricia Eichenbaum. *Court Art of the Tang.* Lanham, MD: Univ. Press of America, 1996.

Kim, Kumja Paik. *Goryeo Dynasty: Korea's Age of Enlightenment, 918–1392.* San Francisco: Asian Art Museum—Chong-Moon Lee Center for Asian Art and Culture in cooperation with the National Museum of Korea and the Nara National Museum, 2003.

Li, Jian, ed. *The Glory of the Silk Road: Art from Ancient China.* Dayton, OH: Dayton Art Institute, 2003.

Little, Stephen, and Shawn Eichman. *Taoism and the Arts of China.* Chicago: Art Institute of Chicago, 2000.

Liu, Cary Y., Dora C.Y. Ching, and Judith G. Smith, eds. *Character & Context in Chinese Calligraphy.* Princeton: Art Museum, Princeton Univ., 1999.

Luo, Zhewen. *Ancient Pagodas in China.* Beijing, China: Foreign Languages Press, 1994.

Ma, Chengyuan. *Ancient Chinese Bronzes.* Ed. Hsio-Yen Shih. Hong Kong: Oxford Univ. Press, 1986.

Murck, Alfreda. *Poetry and Painting in Song China: The Subtle Art of Dissent.* Harvard-Yenching Institute Monograph Series. Cambridge, MA: Harvard Univ. Asia Center for the Harvard-Yenching Institute, 2000.

Ortiz, Valérie Malenfer. *Dreaming the Southern Song Landscape: The Power of Illusion in Chinese Painting.* Studies in Asian Art and Archaeology, vol. 22. Boston: Brill, 1999.

Paludan, Ann. *Chinese Tomb Figurines.* Hong Kong: Oxford Univ. Press, 1994.

Portal, Jane. *Korea: Art and Archaeology.* New York: Thames & Hudson, 2000.

Rawson, Jessica. *Mysteries of Ancient China: New Discoveries from the Early Dynasties.* London: British Museum Press, 1996.

Rhie, Marylin M. *Early Buddhist Art of China and Central Asia.* 2 vols in 3. Handbuch der Orientalistik. Vierte Abteilung; China, 12. Leiden: Brill, 1999.

Scarpari, Maurizio. *Splendours of Ancient China.* London: Thames & Hudson, 2000.

So, Jenny F. ed. *Noble Riders from Pines and Deserts: The Artistic Legacy of the Qidan.* Hong Kong: Art Museum, Chinese Univ. of Hong Kong, 2004.

Sturman, Peter Charles. *Mi Fu: Style and the Art of Calligraphy in Northern Song.* New Haven: Yale Univ. Press, 1997.

Wang, Eugene Y. *Shaping the Lotus Sutra: Buddhist Visual Culture in Medieval China.* Seattle: Univ. of Washington Press, 2005.

Watson, William. *The Arts of China to a.d. 900.* Pelican History of Art. New Haven: Yale Univ. Press, 1995.

———. *The Arts of China 900–1620.* Pelican History of Art. New Haven: Yale Univ. Press, 2000. Reissue ed. 2003.

Watt, James C.Y. *China: Dawn of a Golden Age, 200–750 a.d..* New York: Metropolitan Museum of Art, 2004.

Whitfield, Susan, and Ursula Sims-Williams, eds. *The Silk Road: Trade, Travel, War and Faith.* Chicago: Serindia Publications, 2004.

Wu Hung. *Monumentality in Early Chinese Art and Architecture.* Stanford: Stanford Univ. Press, 1995.

Yang, Xiaoneng, ed. *The Golden Age of Chinese Archaeology: Celebrated Discoveries from the People's Republic of China.* Washington DC: National Gallery of Art, 1999.

Chapter 11 Japanese Art before 1333

Cunningham, Michael R. *Buddhist Treasures from Nara.* Cleveland: Cleveland Museum of Art, 1998.

Harris, Victor, ed. *Shinto: The Sacred Art of Ancient Japan.* London: British Museum Press, 2001.

Izutsu, Shinryu, and Shoryu Omori. *Sacred Treasures of Mount Koya: The Art of Japanese Shingon Buddhism.* Honolulu: Koyasan Reihokan Museum, 2002.

Kurata, Bunsaku. *Horyu-ji, Temple of the Exalted Law: Early Buddhist Art from Japan.* New York: Japan Society, 1981.

Levine, Gregory P.A., and Yukio Lippit. *Awakenings: Zen Figure Painting in Medieval Japan.* New York: Japan Society, 2007.

McCallum, Donald F. *The Four Great Temples: Buddhist Archaeology, Architecture, and Icons of Seventh-Century Japan.* Honolulu: Univ. of Hawai'i Press, 2009.

Mino, Yutaka. *The Great Eastern Temple: Treasures of Japanese Buddhist Art from Todai-ji.* Chicago: Art Institute of Chicago, 1986.

Mizoguchi, Koji. *An Archaeological History of Japan: 30,000 b.c. to a.d. 700.* Philadelphia: Univ. of Pennsylvania Press, 2002.

Murase, Miyeko. *The Tale of Genji: Legends and Paintings.* New York: Braziller, 2001.

Nishiwara, Kyotaro, and Emily J. Sano. *The Great Age of Japanese Buddhist Sculpture, a.d. 60–1300.* Fort Worth, TX: Kimbell Art Museum, 1982.

Pearson, Richard J. *Ancient Japan.* Washington, DC: Sackler Gallery, 1992.

Ten Grotenhuis, Elizabeth. *Japanese Mandalas: Representations of Sacred Geography.* Honolulu: Univ. of Hawai'i Press, 1999.

Washizuka, Hiromitsu, Park Youngbok, and Kang Woo-bang. *Transmitting the Forms of Divinity: Early Buddhist Art from Korea and Japan.* Ed. Naomi Noble Richard. New York: Japan Society, 2003.

Wong, Dorothy C., and Eric M. Field, eds. *Horyuji Reconsidered.* Newcastle: Cambridge Scholars, 2008.

Chapter 12 Art of the Americas before 1300

Benson, Elizabeth P., and Beatriz de la Fuente. *Olmec Art of Ancient Mexico.* Washington, DC: National Gallery of Art, 1996.

Berrin, Kathleen, ed. *Feathered Serpents and Flowering Trees: Reconstructing the Murals of Teotihuacan.* San Francisco: Fine Arts Museums of San Francisco, 1988.

Brody, J. J. *Anasazi and Pueblo Painting.* Albuquerque: Univ. of New Mexico Press, 1991.

———, Catherine J. Scott, and Steven A. LeBlanc. *Mimbres Pottery: Ancient Art of the American Southwest: Essays.* New York: Hudson Hills Press in assoc. with The American Federation of Arts, 1983.

Burger, Richard L. *Chavin and the Origins of Andean Civilization.* New York: Thames & Hudson, 1992.

Clark, John E., and Mary E. Pye, eds. *Olmec Art and Archaeology in Mesoamerica.* Studies in the History of Art, 58: Symposium Papers, 35. Washington, DC: National Gallery of Art, 2000.

Clayton, Lawrence A., Vernon J. Knight, and Edward Moore, eds. *The De Soto Chronicles: The Expedition of Hernando de Soto to North America, 1539–1543.* 2 vols. Tuscaloosa: Univ. of Alabama Press, 1993.

Coe, Michael D. and Rex Koontz. *Mexico: From the Olmecs to the Aztecs.* 5th ed. New York: Thames & Hudson, 2005.

———. *Breaking the Maya Code.* Rev. ed. New York: Thames & Hudson, 1999.

Donnan, Christopher. *Moche Portraits from Ancient Peru.* Austin: Univ. of Texas Press, 2003.

Fagan, Brian M. *Chaco Canyon: Archeologists Explore the Lives of an Ancient Society.* New York: Oxford Univ. Press, 2005.

Hall, Robert L. *An Archaeology of the Soul: North American Indian Belief and Ritual.* Urbana: Univ. of Illinois Press, 1997.

Heyden, Doris, and Paul Gendrop. *Pre-Columbian Architecture of Mesoamerica.* Trans. Judith Stanton. History of World Architecture. New York: Electa/Rizzoli, 1988.

Korp, Maureen. *The Sacred Geography of the American Mound Builders.* Native American Studies. Lewiston, NY: Mellen Press, 1990.

Kubler, George. *The Art and Architecture of Ancient America: The Mexican, Maya, and Andean Peoples.* 3rd ed. with updated bib. Pelican History of Art. New Haven: Yale Univ. Press, 1993.

Labbé, Armand J. *Shamans, Gods, and Mythic Beasts: Colombian Gold and Ceramics in Antiquity.* New York: American Federation of Arts, 1998.

Loendorf, Lawrence L., Christopher Chippindale, and David S. Whitley, eds. *Discovering North American Rock Art.* Tucson: Univ. of Arizona Press, 2005.

Martin, Simon, and Nikolai Grube. *Chronicle of the Maya Kings and Queens: Deciphering the Dynasties of the Ancient Maya.* 2nd ed. New York: Thames & Hudson, 2008.

Miller, Mary Ellen. *The Art of Mesoamerica: From Olmec to Aztec.* 4th ed. World of Art. London: Thames & Hudson, 2006.

———. *Maya Art and Architecture.* World of Art. London: Thames & Hudson, 1999.

———, and Simon Martin. *Courtly Art of the Ancient Maya.* San Francisco: Fine Arts Museums of San Francisco, 2004.

———, and Karl Taube. *The Gods and Symbols of Ancient Mexico and the Maya: An Illustrated Dictionary of Mesoamerican Religion.* London: Thames & Hudson, 1993.

Milner, George R. *The Moundbuilders: Ancient Peoples of Eastern North America.* Ancient Peoples and Places, 110. London: Thames & Hudson, 2004.

Noble, David Grant. *In Search of Chaco: New Approaches to an Archaeological Enigma.* Santa Fe, NM: School of American Research Press, 2004.

O'Connor, Mallory McCane. *Lost Cities of the Ancient Southeast.* Gainesville: Univ. Press of Florida, 1995.

Pasztory, Esther. *Teotihuacan: An Experiment in Living.* Norman: Univ. of Oklahoma Press, 1997.

Pillsbury, Joanne, ed. *Moche Art and Archaeology in Ancient Peru.* Studies in the History of Art: Center for Advanced Study in the Visual Arts, 63: Symposium Papers, 40. Washington, DC: National Gallery of Art, 2001.

Power, Susan C. *Early Art of the Southeastern Indians: Feathered Serpents & Winged Beings.* Athens: Univ. of Georgia Press, 2004.

Rohn, Arthur H., and William M. Ferguson. *Puebloan Ruins of the Southwest.* Albuquerque: Univ. of New Mexico Press, 2006.

Sharer, Robert J., and Loa P. Traxler. *The Ancient Maya.* 6th ed. Stanford, CA: Stanford Univ. Press, 2006.

Stierlin, Henri. *The Maya: Palaces and Pyramids of the Rainforest.* Köln: Taschen, 2001.

Stone-Miller, Rebecca. *Art of the Andes: From Chavin to Inca.* 2nd ed. World of Art. New York: Thames & Hudson, 2002.

———. *To Weave for the Sun: Ancient Andean Textiles.* New York: Thames & Hudson 1994.

Townsend, Richard F., and Robert V. Sharp, eds. *Hero, Hawk, and Open Hand: American Indian Art of the Ancient Midwest and South.* Chicago: Art Institute of Chicago, 2004.

Von Hagen, Adriana, and Craig Morris. *The Cities of the Ancient Andes.* New York: Thames and Hudson, 1998.

Chapter 13 Early African Art

Ben-Amos, Paula. *The Art of Benin.* Rev. ed. Washington, DC: Smithsonian Institution Press, 1995.

Berzock, Kathleen Bickford. *Benin: Royal Arts of a West African Kingdom.* Chicago: Art Institute of Chicago, 2008.

Blier, Suzanne Preston. *The Royal Arts of Africa: The Majesty of Form.* Perspectives. New York: Abrams, 1998.

Cole, Herbert M. *Igbo Arts: Community and Cosmos.* Los Angeles: Fowler Museum of Cultural History, Univ. of California, 1984.

Connah, Graham. *Forgotten Africa: An Introduction to Its Archaeology.* New York: Routledge, 2004.

Darish, Patricia J. "Memorial Head of an Oba: Ancestral Time in Benin Culture." In *Tempus Fugit, Time Flies,* edited by Jan Schall. Kansas City, MO: The Nelson Atkins Museum of Art, 2000: 290–297.

Eyo, Ekpo, and Frank Willett. *Treasures of Ancient Nigeria.* Ed. Rollyn O. Kirchbaum. New York: Knopf, 1980.

Garlake, Peter S. *Early Art and Architecture of Africa.* Oxford History of Art. Oxford: Oxford Univ. Press, 2002.

Grunne, Bernard de. *The Birth of Art in Africa: Nok Statuary in Nigeria.* Paris: A. Biro, 1998.

Huffman, Thomas N. *Symbols in Stone: Unravelling the Mystery of Great Zimbabwe.* Johannesburg: Witwatersrand Univ. Press, 1987.

LaViolette, Adria Jean. *Ethno-Achaeology in Jenné, Mali: Craft and Status among Smiths, Potters, and Masons.* Oxford: Archaeopress, 2000.

M'Bow, Babacar, and Osemwegie Ebohon. *Benin, a Kingdom in Bronze: The Royal Court Art.* Ft. Lauderdale, FL: African American Research Library and Cultural Center, Broward County Library, 2005.

Phillipson, D. W. *African Archaeology.* 3rd ed. Cambridge World Archaeology. New York: Cambridge Univ. Press, 2005.

Schädler, Karl-Ferdinand. *Earth and Ore: 2500 Years of African Art in Terra-Cotta and Metal.* Trans. Geoffrey P. Burwell. München: Panterra, 1997.

Chapter 14 Early Medieval Art in Europe

Alexander, J. J. G. *Medieval Illuminators and Their Methods of Work.* New ed. New Haven: Yale Univ. Press, 1994.

The Art of Medieval Spain, a.d. 500–1200. New York: Metropolitan Museum of Art, 1993.

Backhouse, Janet, D. H. Turner, and Leslie Webster, eds. *The Golden Age of Anglo-Saxon Art, 966–1066.* Bloomington: Indiana Univ. Press, 1984.

Bandmann, Günter. *Early Medieval Architecture as Bearer of Meaning.* New York: Columbia Univ. Press, 2005.

Brown, Michelle P. *The Lindisfarne Gospels: Society, Spirituality and the Scribe.* Toronto: Univ. of Toronto Press, 2003.

Calkins, Robert G. *Illuminated Books of the Middle Ages.* Ithaca, NY: Cornell Univ. Press, 1983.

Carver, Martin. *Sutton Hoo: A Seventh-Century Princely Burial Ground and Its Context.* London: British Museum Press, 2005.

Davis-Weyer, Caecilia. *Early Medieval Art, 300–1150: Sources and Documents.* Upper Saddle River, NJ: Pearson/Prentice Hall, 1971.

Diebold, William J. *Word and Image: An Introduction to Early Medieval Art.* Boulder, CO: Westview Press, 2000.

Dodwell, C. R. *Pictorial Arts of the West, 800–1200.* Pelican History of Art. New Haven: Yale Univ. Press, 1993.

Farr, Carol. *The Book of Kells: Its Function and Audience.* London: British Library, 1997.

Fitzhugh, William W., and Elisabeth I. Ward, eds. *Vikings: The North Atlantic Saga.* Washington, DC: Smithsonian Institution Press, 2000.

Harbison, Peter. *The Golden Age of Irish Art: The Medieval Achievement, 600–1200.* London: Thames & Hudson, 1999.

Henderson, George. *From Durrow to Kells: The Insular Gospel-Books, 650–800.* London: Thames & Hudson, 1987.

Horn, Walter W., and Ernest Born. *Plan of Saint Gall: A Study of the Architecture and Economy of and Life in a Paradigmatic Carolingian Monastery.* California Studies in the History of Art, 19. 3 vols. Berkeley: Univ. of California Press, 1979.

Lasko, Peter. *Ars Sacra, 800–1200.* 2nd ed. Pelican History of Art. New Haven: Yale Univ. Press, 1994.

McClendon, Charles B. *The Origins of Medieval Architecture: Building in Europe, a.d 600–900.* New Haven: Yale Univ. Press, 2005.

Mayr-Harting, Henry. *Ottonian Book Illumination: An Historical Study.* 2nd rev. ed. 2 vols. London: Harvey Miller, 1999.

Mentré, Mireille. *Illuminated Manuscripts of Medieval Spain.* New York: Thames & Hudson, 1996.

Nees, Lawrence. *Early Medieval Art.* Oxford History of Art. Oxford: Oxford Univ. Press, 2002.

Richardson, Hilary, and John Scarry. *An Introduction to Irish High Crosses.* Dublin: Mercier, 1990.

Schapiro, Meyer. *Language of Forms: Lectures on Insular Manuscript Art.* Ed. Jane Rosenthal. New York: Pierpont Morgan Library, 2006.

Stalley, R. A. *Early Medieval Architecture.* Oxford History of Art. Oxford: Oxford Univ. Press, 1999.

Wickham, Chris. *Framing the Early Middle Ages: Europe and the Mediterranean 400–800.* New York: Oxford Univ. Press, 2005.

Williams, John. *Early Spanish Manuscript Illumination.* New York: Braziller, 1977.

Wilson, David M. *Anglo-Saxon Art: From the Seventh Century to the Norman Conquest.* London: Thames & Hudson, 1984.

———, and Ole Klindt-Jensen. *Viking Art.* 2nd ed. Minneapolis: Univ. of Minnesota Press, 1980.

Chapter 15 Romanesque Art

Barral i Altet, Xavier. *The Romanesque: Towns, Cathedrals and Monasteries.* Taschen's World Architecture. New York: Taschen, 1998.

Bernard of Clairvaux. *"Apologia to Abbot William."* In *Treatises I.* The Work of Bernard of Clairvaux, 1: Cistercian Fathers Series, 1. Shannon, Ireland: Irish Univ. Press, 1970: 33–69.

The Book of Sainte Foy. Ed. and trans. Pamela Sheingorn. Philadelphia: Univ. of Pennsylvania Press, 1995.

Cahn, Walter. *Romanesque Manuscripts: The Twelfth Century.* 2nd ed. 2 vols. A Survey of Manuscripts Illuminated in France. London: Harvey Miller, 1996.

Caviness, Madeline H. *"Hildegard as Designer of the Illustrations to her Works."* In *Hildegard of Bingen: The Context of her Thought and Art*, edited by Charles Burnett and Peter Dronke. London: Warburg Institute, 1998: 29–63.

Davis-Weyer, Caecilia. *Early Medieval Art, 300–1150. Sources and Documents.* Upper Saddle River, NJ: Pearson/Prentice Hall, 1971.

Dimier, Anselme. *Stones Laid before the Lord: A History of Monastic Architecture.* Trans. Gilchrist Lavigne. Cistercian Studies Series, no. 152. Kalamazoo, MI: Cistercian Publications, 1999.

Fergusson, Peter. *Architecture of Solitude: Cistercian Abbeys in Twelfth-Century England.* Princeton: Princeton Univ. Press, 1984.

Forsyth, Ilene H. *The Throne of Wisdom: Wood Sculptures of the Madonna in Romanesque France.* Princeton: Princeton Univ. Press, 1972.

Gaud, Henri, and Jean-François Leroux-Dhuys. *Cistercian Abbeys: History and Architecture.* Köln: Könemann, 1998.

Gerson, Paula, ed. *The Pilgrim's Guide to Santiago de Compostela: A Critical Edition.* 2 vols. London: Harvey Miller, 1998.

Grivot, Denis, and George Zarnecki. *Gislebertus: Sculptor of Autun.* New York: Orion Press, 1961.

Hearn, M. F. *Romanesque Sculpture: The Revival of Monumental Stone Sculptures in the Eleventh and Twelfth Centuries.* Ithaca, NY: Cornell Univ. Press, 1981.

Hicks, Carola. *The Bayeux Tapestry: The Life Story of a Masterpiece.* London: Chatto & Windus, 2006.

Hourihane, Colum, ed. *Romanesque Art and Thought in the Twelfth Century: Essays in Honor of Walter Cahn.* The Index of Christian Art Occasional Papers 10. University Park, PA: Penn State Press, 2008.

Kubach, Hans E. *Romanesque Architecture. History of World Architecture.* New York: Electa/Rizzoli, 1988.

Minne-Sève, Viviane, and Hervé Kergall. *Romanesque and Gothic France: Architecture and Sculpture.* Trans. Jack Hawkes and Lory Frankel. New York: Abrams, 2000.

Newman, Barbara. *Sister of Wisdom: St. Hildegard's Theology of the Feminine.* 2nd ed. Berkeley: Univ. of California Press, 1997.

Schapiro, Meyer. *Romanesque Art: Selected Papers.* New York: George Braziller, 1977.

_____. *The Romanesque Sculpture of Moissac.* New York: Braziller, 1985.

_____. *Romanesque Architectural Sculpture: The Charles Eliot Norton Lectures.* Ed. Linda Seidel. Chicago: Univ. of Chicago Press, 2006.

Seidel, Linda. *Legends in Limestone: Lazarus, Gislebertus, and the Cathedral of Autun.* Chicago: Univ. of Chicago Press, 1999.

Sundell, Michael G. *Mosaics in the Eternal City.* Tempe: Arizona Center for Medieval and Renaissance Studies, 2007.

Swanson, R. N. *The Twelfth-Century Renaissance.* Manchester: Manchester Univ. Press, 1999.

Theophilus. *On Divers Arts: The Foremost Medieval Treatise on Painting, Glassmaking, and Metalwork.* Trans. John G. Hawthorne and Cyril Stanley Smith. New York: Dover, 1979.

Toman, Rolf, ed. *Romanesque: Architecture, Sculpture, Painting.* Trans. Fiona Hulse and Ian Macmillan. Köln: Könemann, 1997.

Wilson, David M. *The Bayeux Tapestry: The Complete Tapestry in Color.* London: Thames & Hudson and New York: Knopf, 2004.

Zarnecki, George, Janet Holt, and Tristam Holland, eds. *English Romanesque Art, 1066–1200.* London: Weidenfeld and Nicolson, 1984.

Chapter 16 Gothic Art of the Twelfth and Thirteenth Centuries

Barnes, Carl F. *The Portfolio of Villard de Honnecourt: A New Critical Edition and Color Facsimile.* Burlington, VT: Ashgate, 2009.

Binding, Günther. *High Gothic: The Age of the Great Cathedrals.* Taschen's World Architecture. London: Taschen, 1999.

Binski, Paul. *Becket's Crown: Art and Imagination in Gothic England, 1170–1300.* New Haven: Yale Univ. Press, 2004.

Bony, Jean. *French Gothic Architecture of the 12th and 13th Centuries.* California Studies in the History of Art, 20. Berkeley: Univ. of California Press, 1983.

Camille, Michael. *Gothic Art: Glorious Visions.* Perspectives. New York: Abrams, 1996.

Cennini, Cennino. *The Craftsman's Handbook "Il libro dell'arte".* Trans. D. V. Thompson, Jr. New York: Dover, 1960.

Coldstream, Nicola. *Masons and Sculptors.* Toronto and Buffalo, NY: Univ. of Toronto Press, 1991.

Crosby, Sumner M. *The Royal Abbey of Saint-Denis from Its Beginnings to the Death of Suger, 475–1151.* Yale Publications in the History of Art, 37. New Haven: Yale Univ. Press, 1987.

Erlande-Brandenburg, Alain. *Gothic Art.* Trans. I. Mark Paris. New York: Abrams, 1989.

Favier, Jean. *The World of Chartres.* Trans. Francisca Garvie. New York: Abrams, 1990.

Frankl, Paul. *Gothic Architecture.* Revised. Paul Crossley. Pelican History of Art. New Haven: Yale Univ. Press, 2000.

Frisch, Teresa G. *Gothic Art, 1140–c. 1450: Sources and Documents.* Upper Saddle River, NJ: Pearson/Prentice Hall, 1971.

Grodecki, Louis, and Catherine Brisac. *Gothic Stained Glass, 1200–1300.* Ithaca, NY: Cornell Univ. Press, 1985.

Jordan, Alyce A. *Visualizing Kingship in the Windows of the Sainte-Chapelle.* Turnhout: Brepols, 2002.

Moskowitz, Anita Fiderer. *Nicola & Giovanni Pisano: The Pulpits: Pious Devotion, Pious Diversion.* London: Harvey Miller, 2005.

Nussbaum, Norbert. *German Gothic Church Architecture.* Trans. Scott Kleager. New Haven: Yale Univ. Press, 2000.

Panofsky, Erwin. *Abbot Suger on the Abbey Church of St.-Denis and Its Art Treasures.* 2nd ed. Ed. Gerda Panofsky-Soergel. Princeton: Princeton Univ. Press, 1979.

Parry, Stan. *Great Gothic Cathedrals of France.* New York: Viking Studio, 2001.

Sauerländer, Willibald. *Gothic Sculpture in France, 1140–1270.* Trans. Janet Sandheimer. London: Thames & Hudson, 1972.

Scott, Robert A. *The Gothic Enterprise: A Guide to Understanding the Medieval Cathedral.* Berkeley: Univ. of California Press, 2003.

Simsom, Otto Georg von. *The Gothic Cathedral: Origins of Gothic Architecture and the Medieval Concept of Order.* 3rd ed. exp. Bollingen Series. Princeton: Princeton Univ. Press, 1988.

Suckale, Robert, and Matthias Weniger. *Painting of the Gothic Era.* Ed. Ingo F. Walther. New York: Taschen, 1999.

Wieck, Roger S. *Time Sanctified: The Book of Hours in Medieval Art and Life.* 2nd ed. New York: Braziller, 2001.

Williamson, Paul. *Gothic Sculpture, 1140–1300.* Pelican History of Art. New Haven: Yale Univ. Press, 1995.

Chapter 17 Fourteenth-Century Art in Europe

Alexander, Jonathan, and Paul Binski, eds. *Age of Chivalry: Art in Plantagenet England, 1200–1400.* London: Royal Academy of Arts, 1987.

Backhouse, Janet. *Illumination from Books of Hours.* London: British Library, 2004.

Boehm, Barbara Drake, and Jirí Fajt, eds. *Prague: The Crown of Bohemia, 1347–1437.* New York: Metropolitan Museum of Art, 2005.

Bony, Jean. *The English Decorated Style: Gothic Architecture Transformed, 1250–1350.* The Wrightsman Lectures 10th. Oxford: Phaidon Press, 1979.

Borsook, Eve. *The Mural Painters of Tuscany: From Cimabue to Andrea del Sarto.* 2nd ed. rev. & enlarged. Oxford Studies in the History of Art and Architecture. Oxford: Clarendon Press 1980.

Derbes, Anne, and Mark Sandona, eds. *The Cambridge Companion to Giotto.* Cambridge and New York: Cambridge Univ. Press, 2003.

Fajt, Jirí, ed. *Magister Theodoricus, Court Painter to Emperor Charles IV: The Pictorial Decoration of the Shrines at Karlstejn Castle.* Prague: National Gallery, 1998.

Holt, Elizabeth Gilmore, ed. *A Documentary History of Art.* 2 vols. Princeton, Princeton Univ. Press, 1982–86.

Ladis, Andrew. ed, *The Arena Chapel and the Genius of Giotto: Padua.* Giotto and the World of Early Italian Art, 2. New York: Garland, 1998.

Meiss, Millard. *Painting in Florence and Siena after the Black Death: The Arts, Religion, and Society in the Mid-Fourteenth Century.* 2nd ed. Princeton: Princeton Univ. Press, 1978.

Moskowitz, Anita Fiderer. *Italian Gothic Sculpture: c. 1250–c. 1400.* New York: Cambridge Univ. Press, 2001.

Norman, Diana, ed. *Siena, Florence, and Padua: Art, Society, and Religion 1280–1400.* 2 vols. New Haven: Yale Univ. Press, 1995.

Poeschke, Joachim. *Italian Frescoes, the Age of Giotto, 1280–1400.* New York: Abbeville Press, 2005.

Schleif, Corine. "St. Hedwig's Personal Ivory Madonna: Women's Agency and the Powers of Possessing Portable Figures." In *The Four Modes of Seeing: Approaches to Medieval Imagery in Honor of Madeline Harrison Caviness*, edited by Evelyn Staudinger Lane, Elizabeth Carson Paston, and Ellen M. Shortell. Farnham, Surrey: Ashgate, 2009: 282–403.

Vasari, Giorgio. *The Lives of the Artists.* Trans. Julia Conaway Bondanella and Peter Bondanella. Oxford World's Classics. New York: Oxford Univ. Press, 2008.

Welch, Evelyn S. *Art in Renaissance Italy, 1350–1500.* New ed. Oxford History of Art. Oxford: Oxford Univ. Press, 2000.

White, John. *Art and Architecture in Italy, 1250 to 1400.* 3rd ed. Pelican History of Art. Harmondsworth, UK: Penguin, 1993.

Chapter 18 Fifteenth-Century Art in Northern Europe

Art from the Court of Burgundy: The Patronage of Philip the Bold and John the Fearless 1364–1419. Dijon: Musée des Beaux-Arts and Cleveland: Cleveland Museum of Art, 2004.

Baxandall, Michael. *The Limewood Sculptors of Renaissance Germany.* New Haven: Yale Univ. Press, 1980.

Blum, Shirley. *Early Netherlandish Triptychs: A Study in Patronage.* California Studies in the History of Art, 13. Berkeley: Univ. of California Press, 1969.

Borchert, Till-Holger. *Age of Van Eyck: The Mediterranean World and Early Netherlandish Painting, 1430–1530.* New York: Thames & Hudson, 2002.

Campbell, Lorne. *The Fifteenth-Century Netherlandish Schools* (National Gallery Catalogues). London: National Gallery, 1998.

Cavallo, Adolph S. *The Unicorn Tapestries at the Metropolitan Museum of Art.* New York: Metropolitan Museum of Art, 1998.

Chastel, Andrè. *French Art: The Renaissance, 1430–1620.* Paris: Flammarion, 1995.

Dhanens, Elisabeth. *Van Eyck: The Ghent Altarpiece.* New York: Viking Press, 1973.

Füssel, Stephan. *Gutenberg and the Impact of Printing.* Trans. Douglas Martin. Burlington, VT: Ashgate, 2005.

Koster, Margaret L. "The *Arnolfini Double Portrait*: A Simple Solution." Apollo 157 (September 2003): 3–14.

Lane, Barbara G. *The Altar and the Altarpiece: Sacramental Themes in Early Netherlandish Painting.* New York: Harper & Row, 1984.

Marks, Richard, and Paul Williamson, eds. *Gothic: Art for England 1400–1547.* London: V&A Publications, 2003.

Meiss, Millard. *French Painting in the Time of Jean de Berry: The Limbourgs and their Contemporaries.* 2 vols. New York: Braziller, 1974.

Müller, Theodor. *Sculpture in the Netherlands, Germany, France, and Spain: 1400–1500.* Trans. Elaine and William Robson Scott. Pelican History of Art. Harmondsworth, UK: Penguin, 1966.

Pächt, Otto. *Early Netherlandish Painting: From Rogier van der Weyden to Gerard David.* Ed. Monika Rosenauer. Trans. David Britt. London: Harvey Miller, 1997.

———. *Van Eyck and the Founders of Early Netherlandish Painting.* London: Miller, 1994.

Panofsky, Erwin. *Early Netherlandish Painting. Its Origins and Character.* 2 vols. Cambridge, MA: Harvard Univ. Press, 1966.

Parshall, Peter W., and Rainer Schoch. *Origins of European Printmaking: Fifteenth-Century Woodcuts and their Public.* Washington, DC: National Gallery of Art, 2005.

Plummer, John. *The Last Flowering: French Painting in Manuscripts, 1420–1530, from American Collections.* New York: Pierpont Morgan Library, 1982.

Seidel, Linda. *Jan van Eyck's Arnolfini Portrait: Stories of an Icon.* New York: Cambridge Univ. Press, 1993.

Smith, Jeffrey Chipps. *The Northern Renaissance.* London and New York: Phaidon Press, 2004.

Snyder, James. *Northern Renaissance Art: Painting, Sculpture, the Graphic Arts from 1350 to 1575.* 2nd ed. rev. Larry Silver and Henry Luttikhuizen. Upper Saddle River, NJ: Prentice Hall, 2005.

Vos, Dirk de. *The Flemish Primitives: The Masterpieces.* Princeton: Princeton Univ. Press, 2002.

Zuffi, Stefano. *European Art of the Fifteenth Century.* Trans. Brian D. Phillips. Art through the Centuries. Los Angeles: J. Paul Getty Museum, 2005.

Chapter 19 Renaissance Art in Fifteenth-Century Italy

Adams, Laurie Schneider. *Italian Renaissance Art.* Boulder, CO: Westview Press, 2001.

Ahl, Diane Cole, ed. *The Cambridge Companion to Masaccio.* New York: Cambridge Univ. Press, 2002.

Ames-Lewis, Francis. *Drawing in Early Renaissance Italy.* 2nd ed. New Haven: Yale Univ. Press, 2000.

———. *The Intellectual Life of the Early Renaissance Artist.* New Haven: Yale Univ. Press, 2000.

Baxandall, Michael. *Painting and Experience in Fifteenth-Century Italy: A Primer in the Social History of Pictorial Style.* 2nd ed. Oxford: Oxford Univ. Press, 1988.

Boskovits, Miklós. *Italian Paintings of the Fifteenth Century.* The Collections of the National Gallery of Art. Washington, DC: National Gallery of Art, 2003.

Botticelli and Filippino: Passion and Grace in Fifteenth-Century Florentine Painting. Milano: Skira, 2004.

Brown, Patricia Fortini. *Art and Life in Renaissance Venice.* Perspectives. New York: Abrams, 1997. Reissue ed. Upper Saddle River, NJ: Pearson/Prentice Hall, 2006.

Christiansen, Keith, Laurence B. Kanter, and Carl Brandon Strehlke. *Painting in Renaissance Siena, 1420–1500.* New York: Metropolitan Museum of Art, 1988.

Christine, de Pisan. *The Book of the City of Ladies.* Trans. Rosalind Brown-Grant. London: Penguin Books, 1999.

Gilbert, Creighton, ed. *Italian Art, 1400–1500: Sources and Documents.* Evanston, IL: Northwestern Univ. Press, 1992.

Heydenreich, Ludwig Heinrich. *Architecture in Italy, 1400–1500.* Revised. Paul Davies. Pelican History of Art. New Haven: Yale Univ. Press, 1996.

Hind, Arthur M. *An Introduction to a History of Woodcut.* New York: Dover, 1963.

Hyman, Timothy. *Sienese Painting: The Art of a City-Republic (1278–1477).* World of Art. New York: Thames & Hudson, 2003.

King, Ross. *Brunelleschi's Dome: How a Renaissance Genius Reinvented Architecture.* New York: Walker, 2000.

Lavin, Marilyn Aronberg, ed. *Piero della Francesca and his Legacy.* Studies in the History of Art, 48: Symposium Papers, 28. Washington, DC: National Gallery of Art, 1995.

Pächt, Otto. *Venetian Painting in the 15th Century: Jacopo, Gentile and Giovanni Bellini and Andrea Mantegna.* Ed. Margareta Vyoral-Tschapka and Michael Pächt. Trans. Fiona Elliott. London: Harvey Miller, 2003.

Paoletti, John T., and Gary M. Radke. *Art in Renaissance Italy.* 3rd ed. Upper Saddle River, NJ: Pearson/Prentice Hall, 2005.

Partridge, Loren W. *The Art of Renaissance Rome, 1400–1600.* Perspectives. New York: Abrams, 1996. Reissue ed. Upper Saddle River, NJ: Pearson/Prentice Hall, 2006.

Poeschke, Joachim. *Donatello and His World: Sculpture of the Italian Renaissance.* Trans. Russell Stockman. New York: Abrams, 1993.

Pope-Hennessy, John. *Italian Renaissance Sculpture.* 4th ed. London: Phaidon Press, 1996.

Radke, Gary M., ed. *The Gates of Paradise: Lorenzo Ghiberti's Masterpiece.* New Haven: Yale Univ. Press, 2007.

Randolph, Adrian W. B., *Engaging Symbols: Gender, Politics, and Public Art in Fifteenth-Century Florence.* New Haven: Yale Univ. Press, 2002.

Troncelliti, Latifah. *The Two Parallel Realities of Alberti and Cennini: The Power of Writing and the Visual Arts in the Italian Quattrocento.* Studies in Italian Literature, vol. 14. Lewiston, NY: Mellen Press, 2004.

Turner, Richard. *Renaissance Florence: The Invention of a New Art.* Perspectives. New York: Abrams, 1997. Reissue ed. Upper Saddle River, NJ: Pearson/Prentice Hall, 2006.

Verdon, Timothy, and John Henderson, eds. *Christianity and the Renaissance: Image and Religious Imagination in the Quattrocento.* Syracuse, NY: Syracuse Univ. Press, 1990.

Walker, Paul Robert. *The Feud that Sparked the Renaissance: How Brunelleschi and Ghiberti Changed the Art World.* New York: William Morrow, 2002.

Welch, Evelyn S. *Art and Society in Italy, 1350–1500.* Oxford History of Art. Oxford: Oxford Univ. Press, 1997.

Chapter 20 Sixteenth-Century Art in Italy

Acidini Luchinat, Cristina, et al. *The Medici, Michelangelo, & the Art of Late Renaissance Florence.* New Haven: Yale Univ. Press, 2002.

Bambach, Carmen. *Drawing and Painting in the Italian Renaissance Workshop: Theory and Practice, 1330–1600.* Cambridge: Cambridge Univ. Press, 1999.

Barriault, Anne B., ed. *Reading Vasari.* London: Philip Wilson in assoc. with the Georgia Museum of Art, 2005.

Brambilla Barcilon, Pinin. *Leonardo: The Last Supper.* Chicago: Univ. of Chicago Press, 2001.

Brown, Patricia Fortini. *Art and Life in Renaissance Venice.* Perspectives. New York: Abrams, 1997.

Cellini, Benvenuto. *Autobiography.* Rev. ed. Trans. George Bull. Penguin Classics. New York: Penguin, 1998.

Chelazzi Dini, Giulietta, Alessandro Angelini, and Bernardina Sani. *Sienese Painting: From Duccio to the Birth of the Baroque.* New York: Abrams, 1998.

Cole, Alison. *Virtue and Magnificence: Art of the Italian Renaissance Courts.* Perspectives. New York: Abrams, 1995. Reissue ed. as Art of the Italian Courts. Upper Saddle River, NJ: Pearson/Prentice Hall, 2006.

Franklin, David, ed. *Leonardo da Vinci, Michelangelo, and the Renaissance in Florence.* Ottawa: National Gallery of Canada in assoc. with Yale Univ. Press, 2005.

Freedberg, S. J. *Painting in Italy, 1500 to 1600.* 3rd ed. Pelican History of Art. New Haven: Yale Univ. Press, 1993.

Goffen, Rona. *Renaissance Rivals: Michelangelo, Leonardo, Raphael, Titian.* New Haven: Yale Univ. Press, 2002.

———. *Titian's Venus of Urbino.* Masterpieces of Western Painting. Cambridge: Cambridge Univ. Press, 1997.

———. *Titian's Women.* New Haven: Yale Univ. Press, 1997.

Hall, Marcia B. *After Raphael: Painting in Central Italy in the Sixteenth Century.* New York: Cambridge Univ. Press, 1999.

———, ed. *The Cambridge Companion to Raphael.* New York: Cambridge Univ. Press, 2005.

Hollingsworth, Mary. *Patronage in Sixteenth Century Italy.* London: John Murray, 1996.

Hopkins, Andrew. *Italian Architecture: From Michelangelo to Borromini.* World of Art. New York: Thames & Hudson, 2002.

Hughes, Anthony. *Michelangelo.* Art & Ideas. London: Phaidon Press, 1997.

Huse, Norbert, and Wolfgang Wolters. *Art of Renaissance Venice: Architecture, Sculpture and Painting, 1460–1590.* Trans. Edmund Jephcott. Chicago: Univ. of Chicago Press, 1990.

Joannides, Paul. *Titian to 1518: The Assumption of Genius.* New Haven: Yale Univ. Press, 2001.

Klein, Robert, and Henri Zerner. *Italian Art, 1500–1600: Sources and Documents.* Upper Saddle River, NJ: Pearson/Prentice Hall, 1966.

Kliemann, Julian-Matthias, and Michael Rohlmann. *Italian Frescoes: High Renaissance and Mannerism, 1510–1600.* Trans. Steven Lindberg. New York: Abbeville Press, 2004.

Landau, David, and Peter Parshall. *The Renaissance Print: 1470–1550.* New Haven: Yale Univ. Press, 1994.

Lieberman, Ralph. *Renaissance Architecture in Venice, 1450–1540.* New York: Abbeville Press, 1982.

Lotz, Wolfgang. *Architecture in Italy, 1500–1600.* Revised. Deborah Howard. Pelican History of Art. New Haven: Yale Univ. Press, 1995.

Meilman, Patricia, ed. *The Cambridge Companion to Titian.* New York: Cambridge Univ. Press, 2004.

Mitrovic, Branko. *Learning from Palladio.* New York: Norton, 2004.

Murray, Linda. *The High Renaissance and Mannerism: Italy, the North and Spain, 1500–1600.* World of Art. London: Thames & Hudson, 1995.

Partridge, Loren W. *The Art of Renaissance Rome, 1400–1600.* Perspectives. New York: Abrams, 1996.

———. *Michelangelo, the Last Judgment: A Glorious Restoration.* New York: Abrams, 1997.

Pilliod, Elizabeth. *Pontormo, Bronzino, Allori: A Genealogy of Florentine Art.* New Haven: Yale Univ. Press, 2001.

Pope-Hennessy, John. *Italian High Renaissance and Baroque Sculpture.* 4th ed. London: Phaidon Press, 1996.

Rosand, David. *Painting in Cinquecento Venice: Titian, Veronese, Tintoretto.* Rev. ed. Cambridge: Cambridge Univ. Press, 1997.

Rowe, Colin, and Leon Satkowski. *Italian Architecture of the 16th Century.* New York: Princeton Architectural Press, 2002.

Rowland, Ingrid D. *The Culture of the High Renaissance: Ancients and Moderns in Sixteenth Century Rome.* Cambridge: Cambridge Univ. Press, 1998.

Shearman, John. *Mannerism.* Harmondsworth, UK: Penguin, 1967. Reissue ed. New York: Penguin, 1990.

Vasari, Giorgio. *The Lives of the Artists.* Trans. Julia Conaway Bondanella and Peter Bondanella. Oxford World's Classics. New York: Oxford Univ. Press, 2008.

Verheyen, Egon. *The Paintings in the Studiolo of Isabella d'Este at Mantua.* Monographs on Archaeology and Fine Arts, 23. New York: New York Univ. Press, 1971.

Williams, Robert. *Art, Theory, and Culture in Sixteenth-Century Italy: From Techne to Metateche.* Cambridge: Cambridge Univ. Press, 1997.

Chapter 21 Sixteenth-Century Art in Northern Europe and the Iberian Peninsula

Bartrum, Giulia. *Albrecht Dürer and his Legacy: The Graphic Work of a Renaissance Artist.* London: British Museum Press, 2002.

Bartrum, Giulia. *German Renaissance Prints 1490–1550.* London: British Museum Press, 1995.

Brown, Jonathan. *Painting in Spain, 1500–1700.* Pelican History of Art. New Haven: Yale Univ. Press, 1998.

Buck, Stephanie, and Jochen Sander. *Hans Holbein the Younger: Painter at the Court of Henry VIII.* Trans. Rachel Esner and Beverley Jackson. New York: Thames & Hudson, 2004.

Chapuis, Julien. *Tilman Riemenschneider: Master Sculptor of the Late Middle Ages.* Washington, DC: National Gallery of Art, 1999.

Lovell, Margaretta M. *Art in a Season of Revolution: Painters, Artisans, and Patrons in Early America.* Early American Studies. Philadelphia: Univ. of Pennsylvania Press, 2005.
Monneret, Sophie. *David and Neo-Classicism.* Trans. Chris Miller and Peter Snowdon. Paris: Terrail, 1999.
Montgomery, Charles F., and Patrick E. Kane, eds. *American Art, 1750–1800: Towards Independence.* Boston: New York Graphic Society, 1976.
Natter, Tobias, ed. *Angelica Kauffman: A Woman of Immense Talent.* Ostfildern: Hatje Cantz, 2007.
Porterfield, Todd, and Susan L. Siegfried. *Staging Empire: Napoleon, Ingres, and David.* University Park: Pennsylvania State Univ. Press, 2006.
Poulet, Anne L. *Jean-Antoine Houdon: Sculptor of the Enlightenment.* Washington, DC: National Gallery of Art, 2003.
Summerson, John. *Architecture of the Eighteenth Century.* World of Art. New York: Thames & Hudson, 1986.
Wilton, Andrew, and Ilaria Bignamini, eds. *Grand Tour: The Lure of Italy in the Eighteenth Century.* London: Tate Gallery, 1996.

Chapter 30 Mid to Late Nineteenth Century Art in Europe and the United States

Adams, Steven. *The Barbizon School and the Origins of Impressionism.* London: Phaidon Press, 1994.
Bajac, Quentin. *The Invention of Photography.* Discoveries. New York: Abrams, 2002.
Barger, M. Susan, and William B. White. *The Daguerreotype: Nineteenth-Century Technology and Modern Science.* Washington, DC: Smithsonian Institution Press, 1991.
Benjamin, Roger. *Orientalist Aesthetics: Art, Colonialism, and French North Africa, 1880–1930.* Berkeley: Univ. of California Press, 2003.
Bergdoll, Barry. *European Architecture, 1750–1890.* Oxford History of Art. New York: Oxford Univ. Press, 2000.
Blühm, Andreas, and Louise Lippincott. *Light!: The Industrial Age 1750–1900: Art & Science, Technology & Society.* New York: Thames & Hudson, 2001.
Boime, Albert. *The Academy and French Painting in the Nineteenth Century.* 2nd ed. New Haven: Yale Univ. Press, 1986.
Butler, Ruth, and Suzanne G. Lindsay. *European Sculpture of the Nineteenth Century.* Washington, DC: National Gallery of Art, 2000.
Callen, Anthea. *The Art of Impressionism: Painting Technique & the Making of Modernity.* New Haven: Yale Univ. Press, 2000.
Chu, Petra ten-Doesschate. *Nineteenth Century European Art.* 2nd. ed. Upper Saddle River, NJ: Pearson/Prentice Hall, 2006.
Clark, T. J. *The Painting of Modern Life: Paris in the Art of Manet and His Followers.* Rev. ed. London: Thames & Hudson, 1999.
Conrads, Margaret C. *Winslow Homer and the Critics: Forging a National Art in the 1870s.* Princeton: Princeton Univ. Press in association with the Nelson-Atkins Museum of Art, 2001.
Denis, Rafael Cardoso, and Colin Trodd. *Art and the Academy in the Nineteenth Century.* New Brunswick, NJ: Rutgers Univ. Press, 2000.
Eisenman, Stephen F. *Nineteenth Century Art: A Critical History.* 3rd ed. New York: Thames & Hudson, 2007.
Eitner, Lorenz. *Nineteenth Century European Painting: David to Cezanne.* Rev. ed. Boulder, CO: Westview Press, 2002.
Frazier, Nancy. *Louis Sullivan and the Chicago School.* New York: Knickerbocker Press, 1998.
Fried, Michael. *Manet's Modernism, or, The Face of Painting in the 1860s.* Chicago: Univ. of Chicago Press, 1996.
Gerdts, William H. *American Impressionism.* 2nd ed. New York: Abbeville Press, 2001.
Greenhalgh, Paul, ed. *Art Nouveau, 1890–1914.* London: V&A Publications, 2000.
Grigsby, Darcy Grimaldo. *Extremities: Painting Empire in Post-Revolutionary France.* New Haven: Yale Univ. Press, 2002.
Groseclose, Barbara. *Nineteenth-Century American Art.* Oxford History of Art. Oxford: Oxford Univ. Press, 2000.
Harrison, Charles, Paul Wood, and Jason Gaiger. *Art in Theory 1815–1900: An Anthology of Changing Ideas.* Oxford: Blackwell, 1998.
Herrmann, Luke. *Nineteenth Century British Painting.* London: Giles de la Mare, 2000.
Hirsh, Sharon L. *Symbolism and Modern Urban Society.* New York: Cambridge Univ. Press, 2004.
Kaplan, Wendy. *The Arts & Crafts Movement in Europe & America: Design for the Modern World.* New York: Thames & Hudson in assoc. with the Los Angeles County Museum of Art, 2004.
Kendall, Richard. *Degas: Beyond Impressionism.* London: National Gallery, 1996.
Lambourne, Lionel. *Japonisme: Cultural Crossings between Japan and the West.* New York: Phaidon Press, 2005.
Lemoine, Bertrand. *Architecture in France, 1800–1900.* Trans. Alexandra Bonfante-Warren. New York: Abrams, 1998.
Lewis, Mary Tompkins, ed.. *Critical Readings in Impressionism and Post-Impressionism: An Anthology.* Berkeley: Univ. of California Press, 2007.
Lochnan, Katharine Jordan. *Turner Whistler Monet.* London: Tate Publishing in assoc. with the Art Gallery of Ontario, 2004.
Miller, Angela L., et al. *American Encounters: Art, History, and Cultural Identity.* Upper Saddle River, NJ: Pearson/Prentice Hall, 2008.
Noon, Patrick J. *Crossing the Channel: British and French Painting in the age of Romanticism.* London: Tate Publishing, 2003.
Pissarro, Joachim. *Pioneering Modern Painting: Cézanne & Pissarro 1865–1885.* New York: Museum of Modern Art, 2005.
Rodner, William S. *J. M. W. Turner: Romantic Painter of the Industrial Revolution.* Berkeley: Univ. of California Press, 1997.
Rosenblum, Robert, and H. W. Janson. *19th Century Art.* Rev. & updated ed. Upper Saddle River, NJ: Pearson Prentice Hall, 2005.
Rubin, James H. *Impressionism. Art & Ideas.* London: Phaidon Press, 1999.
Rybczynski, Witold. *A Clearing in the Distance: Frederick Law Olmsted and America in the Nineteenth Century.* New York: Scribner, 1999.
Smith, Paul. *Seurat and the Avant-Garde.* New Haven: Yale Univ. Press, 1997.
Thomson, Belinda. *Impressionism: Origins, Practice, Reception.* World of Art. New York: Thames & Hudson, 2000.
Twyman, Michael. *Breaking the Mould: The First Hundred Years of Lithography.* The Panizzi Lectures, 2000. London: British Library, 2001.
Vaughan, William, and Francoise Cachin. *Arts of the 19th Century.* 2 vols. New York: Abrams, 1998.
Werner, Marcia. *Pre-Raphaelite Painting and Nineteenth-Century Realism.* New York: Cambridge Univ. Press, 2005.
Zemel, Carol M. *Van Gogh's Progress: Utopia, Modernity, and Late-Nineteenth-Century Art.* California Studies in the History of Art, 36. Berkeley: Univ. of California Press, 1997.

Chapter 31 Modern Art in Europe and The Americas, 1900–1950

Ades, Dawn, comp. *Art and Power: Europe under the Dictators, 1930–45.* Stuttgart, Germany: Oktagon in assoc. with Hayward Gallery, 1995.
Antliff, Mark, and Patricia Leighten. *Cubism and Culture. World of Art.* London: Thames & Hudson, 2001.
Bailey, David A. *Rhapsodies in Black: Art of the Harlem Renaissance.* London: Hayward Gallery, 1997.
Balken, Debra Bricker. *Debating American Modernism: Stieglitz, Duchamp, and the New York Avant-Garde.* New York: American Federation of Arts, 2003.
Barron, Stephanie, ed. *Degenerate Art: The Fate of the Avant-Garde in Nazi Germany.* Los Angeles: Los Angeles County Museum of Art, 1991.
———, and Wolf-Dieter Dube, eds. *German Expressionism: Art and Society.* New York: Rizzoli, 1997.
Bochner, Jay. *An American Lens: Scenes from Alfred Stieglitz's New York Secession.* Cambridge, MA: MIT Press, 2005.
Bohn, Willard. *The Rise of Surrealism: Cubism, Dada, and the Pursuit of the Marvelous.* Albany: State Univ. of New York Press, 2002.
Bowlt, John E., and Evgeniia Petrova, eds. *Painting Revolution: Kandinsky, Malevich and the Russian Avant-Garde.* Bethesda, MD: Foundation for International Arts and Education, 2000.
Bown, Matthew Cullerne. *Socialist Realist Painting.* New Haven: Yale Univ. Press, 1998.
Brown, Milton W. *Story of the Armory Show.* 2nd ed. New York: Abbeville Press, 1988.
Chassey, Eric de, ed. *American Art: 1908–1947, from Winslow Homer to Jackson Pollock.* Trans. Jane McDonald. Paris: Réunion des Musées Nationaux, 2001.
Corn, Wanda M. *The Great American Thing: Modern Art and National Identity, 1915–1935.* Berkeley: Univ. of California Press, 1999.
Curtis, Penelope. *Sculpture 1900–1945: After Rodin.* Oxford History of Art. Oxford: Oxford Univ. Press, 1999.
Dachy, Marc. *Dada: The Revolt of Art.* Trans. Liz Nash. New York: Abrams, 2006.
Elger, Dietmar. *Expressionism: A Revolution in German Art.* Ed. Ingo F. Walther. Trans. Hugh Beyer. New York: Taschen, 1998.
Fer, Briony. *On Abstract Art.* New Haven: Yale Univ. Press, 1997.
Fletcher, Valerie J. *Crosscurrents of Modernism: Four Latin American Pioneers: Diego Rivera, Joaquín Torres-García, Wifredo Lam, Matta.* Washington, DC: Hirshhorn Museum and Sculpture Garden in assoc. with the Smithsonian Institution Press, 1992.
Folgarait, Leonard. *Mural Painting and Social Revolution in Mexico, 1920–1940: Art of the New Order.* New York: Cambridge Univ. Press, 1998.
Forgács, Eva. *The Bauhaus Idea and Bauhaus Politics.* Trans. John Bátki. New York: Central European Univ. Press, 1995.
Frampton, Kenneth. *Modern Architecture: A Critical History.* 4th ed. World of Art. London: Thames & Hudson, 2007.
Gooding, Mel. *Abstract Art.* Movements in Modern Art. Cambridge: Cambridge Univ. Press, 2001.
Grant, Kim. *Surrealism and the Visual Arts: Theory and Reception.* New York: Cambridge Univ. Press, 2005.
Green, Christopher. *Art in France: 1900–1940.* Pelican History of Art. New Haven: Yale Univ. Press, 2000.
Harris, Jonathan. *Federal Art and National Culture: The Politics of Identity in New Deal America.* Cambridge Studies in American Visual Culture. New York: Cambridge Univ. Press, 1995.
Harrison, Charles, Francis Frascina, and Gill Perry. *Primitivism, Cubism, Abstraction: The Early Twentieth Century.* New Haven: Yale Univ. Press, 1993.
Haskell, Barbara. *The American Century: Art & Culture, 1900–1950.* New York: Whitney Museum of American Art, 1999.
Herskovic, Marika, ed. *American Abstract Expressionism of the 1950s: An Illustrated Survey: With Artists' Statements, Artwork and Biographies.* New York: New York School Press, 2003.
Hill, Charles C. *The Group of Seven: Art for a Nation.* Ottawa: National Gallery of Canada, 1995.
James-Chakraborty, Kathleen, ed. *Bauhaus Culture: From Weimar to the Cold War.* Minneapolis: Univ. of Minnesota Press, 2006.
Karmel, Pepe. *Picasso and the Invention of Cubism.* New Haven: Yale Univ. Press, 2003.
Lista, Giovanni. *Futurism.* Trans. Susan Wise. Paris: Terrail, 2001.
Lucie-Smith, Edward. *Latin American Art of the 20th Century.* 2nd ed. World of Art. London: Thames & Hudson, 2005.
McCarter, Robert, ed. *On and by Frank Lloyd Wright: A Primer of Architectural Principles.* New York: Phaidon Press, 2005.
Moudry, Roberta, ed. *The American Skyscraper: Cultural Histories.* New York: Cambridge Univ. Press, 2005.
Rickey, George. *Constructivism: Origins and Evolution.* Rev. ed. New York: Braziller, 1995.
Taylor, Brandon. *Collage: The Making of Modern Art.* London: Thames & Hudson, 2004.
Weston, Richard. *Modernism.* London: Phaidon Press, 1996.
White, Michael. *De Stijl and Dutch Modernism.* Critical Perspectives in Art History. New York: Manchester Univ. Press, 2003.
Whitfield, Sarah. *Fauvism.* World of Art. New York: Thames & Hudson, 1996.
Whitford, Frank. *The Bauhaus: Masters and Students by Themselves.* Woodstock, NY: Overlook Press, 1993.
Zurier, Rebecca, Robert W. Snyder, and Virginia M. Mecklenburg. *Metropolitan Lives: The Ashcan Artists and Their New York.* Washington, DC: National Museum of American Art, 1995.

Chapter 32 The International Scene since 1950

Alberro, Alexander, and Blake Stimson, eds. *Conceptual Art: A Critical Anthology.* Cambridge, MA: MIT Press, 1999.
Archer, Michael. *Art Since 1960.* 2nd ed. World of Art. New York: Thames & Hudson, 2002.
Atkins. Robert. *Artspeak: A Guide to Contemporary Ideas, Movements, and Buzzwords.* 2nd ed. New York: Abbeville Press, 1997.
Ault, Julie. *Art Matters: How the Culture Wars Changed America.* Ed. Brian Wallis, Marianne Weems, and Philip Yenawine. New York: New York Univ. Press, 1999.
Battcock, Gregory. *Minimal Art: A Critical Anthology.* Berkeley: Univ. of California Press, 1995.
Beardsley, John. *Earthworks and Beyond: Contemporary Art in the Landscape.* 4th ed. ebook. New York: Abbeville Press, 2006.
Bird, Jon, and Michael Newman, eds. *Rewriting Conceptual Art.* Critical Views. London: Reaktion Books, 1999.
Bishop, Claire. *Installation Art: A Critical History.* New York: Routledge, 2005.
Blais, Joline, and Jon Ippolito. *At the Edge of Art.* London: Thames & Hudson, 2006.

Buchloh, Benjamin H. D. *Neo-Avantgarde and Culture Industry: Essays on European and American Art from 1955 to 1975.* Cambridge, MA: MIT Press, 2000.

Carlebach, Michael L. *American Photojournalism Comes of Age.* Washington, DC: Smithsonian Institution Press, 1997.

Causey, Andrew. *Sculpture since 1945.* Oxford History of Art. Oxford: Oxford Univ. Press, 1998.

Corris, Michael, ed. *Conceptual Art: Theory, Myth, and Practice.* New York: Cambridge Univ. Press, 2004.

De Oliveira, Nicolas, Nicola Oxley, and Michael Petry. *Installation Art in the New Millennium: The Empire of the Senses.* New York: Thames & Hudson, 2003.

De Salvo, Donna, ed. *Open Systems: Rethinking Art c. 1970.* London: Tate Gallery, 2005.

Fabozzi, Paul F. *Artists, Critics, Context: Readings In and Around American Art Since 1945.* Upper Saddle River, NJ: Pearson/Prentice Hall, 2002.

Fineberg, Jonathan. *Art Since 1940: Strategies of Being.* 2nd ed. New York: Abrams, 2000.

Flood, Richard, and Frances Morris. *Zero to Infinity: Arte Povera, 1962–1972.* Minneapolis, MN: Walker Art Center, 2001.

Goldberg, RoseLee. *Performance Art: From Futurism to the Present.* Rev. and exp. ed. World of Art. London: Thames & Hudson, 2001.

Goldstein, Ann. *A Minimal Future? Art as Object 1958–1968.* Los Angeles: Museum of Contemporary Art, 2004.

Grande, John K. *Art Nature Dialogues: Interviews with Environmental Artists.* Albany: State Univ. of New York Press, 2004.

Grosenick, Uta, ed. *Women Artists in the 20th and 21st Century.* New York: Taschen, 2001.

———, and Burkhard Riemschneider, eds. *Art at the Turn of the Millennium.* New York: Taschen, 1999.

Grunenberg, Christoph, ed. *Summer of Love: Art of the Psychedelic Era.* London: Tate Gallery, 2005.

Hitchcock, Henry Russell, and Philip Johnson. *The International Style.* New York: Norton, 1995.

Hopkins, David. *After Modern Art: 1945–2000.* Oxford History of Art. Oxford: Oxford Univ. Press, 2000.

Jencks, Charles. *The New Paradigm in Architecture: The Language of Post-Modernism.* New Haven: Yale Univ. Press, 2002.

Jodidio, Philip. *New Forms: Architecture in the 1990s.* Taschen's World Architecture. New York: Taschen, 2001.

Johnson, Deborah, and Wendy Oliver, eds. *Women Making Art: Women in the Visual, Literary, and Performing Arts Since 1960.* Eruptions, vol. 7. New York: Peter Lang, 2001.

Jones, Caroline A. *Machine in the Studio: Constructing the Postwar American Artist.* Chicago: Univ. of Chicago Press, 1996.

Joselit, David. *American Art Since 1945.* World of Art. London: Thames & Hudson, 2003.

Legault, Réjean, and Sarah Williams Goldhagen, eds. *Anxious Modernisms: Experimentation in Postwar Architectural Culture.* Montréal: Canadian Centre for Architecture, 2000.

Lucie-Smith, Edward. *Movements in Art since 1945.* New ed. World of Art. London: Thames & Hudson, 2001.

Madoff, Steven Henry, ed. *Pop Art: A Critical History.* The Documents of Twentieth Century Art. Berkeley: Univ. of California Press, 1997.

Moos, David, ed. *The Shape of Colour: Excursions in Colour Field Art, 1950–2005.* Toronto: Art Gallery of Ontario, 2005.

Paul, Christiane. *Digital Art.* 2nd ed. World of Art. London: Thames & Hudson, 2008.

Phillips, Lisa. *The American Century: Art and Culture, 1950–2000.* New York: Whitney Museum of American Art, 1999.

Pop Art: Contemporary Perspectives. Princeton: Princeton Univ. Art Museum, 2007.

Ratcliff, Carter. *The Fate of a Gesture: Jackson Pollock and Postwar American Art.* New York: Farrar, Straus, Giroux, 1996.

Reckitt, Helena, ed. *Art and Feminism.* Themes and Movements. London: Phaidon Press, 2001.

Robertson, Jean, and Craig McDaniel. *Themes of Contemporary Art: Visual Art after 1980.* 2nd ed. New York: Oxford Univ. Press, 2009.

Robinson, Hilary, ed. *Feminism-Art-Theory: An Anthology, 1968–2000.* Malden, MA: Blackwell, 2001.

Rorimer, Anne. *New Art in the 60s and 70s: Redefining Reality.* New York: Thames & Hudson, 2001.

Rush, Michael. *New Media in Late 20th-Century Art.* 2nd ed. World of Art. London: Thames & Hudson, 2005.

———. *Video Art.* 2nd ed. London: Thames & Hudson, 2007.

Sandler, Irving. *Art of the Postmodern Era: From the Late 1960s to the Early 1990s.* New York: Icon Editions, 1996.

Shohat, Ella. *Talking Visions: Multicultural Feminism in a Transnational Age.* Documentary Sources in Contemporary Art, vol. 5. New York: New Museum of Contemporary Art, 1998.

Stiles, Kristine, and Peter Selz. *Theories and Documents of Contemporary Art: A Sourcebook of Artists' Writings.* California Studies in the History of Art, 35. Berkeley: Univ. of California, 1996.

Sylvester, David. *About Modern Art.* 2nd ed. New Haven: Yale Univ. Press, 2001.

Varnedoe, Kirk, Paola Antonelli, and Joshua Siegel, eds. *Modern Contemporary: Art Since 1980 at MoMA.* Rev. ed. New York: Museum of Modern Art, 2004.

Waldman, Diane. *Collage, Assemblage, and the Found Object.* New York: Abrams, 1992.

Weintraub, Linda, Arthur Danto, and Thomas McEvilley. *Art on the Edge and Over: Searching for Art's Meaning in Contemporary Society, 1970s–1990s.* Litchfield, CT: Art Insights, 1996.

CREDITS

Introduction

Intro 1 © 2010 Digital Image, The Museum of Modern Art, New York/Scala, Florence; Intro 2 object no 1997.007.0697; Art and its Contexts © Achim Bednorz; Closer Look a British Library, London; Closer Look b © Quattrone, Florence; Closer Look © The Frick Collection, New York; Closer Look The British Library, London; Intro 3 Su concessione del Ministero per il Beni e le Attività Culturali – photo Index/Tosi; Intro 4 © 2007 Image copyright The Metropolitan Museum of Art/Art Resource, NY/Scala, Florence; Closer Look a Ashmolean Museum, Oxford, England, U.K.; Closer look b Princeton University Art Museum. Photo: Bruce M. White; Intro 5, Intro 9 © 2004 Photo The Philadelphia Museum of Art/Scala, Florence; Intro 6 Kunsthistorisches Museum, Vienna; Intro 8 © Quattrone, Florence

Chapter 17

17.1 Scala, Florence/Art Resource, NY; 17.2, 17.21a © Achim Bednorz, Koln; 17.3 Tosi/Index Ricerca Iconografica; 17.5 Cimabue (Cenni di Pepi)/Index Ricerca Iconografica; 17.6 Galleria degli Uffizi; 17.7 Assessorato ai Musei. Politiche Culturali e Spettacolo del Comune di Padova; 17.8, 17.10, 17.13 © Quattrone, Florence; 17.9 © Studio Deganello, Padua; 17.12 © Kimbell Art Museum, Fort Worth, Texas/Art Resource/Scala, Florence; 17.14 © Archivi Alinari, Florence; 17.15 a, b Scala, Florence/Art Resource, NY; Art and its Contexts © Quattrone, Florence; 17.16 M. Beck-Coppola/Louvre, Paris/Art Resource, NY; Closer Look The Metropolitan Museum of Art/Art Resource, NY; 17.17 Art Resource/The Metropolitan Museum of Art; Object Speaks a, b, c The Walters Art Museum, Baltimore; 17.18 The Walters Art Museum, Baltimore; 17.19 Landschaftsverband Rheinland/Rheinisches Landesmuseum Bonn

Chapter 18

18.1 © National Gallery, London/Scala, Florence; 18.2a, b Scala, Florence/Art Resource, NY; 18.3 Erich Lessing/Chartreuse de Champmol/Art Resource, NY; Art and its Contexts Bibliothèque Nationale de France; 18.4, 18.5 R.G. Ojeda/RMN/Art Resource/Musée Conde, Chantilly, France; 18.6 Bildarchiv der Osterreichische Nationalbibliothek; 18.7 Art Resource/The Metropolitan Museum of Art; 18.8 Kunsthistorisches Museum, Vienna, Austria; 18.9, 18.10 Art Resource/The Metropolitan Museum of Art; 18.11, 18.12 © National Gallery, London/Scala, Florence; Object Speaks a, b Erich Lessing/Art Resource, NY; 18.13 Derechos reservados © Museo Nacional Del Prado - Madrid; 18.14 Photograph © Museum of Fine Arts, Boston; 18.15 © 2007 Image copyright The Metropolitan Museum of Art/Art Resource, NY/Scala, Florence; Closer Look Art Resource/The Metropolitan Museum of Art; 18.16a © Quattrone, Florence; 18.16b, c Galleria degli Uffizi; 18.17 AKG Images/Erich Lessing; 18.18a Joerg P. Anders/ Art Resource/Bildarchiv Preussicher Kulturbesitz; 18.18b Image Courtesy of Reproductiefonds Vlaamse Musea NV.; 18.19 © 2007 Image copyright The Metropolitan Museum of Art/Art Resource, NY/Scala, Florence; 18.20, 18,24 © Achim Bednorz, Koln; 18.22 Art Resource, NY/Giraudon; 18.23 Musee d'art et d'histoire, Genève; 18.25 John Rylands University Library of Manchester; 18.26 Art Resource, NY/The Metropolitan Museum of Art; 18.27 Bibliothèque Mazarine, Paris, France/Archives Charmet/The Bridgeman Art Library

Chapter 19

19.1 © National Gallery, London; 19.2, 19.4a Scala, Florence/Art Resource, NY; 19.3 Dorling Kindersley; Object Speaks a Canali Photobank; Object Speaks b Scala, Florence/Art Resource, NY; 19.5, 19.13, 19.35 © Achim Bednorz, Koln; 19.6 Index Ricerca Iconografica; Art and its Contexts a © Corbis; Art and its Contexts b Scala, Florence/Art Resource, NY; 19.7, 19.19, 19.33 © Quattrone, Florence; 19.8, 19.9, 19.12, 19.22, 19.29a, b Canali Photobank; 19.10 AKG-Images; 19.11 The Bridgeman Art Library; 19.14, 19.16, 19.20, 19.25, 19.27, 19.34 Scala, Florence/Art Resource, NY; Technique b Canali Photobank; 19.15 Cincinnati Art Museum; 19.18, 19.28 Erich Lessing/Art Resource, NY; 19.21 © National Gallery, London/Scala, Florence; 19.23 © 2007 Image © The Metropolitan Museum of Art/Art Resource, NY/Scala, Florence; Art and its Contexts © Courtauld Institue of Art Gallery, London; 19.24 Alinari/Art Resource, NY; 19.26 © National Gallery, London/Scala, Florence; 19.30 © Photo Vatican Museums; 19.32 Archivi Alinari, Firenze; Closer Look Canali Photobank; 19.36, 19.37 © Cameraphoto Arte, Venice; 19.38 © The Frick Collection, New York

Chapter 20

20.1 © Photo Vatican Museums; 20.2 Art Resource/Musée du Louvre, Paris; 20.3 Ghigo Roli/Index Ricerca Iconografica; 20.4, 20.14, 20.15 © Quattrone, Florence; 20.5 Art Resource/Musée du Louvre, Paris; Art and its Contexts Cameraphoto Arte, Venice; 20.6 Photograph © Board of Trustees National Gallery of Art, Washington, D.C.; 20.7, 20.8 © Staatliche Museen zu Berlin-Preussischer Kulturbesitz Gemäldegalerie, Photo Jörg P. Anders; Closer Look © Photo Vatican Museums; 20.9, 20.13, 20.25, 20.26, 20.31, 20.35 Canali Photobank; 20.10 Galleria dell' Accademia, Florence/Scala, Florence/Art Resource, NY; 20.11 Zigrossi Bracchetti/Vatican Museums/Ikona; 20.12a © Photo Vatican Museums; Object Speaks a The Royal Collection © 2010 Her Majesty Queen Elizabeth II; Object Speaks b V&A Images; Object Speaks c © Photo Vatican Museums; 20.16, 20.40 © Achim Bednorz, Koln; 20.17 Super-Stock, Inc.; 20.18, 20.19 Scala, Florence/Art Resource, NY; 20.20 Ikona; 20.21 Cameraphoto/Art Resource, NY; 20.22 Musée du Louvre, Paris/RMN Réunion des Musées Nationaux, France. Erich Lessing/Art Resource, NY; 20.23 Embassy of Italy; Art and its Contexts Kunsthistorisches Museum Wien; 20.24 Index Ricerca Iconografica/Summerfield/Galleria degli Uffizi, Florence; 20.27 Galleria degli Uffizi; 20.28 Art Resource/The Metropolitan Museum of Art; 20.29 © National Gallery, London/Scala, Florence; 20.30 Photograph © 2008 Museum of Fine Arts, Boston; 20.32, 20.33 Kunsthistorisches Museum, Vienna, Austria; 20.34 © Photo Vatican Museums/A. Braccetti - P. Zigrossi; 20.36a Scala, Florence/Art Resource, NY; Art and its Contexts Alinari/Art Resource, NY; 20.37 Cameraphoto/Art Resource, NY; 20.38 Erich Lessing/Art Resource, NY; 20.39 L. Hammel/A. van der Voort/Bildarchiv Monheim GmbH/Alamy Images

Chapter 21

21.1 Scala, Florence/Alte Pinakothek, Munich/Art Resource, NY; 21.2 Erich Lessing/Art Resource, NY; Technique Germanisches Nationalmuseum Nurnberg; 21.3, 21.4, 21.5 Musée d'Unterlinden; 21.6 Laurie Platt Winfrey, Inc./The Metropolitan Museum of Art, New York; 21.7 Philadelphia Museum of Art/Scala, Florence/Art Resource, NY; 21.8 Artothek; 21.9 Photograph © Board of Trustees, National Gallery of Art, Washington D.C.; 21.10 Kunstmuseum Basel, Martin P. Buhler; 21.11 Bayerische Staatsgemaldesammlungen, Neue Pinakothek, Munich; 21.12 Art Resource/Musée du Louvre; Art and its Contexts L. B. Foy/Global Quest Photography; 21.13 © RMN/Jean-Pierre Lagiewski; 21.14 Erich Lessing/Art Resource, NY; Art and its Contexts Scala, Florence/Art Resource, NY; 21.15 Laurie Platt Winfrey, Inc.; 21.16 Scala, Florence/Art Resource, NY; 21.17 Museo Nacional del Prado/Oronoz; 21.18 © 1990 Photo Scala Florence; 21.19 Eric Lessing/Kunsthistorisches Museum, Vienna/Art Resource, NY; 21.20 Kunsthistorisches Museum, Vienna; 21.21 Kunstmuseum Basel. Photo: Martin Buhler/Kunstmuseum Basel; Object Speaks a Erich Lessing/Art Resource, NY; Object Speaks b Metropolitan Museum of Art, New York/Art Resource, NY/Scala, Florence; Closer Look © National Gallery, London/Scala, Florence; 21.22 © National Portrait Gallery, London; 21.23 The Nelson-Atkins Museum of Art; Art and its Contexts Photograph © 2007 The Metropolitan Museum of Art; 21.24 Bridgeman Art Library; 21.25 A.F. Kersting/AKG Images

Chapter 22

22.1, 22.9 Canali Photobank; 22.2 © Alinari Archives/Corbis. All Rights Reserved; 22.3 © Achim Bednorz, Koln; 22.4 Scala, Florence/Art Resource, NY; 22.5, 22.12 © Vincenzo Pirozzi, Rome; 22.6 Ikona; 22.8 Alinari/Art Resource, NY; 22.10 © ADP - Management Fratelli Alinari/Art Resource, NY; 22.11 Galleria degli Uffizi, Florence/Dagli Orgi/Art Archive; Object Speaks a, b Canali Photobank; 22.13 AKG-Images/Electa; 22.14 The Royal Collection © Her Majesty Queen Elizabeth II. Photo by A. C. Cooper Ltd.; 22.15 The Cleveland Museum of Art; 22.16 Palazzo Barberini, Italy/Canali Photobank; 22.17 Scala, Florence/Art Resource, NY; 22.18 San Diego Museum of Art.; 22.19 Photo: Bob Grove © Board of Trustees, National Gallery of Art, Washington D.C; 22.20 Courtesy Wadsworth Atheneum, Hartford, Connecticut; 22.21 V & A Picture Library; 22.22, 22.32 Derechos reservados © Museo Nacional Del Prado - Madrid; 22.23 Derechos reservados © Museo Nacional Del Prado - Madrid/Scala, Florence; 22.24 © Prado Museum, Madrid; 22.27 Fotodienst/Mayer van den Bergh Museum; 22.26 Blauel/Gnamm/Artothek; 22.28a, b, c © IRPA-KIK, Brussels, Belgium; 22.29 Photo: Ojeda/Le Mage. Louvre, Paris, © Réunion des Musées Nationaux/Art Resource, NY; 22.30 Museo del Prado, Madrid, Spain. Art Resource, NY/Scala, Florence; Closer Look Museo del Prado, Madrid, Spain. Scala/Art Resource, NY; 22.31 Musée du Louvre, Paris. RMN Reunion des Musées Nationaux, France. Scala/Art Resource, NY; 22.33 Allen Memorial Art Museum; 22.34 Staatliche Museen zu Berlin, Preussischer Kulturbesitz, Gemäldegalerie.; 22.35 Frans Hals Museum De Hallen; 22.36 Photograph © Board of Trustees, National Gallery of Art, Washington, D.C.; 22.37 Mauritshuis, The Hague, The Netherlands. SCALA/Art Resource, NY; 22.38, 22.39 Rijksmuseum, Amsterdam; 22.40 © The Frick Collection, New York; 22.41 Royal Cabinet of Paintings, Mauritshuis The Hague; 22.42 Photo: Richard Carafelli © Board of Trustees, National Gallery of Art, Washington, D.C.; 22.43 Photograph Richard Carafelli/© Board of Trustees, National Gallery of Art, Washington, D.C.; 22.44 The J. Paul Getty Museum, Los Angeles.; 22.45 Rijksmuseum, Amsterdam; 22.46, 22.47 Royal Cabinet of Paintings, Mauritshius, The Hague; 22.48 The Toledo Museum of Art, Toledo, Ohio (1956.57); Art and its Contexts National Museum of Women in the Arts, Washington, DC; 22.49 Photo: Hervé Lewandowski. Louvre, Paris, France. Réunion des Musées Nationaux/Art Resource, NY; 22.50 Paul M.R. Maeyaert; 22.51 © Massimo Listri/Corbis; 22.52 Los Angeles County Museum of Art. Photograph © 2000 Museum Associates/LACMA. All Rights Reserved; 22.53 © Musée du Louvre, Paris/RMN/Art Resource, NY; 22.54 Staatliche Museen, Berlin/BPK; 22.55 Photograph © 2007, The Art Institute of Chicago. All Rights Reserved; 22.56 Art Resource, NY/Yale University Art Gallery; 22.57 A.F. Kersting/AKG Images; 22.58 Historic Royal Palaces Enterprises Ltd; 22.59 St. Paul's Cathedral

Chapter 23

23.1 © Peter Adams/Corbis; 23.2 © Dirk Bakker; 23.3 Prince of Wales Museum of Western India; 23.4 Courtesy of Marilyn Stokstad, Private Collection; Art and its Contexts a Thierry Ollivier. Musée des Arts Asiatiques-Guimet, Paris, France. Réunion des Musées Nationaux/Art Resource, NY; Art and its Contexts b Rene-Gabriel Ojeda/RMN/Art Resource, NY; 23.6 The Walters Art Museum, Baltimore; 23.7 Collection of Phoenix Art Museum. Photographed by Craig Smith; 23.8 Bernard O'Kane/Alamy; Closer Look © Sheldan Collins/Corbis; 23.10, 23.12 V&A Images; 23.11 Freer Gallery of Art, Smithsonian Institution, Washington, D.C.; Object Speaks Katherine Wetzel/Virginia Museum of Fine Arts; 23.13 B.P. Mathur/Pierre/Dinodia Picture Agency; 23.14 Photograph © 2008 Museum of Fine Arts, Boston.; 23.15 David Ball/Alamy Images; 23.16 Courtesy of Marilyn Stokstad, Private Collection; 23.17 Rick Asher; 23.18 Photograph courtesy Peabody Essex Museum. Photo: Sexton/Dykes; 23.19 © Tate, London 2010 © Anish Kapoor

Chapter 24

24.1, 24.2, 24.3 National Palace Museum Taiwan, Republic of China; 24.4 The Cleveland Museum of Art; 24.5, 24.6 National Palace Museum, Taipei, Republic of China; Closer Look National Palace Museum Taipei, Republic of China; 24.7 Palace Museum, Beijing; 24.8 PanoramaStock/Robert Harding World Imagery; 24.9 The Nelson-Atkins Museum of Art, Kansas City, Missouri. Photograph by Jamison Miller; 24.10 © Wolfgang Kaehler 2007 www.wkaehlerphoto.com; Object Speaks The Nelson-Atkins Museum of Art, Kansas City, Missouri. Photograph Robert Newcombe; 24.11 The Cleveland Museum of Art; 24.12 Collection of Phoenix Art Museum; 24.13 Collection C. C. Wang family; 24.14 Spencer Museum of Art, The University of Kansas; 24.15 Museum of Oriental Ceramics, Osaka. Gift of the Sumitomo Group [20773]; 24.16 Ewha Woman's University Museum, Seoul, Korea; 24.17 Photo Courtesy of Central Library, Tenri University, Tenri, Japan; 24.18 National Treasure # 217. Samsung Museum, Lee'um, Seoul, Republic of Korea; 24.19 National Museum of Korea; 24.20 Whanki Foundation/Whanki Museum

Chapter 25

25.1 Photograph © The Art Institute of Chicago; 25.2 Reproduced with permission. © 2005 Museum of Fine Arts, Boston. All Rights Reserved; 25.3 TNM Image Archives/DNP; 25.4 Michael S. Yamashita, Inc.; 25.5 Steve Vidler/SuperStock, Inc.; 25.6 Sakamoto Manschichi Photo Research Library, Tokyo; 25.7 Myoki-an/Pacific Press Service; 25.8 Sakai Collection, Tokyo. Photo: Stephen Addiss; Object Speaks a, b TNM Image Archives/DNP; 25.9a, b Smithsonian Institution; 25.10 Los Angeles County Museum of Art. Photograph © 2003 Museum Associates/LACMA; 25.11 Hosomi Museum; Technique © The Trustees of the British Museum; 25.12 Honolulu Academy of Arts; 25.13 Gitter-Yelen Foundation; 25.14 The Nelson-Atkins Museum of Art, Kansas City, Missouri. Photograph by John Lamberton; Closer Look The Nelson-Atkins Museum of Art, Kansas City, Missouri; 25.15 © Shokodo, Ltd. & Japan Artists Association, Inc. 2006; 25.16 Courtesy Hiroshima Peace Memorial Museum; Recovering the Past Courtesy Koukei Eri; 25.17 Toyobi Far Eastern Art

Chapter 26

26.2 Bodleian Library, University of Oxford; 26.3 Werner Forman/Art Resource, NY; 26.4 © Michel Zabe; Closer Look Museo Nacional de Arqueologia, Mexico City, Mexico/Photo © AISA/The Bridgeman Art Library; 26.5 World Museum Liverpool, National Museums Liverpool; 26.6 Chris Rennie/Robert Harding World Imagery; 26.7 © Art Archive/Dagli Orti; 26.8 Justin Kerr/Dumbarton Oaks, Byzantine Photograph and Fieldwork Archives, Washington, D.C.; 26.9 Photo by John Bigelow Taylor, NY. Courtesy Dept. of Library Services, American Museum of Natural History; Technique Philbrook Museum, Tulsa, Oklahoma; 26.10 With permission of the Royal Ontario Museum © ROM; 26.11

INDEX

Page numbers in *italics* refer to illustrations and maps

A